THE COMPLETE WORKS OF ROBERT BROWNING, VOLUME XII

"Modern Poetry"

Robert Browning, caricatured as "Modern Poetry"
by Carlo Pellegrini ("Ape") for Vanity Fair *Magazine, 1875.*

The Complete works of Robert Browning

With Variant Readings & Annotations

Volume XII

EDITED BY

RITA S. PATTESON

PAUL D. L. TURNER

BAYLOR UNIVERSITY
WACO, TEXAS
OHIO UNIVERSITY PRESS
ATHENS, OHIO
2001

THE COMPLETE WORKS OF ROBERT BROWNING

Editorial Board

ALLAN C. DOOLEY, General Editor

SUSAN CROWL

PARK HONAN, Founding Editor

ROMA A. KING, Founding Editor
General Editor, 1967–1985

JACK W. HERRING (1925–1999)
General Editor, 1985–1999

Contributing Editors

JOHN C. BERKEY

MICHAEL BRIGHT

ASHBY BLAND CROWDER

SUSAN E. DOOLEY

DAVID EWBANK

RITA S. PATTESON

PAUL D.L. TURNER

Ohio University Press, Athens, Ohio 45701
© 2001 by Ohio University Press and Baylor University
Printed in the United States of America
All rights reserved

06 05 04 03 02 01   5 4 3 2 1

Ohio University Press books are printed on acid-free paper ∞ ™

Library of Congress Cataloging-in-Publication data
(Revised for vol. 12)

Browning, Robert, 1812–1889.
The complete works of Robert Browning, with variant readings & annotations.

Vol. 12 edited by Rita S. Patteson and Paul D. L. Turner
Includes bibliographical references and indexes.
I. King, Roma A., 1914–   , ed.
II. Title.
PR4201.K5 1969 821'.8   68-18389
ISBN 0-8214-1359-7 (v. 12)

CONTENTS

PREFACE

I CONTENTS

This edition of the works of Robert Browning is intended to be complete. It will comprise at least seventeen volumes and will contain:

1. The entire contents of the first editions of Browning's works, arranged in their chronological order of publication. (The poems included in *Dramatic Lyrics, Dramatic Romances and Lyrics,* and *Men and Women,* for example, appear in the order of their first publication rather than in the order in which Browning rearranged them for later publication.)

2. All prefaces and dedications which Browning is known to have written for his own works and for those of Elizabeth Barrett Browning.

3. The two prose essays that Browning is known to have published: the review of a book on Tasso, generally referred to as the "Essay on Chatterton," and the preface for a collection of letters supposed to have been written by Percy Bysshe Shelley, generally referred to as the "Essay on Shelley."

4. The front matter and the table of contents of each of the collected editions (1849, 1863, 1865, 1868 [70, 75], 1888-1889) which Browning himself saw through the press.

5. Poems published during Browning's lifetime but not collected by him.

6. Poems not published during Browning's lifetime which have come to light since his death.

7. John Forster's *Thomas Wentworth, Earl of Strafford,* to which Browning contributed significantly, though the precise extent of his contribution has not been determined.

8. Variants appearing in primary and secondary materials as defined in Section II below.

9. Textual emendations.

10. Informational and explanatory notes for each work.

II PRIMARY AND SECONDARY MATERIALS

Aside from a handful of uncollected short works, all of Browning's works but *Asolando* (1889) went through two or more editions during his lifetime. Except for *Pauline* (1833), *Strafford* (1837), and *Sordello*

(1840), all the works published before 1849 were revised and corrected for the 1849 collection. *Strafford* and *Sordello* were revised and corrected for the collection of 1863, as were all the other works in that edition. Though no further poems were added in the collection of 1865, all the works were once again corrected and revised. The 1868 collection added a revised *Pauline* and *Dramatis Personae* (1864) to the other works, which were themselves again revised and corrected. A new edition of this collection in 1870 contained further revisions, and Browning corrected his text again for an 1875 reimpression. The printing of the last edition of the *Poetical Works* over which Browning exercised control began in 1888, and the first eight volumes are dated thus on their title-pages. Volumes 9 through 16 of this first impression are dated 1889, and we have designated them 1889a to distinguish them from the second impression of all 16 volumes, which was begun and completed in 1889. Some of the earlier volumes of the first impression sold out almost immediately, and in preparation for a second impression, Browning revised and corrected the first ten volumes before he left for Italy in late August,1889. The second impression, in which all sixteen volumes bear the date 1889 on their title-pages, consisted of a revised and corrected second impression of volumes 1-10, plus a second impression of volumes 11-16 altered by Browning in one instance. This impression we term 1889 (see section III below).

Existing manuscripts and editions are classified as either primary or secondary material. The primary materials include the following:

1. The manuscript of a work when such is known to exist.

2. Proof sheets, when known to exist, that contain authorial corrections and revisions.

3. The first and subsequent editions of a work that preserve evidence of Browning's intentions and were under his control.

4. The collected editions over which Browning exercised control:

1849—*Poems.* Two Volumes. London: Chapman and Hall.

1863—*The Poetical Works.* Three Volumes. London: Chapman and Hall.

1865—*The Poetical Works.* Three Volumes. London: Chapman and Hall.

1868—*The Poetical Works.* Six Volumes. London: Smith, Elder and Company.

1870—*The Poetical Works.* Six Volumes. London: Smith, Elder and Company. This resetting constituted a new edition, which was stereotyped and reimpressed several times; the 1875 impression contains revisions by Browning.

1888-1889—*The Poetical Works.* Sixteen Volumes. London: Smith,

Elder and Company. Exists in numerous stereotype impressions, of which two are primary material:

1888-1889a—The first impression, in which volumes 1-8 are dated 1888 and volumes 9-16 are dated 1889.

1889—The corrected second impression of volumes 1-10 and a second impression of volumes 11-16 altered by Browning only as stated in section III below; all dated 1889 on the title pages.

5. The corrections in Browning's hand in the Dykes Campbell copy of 1888-1889a, and the manuscript list of corrections to that impression in the Brown University Library (see section III below).

Other materials (including some in the poet's handwriting) that affected the text are secondary. Examples are: the copy of the first edition of *Pauline* which contains annotations by Browning and John Stuart Mill; the copies of the first edition of *Paracelsus* which contain corrections in Browning's hand; a very early manuscript of *A Blot in the 'Scutcheon* which Browning presented to William Macready, but not the one from which the first edition was printed; informal lists of corrections that Browning included in letters to friends, such as the corrections to *Men and Women* he sent to D. G. Rossetti; verbal and punctuational changes Browning essayed in presentation copies of his works or in his own copies, if not used by his printers; Elizabeth Barrett's suggestions for revisions in *A Soul's Tragedy* and certain poems in *Dramatic Romances and Lyrics;* and the edition of *Strafford* by Emily Hickey for which Browning made suggestions.

The text and variant readings of this edition derive from collation of primary materials as defined above. Secondary materials are occasionally discussed in the notes and sometimes play a part when emendation is required.

III COPY-TEXT

The copy-text for this edition is Browning's final text: the first ten volumes of 1889 and the last six volumes of 1888-1889a, as described above. For this choice we offer the following explanation.

Manuscripts used as printer's copy for twenty of Browning's thirty-four book publications are known to exist; others may yet become available. These manuscripts, or, in their absence, the first editions of the works, might be considered as the most desirable copy-text. And this would be the case for an author who exercised little control over his text after the manuscript or first edition stage, or whose text clearly became corrupted in a succession of editions. To preserve the intention of such an author, one would have to choose an early text and emend it as evidence and judgment demanded.

With Browning, however, the situation is different, and our copy-text choice results from that difference. Throughout his life Browning continually revised his poetry. He did more than correct printer's errors and clarify previously intended meanings; his texts themselves remained fluid, subject to continuous alteration. As the manuscript which he submitted to his publisher was no doubt already a product of revision, so each subsequent edition under his control reflects the results of an ongoing process of creating, revising, and correcting. If we were to choose the manuscript (where extant) or first edition as copy-text, preserving Browning's intention would require extensive emendation to capture the additions, revisions, and alterations which Browning demonstrably made in later editions. By selecting Browning's final corrected text as our copy-text, emending it only to eliminate errors and the consequences of changing house-styling, we present his works in the form closest to that which he intended after years of revision and polishing.

But this is true only if Browning in fact exercised extensive control over the printing of his various editions. That he intended and attempted to do so is apparent in his comments and his practice. In 1855, demanding accuracy from the printers, he pointed out to his publisher Chapman, "I attach importance to the mere stops . . ." (De-Vane and Knickerbocker, p. 83). There is evidence of his desire to control the details of his text as early as 1835, in the case of *Paracelsus*. The *Paracelsus* manuscript, now in the Forster and Dyce collection in the Victoria and Albert Museum Library, demonstrates a highly unconventional system of punctuation. Of particular note is Browning's unrestrained use of dashes, often in strings of two or three, instead of more precise or orthodox punctuation marks. It appears that this was done for its rhetorical effect. One sheet of Part 1 of the manuscript and all but the first and last sheets of Part 3 have had punctuation revised in pencil by someone other than Browning, perhaps J. Riggs, whose name appears three times in the margins of Part 3. In addition to these revisions, there are analogous punctuation revisions (in both pencil and ink) which appear to be in Browning's hand, and a few verbal alterations obviously in the poet's script.

A collation of the first edition (1835) with the manuscript reveals that a major restyling of punctuation was carried out before *Paracelsus* was published. However, the revisions incorporated into the first edition by no means slavishly follow the example set by the pencilled revisions of Parts 1 and 3 of the manuscript. Apparently the surviving manuscript was not used as printer's copy for the first edition. Browning may have submitted a second manuscript, or he may have revised extensively in proof. The printers may have carried out the revisions to punctuation, with or without the poet's point by point involvement. With the present evidence, we cannot be conclusive about the extent of Browning's control over the first edition of *Paracelsus*. It can be stated, however, in the light of the incompleteness of the pencilled revisions and the frequent lack or correspondence between the pencilled revisions and the lines as printed in 1835, that Browning himself may have been responsible for the punctuation of the first edition of *Paracelsus*. Certainly he was responsible for the frequent instances in the first and subsequent editions where the punctuation defies conventional rules, as in the following examples:

> What though
> It be so?—if indeed the strong desire
> Eclipse the aim in me—if splendour break
> (Part I, ll. 329-331)

> I surely loved them—that last night, at least,
> When we . . . gone! gone! the better: I am saved
> (Part II, ll. 132-133)

> Of the body, even,)—what God is, what we are,
> (Part V, l. 642, 1849 reading)

The manuscripts of *Colombe's Birthday* (1844) and *Christmas-Eve and Easter-Day* (1850) were followed very carefully in the printing of the first editions. There are slight indications of minor house-styling, such as the spellings *colour* and *honour* for the manuscripts' *color* and *honor*. But the unorthodox punctuation, used to indicate elocutionary and rhetorical subtleties as well as syntactical relationships, is carried over almost unaltered from the manuscripts to the first editions. Similar evidence of Browning's painstaking attention to the smallest details in the printing of his poems can be seen in the manuscript and proof sheets of *The Ring and the Book* (1868-69). These materials reveal an interesting and significant pattern. It appears that Browning wrote swiftly, giving primary attention to wording and less to punctuation, being satisfied to use dashes to indicate almost any break in thought, syntax, or rhythm. Later, in the proof sheets for Books 1-6 of the poem and in the manuscript itself for Books 7-12, he changed the dashes to more specific and purposeful punctuation marks. The revised punctuation is what was printed, for the most part, in the first edition of *The Ring and the Book*; what further revisions there are conform to Browning's practice, though hardly to standard rules. Clearly Browning was in control of nearly every aspect of the published form of his works, even to the "mere stops."

Of still greater importance in our choice of copy-text is the substantial evidence that Browning took similar care with his collected editions. Though he characterized his changes for later editions as trivial and few in number, collations reveal thousands of revisions and corrections in each successive text. *Paracelsus*, for example, was extensively revised for the 1849 *Poems;* it was again reworked for the *Poetical Works* of 1863. *Sordello*, omitted in 1849, reappeared in 1863 with 181 new lines and short marginal glosses; Browning admitted only that it was "corrected *throughout*" (DeVane and Knickerbocker, p. 157). The poems of *Men and Women* (1855) were altered in numerous small but meaningful ways for both the 1863 and 1865 editions of the *Poetical Works* (see Allan C. Dooley, "The Textual Significance of Robert Browning's 1865 *Poetical Works*," *PBSA* 71 [1977], 212-18). Michael Hancher cites evidence of the poet's close supervision of the 1868 collected edition ("Browning and the *Poetical Works* of 1888-1889," *Browning Newsletter,* Spring, 1971, 25-27), and Michael Meredith has traced Browning's attentions to his text in the 1870 edition and an 1875 reimpression of it ("Learning's Crabbed Text," *SBHC* 13 [1985], 97-107); another perspective is offered in Allan C. Dooley's *Author and Printer in Victorian England* (1992), Ch. 4-5. Mrs. Orr, writing of the same period in Browning's life, reports his resentment of those who garbled his text by misplacing his stops (*Life*, pp. 357-58).

There is plentiful and irrefutable evidence that Browning controlled, in the same meticulous way, the text of his last collected edition, that which we term 1888-1889. Hancher has summarized the relevant information:

> The evidence is clear that Browning undertook the 1888-1889 edition of his *Poetical Works* intent on controlling even the smallest minutiae of the text. Though he at one time considered supplying biographical and explanatory notes to the poems, he finally decided against such a scheme, concluding, in his letter to Smith of 12 November 1887, "I am correcting them carefully, and *that* must suffice." On 13 January 1888, he wrote, regarding the six-volume edition of his collected works published in 1868 which was to serve as the printer's copy for the final edition: "I have thoroughly corrected the six volumes of the Works, and can let you have them at once." . . . Browning evidently kept a sharp eye on the production of all sixteen of the volumes, including those later volumes. . . . Browning returned proof for Volume 3 on 6 May 1888, commenting, "I have had, as usual, to congratulate myself on

the scrupulous accuracy of the Printers"; on 31 December he returned proofs of Volume 11, "corrected carefully"; and he returned "the corrected Proofs of Vol. XV" on 1 May 1889.

Throughout his long career, then, Browning continuously revised and corrected his works. Furthermore, his publishers took care to follow his directions exactly, accepting his changes and incorporating them into each successive edition. This is not to say that no one else had any effect whatsoever on Browning's text: Elizabeth Barrett made suggestions for revisions to *A Soul's Tragedy* and *Dramatic Romances and Lyrics*. Browning accepted some suggestions and rejected others, and those which he accepted we regard as his own. Mrs. Orr reports that Browning sent proof sheets to Joseph Milsand, a friend in France, for corrections (*Life*, p. 183), and that Browning accepted suggestions from friends and readers for the corrections of errors in his printed works. In some of the editions, there are slight evidences of minor house-styling in capitalization and the indication of quotations. But the evidence of Browning's own careful attention to revisions and corrections in both his manuscripts and proof sheets assures us that other persons played only a very minor role in the development of his text. We conclude that the vast majority of the alterations in the texts listed above as Primary Materials are Browning's own, and that only Browning's final corrected text, the result of years of careful work by the poet himself, reflects his full intentions.

The first impression of Browning's final collected edition (i.e., 1888-1889a) is not in and of itself the poet's final corrected text. By the spring of 1889 some of the early volumes of the first impression were already sold out, and by mid-August it was evident that a new one would be required. About this time James Dykes Campbell, Honorary Secretary of the London Browning Society, was informed by Browning that he was making further corrections to be incorporated into the new impression. According to Dykes Campbell, Browning had corrected the first ten volumes and offered to transcribe the corrections into Dykes Campbell's copy of 1888-1889a before leaving for Italy. The volumes altered in Browning's hand are now in the British Library and contain on the flyleaf of Volume I Dykes Campbell's note explaining precisely what happened. Of course, Dykes Campbell's copy was not the one used by the printer for the second impression. Nevertheless, these changes are indisputably Browning's and are those which, according to his own statement, he proposed to make in the new impression. This set of corrections carries, therefore, great authority.

Equally authoritative is a second set of corrections, also in Browning's hand, for part of 1888-1889a. In the poet's possession at the time of his death, this handwritten list was included in lot 179 of Sotheby, Wilkinson, and Hodge's auction of Browning materials in 1913; it is today located in the Brown University Library. The list contains corrections only to Volumes 4-10 of 1888-1889a. We know that Browning, on 26 July 1889, had completed and sent to Smith "the corrections for Vol. III in readiness for whenever you need them." By the latter part of August, according to Dykes Campbell, the poet had finished corrections for Volumes 1-10. Browning left for Italy on 29 August. The condition of the Brown University list does not indicate that it was ever used by the printer. Thus we surmise that the Brown list (completing the corrections through volume 10) may be the poet's copy of another list sent to his publisher. Whatever the case, the actual documents used by the printers—a set of marked volumes or handwritten lists—are not known to exist. A possible exception is a marked copy of *Red Cotton Night-Cap Country* (now in the Berg Collection of the New York Public Library) which seems to have been used by printers. Further materials used in preparing Browning's final edition may yet appear.

The matter is complicated further because neither set of corrections of 1888-1889a corresponds exactly to each other nor to the 1889 second impression. Each set contains corrections the other omits, and in a few cases the sets present alternative corrections of the same error. Our study of the Dykes Campbell copy of 1888-1889a reveals fifteen discrepancies between its corrections and the 1889 second impression. The Brown University list, which contains far fewer corrections, varies from the second impression in thirteen instances. Though neither of these sets of corrections was used by the printers, both are authoritative; we consider them legitimate textual variants, and record them as such. The lists are, of course, useful when emendation of the copy-text is required.

The value of the Dykes Campbell copy of 1888-1889a and the Brown University list is not that they render Browning's text perfect. The corrections to 1888-1889a must have existed in at least one other, still more authoritative form: the documents which Browning sent to his publisher. That this is so is indicated by the presence of required corrections in the second impression which neither the Dykes Campbell copy nor the Brown University list calls for. The significance of the existing sets of corrections is that they clearly indicate two important points: Browning's direct and active interest in the preparation of a corrected second impression of his final collected edition; and, given the high degree of correspondence between the two sets of corrections and the affected lines of the second impression, the concern of the printers to follow the poet's directives.

The second impression of 1888-1889 incorporated most of Browning's corrections to the first ten volumes of the first impression. There is no evidence whatever that any corrections beyond those which Browning sent to his publisher in the summer of 1889 were ever made. We choose, therefore, the 1889 corrected second impression of volumes 1-10 as copy-text for the works in those volumes. Corrections to the first impression were achieved by cutting the affected letters or punctuation out of the stereotype plates and pressing or soldering in the correct pieces of type. The corrected plates were then used for many copies, without changing the date on the title pages (except, of course, in volumes 17 [*Asolando*] and 18 [*New Poems*], added to the set by the publishers in 1894 and 1914 respectively). External evidence from publishers' catalogues and the advertisements bound into some volumes of 1889 indicate that copies of this impression were produced as late as 1913, although the dates on the title pages of volumes 1-16 remained 1889. Extensive plate deterioration is characteristic of the later copies, and use of the Hinman collator on early and late examples of 1889 reveals that the inserted corrections were somewhat fragile, some of them having decayed or disappeared entirely as the plates aged. (See Allan C. Dooley, "Browning's *Poetical Works* of 1888-1889," *SBHC* 7:1 [1978], 43-69.)

We do not use as copy-text volumes 11-16 of 1889, because there is no present evidence indicating that Browning exercised substantial control over this part of the second impression of 1888-1889. We do know that he made one correction, which he requested in a letter to Smith quoted by Hancher:

> I have just had pointed out to [me] that an error, I supposed corrected, still is to be found in the 13th Volume—(Aristophanes' Apology) page 143, line 9, where the word should be Opora—without an i. I should like it altered, if that may be possible.

This correction was indeed made in the second impression. Our collations of copies of volumes 11-16 of 1889a and 1889 show no other intentional changes. The later copies do show, however, extensive type batter, numerous scratches, and irregular inking. Therefore our copy-text for the works in the last six volumes of 1888-1889 is volumes 11-16 of 1888-1889a.

IV VARIANTS

In this edition we record, with a very few exceptions discussed below, all variants from the copy text appearing in the manuscripts and in the editions under Browning's control. Our purpose in doing this is two-fold.

1. We enable the reader to reconstruct the text of a work as it stood at the various stages of its development.

2. We provide the materials necessary to an understanding of how Browning's growth and development as an artist are reflected in his successive revisions to his works.

As a consequence of this policy our variant listings inevitably contain some variants that were not created by Browning; printer's errors and readings that may result from house-styling will appear occasionally. But the evidence that Browning assumed responsibility for what was printed, and that he considered and used unorthodox punctuation as part of his meaning, is so persuasive that we must record even the smallest and oddest variants. The following examples, characteristic of Browning's revisions, illustrate the point:

> *Pauline,* l. 700:
>> 1833: I am prepared—I have made life my own—
>> 1868: I am prepared: I have made life my own.
> "Evelyn Hope," l. 41:
>> 1855: I have lived, I shall say, so much since then,
>> 1865: I have lived (I shall say) so much since then,
> "Bishop Blougram's Apology," l. 267:
>> 1855: That's the first cabin-comfort I secure—
>> 1865: That's the first-cabin comfort I secure:
> *The Ring and the Book,* Book 11 ("Guido"), l. 1064:
>> 1869: What if you give up boys' and girls' fools'-play
>> 1872: What if you give up boy and girl fools'-play
>> 1889a: What if you give up boy-and-girl-fools' play

We have concluded that Browning himself is nearly always responsible for such changes. But even if he only accepted these changes (rather than originating them), their effect on syntax, rhythm, and meaning is so significant that they must be recorded in our variant listings.

The only variants we do not record are those which strongly appear to result from systematic house-styling. For example, Browning nowhere indicated that he wished to use typography to influence meaning, and our inference is that any changes in line-spacing, depth of paragraph indentation, and the like, were the responsibility of the printers of the various editions, not the poet himself. House-styling was also very probably the cause of certain variants in the apparatus of Browning's plays, including variants in stage directions which involve a change only in manner of statement, such as *Enter Hampden* instead of

Hampden enters; variants in the printing of stage directions, such as *Aside* instead of *aside,* or [*Aside.*] instead of [*Aside*], or [*Strafford.*] instead of [*Strafford*]; variants in character designations, such as *Lady Carlisle* instead of *Car* or *Carlisle.* Browning also accepted current convention for indicating quotations (see section V below). Neither do we list changes in type face (except when used for emphasis), nor the presence or absence of a period at the end of the title of a work.

V ALTERATIONS TO THE COPY-TEXT

We have rearranged the sequence of works in the copy-text, so that they appear in the order of their first publication. This process involves the restoration to the original order of the poems included in *Dramatic Lyrics, Dramatic Romances and Lyrics,* and *Men and Women.* We realize, of course, that Browning himself was responsible for the rearrangement of these poems in the various collected editions; in his prefatory note for the 1888-1889 edition, however, he indicates that he desired a chronological presentation:

> The poems that follow are again, as before, printed in chronological order; but only so far as proves compatible with the prescribed size of each volume, which necessitates an occasional change in the distribution of its contents.

We would like both to indicate Browning's stated intentions about the placement of his poems and to present the poems in the order which suggests Browning's development as a poet. We have chosen, therefore, to present the poems in order of their first publication, with an indication in the notes as to their respective subsequent placement. We also include the tables of contents of the editions listed as Primary Materials above.

We have regularized or modernized the copy-text in the following minor ways:

1. We do not place a period at the end of the title of a work, though the copy-text does.

2. In some of Browning's editions, including the copy-text, the first word of each work is printed in capital letters. We have used the modern practice of capitalizing only the first letter.

3. The inconsistent use of both an ampersand and the word *and* has been regularized to the use of *and.*

4. We have eliminated the space between the two parts of a contraction; thus the copy-text's *it 's* is printed as *it's,* for example.

5. We uniformly place periods and commas within closing quotation marks.

6. We have employed throughout the modern practice of indicating quoted passages with quotation marks only at the beginning and end of the quotation. Throughout Browning's career, no matter which publisher or printer was handling his works, this matter was treated very inconsistently. In some of the poet's manuscripts and in most of his first editions, quotations are indicated by quotation marks only at the beginning and end. In the collected editions of 1863 and 1865, issued by Chapman and Hall, some quoted passages have quotation marks at the beginning of each line of the quotation, while others follow modern practice. In Smith, Elder's collected editions of 1868 and 1888-1889, quotation marks usually appear at the beginning of each line of a quotation. We have regularized and modernized what seems a matter of house-styling in both copy-text and variants.

The remaining way in which the copy-text is altered is by emendation. Our policy is to emend the copy-text to eliminate apparent errors of either Browning or his printers. It is evident that Browning did make errors and overlook mistakes, as shown by the following example from "One Word More," the last poem in *Men and Women*. Stanza sixteen of the copy-text opens with the following lines:

What, there's nothing in the moon noteworthy?
Nay: for if that moon could love a mortal,
Use, to charm him (so to fit a fancy,
All her magic ('tis the old sweet mythos)
She . . .

Clearly the end punctuation in the third line is incorrect. A study of the various texts is illuminating. Following are the readings of the line in each of the editions for which Browning was responsible:

MS:	fancy)	1855:	fancy)	1865:	fancy)	1888:	fancy
P:	fancy)	1863:	fancy)	1868:	fancy)	1889:	fancy,

The omission of one parenthesis in 1888 was almost certainly a printer's error. Browning, in the Dykes Campbell copy corrections to 1888-1889a, missed or ignored the error. However, in the Brown University list of corrections, he indicated that *fancy* should be followed by a comma. This is the way the line appears in the corrected second impression of Volume 4, but the correction at best satisfies the demands of syntax only partially. Browning might have written the line:

> Use, to charm him, so to fit a fancy,

or, to maintain parallelism between the third and fourth lines:

> Use, to charm him (so to fit a fancy),

or he might simply have restored the earlier reading. Oversights of this nature demand emendation, and our choice would be to restore the punctuation of the manuscript through 1868. All of our emendations will be based, as far as possible, on the historical collation of the passage involved, the grammatical demands of the passage in context, and the poet's treatment of other similar passages. Fortunately, the multiple editions of most of the works provide the editor with ample textual evidence to make an informed and useful emendation.

All emendations to the copy-text are listed at the beginning of the Editorial Notes for each work. The variant listings for the copy-text also incorporate the emendations, which are preceded and followed there by the symbol indicating an editor's note.

VI APPARATUS

1. *Variants.* In presenting the variants from the copy-text, we list at the bottom of each page readings from the known manuscripts, proof sheets of the editions when we have located them, and the first and subsequent editions.

A variant is generally preceded and followed by a pickup and a drop word (example a). No note terminates with a punctuation mark unless the punctuation mark comes at the end of the line; if a variant drops or adds a punctuation mark, the next word is added (example b). If the normal pickup word has appeared previously in the same line, the note begins with the word preceding it. If the normal drop word appears subsequently in the line, the next word is added (example c). If a capitalized pickup word occurs within the line, it is accompanied by the preceding word (example d). No pickup or drop words, however, are used for any variant consisting of an internal change, for example a hyphen in a compounded word, an apostrophe, a tense change or a spelling change (example e). A change in capitalization within a line of poetry will be preceded by a pickup word, for which, within an entry containing other variants, the < > is suitable (example f). No drop word is used when the variant comes at the end of a line (example g).

a. 611| *1840*:but that appeared   *1863*:but this appeared
b. variant at end of line: 109| *1840*:intrigue:" *1863*:intrigue.
    variant within line: 82| *1840*:forests like *1863*:forests, like
c. 132| *1840*:too sleeps; but *1863*:too sleeps: but   77| *1840*:that night
    by *1863*:that, night by night, *1888*:by night
d. 295| *1840*:at Padua to repulse the *1863*:at Padua who repulsed the
e. 284| *1840*:are *1863*:were
    344| *1840*:dying-day, *1863*:dying day,
f. capitalization change with no other variants: 741| *1840*:
    retaining Will, *1863*:will,
    with other variants: 843| *1840*:Was < > Him back! Why *1863*:Is
    < > back!" Why *1865*:him
g. 427| *1840*:dregs: *1863*:dregs.

Each recorded variant will be assumed to be incorporated in the next edition if there is no indication otherwise. This rule applies even in cases where the only change occurs in 1888-1889, although it means that the variant note duplicates the copy-text. A variant listing, then, traces the history of a line and brings it forward to the point where it matches the copy-text.

With regard to manuscript readings, our emphasis is on the textual development and sequence of revisions; visual details of the manuscripts are kept to a minimum. For economy of space, we use formulae such as §crossed out and replaced above by§, but these often cannot report fine details such as whether, when two words were crossed out, the accompanying punctuation was precisely cancelled also. Our MS entries provide enough information to reconstruct with reasonable accuracy B's initial and revised manuscript readings, but they cannot substitute for direct scrutiny of the documents themselves.

It should be noted that we omit drop words in manuscript entries where the final reading is identical to the printed editions—thus

MS:Silence, and all that ghastly §crossed out and replaced above by§ tinted pageant, base

Printed editions: Silence, and all that tinted pageant, base

is entered as

MS:that ghastly §crossed out and replaced above by§ tinted

in our variant listings.

An editor's note always refers to the single word or mark of punctuation immediately preceding or following the comment, unless otherwise specified.

In Browning's plays, all character designations which happen to occur in variant listings are standardized to the copy-text reading. In listing variants in the plays, we ignore character designations unless the designation comes within a numbered line. In such a case, the character designation is treated as any other word, and can be used as a pickup or drop word. When a character designation is used as a pickup word, however, the rule excluding capitalized pickup words (except at the beginning of a line) does not apply, and we do not revert to the next earliest uncapitalized pickup word.

2. *Line numbers.* Poetic lines are numbered in the traditional manner, taking one complete poetic line as one unit of counting. In prose passages the unit of counting is the type line of this edition.

3. *Table of signs in variant listings.* We have avoided all symbols and signs used by Browning himself. The following is a table of the signs used in the variant notes:

§ . . . §	Editor's note
< >	Words omitted
/	Line break
/ / , / / / , . . .	Line break plus one or more lines without internal variants

4 *Annotations.* In general principle, we have annotated proper names, phrases that function as proper names, and words or groups of words the full meaning of which requires factual, historical, or literary background. Thus we have attempted to hold interpretation to a minimum, although we realize that the act of selection itself is to some extent interpretive.

Notes, particularly on historical figures and events, tend to fullness and even to the tangential and unessential. As a result, some of the information provided may seem unnecessary to the scholar. On the other hand, it is not possible to assume that all who use this edition are fully equipped to assimilate unaided all of Browning's copious literary, historical, and mythological allusions. Thus we have directed our efforts toward a diverse audience.

TABLES

1. *Manuscripts.* We have located manuscripts for the following of Browning's works; the list is chronological.

Paracelsus
    Forster and Dyce Collection,
    Victoria and Albert Museum, London
Colombe's Birthday
    New York Public Library
Christmas-Eve and Easter-Day
    Forster and Dyce Collection,
    Victoria and Albert Museum, London
"Love Among the Ruins"
    Lowell Collection,
    Houghton Library, Harvard University
"The Twins"
    Pierpont Morgan Library, New York
"One Word More"
    Pierpont Morgan Library, New York
"James Lee's Wife," ll. 244-69
    Armstrong Browning Library, Baylor University
"May and Death"
    Armstrong Browning Library, Baylor University
"A Face"
    Armstrong Browning Library, Baylor University
Dramatis Personae
    Pierpont Morgan Library, New York
The Ring and the Book
    British Library, London
Balaustion's Adventure
    Balliol College Library, Oxford
Prince Hohenstiel-Schwangau
    Balliol College Library, Oxford
Fifine at the Fair
    Balliol College Library, Oxford
Red Cotton Night-Cap Country
    Balliol College Library, Oxford
Aristophanes' Apology
    Balliol College Library, Oxford
The Inn Album
    Balliol College Library, Oxford
Of Pacchiarotto, and How He Worked in Distemper
    Balliol College Library, Oxford
"Hervé Riel"
    Pierpont Morgan Library, New York

The Agamemnon of Aeschylus
    Balliol College Library, Oxford
La Saisiaz and The Two Poets of Croisic
    Balliol College Library, Oxford
Dramatic Idylls
    Balliol College Library, Oxford
Dramatic Idylls, Second Series
    Balliol College Library, Oxford
Jocoseria
    Balliol College Library, Oxford
Ferishtah's Fancies
    Balliol College Library, Oxford
Parleyings With Certain People of Importance in Their Day
    Balliol College Library, Oxford
Asolando
    Pierpont Morgan Library, New York

We have been unable to locate manuscripts for the following works, and request that persons with information about any of them communicate with us.

Pauline   *The Return of the Druses*
Strafford   *A Blot in the 'Scutcheon*
Sordello   *Dramatic Romances and Lyrics*
Pippa Passes   *Luria*
King Victor and King Charles   *A Soul's Tragedy*
"Essay on Chatterton"   "Essay on Shelley"
Dramatic Lyrics   *Men and Women*

   2. *Editions referred to in Volume XII.* The following editions have been used in preparing the text and variants presented in this volume. The dates given below are used as symbols in the variant listings at the foot of each page.

   1875   *Aristophanes' Apology; Including a Transcript from Euripides:
           Being the Last Adventure of Balaustion.*
               London: Smith, Elder and Company.

   1889a   *The Poetical Works.*
               Volumes 9-16. London: Smith, Elder and Company.

3. *Short titles and abbreviations.* The following short forms of reference have been used in the Editorial Notes:

Athenaeus	Athenaeus, *Deipnosophists.*
B	Browning
Correspondence	*The Brownings' Correspondence*, ed. P. Kelley et al. Winfield, KS, 1984-.
DeVane, *Hbk.*	W. C. DeVane. *A Browning Handbook*, 2nd ed. New York, 1955.
EBB	Elizabeth Barrett Browning
Fragmenta	*Tragicorum Graecorum Fragmenta*, ed. A. Nauck, 2nd ed. [1856] Leipsig, 1889.
HL	*Heracles*, in *Euripides*, Vol. 3 (Loeb Classical Library), ed. and tr. D. Kovacs. London, 1998. [Greek text only.]
HN	*Heracles*, in *Euripidis Tragoediae*, ed. A. Nauck, 2nd ed. Leipsig, 1866.
HP	*Heracles*, in *Euripides With an English Commentary, by F. A. Paley*, 3 vols. London, 1857-60.
Hood	*Letters of Robert Browning Collected by Thomas J. Wise*, ed. T. L. Hood. New Haven, CT, 1933.
Irvine and Honan	W. Irvine and P. Honan. *The Book, the Ring, and the Poet.* New York, 1974.
Lemprière	*Lemprière's Classical Dictionary* [1788], ed. F. A. Wright. London, 1949.
Liddell and Scott	*A Greek-English Lexicon*, comp. H. G. Liddell and R. Scott, et al. Oxford, eds. of 1843, 1871, 1996.
Life of Sophocles	*Life of Sophocles* in *Sophoclis Fabulae*, ed. A. C. Pearson. Oxford, 1957.
Meineke	*Fragmenta Comicorum Graecorum*, ed. A. Meineke, 5 vols. Berlin, 1839-57.
Nauck	*Euripidis Tragoediae*, Vol. 1, ed. A. Nauck. Leipsig, 1866.
OED	*The Oxford English Dictionary*, 2nd ed. Oxford, 1989.
Orr, *Life*	Mrs. Sutherland Orr. *Life and Letters of Robert Browning.* 2nd ed. London, 1891.
Reconstruction	*The Browning Collections, a Reconstruction, with Other Memorabilia*, comp. P. Kelley and B. A. Coley. Waco, TX; New York; Winfield, KS; and London, 1984.

Scholia	*Scholia Graeca in Aristophanem,* ed. Fr. Düb-ner. Paris, 1842.

Citations and quotations from the Bible refer to the King James Version unless otherwise specified.

Citations and quotations from Shakespeare refer to T*he Riverside Shakespeare,* 2nd ed., ed. G. B. Evans, et al., Boston, 1997.

ACKNOWLEDGMENTS

For providing services and money which have made it possible for us to prepare this volume, the following institutions have our gratitude: Baylor University; the Armstrong Browning Library and its director, Mairi Rennie; the Kent State University Research Council, Department of English, and Institute for Bibliography and Editing; and the Ohio University Press.

For making available to us materials under their care we thank the Armstrong Browning Library, Baylor University; the Balliol College Library, the Bodleian Library, the English Faculty Library, and the Classics section of the Ashmolean Library, all of Oxford University; the London Library; the Alexander H. Turnbull Library, Wellington, New Zealand; Mairi Rennie, Director, Armstrong Browning Library; Penelope Bulloch, Librarian of Balliol; and Philip Kelley.

For scholarly assistance in preparing this volume, we particularly thank the following: Tony Dodd, Nan Dunbar, Philip Kelley, David Kovacs, S. W. Reid.

ARISTOPHANES' APOLOGY; INCLUDING A
TRANSCRIPT FROM EURIPIDES:
BEING THE LAST ADVENTURE OF BALAUSTION

Text edited by Rita S. Patteson
Annotations by Paul D. L. Turner

PERSONS IN THE
TRANSCRIBED PLAY OF "HERAKLES"

AMPHITRUON
MEGARA
LUKOS
HERAKLES
IRIS
LUTTA (*Madness*)
Messenger
THESEUS
Choros of Aged Thebans

ARISTOPHANES' APOLOGY; INCLUDING A
TRANSCRIPT FROM EURIPIDES:
BEING THE LAST ADVENTURE OF BALAUSTION

Title| *P1875:ARISTOPHANES' APOLOGY / INCLUDING / A TRANSCRIPT FROM
EURIPIDES / BEING THE / LAST ADVENTURE OF BALAUSTION / BY / ROBERT
BROWNING / IN TWO VOLUMES / VOL. I   CP1875:*§last two lines cancelled§

ϑὺκ ἔσθω κενέβρει· ὁπόταν δὲ θύῃς τι, κάλει με.
I eat no carrion; when you sacrifice
Some cleanly creature—call me for a slice!

Epigraph| MS:slice!   *P1875*:slice.   *CP1875*:slice!

ARISTOPHANES' APOLOGY

1875

Wind, wave, and bark, bear Euthukles and me,
Balaustion, from—not sorrow but despair,
Not memory but the present and its pang!
Athenai, live thou hearted in my heart:
₅ Never, while I live, may I see thee more,
Never again may these repugnant orbs
Ache themselves blind before the hideous pomp,
The ghastly mirth which mocked thine overthrow
—Death's entry, Haides' outrage!

                       Doomed to die,—
₁₀ Fire should have flung a passion of embrace
About thee till, resplendently inarmed,
(Temple by temple folded to his breast,
All thy white wonder fainting out in ash)
Lightly some vaporous sigh of soul escaped,
₁₅ And so the Immortals bade Athenai back!
Or earth might sunder and absorb thee, save,
Buried below Olumpos and its gods,
Akropolis to dominate her realm
For Koré, and console the ghosts; or, sea,
₂₀ What if thy watery plural vastitude,
Rolling unanimous advance, had rushed,
Might upon might, a moment,—stood, one stare,
Sea-face to city-face, thy glaucous wave

---

§MS in Balliol College Library, Oxford. Ed. P1875, CP1875, 1875, 1889a; see Editorial Notes§
¹| MS:Bark, §crossed out and replaced above by§ Bank §crossed out§ wind, §altered to§
Wind, and §crossed out§ wave, and, bark, §last two words and comma inserted above§
³| MS:memory, but *P1875:*memory but   ⁵| MS:while I *P1875:*while I
⁹| MS:entry, Hades' *P1875:*entry, Haides'   ¹²| MS:Temple *P1875:*(Temple
¹³| MS:fainted §altered to§ fainting < > ash, *P1875:*ash)
¹⁴| MS:Some < > soul went §crossed out and replaced above by§ had lightly up, §crossed out
and replaced above by§ 'scaped, *1889a:*Lightly some < > soul escaped,
¹⁶| MS:Or Earth could §crossed out and replaced above by§ might *P1875:*earth
¹⁹| MS:or, Sea, *P1875:*sea,   ²²| MS:stare— *P1875:*stare,

Glassing that marbled last magnificence,—
25 Till fate's pale tremulous foam-flower tipped the grey,
And when wave broke and overswarmed and, sucked
To bounds back, multitudinously ceased,
Let land again breathe unconfused with sea,
Attiké was, Athenai was not now!

30 Such end I could have borne, for I had shared.
But this which, glanced at, aches within my orbs
To blinding,—bear me thence, bark, wind and wave!
Me, Euthukles, and, hearted in each heart,
Athenai, undisgraced as Pallas' self,
35 Bear to my birthplace, Helios' island-bride,
Zeus' darling: thither speed us, homeward-bound,
Wafted already twelve hours' sail away
From horror, nearer by one sunset Rhodes!

Why should despair be? Since, distinct above
40 Man's wickedness and folly, flies the wind
And floats the cloud, free transport for our soul
Out of its fleshly durance dim and low,—
Since disembodied soul anticipates
(Thought-borne as now, in rapturous unrestraint)
45 Above all crowding, crystal silentness,
Above all noise, a silver solitude:—
Surely, where thought so bears soul, soul in time
May permanently bide, "assert the wise,"
There live in peace, there work in hope once more—
50 O nothing doubt, Philemon!   Greed and strife,
Hatred and cark and care, what place have they
In yon blue liberality of heaven?
How the sea helps!   How rose-smit earth will rise

24| MS:magnificence, *P1875*:magnificence,—   28| MS:And land < > breathed
1889a:Let land < > breathe   32| MS:bark §crossed out and restored§ < > wave—
P1875:wave!   34| MS:self,— *P1875*:self,   38| MS:horror, and a sunset
nearer Rhodes!   *1889a*:horror, nearer by one sunset Rhodes!
45-46| MS:§lines marked for transposition§   45| MS:chrystal *P1875*:crystal
46| MS:solitude,— *P1875*:solitude:—   49| MS:more, *1889a*:more—

Breast-high thence, some bright morning, and be Rhodes!
55 Heaven, earth and sea, my warrant—in their name,
Believe—o'er falsehood, truth is surely sphered,
O'er ugliness beams beauty, o'er this world
Extends that realm where, "as the wise assert,"
Philemon, thou shalt see Euripides
60 Clearer than mortal sense perceived the man!

A sunset nearer Rhodes, by twelve hours' sweep
Of surge secured from horror?   Rather say,
Quieted out of weakness into strength.
I dare invite, survey the scene my sense
65 Staggered to apprehend: for, disenvolved
From the mere outside anguish and contempt,
Slowly a justice centred in a doom
Reveals itself.   Ay, pride succumbed to pride,
Oppression met the oppressor and was matched.
70 Athenai's vaunt braved Sparté's violence
Till, in the shock, prone fell Peiraios, low
Rampart and bulwark lay, as,—timing stroke
Of hammer, axe, and beam hoist, poised and swung,—
The very flute-girls blew their laughing best,
75 In dance about the conqueror while he bade
Music and merriment help enginery
Batter down, break to pieces all the trust
Of citizens once, slaves now.   See what walls
Play substitute for the long double range
80 Themistoklean, heralding a guest
From harbour on to citadel!   Each side
Their senseless walls demolished stone by stone,

---

[61]| MS:nearer Rhodes; by twelve-hours'   *P1875:*nearer Rhodes, by twelve hours'
[67]| MS:in the §crossed out and replaced above by§ a   [69]| MS:and its match.   *1889a:*and
was matched.   [73]| MS:hammer, pickaxe, beam hoist, §last word and comma inserted
above§ poised   *P1875:*hammer, axe, <> and poised   *1889a:*hammer, <> hoist, poised
[77]| MS:all that trust   *P1875:*all their trust,   *1889a:*all the trust   [78]| *P1875:*Those
citizens   *1889a:*Of citizens   [80]| MS:heralding §last three letters added§ of §crossed out
and replaced above by crossed-out word, *all*§ the way §last two words crossed out and replaced
above by one word§ a   [81]| MS:side,   *P1875:*side   [82]| MS:Witnessing §crossed out
and replaced above by two words§ The §crossed out and replaced above by§ Of senseless

See,—outer wall as stonelike,—heads and hearts,—
Athenai's terror-stricken populace!
85 Prattlers, tongue-tied in crouching abjectness,—
Braggarts, who wring hands wont to flourish swords—
Sophist and rhetorician, demagogue,
(Argument dumb, authority a jest)
Dikast and heliast, pleader, litigant,
90 Quack-priest, sham-prophecy-retailer, scout
O' the customs, sycophant, whate'er the style,
Altar-scrap-snatcher, pimp and parasite,—
Rivalities at truce now each with each,
Stupefied mud-banks,—such an use they serve!
95 While the one order which performs exact
To promise, functions faithful last as first,
What is it but the city's lyric troop,
Chantress and psaltress, flute-girl, dancing-girl?
Athenai's harlotry takes laughing care
100 Their patron miss no pipings, late she loved,
But deathward tread at least the kordax-step.

Die then, who pulled such glory on your heads!
There let it grind to powder!   Perikles!
The living are the dead now: death be life!
105 Why should the sunset yonder waste its wealth?
Prove thee Olympian!   If my heart supply
Inviolate the structure,—true to type,

---

*P1875:*The senseless   *1889a:*Their senseless   83| MS:See, §word and comma in margin§
An §crossed out and replaced below by dash§ outer wall of §crossed out and replaced above
by§ as   84| MS:populace: *P1875:*populace!   86| MS:sword,—   *P1875:*swords—
88| MS:jest)—   *P1875:*jest)   89| MS:§line added§   91| MS:customs; sycophant
<> style;   *P1875:*customs, sycophant <> style,   92| MS:parasite,   *P1875:*parasite,—
93| MS:Obscenities at   *P1875:*Rivalities at   94| MS:mud-banks,—that's the use   *1889a:*
mud-banks,—such an use   95| MS:order that performs   *P1875:*order which performs
96| MS:Its §over To§ promise   *P1875:*To promise   97| MS:§line added§
98| MS:§line added in margin§ dancing girl?   *P1875:*dancing-girl?   99| MS:The lyric
§last two words crossed out and replaced below by one word§ Athenai's   100| MS:Their
city §crossed out and replaced above by§ patron <> pipings, late §inserted above§ she so
§crossed out§ loved,   101| MS:But dance §crossed out and replaced above by two words§
deathward tread <> kordax-step. to death. §last two words and period crossed out§
102| MS:heads, §comma altered to exclamation point§   103| MS:And §crossed out and
replaced above by§ There let   105| MS:§line added§

Build me some spirit-place no flesh shall find,
As Pheidias may inspire thee: slab on slab,
110   Renew Athenai, quarry out the cloud,
Convert to gold yon west extravagance!
'Neath Propulaia, from Akropolis
By vapoury grade and grade, gold all the way,
Step to thy snow-Pnux, mount thy Bema-cloud,
115   Thunder and lighten thence a Hellas through
That shall be better and more beautiful
And too august for Sparté's foot to spurn!
Chasmed in the crag, again our Theatre
Predominates, one purple: Staghunt-month,
120   Brings it not Dionusia?   Hail, the Three!
Aischulos, Sophokles, Euripides
Compete, gain prize or lose prize, godlike still.
Nay, lest they lack the old god-exercise—
Their noble want the unworthy,—as of old,
125   (How otherwise should patience crown their might?)
What if each find his ape promoted man,
His censor raised for antic service still?
Some new Hermippos to pelt Perikles,
Kratinos to swear Pheidias robbed a shrine,
130   Eruxis—I suspect, Euripides,
No brow will ache because with mop and mow
He gibes my poet!   There's a dog-faced dwarf
That gets to godship somehow, yet retains
His apehood in the Egyptian hierarchy,
135   More decent, indecorous just enough:
Why should not dog-ape, graced in due degree,

108| MS:me the §crossed out and replaced above by§ some   109| MS:thee! slab *P1875:*
thee; slab *1889a:*thee: slab   112| MS:'Neath *1889a:*'Neath §emended to§ 'Neath
§see Editorial Notes§   115| MS:thence some §crossed out and replaced above by§ a
117| MS:And greater than Lusandros' §last three words crossed out and replaced above by
four words§ too august for Sparte's foot dares §crossed out and replaced above by§ to
119| MS:staghunt-month— *P1875:*purple: Staghunt-month,   124| MS:noble by the
unworthier §altered to§ unworthy *P1875:*noble want the   125| MS:—How < >
might?— *P1875:*(How < > might?)   127| MS:still, *P1875:*still?
129| MS:Krateinos *P1875:*Kratinos   130| MS:Or Platon—I *P1875:*Eruxis—I
132| MS:poet? There's *1889a:*poet! There's   135| MS:decent yet < > enough—
*P1875:*enough: *1889a:*decent, indecorous just enough: 136| MS:not Platon, graced

Grow Momos as thou Zeus?   Or didst thou sigh
Rightly with thy Makaria?   "After life,
Better no sentiency than turbulence;
140   Death cures the low contention."   Be it so!
Yet progress means contention, to my mind.

Euthukles, who, except for love that speaks,
Art silent by my side while words of mine
Provoke that foe from which escape is vain
145   Henceforward, wake Athenai's fate and fall,—
Memories asleep as, at the altar-foot
Those Furies in the Oresteian song,—
Do I amiss who, wanting strength, use craft,
Advance upon the foe I cannot fly,
150   Nor feign a snake is dormant though it gnaw?
That fate and fall, once bedded in our brain,
Roots itself past upwrenching; but coaxed forth,
Encouraged out to practise fork and fang,—
Perhaps, when satiate with prompt sustenance,
155   It may pine, likelier die than if left swell
In peace by our pretension to ignore,
Or pricked to threefold fury, should our stamp

---

*P1875:*not dog-ape, graced   137| MS:thou, §comma crossed out§ Zeus? Or
138| MS:thy Makaria "After   *P1875:*thy Makaria? "After   139| MS:turbulence: *P1875:*
turbulence;   142| MS:except for love   *1889a:*except a love   144| MS:escape were
vain   *1889a:*escape is vain   145-48| MS:Henceforward,—our Athenai's <> fall,— / Do
<> who measures wile with strength, §last four words crossed out and replaced above by four
words§ wanting strength use craft,   *P1875:*Henceforward, wake Athenai's <> / Do   *1889a:*/
Memories <> altar-foot / Those <> song,— / <> strength, use   149| MS:§line added§   150| MS:feign the §crossed out and replaced above by§ a
151| MS:in the §crossed out and replaced above by§ our   152| MS:upwrenching: but
§inserted above§ coaxed it §crossed out§ forth,   *P1875:*upwrenching; but   153| MS:Encouraged it §crossed out and replaced above by§ thus to   *P1875:*Encouraged out to
154| MS:Possibly, satiate *1889a:*Perhaps, when satiate   155| MS:It may §inserted above§
pines §altered to§ pine off far §inserted above§ likelier than left   *1889a:*pine, likelier die
than if left   156| MS:§solidus and line added in margin§ in §altered to§ In peace, by
*P1875:*peace by   157| MS:to threefold §inserted above§ fury. §period altered to comma§
Treat the tragic theme §last four words crossed out§ should our stamp

Bruise and not brain the pest.

A middle course!
What hinders that we treat this tragic theme
160 As the Three taught when either woke some woe,
—How Klutaimnestra hated, what the pride
Of Iokasté, why Medeia clove
Nature asunder.   Small rebuked by large,
We felt our puny hates refine to air,
165 Our poor prides sink, prevent the humbling hand,
Our petty passions purify their tide.
So, Euthukles, permit the tragedy
To re-enact itself, this voyage through,
Till sunsets end and sunrise brighten Rhodes!
170 Majestic on the stage of memory,
Peplosed and kothorned, let Athenai fall
Once more, nay, oft again till life conclude,
Lent for the lesson: Choros, I and thou!
What else in life seems piteous any more
175 After such pity, or proves terrible
Beside such terror?

Still—since Phrunichos
Offended, by too premature a touch
Of that Milesian smart-place freshly frayed—
(Ah, my poor people, whose prompt remedy
180 Was—fine the poet, not reform thyself!)
Beware precipitate approach!   Rehearse
Rather the prologue, well a year away,

158-59| MS:§lines added§   159| MS:theme, *P1875:*theme   160| MS:taught, when
<> woe   *P1875:* taught when <> woe,   163| MS:asunder? Small   *P1875:*asunder.
Small   164| MS:We §over illegible word, perhaps *I*§ felt my §crossed out and replaced
above by§ our   165| MS:My §crossed out and replaced above by§ Our prides as poor
prevent   *1889a:*Our poor prides sink, prevent   166| MS:My §crossed out and replaced
above by§ Our <> passion <> its   *1889a:*passions <> their   172| MS:more—nay
*P1875:*more, nay   173| MS:choros   *P1875:*choros   174| MS:Since what in
*P1875:*What else in   176| MS:§¶§Still—for §crossed out and replaced above by§ since
177| MS:Offended by a touch too premature §last two words marked for transposition to
follow by§   *P1875:*Offended, by   181| MS:rehearse §altered to§ Rehearse

Than the main misery, a sunset old.
What else but fitting prologue to the piece
185 Style an adventure, stranger than my first
By so much as the issue it enwombed
Lurked big beyond Balaustion's littleness?
Second supreme adventure!   O that Spring,
That eve I told the earlier to my friends!
190 Where are the four now, with each red-ripe mouth
Crumpled so close, no quickest breath it fetched
Could disengage the lip-flower furled to bud
For fear Admetos,—shivering head and foot,
As with sick soul and blind averted face
195 He trusted hand forth to obey his friend,—
Should find no wife in her cold hand's response,
Nor see the disenshrouded statue start
Alkestis, live the life and love the love!
I wonder, does the streamlet ripple still,
200 Outsmoothing galingale and watermint
Its mat-floor? while at brim, 'twixt sedge and sedge,
What bubblings past Baccheion, broadened much,
Pricked by the reed and fretted by the fly,
Oared by the boatman-spider's pair of arms!
205 Lenaia was a gladsome month ago—
Euripides had taught "Andromedé:"
Next month, would teach "Kresphontes"—which same month
Someone from Phokis, who companioned me
Since all that happened on those temple-steps,
210 Would marry me and turn Athenian too.
Now! if next year the masters let the slaves
Do Bacchic service and restore mankind

183| MS:Than that main   *P1875:*Than the main   193| MS:fear Admetos, shivering
*P1875:*fear Admetos,—shivering   194| MS:face,   *P1875:*face   195| MS:to please
Herakles, §last two words and comma crossed out and replaced above by three words and
comma§ obey his friend,   *P1875:*friend,—   200| MS:Out smoothing   *P1875:*Out-
smoothing   *1889a:*Outsmoothing   201| MS:Its mat- §word and hyphen inserted above§
floorage, §last three letters crossed out, forming§ mat-floor, while   *P1875:*mat-floor? while
203| MS:reed, and   *P1875:*reed and   204| MS:arms?   *P1875:*arms!
205| MS:a glorious month   *P1875:*a gladsome month   207| MS:month,   *P1875:*month
211| MS:next month §crossed out and replaced above by§ year

That trilogy whereof, 'tis noised, one play
Presents the Bacchai,—no Euripides
215   Will teach the choros, nor shall we be tinged
By any such grand sunset of his soul,
Exiles from dead Athenai,—not the live
That's in the cloud there with the new-born star!

Speak to the infinite intelligence,
220   Sing to the everlasting sympathy!
Winds belly sail, and drench of dancing brine
Buffet our boat-side, so the prore bound free!
Condense our voyage into one great day
Made up of sunset-closes: eve by eve,
225   Resume that memorable night-discourse
When,—like some meteor-brilliance, fire and filth,
Or say, his own Amphitheos, deity
And dung, who, bound on the gods' embassage,
Got men's acknowledgment in kick and cuff—
230   We made acquaintance with a visitor
Ominous, apparitional, who went
Strange as he came, but shall not pass away.
Let us attempt that memorable talk,
Clothe the adventure's every incident
235   With due expression: may not looks be told,
Gesture made speak, and speech so amplified
That words find blood-warmth which, cold-writ, they lose?

Recall the night we heard the news from Thrace,
One year ago, Athenai still herself.

213| MS:where it §altered to§ of *P1875:*whereof   215| MS:be taught *P1875:*be tinged
217| MS:from §next word illegibly crossed out, perhaps *their*§ dead §inserted above§ <> not
our own,— §last two words and punctuation crossed out and replaced above by two words§
the new *P1875:*the live   218| MS:the star above! *1889a:*the new-born star!
221| MS:dancing spray *P1875:*dancing brine   224| MS:sunset closes *CP1875:*sunset-
closes   228| MS:who sent §crossed out and replaced above by§ bound *P1875:*who,
bound   229| MS:Got his deserts in human §last four words crossed out and replaced
above by three words§ men's acknowledgement in <> cuff,— *P1875:*cuff—
233| MS:us preserve §crossed out and replaced above by§ attempt
234| MS:Dare, the <> incident, *P1875:*Clothe the <> incident   235| MS:Its due
expression: should §crossed out and replaced above by§ may *P1875:*With due

240 　We two were sitting silent in the house,
　　　Yet cheerless hardly.　Euthukles, forgive!
　　　I somehow speak to unseen auditors.
　　　Not *you*, but—Euthukles had entered, grave,
　　　Grand, may I say, as who brings laurel-branch
245 　And message from the tripod: such it proved.

　　　He first removed the garland from his brow,
　　　Then took my hand and looked into my face.

　　　"Speak good words!" much misgiving faltered I.

　　　"Good words, the best, Balaustion! He is crowned,
250 　Gone with his Attic ivy home to feast,
　　　Since Aischulos required companionship.
　　　Pour a libation for Euripides!"

　　　When we had sat the heavier silence out—
　　　"Dead and triumphant still!" began reply
255 　To my eye's question.　"As he willed he worked:
　　　And, as he worked, he wanted not, be sure,
　　　Triumph his whole life through, submitting work
　　　To work's right judges, never to the wrong—
　　　To competency, not ineptitude.
260 　When he had run life's proper race and worked
　　　Quite to the stade's end, there remained to try
　　　The stade's turn, should strength dare the double course.
　　　Half the diaulos reached, the hundred plays
　　　Accomplished, force in its rebound sufficed

241| 　MS:hardly. Euthukles (. . §parenthesis crossed out§ forgive!　*P1875:*hardly. Euthukles,
forgive!　　　242| 　MS:to §next word illegibly crossed out§ unseen auditors):— §parenthesis
crossed out§　*P1875:*auditors.　　　243| 　MS:but—Euthukles) §parenthesis crossed out§
244| 　MS:brings oracle §crossed out§ laurel-branch　　　245| 　MS:§line added§
248| 　MS: much-misgiving faultered　*P1875:*much misgiving　*1889a:*faltered
252| 　MS:for Euripides!'　*P1875:*for Euripides!"　　　253| 　MS:out,—　*P1875:*out—
254| 　MS:still" began　*P1875:*still!" began　　　255| 　MS:willed, he　*1889a:*willed he
258| 　MS:wrong,　*1889a:*wrong—　　　262| 　MS:Its turning, < > strength last §crossed out
and replaced above by§ dare　*1889a:*The stade's turn　　　264| 　MS:Gained him, enough
that §last four words crossed out and replaced above by one word and comma§ Accomplished,

²⁶⁵ To lift along the athlete and ensure
     A second wreath, proposed by fools for first,
     The statist's olive as the poet's bay.
     Wiselier, he suffered not a twofold aim
     Retard his pace, confuse his sight; at once
²⁷⁰ Poet and statist; though the multitude
     Girded him ever 'All thine aim thine art?
     The idle poet only?   No regard
     For civic duty, public service, here?
     We drop our ballot-bean for Sophokles!
²⁷⁵ Not only could he write "Antigoné,"
     But—since (we argued) whoso penned that piece
     Might just as well conduct a squadron,—straight
     Good-naturedly he took on him command,
     Got laughed at, and went back to making plays,
²⁸⁰ Having allowed us our experiment
     Respecting the fit use of faculty.'
     No whit the more did athlete slacken pace.
     Soon the jeers grew: 'Cold hater of his kind,
     A sea-cave suits him, not the vulgar hearth!
²⁸⁵ What need of tongue-talk, with a bookish store
     Would stock ten cities?'   Shadow of an ass!
     No whit the worse did athlete touch the mark
     And, at the turning-point, consign his scorn
     O' the scorners to that final trilogy

<> sufficed. §period crossed out§   ²⁶⁵| MS:To §in margin§ Lifted §altered to§ lift <>
athlete to §crossed out and replaced above by§ and   ²⁶⁶| MS:The §crossed out and
replaced above by§ A second   ²⁶⁸| MS:not confuse his sight,   *1889a:*not a twofold
aim   ²⁶⁹| MS:pace a two-fold aim, at   *1889a:*pace, confuse his sight; at
²⁷⁴| MS:We §over illegible word, perhaps *I*§ drop my §crossed out and replaced above by§ our
²⁷⁵| MS:only did §crossed out and replaced above by§ could <> write 'Antigoné,'   *1889a:*
write "Antigoné,"   ²⁷⁶| MS:But, §next word and punctuation inserted above§ —since, we
argued, whoso   *P1875:*But—since   *1889a:*since (we argued) whoso
²⁷⁷| MS:conduct an armament, §last two words and comma crossed out and replaced above
by three words§ a squadron,—straight   ²⁷⁸| MS:Goodnaturedly   *P1875:*Good-naturedly
²⁷⁹| MS:at and   *1889a:*at, and   ²⁸¹| MS:the §inserted above§ fittest §altered to§ fit
²⁸²| MS:§line added§ more the §crossed out and replaced above by§ did <> slackened
§altered to§ slacken   ²⁸⁴| MS:hearth;   *P1875:*hearth!   ²⁸⁵| MS:tongue-talk with
his §crossed out and replaced above by§ a   *P1875:*tongue-talk, with   ²⁸⁷| MS:worse the
athlete touched   *P1875:*worse did athlete touch   ²⁸⁸| MS:consigned   *P1875:*consign
²⁸⁹| MS:to §over illegible word§ that closing §crossed out§ that final §inserted above§

290 'Hupsipule,' 'Phoinissai,' and the Match
Of Life Contemplative with Active Life,
Zethos against Amphion.   Ended so?
Nowise!—began again; for heroes rest
Dropping shield's oval o'er the entire man,
295 And he who thus took Contemplation's prize
Turned stade-point but to face Activity.
Out of all shadowy hands extending help
For life's decline pledged to youth's labour still,
Whatever renovation flatter age,—
300 Society with pastime, solitude
With peace,—he chose the hand that gave the heart,
Bade Macedonian Archelaos take
The leavings of Athenai, ash once flame.
For fifty politicians' frosty work,
305 One poet's ash proved ample and to spare:
He propped the state and filled the treasury,
Counselled the king as might a meaner soul,
Furnished the friend with what shall stand in stead
Of crown and sceptre, star his name about

---

*P1875:*to that final   290| MS:'Hupsipilé,' <> the Strife   *P1875:*'Hupsipule,' <> the
Match   291| MS:Of contemplation §altered to§ Contemplation with Activity,   *P1875:*Of
Life Contemplative with Active Life,   294| MS:Dropping §last three letters crossed out
and replaced above by two illegibly crossed-out words and then original reading restored§ <>
man;   *1889a:*man,   295| MS:And he §last two words in margin§ Who §altered to§ who
took triumphant §crossed out and replaced above by§ thus §marked for transposition to
follow *who*§ contemplation's §altered to§ Contemplation's prize,   *1889a:*prize
296| MS:And, §crossed out and replaced above by two words§ Then §crossed out§ turned
§altered to§ Turned stade-point turned, full faced §last three words crossed out and replaced
above by three words§ but to face activity §altered to§ Activity.   297| MS:As, from §last
two words crossed out and replaced above by two words§ Out of   298| MS:For the
§crossed out and replaced above by§ such declining §altered to§ decline heros final feat,—
§last three words and punctuation crossed out and replaced above by four words and comma§
pledged to such enterprise,   *P1875:*For life's decline <> to youth's enterprise,   *1889a:*
youth's labour still,   299| MS:§line added§   300| MS:Society and §crossed out and
replaced above by§ with   301| MS:And §crossed out and replaced above by§ With
302| MS:Bade Macedonia's §altered to§ Macedonian §next word inserted above and illegibly
crossed out§ Archelaos   303| MS:flame,— §punctuation altered to period§
304| MS:frosty make,   *1889a:*frosty work,   305| MS:ash found ample <> spare,
*1889a:*ash proved ample <> spare: 306| MS:treasury: *1889a:*treasury,
307| MS:Counseled his king   *1889a:*Counselled the king   308| MS:Furnished his friend
*1889a:*Furnished the friend   309| MS:about—   *P1875:*about

310 When these are dust; for him, Euripides
Last the old hand on the old phorminx flung,
Clashed thence 'Alkaion,' maddened 'Pentheus' up;
Then music sighed itself away, one moan
Iphigeneia made by Aulis' strand;
315 With her and music died Euripides.

"The poet-friend who followed him to Thrace,
Agathon, writes thus much: the merchant-ship
Moreover brings a message from the king
To young Euripides, who went on board
320 This morning at Mounuchia: all is true."

I said "Thank Zeus for the great news and good!"

"Nay, the report is running in brief fire
Through the town's stubbly furrow," he resumed:
—"Entertains brightly what their favourite styles
325 'The City of Gapers' for a week perhaps,
Supplants three luminous tales, but yesterday
Pronounced sufficient lamps to last the month:
How Glauketes, outbidding Morsimos,
Paid market-price for one Kopaic eel
330 A thousand drachmai, and then cooked his prize
Not proper conger-fashion but in oil
And nettles, as man fries the foam-fish-kind;
How all the captains of the triremes, late
Victors at Arginousai, on return
335 Will, for reward, be straightway put to death;

310| MS:for whom §crossed out and replaced above by§ him
312| MS:up, *P1875:*up; 313| MS:music §inserted above§
316| MS:The *P1875:*"The 317| MS:writes §altered to *wrote* and then restored§
*P1875:*wrote *1889a:*writes 318| MS:brought *1889a:*brings
320| MS:true. *P1875:*true." 323| MS:furrow," like to last, §last three words and comma
crossed out§ he 324| MS:—Entertains *P1875:*—"Entertains 325| MS:week,
indeed §comma and last word crossed out§ perhaps *P1875:*perhaps,
327| MS:sufficient lights §crossed out and replaced above by§ lamps to lamp §crossed out and
replaced above by§ last 328| MS:How Glauketes, the harp-player §last two words crossed
out§ outbidding 332| MS:nettles as *P1875:*nettles, as 333| MS:triremes late
*P1875:*triremes, late 334| MS:Victors off §crossed out and replaced above by§ at

How Mikon wagered a Thessalian mime
Trained him by Lais, looked on as complete,
Against Leogoras' blood-mare koppa-marked,
Valued six talents,—swore, accomplished so,
340   The girl could swallow at a draught, nor breathe,
A choinix of unmixed Mendesian wine;
And having lost the match will—dine on herbs!
Three stories late a-flame, at once extinct,
Outblazed by just 'Euripides is dead'!

345   "I met the concourse from the Theatre,
The audience flocking homeward: victory
Again awarded Aristophanes
Precisely for his old play chopped and changed
'The Female Celebrators of the Feast'—
350   That Thesmophoria, tried a second time.
'Never such full success!'—assured the folk,
Who yet stopped praising to have word of mouth
With 'Euthukles, the bard's own intimate,
Balaustion's husband, the right man to ask.'

355   "'Dead, yes, but how dead, may acquaintance know?
You were the couple constant at his cave:
Tell us now, is it true that women, moved
By reason of his liking Krateros . . .'

"I answered 'He was loved by Sokrates.'

360   "'Nay,' said another, 'envy did the work!

336| MS:wagered his Thessalian   *P1875:*wagered a Thessalian   339| MS:talents,—that,
§crossed out and replaced above by§ swore   340| MS:draught nor breathe
P1875: draught, nor breathe,   342| MS:will hang himself. §last two words and period
crossed out and replaced above by dash, three words and exclamation point§ —dine on herbs!
344| MS:Out-blazed   *CP1875:*Outblazed §not B§   1875:Out-blazed   *1889a:*Outblazed
345| MS:the Theatre   *P1875:*the Theatre,   346| MS:homewards   *P1875:*homeward
350| MS:That Thesmophoria: <> time,   *1889a:*That Thesmophoria, <> time.
351| MS:Never <> success!—assured   *P1875:*'Never <> success!'—assured
353| MS:With Euthukles   *P1875:*With 'Euthukles   354| MS:ask—   *P1875:*ask.'
355| MS:'Dead   *P1875:* "'Dead   358| MS:§line added§ liking Krateros..   *P1875:*liking
Krateros...'   359| MS:I   *P1875:*"I   360| MS:'Nay <> work!'   *1889a:*"'Nay <> work!

For, emulating poets of the place,
One Arridaios, one Krateues, both
Established in the royal favour, these . . .'

"Protagoras instructed him," said I.

³⁶⁵   "'*Phu*,' whistled Comic Platon, 'hear the fact!
'Twas well said of your friend by Sophokles
"He hate our women?   In his verse, belike:
But when it comes to prose-work,—ha, ha, ha!"
New climes don't change old manners: so, it chanced,
³⁷⁰   Pursuing an intrigue one moonless night
With Arethousian Nikodikos' wife,
(Come now, his years were simply seventy-five)
Crossing the palace-court, what haps he on
But Archelaos' pack of hungry hounds?
³⁷⁵   Who tore him piecemeal ere his cry brought help.'

"I asked: Did not you write 'The Festivals'?
You best know what dog tore him when alive.
You others, who now make a ring to hear,
Have not you just enjoyed a second treat,
³⁸⁰   Proclaimed that ne'er was play more worthy prize
Than this, myself assisted at, last year,
And gave its worth to,—spitting on the same?
Appraise no poetry,—price cuttlefish,
Or that seaweed-alphestes, scorpion-sort,

---

^{361-63|} MS:§lines added§   ^{361|} MS:For emulating *P1875:*For, emulating
^{363|} MS:favor, these... *1889a:*favour, these...'   ^{365|} MS:"Phu," pushed up §last two
words crossed out and replaced above by one word§ whistled <> "hear <> facts! *P1875:*
'*Phu*,' <> 'hear <> fact! *1889a:*"'*Phu*,' whistled   ^{366|} MS:of the man by *P1875:*of
your friend by   ^{367|} MS:hate the §crossed out and replaced above by§ our *P1875:*
belike. *1889a:*belike: ^{371|} MS:§line added§   ^{373|} MS:what comes he *P1875:*
what haps he   ^{374|} MS:hounds *P1875:*hounds?   ^{375|} MS:help?" *P1875:*help.'
^{376|} MS:I asked "Did <> "The Festivals?" *P1875:*"I asked: Did <> 'The Festivals?'
*1889a:*Festivals'?   ^{377|} MS:him while alive. *P1875:*him when alive.
^{380|} MS:that §inserted above§ was never §altered to§ ne'er §last two words marked for
transposition§   ^{383|} MS:Talk §crossed out and replaced above by§ Appraise not §altered
to§ no of §crossed out§ poetry, but §crossed out and replaced above by§ —price
^{384|} MS:scorpion fish §last two words altered to one word§ scorpion-sort,

385 Much famed for mixing mud with fantasy
     On midnights! I interpret no foul dreams."

     If so said Euthukles, so could not I,
     Balaustion, say. After "Lusistraté"
     No more for me of "people's privilege,"
390 No witnessing "the Grand old Comedy
     Coëval with our freedom, which, curtailed,
     Were freedom's deathblow: relic of the past,
     When Virtue laughingly told truth to Vice,
     Uncensured, since the stern mouth, stuffed with flowers,
395 Through poetry breathed satire, perfumed blast
     Which sense snuffed up while searched unto the bone!"
     I was a stranger: "For first joy," urged friends,
     "Go hear our Comedy, some patriot piece
     That plies the selfish advocates of war
400 With argument so unevadable
     That crash fall Kleons whom the finer play
     Of reason, tickling, deeper wounds no whit
     Than would a spear-thrust from a savory-stalk!
     No: you hear knave and fool told crime and fault,
405 And see each scourged his quantity of stripes.
     'Rough dealing, awkward language,' whine our fops:
     The world's too squeamish now to bear plain words
     Concerning deeds it acts with gust enough:
     But, thanks to wine-lees and democracy,

385| MS:Bad §crossed out and replaced above by§ Much <> with soul, they say. §last three words and period crossed out and replaced by one word§ fantasy   386| MS:§line added§ O' midnights *P1875:*Of midnights *1889a:*On midnights   388| MS:say. After 'Lusistraté' *1889a:*say. After "Lusistraté"   390| MS:§line added§ No §in margin§ Of §crossed out§ witnessing <> grand <> comedy §altered to§ Comedy *1889a:*the Grand
391| MS:freedom,—which *P1875:*freedom, which   392| MS:the Past, *P1875:*past,
393| MS:laughingly dared tell Vice truth, *P1875:*laughingly told truth to Vice,
394| MS:Uncensored, since §crossed out and replaced above by§ for §crossed out and *since* restored§   397| MS:"for §altered to§ "For   398| MS: Go <> patriot-piece *P1875:* "Go <> patriot piece   400| MS:unevadible *1889a:*unevadable   402| MS:reason tickling *P1875:*reason, tickling   403| MS:would a §last two words inserted above§ spear thrust <> stalk of §crossed out§ savory-! §word and hyphen marked for transposition to precede *stalk*§ *P1875:*spear-thrust   406| MS:"Rough <> language," whine *P1875:*

410   We've still our stage where truth calls spade a spade!
Ashamed?   Phuromachos' decree provides
The sex may sit discreetly, witness all,
Sorted, the good with good, the gay with gay,
Themselves unseen, no need to force a blush.
415   A Rhodian wife and ignorant so long?
Go hear next play!"
                              I heard "Lusistraté."
Waves, said to wash pollution from the world,
Take that plague-memory, cure that pustule caught
As, past escape, I sat and saw the piece
420   By one appalled at Phaidra's fate,—the chaste,
Whom, because chaste, the wicked goddess chained
To that same serpent of unchastity
She loathed most, and who, coiled so, died distraught
Rather than make submission, loose one limb
425   Love-wards, at lambency of honeyed tongue,
Or torture of the scales which scraped her snow
   —I say, the piece by him who charged this piece
(Because Euripides shrank not to teach,
If gods be strong and wicked, man, though weak,
430   May prove their match by willing to be good)
With infamies the Scythian's whip should cure—
"Such outrage done the public—Phaidra named!
Such purpose to corrupt ingenuous youth,
Such insult cast on female character!"—

'Rough <> language,' whine   410| MS:We've §over illegible erasure§ still the §crossed
out and replaced above by§ our <> where man calls   *P1875:*where truth calls
411| MS:Besides, Phuromachos'   *P1875:*Ashamed? Phuromachos'   416| *P1875:*heard
'Lusistraté.'   *1889a:*heard "Lusistraté."   418| MS:cure the §altered to§ that
419| MS:saw that §altered to§ the   420| MS:By him whose charge was—Phaidra's fate,
the   *P1875:*By one appalled at Phaidra's fate,—the   421| MS:wicked Goddess   *P1875:*
goddess   423| MS:loathed the most and, coiled   *P1875:*loathed most, and who, coiled
424| MS:Rather §over illegible word§   425| MS:at §inserted above§ by §crossed out§
lambency of honeyed §last two words inserted above§ tongue solicited, §word and comma
crossed out§   *P1875:*tongue,   426| MS:which §over illegible word§   427| MS:say,
that §altered to§ the <> piece—   *P1875:*this piece   428| MS:to show,   *P1875:*to teach,
430| MS:good)—   *P1875:*good)   432| MS:"Such <> public decency, §word and comma
crossed out and replaced above by§ —Phaidra   *P1875:*'Such   *1889a:*"Such
434| MS:character!"   *P1875:*character!'—   *1889a:*character!"—

435 Why, when I saw that bestiality—
     So beyond all brute-beast imagining,
     That when, to point the moral at the close,
     Poor Salabaccho, just to show how fair
     Was "Reconciliation," stripped her charms,
440 That exhibition simply bade us breathe,
     Seemed something healthy and commendable
     After obscenity grotesqued so much
     It slunk away revolted at itself.
     Henceforth I had my answer when our sage
445 Pattern-proposing seniors pleaded grave
     "You fail to fathom here the deep design!
     All's acted in the interest of truth,
     Religion, and those manners old and dear
     Which made our city great when citizens
450 Like Aristeides and like Miltiades
     Wore each a golden tettix in his hair."
     What do they wear now under—Kleophon?

     Well, for such reasons,—I am out of breath,
     But loathsomeness we needs must hurry past,—
455 I did not go to see, nor then nor now,
     The "Thesmophoriazousai." But, since males
     Choose to brave first, blame afterward, nor brand
     Without fair taste of what they stigmatize,
     Euthukles had not missed the first display,
460 Original portrait of Euripides
     By "Virtue laughingly reproving Vice":

439| MS:Was 'Reconciliation,' stripped herself, §last four letters and comma crossed out§ charms,   *1889a:*Was "Reconciliation," stripped   445| MS:And §crossed out§ Pattern-proposing   448| MS:Religion and   *P1875:*Religion, and   450| MS:and Miltiades *1889a:*and like Miltiades   451| MS:each one a   *P1875:*each a   453| MS:breath *P1875:*breath,   454| MS:But certain §crossed out§ loathsomeness we have §over illegible erasure§ to §last two words inserted above§ hurry   *P1875:*we needs must hurry 455| MS:did §over illegible word, perhaps *had*§ not gone §altered to§ go <> nor for §crossed out§ then   457| MS:Take §crossed out and replaced above by two words§ Choose to braving §altered to *braved*, then altered to§ brave bestiality, nor   *P1875:*brave first, blame afterward, nor   458| MS:Without a §crossed out and replaced above by§ fair 459| MS:the filth's §crossed out§ first fling, §crossed out and replaced above by§ display— *P1875:*display,   461| MS:reproving Vice"—   *P1875:* reproving Vice":

"Virtue,"—the author, Aristophanes,
Who mixed an image out of his own depths,
Ticketed as I tell you.   Oh, this time
465 No more pretension to recondite worth!
No joke in aid of Peace, no demagogue
Pun-pelleted from Pnux, no kordax-dance
Overt helped covertly the Ancient Faith!
All now was muck, home-produce, honestman
470 The author's soul secreted to a play
Which gained the prize that day we heard the death.

I thought "How thoroughly death alters things!
Where is the wrong now, done our dead and great?
How natural seems grandeur in relief,
475 Cliff-base with frothy spites against its calm!"

Euthukles interposed—he read my thought—

"O'er them, too, in a moment came the change.
The crowd's enthusiastic, to a man:
Since, rake as such may please the ordure-heap
480 Because of certain sparkles presumed ore,
At first flash of true lightning overhead,
They look up, nor resume their search too soon.
The insect-scattering sign is evident,
And nowhere winks a fire-fly rival now,

462| MS:author, Aristophanes *P1875:*author, Aristophanes,   163| MS:Who made
§crossed out and replaced above by§ mixed <> of excrement §crossed out and replaced
above by three words and comma§ his own filth, *P1875:*own depths,
464| MS:And called §crossed out and replaced above by§ named it §last three words crossed
out and replaced below by one word§ Ticketed <> you: <> this time play §last two words
crossed out and *time* restored§ *P1875:*you. Oh   475| MS: The rock §last two words
crossed out and replaced above by one word§ Cliff-base   476| MS:Euthukles ended—for
he *P1875:*Euthukles interposed—he   478| MS:man, *P1875:*man:
479| MS:Since, §next word illegibly crossed out and replaced above by§ rake as man §crossed
out and replaced above by§ fools may <> the §over illegible word§ ordure-heap *P1875:*as
such may <> ordure heap *1889a:*ordure-heap   482| MS:He §altered to§ They looks
§altered to§ look <> resumes §altered to§ resume the §altered to§ their
483| MS:sign was §crossed out and replaced above by§ is
484| MS:nowhere winked §altered to§ winks <> firefly-rival *P1875:*fire-fly rival

⁴⁸⁵ Nor bustles any beetle of the brood
With trundled dung-ball meant to menace heaven.
Contrariwise, the cry is 'Honour him!'
'A statue in the theatre!' wants one;
Another 'Bring the poet's body back,
⁴⁹⁰ Bury him in Peiraios: o'er his tomb
Let Alkamenes carve the music-witch,
The songstress-seiren, meed of melody:
Thoukudides invent his epitaph!'
To-night the whole town pays its tribute thus."

⁴⁹⁵ Our tribute should not be the same, my friend!
Statue?   Within our heart he stood, he stands!
As for the vest outgrown now by the form,
Low flesh that clothed high soul,—a vesture's fate—
Why, let it fade, mix with the elements
⁵⁰⁰ There where it, falling, freed Euripides!
But for the soul that's tutelary now
Till time end, o'er the world to teach and bless—
How better hail its freedom than by first
Singing, we two, its own song back again,
⁵⁰⁵ Up to that face from which flowed beauty—face
Now abler to see triumph and take love
Than when it glorified Athenai once?

The sweet and strange "Alkestis," which saved me,
Secured me—you, ends nowise, to my mind,
⁵¹⁰ In pardon of Admetos. Hearts are fain

---

⁴⁸⁵| MS:bustled §altered to§ bustles   ⁴⁸⁶| MS:dung ball like §crossed out and
replaced above by§ meant   *P1875:* dung-ball   ⁴⁸⁷| MS:is 'Honor   *1889a:*is 'Honour
⁴⁸⁸| MS:one: *P1875:*one;   ⁴⁹⁰⁻⁹²| MS:§lines added in margin§   ⁴⁹⁰| MS:his Tomb
*P1875:*tomb   ⁴⁹¹| MS:Let Alcamenes carve §crossed out and replaced above by§ set
*P1875:*Let Alcamenes carve   ⁴⁹³| MS:Thoukudides shall write §crossed out and replaced
above by§ pen his   *P1875:* Thoukudides invent his   ⁵⁰⁰| MS:it, fall §altered to§ falling
down, §crossed out; comma retained§ freed   ⁵⁰²| MS:Till time's §altered to§ time
⁵⁰³| MS:by back §crossed out§ first   ⁵⁰⁴| MS:song to that face §last three words crossed
out§ back   ⁵⁰⁵| MS:§line added§ beauty—now   *P1875:*beauty—face   ⁵⁰⁶| MS:Abler
< > see the triumph, take the love,   *P1875:*Now abler < > see triumph and take love
⁵⁰⁸| MS:me   *P1875:*me,   ⁵¹⁰| MS:of Admetos: hearts   *P1875:*of Admetos. Hearts

To follow cheerful weary Herakles
Striding away from the huge gratitude,
Club shouldered, lion-fleece round loin and flank,
Bound on the next new labour "height o'er height
515   Ever surmounting,—destiny's decree!"
Thither He helps us: that's the story's end;
He smiling said so, when I told him mine—
My great adventure, how Alkestis helped.
Afterward, when the time for parting fell,
520   He gave me, with two other precious gifts,
This third and best, consummating the grace,
"Herakles," writ by his own hand, each line.

"If it have worth, reward is still to seek.
Somebody, I forget who, gained the prize
525   And proved arch-poet: time must show!" he smiled:
"Take this, and, when the noise tires out, judge me—
Some day, not slow to dawn, when somebody—
Who? I forget—proves nobody at all!"

Is not that day come?   What if you and I
530   Re-sing the song, inaugurate the fame?
We have not waited to acquaint ourselves
With song and subject; we can prologuize
How, at Eurustheus' bidding,—hate strained hard,—
Herakles had departed, one time more,
535   On his last labour, worst of all the twelve;
Descended into Haides, thence to drag
The triple-headed hound, which sun should see

518| MS:adventure, what §crossed out and replaced above by§ how Alkestis did §crossed out§ helped.   519| MS:fell, §over illegible word§   523| MS:seek: *P1875*:seek.
525| MS:proved the poet: §last two words altered to§ arch-poet: <> show!"—he   *P1875*:show!"
he   526| MS:this, §over illegible erasure§ <> noise desists, §crossed out and replaced
above by two words§ tires out   527| MS:That §crossed out and replaced above by§ Some
<> not long §crossed out and replaced above by§ slow to wait, §crossed out and replaced
above by§ dawn   528| MS:Who, I   *P1875*:Who? I   532| MS:subject; and §crossed
out and replaced above by§ we   534| MS:Herakles made §crossed out and replaced
above by§ had departure, §altered to§ departed   535| MS:the Twelve;   *P1875*:twelve;
536| MS:into Hades   *P1875*:into Haides   537| MS:triple-headed Hound   *P1875*:hound

Spite of the god whose darkness whelped the Fear.
Down went the hero, "back—how should he come?"
540 So laughed King Lukos, an old enemy,
Who judged that absence testified defeat
Of the land's loved one,—since he saved the land
And for that service wedded Megara
Daughter of Thebai, realm her child should rule.
545 Ambition, greed and malice seized their prey,
The Heracleian House, defenceless left,
Father and wife and child, to trample out
Trace of its hearth-fire: since extreme old age
Wakes pity, woman's wrong wins championship,
550 And child may grow up man and take revenge.
Hence see we that, from out their palace-home
Hunted, for last resource they cluster now
Couched on the cold ground, hapless suppliants
About their courtyard altar,—Household Zeus
555 It is, the Three in funeral garb beseech,
Delaying death so, till deliverance come—
When did it ever?—from the deep and dark.
And thus breaks silence old Amphitruon's voice. . . .
Say I not true thus far, my Euthukles?

560 Suddenly, torch-light! knocking at the door,
Loud, quick, "Admittance for the revels' lord!"
Some unintelligible Komos-cry—
Raw-flesh red, no cap upon his head,
Dionusos, Bacchos, Phales, Iacchos,

538| MS:the God *P1875:*god 541| MS:Who in that prolonged absence, plain defeat *1889a:*Who judged that absence testified defeat 542| MS:one,—for he *1889a:*
one,—since he 544| MS:rule,— *1889a:*rule. 545| MS:Saw his occasion, seized
the tempting prey, *1889a:*Ambition, greed and malice seized their prey,
546| MS:defenceless now, *P1875:*defenceless left, 550| MS:And the child grow the
man <> takes *1889a:*And child may grow up man <> take 553| MS:ground, §next
word illegibly crossed out and replaced above by§ hapless §over illegibly erased word§
554-56| MS:About <> altar,—Household Zeus / Delaying *1889a:*altar,—Household Zeus
/ It <> beseech, / Delaying 557| MS:the Deep <> Dark. *P1875:*deep <> dark.
558| MS:voice... *1889a:*voice.... 560| MS:knockings §altered to§ knocking
563| MS:*Raw-flesh-red* *P1875:Raw-flesh red*

26

565   *In let him reel with the kid-skin at his heel,*
       Where it buries in the spread of the bushy myrtle-bed!
       (Our Rhodian Jackdaw-song was sense to that!)
       Then laughter, outbursts ruder and more rude,
       Through which, with silver point, a fluting pierced,
570   And ever "Open, open, Bacchos bids!"

       But at last—one authoritative word,
       One name of an immense significance:
       For Euthukles rose up, threw wide the door.

       There trooped the Choros of the Comedy
575   Crowned and triumphant; first, those flushed Fifteen
       Men that wore women's garb, grotesque disguise.
       Then marched the Three,—who played Mnesilochos,
       Who, Toxotes, and who, robed right, masked rare,
       Monkeyed our Great and Dead to heart's content
580   That morning in Athenai. Masks were down
       And robes doffed now; the sole disguise was drink.

       Mixing with these—I know not what gay crowd,
       Girl-dancers, flute-boys, and pre-eminent
       Among them,—doubtless draped with such reserve
585   As stopped fear of the fifty-drachma fine
       (Beside one's name on public fig-tree nailed)
       Which women pay who in the streets walk bare,—
       Behold Elaphion of the Persic dance!

566| MS:*the black thick* §last two words crossed out and replaced above by one word§ *bushy*
567| MS:(Our Rhodian Jack-daw-song §altered to§ Jackdaw-song was §over illegible word,
perhaps *is*§   571| MS:§line added§word!   *1889a:*word,   572| MS:§line added in
margin§ significance—   *P1875:*significance: 573| MS:And §in margin; crossed out and
replaced in margin by§ For < > up, and §crossed out§ threw   576| MS:that played
§crossed out and replaced above by illegibly crossed-out word, perhaps *danced*§ wore §inserted
above§ women garbed §inserted above and last two words altered to§ women's garb, the
§crossed out§ grotesque   577| MS:Then came §crossed out and replaced above by§
marched   579| MS:Monkeyed the §crossed out and replaced above by§ our
581-82| MS:§no ¶ called for§   *P1875:*§page ends§   *1889a:*§¶§
582| MS:what the §crossed out and replaced above by§ gay
583| MS:flutists §altered to§ flute-boys   586| MS:figtree   *P1875:*fig-tree

Who lately had frisked fawn-foot, and the rest,
590 —All for the Patriot Cause, the Antique Faith,
The Conservation of True Poesy—
Could I but penetrate the deep design!
Elaphion, more Peiraios-known as "Phaps,"
Tripped at the head of the whole banquet-band
595 Who came in front now, as the first fell back;
And foremost—the authoritative voice,
The revels-leader, he who gained the prize,
And got the glory of the Archon's feast—
There stood in person Aristophanes.

600 And no ignoble presence!   On the bulge
Of the clear baldness,—all his head one brow,—
True, the veins swelled, blue network, and there surged
A red from cheek to temple,—then retired
As if the dark-leaved chaplet damped a flame,—
605 Was never nursed by temperance or health.
But huge the eyeballs rolled back native fire,
Imperiously triumphant: nostrils wide
Waited their incense; while the pursed mouth's pout
Aggressive, while the beak supreme above,
610 While the head, face, nay, pillared throat thrown back,
Beard whitening under like a vinous foam,
These made a glory, of such insolence—
I thought,—such domineering deity
Hephaistos might have carved to cut the brine
615 For his gay brother's prow, imbrue that path
Which, purpling, recognized the conqueror.
Impudent and majestic: drunk, perhaps,
But that's religion; sense too plainly snuffed:

589| MS: Who late had §last two words inserted above§ after §altered to§ afterwards frisked
her §crossed out§ fawn-foot   *P1875:*lately   592| MS:Could we §crossed out and replaced
above by§ I   597| MS:revel-leader   *1889a:*revels-leader   602| MS:surged §over
illegible erasure§   604| MS:damped the §crossed out and replaced above by§ a
605| MS:Was rarely §crossed out and replaced above by§ never < > health;   *P1875:*health.
611| MS: vinous §inserted above§ foam, to wine, §last two words and comma crossed out§
616| MS:recognized   *P1875:*recognised   *CP1875:*recognized §not B§   618| MS:too plain
§altered to§ plainly §word illegibly crossed out§ snuff §altered to§ snuffed,   *P1875:*snuffed:

Still, sensuality was grown a rite.

620   What I had disbelieved most proved most true.
There was a mind here, mind a-wantoning
At ease of undisputed mastery
Over the body's brood, those appetites.
Oh but he grasped them grandly, as the god
625   His either struggling handful,—hurtless snakes
Held deep down, strained hard off from side and side!
Mastery his, theirs simply servitude,
So well could firm fist help intrepid eye.
Fawning and fulsome, had they licked and hissed?
630   At mandate of one muscle, order reigned.
They had been wreathing much familiar now
About him on his entry; but a squeeze
Choked down the pests to place: their lord stood free.

Forward he stepped: I rose and fronted him.

635   "Hail, house, the friendly to Euripides!"
(So he began) "Hail, each inhabitant!
You, lady? What, the Rhodian? Form and face,
Victory's self upsoaring to receive
The poet? Right they named you .. some rich name,
640   Vowel-buds thorned about with consonants,
Fragrant, felicitous, rose-glow enriched

619| MS:sensuality was §crossed out and replaced above by illegibly crossed-out word and then restored§   620| MS:disbelieved in, was the mind §last four words crossed out and replaced above by one word and comma§ most, proved   621| MS:§line added§ mind in Aristophanes §last two words crossed out§   *1889a:*most proved   623| MS:appetites, *P1875:*appetites.   624| MS:Oh, but   *1889a:*Oh but   628| MS:So long as firm < > helped < > eye!   *P1875:*So well could firm < > help < > eye.   629| MS:and played §crossed out and replaced above by§ hissed?   630| MS:One §crossed out and replaced above by four words§ At mandate of one muscle's §altered to§ muscle, knitting, and each pest resigned §last five words crossed out and replaced above by two words§ order reigned.   631| MS:Shrunk to its §last three words crossed out and replaced above by four words§ They had been wreathing   632| MS:entry: but   *P1875:*entry; but   633| MS:Choaked down the §crossed out and replaced above by§ each §crossed out and *the* restored§ pests §altered to *pest* and original reading restored§ < > place; their < > stood §over illegible erasure§ *P1875.*place: their   *1889a:*Choaked   634| MS:stepped, I   *1889a:*stepped: I   639| MS:you...some   *1889a:*you..some   641| MS:Fragrant, §crossed out and restored§

By the Isle's unguent: some diminished end
In *ion*, Kallistion? delicater still,
Kubelion or Melittion,—or, suppose
645 (Less vulgar love than bee or violet)
Phibalion, for the mouth split red-fig-wise,
Korakinidion for the coal-black hair,
Nettarion, Phabion for the darlingness?
But no, it was some fruit-flower, Rhoidion . . . ha,
650 We near the balsam-bloom—Balaustion!   Thanks,
Rhodes!   Folk have called me Rhodian, do you know?
Not fools so far!   Because, if Helios wived,
As Pindaros sings somewhere prettily,
Here blooms his offspring, earth-flesh with sun-fire,
655 Rhodes' blood and Helios' gold. My phorminx, boy!
Why does the boy hang back and baulk an ode
Tiptoe at spread of wing?   But like enough,
Sunshine frays torchlight.   Witness whom you scare,
Superb Balaustion!   Look outside the house!
660 *Pho*, you have quenched my Komos by first frown,
Struck dead all joyance: not a fluting puffs
From idle cheekband!   Ah, my Choros too?
You've eaten cuckoo-apple?   Dumb, you dogs?
So much good Thasian wasted on your throats
665 And out of them not one *Threttanelo?*
Neblaretai! Because this earth-and-sun
Product looks wormwood and all bitter herbs?
Well, do I blench, though me she hates the most
Of mortals?   By the cabbage, off they slink!
670 You, too, my Chrusomelolonthion-Phaps,
Girl-goldling-beetle-beauty?   You, abashed,
Who late, supremely unabashable,

---

felicitous, §next word illegibly crossed out§ rose-glow   644| MS:or, Melittion < >
suppose,   *P1875:*or Melittion   *1889a:*suppose   647| MS:Korakinidion, for   *1889a:*
Korakinidion for   648| MS:Nettarion, Phabion, for   *1889a:*Nettarion, Phabion for
649| MS:But §over illegible erasure§ < > fruit-flower, Rhodian . . ha, §over illegible erasure§
*P1875:*fruit flower, Rhoidion...ha,   655| MS:gold! My   *P1875:*gold. My
660| MS:Why, §crossed out and replaced above by§ Pho, you < > frown,   *P1875:Pho   1889a:*
frown §emended to§ frown, §see Editorial Notes§   665| MS:one Threttanelo?   *P1875:*
one *Threttanelo?*   666| MS:Neblaretai! Because   *P1875:Neblaretai!* Because

Propped up my play at that important point
When Artamouxia tricks the Toxotes?
675 Ha, ha,—thank Hermes for the lucky throw,—
We came last comedy of the whole seven,
So went all fresh to judgment well-disposed
For who should fatly feast them, eye and ear,
We two between us!   What, you fail your friend?
680 Away then, free me of your cowardice!
Go, get you the goat's breakfast!   Fare afield,
Ye circumcised of Egypt, pigs to sow,
Back to the Priest's or forward to the crows,
So you but rid me of such company!
685 Once left alone, I can protect myself
From statuesque Balaustion pedestalled
On much disapprobation and mistake!
She dares not beat the sacred brow, beside!
Bacchos' equipment, ivy safeguards well
690 As Phoibos' bay.

              "They take me at my word!
One comfort is, I shall not want them long,
The Archon's cry creaks, creaks, 'Curtail expense!'
The war wants money, year the twenty-sixth!
Cut down our Choros number, clip costume,
695 Save birds' wings, beetles' armour, spend the cash
In three-crest skull-caps, three days' salt-fish-slice,
Three-banked-ships for these sham-ambassadors,
And what not: any cost but Comedy's!
'No Chorus'—soon will follow; what care I?

675| MS:thanks §altered to§ thank   678| MS:Since §crossed out and replaced above by§
For < > should §over illegible erasure§ fatly feasted §altered to§ feast them §word and comma
inserted above§   685| MS:myself—   *P1875:*myself   691| MS:long   *P1875:*long,
692| MS:cry is to §last two words crossed out and replaced above by two words and
punctuation§ creaks, creaks, curtail §altered to§ 'Curtail expense!   *P1875:*expense!'
693| MS:§line added§ twenty sixth: *P1875:*twenty-sixth!   694| MS:down the §crossed
out and replaced below by§ your Choros' < > costume   *P1875:* down our Choros < >
costume,   695| MS:Of birds'-wings   *P1875:*Save birds' wings   696| MS:scull-caps
<,> salt-fish-sliced, §altered to§ salt-fish-slice,   *1889a:*skull-caps   697| MS:§line added§
698| MS:comedy!   *P1875:*but Comedy's!   699| MS:follow: what   *P1875:*follow; what

31

700 Archinos and Agurrhios, scrape your flint,
     Flay your dead dog, and curry favour so!
     Choros in rags, with loss of leather next,
     We lose the boys' vote, lose the song and dance,
     Lose my Elaphion!   Still, the actor stays.
705 Save but my acting, and the baldhead bard
     Kudathenaian and Pandionid,
     Son of Philippos, Aristophanes
     Surmounts his rivals now as heretofore,
     Though stinted to mere sober prosy verse—
710 'Manners and men,' so squeamish gets the world!
     No more 'Step forward, strip for anapæsts!'
     No calling naughty people by their names,
     No tickling audience into gratitude
     With chickpease, barleygroats and nuts and plums,
715 No setting Salabaccho . . . "

                         As I turned—

     "True, lady, I am tolerably drunk:
     The proper inspiration!   Otherwise,—
     Phrunichos, Choirilos!—had Aischulos
     So foiled you at the goat-song?   Drink's a god.
720 How else did that old doating driveller
     Kratinos foil me, match my masterpiece
     The 'Clouds'? I swallowed cloud-distilment—dew
     Undimmed by any grape-blush, knit my brow
     And gnawed my style and laughed my learnedest;

700| MS:flint! *P1875:*flint,   701| MS:dog—and <> favor so— *P1875:*dog, and <> so! *1889a:*favour   705| MS:but §over illegible erasure§   707| MS:of Philippos, Aristophanes, §comma crossed out§   712| MS:name, *P1875:*names,   713| MS:No pelting audience *P1875:*No tickling audience   714| MS:and sugar §crossed out and replaced above by two words§ nuts and   715| MS:setting Salabaccho . ." *P1875:*setting Salabaccho..."   716| MS:drunk— *P1875:*drunk: 718| MS:Phrunuchos *P1875:* Phrunichos   720| MS:driveler *1889a:*driveller   721| MS:Foil §altered to§ foil me—Krateinos §marked for transposition to precede *foil*§ match *P1875:*Kratinos <> me, match   722| MS:The 'Clouds?' I swallowed their distilment *P1875:*swallowed cloud-distilment *1889a:*The 'Clouds'? I   723| MS:any §inserted above§ grape-blush, while §crossed out§ I knit *P1875:*grape-blush, knit   724| MS:learnedest: *P1875:*learnedest;

⁷²⁵ While he worked at his 'Willow-wicker-flask,'
Swigging at that same flask by which he swore,
Till, sing and empty, sing and fill again,
Somehow result was—what it should not be
Next time, I promised him and kept my word!
⁷³⁰ Hence, brimful now of Thasian . . . I'll be bound,
Mendesian, merely: triumph-night, you know,
The High Priest entertains the conqueror,
And, since war worsens all things, stingily
The rascal starves whom he is bound to stuff,
⁷³⁵ Choros and actors and their lord and king
The poet; supper, still he needs must spread—
And this time all was conscientious fare:
He knew his man, his match, his master—made
Amends, spared neither fish, flesh, fowl nor wine:
⁷⁴⁰ So merriment increased, I promise you,
Till—something happened."

               Here he strangely paused.

"After that,—well, it either was the cup
To the Good Genius, our concluding pledge,
That wrought me mischief, decently unmixed,—
⁷⁴⁵ Or, what if, when *that* happened, need arose
Of new libation?   Did you only know
What happened!   Little wonder I am drunk."

Euthukles, o'er the boat-side, quick, what change,
Watch, in the water!   But a second since,
⁷⁵⁰ It laughed a ripply spread of sun and sea,

---

^{725|} MS:his "Willow-wicker-flask," *P1875:*his 'Willow-wicker-flask,' ^{727|} MS:And, §crossed out and replaced above by§ Till, sing ^{733|} MS:all, more §comma and last word crossed out and replaced above by word and comma§ things §over illegible word§ ^{736|} MS:poet: supper *P1875:*poet; supper ^{738-39|} MS:§lines added§ ^{739|} MS:nor—wine: *P1875:*nor wine: ^{741|} 1875:paused *1889a:*paused. ^{743|} MS:the Good Genius, the §crossed out and replaced above by§ our ^{746|} MS:libation? If you <> knew *P1875:*libation? Did you <> know ^{748|} MS:§line added§ Euthukles, take your eyes away, §last four words crossed out and replaced above by four words§ o'er the boat-side, quick ^{749|} MS:See, in *P1875:*Watch, in

Ray fused with wave, to never disunite.
Now, sudden all the surface, hard and black,
Lies a quenched light, dead motion: what the cause?
Look up and lo, the menace of a cloud
755 Has solemnized the sparkling, spoiled the sport!
Just so, some overshadow, some new care
Stopped all the mirth and mocking on his face
And left there only such a dark surmise
—No wonder if the revel disappeared,
760 So did his face shed silence every side!
I recognized a new man fronting me.

"So!" he smiled, piercing to my thought at once,
"You see myself?   Balaustion's fixed regard
Can strip the proper Aristophanes
765 Of what our sophists, in their jargon, style
His accidents?   My soul sped forth but now
To meet your hostile survey,—soul unseen,
Yet veritably cinct for soul-defence
With satyr sportive quips, cranks, boss and spike,
770 Just as my visible body paced the street,
Environed by a boon companionship
Your apparition also puts to flight.
Well, what care I if, unaccoutred twice,
I front my foe—no comicality
775 Round soul, and body-guard in banishment?
Thank your eyes' searching, undisguised I stand:
The merest female child may question me.

751| MS:Ray §over illegible word§ <> wave, no fear they §last three words crossed out and replaced above by two words§ to never   755| MS:the dance! *P1875:*the sport!
756| MS:so, the §crossed out and replaced above by§ some overshadow, the §crossed out and replaced above by§ some new thought *P1875:*new care   760| MS:So did it §last two words crossed out and replaced above by two words§ his face ray §altered to§ rayed for the silence *P1875:*did his face shed silence   768| MS:for soul's defence *P1875:*for soul-defence   769| MS:satyr sportivenesses, boss *P1875:*satyr sportive quips, cranks, boss 770| MS:While this my <> street *P1875:*Just as my <> street,   773| MS:unaccoutred thus *P1875:*unaccoutred twice,   776| MS:eyes' service, undisguised <> stand— *P1875:*eyes' searching, undisguised <> stand: 777| MS:me: *P1875:*me.

Spare not, speak bold, Balaustion!"

I did speak:

"Bold speech be—welcome to this honoured hearth,
780   Good Genius!   Glory of the poet, glow
O' the humourist who castigates his kind,
Suave summer-lightning lambency which plays
On stag-horned tree, misshapen crag askew,
Then vanishes with unvindictive smile
785   After a moment's laying black earth bare.
Splendour of wit that springs a thunderball—
Satire—to burn and purify the world,
True aim, fair purpose: just wit justly strikes
Injustice,—right, as rightly quells the wrong,
790   Finds out in knaves', fools', cowards' armoury
The tricky tinselled place fire flashes through,
No damage else, sagacious of true ore;
Wit, learned in the laurel, leaves each wreath
O'er lyric shell or tragic barbiton,—
795   Though alien gauds be singed,—undesecrate,
The genuine solace of the sacred brow.
Ay, and how pulses flame a patriot-star
Steadfast athwart our country's night of things,
To beacon, would she trust no meteor-blaze,
800   Athenai from the rock she steers for straight!
O light, light, light, I hail light everywhere,
No matter for the murk that was,—perchance,
That will be,—certes, never should have been

778| MS:Do not you speak, Balaustion?" *P1875:*Spare not, speak bold, Balaustion!"
779| MS:"My speech *P1875:*"Bold speech   780| MS:genius *P1875:*Good Genius
781| MS:Of *P1875:*O'   783| MS:stag horned *P1875:*stag-horned
786| MS:Splendor *1889a:*Splendour   788| MS:aim, fit purpose: just, wit *P1875:*aim,
fair purpose: just wit   790| MS:Finding in *P1875:*Finds out in
791| MS:through *P1875:*through,   792| MS:Nor touches gold, sagacious *P1875:*No
damage else, sagacious   795| MS:alien leaf be *P1875:*alien gauds be

Such orb's associate!

"Aristophanes!
805 'The merest female child may question you?'
Once, in my Rhodes, a portent of the wave
Appalled our coast: for many a darkened day,
Intolerable mystery and fear.
Who snatched a furtive glance through crannied peak,
810 Could but report of snake-scale, lizard-limb,—
So swam what, making whirlpools as it went,
Madded the brine with wrath or monstrous sport.
''Tis Tuphon, loose, unmanacled from mount,'
Declared the priests, 'no way appeasable
815 Unless perchance by virgin-sacrifice!'
Thus grew the terror and o'erhung the doom—
Until one eve a certain female-child
Strayed in safe ignorance to seacoast edge,
And there sat down and sang to please herself.
820 When all at once, large-looming from his wave,
Out leaned, chin hand-propped, pensive on the ledge,
A sea-worn face, sad as mortality,
Divine with yearning after fellowship.
He rose but breast-high.   So much god she saw;
825 So much she sees now, and does reverence!"

Ah, but there followed tail-splash, frisk of fin!
Let cloud pass, the sea's ready laugh outbreaks.

804-06| MS:Such <> §¶§ "Aristophanes! / Once   *P1875:*Such <> "Aristophanes! / 'The <>
you?' / Once   811| MS:swam he, making <> as he went   *P1875:*swam what, making
<> as it went,   812| MS:Madding   *P1875:*Madded   814| MS:way appears able §last
two words altered to§ appeasable   815| MS:Unless it prove by   *P1875:*Unless perchance
by   816| MS:doom,   *P1875:*doom—   817| MS:Until it chanced a   *P1875:*Until
one eve a   818| MS:in its ignorance   *P1875:*in safe ignorance
819| MS:sate <> itself.   *P1875:*herself.   *1889a:*sat   820-21| MS:§lines added§
822| MS:sea-god §last three letters crossed out and replaced above by§ -worn   824|
MS:breast high, §comma altered to period§ just §crossed out§ so §altered to§ So <> god
§inserted above§   *P1875:*breast-high   825| MS she §over illegible word, perhaps *I*§ see
§altered to§ sees <> and do §altered to§ does   827| MS:The §crossed out and replaced
above by§ Let <> passed §altered to§ pass <> outbroke, §last three letters crossed out and
replaced above by four letters, *eaks,* and comma altered to period, forming§ outbreaks.

No very godlike trace retained the mouth
Which mocked with—

         "So, He taught you tragedy!
830   I always asked 'Why may not women act?'
Nay, wear the comic visor just as well;
Or, better, quite cast off the face-disguise
And voice-distortion, simply look and speak,
Real women playing women as men—men!
835   I shall not wonder if things come to that,
Some day when I am distant far enough.
Do you conceive the quite new Comedy
When laws allow? laws only let girls dance,
Pipe, posture,—above all, Elaphionize,
840   Provided they keep decent—that is, dumb.
Ay, and, conceiving, I would execute,
Had I but two lives: one were overworked!
How penetrate encrusted prejudice,
Pierce ignorance three generations thick
845   Since first Sousarion crossed our boundary?
He battered with a big Megaric stone;
Chionides felled oak and rough-hewed thence
This club I wield now, having spent my life
In planing knobs and sticking studs to shine;
850   Somebody else must try mere polished steel!"

Emboldened by the sober mood's return,
"Meanwhile," said I, "since planed and studded club

830| MS:asked 'Why should §crossed out and replaced above by§ may
831| MS:well—   *P1875:*well;   834| MS:men?   *P1875:*men!   837| MS:new comic
play—   *P1875:*new Comedy   838| MS:let you §altered to§ girls   840| MS:Provided
you §crossed out and replaced above by§ they   844| MS:Through §in margin over
illegible erasure§ Ignorance §altered to§ ignorance now §crossed out§ three   *P1875:*Pierce
ignorance   847| MS:felled §over illegible word§ <> rough hewed club §crossed out and
replaced above by dash and word§ —thence   *P1875:*rough-hewed thence
848| MS:This which §crossed out and replaced above by§ club   849| MS:In smoothing
§crossed out and replaced above by§ planing   851| MS:§line added§
852| MS:May I enquire? What smoothed §last five words crossed out and replaced above by
five words§ "Meanwhile" said I. "since planed   *P1875:*"Meanwhile," said I, "since

Once more has pashed competitors to dust,
And poet proves triumphant with that play
855 Euthukles found last year unfortunate,—
Does triumph spring from smoothness still more smoothed,
Fresh studs sown thick and threefold? In plain words,
Have you exchanged brute-blows,—which teach the brute
Man may surpass him in brutality,—
860 For human fighting, or true god-like force
Which breathes persuasion nor needs fight at all?
Have you essayed attacking ignorance,
Convicting folly, by their opposites,
Knowledge and wisdom? not by yours for ours,
865 Fresh ignorance and folly, new for old,
Greater for less, your crime for our mistake!
If so success at last have crowned desert,
Bringing surprise (dashed haply by concern
At your discovery such wild waste of strength
870 —And what strength!—went so long to keep in vogue
Such warfare—and what warfare!—shamed so fast,
So soon made obsolete, as fell their foe
By the first arrow native to the orb,
First onslaught worthy Aristophanes)—

853| MS:Again §crossed out and replaced above by two words§ Once more
854| MS:And §in margin§ The §crossed out§ poet has just §last two words crossed out and
replaced above by one word§ proved §altered to§ proves triumphed §altered to§ triumphant
with a play, *P1875:*with that play, *1889a:*play   855| MS:Euthukles §crossed out and
replaced above by§ Athenai §crossed out and original reading restored§
860| MS:fighting, if not godlike force? §over illegible word; question mark crossed out§
*P1875:*fighting, or true god-like   861| MS:§line added§ That breathes *P1875:*Which
breathes   862| MS:Have you §last two words in margin§ Essayed §altered to§ essayed at
last §last two words crossed out§ attacking   864| MS:§line added§ wisdom, not *P1875:*
wisdom? not   865| MS:Not §crossed out and replaced below by§ Fresh §over illegible
word§   866| MS:for their §crossed out and replaced above by§ our mistake? *P1875:*
mistake!   867| MS:success for once §last two words crossed out and replaced above by
two words§ at last   868| MS:surprise, dashed *P1875:*surprise (dashed
869| MS:At late discovery, such §crossed out and replaced above by illegibly erased word and
such restored§ *P1875:*discovery—such *1889a:*At your discovery such   870| MS:(And
<> strength!) went *1889a:*—And <> strength!—went   871| MS:warfare (and <>
warfare!)—shamed at last, §last two words crossed out and replaced above by one word§ away,
*P1875:*warfare!) shamed *1889a:*warfare—and <> warfare!—shamed so fast,
872| MS:§line added§ Made obsolete for ever, as foe fell *1889a:*So soon made obsolete, as fell
their foe   874| MS:§line added§ worthy Aristophanes,— *P1875:*worthy Aristophanes)—

875 Was this conviction's entry that same strange
'Something that happened' to confound your feast?"

"Ah, did he witness then my play that failed,
First 'Thesmophoriazousai'?   Well and good!
But did he also see,—your Euthukles,—
880 My 'Grasshoppers' which followed and failed too,
Three months since, at the 'Little-in-the-Fields'?"

"To say that he did see that First—should say
He never cared to see its following."

"There happens to be reason why I wrote
885 First play and second also.   Ask the cause!
I warrant you receive ere talk be done,
Fit answer, authorizing either act.
But here's the point: as Euthukles made vow
Never again to taste my quality,
890 So I was minded next experiment
Should tickle palate—yea, of Euthukles!
Not by such utter change, such absolute
A topsyturvy of stage-habitude
As you and he want,—Comedy built fresh,
895 By novel brick and mortar, base to roof,—
No, for I stand too near and look too close!
Pleasure and pastime yours, spectators brave,
Should I turn art's fixed fabric upside down!
Little you guess how such tough work tasks soul!

877| MS:then the §crossed out and replaced above by§ my   878| MS:First
Thesmophoriazousai? Well   *P1875*:First 'Thesmophoriazousai?' Well   *1889a*:First
'Thesmophoriazousai'? Well   884| MS:"There may have been good reason
P1875:"There happens to be reason   886-87| MS:§these two lines transposed§
886| MS:done.   *1889a*:done,   887| MS:act,   *1889a*:act.   888| MS:But I resume,—
§comma and dash altered to colon§ as   *P1875*:But here's the point: as
893| MS:topsyturvey   *P1875*:topsyturvy   896| MS:No! for   *P1875*:No, for
897| MS:An §over illegible erasure, perhaps *All*§ easy sport §over illegibly erased word§ for
you, spectators brave, §over illegible word§   *P1875*:Pleasure and pastime yours, spectators
898| MS:This turning art's   *P1875*:Should turn art's   *CP1875*:Should I turn

900   Not overtasks, though: give fit strength fair play,
      And strength's a demiourgos!   Art renewed?
      Ay, in some closet where strength shuts out—first
      The friendly faces, sympathetic cheer:
      'More of the old provision none supplies
905   So bounteously as thou,—our love, our pride,
      Our author of the many a perfect piece!
      Stick to that standard, change were decadence!'
      Next, the unfriendly: 'This time, strain will tire,
      He's fresh, Ameipsias thy antagonist!'
910   —Or better, in some Salaminian cave
      Where sky and sea and solitude make earth
      And man and noise one insignificance,
      Let strength propose itself,—behind the world,—
      Sole prize worth winning, work that satisfies
915   Strength it has dared and done strength's uttermost!
      After which,—clap-to closet and quit cave,—
      Strength may conclude in Archelaos' court,
      And yet esteem the silken company

900| MS:overtasks, §next word illegibly crossed out and replaced above by§ though
901| MS:And §in margin§ Strength §altered to§ strength cries 'Lay on, care §altered to§ spare nowise §altered to§ not!' §¶ called for in margin§ "Art   *P1875:*And strength's a demiourgos!' §no ¶§ "Art   *1889a:*demiourgos! Art   902| MS:in the §crossed out and replaced above by§ some <> Strength   *P1875:*strength   903| MS:cheer,   *P1875:*cheer:
904| MS:"More   *P1875:*'More   906| MS:a pleasant piece!   *P1875:*a perfect piece!
907| MS:decadence!"   *P1875:*decadence!'   908| MS:Then, the unfriendly: "This   *P1875:*Next, the unfriendly: 'This   909| MS:This time, Ameipsias for §crossed out and replaced above by§ thy antagonist!"   *P1875:*He's fresh, Ameipsias <> antagonist!'   910| MS:—Ay, §word and comma crossed out and replaced above by§ Or <> in the §crossed out and replaced above by§ some   912| MS:And transiency seem §crossed out and replaced above by§ grow insignificance;   *P1875:*And man and noise one insignificance,
913| MS:And §crossed out and replaced above by§ Let Strength says §altered to§ say,— weakness well behind the back §crossed out and replaced above by§ world,—   *P1875:*strength propose itself,—behind   914| MS:'Sole prize, worth winning, is §crossed out and replaced above by§ work to satisfy   *P1875:*Sole prize worth <> work that satisfies
915| MS:done strength's §altered to§ Strength's uttermost!'   *P1875:*strength's uttermost!
916| MS:Nay, I'll add, close the §last two words crossed out and replaced above by one word§ leave §crossed out§ clap-to §inserted above§ closet, §comma crossed out and §inserted above§ quit the §crossed out§ cave,   *P1875:*After which,—clap-to <> cave,—
917| MS:Strength best §crossed out and replaced above by§ may concludes §altered to§ conclude   918| MS:Counting §crossed out and replaced above by two words§ Esteeming all the silken §next word illegibly crossed out§ company   *P1875:*And yet esteem the

So much sky-scud, sea-froth, earth-thistledown,
920 For aught their praise or blame should joy or grieve.
Strength amid crowds as late in solitude
May lead the still life, ply the wordless task:
Then only, when seems need to move or speak,
Moving—for due respect, when statesmen pass,
925 (Strength, in the closet, watched how spiders spin)
Speaking—when fashion shows intelligence,
(Strength, in the cave, oft whistled to the gulls)
In short, has learnt first, practised afterwards!
Despise the world and reverence yourself,—
930 Why, you may unmake things and remake things,
And throw behind you, unconcerned enough,
What's made or marred: 'you teach men, are not taught!'
So marches off the stage Euripides!

"No such thin fare feeds flesh and blood like mine
935 No such faint fume of fancy sates my soul,
No such seclusion, closet, cave or court,
Suits either: give me Iostephanos
Worth making happy what coarse way she will—
O happy-maker, when her cries increase
940 About the favourite! 'Aristophanes!
More grist to mill, here's Kleophon to grind!
He's for refusing peace, though Sparté cede

919| MS:As §in margin, crossed out and replaced in margin by two words§ So much Sky-scud
§altered to§ sky-scud, and §crossed out§ sea-froth, and §crossed out§ earth-thistledown,
920-22| MS:For <> grieve:— / May §in margin§ Leading §altered to§ lead <> life, at the
wordless work: *P1875:*grieve: / <> life, ply the wordless task: *1889a:*grieve. / Strength <>
solitude / May   923| MS:Strength §in margin§ And, §crossed out§ only when is need
*P1875:*Then only, when seems need   924| MS:respect since statesmen *P1875:*respect,
since *1889a:*respect, when statesmen   925| *P1875:*spin!) *1889a:*spin)
927-29| MS:(Strength <> cave, oft §crossed out and replaced above by§ has whistled <> gulls.)
/ Despise *P1875:*cave, had whistled <> gulls!) / Despise *1889a:*cave, oft whistled <>
gulls) / In <> afterwards! / Despise   934| MS:mine, *1889a:*mine
935| MS:fume the Aristophanic soul, *1889a:*fume of fancy sates my soul,
937| MS:either like this Iostephanos *P1875:*like our Iostephanos *1889a:*either:give me
Iostephanos   938| MS:happy in what way it will— *P1875:*happy what coarse way she
will—   939| MS:Ever Athenai, when §over illegible word§ the crowds increase *P1875:*
The happy-maker, when the cries increase *1889a:*O happy-maker, when her cries
940| MS:the victor! 'Aristophanes! *P1875:*the favourite! 'Aristophanes!

41

Even Dekeleia! Here's Kleonumos
Declaring—though he threw away his shield,
945   He'll thrash you till you lay your lyre aside!
Orestes bids mind where you walk of nights—
He wants your cloak as you his cudgelling:
Here's, finally, Melanthios fat with fish,
The gormandizer-spendthrift-dramatist!
950   So, bustle!   Pounce on opportunity!
Set fun a-screaming in Parabasis,
Find food for folk agape at either end,
Mad for amusement!   Times grow better too,
And should they worsen, why, who laughs, forgets.
955   In no case, venture boy-experiments!
Old wine's the wine: new poetry drinks raw:
Two plays a season is your pledge, beside;
So, give us "Wasps" again, grown hornets now!' "

Then he changed.

                "Do you so detect in me—
960   Brow-bald, chin-bearded, me, curved cheek, carved lip,
Or where soul sits and reigns in either eye—
What suits the—stigma, I say,—style say you,
Of 'Wine-lees-poet'?   Bravest of buffoons,
Less blunt than Telekleides, less obscene
965   Than Murtilos, Hermippos: quite a match

944| MS:Declaring—if he   *1889a:*Declaring—though he   946| MS:nights: *P1875:*
nights   *1889a:*nights—   947| MS:cudgeling.   *1889a:*cudgelling:
948| MS:Here's—finally—Melanthios   *P1875:*Here's, finally, Melanthios
951| MS:Set fun   *P1875:*Let fun §emended to§ Set fun §see Editorial Notes§
953| MS:amusement: times are mending §last two words crossed out and replaced above by
two words§ grow better   *P1875:*amusement! Times   954| MS:forgets!   *P1875:*forgets.
955| MS:venture play-experiments: *P1875:*venture boy-experiments!
957| MS:is child's play beside;   *P1875:*is your pledge, beside;   958| MS:grown Hornets
now!'   *P1875:*hornets now!"   *1889a:*now!' "   960| MS:Brow-baldness, chin-beard §last
two words altered to§ Brow-bald, chin-bearded,—me, §dash, word and comma inserted above§
<> carven §altered to§ carved   *P1875:*chin-bearded, me
962| MS:say,—you say, style §last three words transposed to§ style say you,
963| *P1875:*Of 'Wine-lees-poet?' Bravest   *1889a:*Of 'Wine-lees-poet'? Bravest
965| MS:Than Murtilos, Hermippos: while a   *P1875:*Than Murtilos, Hermippos: quite a

In elegance for Eupolis himself,
Yet pungent as Kratinos at his best?
Graced with traditional immunity
Ever since, much about my grandsire's time,
970   Some funny village-man in Megara,
Lout-lord and clown-king, used a privilege,
As due religious drinking-bouts came round,
To daub his phyz,—no, that was afterward,—
He merely mounted cart with mates of choice
975   And traversed country, taking house by house,
At night,—because of danger in the freak,—
Then hollaed 'Skin-flint starves his labourers!
Clench-fist stows figs away, cheats government!
Such an one likes to kiss his neighbour's wife,
980   And beat his own; while such another . . . Boh!'
Soon came the broad day, circumstantial tale,
Dancing and verse, and there's our Comedy,
There's Mullos, there's Euetes, there's the stock
I shall be proud to graft my powers upon!
985   Protected? Punished quite as certainly
When Archons pleased to lay down each his law,—
Your Morucheides-Surakosios sort,—
Each season, 'No more naming citizens,
Only abuse the vice, the vicious spare!
990   Observe, henceforth no Areopagite
Demean his rank by writing Comedy!'
(They one and all could write the 'Clouds' of course.)
'Needs must we nick expenditure, allow

967| MS:And §crossed out and replaced above by§ Yet <> Krateinos   *P1875:*as Kratinos
970| MS:In Megara, §last two words and comma marked for transposition to follow *village-man*§ The funny village-man,   *P1875:*Some funny village-man in   971| MS: used his §crossed out and replaced above by§ a   975| *P1875:*travers'd   *1889a:*traversed
976| MS:By night   *P1875:*At night   977| MS:hollaing §altered to§ hollaed 'Skin flint *P1875:* hollaed 'Skin-flint   978| MS:Clench fist   *P1875:*Clench-fist   980| MS:own: while §inserted above§ such an §inserted above§ other..Boh!'   *P1875:*own; <> another *1889a:*another...Boh!'   981| MS:Soon §in margin§ Next §crossed out§ <> broad §inserted above§ day, light §crossed out§circumstantial   982| MS:there's your §altered to§ our   987| MS:Your Morucheides-Surakosios-sort,—   *P1875:*Your Morucheides-Surakosios sort,—   990| MS:Caution §crossed out and replaced above by§ Observe! henceforth   *P1875:*Observe, henceforth   992| MS:course)   *1889a:*course.)

Comedy half a choros, supper—none,
995   Times being hard, while applicants increase
For, what costs cash, the Tragic Trilogy.'
Lofty Tragedians!   How they lounge aloof
Each with his Triad, three plays to my one,
Not counting the contemptuous fourth, the frank
1000 Concession to mere mortal levity,
Satyric pittance tossed our beggar-world!
Your proud Euripides from first to last
Doled out some five such, never deigned us more!
And these—what curds and whey for marrowy wine!
1005 That same 'Alkestis' you so rave about
Passed muster with him for a Satyr-play,
The prig!—why trifle time with toys and skits
When he could stuff four ragbags sausage-wise
With sophistry, with bookish odds and ends,
1010 Sokrates, meteors, moonshine, 'Life's not Life,'
'The tongue swore, but unsworn the mind remains,'
And fifty such concoctions, crab-tree-fruit
Digested while, head low and heels in heaven,
He lay, let Comics laugh—for privilege!
1015 Looked puzzled on, or pityingly off,
But never dreamed of paying gibe by jeer,
Buffet by blow: plenty of proverb-pokes
At vice and folly, wicked kings, mad mobs!

999| MS:counting the §over illegible erasure§ <> Fourth, the §over illegible erasure§
P1875:fourth   1000| MS:to poor §crossed out and replaced above by§ mere
1001| MS:our §over illegible erasure§   1002| MS:Why, your §last two words crossed out
and replaced above by two words and comma§ I find, Euripides   *P1875*:Your proud Euripides
1005| MS:you have §crossed out and replaced above by§ so raved §altered to§ rave
1009| MS:sophistry, and §crossed out and replaced above by§ with   1011| MS:but the
mind remained §altered to§ remains unsworn' §transposed to§ but unsworn the mind
remains'   *1889a*:remains,'   1012| MS:concoctions, just-the-fruit §altered to§ crab-tree-fruit
1013| MS:Of dreaming with §last three words crossed out and replaced above by two words§
Culled while §last two words crossed out and replaced by two words and comma§ Digested
while, head down §crossed out and replaced above by§ low <> heaven, §over illegible
erasure§   1014| MS:lay, and §crossed out§ let comics §altered to§ Comics <> privilege—
P1875:privilege!   1016| MS:paying joke §crossed out and replaced above by§ gibe
1017| MS:blow: a §crossed out§ <> proverb-thrusts §altered to§ proverb-pokes

No sign of wincing at my Comic lash,
1020 No protest against infamous abuse,
Malignant censure,—nought to prove I scourged
With tougher thong than leek-and-onion-plait!
If ever he glanced gloom, aggrieved at all,
The aggriever must be—Aischulos perhaps:
1025 Or Sophokles he'd take exception to.
—Do you detect in me—in me, I ask,
The man like to accept this measurement
Of faculty, contentedly sit classed
Mere Comic Poet—since I wrote 'The Birds'?"

1030 I thought there might lurk truth in jest's disguise.

"Thanks!" he resumed, so quick to construe smile!
"I answered—in my mind—these gapers thus:
Since old wine's ripe and new verse raw, you judge—
What if I vary vintage-mode and mix
1035 Blossom with must, give nosegay to the brew,
Fining, refining, gently, surely, till
The educated taste turns unawares
From customary dregs to draught divine?
Then answered—with my lips: More 'Wasps' you want?

---

¹⁰¹⁹| MS:No word like §crossed out and replaced above by§ nor wincing at the Comic Muse,
*P1875:*No sign of wincing at my Comic lash, ¹⁰²⁰| MS:§line added§ against 'infamous
*P1875:*against infamous ¹⁰²¹| MS:censure,'—nought §over illegible word§ that §crossed
out and replaced above by§ to proves §altered to§ prove you §crossed out and
replaced above by§ I scourge §altered to§ scourged *P1875:*censure,—nought
¹⁰²²| MS:With no more §last two words crossed out and replaced above by one word§ tougher
thong of §crossed out and replaced above by§ than ¹⁰²⁴| MS:aggriever might §crossed
out and replaced above by§ must ¹⁰²⁵| MS:§line added§ he took exception to!
*P1875:*he'd take exception to. ¹⁰²⁶| MS:— §dash in margin§ Do you perce §last five letters
crossed out§ detect in Aristophanes §crossed out and replaced above by three words and
comma§ me—in me ¹⁰²⁷| MS:like §inserted above§ to take §crossed out and replaced
above by§ accept this §next word illegibly crossed out§ measurement
¹⁰²⁸| MS:classed §over illegible erasure§ ¹⁰²⁹| MS:'Mere <> Poet'—since §crossed out
and replaced above by§ for he wrote <> Birds'? *P1875:*Mere <> Poet—since I wrote <>
Birds'?" ¹⁰³¹| MS:"So" §crossed out and replaced above by§ Thanks! <> smile,
§comma altered to exclamation point§ ¹⁰³⁵| MS:must, new §crossed out and replaced
above by§ give <> to old §crossed out and replaced above by§ the ¹⁰³⁷| MS:turn
*1889a:*turns ¹⁰³⁹| MS:Then §over illegible word§

45

¹⁰⁴⁰ Come next year and I give you 'Grasshoppers'!
And 'Grasshoppers' I gave them,—last month's play.
They formed the Choros. Alkibiades,
No longer Triphales but Trilophos,
(Whom I called Darling-of-the-Summertime,
¹⁰⁴⁵ Born to be nothing else but beautiful
And brave, to eat, drink, love his life away)
Persuades the Tettix (our Autochthon-brood,
That sip the dew and sing on olive-branch
Above the ant-and-emmet populace)
¹⁰⁵⁰ To summon all who meadow, hill and dale
Inhabit—bee, wasp, woodlouse, dragonfly—
To band themselves against red nipper-nose
Stagbeetle, huge Taügetan (you guess—
Sparté) Athenai needs must battle with,
¹⁰⁵⁵ Because her sons are grown effeminate
To that degree—so morbifies their flesh
The poison-drama of Euripides,
Morals and music—there's no antidote
Occurs save warfare which inspirits blood,
¹⁰⁶⁰ And brings us back perchance the blessed time
When (Choros takes up tale) our commonalty
Firm in primæval virtue, antique faith,

---

^{1042|} MS:They made §crossed out and replaced above by§ formed < > Choros: Alkibiades,
*P1875:*the Choros. Alkibiades,   ^{1043|} MS:§line added§   ^{1044|} MS:(§parenthesis in
margin§   ^{1046|} MS:away, §comma altered to closing parenthesis§   ^{1047|} MS:the
Tettix,— §comma and dash altered to parenthesis§ (our   ^{1049|} MS:populace— §dash
altered to closing parenthesis§   ^{1051|} MS:wasp, pismire §crossed out and replaced above
by§ woodlouse, dragonfly,   *1889a:*dragonfly—   ^{1052|} MS:against the §crossed out and
replaced above by§ red nippered §last two words altered to§ Red Nippered foe §last word and
preceding two letters crossed out and replaced above by hyphen, word and comma, forming§
Nipper-nose,   *P1875:*red nipper-nose   ^{1053|} MS:Stagbeetle, the §crossed out and
replaced above by§ huge Taügetan,— §comma and dash altered to parenthesis§ (you guess—
§over illegible word§   ^{1054|} MS:Sparté,— §comma and dash altered to closing
parenthesis§ Athenai   ^{1055|} MS:her youth is §last two words crossed out and replaced
above by two words§ sons are   ^{1056|} MS:so eats the heart §last three words crossed out
and replaced above by four words§ morbifies into §crossed out§ their flesh
^{1057|} MS:That §altered to§ The   ^{1058|} MS:music—that §crossed out and replaced above
by§ there's no remedy §crossed out and replaced above by§ antidote   ^{1059|} MS:Remains
but §last two words crossed out and replaced above by two words§ Occurs save < > which
renews the §last two words crossed out and replaced above by one word§ inspirits

Ere earwig-sophist plagued or pismire-sage,
Cockered no noddle up with A, b, g,
1065 Book-learning, logic-chopping, and the moon,
But just employed their brains on '*Ruppapai*,
Row, boys, munch barley-bread, and take your ease—
Mindful, however, of the tier beneath!'
Ah, golden epoch! while the nobler sort
1070 (Such needs must study, no contesting that!)
Wore no long curls but used to crop their hair,
Gathered the tunic well about the ham,
Remembering 'twas soft sand they used for seat
At school-time, while—mark this—the lesson long,
1075 No learner ever dared to cross his legs!
Then, if you bade him take the myrtle-bough
And sing for supper—'twas some grave romaunt
How man of Mitulené, wondrous wise,
Jumped into hedge, by mortals quickset called,
1080 *And there, anticipating Oidipous,*
Scratched out his eyes and scratched them in again.
None of your Phaidras, Augés, Kanakés,
To mincing music, turn, trill, tweedle-trash,
Whence comes that Marathon is obsolete!
1085 Next, my Antistrophé was—praise of Peace:
Ah, could our people know what Peace implies!
Home to the farm and furrow! Grub one's vine,
Romp with one's Thratta, pretty serving-girl,
When wife's busy bathing! Eat and drink,
1090 And drink and eat, what else is good in life?

1063| MS:§line added§   1065| *P1875:*and, the   *CP1875:*and the
1066| MS:on '*Ruppapai*,   *P1875:*on '*Ruppapai*,   1072| MS:Gathered their §altered to§
the tunics §altered to§ tunic <> about their §altered to§ the hams §altered to§ ham   *P1875:*
ham,   1073| MS:they sat upon §last two words crossed out and replaced above by three
words§ used for seat   1074| MS:while— §over illegible word§ mark §next word illegibly
crossed out, perhaps *your,* and replaced above by two words§ this! the   *P1875:*this—the
1080| MS:anticipated   *P1875:* anticipating   1085| MS:Antistrophé—the §dash and word
crossed out and replaced above by word and dash§ was— <> of Peace,—ah, Peace,   *P1875:*
Next my Antistrophé <> of Peace: 1086| MS:Peace, if our <>
knew   *P1875:*Ah, could our <> know   1088| MS:serving-girl   *P1875:*serving-girl,
1089| MS:busy washing! Eat   *P1875:*busy bathing! Eat

Slice hare, toss pancake, gaily gurgle down
The Thasian grape in celebration due
Of Bacchos!   Welcome, dear domestic rite,
When wife and sons and daughters, Thratta too,
1095   Pour peasoup as we chant delectably
In Bacchos reels, his tunic at his heels!
Enough, you comprehend,—I do at least!
Then,—be but patient,—the Parabasis!
Pray!   For in that I also pushed reform.
1100   None of the self-laudation, vulgar brag,
Vainglorious rivals cultivate so much!
No!   If some merest word in Art's defence
Justice demanded of me,—never fear!
Claim was preferred, but dignifiedly.
1105   A cricket asked a locust (winged, you know)
What he had seen most rare in foreign parts?
'I have flown far,' chirped he, 'North, East, South, West,
And nowhere heard of poet worth a fig
If matched with Bald-head here, Aigina's boast,
1110   Who in this play bids rivalry despair
Past, present, and to come, so marvellous
His Tragic, Comic, Lyric excellence!
Whereof the fit reward were (not to speak
Of dinner every day at public cost
1115   I' the Prutaneion) supper with yourselves,
My Public, best dish offered bravest bard!'

No more! no sort of sin against good taste!
Then, satire,—Oh, a plain necessity!
But I won't tell you: for—could I dispense
1120 With one more gird at old Ariphrades?
How scorpion-like he feeds on human flesh—
Ever finds out some novel infamy
Unutterable, inconceivable,
Which all the greater need was to describe
1125 Minutely, each tail-twist at ink-shed time . . .
Now, what's your gesture caused by?   What you loathe,
Don't I loathe doubly, else why take such pains
To tell it you?   But keep your prejudice!
My audience justified you!   Housebreakers!
1130 This pattern-purity was played and failed
Last Rural Dionusia—failed! for why?
Ameipsias followed with the genuine stuff.
He had been mindful to engage the Four—
Karkinos and his dwarf-crab-family—
1135 Father and sons, they whirled like spinning-tops,
Choros gigantically poked his fun,
The boys' frank laugh relaxed the seniors' brow,
The skies re-echoed victory's acclaim,
Ameipsias gained his due, I got my dose
1140 Of wisdom for the future.   Purity?
No more of that next month, Athenai mine!
Contrive new cut of robe who will,—I patch
The old exomis, add no purple sleeve!
The Thesmophoriazousai, smartened up

1117| MS:more—no *P1875:*more! no   1018| MS:Then,—Satire *P1875:*Then, satire
1119| MS:you: how §crossed out and replaced above by word and dash§ for
1125| MS:time,— *P1875:*time...   1125-26| MS:§¶ called for in margin§ *P1875:*§page
ends§ *1889a:*§no ¶§   1126| MS:what's the §crossed out and replaced above by§ your
1129| MS:you; never fear! *P1875:*you! Housebreakers!   1130| MS:This play, this purity,
was *P1875:*This pattern-purity was   1131| MS:Last Rural Dionusia, since, at end,
*P1875:*Last Rural Dionusia—failed! for why?   1132| MS:Followed Ameipsias with *P1875:*
Ameipsias followed with   1134| MS:his §inserted above§   1138| MS:So, skies
reechoed *P1875:*The skies re-echoed   1139| MS:gained the prize, I *P1875:*gained his
due, I   1140| MS:future—'Purity? *P1875:*future. Purity?   1143| MS:exomis §over
partial erasure§   1144| MS:Next month, the <> smart *P1875:*The <> smartened up

1145   With certain plaits, shall please, I promise you!

"Yes, I took up the play that failed last year,
And re-arranged things; threw adroitly in,—
No Parachoregema,—men to match
My women there already; and when these
1150   (I had a hit at Aristullos here,
His plan how womankind should rule the roast)
Drove men to plough—'A-field, ye cribbed of cape!'
Men showed themselves exempt from service straight
Stupendously, till all the boys cried 'Brave!'
1155   Then for the elders, I bethought me too,
Improved upon Mnesilochos' release
From the old bowman, board and binding-strap:
I made his son-in-law Euripides
Engage to put both shrewish wives away—
1160   'Gravity' one, the other 'Sophist-lore'—
And mate with the Bald Bard's hetairai twain—
'Goodhumour' and 'Indulgence': on they tripped,
Murrhiné, Akalanthis,—'beautiful
Their whole belongings'—crowd joined choros there!
1165   And while the Toxotes wound up his part
By shower of nuts and sweetmeats on the mob,
The woman-choros celebrated New
Kalligeneia, the frank last-day rite.
Brief, I was chairéd and caressed and crowned
1170   And the whole theatre broke out a-roar,

1145| MS:plaits shall   *P1875:*plaits, shall   1146| MS:Yes   *P1875:*"Yes   1147| MS:I §altered to§ And <> things: <> in,   *P1875:*things; <> in,—   1148| MS:As parachoregema, men   *P1875:*No Parachoregema,—men   1149| MS:My §over illegible erasure§ <> already: <> these,   *CP1875:*already; <> these §not B§   1151| MS:plan for §crossed out and replaced above by§ how womankind to §crossed out and replaced above by§ should   1153| MS:They showed   *P1875:*Men showed   1155| MS:Then, for   *P1875:* Then for   1157| MS:From Skuthian bowman   *P1875:*From the old bowman   1158| MS:His son-in-law engaged—Euripides,   *P1875:*I made his son-in-law Euripides   1159| MS:Imagine!—to <> both his wives away,   *P1875:*Engage to <> both shrewish wives   *1889a:* away—   1160| MS:'Gravity', one, the other 'Sophist-lore,'   *P1875:*'Gravity,' <> other, 'Sophist-lore,'   *1889a:*'Gravity' one <> other 'Sophist-lore'   1162| MS:and 'Indulgence'—on   *P1875:*and 'Indulgence': on   1164| MS:In all belongings'   *P1875:* Their whole belongings'   1170| MS:whole Theatre <> a-roar   *P1875:*theatre <> a-roar,

Echoed my admonition—choros-cap—
Rivals of mine, your hands to your faces!
Summon no more the Muses, the Graces,
Since here by my side they have chosen their places!

1175 And so we all flocked merrily to feast,
I, my choragos, choros, actors, mutes
And flutes aforesaid, friends in crowd, no fear,
At the Priest's supper; and hilarity
Grew none the less that, early in the piece,
1180 Ran a report, from row to row close-packed,
Of messenger's arrival at the Port
With weighty tidings, 'Of Lusandros' flight,'
Opined one; 'That Euboia penitent
Sends the Confederation fifty ships,'
1185 Preferred another; while 'The Great King's Eye
Has brought a present for Elaphion here,
That rarest peacock Kompolakuthes!'
Such was the supposition of a third.
'No matter what the news,' friend Strattis laughed,
1190 'It won't be worse for waiting: while each click
Of the klepsudra sets a-shaking grave
Resentment in our shark's-head, boiled and spoiled
By this time: dished in Sphettian vinegar,

1171| MS:With my last admonition—choros-end— *P1875:*Echoed my admonition—choros-
cap— 1174-75| MS:§¶ called for in margin§ *P1875:*§no ¶§ 1175| MS:to sup
§crossed out§ feast,— *1889a:*feast, 1176| MS:my Choragos, Choros, Actors three,
*P1875:*choragos, choros, actors, mutes 1177| MS:Mute-girls aforesaid < > fear,—
*P1875:*And flutes aforesaid < > fear, 1178| MS:supper: and *P1875:*supper; and
1179| MS:the day, *P1875:*the piece, 1182| MS:tidings 'Of < > flight' *P1875:*tidings,
'Of < > flight,' 1183| MS:one: 'How the §crossed out§ repentant Euboia
*P1875:*one; 'That Euboia penitent 1185| MS:Assured §crossed out and replaced above
by§ Supposed another, while *P1875:*Preferred another; while 1187-89| MS:That < >
Kompolakuthes!' / Laughed Strattis: "Well, §last three words and comma crossed out§ "no
§altered to§ No < > news," friend *P1875:*peacock Kompolakuthes!' / Such < > third. / 'No
< > news,' friend 1190| MS:"It < > waiting—what don't wait §last three words crossed
out and replaced above by three words§ while each §over illegible word§ click
P1875:'It < > waiting: while 1191| MS:klepsudra but wakes §last two words crossed out
and replaced above by one word§ sets resentment grave *P1875:*sets a-shaking grave
1192-93| MS:§one line expanded to two lines§ Put in the §last three words crossed out and
replaced above by two words§ Shaking our shark's-head fried with §crossed out and replaced
above by§ in vinegar, *P1875:*§lines 1192-93 added§

Silphion and honey, served with cocks'-brain-sauce!
1195 So, swift to supper, Poet! No mistake,
This play; nor, like the unflavoured "Grasshoppers,"
Salt without thyme!' Right merrily we supped,
Till—something happened.

"Out it shall, at last!

"Mirth drew to ending, for the cup was crowned
1200 To the Triumphant! 'Kleonclapper erst,
Now, Plier of a scourge Euripides
Fairly turns tail from, flying Attiké
For Makedonia's rocks and frosts and bears,
Where, furry grown, he growls to match the squeak
1205 Of girl-voiced, crocus-vested Agathon!
Ha ha, he he!' When suddenly a knock—
Sharp, solitary, cold, authoritative.

"*Babaiax!* Sokrates a-passing by,
A-peering in for Aristullos' sake,
1210 To put a question touching Comic Law?'
"No! Enters an old pale-swathed majesty,
Makes slow mute passage through two ranks as mute,
(Strattis stood up with all the rest, the sneak!)
Grey brow still bent on ground, upraised at length
1215 When, our Priest reached, full-front the vision paused.

1196| MS:This Play,—like that unlucky §crossed out and replaced above by§ unflavored 'Grasshoppers'— *P1875:*play; nor, like the unflavoured 'Grasshoppers,' *1889a:* unflavoured "Grasshoppers,"   1197| MS:thyme!" This §crossed out and replaced above by§ And merry way §last two words altered to one word§ merrily *P1875:*thyme!' Right merrily *1889a:*thyme! Right §emended to§ thyme!' Right §see Editorial Notes§
1199| MS:ending—for *P1875:*ending, for   1202| MS:from, flies warm Attiké *P1875:* from, flying Attiké   1205| MS:girl-voiced crocus-vested §inserted above§ Agathon— *P1875:*girl-voiced, crocus-vested Agathon!   1206| MS:he!' §¶ called for in margin§ When *P1875:*§no ¶§   1208| MS:"Babaiax *P1875:*'Babaiax *1889a:*"'Babaiax
1210| MS:touching Comic Law?" *P1875:*touching Comic Law?'   1211| MS:Slow enters *P1875:*"No! Enters   1212| MS:Makes a mute *P1875:*Makes slow mute
1213| MS:§line added§   1215| MS:When, the §crossed out and replaced above by§ our

52

"'Priest!'—the deep tone succeeded the fixed gaze—
'Thou carest that thy god have spectacle
Decent and seemly; wherefore I announce
That, since Euripides is dead to-day,
1220   My Choros, at the Greater Feast, next month,
Shall, clothed in black, appear ungarlanded!'

"Then the grey brow sank low, and Sophokles
Re-swathed him, sweeping doorward: mutely passed
'Twixt rows as mute, to mingle possibly
1225   With certain gods who convoy age to port;
And night resumed him.

                    "When our stupor broke,
Chirpings took courage, and grew audible.

'Dead—so one speaks now of Euripides!
Ungarlanded dance Choros, did he say?
1230   I guess the reason: in extreme old age
No doubt such have the gods for visitants.
Why did he dedicate to Herakles
An altar else, but that the god, turned Judge,
Told him in dream who took the crown of gold?
1235   He who restored Akropolis the theft,
Himself may feel perhaps a timely twinge
At thought of certain other crowns he filched

1216| MS:"Priest!"—the   *P1875:*'Priest!'—the   *1889a:*"'Priest!'—the   1217| MS:"Thou
< > thy God   *P1875:*Thou < > god   *1889a:*Thou §emended to§ 'Thou §see Editorial Notes§
1218| MS:wherefore, I   *1889a:*wherefore I   1221| MS:in sable, go §last two words crossed
out and replaced above by two words§ black, appear ungarlanded!"   *P1875:*ungarlanded!'
1222| MS:sank back, and   *P1875:*sank low, and   1224| MS:mute, then §crossed out and
replaced above by§ to mingled §altered to§ mingle   1225| MS:certain Gods   *P1875:*gods
1227| MS:and grew §last two words inserted above§ audible. §period inserted§ ere long— §last
two words and dash crossed out§   1228| MS:"Dead < > Euripides!"   *P1875:*'Dead < >
Euripides!'   *1889a:*Euripides!   1229| MS:"Ungarlanded his Choros   *P1875:*'Ungarlanded
*1889a:*Ungarlanded dance Choros   1231| MS:doubt §next word illegibly crossed out and
replaced above by§ such has §altered to§ have the Gods   *P1875:*gods   1233| MS:the deity
§crossed out§ God   *P1875:*god   1234| MS:Told §over illegible word§ him §inserted above§
in a §crossed out§ < > crown away §crossed out and replaced above by two words§ of gold,
*P1875:*gold?   1235| MS:And so restored < > theft.   *P1875:*He who restored < > theft,

From—who now visits Herakles the Judge.
Instance "Medeia"! that play yielded palm
1240 To Sophokles; and he again—to whom?
Euphorion!   Why?   Ask Herakles the Judge!'

'Ungarlanded, just means—economy!
Suppress robes, chaplets, everything suppress
Except the poet's present! An old tale
1245 Put capitally by Trugaios—eh?
—News from the world of transformation strange!
How Sophokles is grown Simonides,
And,—aged, rotten,—all the same, for greed
Would venture on a hurdle out to sea!—
1250 So jokes Philonides.   Kallistratos
Retorts—Mistake!   Instead of stinginess,
The fact is, in extreme decrepitude,
He has discarded poet and turned priest,
Priest of Half-Hero Alkon: visited
1255 In his own house too by Asklepios' self,
So he avers.   Meanwhile, his own estate
Lies fallow; Iophon's the manager,—
Nay, touches up a play, brings out the same,
Asserts true sonship. See to what you sink
1260 After your dozen-dozen prodigies!
Looking so old—Euripides seems young,

1238| MS:the Judge— *P1875:* the Judge.   1239| MS:'Medeia,' for instance: that
*P1875:*Instance 'Medeia'! that   *1889a:*Instance "Medeia"! that   1240| MS:To
Sophokles—and *P1875:*To Sophokles; and   1241| MS:the Judge!" *P1875:*the Judge.'
1242| MS:"Mistake! The measure means economy! *P1875:*Ungarlanded, just, means—
economy! *CP1875:*just means   *1889a:*'Ungarlanded   1245| MS:§line added§
1246| MS:'News *P1875:*"News   *1889a:*—News   1249-51| MS:Would <> sea'!" §¶ called
for§ "Quite otherwise! Instead <> stinginess— *P1875:*sea!" §no ¶§ So jokes Philonides.
Kallistratos / Retorts 'Mistake! Instead   *1889a:*sea!— / / <> stinginess,
1252| MS:in this last §last two words crossed out and replaced above by
one word§ extreme   1253| MS:has left off the §last three words crossed out and replaced
above by one word§ discarded poet, §comma crossed out§ and §inserted above§ turned the
§crossed out§ priest— *P1875:*priest,   1256| MS:avers. §period added§ meanwhile
§altered to§ Meanwhile   1257| MS:manager: *P1875:*manager,—
1259| MS:Asserting §altered to§ Asserts true §inserted above§ sonship. see §altered to§ See
1261| MS:Looking §in margin§ So old he looks, §last two words and comma crossed out; dash
inserted above§ <> young. §period altered to comma§ *P1875:*so

Born ten years later.'

                      'Just his tricky style!
Since, stealing first away, he wins first word
Out of good-natured rival Sophokles,
1265   Procures himself no bad panegyric.
Had fate willed otherwise, himself were taxed
To pay survivor's-tribute,—harder squeezed
From anybody beaten first to last,
Than one who, steadily a conqueror,
1270   Finds that his magnanimity is tasked
To merely make pretence and—beat itself!'

"So chirped the feasters though suppressedly.

"But I—what else do you suppose?—had pierced
Quite through friends' outside-straining, foes' mock-praise,
1275   And reached conviction hearted under all.
Death's rapid line had closed a life's account,
And cut off, left unalterably clear
The summed-up value of Euripides.

1262| MS:Dead §crossed out and replaced above by§ Born < > years sooner, §crossed out and replaced above by§ later." §over illegible word§ §¶§ "Just < > tricky §inserted above§ style! of trick! §last two words and exclamation point crossed out§ *P1875:*later.' §¶§ 'Just
1263| MS:Since §in margin§ For, §crossed out§ < > wins good §crossed out and replaced above by§ first   1264| MS:goodnatured easy §crossed out and replaced above by§ rival
1265| MS:Procures §over illegible erasure§   *1889a:*good-natured   1267| MS:pay such tribute < > squeezed §inserted above§ from §over illegible word§ man,   *P1875:*pay survivors tribute,—harder squeezed   *CP1875:*survivor's-tribute   1268| MS:Beaten and §last two words crossed out and replaced above by four words§ I fancy, who was beaten from the §last two words crossed out§ first   *P1875:*From anybody beaten   1269| MS:Than when, as §last two words crossed out and replaced above by two words and comma§ one who
1270| MS:Your §crossed out and replaced above by§ Finds magnanimity is simply §crossed out and replaced above by§ merely tasked   *P1875:*Finds that his magnanimity is tasked
1271| MS:To make < > and, this time, beat yourself §altered to§ himself!"   *P1875:*To merely make < > and—beat itself!'   1272| MS:So *P1875:*"So
1274| MS:friends' §over illegible word§ outside mocking meant for §last three words crossed out and replaced above by three words and hyphen§ straining and mock-   *P1875:*outside-straining, foes' mock-praise,   1276| MS:line ran, §word and comma altered to§ had closing §altered to§ closed a §inserted above§   1277| MS:Leaving henceforth §last two words crossed out and replaced above by four words§ And cut off, and §crossed out§ left

"Well, it might be the Thasian!   Certainly
1280 There sang suggestive music in my ears;
And, through—what sophists style—the wall of sense
My eyes pierced: death seemed life and life seemed death,
Envisaged that way, now, which I, before,
Conceived was just a moonstruck mood.   Quite plain
1285 There re-insisted,—ay, each prim stiff phrase
Of each old play, my still-new laughing-stock,
Had meaning, well worth poet's pains to state,
Should life prove half true life's term,—death, the rest.
As for the other question, late so large
1290 Now all at once so little,—he or I,
Which better comprehended playwright craft,—
There, too, old admonition took fresh point.
As clear recurred our last word-interchange
Two years since, when I tried with 'Ploutos.' 'Vain!'
1295 Saluted me the cold grave-bearded bard—
'Vain, this late trial, Aristophanes!
None baulks the genius with impunity!
You know what kind's the nobler, what makes grave
Or what makes grin; there's yet a nobler still,
1300 Possibly,—what makes wise, not grave,—and glad,

1279| MS:"Well <> the Thasian! Certainly §over *certainly*§   *1889a:*Well §emended to§ "Well
§see Editorial Notes§   1280| MS:There grew §altered to§ sang <> singing §altered to§
music   1281| MS:through the wall of sense—what sophists style— §last three words and
dashes marked for transposition to follow *through*§   1282| MS:eyes saw: §crossed out and
replaced above by§ pierced   1283| MS:Envisaged this §altered to§ that <> now; as
§crossed out and replaced above by§ which mine, before,   *P1875:*which I, before,
1284| MS:Made out §last two words crossed out and replaced above by three words§ Conceived
was just <> moonstruck man's §period inserted above§ with work to match: §last four words
and colon crossed out§ No, no!   *P1875:*moon-struck mood. Quite plain   *1889a:*moonstruck
1285| MS:re-insisted in each   *P1875:*re-insisted,—ay, each   1287| MS:A meaning
*P1875:*Had meaning   1288| MS:Were §crossed out and replaced above by§ Should life
but §crossed out and replaced above by§ prove half real §inserted above§ life's term, and
§crossed out and replaced above by dash§   *P1875:*half true life's term—death   *1889a:*
term,—death   1288-89| MS:§¶ called for in margin§   *P1875:*§no ¶§
1290| MS:And all   *P1875:*Now all   1293| MS:Again §crossed out and replaced above by
two words§ As clear   1294| MS:with 'Ploutos.' "Vain!"   *P1875:*with 'Ploutos.' 'Vain!'
1295| MS:grave bearded age—   *P1875:*grave-bearded   *1889a:*grave-bearded bard—
1296| MS:"Vain, this new trial   *P1875:*'Vain, this late trial
1297| MS:No quitting nature with   *P1875:*None baulks the genius with

---

56

Not grinning: whereby laughter joins with tears,
Tragic and Comic Poet prove one power,
And Aristophanes becomes our Fourth—
Nay, greatest! Never needs the Art stand still,
1305 But those Art leans on lag, and none like you,
Her strongest of supports, whose step aside
Undoes the march: defection checks advance
Too late adventured!   See the "Ploutos" here!
This step decides your foot from old to new—
1310 Proves you relinquish song and dance and jest,
Discard the beast, and, rising from all-fours,
Fain would paint, manlike, actual human life,
Make veritable men think, say and do.
Here's the conception: which to execute,
1315 Where's force? Spent!   Ere the race began, was breath
O' the runner squandered on each friendly fool—
Wit-fireworks fizzed off while day craved no flame:
How should the night receive her due of fire
Flared out in Wasps and Horses, Clouds and Birds,
1320 Prodigiously a-crackle?   Rest content!

1301| MS:grinning: so should §last two words crossed out and replaced above by one word§
whereby   1304| MS:Our §over illegible erasure§ greatest. never §altered to§ Never
P1875:Nay, greatest! Never   1306| MS:Her §over illegible erasure§
1307| MS:march: §colon altered to semi-colon§ defection for §crossed out and replaced above
by§ checks   P1875:march: defection   1308| MS:§line added§ adventured. <> 'Ploutos'
here—   P1875:adventured! <> "Ploutos" here!   1310| MS:There §crossed out and
replaced above by§ Frank you   P1875:Proves you   1311| MS:Forego §crossed out and
replaced above by§ Discard the §next word illegibly crossed out§ nay, unobscene, §last three
words crossed out and replaced above by six words§ beast, and, rising from all fours,   P1875:
all-fours,   1312| MS:Try to §last two words crossed out and replaced above by two words§
Fain would paint, simply present §last two words crossed out and replaced above by two
words§ manlike, actual   1313| MS:Make §in margin§ How actual §last two words crossed
out and replaced above by one word§ veritable men about us say and do. §last five words
crossed out and replaced above by four words§ think, speak, not act §last four words crossed
out and replaced below by one word and comma§ think §*say and do* and punctuation
restored§   1314| MS:§line added in margin§ conception: but, to   P1875:conception:
which to   1315| MS:Where's §over illegible erasure§ force? Spent! breathless §crossed out§
ere §altered to§ Ere <> began,—the breath   P1875:began, was breath
1316| MS:§line added§   1317| MS:off before night §last two words crossed out§ and
§inserted below and crossed out§ while day §inserted below§ craved no §inserted above§
1318| MS:§line added in margin§   1319| MS:All gone in <> Horses §over illegibly erased
word§   P1875:Flared out in   1320| MS:Prodigiously achieved! §crossed out and replaced
above by§ a-crackle? There §crossed out§ rest §altered to§ Rest

The new adventure for the novel man
Born to that next success myself foresee
In right of where I reach before I rest.
At end of a long course, straight all the way,
1325   Well may there tremble somewhat into ken
The untrod path, clouds veiled from earlier gaze!
None may live two lives: I have lived mine through,
Die where I first stand still. You retrograde.
I leave my life's work. *I* compete with you,
1330   My last with your last, my 'Antiope'—
'Phoinissai'—with this 'Ploutos'? No, I think!
Ever shall great and awful Victory
Accompany my life—in Maketis
If not Athenai. Take my farewell, friend!
1335   Friend,—for from no consummate excellence
Like yours, whatever fault may countervail,
Do I profess estrangement: murk the marsh,
Yet where a solitary marble block
Blanches the gloom, there let the eagle perch!
1340   You show—what splinters of Pentelikos,
Islanded by what ordure! Eagles fly,
Rest on the right place, thence depart as free;
But 'ware man's footstep, would it traverse mire

1321| MS:The next §crossed out and replaced above by§ new   1322| MS:Born for that last
§crossed out and replaced above by§ next   *P1875:*Born to that   1324| MS:At far
§crossed out§ end <> a §inserted above§   1325| MS:§word illegibly crossed out, perhaps
Expect, and replaced above by§ Well <> there §inserted above§ <> into view   *P1875:*into ken
1328| MS:Fall §crossed out and replaced above by§ Die where   1330| MS:my §inserted above§
*P1875:*my 'Antiope'—   *1889a:*my Antiope—   1331| MS:Orestes §crossed out and
replaced above by§ Phoinissai <> 'Ploutos'? No   *P1875:*'Phoinissai'—with   *1889a:*
Phoinissai <> Ploutos? No   1332| MS:shall 'Great   *P1875:*great   *1889a:*shall great
1333| MS:life'—in Maketis §over partial erasure§   *1889a:*life—in   1336| MS:counterfoil,
*P1875:*countervail,   1337| MS:May §crossed out and replaced above by§ Do <>
estrangement: wide §crossed out and replaced above by§ murk the waste §crossed out and
replaced above by§ marsh,   1339| MS:there should §crossed out and replaced above by§
let §illegibly crossed-out word inserted above§   1340| MS:While you §last two words crossed
out and replaced above by two words§You show   1342| MS:§line added in margin§ Find
out §last two words crossed out and replaced above by two words§ Rest §over illegible word§
on   1343| MS:ware man's §crossed out and restored§ footstep, that §crossed out§ would
it §inserted above§ traverse filth   *P1875:*traverse mire   *1889a:* 'ware

Untainted!   Mire is safe for worms that crawl.'

¹³⁴⁵   "Balaustion!   Here are very many words,
All to portray one moment's rush of thought,—
And much they do it!   Still, you understand.
The Archon, the Feast-master, read their sum
And substance, judged the banquet-glow extinct,
¹³⁵⁰   So rose, discreetly if abruptly, crowned
The parting cup,—'To the Good Genius, then!'

"Up starts young Strattis for a final flash:
'Ay, the Good Genius!   To the Comic Muse,
She who evolves superiority,
¹³⁵⁵   Triumph and joy from sorrow, unsuccess
And all that's incomplete in human life;
Who proves such actual failure transient wrong,
Since out of body uncouth, halt and maimed—
Since out of soul grotesque, corrupt or blank—
¹³⁶⁰   Fancy, uplifted by the Muse, can flit
To soul and body, re-instate them Man:
Beside which perfect man, how clear we see
Divergency from type was earth's effect!
Escaping whence by laughter,—Fancy's feat,—
¹³⁶⁵   We right man's wrong, establish true for false,—
Above misshapen body, uncouth soul,
Reach the fine form, the clear intelligence—
Above unseemliness, reach decent law,—

---

¹³⁴⁴| MS:Untainted! Filth belongs to §last two words crossed out and replaced below by three words§ is safe for <> crawl."   *P1875*:Untainted! Mire is   *1889a*:crawl.'
¹³⁴⁷| MS:understand—   *P1875*:understand.   ¹³⁴⁸| MS:For even §last two words crossed out and replaced above by two words and comma§ The Archon   ¹³⁵¹| MS:The final §crossed out and replaced above by§ parting   ¹³⁵³| MS:'Ay, the   *1889a*:'Ay the §emended to§ 'Ay, the §see Editorial Notes§   ¹³⁵⁴| MS:superiority;   *P1875*:superiority,
¹³⁵⁶| MS:all the §altered to§ that's incomplete of §crossed out and replaced above by§ in
¹³⁵⁷| MS:So proving actual   *P1875*:Who proves such actual   ¹³⁵⁸| MS:body, uncouth   *P1875*:body uncouth   ¹³⁵⁹| MS:Since out §last two words inserted above§ Of <> blank   *P1875*:of <> blank—   ¹³⁶¹| MS:re-instated Man: *P1875*:re-instate them Man:
¹³⁶²| MS:§line added§   ¹³⁶³| MS:effect, §comma altered to exclamation point§
¹³⁶⁵| MS:right the §crossed out and replaced above by§ man's   ¹³⁶⁶| MS:Above §over partial erasure§   ¹³⁶⁸| MS:unseemliness, the §crossed out and replaced above by§ reach

59

By laughter: attestation of the Muse
¹³⁷⁰ That low-and-ugsome is not signed and sealed
Incontrovertibly man's portion here,
Or, if here,—why, still high-and-fair exists
In that ethereal realm where laughs our soul
Lift by the Muse. Hail thou her ministrant!
¹³⁷⁵ Hail who accepted no deformity
In man as normal and remediless,
But rather pushed it to such gross extreme
That, outraged, we protest by eye's recoil
The opposite proves somewhere rule and law!
¹³⁸⁰ Hail who implied, by limning Lamachos,
Plenty and pastime wait on peace, not war!
Philokleon—better bear a wrong than plead,
Play the litigious fool to stuff the mouth
Of dikast with the due three-obol fee!
¹³⁸⁵ The Paphlagonian—stick to the old sway
Of few and wise, not rabble-government!
Trugaios, Pisthetairos, Strepsiades,—
Why multiply examples? Hail, in fine,

---

¹³⁶⁹| MS:laughter—attestation *P1875:*laughter: attestation ¹³⁷⁰| MS:low-and-ugly §altered to§ low-and-ugsome ¹³⁷²| MS:why, that §crossed out and replaced above by§ still ¹³⁷³| MS:etherial <> laughs the §crossed out and replaced above by§ our soul §over illegible erasure§ *1889a:*ethereal ¹³⁷⁴| MS:the Muse. Hail then her *1889a:*the Muse. Hail thou her ¹³⁷⁵| MS:Hail §over illegible word, perhaps *He*§ ¹³⁷⁸| MS:That dullest eye §last three words crossed out and replaced above by four words§ That §next word illegibly crossed out§ outraged we protested §altered to§ protest <> eye's §inserted above§ *1889a:*That, outraged, we ¹³⁷⁹| MS:opposite was §crossed out and replaced above by§ proves <> law and rule! §last three words marked for transposition§ ¹³⁸⁰| MS:Hail §over illegible word, perhaps *He*§ ¹³⁸¹| MS:'Peace, were §crossed out and replaced above by§ proves the better: that §crossed out and replaced above by§ by litigious fool §last six words crossed out and replaced below by six words§ plenty, pastime a §altered to dash§ quick exchange for war!' *P1875:*'Plenty and pastime wait on peace, not war!' *1889a:* Plenty <> war! ¹³⁸²| MS:Philokleon—'better <> a loss §crossed out and replaced above by§ wrong *1889a:*Philokleon—better ¹³⁸³| MS:§line added§ Act §in margin§ Play §crossed out§ the *P1875:*Play the ¹³⁷⁴| MS:§line added in margin§ dikasts §altered to§ dikast <> fee!' *1889a:*fee! ¹³⁸⁵| MS:The Paphlagonian—better §crossed out and replaced below by two words§ 'stick to *1889a:*The Paphlagonian—stick ¹³⁸⁶| MS:wise, than §crossed out and replaced above by§ not mad mob government!' *P1875:* not rabble-government!' *1889a:*rabble-government! ¹³⁸⁷| MS:Strepsiades, §dash inserted§ Pisthetairos, Trugaios §last three words marked for transposition§

The hero of each painted monster—so
1390 Suggesting the unpictured perfect shape!
Pour out!   A laugh to Aristophanes!'

"'Stay, my fine Strattis'—and I stopped applause—
'To the Good Genius—but the Tragic Muse!
She who instructs her poet, bids man's soul
1395 Play man's part merely nor attempt the gods'
Ill-guessed of!   Task humanity to height,
Put passion to prime use, urge will, unshamed
When will's last effort breaks in impotence!
No power forego, elude: no weakness,—plied
1400 Fairly by power and will,—renounce, deny!
Acknowledge, in such miscalled weakness strength
Latent: and substitute thus things for words!
Make man run life's race fairly,—legs and feet,
Craving no false wings to o'erfly its length!
1405 Trust on, trust ever, trust to end—in truth!
By truth of extreme passion, utmost will,
Shame back all false display of either force—
Barrier about such strenuous heat and glow,
That cowardice shall shirk contending,—cant,
1410 Pretension, shrivel at truth's first approach!
Pour to the Tragic Muse's ministrant
Who, as he pictured pure Hippolutos,

1389| MS:The glory §crossed out and replaced above by§ hero of the §crossed out and
replaced above by§ each written §crossed out and replaced above by§ painted
1390| MS:Suggesting plain §crossed out§ the   1391| MS:to Aristophanes!" *P1875:*to
Aristophanes!'   1392| MS:"Stay, my good Strattis"—and §over illegible word§ *P1875:*my
fine Strattis §emended to§ "'Stay < > Strattis' §see Editorial Notes§   1393| MS:"To the
Good Genius—to §crossed out and replaced above by§ but   *1889a:*'To
1394| MS:poet 'Bid   *1889a:*poet, bids   1395| MS:the Gods'   *P1875:*gods'
1396| MS:of: task   *P1875:*of! Task   1397| MS:use, work will   *P1875:*use, urge will
1399| MS:elude—no weakness, plied   *P1875:*elude: no weakness,—plied   1400| MS:Vainly
by < > will, renounce, deny— §dash altered to exclamation point§   *P1875:*Fairly by < >
will,—renounce   1402| MS:Latent: still §crossed out and replaced above by§ and
substituting §altered to§ substitute thus §inserted above§   1409| MS:§line added§ shirk §over
partial erasure§   1410| MS:Pretension, shall §crossed out§ shrivel at their first approach!
*P1875:*at truth's first   1412| MS:pictured a §crossed out and replaced above by§ pure

Abolished our earth's blot Ariphrades;
Who, as he drew Bellerophon the bold,
1415 Proclaimed Kleonumos incredible;
Who, as his Theseus towered up man once more,
Made Alkibiades shrink boy again!
A tear—no woman's tribute, weak exchange
For action, water spent and heart's-blood saved—
1420 No man's regret for greatness gone, ungraced
Perchance by even that poor meed, man's praise—
But some god's superabundance of desire,
Yearning of will to 'scape necessity,—
Love's overbrimming for self-sacrifice,
1425 Whence good might be, which never else may be,
By power displayed, forbidden this strait sphere,—
Effort expressible one only way—
Such tear from me fall to Euripides!'

"The Thasian!—All, the Thasian, I account!

1413| MS:Abolished by a §last two words crossed out and replaced above by two words§ our earth's < > Ariphrades: *P1875:*blot Ariphrades; 1414| MS:bold *P1875:*bold, 1415| MS:Proved a Kleonumos impossible: *P1875:*Proclaimed Kleonumos incredible; 1416| MS:his Theseus grew above again §last three words crossed out and replaced above by two words§ faced his §last two words crossed out and replaced above by two words and comma§ towered up, man once more, §last three words and comma inserted above§ *P1875:* up man 1417| MS:shrink §over illegible erasure§ 1419| MS:spent for §crossed out and replaced above by§ and §over illegible word§ 1420| MS:No mere §crossed out§ man's §next word illegibly crossed out§ regret for greatness §crossed out and replaced above by§ glory gone *P1875:*for greatness gone 1421| MS:Perchance, §word and comma in margin§ by §over partial erasure§ *P1875:*Perchance by 1422| MS:But—some §inserted above§ God's raw §crossed out§ superabundance §following this line§ go on overleaf *P1875:* But some god's 1423-29| MS:§these lines composed on verso of leaf bearing ll. 1392-1422§ 1423| MS:will, beyond §comma and word crossed out and replaced above by two words§ to 'scape 1424| MS:Of §crossed out and replaced above by§ God's aspiration for §over illegible erasure§ *P1875:*Love's overbrimming for 1425| MS:Whence §in margin§ For §crossed out§ good to §crossed out and replaced above by§ might < > never could have §last two words crossed out and replaced above by two words§ else may be, §over *been*§ 1426| MS:By §in margin§ powers §over partial erasure§ to §crossed out§ displayed < > sphere, *P1875:*power < > sphere,— 1427| MS:expressible this §crossed out and replaced above by§ one 1428| MS:Such §in margin§ A §crossed out§ tear < > me then §crossed out and replaced above by§ fall < > Euripides!'" *P1875:* Euripides!' *1889a:*Euripides!" §emended to§ Euripides!' §see Editorial Notes§ 1429| MS:the Thasian, possibly! §word and exclamation point crossed out§ I *P1875:*"The *1889a:*The §emended to§ "The §see Editorial Notes§

62

1430   "Whereupon outburst the whole company
      Into applause and—laughter, would you think?

      "'The unrivalled one! How, never at a loss,
      He turns the Tragic on its Comic side
      Else imperceptible! Here's death itself—
1435   Death of a rival, of an enemy,—
      Scarce seen as Comic till the master-touch
      Made it acknowledge Aristophanes!
      Lo, that Euripidean laurel-tree
      Struck to the heart by lightning! Sokrates
1440   Would question us, with buzz of how and why,
      Wherefore the berry's virtue, the bloom's vice,
      Till we all wished him quiet with his friend;
      Agathon would compose an elegy,
      Lyric bewailment fit to move a stone,
1445   And, stones responsive, we might wince, 'tis like;
      Nay, with most cause of all to weep the least,
      Sophokles ordains mourning for his sake
      While we confess to a remorseful twinge:—
      Suddenly, who but Aristophanes,
1450   Prompt to the rescue, puts forth solemn hand,
      Singles us out the tragic tree's best branch,
      Persuades it groundward and, at tip, appends,
      For votive-visor, Faun's goat-grinning face!

1430| *P1875:*"Whereupon *1889a:*Whereupon §emended to§ "Whereupon §see Editorial Notes§ 1432| MS:one! How §over illegible erasure§ *P1875:*'The *1889a:*"The §emended to§ "'The §see Editorial Notes§ 1433| MS:He §over illegible word§ 1436| MS:Yet §crossed out and replaced above by§ How §crossed out§ scarce §altered to§ Scarce §crossed out and restored§ <> as §inserted above§ 1438| MS:Here's §crossed out and replaced above by word and comma§ Lo 1440| MS:with §over illegible word§ *P1875:*of 'how' and 'why,' *1889a:*of how and why, 1442| MS:Till §in margin§ And §crossed out§ we should §crossed out and replaced above by§ all wish §altered to§ wished 1445| MS:we should §crossed out and replaced above by§ might wince, at least: §last two words crossed out and replaced above by two words§ tis like *P1875:*'tis like; 1446| MS:He §crossed out and replaced above by word and comma§ Nay 1447| MS:Sophokles puts on §last two words crossed out and replaced above by one word§ ordains 1448| MS:While §in margin§ And §crossed out§ we <> twinge *P1875:*twinge:— 1449| MS:but Aristophanes *P1875:*but Aristophanes, 1451| MS:Singles him §crossed out and replaced above by§ us 1452| MS:it towards ground, and *P1875:*it groundward and

Back it flies, evermore with jest a-top,
1455 And we recover the true mood, and laugh!'

"I felt as when some Nikias,—ninny-like
Troubled by sunspot-portent, moon-eclipse,—
At fault a little, sees no choice but sound
Retreat from foeman; and his troops mistake
1460 The signal, and hail onset in the blast,
And at their joyous answer, *alalé,*
Back the old courage brings the scattered wits;
He wonders what his doubt meant, quick confirms
The happy error, blows the charge amain.
1465 So I repaired things.

          "'Both be praised' thanked I.
'You who have laughed with Aristophanes,
You who wept rather with the Lord of Tears!
Priest, do thou, president alike o'er each,
Tragic and Comic function of the god,
1470 Help with libation to the blended twain!
Either of which who serving, only serves—
Proclaims himself disqualified to pour
To that Good Genius—complex Poetry,
Uniting each god-grace, including both:
1475 Which, operant for body as for soul,
Masters alike the laughter and the tears,
Supreme in lowliest earth, sublimest sky.

1454| MS:ever more §last two words altered to§ evermore   1455| *P1875:*laugh!'   *1889a:*
laugh!" §emended to§ laugh!' §see Editorial Notes§   1456| MS:I < > some Nikias, ninny-
like   *P1875:*"I < > some Nikias,—ninny-like   1457| MS:by portent-sunspot, or §crossed
out and replaced above by§ moon eclipse—   *P1875:*by sunspot-portent, moon-eclipse,—
1462| MS:Back his old   *P1875:*Back the old   1463| MS:what the doubt   *P1875:*what his
doubt   1465| MS:things. §¶§ "You §crossed out and replaced above by§ Both say well"
laughed §crossed out and replaced above by§ joined I.   *P1875:*things. §¶§ "Both be praised"
thanked I. §emended to§ "'Both < > praised' §see Editorial Notes§   1466| MS:"You
1889a:"You §emended to§ 'You §see Editorial Notes§
1468| MS:Priest! Do < > o'er both §crossed out§ each,   *P1875:*Priest, do
1469| MS:the God,   *P1875:*god,   1470| MS:twain: *P1875:*twain!   1471| MS:who
serves exclusively   *P1875:*who serving, only serves—   1474| MS:both:—   *P1875:*both:

Who dares disjoin these,—whether he ignores
Body or soul, whichever half destroys,—
1480 Maims the else perfect manhood, perpetrates
Again the inexpiable crime we curse—
Hacks at the Hermai, halves each guardian shape
Combining, nowise vainly, prominence
Of august head and enthroned intellect,
1485 With homelier symbol of asserted sense,—
Nature's prime impulse, earthly appetite.
For, when our folly ventures on the freak,
Would fain abolish joy and fruitfulness,
Mutilate nature—what avails the Head
1490 Left solitarily predominant,—
Unbodied soul,—not Hermes, both in one?
I, no more than our City, acquiesce
In such a desecration, but defend
Man's double nature—ay, wert thou its foe!
1495 Could I once more, thou cold Euripides,
Encounter thee, in nought would I abate
My warfare, nor subdue my worst attack
On thee whose life-work preached "Raise soul, sink sense!
Evirate Hermes!"—would avenge the god,
1500 And justify myself.   Once face to face,
Thou, the argute and tricksy, shouldst not wrap,
As thine old fashion was, in silent scorn
The breast that quickened at the sting of truth,
Nor turn from me, as, if the tale be true,
1505 From Lais when she met thee in thy walks,

1478| MS:ignore *P1875*:ignores   1479| MS:destroy,— *P1875*:destroys,—
1480| MS:He maims the perfect *P1875*:Maims the else perfect   1484| MS:head, and
§inserted above§ *P1875*:head and   1485| MS:sense, *P1875*:sense,—
1487| MS:And when *P1875*:For, when   1494| MS:nature—Ay §altered to§ ay <> thou
my foe, *P1875*:thou its foe!   1496| MS:thee, I would in nought abate §last five words
marked for transposition to§ in nought would I abate   1498| MS:life-work was—'raise
§altered to§ 'Raise *P1875*:life-work preached 'Raise §emended to§ preached "Raise §see
Editorial Notes§   1499| MS:Evirate Hermes!' <> God, *P1875*:god, §emended to§
Evirate Hermes!"—would §see Editorial Notes§   1500| MS:And vendicate myself,
§comma altered to period§ once §altered to§ Once *P1875*:And justify myself
1503| MS:Those breast-beats quickened <> truth; *1889a*:The breast that quickened <>
truth,   1504| MS:as §over illegible erasure§

And questioned why she had no rights as thou:
Not so shouldst thou betake thee, be assured,
To book and pencil, deign me no reply!
I would extract an answer from those lips
1510 So closed and cold, were mine the garden-chance!
Gone from the world! Does none remain to take
Thy part and ply me with thy sophist-skill?
No sun makes proof of his whole potency
For gold and purple in that orb we view:
1515 The apparent orb does little but leave blind
The audacious, and confused the worshipping;
But, close on orb's departure, must succeed
The serviceable cloud,—must intervene,
Induce expenditure of rose and blue,
1520 Reveal what lay in him was lost to us.
So, friends, what hinders, as we homeward go,
If, privileged by triumph gained to-day,
We clasp that cloud our sun left saturate,
The Rhodian rosy with Euripides?
1525 Not of my audience on my triumph-day,
She nor her husband! After the night's news
Neither will sleep but watch; I know the mood.
Accompany! my crown declares my right!'

"And here you stand with those warm golden eyes!

1506| MS:Demanding §altered to§ Demanded why *P1875:*thou. *1889a:*And questioned why
< > thou: 1508| MS:deigning §last three letters crossed out and replaced above by one
word§ me   1514| *P1875:*view;   *1889a:*view: 1515| MS:does nothing §crossed out
and replaced above by§ little   1516| MS:worshipping.   *1889a:*worshipping;
1517| MS:But, §word and comma in margin§ Close on that §crossed out§ orb's departure, still
§crossed out and replaced above by§ must succeeds §altered to§ succeed   *P1875:*close
1518| MS:cloud, to §crossed out and replaced above by dash and word§ —must
1519| MS:Prove his §last two words crossed out and replaced below by one word§ Induce
1520| MS:him, was   *1889a:*him was   1522| MS:By §crossed out and replaced above by
word and comma§ If, privileged of §crossed out and replaced above by§ by   1523| MS:We
hail that   *P1875:*We clasp that   1525| MS:None of   *P1875:*Not of   1526| MS:She
and her   *1889a:*She nor her   1527| MS:sleep, but < > the way §crossed out§ mood.
*1889a:*sleep but   1528| MS:right!"   *1889a:*right! §emended to§ right.' §see Editorial
Notes§   1529| MS:"And   *1889a:*And §emended to§ "And §see Editorial Notes§

¹⁵³⁰ "In honest language, I am scarce too sure
Whether I really felt, indeed expressed
Then, in that presence, things I now repeat:
Nor half, nor any one word,—will that do?
May be, such eyes must strike conviction, turn
¹⁵³⁵ One's nature bottom upwards, show the base—
The live rock latent under wave and foam:
Superimposure these! Yet solid stuff
Will ever and anon, obeying star,
(And what star reaches rock-nerve like an eye?)
¹⁵⁴⁰ Swim up to surface, spout or mud or flame,
And find no more to do than sink as fast.

"Anyhow, I have followed happily
The impulse, pledged my Genius with effect,
Since, come to see you, I am shown—myself!"

¹⁵⁴⁵ I answered:

"One of us declared for both
'Welcome the glory of Aristophanes.'
The other adds: and,—if that glory last,
Nor marsh-born vapour creep to veil the same,—
Once entered, share in our solemnity!
¹⁵⁵⁰ Commemorate, as we, Euripides!"

---

¹⁵³²| MS:repeat— *P1875:*repeat: ¹⁵³³| MS:half—nor *P1875:*half, nor
¹⁵³⁶| MS:Was §crossed out and replaced above by§ True live <> under sand §crossed out and replaced above by§ waves <> foam— *P1875:*The live <> wave <> foam:
¹⁵³⁷| MS:Superimposure of me, §last two words and comma crossed out and replaced above by one word and comma§ these, not myself the §last two words crossed out§ solid soul *P1875:* these! Yet solid stuff   ¹⁵³⁸| MS:That §crossed out and replaced above by§ Which ever *P1875:*Will ever   ¹⁵⁴⁰| MS:Swims <> spouts *P1875:*Swim <> spout
¹⁵⁴¹| MS:finds *P1875:*find   ¹⁵⁴⁴| MS:Since, come *1889a:*Since. come §emended to§ Since, come §see Editorial Notes§   ¹⁵⁴⁵| MS:answered: §¶§ Euthukles has said §last three words crossed out and replaced above by four words§ "One of us declared <> both— *P1875:*both   ¹⁵⁴⁷| MS:The other §last two words in margin§ I §crossed out§ add §altered to§ adds,—and, if <> last, §comma inserted§ the while, §last two words and comma crossed out§ *P1875:*adds 'and,—if *1889a:*adds: and   ¹⁵⁴⁸| MS:§line added§ vapour haste to *P1875:*vapour creep to   ¹⁵⁵⁰| MS:Commemorate, with us, §last two words crossed out and replaced above by two words§ as we

67

"What?" he looked round, "I darken the bright house?
Profane the temple of your deity?
That's true!   Else wherefore does he stand portrayed?
What Rhodian paint and pencil saved so much,
1555   Beard, freckled face, brow—all but breath, I hope!
Come, that's unfair: myself am somebody,
Yet my pictorial fame's just potter's-work,—
I merely figure on men's drinking-mugs!
I and the Flat-nose, Sophroniskos' son,
1560   Oft make a pair.   But what's this lies below?
His table-book and graver, playwright's tool!
And lo, the sweet psalterion, strung and screwed,
Whereon he tried those *le-é-é-és*
And *ke-é-é-és* and turns and trills,
1565   Lovely lark's tirra-lirra, lad's delight!
Aischulos' bronze-throat eagle-bark at blood
Has somehow spoiled my taste for twitterings!
With . . . what, and did he leave you 'Herakles'?
The 'Frenzied Hero,' one unfractured sheet,
1570   No pine-wood tablets smeared with treacherous wax—
Papuros perfect as e'er tempted pen!

1551| MS:"What?" §inserted above§ he §over partial erasure§ looked around §altered to§
round, "I in Balaustion's §last two words crossed out and replaced above by three words§
darken the bright   1552| MS:Profane §over illegible erasure§ <> of her §crossed out
and replaced above by§ your diety, §comma altered to question mark§
1553| MS:wherefore should §crossed out and replaced above by§ does <> portrayed,—
*P1875:*portrayed?   1554| MS:paint and §last two words inserted above§ pencil was it §last
two words crossed out§ saved   1557| MS:pictorial fame §altered to§ fame's proves
§crossed out and replaced above by§ just potter's work,—   *1889a:*potter's-work,—
1558| MS:When §crossed out§ I cut §crossed out and replaced above by§ barely figure <> on
the §crossed out and replaced above by§ men's   *1889a:*I merely figure   1560| MS:Oft
§over illegible word§ <> pair. But §over illegible word§   1561| MS:and stulos, §crossed
out and replaced above by§ graver, playwright's ware §crossed out and replaced above by§
tool!   1565| MS:Lark's lovely §last two words transposed and altered to§ Lovely lark's
tirra-lirra, which made tame §last three words crossed out and replaced above by two words§
lad's delight—   *P1875:*delight!   1566| MS:eagle-bark for §crossed out and replaced
above by§ at blood,   *P1875:*blood   1567| MS:§line added§ my ear, §word and comma
crossed out and replaced above by§ taste for §over illegible word§
1568| MS:With . . what <> 'Herakles?'   *1889a:*With...what <> 'Herakles'?
1570| MS:§line added§ pine wood   *P1875:*pine-wood
1571| MS:Perfect papuros §last two words transposed and altered to§ Papuros perfect

This sacred twist of bay-leaves dead and sere
Must be that crown the fine work failed to catch,—
No wonder! This might crown 'Antiope.'

1575 'Herakles' triumph? In your heart perhaps!
But elsewhere? Come now, I'll explain the case,
Show you the main mistake. Give me the sheet!"

I interrupted:

"Aristophanes!
The stranger-woman sues in her abode—
1580 'Be honoured as our guest!' But, call it—shrine,
Then 'No dishonour to the Daimon!' bids
The priestess 'or expect dishonour's due!'
You enter fresh from your worst infamy,
Last instance of long outrage; yet I pause,
1585 Withhold the word a-tremble on my lip,
Incline me, rather, yearn to reverence,—
So you but suffer that I see the blaze
And not the bolt,—the splendid fancy-fling,
Not the cold iron malice, the launched lie
1590 Whence heavenly fire has withered; impotent,
Yet execrable, leave it 'neath the look
Of yon impassive presence! What he scorned,
His life long, need I touch, offend my foot,
To prove that malice missed its mark, that lie

1572| MS:This twist §over illegible erasure§ beside it, §word and comma altered to§ of bay
leaves <> sere, *P1875:*This sacred twist <> bay-leaves <> sere   1573| MS:What should
it §last three words crossed out and replaced above by one word§ Must <> that §over illegible
word§ <> work §inserted above§ <> to win,—   *P1875:*to catch,—
1574| MS:wonder! This was for §last two words crossed out and replaced above by two words§
might crown 'Antiopé.' *P1875:*crown 'Antiope.'   1577| MS:mistake, §comma altered to
period§ just §crossed out§ give §altered to§ Give it §crossed out§ me
1579| MS:stranger-woman speaks §crossed out and replaced above by§ sues
1581| MS:'Dare no dishonor   *P1875:*Then 'No   *1889a:*dishonour   1582| MS:dishonor's
*1889a:*dishonour's   1586| MS:reverence—   *P1875:*reverence,—
1590| MS:withered: impotent,   *P1875:*withered; impotent,   1592| MS:Of the §crossed
out and replaced above by§ yon <> Presence   *P1875:*presence   1593| MS:life-long <>
offend §altered to§ offending the §crossed out§ foot,   *P1875:*life long   *1889a:*offend my foot,

1595   Cumbers the ground, returns to whence it came?
I marvel, I deplore,—the rest be mute!
But, throw off hate's celestiality,—
Show me, apart from song-flash and wit-flame,
A mere man's hand ignobly clenched against
1600   Yon supreme calmness,—and I interpose,
Such as you see me!   Silk breaks lightning's blow!"

He seemed to scarce so much as notice me,
Aught I had spoken, save the final phrase:
Arrested there.

              "Euripides grown calm!
1605   Calmness supreme means dead and therefore safe,"
He muttered; then more audibly began—

"Dead! Such must die! Could people comprehend!
There's the unfairness of it!   So obtuse
Are all: from Solon downward with his saw
1610   'Let none revile the dead,—no, though the son,
Nay, far descendant, should revile thyself!'—
To him who made Elektra, in the act
Of wreaking vengeance on her worst of foes,
Scruple to blame, since speech that blames insults
1615   Too much the very villain life-released.
Now, *I* say, only after death, begins

1595| MS:returned §altered to§ returns   1597| MS:But, unclothed §crossed out and replaced above by two words§ throw off < > celestiality, *P1875:*celestiality,—
1600| MS:The §crossed out and replaced above by§ Yon < > calmness, and *P1875:* calmness,—and   1601-02| MS:§between these two lines§ Calmness supreme—Euripides is dead!" §entire line crossed out§   1602| MS:to not §crossed out and replaced above by§ scarce   1603| MS:Aught I had spoken < > phrase— *P1875:*phrase: *1889a:*Aught had I spoken §emended to§ Aught I had spoken §see Editorial Notes§
1604| MS:there. §¶§ "Euripides is dead §last two words crossed out§ the §crossed out and replaced above by§ grown calm!   1605| MS:§line added§   1606| MS:muttered; more §crossed out§ then §over *than*§ more §inserted below§ < > began *P1875:*began—
1607| MS:"Dead! They all §last two words crossed out and replaced above by two words§ Such must   1609| MS:all—from < > saw' §quotation mark crossed out§ *P1875:*all: from
1611| MS:Nay, §word and comma in margin§ The §crossed out§ far   1612| MS:Down §in margin§ To §altered to§ to *Him* and crossed out§ who *P1875:*To him who
1614-16| MS:Scruples §altered to§ Scruple to speak, lest §crossed out and replaced above by§

70

That formidable claim,—immunity
Of faultiness from fault's due punishment!
The living, who defame me,—why, they live:
1620 Fools,—I best prove them foolish by their life,
Will they but work on, lay their work by mine,
And wait a little, one Olympiad, say!
Then—where's the vital force, mine froze beside?
The sturdy fibre, shamed my brittle stuff?
1625 The school-correctness, sure of wise award
When my vagaries cease to tickle taste?
Where's censure that must sink me, judgment big
Awaiting just the word posterity
Pants to pronounce? Time's wave breaks, buries—*whom,*
1630 Fools, when myself confronts you four years hence?
But die, ere next Lenaia,—safely so
You 'scape me, slink with all your ignorance,
Stupidity and malice, to that hole
O'er which survivors croak 'Respect the dead!'
1635 Ay, for I needs must! But allow me clutch
Only a carrion-handful, lend it sense,

since speech insults the slain. / Now <> say—only   *P1875:*to lame, since speech that blames insults / Too <> released / <> say, only   *CP1875:*to blame, since <> insults / Too §not B§
1617| MS:formidable power §crossed out and replaced above by§ claim
1619| MS:defame you §crossed out and replaced above by§ me   1620| MS:Fools,—you §crossed out and replaced above by§ I   1621| MS:by yours §crossed out and replaced above by§ mine,   1622| MS:§line added§ say: *P1875:*say!   1623| MS:vital fire, you §crossed out and replaced above by§ I froze   *P1875:*vital force, mine froze
1624| MS:fibre,— §over illegible erasure§ fie on §dash and last two words crossed out and replaced above by two words§ shamed your §crossed out§ my §inserted above§ <> stuff!   *P1875:*stuff?   1625| MS:school-correct §altered to§ school-correctness secure §crossed out and replaced above by§ sure   *P1875:*school-correctness, sure   1626| MS:When your §crossed out and replaced above by§ my   1627| MS:sink you §crossed out and replaced above by§ me   1628| MS:—Awaiting   *P1875:*Awaiting   1629| MS:pronounce,— §punctuation altered to question mark§ then §crossed out and replaced above by§ Time's   1630| MS:Fools, should §crossed out and replaced above by§ when himself §altered to§ myself <> four §over illegible erasure§   1631| MS:next Panathenaia,—ha, §last two words crossed out and replaced above by one word§ Lenaia, safely   *P1875:*Lenaia,—safely   1632| MS:'scape §over illegible erasure§ me—slink §over illegible erasure§   1634| MS:Where good §last two words crossed out and replaced above by two words§ Oer which survivors cry §crossed out and replaced above by§ croak "Respect <> dead!"   *P1875:*O'er <> 'Respect <> dead!'

(Mine, not its own, or could it answer me?)
And question 'You, I pluck from hiding-place,
Whose cant was, certain years ago, my "Clouds"
1640 Might last until the swallows came with Spring—
Whose chatter, "Birds" are unintelligible,
Mere psychologic puzzling: poetry?
List, the true lay to rock a cradle with!
O man of Mitulené, wondrous wise!'
1645 —Would not I rub each face in its own filth
To tune of 'Now that years have come and gone,
How does the fact stand?   What's demonstrable
By time, that tries things?—your own test, not mine
Who think men are, were, ever will be fools,
1650 Though somehow fools confute fools,—as these, you!
Don't mumble to the sheepish twos and threes
You cornered and called "audience"! Face this *me*
Who know, and can, and—helped by fifty years—
Do pulverize you pygmies, then as now!'

1655 "Ay, now as then, I pulverize the brood,
Balaustion!   Mindful, from the first, where foe
Would hide head safe when hand had flung its stone,

1637| MS:— §dash altered to parenthesis§ (Mine <> me?— §dash altered to closing parenthesis§   1638| MS:question "You, the §crossed out and replaced above by§ I plucked §altered to§ pluck   1639| MS:was, twenty §altered to§ fifty years   *P1875:*was, certain years   1641| MS:Whose cry §crossed out and replaced above by§ chatter "The §quotation mark and word crossed out§ 'Birds'   *P1875:*chatter, 'Birds'   1643-45| MS:List, the sweet §crossed out and replaced above by§ true <> rock my §crossed out and replaced above by§ a <> with!" / —Would   *P1875:* with! / *O* <> *wise!'* / —Would   1646| MS:of 'Now the §over partial erasure§ fifty §crossed out§ years are §altered to§ have come and §last two words inserted above§   *P1875:*of 'Now that years   1647| MS:fact prove §crossed out and replaced above by§ stand   1649| MS:fools; *P1875:*fools,   1650-51| MS:§between these two lines§ These §altered to§ The novel generation, mine not yours! In virtue of my fools succeeding yours. §all but first word of line crossed out§   1651| MS:to your §crossed out and replaced below by§ the   1652| MS:'audience',— §comma and dash altered to exclamation point§ face   *1889a:*'audience'! Face   1654| MS:Will §crossed out and replaced above by§ Do pulverize the §crossed out and replaced above by§ you <> now!" *P1875:*now!'   1654-55| MS:§no ¶ called for§   *P1875:*§¶§   1655| MS:Ay §over illegible word§   *1889a:*"Ay   1656| MS:Balaustion! Mindful §over partial erasure§   1657| MS:head when safe §last two words marked for transposition§

I did not turn cheek and take pleasantry,
But flogged while skin could purple and flesh start,
1660 To teach fools whom they tried conclusions with.
First face a-splutter at me got such splotch
Of prompt slab mud as, filling mouth to maw,
Made its concern thenceforward not so much
To criticize me as go cleanse itself.
1665 The only drawback to which huge delight,—
(He saw it, how he saw it, that calm cold
Sagacity you call Euripides!)
—Why, 'tis that, make a muckheap of a man,
There, pillared by your prowess, he remains,
1670 Immortally immerded.   Not so he!
Men pelted him but got no pellet back.
He reasoned, I'll engage,—'Acquaint the world
Certain minuteness butted at my knee?
Dogface Eruxis, the small satirist,—
1675 What better would the manikin desire
Than to strut forth on tiptoe, notable
As who, so far up, fouled me in the flank?'

1658| MS:turn cheek, and §last three words inserted above§ take the §crossed out§ pleasantry,
P1875: cheek and   1659| MS:purple and flesh §last three words inserted above§ smart,
*P1875:*flesh start,   1660| MS:And teach §altered to§ taught §last two words crossed out
and replaced above by two words§ To teach   1661| MS:First mouth §crossed out and
replaced above by§ face   1662| MS:Of good §crossed out§ prompt slab §inserted above§
mud that §crossed out and replaced above by§ as, filling it §crossed out and replaced above
by§ mouth   1664| MS:as to §crossed out and replaced above by§ go <> itself, §comma
altered to period§   1666| MS:it, your calm   *P1875:*it, that calm
1667| MS:Sagacity that's §crossed out and replaced above by§ you called §altered to§ call
1669-70| MS:§one line expanded to two lines§ pillared by your prowess §last four words and
comma inserted above§ <> §solidus added§ immortal §altered to§ Immortally immerded.
No, §word and comma altered to§ Not indeed §crossed out and replaced above by two words§
so he, §comma altered to exclamation point§   1673| MS:That little Strattis §last three
words crossed out and replaced above by two words§ Certain minuteness
1674| MS:§line added§ Dogface, the dying little satirist, §entire line crossed out and replaced
in margin§ Dogface Eruxis the dwarf §crossed out and replaced above by§ small satirist,
*P1875:*Dogface Eruxis, the <> satirist,—   1675| MS:better portion §crossed out§ would
1676| MS:to become forever §last two words crossed out and replaced above by four words and
comma§ strut forth on tiptoe   1677| MS:who so high had §last two words crossed out and
replaced above by two words§ far up touched §crossed out and replaced above by§ fouled
Euripides?' §word and punctuation crossed out and replaced above by four words and
punctuation§ me in the flank?'   *1889a:*who, so <> up, fouled

So dealt he with the dwarfs: we giants, too,
Why must we emulate their pin-point play?
1680 Render imperishable—impotence,
For mud throw mountains? Zeus, by mud unreached,—
Well, 'twas no dwarf he heaved Olumpos at!"

My heart burned up within me to my tongue.

"And why must men remember, ages hence,
1685 Who it was rolled down rocks, but refuse too—
Strattis might steal from! mixture-monument,
Recording what? 'I, Aristophanes,
Who boast me much inventive in my art,
Against Euripides thus volleyed muck
1690 Because, in art, he too extended bounds.
I—patriot, loving peace and hating war,—
Choosing the rule of few, but wise and good,
Rather than mob-dictature, fools and knaves
However multiplied their mastery,—
1695 Despising most of all the demagogue,
(Noisome air-bubble, buoyed up, borne along
By kindred breath of knave and fool below,
Whose hearts swell proudly as each puffing face
Grows big, reflected in that glassy ball,
1700 Vacuity, just bellied out to break

1678| MS:No matter for §last three words crossed out and replaced above by four words§ So dealt he with the §crossed out§ dwarfs: the §crossed out and replaced above by§ we   *P1875:* with the dwarfs   1680| MS:§word and comma in margin and illegibly crossed out§ §next two words illegibly crossed out and replaced above by dash and word§ —Render imperishable— §dash inserted above§   1681-83| MS:For Not §crossed out§ mud, but §crossed out and replaced above by§ throw mountains? §question mark inserted§ §next word illegibly crossed out and replaced above by illegibly crossed-out word§ Zeus by mud §last two words inserted above§ unreached!"— §*un* crossed out§ / My   *P1875:*mountains? Zeus, by mud unreached,— / Well <> at! / My   *1889a:* / / <> at!"   1684| MS:"So §altered to§ And shall it be §last three words crossed out and replaced above by three words§ why must men remembered §altered to§ remember   1685| MS:Who rolled the rocks up,—rocks *P1875:*Who it was rolled down rocks   1687| MS:what? but §crossed out§ 'I
1689| MS:Against Euripides have §crossed out and replaced above by§ thus volleyed §altered to§ volley   *P1875:*volleyed   1692| MS:few, the §crossed out and replaced above by§ but
1696| MS:Noisome   *P1875:*(Noisome   1700| MS:to burst §crossed out§ break

And righteously bespatter friends the first)—
I loathing,—beyond less puissant speech
Than my own god-grand language to declare,—
The fawning, cozenage and calumny
1705 Wherewith such favourite feeds the populace
That fan and set him flying for reward:—
I who, detecting what vice underlies
Thought's superstructure,—fancy's sludge and slime
'Twixt fact's sound floor and thought's mere surface-growth
1710 Of hopes and fears which root no deeplier down
Than where all such mere fungi breed and bloat—
Namely, man's misconception of the God:—
I, loving, hating, wishful from my soul
That truth should triumph, falsehood have defeat,
1715 —Why, all my soul's supremacy of power
Did I pour out in volley just on him
Who, his whole life long, championed every cause
I called my heart's cause, loving as I loved,
Hating my hates, spurned falsehood, championed truth,—
1720 Championed truth not by flagellating foe

---

¹⁷⁰¹| MS:first:— *P1875:*first) *1889a:*first)— ¹⁷⁰²| MS:Loathing,—beyond all
§altered to§ a less *1889a:*I loathing,—beyond less ¹⁷⁰⁴| MS:fawning, craftiness and
*P1875:*fawning, cozenage and ¹⁷⁰⁵| MS:favorite *1889a:*favourite
¹⁷⁰⁸| MS:Tho §altered to§ Thought's unsound §crossed out§ superstructure, fancy §word
and dash inserted above§ sludge *P1875:*fancy's sludge ¹⁷⁰⁹| MS:sound §inserted
above§ <> and the fungous §last two words crossed out and replaced above by two words§
thought's mere fancy-growth §altered to§ surface-growth ¹⁷¹⁰| MS:which root no
otherwise §last two words crossed out§ and flourish there §last four words crossed out and
replaced above by four words§ strike no deeper root §punctuation illegibly crossed out§
*P1875:*which root no deeplier down ¹⁷¹¹| MS:That §altered to§ Than fancy §crossed
out§ where all <> mere §last two words inserted above§ ¹⁷¹¹⁻¹²| MS:§between these two
lines§ And find all cheats and shams in breeding place §entire line crossed out§
¹⁷¹²| MS:To wit, §last two words and comma crossed out and replaced
above by one word and comma§ Namely <> Gods:— *P1875:*God:—
¹⁷¹⁴| MS:Such §crossed out and replaced above by§ That truths §altered to§ truth <>
triumph, §comma inserted§ and such falsehoods §altered to§ falsehood flee, §last four words
crossed out and replaced below by two words§ have defeat, §*falsehood* restored§
¹⁷¹⁵| MS:all that §crossed out and replaced above by§ my ¹⁷¹⁷| MS:championed just the
§last two words crossed out and replaced above by one word§ every ¹⁷¹⁹| MS:hates, one
false, one true for both,— *P1875:*false one *1889a:*hates, spurned falsehood, championed
truth,— ¹⁷²⁰| MS:Championed it too §last two words crossed out and replaced above by
two words§ my cause—not as I laughing say §last four words crossed out and replaced above
by two words§ flagellating foe *1889a:*Championed truth not by flagellating

---

With simple rose and lily, gibe and jeer,
Sly wink of boon-companion o'er his bowze
Who, while he blames the liquor, smacks the lip,
Blames, doubtless, but leers condonation too,—
1725   No, the balled fist broke brow like thunderbolt,
Battered till brain flew!   Seeing which descent,
None questioned that was first acquaintanceship,
The avenger's with the vice he crashed through bone.
Still, he displeased me; and I turned from foe
1730   To fellow-fighter, flung much stone, more mud,—
But missed him, since he lives aloof, I see.'
Pah! stop more shame, deep-cutting glory through,
Nor add, this poet, learned,—found no taunt
Tell like 'That other poet studies books!'
1735   Wise,—cried 'At each attempt to move our hearts,
He uses the mere phrase of daily life!'
Witty,—'His mother was a herb-woman!'
Veracious, honest, loyal, fair and good,—

---

^{1721|}   MS:With whip of §last two words crossed out and replaced above by one word§ simple
leeks and onions, gibe   *P1875:*simple rose and lily, gibe   ^{1722|}   MS:wink, of §comma
and word crossed out and replaced above by crossed-out word, *the,* and then *of* restored§
^{1724|}   MS:Blame, doubtlessly, but condonation   *P1875:*Blames, doubtless, but leers
condonation   ^{1725|}   MS:No, but §crossed out§ the balled fist's §altered to§ fist fell like
§last two words crossed out and replaced above by one word§ descent §crossed out§ broke
brow, §over illegible erasure§ a §last three words inserted above§ thunderbolt—   *P1875:*brow
like thunderbolt,   ^{1726|}   MS:Battering §altered to§ Battered < > flew §exclamation point
inserted§ in §crossed out and replaced above by§ Seeing which dread §crossed out§ descent,
^{1727|}   MS:None doubted §crossed out and replaced above by§ questioned that was §last two
words crossed out and replaced above by two illegibly crossed-out words and then restored§
< > acquaintanceship,—   *P1875:*acquaintanceship,   ^{1728|}   MS:The avenger's §altered
to§ avenger with the §altered to§ that vice < > thro bone!   *P1875:*avenger's with the vice < >
through bone.   ^{1730|}   MS:flung thus §crossed out and replaced above by§ much stone,
and §crossed out and replaced above by§ more trash,—   *P1875:*more mud,—
^{1731|}   MS:But §in margin§ And §crossed out§ missed < > he stands aloof < > see."   *P1875:*he
lives aloof < > see.'   ^{1732|}   MS:shame deep cutting the §crossed out§ glory through!
*P1875:*deep-cutting < > through,   *1889a:*shame, deep-cutting   ^{1733|}   MS:Nor §in
margin§ Add not, §crossed out§ 'This §quotation mark crossed out§   *P1875:*add, this
^{1734|}   MS:other busied him with §last three words crossed out and
replaced above by two words§ poet studies   ^{1735|}   MS:Wise—thou §crossed out and
replaced above by§ cried < > move the §crossed out and replaced above by§ our   *P1875:*
Wise,—cried   ^{1737|}   MS:Witty—'His   *P1875:*Witty,—'His
^{1738|}   MS:fair-and-good—   *P1875:*fair-and-good,—   *1889a:*fair and good,—

'It was Kephisophon who helped him write!'

1740   "Whence,—O the tragic end of comedy!—
Balaustion pities Aristophanes.
For, who believed him?   Those who laughed so loud?
They heard him call the sun Sicilian cheese!
Had he called true cheese—curd, would muscle move?
1745   What made them laugh but the enormous lie?
'Kephisophon wrote "Herakles"? ha, ha,
What can have stirred the wine-dregs, soured the soul
And set a-lying Aristophanes?
Some accident at which he took offence!
1750   The Tragic Master in a moody muse
Passed him unhailing, and it hurts—it hurts!
Beside, there's licence for the Wine-lees-song!'"

Blood burnt the cheek-bone, each black eye flashed fierce.

"But this exceeds our licence!   Stay awhile—
1755   That's the solution! both are foreigners,
The fresh-come Rhodian lady and her spouse
The man of Phokis: newly resident,
Nowise instructed—that explains it all!
No born and bred Athenian but would smile,

1739| MS:'It §in margin§ Than §crossed out§ ''Twas §punctuation crossed out and word altered to§ was Kephisophon that §crossed out and replaced above by§ who
1740| MS:§line added§   1742| MS:so much §crossed out and replaced above by§ loud?
1744| MS:true §inserted above§ cheese— §dash inserted§ <> would a §crossed out§ muscle
1745| MS:§line added in margin§   1746| MS:wrote 'Herakles?' ha, ha! *P1875:*ha, ha, *1889a:*wrote Herakles? ha, ha,   1747| MS:have nettled Aristophanes? §last two words and question mark crossed out and replaced above by six words§ stirred the wine-dregs, thick and §last two words crossed out§ soured the soul, *1889a:*soul   1748-49| MS:§lines added in margin§   1750| MS:a musing-mood *P1875:*a moody muse   1752| MS:Besides,— the §altered to§ there's licence of §altered to§ for *P1875:*Beside, there's
1753| MS:fierce §over illegible erasure§   1754| MS:exceeds fair §crossed out and replaced above by§ our license §over illegible erasure§ *P1875:*licence
1755| MS:solution! you §crossed out and replaced above by§ both   1756| MS:The famous §crossed out and replaced above by§ fresh-come §*fresh* over illegible erasure§ *P1875:*lady, and *1889a:*lady and   1757| MS:of Phokis: both §crossed out§ new §altered to§ newly   1758| MS:instructed: that *P1875:*instructed—that

¹⁷⁶⁰ Unless frown seemed more fit for ignorance.
These strangers have a privilege!

"You blame"
(Presently he resumed with milder mien)
"Both theory and practice—Comedy:
Blame her from altitudes the Tragic friend
¹⁷⁶⁵ Rose to, and upraised friends along with him,
No matter how.   Once there, all's cold and fine,
Passionless, rational; our world beneath
Shows (should you condescend to grace so much
As glance at poor Athenai) grimly gross—
¹⁷⁷⁰ A population which, mere flesh and blood,
Eats, drinks and kisses, falls to fisticuffs,
Then hugs as hugely: speaks too as it acts,
Prodigiously talks nonsense,—townsmen needs
Must parley in their town's vernacular.
¹⁷⁷⁵ Such world has, of two courses, one to choose:
Unworld itself,—or else go blackening off
To its crow-kindred, leave philosophy
Her heights serene, fit perch for owls like you.
Now, since the world demurs to either course,
¹⁷⁸⁰ Permit me,—in default of boy or girl,

---

¹⁷⁶⁰| MS:Unless a §crossed out§ frown <> more §inserted above§   ¹⁷⁶¹| MS:But §in margin§ Still, §word and comma crossed out§ strangers <> privilege. §¶§ <> blame"— *P1875:*These strangers <> privilege! §¶§ <> blame"   ¹⁷⁶²| MS:§line added in margin§ ¹⁷⁶³| MS:"Both §over illegible word§   ¹⁷⁶⁴| MS:Speaking from §inserted above§ altitudes §altered to§ altitude your §crossed out and replaced above by§ the   *P1875:*Blame her from altitudes   ¹⁷⁶⁵| MS:raised §altered to§ upraised you §crossed out and replaced above by§ friends up §crossed out§ along   ¹⁷⁶⁸| MS:Glooms (when §crossed out and replaced above by§ should   *P1875:*Shows (should   ¹⁷⁷⁰| MS:A §in margin§ With §over illegible word and crossed out§ population which, all §crossed out and replaced above by§ mere   ¹⁷⁷²| MS:hugely, then with §last two words crossed out§ speaks §over illegible erasure§ like §crossed out and replaced above by three words§ too as it   *P1875:*hugely: speaks   ¹⁷⁷³| MS:needs §over illegible erasure§   ¹⁷⁷⁵⁻⁷⁶| MS:§between these two lines§ Either to fine, refine, turn faint, and §crossed out and replaced above by§ fall, freeze,
¹⁷⁷⁸| MS:Her §in margin§ Its §crossed out§ And §inserted above and crossed out§ cloudy heights, where §crossed out and replaced above by three words§ fit perch for friends like you. §period inserted§ may perch. §last two words and period crossed out§   *P1875:*Her heights serene, fit <> for owls like   ¹⁷⁷⁹| MS:Now, seeing that §last two words crossed out and replaced above by one word§ since <> to both, §word and comma crossed out§ either course,

So they be reared Athenian, good and true,—
To praise what you most blame! Hear Art's defence!
I'll prove our institution, Comedy,
Coëval with the birth of freedom, matched
1785 So nice with our Republic, that its growth
Measures each greatness, just as its decline
Would signalize the downfall of the pair.
Our Art began when Bacchos . . . never mind!
You and your master don't acknowledge gods:
1790 'They are not, no, they are not!' well,—began
When the rude instinct of our race outspoke,
Found,—on recurrence of festivity
Occasioned by black mother-earth's good will
To children, as they took her vintage-gifts,—
1795 Found—not the least of many benefits—
That wine unlocked the stiffest lip, and loosed
The tongue late dry and reticent of joke,
Through custom's gripe which gladness thrusts aside.
So, emulating liberalities,
1800 Heaven joined with earth for that god's day at least,

---

¹⁷⁸²| MS:most §inserted above§ blame! §exclamation point inserted§ first §crossed out§ hear §altered to§ Hear   ¹⁷⁸³| MS:prove the §crossed out and replaced above by§ our
¹⁷⁸⁴| MS:freedom, plain §crossed out§ matched   ¹⁷⁸⁵| MS:So matched §crossed out and replaced above by§ nice   ¹⁷⁸⁶| MS:Measures their greatness   *P1875:*Measures each greatness   ¹⁷⁸⁸| MS:Our §in margin§ The §crossed out§ Art < > Bacchos...I forget! §last two words and exclamation point crossed out§ never mind!   ¹⁷⁸⁹| MS:gods—   *P1875:* gods: ¹⁷⁹⁰| MS:not!' Well   *P1875:*well   ¹⁷⁹¹| MS:When §in margin§ With §crossed out§ the §inserted above§ rude outspoken §crossed out§ instinct
¹⁷⁹²| MS:Found §in margin§ That,— §word crossed out; punctuation inserted§ on
¹⁷⁹³| MS:Occasioned of §crossed out and replaced above by§ by man's §crossed out and replaced above by§ black   ¹⁷⁹⁴| MS:they gathered vintage-gifts,—   *P1875:*they took her vintage-gifts,—   ¹⁷⁹⁵| MS:Found §in margin§ Since— §crossed out and replaced above by crossed-out word, *That*§ not < > benefits   *P1875:*benefits—
¹⁷⁹⁶| MS:Was—wine's unlocking stiffest lip, that §crossed out and replaced above by§ which loose   *P1875:*That wine unlocked the stiffest lip, and loosed   ¹⁷⁹⁷| MS:Tongue §altered to *tongue* and marked for transposition to follow the§ Might §over *might*§ wag the §over *too*§ long §crossed out and replaced above by§ late < > reticent   *P1875:*The tongue late < > reticent of joke,   ¹⁷⁹⁹| MS:Why §crossed out and replaced above by§ So
¹⁸⁰⁰| MS:Heaven joined §last two words in margin§ Of §crossed out and replaced above by§ with earth; man claimed, §last two words and comma crossed out§ for   *P1875:*earth for

Renewed man's privilege, grown obsolete,
Of telling truth nor dreading punishment.
Whereon the joyous band disguised their forms
With skins, beast-fashion, daubed each phyz with dregs,
1805 Then hollaed 'Neighbour, you are fool, you—knave,
You—hard to serve, you—stingy to reward!'
The guiltless crowed, the guilty sunk their crest,
And good folk gained thereby, 'twas evident.
Whence, by degrees, a birth of happier thought,
1810 The notion came—not simply this to say,
But this to do—prove, put in evidence,
And act the fool, the knave, the harsh, the hunks,
Who *did* prate, cheat, shake fist, draw pursestring tight,
As crowd might see, which only heard before.

1815 "So played the Poet, with his man of parts;
And all the others, found unqualified
To mount cart and be persons, made the mob,
Joined choros, fortified their fellows' fun,
Anticipated the community,
1820 Gave judgment which the public ratified.
Suiting rough weapon doubtless to plain truth,
They flung, for word-artillery, why—filth;
Still, folk who wiped the unsavoury salute
From visage, would prefer the mess to wit—

1801| MS:Return to liberty §last three words crossed out and replaced above by three words§
Renewed man's privilege grown   *P1875:*privilege, grown   1803| MS:disguised themselves
§altered to two words§ their forms   1804| *P1875:*phiz   *1889a:*phyz   1807| MS:guilty
couched §crossed out and replaced above by§ sunk   1809| MS:Whence §over partial
erasure§ <> a §over illegible erasure§ spring §crossed out and replaced above by§ birth
1812| MS:With §crossed out§ Here's §crossed out and replaced above by§ Acting the   *P1875:*
And act the   1813-15| MS:Who did §over illegible erasure§ laugh, cheat <> tight! / §line
added§ So <> parts,   *P1875: did* prate, cheat <> tight, / As <> before. / <> parts;
1889a: / / "So   1816| MS:And §in margin§ While §crossed out§ all   1817| MS:and
play §crossed out and replaced above by§ be §crossed out and *play* restored§ persons   *P1875:*
and be persons   1818| MS:Joined §in margin§ As §crossed out§ choros
1823| MS:You say §last two words crossed out and replaced above by two words§ Still, folks
*1889a:*folk   1824| MS:visage, would §crossed out and replaced above by two illegible
words; *would* restored§ prefer §over illegible erasure§ <> to steel §crossed out§ wit—

¹⁸²⁵   Steel, poked through midriff with a civil speech,
As now the way is: then, the kindlier mode
Was—drub not stab, ribroast not scarify!
So did Sousarion introduce, and so
Did I, acceding, find the Comic Art:
¹⁸³⁰   Club,—if I call it,—notice what's implied!
An engine proper for rough chastisement,
No downright slaying: with impunity—
Provided crabtree, steeped in oily joke,
Deal only such a bruise as laughter cures.
¹⁸³⁵   I kept the gained advantage: stickled still
For club-law—stout fun and allowanced thumps:
Knocked in each knob a crevice to hold joke
As fig-leaf holds the fat-fry.

"Next, whom thrash?
Only the coarse fool and the clownish knave?
¹⁸⁴⁰   Higher, more artificial, composite
Offence should prove my prowess, eye and arm!
Not who robs henroost, tells of untaxed figs,

---

^{1825|}   MS:Steel, §word and comma in margin§ poked §over partial erasure§ through one's §crossed out§ midriff with civility,—   *P1875:*with a civil speech,   ^{1826|}   MS:is—but §crossed out and replaced above by word and comma§ then   *P1875:*is: then
^{1827|}   MS:not scorticate!   *P1875:*not scarify!   ^{1828|}   MS:did §inserted above§ introduced §altered to§ introduce Sousarion §last two words transposed§ Comedy, §word crossed out and comma retained§ and   *P1875:*so,   *1889a:*so   ^{1829|}   MS:And so §last two words crossed out§ Did §over *did*§ <> find my §crossed out and replaced above by two words§ the Comic Art:—   *P1875:*the Comic Art: ^{1831|}   MS:An §in margin§ Enginery §altered to§ engine
^{1832|}   MS:slaying, with §crossed out and replaced above by illegible erasure; *with* restored§ impunity   *P1875:*slaying: with impunity—   ^{1834|}   MS:such a §last two words inserted above§ <> laughter is like to §last three words crossed out§ cure §altered to§ cures.
^{1835|}   MS:I §in margin§ kept §over illegible word§ I said §last two words crossed out§ the §inserted above§   ^{1836|}   MS:club-law—stoutness and   *P1875:*club-law—stout fun and
^{1837|}   MS:And §in margin and crossed out§ Knocked <> each §crossed out and restored§ knob its §crossed out and replaced above by§ a <> hold fun   *P1875:*hold joke
^{1838|}   MS:figleaf <> fat-fry, §comma altered to period§ §¶§ but §altered to§ But §crossed out and replaced above by§ "Next   *P1875:*fig-leaf   ^{1839|}   MS:coarser folly, §word and comma crossed out and replaced above by two words§ fool, the clownish vice §crossed out and replaced above by§ knave?   *P1875:*coarse fool and the   ^{1841|}   MS:Offence shall §crossed out and replaced above by§ should   ^{1842|}   MS:untaxed hoard,   *P1875:*untaxed figs,

Spends all his substance on stewed ellops-fish,
Or gives a pheasant to his neighbour's wife:
1845   No! strike malpractice that affects the State,
The common weal—intriguer or poltroon,
Venality, corruption, what care I
If shrewd or witless merely?—so the thing
Lay sap to aught that made Athenai bright
1850   And happy, change her customs, lead astray
Youth or age, play the demagogue at Pnux,
The sophist in Palaistra, or—what's worst,
As widest mischief,—from the Theatre
Preach innovation, bring contempt on oaths,
1855   Adorn licentiousness, despise the Cult.
Are such to be my game? Why, then there wants
Quite other cunning than a cudgel-sweep!
Grasp the old stout stock, but new tip with steel
Each boss, if I would bray—no callous hide
1860   Simply, but Lamachos in coat of proof,
Or Kleon cased about with impudence!
Shaft pushed no worse while point pierced sparkling so
That none smiled 'Sportive, what seems savagest,
—Innocuous anger, spiteless rustic mirth!'
1865   Yet spiteless in a sort, considered well,

1843| MS:his money §crossed out and replaced above by§ substance <> stewed cuttlefish, *P1875:* stewed ellops-fish,   1844| MS:wife—   *P1875:*wife: 1845| MS:No! Some §crossed out and replaced above by§ strike malpractice touched §crossed out and replaced above by§ that   1846| MS:weal—the §crossed out§ intriguer, the §crossed out and replaced above by§ or   *P1875:*intriguer or   1848| MS:thing §over illegible word§   1849| MS:to all §crossed out and replaced above by§ aught <> Athenai grand §over *great*§ *P1875:*made Athenai bright   1851| MS:And glorious, change   *P1875:*And happy, change   1852| MS:or,—what's   *P1875:*or—what's   1853| MS:theatre   *P1875:*the Theatre   1855| MS:the Gods §crossed out§ cult §altered to§ Cult—   *P1875:*the Cult.   1859| MS:if you §crossed out and replaced above by§ I <> hide,   *P1875:*hide   1861| MS:Or §in margin§ Kleon the crust of §last three words crossed out and replaced above by two words§ cased with stolid impudence!   *P1875:*cased about with impudence!   1862| MS:pierced, sparkling   *P1875:*pierced sparkling   1863| MS:smiled 'Sportive, spiteless rustic mirth,' §comma altered to exclamation point and last three words marked for transposition to end of line 1864§   1864| MS:—Ignorant anger, what the §crossed out and replaced above by§ seems savagest, §last three words marked for transposition to end of line 1863§   *P1875:*—Innocuous anger   1865| MS:well, §crossed out and replaced above by illegibly crossed-out word and then restored§

Since I pursued my warfare till each wound
Went through the mere man, reached the principle
Worth purging from Athenai.   Lamachos?
No, I attacked war's representative;
1870 Kleon?   No, flattery of the populace;
Sokrates?   No, but that pernicious seed
Of sophists whereby hopeful youth is taught
To jabber argument, chop logic, pore
On sun and moon, and worship Whirligig.
1875 O your tragedian, with the lofty grace,
Aims at no other and effects as much?
Candidly: what's a polished period worth,
Filed curt sententiousness of loaded line,
When he who deals out doctrine, primly steps
1880 From just that selfsame moon he maunders of,
And, blood-thinned by his pallid nutriment,
Proposes to rich earth-blood—purity?
In me, 'twas equal-balanced flesh rebuked
Excess alike in stuff-guts Glauketes
1885 Or starveling Chairephon; I challenged both,—
Strong understander of our common life,
I urged sustainment of humanity.
Whereas when your tragedian cries up Peace—
He's silent as to cheesecakes Peace may chew;
1890 Seeing through rabble-rule, he shuts his eye
To what were better done than crowding Pnux—

1866| MS:Since I refined §crossed out and replaced above by§ pursued   1872| MS:Of
sophistry §altered to§ sophists whereby our §crossed out and replaced above by§ hopeful
1875| MS:Oh, your   *1889a:*O your   1876| MS:much! §punctuation altered to question
mark§   1878| MS:Of §over illegible erasure§ loaded line, filed §altered to§ Filed curt
sententiousness §last three words marked for transposition to beginning of line§   *P1875:*of
1881| MS:And, pulse-thinned §*pulse* crossed out and replaced above by§ blood
1882| MS:Proposes ruddy §crossed out and replaced above by two words§ to rich earth-blood
§*blood* over illegible erasure§ —purity! §dash inserted; exclamation point altered to question
mark§   1883| MS:me §next word illegibly crossed out, perhaps *'twas,* and replaced above
by§ 'twas   *P1875:*me, 'twas   1886| MS:of man's common   *P1875:*of our common
1887| MS:Staple sustainment   *1889a:*I urged sustainment   1889| MS:cheesecake Peace
should §over partial erasure§ chew;   *P1875:*cheesecake Peace may chew;   *1889a:*cheesecakes
1890| MS:through mob-rule, oh, he shuts each §crossed out and replaced above by§ his
*P1875:*through rabble-rule, he   1891| MS:To—what   *P1875:*To what

83

That's—dance '*Threttanelo,* the Kuklops drunk!'

"My power has hardly need to vaunt itself!
Opposers peep and mutter, or speak plain:
¹⁸⁹⁵ 'No naming names in Comedy!' votes one,
'Nor vilifying live folk!' legislates
Another, 'urge amendment on the dead!'
'Don't throw away hard cash,' supplies a third,
'But crib from actor's dresses, choros-treats!'
¹⁹⁰⁰ Then Kleon did his best to bully me:
Called me before the Law Court: 'Such a play
Satirized citizens with strangers there,
Such other,'—why, its fault was in myself!
I was, this time, the stranger, privileged
¹⁹⁰⁵ To act no play at all,—Egyptian, I—
Rhodian or Kameirensian, Aiginete,
Lindian, or any foreigner he liked—
Because I can't write Attic, probably!
Go ask my rivals,—how they roughed my fleece,
¹⁹¹⁰ And how, shorn pink themselves, the huddled sheep
Shiver at distance from the snapping shears!
Why must they needs provoke me?

                              "All the same,

---

¹⁸⁹²| MS:Dancing 'Threttanelo <> drunk!'   *P1875:*Dancing '*Threttanelo*   *1889a:*That's—
dance '*Threttanelo* <> drunk! §emended to§ drunk!' §see Editorial Notes§
¹⁸⁹³| MS:"Not that my <> has need   *P1875:*"My <> has hardly need
¹⁸⁹⁴| MS:plain   *P1875:*plain: ¹⁸⁹⁵| MS:in Comedy,' votes   *P1875:*in Comedy!' votes
¹⁸⁹⁶| MS:folk §crossed out and replaced above by illegibly crossed-out word and then
restored§   ¹⁸⁹⁷| MS:Another! §exclamation point altered to comma§ 'urge
¹⁸⁹⁸| MS:supplies §over illegible word§   ¹⁸⁹⁹| MS:'On §crossed out and replaced above
by§ Crib actor's dresses and the choros-treat!'   *P1875:*'But crib from actor's dresses, choros-
treats!'   ¹⁹⁰¹| MS:the Law-Court   *P1875:*the Law Court
¹⁹⁰³| MS:myself: *P1875:*myself!   ¹⁹⁰⁸⁻⁰⁹| MS:§¶ called for in margin§   *P1875:*§no ¶§
¹⁹⁰⁹| MS:"As for §last two words crossed out and replaced above by two words§ "Go ask
*P1875:*Go   ¹⁹¹⁰| MS:And, §comma crossed out§ how, §inserted above§ shorn to
§crossed out§ pink themselves, now, §word and comma crossed out and replaced above by§ the
¹⁹¹¹| MS:from my clapping shears,   *P1875:*from the clapping shears!
*1889a:*the snapping shears!   ¹⁹¹²| MS:Go ask §last two words crossed out§ Why must
§inserted above§ <> needs §inserted above§ provoked §altered to§ provoke

No matter for my triumph, I foretell
Subsidence of the day-star: quench his beams?
1915 No Aias e'er was equal to the feat
By throw of shield, tough-hided seven times seven,
'Twixt sky and earth! 'tis dullards soft and sure
Who breathe against his brightest, here a sigh
And there a 'So let be, we pardon you!'
1920 Till the minute mist hangs a block, has tamed
Noonblaze to 'twilight mild and equable,'
Vote the old women spinning out of doors.
Give me the earth-spasm, when the lion ramped
And the bull gendered in the brave gold flare!
1925 O you shall have amusement,—better still,
Instruction! no more horse-play, naming names,
Taxing the fancy when plain sense will serve!
Thearion, now, my friend who bakes you bread,
What's worthier limning than his household life?
1930 His whims and ways, his quarrels with the spouse,
And how the son, instead of learning knead
Kilikian loaves, brings heart-break on his sire
By buying horseflesh branded *San,* each flank,
From shrewd Menippos who imports the ware:

1913| MS:for §over illegible erasure§ its §inserted above over illegible word§ triumphant §altered to§ triumph   *1889a:*for my triumph   1914| MS:day star: blank §crossed out and replaced above by§ quench <> beams?   *P1875:*day-star   *1889a:*beams §emended to§ beams? §see Editorial Notes§   1915| MS:No Aias e'er §last two words over illegible erasures§   1917| MS:'Twixt sun and earth! the §crossed out and replaced above by§ 'tis   *P1875:*'Twixt sky and   1918| MS:Who §in margin§ Breathe §altered to§ breathe up §crossed out§ against   1920| MS:mist makes §crossed out§ hangs entire, §over partial erasure§ has *1889a:*hangs a block, has   1922| MS:Say the §last two words in margin§ old §over partial erasure§ women say, a- §last two words and hyphen crossed out§ spinning   *P1875:*Vote the   1923| MS:the gold-spasm §*gold* crossed out and replaced above by§ earth   1926| MS:more rough §crossed out and replaced above by word and hyphen§ horse-   1927| MS:serve—   *P1875:*serve!   1928-29| MS:§between these two lines§ Or Sporgilos the barber or belike §solidus added§ Heiron, the dapper at appraising goods §entire line crossed out§   1929| MS:limning §inserted below§ than to show §last two words crossed out§ their §over illegible word; crossed out and replaced below by§ his <> life,   *P1875:*life?   1930| MS:His §over illegible erasure§ <> his §over *the*§ <> the §over *his*§   1931| MS:the §over illegible erasure§ <> learning bake §crossed out§ knead   1932| MS:loaves, spends §crossed out and replaced above by§ brings   1933| MS:buying horses §altered to§ horseflesh   1934| MS:§line added in margin§ ware,   *P1875:*ware:

¹⁹³⁵ While pretty daughter Kepphé too much haunts
The shop of Sporgilos the barber! brave!
Out with Thearion's meal-tub politics
In lieu of Pisthetairos, Strepsiades!
That's your exchange?   O Muse of Megara!
¹⁹⁴⁰ Advise the fools *'Feed babe on weasel-lap*
For wild-boar's marrow, Cheiron's hero-pap,
And rear, for man—Ariphrades, mayhap!'
Yes, my Balaustion, yes, my Euthukles,
That's *your* exchange,—who, foreigners in fact
¹⁹⁴⁵ And fancy, would impose your squeamishness
On sturdy health, and substitute such brat
For the right offspring of us Rocky Ones,
Because babe kicks the cradle,—crows, not mewls!

"Which brings me to the prime fault, poison-speck
¹⁹⁵⁰ Whence all the plague springs—that first feud of all
'Twixt me and you and your Euripides.
'Unworld the world' frowns he, my opposite.
I cry, 'Life!'   'Death,' he groans, 'our better Life!'
Despise what is—the good and graspable,
¹⁹⁵⁵ Prefer the out of sight and in at mind,
To village-joy, the well-side violet-patch,
The jolly club-feast when our field's in soak,

---

^{1935|}   MS:pretty §inserted above§   ^{1936|}   MS:§line added in margin§ barber: brave!
*P1875:*barber! brave!   ^{1937|}   MS:Out with §last two words in margin§ Baker §crossed
out§ Thearion's household §crossed out and replaced above by§ meal-tub
^{1938|}   MS:of Pisthetairos, Strepsiades,—   *P1875:*of Pisthetairos, Strepsiades!
^{1939|}   MS:That's your §crossed out and replaced above by illegible erasure, perhaps *it*, and
your restored§ exchanged §altered to§ exchange! O   *P1875:*exchange? O
^{1940|}   MS:Sing to §last two words crossed out and replaced above by one word§ Advise < >
*"Feed   P1875:*fools '*Feed*   ^{1942|}   MS:*rear thereby* §crossed out and replaced above by five
illegibly crossed-out alternate words, perhaps *for the for man from*; these five words replaced
below by two words and dash§ *for man—* < > *mayhap!   P1875:mayhap!'*
^{1943|}   MS:§line added in margin§   ^{1944|}   MS:Yes, *your   P1875:*That's *your*
^{1945|}   MS:Are §altered to§ And fancy, dare §crossed out and replaced above by§ would
^{1946|}   MS:§line added§ and §next word illegibly crossed out, perhaps *first*§ substitute such
§over illegible word§   ^{1947|}   MS:For §in margin§ On §crossed out§ the < > of the
§crossed out and replaced below by§ us   ^{1948|}   MS:Because it §crossed out and replaced
above by§ babe < > cradle,—lives §crossed out and replaced above by§ laughs, not dies
§crossed out and replaced above by§ mewls!   *P1875:*cradle,—crows, not
^{1956|}   MS:wellside   *P1875:*well-side   ^{1957|}   MS:jolly-club feast   *P1875:*jolly club-feast

Roast thrushes, hare-soup, pea-soup, deep washed down
With Peparethian; the prompt paying off
1960 That black-eyed brown-skinned country-flavoured wench
We caught among our brushwood foraging:
On these look fig-juice, curdle up life's cream,
And fall to magnifying misery!
Or, if you condescend to happiness,
1965 Why, talk, talk, talk about the empty name
While thing's self lies neglected 'neath your nose!
I need particular discourtesy
And private insult from Euripides
To render contest with him credible?
1970 Say, all of me is outraged! one stretched sense,
I represent the whole Republic,—gods,
Heroes, priests, legislators, poets,—prone,
And pummelled into insignificance,
If will in him were matched with power of stroke.
1975 For see what he has changed or hoped to change!
How few years since, when he began the fight,
Did there beat life indeed Athenai through!
Plenty and peace, then! Hellas thundersmote
The Persian.   He himself had birth, you say,
1980 That morn salvation broke at Salamis,
And heroes still walked earth.   Themistokles—

1958| MS:Roast pippits, haresoup, peasoup, well §crossed out and replaced above by§ deep
*P1875:*Roast thrushes, haresoup   *1889a:*hare-soup, pea-soup   1959| MS:With
Peparethian, the < > paying-off   *P1875:*With Peparethian; the < > paying off
1960| MS:The §altered to§ That black eyed brown skinned country piece of health §last three
words crossed out and replaced above by two words§ -tasting §crossed out and replaced below
by§ -flavoured wench   *P1875:*black-eyed brown-skinned   1961| MS:among the §crossed
out and replaced above by§ our < > foraging—   *P1875:*foraging: 1962| MS:fig juice
*P1875:*fig-juice   1963| MS:misery!—   *P1875:*misery!   1964| MS:happiness,—
*P1875:*happiness,   1966| MS:While the §crossed out§ thing's self §inserted above§ < >
neglected under §crossed out and replaced above by two words§ 'neath your
1968| MS:And §in margin§ private §over *Private*§ insulting §altered to§ insult
1970| MS:outraged,—one   *P1875:*outraged! one   1973| MS:§line added in margin§
1975| MS:has done §crossed out and replaced above by§ changed < > to do§crossed out and
replaced above by§ change!   1979| MS:The Persian, §comma altered to period§ he
§altered to§ He himself was born §last two words crossed out and replaced above by two words§
had birth   1981| MS:Why, §word and comma crossed out and replaced above by§ And

Surely his mere back-stretch of hand could still
Find, not so lost in dark, Odusseus?—he
Holding as surely on to Herakles,—
1985   Who touched Zeus, link by link, the unruptured chain!
Were poets absent?   Aischulos might hail—
With Pindaros, Theognis,—whom for sire?
Homeros' self, departed yesterday!
While Hellas, saved and sung to, then and thus,—
1990   Ah, people,—ah, lost antique liberty!
We lived, ourselves, undoubted lords of earth:
Wherever olives flourish, corn yields crop
To constitute our title—ours such land!
Outside of oil and breadstuff,—barbarism!
1995   What need of conquest?   Let barbarians starve!
Devote our whole strength to our sole defence,
Content with peerless native products, home,
Beauty profuse in earth's mere sights and sounds,
Such men, such women, and such gods their guard!
2000   The gods? he worshipped best who feared them most,

1982| MS:his §over illegible word, perhaps *has*§ <> hand had §crossed out and replaced above by§ could   1983| MS:Find §over illegible erasure§ <> dark, Odusseus,— §comma altered to question mark§ he   1985| MS:Who, link and link, touched Zeus, the §transposed to§ Who touched Zeus, link and link, the   *1889a:*link by link   1987| MS:With Pindaros, for sire §last two words crossed out and replaced above by four words§ Theognis,—whom for sire? 1988| MS:§solidus and line added in margin§   1989| MS:While who were, §last two words crossed out and replaced above by one word§ Hellas   1990| MS:Ah §over illegible erasure§ <> ah, that §crossed out and replaced above by§ lost   1991| MS:lived §over illegible erasure§ <> of land §over illegible word and crossed out§ earth—   *P1875:*earth: 1992| MS:Let but the §last three words crossed out and replaced above by one word§ Wherever <> crop,   *P1875:*crop   1993| MS:To §in margin§ That §crossed out and replaced above by§ And §crossed out§ constituted §altered to§ constitute <> title, §comma altered to exclamation point§ to the §last two words crossed out and replaced above by two words§ ours such   *P1875:*title—ours   1994| MS:Outside the §crossed out and replaced above by§ of §over illegible word§ oil, the §comma and word crossed out and replaced above by§ and   1995| MS:conquest, §comma altered to question mark§ let §altered to§ Let <> starve! §over illegible erasure§   1997| MS:Content us §crossed out§ with the §crossed out and replaced above by§ peerless native home-delight, §crossed out and replaced above by two words§ products, home,—   *P1875:*home,   1998| MS:in all §crossed out§ earth's mere §inserted above§ <> sounds—   *P1875:*sounds,   2000| MS:For §crossed out§ the §altered to§ The Gods,— §punctuation altered to question mark§ he §inserted above§ worship §altered to§ worshiped <> who fears §altered to§ feared   *P1875:*gods <> worshipped

88

And left their nature uninquired into,
—Nature? their very names! pay reverence,
Do sacrifice for our part, theirs would be
To prove benignantest of playfellows.
2005 With kindly humanism they countenanced
Our emulation of divine escapes
Through sense and soul: soul, sense are made to use;
Use each, acknowledging its god the while!
Crush grape, dance, drink, indulge, for Bacchos' sake!
2010 'Tis Aphrodité's feast-day—frisk and fling,
Provided we observe our oaths, and house
Duly the stranger: Zeus takes umbrage else!
Ah, the great time—had I been there to taste!
Perikles, right Olumpian,—occupied
2015 As yet with getting an Olumpos reared
Marble and gold above Akropolis,—
Wisely so spends what thrifty fools amassed
For cut-throat projects.   Who carves Promachos?
Who writes the Orestcia?

                    "Ah, the time!
2020 For, all at once, a cloud has blanched the blue,
A cold wind creeps through the close vineyard-rank,
The olive-leaves curl, violets crisp and close

2001| MS:And §in margin§ left §over illegible erasure§   2002| MS:—Nature? their
§crossed out and replaced above by word and comma§ nay, very   *P1875:*—Nature? their very
2003| MS:part,—theirs will §crossed out and replaced above by§ would   *P1875:*part, theirs
2005| MS:Their §crossed out and replaced above by§ With <> they §over illegible erasure§
2007| MS:are §over illegible erasure§   2008| MS:its God   *P1875:*god
2010| MS:feast-day—§next word illegibly crossed out§ frisk   2011| MS:Provided you
§crossed out and replaced above by§ we   2012| MS:takes honor so §last two words
crossed out and replaced above by one word§ umbrage   2013| MS:O the   *P1875:*Ah, the
2014| MS:right Olympian, occupied   *1889a:*right Olumpian,—occupied
2016| MS:above §over illegible word§   2017| MS:spends the savings fools
*P1875:*spends what thrifty fools   2018| MS:projects. §period inserted§ Rheidias §crossed
out and replaced above by§ Who   2019| MS:Sophokles §crossed out and replaced above
by§ Who writes the Oresteia? / And §crossed out§ / Are secondary poets §last three words
crossed out§ §¶§ O the   *P1875:*<> §¶§ "Ah, the   2020| MS:When §crossed out and
replaced above by word and comma§ For   2021| MS:vineyard rank,
§over illegible erasure§   *P1875:*vineyard-rank,   2022| MS:olive-leaves turn white,—the
§last three words crossed out and replaced above by one word and comma§ curl

Like a nymph's wrinkling at the bath's first splash
On breast. (Your pardon!) There's a restless change,
2025 Deterioration.   Larks and nightingales
Are silenced, here and there a gor-crow grim
Flaps past, as scenting opportunity.
Where Kimon passaged to the Boulé once,
A starveling crew, unkempt, unshorn, unwashed,
2030 Occupy altar-base and temple-step,
Are minded to indoctrinate our youth!
How call these carrion kill-joys that intrude?
'Wise men,' their nomenclature! Prodikos—
Who scarce could, unassisted, pick his steps
2035 From way Theseia to the Tripods' way,—
This empty noddle comprehends the sun,—
How he's Aigina's bigness, wheels no whit
His way from east to west, nor wants a steed!
And here's Protagoras sets wrongheads right,
2040 Explains what virtue, vice, truth, falsehood mean,
Makes all we seemed to know prove ignorance

2023| MS:nymph's §next word illegibly crossed out and replaced above by§ graces at   *P1875:*
nymph's wrinkling at   2024| MS:(Your <> a restlessness, a change,   *1889a:*On breast.
(Your <> a restless change.   2025| MS:Deterioration: Larks §over *larks*§   *P1875:*
Deterioration. Larks   2026| MS:a carrion crow §last two words altered to§ gor-crow
2027| MS:as finding §crossed out and replaced above by§ scenting   2028| MS:Where
Kimon walked §crossed out and replaced above by§ passaged   2028-29| MS:§between
these two lines§ Where taught his choros §last four words crossed out at top of page§
2029| MS:Unkempt, unshorn, unwashed, a starveling crew   *P1875:*A starveling crew,
unkempt, unshorn, unwashed,   2030| MS:Occupy pillar-base §altered to§ altar-base
2031| MS:Are §in margin§ Minded to just §crossed out§ indoctrinate <> Youth!   *P1875:*
minded <> youth!   2032| MS:How may one §last two words crossed out§ call these
scarecrows §crossed out and replaced above by two words§ carrion kill-joys
2033| MS:'Wise Men'— their   *P1875:*men,' their   2034| MS:Who could scarce,
unassisted <> his way §crossed out§ path §crossed out§ steps   *P1875:*Who scarce could,
unassisted   2035| MS:From Way Theseia §over illegible erasure§ to Peiraid §crossed out
and replaced above by two words§ The Tripods' Way,—   *P1875:*way <> the <> way,—
2036| MS:This worthy's §crossed out and replaced above by§ empty noddle understands
§crossed out and replaced above by§ comprehends   2037| MS:How §in margin§ He's
§altered to§ he's just §crossed out§   2038| MS:from East <> West, and §crossed out and
replaced above by§ nor <> a §over illegible word§   *P1875:*east <> west
2039| MS:And §in margin§ Here's §altered to§ here's Anaxagoras §altered to Protagoras
2040| MS:As to §last two words crossed out and replaced above by one word§ Explains
2041| MS:Since what you §last three words crossed out and replaced above by three words§
Makes all they §crossed out§ we <> know, proves §altered to§ prove

Yet knowledge also, since, on either side
Of any question, something is to say,
Nothing to 'stablish, all things to disturb!
2045 And shall youth go and play at kottabos,
Leaving unsettled whether moon-spots breed?
Or dare keep Choes ere the problem's solved—
Why should I like my wife who dislikes me?
'But sure the gods permit this, censure that?'
2050 So tell them! straight the answer's in your teeth:
'You relegate these points, then, to the gods?
What and where are they?'   What my sire supposed,
And where yon cloud conceals them!   'Till they 'scape
And scramble down to Leda, as a swan,
2055 Europa, as a bull! why not as—ass
To somebody? Your sire was Zeus perhaps!
Either—away with such ineptitude!
Or, wanting energy to break your bonds,
Stick to the good old stories, think the rain
2060 Is—Zeus distilling pickle through a sieve!
Think thunder's thrown to break Theoros' head
For breaking oaths first! Meanwhile let ourselves
Instruct your progeny you prate like fools

---

^{2042|} MS:Yet also knowledge §last two words marked for transposition§
^{2043|} MS:something §altered to§ something's is §crossed out and replaced above by§ straight
to *1889a:*something is to   ^{9044|} MS:to know,—but §last two words crossed out and
replaced above by one word§ stablish   *P1875:*'stablish   ^{2045|} MS:shall you §altered to§
Youth dare §crossed out§ go and §inserted above§   *P1875:*youth
^{2046|} MS:breed,—   *P1875:*breed?   ^{2047|} MS:dare §inserted above§ keep the §crossed
out§ Choes §over *choes*§   ^{2048|} MS:Why do §crossed out§ should
^{2049|} MS:the Gods <> this, enjoin that?'   *P1875:*god <> this, censure that?'
^{2050|} MS:§line added§ straight their answer's   *P1875:*straight the answer's
^{2051|} MS:the Gods?   *P1875:*gods?   ^{2052|} MS:where find them §last two words crossed
out and replaced above by two words§ are they?' 'What—my   *P1875:*they?' 'What my
*1889a:*they?' What   ^{2053|} MS:where—yon <> them!'...'Till   *P1875:*where yon
*1889a:*them! 'Till   ^{2057|} MS:ineptitude, §comma altered to exclamation point§
^{2059|} MS:Stick, you, §word and commas crossed out§ to <> good §inserted above§ <> think
the §altered to§ that rain   *P1875:*think the rain   ^{2060|} MS:pickle §over illegible
erasure§ <> sieve,   *P1875:*sieve!   ^{2061|} MS:While §crossed out and replaced above by§
And thunder's   *P1875:*Think thunder's   ^{2062|} MS:first! only §crossed out and replaced
above by two words§ so you let the sage   *P1875:*first! So you let ourselves   *1889a:*first!
Meanwhile let   ^{2063|} MS:progeny what fools are you   *1889a:*progeny you prate like fools

Of father Zeus, who's but the atmosphere,
2065   Brother Poseidon, otherwise called—sea,
And son Hephaistos—fire and nothing else!
Over which nothings there's a something still,
"Necessity," that rules the universe
And cares as much about your Choes-feast
2070   Performed or intermitted, as you care
Whether gnats sound their trump from head or tail!'
When, stupefied at such philosophy,
We cry—Arrest the madmen, governor!
Pound hemlock and pour bull's-blood, Perikles!—
2075   Would you believe? The Olumpian bends his brow,
Scarce pauses from his building! 'Say they thus?
Then, they say wisely.   Anaxagoras,
I had not known how simple proves eclipse
But for thy teaching!   Go, fools, learn like me!'

2080   "Well, Zeus nods: man must reconcile himself,
So, let the Charon's-company harangue,
And Anaxagoras be—as we wish!
A comfort is in nature: while grass grows
And water runs, and sesame pricks tongue,
2085   And honey from Brilesian hollow melts
On mouth, and Bacchis' flavorous lip beats both,

2064| MS:Who §crossed out and replaced above by§ For fear §altered to§ fearing Zeus, who is just §crossed out§ the   *1889a:*Of father Zeus, who's but the   2068| MS:'Necessity', that *P1875:*'Necessity,' that   *1889a:*"Necessity," that   2071| MS:Whether gnat §altered to§ gnats sound their §last two words inserted above§ trumpet §altered to§ trump from the §crossed out§ head <> tail!   *P1875:*tail!'   2073| MS:cry "Arrest the madness §altered to§ madmen   *P1875:*cry 'Arrest   *1889a:*cry—Arrest   2074| MS:bulls' blood, Perikles! *P1875:*bull's-blood, Perikles!'   *1889a:*bull's-blood, Perikles!—   2075| MS:believe? The Olympian   *1889a:*believe? The Olumpian   2076| MS:Scarces   *P1875:*Scarce 2078| MS:simple is §crossed out and replaced above by§ proves   2079| MS:teaching! Go, and §crossed out and replaced above by§ men, learn <> me!"   *P1875:*me!'   *1889a:* teaching! Go, fools, learn   2080| MS:"Well: §word and punctuation in margin; double quotation mark crossed out§ Zeus <> man needs §crossed out§ must   *P1875:*"Well, Zeus *1889a:*"Well   2081| MS:Why §crossed out and replaced above by§ So 2082| MS:be— §dash inserted§ as I §crossed out and replaced above by§ we 2083| MS:A §in margin§ The §crossed out§ comfort 2084| MS:runs; while §crossed out and replaced above by§ and   *P1875:*runs, and 2085| MS:And, honey <> hollows   *P1875:*And honey <> hollow

You will not be untaught life's use, young man?
Pho! My young man just proves that panniered ass
Said to have borne Youth strapped on his stout back,
2090 With whom a serpent bargained, bade him swap
The priceless boon for—water to quench thirst!
What's youth to my young man? In love with age,
He Spartanizes, argues, fasts and frowns,
Denies the plainest rules of life, long since
2095 Proved sound; sets all authority aside,
Must simply recommence things, learn ere act,
And think out thoroughly how youth should pass—
Just as if youth stops passing, all the same!

"One last resource is left us—poetry!
2100 Vindicate nature, prove Plataian help,
Turn out, a thousand strong, all right and tight,
To save Sense, poet! Bang the sophist-brood
Would cheat man out of wholesome sustenance
By swearing wine is water, honey—gall,
2105 Saperdion—the Empousa!   Panic-smit,
Our juveniles abstain from Sense and starve:
Be yours to disenchant them!   Change things back!
Or better, strain a point the other way

2086| MS:and Bacchis' lip beats both, my boy,   *1889a:*and Bacchis' flavorous lip beats both,
2087| MS:untaught their §crossed out and replaced above by§ life's <> man?'   *1889a:*man?
2088| MS:Pho! The §crossed out and replaced above by§ My   *P1875:*Pho!
2089| MS:his broad §crossed out and replaced above by§ stout
2090| MS:Who bargained with the §crossed out and replaced above by§ a serpent, let him filch §crossed out§ swap   *1889a:*With whom a serpent bargained, bade him   2091| MS:for— §dash inserted§   2092| MS:to our §crossed out and replaced above by§ my
2093| MS:and prates,   *1889a:*and frowns,   2094| MS:Questions §crossed out and replaced above by§ Denies the soundest §altered to§ plainest   2095| MS:Proved so §altered to§ sound, and §crossed out§ sets all §inserted above§   *P1875:*sound; sets
2096| MS:Must §in margin§ To §crossed out§ simply   2098| MS:youth stopped §altered to§ stops <> the while §crossed out and replaced above by§ same!   2100| MS:§line added§ 'Vindicate   *P1875:*prove Plataian   *CP1875:*prove Plataian   *1889a:*Vindicate
2101| MS:§line added in margin§   2102| MS:To save §last two words in margin§ Help §crossed out§ sense §altered to§ Sense, thou §crossed out§ poet! §exclamation point altered to comma§ Here's §crossed out and replaced below by§ from the §over illegible word§   *P1875:*poet! Bang the   2105| MS:And Bacchis §last two words crossed out and replaced above by one word§ Saperdion   2106| MS:starve;   *P1875:*starve.   *1889a:*starve:

And handsomely exaggerate wronged truth!
2110   Lend wine a glory never gained from grape,
Help honey with a snatch of him we style
The Muses' Bee, bay-bloom-fed Sophokles,
And give Saperdion a Kimberic robe!

"'I, his successor,' gruff the answer grunts,
2115   'Incline to poetize philosophy,
Extend it rather than restrain; as thus—
Are heroes men?   No more, and scarce as much,
Shall mine be represented.   Are men poor?
Behold them ragged, sick, lame, halt and blind!
2120   Do they use speech?   Ay, street-terms, market-phrase!
Having thus drawn sky earthwards, what comes next
But dare the opposite, lift earth to sky?
Mere puppets once, I now make womankind,
For thinking, saying, doing, match the male.
2125   Lift earth?   I drop to, dally with, earth's dung!
—Recognize in the very slave—man's mate,
Declare him brave and honest, kind and true,
And reasonable as his lord, in brief.
I paint men as they are—so runs my boast—
2130   Not as they should be: paint—what's part of man

---

^{2107|}   MS:them! Change §over *change*§ <> back,— *P1875:*back!   ^{2112-14|}   MS:The <>
bay-bloom-fed Sophokles!" / 'I <> successor,' the gruff §last two words marked for
transposition§ <> grunts §over illegible erasure§   *P1875:*bay-bloom-fed Sophokles, / And
<> robe!' / "'I <> grunts,   *1889a:*/ robe! /   ^{2115|}   MS:'Rather will §last two words
crossed out and replaced above by two words§ 'Incline to   ^{2117|}   MS:Heroes are §altered
to§ Are men §last three words transposed to§ Are heroes men   ^{2118|}   MS:represented;
are   *P1875:*represented. Are   ^{2119|}   MS:ragged! sick? lame   *1889a:*ragged, sick, lame
^{2120|}   MS:Do they §last two words in margin§ Use <> Ay, town-talk, §word and comma crossed
out§ street-terms   *P1875:*use   ^{2121|}   MS:Thus having §last two words transposed and
altered to§ Having thus   ^{2122|}   MS:But try §crossed out and replaced above by illegible
word, perhaps *aim*; crossed out and replaced below by§ dare   ^{2123|}   MS:womankind
*P1875:*womankind,   ^{2125|}   MS:dung,—   *P1875:*dung!   ^{2126|}   MS:—Who §crossed
out§ recognize §altered to§ Recognize in §inserted above§   ^{2127|}   MS:Declare §in
margin§ Show §crossed out§ him as §crossed out§ brave   ^{2129|}   MS:'I <> are'—so
P1875:"I <> are"—so   *1889a:*I <> are—so   ^{2130|}   MS:'Not <> be:' ay, and §last two
words crossed out and replaced above by crossed-out word, *therefore*§ paint, beside, no less §last
three words crossed out and replaced above by four words and punctuation§ —what's part of
'man',   *P1875:*"Not <> be:" paint <> of "man,"   *1889a:*Not <> be: paint <> of man

94

—Women and slaves—not as, to please your pride,
They should be, but your equals, as they are.
O and the Gods! Instead of abject mien,
Submissive whisper, while my Choros cants
2135   "Zeus,—with thy cubit's length of attributes,—
May I, the ephemeral, ne'er scrutinize
Who made the heaven and earth and all things there!"
Myself shall say'. . . Ay, 'Herakles' may help!
Give me,—I want the very words,—attend!"

2140   He read. Then "Murder's out,—'There are no Gods,'
Man has no master, owns, by consequence,
No right, no wrong, except to please or plague
His nature: what man likes be man's sole law!
Still, since he likes Saperdion, honey, figs,
2145   Man may reach freedom by your roundabout.
'Never believe yourselves the freer thence!
There are no gods, but there's "Necessity,"—
Duty enjoined you, fact in figment's place,

---

²¹³¹| MS:Women <> slaves,—not *P1875:*—Women *1889a:*slaves—not
²¹³⁴| MS:my Choros croons *P1875:*my Choros cants   ²¹³⁵| *P1875:*"Zeus *1889a:*'Zeus
§emended to§ "Zeus §see Editorial Notes§   ²¹³⁷| MS:heaven, the §comma and word
crossed out and replaced above by§ and <> there,' §comma altered to exclamation point§
*P1875:*there!" *1889a:*there!' §emended to§ there!" §see Editorial Notes§
²¹³⁸| MS:Myself §in margin§ No, I §last two words crossed out§ shall say'... §¶ called for in
margin§ Ay 'Herakles' may *P1875:*say'.. §no ¶§ Ay *1889a:*say'... Ay, Herakles may
²¹³⁹| MS:very §inserted above§ words—attend! §following this line in margin§ insert the
passage from / the translation §entire line crossed out§ *P1875:*words,—attend!"
²¹³⁹⁻⁴⁰| MS:§no ¶ called for§ *P1875:*§¶§   ²¹⁴⁰| MS:Read here! §last two words and
punctuation in margin§ Good, then,— §last two words and punctuation crossed out§ the
murder's out,—'there §altered to§ 'There *P1875:*He read. Then—"Murder's *1889a:*read.
Then "Murder's   ²¹⁴¹| MS:master, then §crossed out and replaced above by§ and, by
*P1875:*master, owns, by   ²¹⁴²| MS:What's §crossed out and replaced above by§ No right
nor wrong <> to §inserted above§ *P1875:*right, no wrong
²¹⁴³| MS:His §over illegible word§ <> likes should §altered to§ shall be man's law! *P1875:*
likes be man's sole law!   ²¹⁴⁴| MS:And does not §last two words crossed out and replaced
above by one word§ since he like §altered to§ likes Bacchis §crossed out and replaced above
by§ Saperdion <> figs, §over illegible erasure§ *P1875:*"Still, since *CP1875:*Still
²¹⁴⁵| MS:We shall §last two words crossed out and replaced above by two words§ Man may <>
roundabout! *P1875:*roundabout!" *CP1875:*roundabout! *1889a:*roundabout.
²¹⁴⁷| MS:but §inserted above§ there is §last two words altered to§
there's—'Necessity,'— *P1875:*there's 'Necessity,'— *1889a:*there's "Necessity,"—

95

Throned on no mountain, native to the mind!
2150 Therefore deny yourselves Saperdion, figs
And honey, for the sake of—what I dream,
A-sitting with my legs up!'

"Infamy!
The poet casts in calm his lot with these
Assailants of Apollon!   Sworn to serve
2155 Each Grace, the Furies call him minister—
He, who was born for just that roseate world
Renounced so madly, where what's false is fact,
Where he makes beauty out of ugliness,
Where he lives, life itself disguised for him
2160 As immortality—so works the spell,
The enthusiastic mood which marks a man
Muse-mad, dream-drunken, wrapt around by verse,
Encircled with poetic atmosphere,
As lark emballed by its own crystal song,
2165 Or rose enmisted by that scent it makes!
No, this were unreality! the real
He wants, not falsehood,—truth alone he seeks,
Truth, for all beauty!   Beauty, in all truth—

2149| MS:no mountain, §last three letters and comma crossed out and replaced above by one word§ but native   *P1875:*no mountain, native   2150| MS:deny the body, honey, wine §crossed out§ figs,   *P1875:*deny yourselves Saperdion, figs,   2151| MS:And Bacchis §last two words crossed out and replaced above by one word§ Saperdion, for < > dream, §over partial erasure§   *P1875:*And honey, for   2152| MS:A- §letter and hyphen in margin§ When §over *A-*§ sitting < > up!" §¶§ Infamy!   *P1875:*up!' §¶§ "Infamy!   2154| MS:of Apollon! Sworn §over *sworn*§   2155| MS:minister: *P1875:*minister—   2156| MS:He who < > just §inserted above§ that rosy world   *P1875:*He, who   *1889a:*that roseate world   2157| MS:where the §crossed out and replaced above by§ what's   2161| MS:Of that §last two words crossed out§ Enthusiastic §over *enthusiastic*§ mood   *1889a:*The enthusiastic mood   2162| MS:The §crossed out§ Muse-mad, §over partial erasure§ and §crossed out§ dream-drunken, §next two words illegibly crossed out, perhaps *verse maker,* and replaced above by four words§ wrapt around by verse,   2163| MS:Encircled still with §over *in*§ his own §last two words crossed out and replaced above by one word and hyphen, forming§ poet-atmosphere,   *1889a:*Encircled with poetic atmosphere,   2164| MS:emballed with §crossed out and replaced above by§ by < > chrystal   *P1875:*crystal   2165| MS:enmisted §over illegible word§ by the §altered to§ that it breathes §crossed out and replaced above by§ makes!   2166| MS:No, that §crossed out and replaced above by§ this were §over partial erasure§ unreality—the   *P1875:*unreality! the   2168| MS:truth!   *P1875:*truth—

That's certain somehow! Must the eagle lilt
2170   Lark-like, needs fir-tree blossom rose-like? No!
Strength and utility charm more than grace,
And what's most ugly proves most beautiful.
So much assistance from Euripides!

    "Whereupon I betake me, since needs must,
2175   To a concluding—'Go and feed the crows!
Do!   Spoil your art as you renounce your life,
Poetize your so precious system, do,
Degrade the hero, nullify the god,
Exhibit women, slaves and men as peers,—
2180   Your castigation follows prompt enough!
When all's concocted upstairs, heels o'er head,
Down must submissive drop the masterpiece
For public praise or blame: so, praise away,
Friend Socrates, wife's-friend Kephisophon!
2185   Boast innovations, cramp phrase, uncouth song,
Hard matter and harsh manner, gods, men, slaves
And women jumbled to a laughing-stock
Which Hellas shall hold sides at lest she split!
Hellas, on these, shall have her word to say!'

2169| MS:somehow. Does §crossed out and replaced above by§ Must   *P1875:*somehow! Must
2170| MS:Larklike, the §crossed out and replaced above by§ should fir-tree <> rose-like?
Strength— §word and dash crossed out and replaced above by word and punctuation§ No!
*P1875:*Lark-like, needs fir-tree   2171| MS:§line added§ utility are §crossed out§ charms
past §crossed out and replaced below by two words§ more than   *P1875:*charm
2172| MS:And §over illegible erasure§ what's past beauty §last two words crossed out and
replaced below by two words§ most ugly or §crossed out and replaced below by§ proves
2174| MS:Whereupon   *P1875:*"Whereupon   2175| MS:concluding 'Go   *1889a:*
concluding—'Go   2177| MS:system, pray! §crossed out and replaced above by§ do,
2179| MS:slaves, and   *P1875:*slaves and   2181| *P1875:*o'er-head,   *1889a:*o'er head,
2183| MS:or censure: §word and colon crossed out and replaced above by two words§ blame:
so   2185| MS:Boast §in margin§ Those §crossed out and replaced above by§ Praise
§crossed out§ innovations   2186| MS:manner, Gods <> slaves,   *P1875:*gods <> slaves
2187| MS:laughing stock   *P1875:*laughing-stock   2188| MS:She §crossed out and
replaced above by three words§ Hellas shall soon holds §altered to§ hold her §crossed out§
sides <> split! before, §word and comma crossed out§   *P1875:*Which Hellas shall hold
2189| MS:these, §over illegible word§ may §crossed out and replaced
above by§ shall <> say!'   *1889a:*say! §emended to§ say!' §see Editorial Notes§

2190   "She has it and she says it—there's the curse!—
        She finds he makes the shag-rag hero-race,
        The noble slaves, wise women, move as much
        Pity and terror as true tragic types:
        Applauds inventiveness—the plot so new,
2195   The turn and trick subsidiary so strange!
        She relishes that homely phrase of life,
        That common town-talk, more than trumpet-blasts:
        Accords him right to chop and change a myth:
        What better right had he, who told the tale
2200   In the first instance, to embellish fact?
        This last may disembellish yet improve!
        Both find a block: this man carves back to bull
        What first his predecessor cut to sphynx:
        Such genuine actual roarer, nature's brute,
2205   Intelligible to our time, was sure
        The old-world artist's purpose, had he worked
        To mind; this both means and makes the thing!
        If, past dispute, the verse slips oily-bathed
        In unctuous music—say, effeminate—
2210   We also say, like Kuthereia's self,

2190| MS:She *P1875:*"She   2191| MS:She §crossed out§ finds §altered to§ Finds him §crossed out and replaced above by two words§ he can make the shagrag §inserted above§ hero-race, in rags, §last two words and comma crossed out§ *P1875:*She finds he makes <> shag-rag   2192| MS:The noble §last two words in margin§ Slaves, wise §inserted above§ women, in heroics §last two words crossed out§ move *P1875:*slaves

2195| MS:so §over partial erasure§ tricky the §last two words crossed out and replaced above by one word and exclamation point§ strange! subsidiary §over partial erasure§ The §inserted above§ turn and trick §line marked for transposition to 1889a reading§   2196| MS:that common §crossed out and replaced above by§ homely   2197| MS:That common §last two words in margin§ Town-talk §altered to§ town-talk, street-times, instead of §last three words crossed out and replaced above by two words§ more than *P1875:*trumpet-blasts; *1889a:*trumpet-blasts: 2198| MS:She recognizes §last two words crossed out and replaced above by two words§ Accords him <> chop and §last two words inserted above§ *P1875:*myth; *1889a:*myth: 2200| MS:to §over illegible erasure§ embellished §altered to§ embellish fact, §comma altered to question mark§

2201| MS:This man §crossed out and replaced above by§ bard may *1889a:*This last may   2203| MS:sphynx; *P1875:*sphynx: 2204| MS:A genuine *P1875:*Such genuine   2206| MS:old world *P1875:*old-world   2207| MS:this other §crossed out and replaced above by§ artist means *1889a:*this both means   2208| MS:Then, past *1889a:*If, past   2209| MS:music: say, effeminate— §over illegible word§ *1889a:*music—say   2210| MS:You also say—like <> self! *P1875:*say, like <> self, *1889a:*We also

A lulling effluence which enswathes some isle
Where hides a nymph, not seen but felt the more.
That's Hellas' verdict!

　　　　　　"Does Euripides
　　Even so far absolved, remain content?
2215　Nowise!　His task is to refine, refine,
　　Divide, distinguish, subtilize away
　　Whatever seemed a solid planting-place
　　For foot-fall,—not in that phantasmal sphere
　　Proper to poet, but on vulgar earth
2220　Where people used to tread with confidence.
　　There's left no longer one plain positive
　　Enunciation incontestable
　　Of what is good, right, decent here on earth.
　　Nobody now can say 'this plot is mine,
2225　Though but a plethron square,—my duty!'—'Yours?
　　Mine, or at least not yours,' snaps somebody!
　　And, whether the dispute be parent-right
　　Or children's service, husband's privilege
　　Or wife's submission, there's a snarling straight,
2230　Smart passage of opposing 'yea' and 'nay,'
　　'Should,' 'should not,' till, howe'er the contest end,
　　Spectators go off sighing—Clever thrust!
　　Why was I so much hurried to pay debt,
　　Attend my mother, sacrifice an ox,
2235　And set my name down 'for a trireme, good'?
　　Something I might have urged on t' other side!
　　No doubt, Chresphontes or Bellerophon

2211| MS:effluence,—such enswathes　*P1875*:effluence which enswathes　2212| MS:more.'
1889a:more.　2213| MS:verdict, §comma altered to exclamation point§ so contend no
more! §last four words and exclamation point crossed out and replaced above by two words; ¶
inserted§ "Does Euripedes　2215| MS:Nowise! He §altered to§ His goes on §last two
words crossed out and replaced above by two words§ task is　2218| MS:footfall,—not on
§altered to§ in　*P1875*:foot-fall　2223| MS:what's <> right and decent　*1889a*:what is
<> right, decent　2226| MS:somebody, §comma altered to exclamation point§
2227| MS:parent-rights　*P1875*:parent-right　2230| MS:opposing 'Yea' <> 'Nay,'
P1875:'yea' <> 'nay,'　2232| MS:sighing 'Clever　*1889a*:sighing—Clever
2235| MS:down 'For <> Trireme, good?'　*P1875*:'for <> trireme　*1889a*:good'?

We don't meet every day; but Stab-and-stitch
The tailor—ere I turn the drachmas o'er
2240　I owe him for a chiton, as he thinks,
I'll pose the blockhead with an argument!

"So has he triumphed, your Euripides!
Oh, I concede, he rarely gained a prize:
That's quite another matter! cause for that!
2245　Still, when 'twas got by Ions, Iophons,
Off he would pace confoundedly superb,
Supreme, no smile at movement on his mouth
Till Sokrates winked, whispered: out it broke!
And Aristullos jotted down the jest,
2250　While Iophons or Ions, bay on brow,
Looked queerly, and the foreigners—like you—
Asked o'er the border with a puzzled smile
—'And so, you value Ions, Iophons,
Euphorions!　How about Euripides?'
2255　(Eh, brave bard's-champion?　Does the anger boil?
Keep within bounds a moment,—eye and lip
Shall loose their doom on me, their fiery worst!)
What strangers?　Archelaos heads the file!

2238|　MS:day: but §next word illegibly crossed out, perhaps *Tupaides*§ stitch-and-stab §altered
to *Stitch-and-stab*, then crossed out and replaced above by§ Stab-and-stitch,　*P1875:*day; but
Stab-and-stitch　　　2239|　MS:tailor, ere <> drachma's　*P1875:*tailor—ere <> drachmas
2240|　MS:for the §crossed out and replaced above by§ a　　　2241|　MS:argument!'　*1889a:*
argument!　　　2242|　MS:So　*1889a:*"So　　　2243|　MS:Oh, understand §crossed out and
replaced above by two words§ I concede!—he <> prize—　*P1875:*concede, he <> prize:
2245|　MS:by Ion, Iophon, §last two words altered to§ Ions, Iophons,　　　2246|　MS:would go
confoundely　*P1875:*would pace confoundedly　　　2248|　MS:Till Sokrates would §crossed
out and replaced above by§ winked, whispered—out　*P1875:*whispered: out
2249|　MS:the joke §crossed out§ jest,　　　2250|　MS:While §over illegible word, perhaps *And*§
poor §crossed out and replaced above by§ Iophon <> Ion, crown §crossed out and replaced
above by§ bays　*P1875:*While Iophons <> Ions, bay　　　2251|　MS:queerly: and　*P1875:*
queerly, and　　　2252|　MS:Looked across §crossed out and replaced above by two words§
o'er the barriers §altered to§ barrier with <> puzzled stare §crossed out§ smile　*P1875:*
Asked o'er the border with　　　2253|　MS:so you <> Ion, Iophon,　*P1875:*so, you <> Ions,
Iophons,　　　2254|　MS:Euphorion! How　*P1875:*Euphorions! How　　　2255|　MS:brave
Balaustion? Does　*P1875:*brave bard's-champion? Does　　　2256|　MS:Keep just in bounds
<> eyes <> lips §last two words altered to§ eye <> lip　*P1875:*Keep within bounds
2257|　MS:me—their　*P1875:*me, their　　　2258|　MS:strangers? King §crossed out§ Archelaos

He sympathizes, he concerns himself,
2260 He pens epistle, each successless play:
'Athenai sinks effete; there's younger blood
In Makedonia. Visit where I rule!
Do honour to me and take gratitude!
Live the guest's life, or work the poet's way,
2265 Which also means the statesman's: he who wrote
"Erechtheus" may seem rawly politic
At home where Kleophon is ripe; but here
My council-board permits him choice of seats.'

"Now this was operating,—what should prove
2270 A poison-tree, had flowered far on to fruit
For many a year,—when I was moved, first man,
To dare the adventure, down with root and branch.
So, from its sheath I drew my Comic steel,
And dared what I am now to justify.
2275 A serious question first, though!

                             "Once again!
Do you believe, when I aspired in youth,
I made no estimate of power at all,
Nor paused long, nor considered much, what class
Of fighters I might claim to join, beside
2280 That class wherewith I cast in company?
Say, you—profuse of praise no less than blame—
Could not I have competed—franker phrase
Might trulier correspond to meaning—still,

2260| MS:He §over illegible word§ <> play— *P1875*:play: ²²⁶¹| MS:"Athenai sinks §over illegible word§ effete: there's *P1875*:'Athenai <> effete; there's ²²⁶²| MS:In Makedonia: visit *P1875*:In Makedonia. Visit ²²⁶³| MS:honor *1889a*:honour ²²⁶⁴| MS:way— *P1875*:way, ²²⁶⁶| MS:'Erectheus' may be raw §altered to§ rawly at §crossed out§ politics §altered to§ politic *1889a*:Erechtheus may seem rawly ²²⁶⁷| MS:ripe: but *P1875*:ripe; but ²²⁶⁸| MS:The §crossed out and replaced above by§ My ²²⁷²| MS:branch, *P1875*:branch. ²²⁷³| MS:As from <> steel— *P1875*:So, from <> steel, ²²⁷⁴| MS:§first two words illegibly crossed out and replaced above by three words§ And dared what ²²⁷⁵| MS:§line added in margin§ though! §¶§ Look at me! *P1875*:though! §¶§ "Once again! ²²⁷⁷| MS:all— *P1875*:all, ²²⁷⁹| MS:besides *P1875*:beside ²²⁸⁰| MS:With what class I would cast *P1875*:That class wherewith I cast

Competed with your Tragic paragon?
2285 Suppose me minded simply to make verse,
To fabricate, parade resplendent arms,
Flourish and sparkle out a Trilogy,—
Where was the hindrance?   But my soul bade 'Fight!
Leave flourishing for mock-foe, pleasure-time;
2290 Prove arms efficient on real heads and hearts!'
How?   With degeneracy sapping fast
The Marathonian muscle, nerved of old
To maul the Mede, now strung at best to help
—How did I fable?—War and Hubbub mash
2295 To mincemeat Fatherland and Brotherhood,
Pound in their mortar Hellas, State by State,
That greed might gorge, the while frivolity
Rubbed hands and smacked lips o'er the dainty dish!
Authority, experience—pushed aside
2300 By any upstart who pleads throng and press
O' the people! 'Think, say, do thus!' Wherefore, pray?
'We are the people: who impugns our right
Of choosing Kleon that tans hide so well,
Huperbolos that turns out lamps so trim,
2305 Hemp-seller Eukrates or Lusikles
Sheep-dealer, Kephalos the potter's son,
Diitriphes who weaves the willow-work

2284| MS:Competed—with *P1875:*Competed with   2286| MS:To §in margin§ fabricate,
§over partial erasure§ and §crossed out§ parade   2288| MS:Where hides the   *P1875:*
Where was the   2289| MS:pleasure-time: *P1875:*pleasure-time;   2291| MS:What?
With < > sapping fast §last two words crossed out and replaced above by two illegibly crossed-
out words and then restored§ *P1875:*How? With   2296| MS:That §crossed out§ Pound
Hellas, in their mortar, §last five words transposed to§ Pound in their mortar Hellas, state < >
state, §last two words altered to§ State < > State,   2297| MS:greed may §altered to§ might
gorge the   *P1875:*gorge, the   2298| MS:Rubs hand §last two words altered to§ Rubbed
hands < > smacks lip §last two words altered to§ smacked lips
2300| MS:upstart through the §last two words crossed out and replaced above by two words§
helped by throng *P1875:*upstart pleading throng   *1889a:*upstart who pleads throng
2303| MS:Of §over illegible word§ choosing §over *choose*§ good §crossed out§ Kleon, who tans
*P1875:*choosing Kleon that tans   2304| MS:§line added§ Of plain §last two words crossed
out§ Huperbolos, who turns   *P1875:*Huperbolos that turns
2305-09| MS:§lines added in margin§   2305| MS:Hemp-seller Eukrates and Lusikles
*P1875:*Hemp-seller Eukrates or Lusikles   2306| MS:Sheep-seller §altered to§ Sheep-dealer
2307| MS:who §next word illegibly crossed out and replaced above by§ weaves

To go round bottles, and Nausikudes
The meal-man? Such we choose and more, their mates,
2310 To think and say and do in our behalf!'
While sophistry wagged tongue, emboldened still,
Found matter to propose, contest, defend,
'Stablish, turn topsyturvy,—all the same,
No matter what, provided the result
2315 Were something new in place of something old,—
Set wagging by pure insolence of soul
Which needs must pry into, have warrant for
Each right, each privilege good policy
Protects from curious eye and prating mouth!
2320 Everywhere lust to shape the world anew,
Spurn this Athenai as we find her, build
A new impossible Cloudcuckooburg
For feather-headed birds, once solid men,
Where rules, discarding jolly habitude,
2325 Nourished on myrtle berries and stray ants,
King Tereus who, turned Hoopoe Triple-Crest,
Shall terrify and bring the gods to terms!

---

²³⁰⁸| MS:and Nausikudes,   *P1875:*and Nausikudes   ²³⁰⁹| MS:meal man—choosing
these and   *P1875:*meal-man? Such we choose and   ²³¹⁰| MS:behalf?'   *P1875:*behalf!'
²³¹¹| MS:Sophistry's tongue that wagged, §last two words inserted above§ emboldened more
and more §last three words crossed out and replaced above by one word§ still,   *P1875:*While
sophistry wagged tongue, emboldened   ²³¹²| MS:To question, §last two words and
comma crossed out and replaced above by two words§ With matter   *P1875:*Found matter
²³¹³| MS:Establish §altered to§ 'Stablish, or §crossed out§ turn topsyturvy, well, §word and
comma crossed out§ —all   ²³¹⁵| MS:Be something   *P1875:*Were something
²³¹⁶| MS:by an §crossed out and replaced above by§ pure   ²³¹⁸| MS:privilege that policy
*P1875:*privilege good policy   ²³¹⁹| MS:prating tongue!   *P1875:*prating mouth!
²³²⁰| MS:In short, that §crossed out and replaced above by§ a lust to chop and change the
world,   *P1875:*Everywhere lust to shape the world anew,   ²³²²| MS:impossible
Cloudcuckooborough §altered to§ Cloudcuckooburg   ²³²³| MS:For bird-like §crossed
out and replaced above by§ foolish feather heads §altered to§ headed birds, §word and
comma inserted above§ once men, of flesh, §last two words and comma crossed out§   *P1875:*
For feather-headed <> once solid men,   ²³²⁴| MS:Wherein, §last two letters and comma
crossed out§ such, §word and comma inserted above and crossed out§ rules, §word and
comma inserted above§ discarding earthly §crossed out and replaced above by§ jolly
habitudes §altered to§ habitude,   ²³²⁵| MS:And fed with §last three words crossed out
and replaced above by two words§ Nourished on myrtle berries   *P1875:*myrtle-berries
²³²⁶| MS:King Tereus, who, §word and comma inserted above§ turned to §crossed out§
Hoopoe   *P1875:*King Tereus who   ²³²⁷| MS:the Gods   *P1875:*gods

"Where was I? Oh! Things ailing thus—I ask,
What cure?   Cut, thrust, hack, hew at heap-on-heaped
2330 Abomination with the exquisite
Palaistra-tool of polished Tragedy?
'Erechtheus' shall harangue Amphiktuon,
And incidentally drop word of weight
On justice, righteousness, so turn aside
2335 The audience from attacking Sicily!—
The more that Choros, after he recounts
How Phrixos rode the ram, the far-famed Fleece,
Shall add—at last fall of grave dancing-foot—
'Aggression never yet was helped by Zeus!'
2340 That helps or hinders Alkibiades?
As well expect, should Pheidias carve Zeus' self
And set him up, some half a mile away,
His frown would frighten sparrows from your field!
Eagles may recognize their lord, belike,
2345 But as for vulgar sparrows,—change the god,
And plant some big Priapos with a pole!
I wield the Comic weapon rather—hate!
Hate! honest, earnest and directest hate—

2328| MS:§line added§ was I? O, with all §last two words crossed out§ things being thus
P1875:'Where <> Oh! Things ailing thus   *1889a:*"Where   2329| MS:What? Cut <>
hack and hew at all this §last two words crossed out and replaced below by two hyphenated
words, forming§ heap-on-heaped   *P1875:*What cure? Cut <> hack, hew
2331| MS:Palestra-weapon §*weapon* crossed out and replaced above by two words§ -tool of <>
Tragedy? §over *tragedy*§   *P1875:*Palaistra-tool   2332| MS:'Erechtheus' while §crossed out
and replaced above by§ shall haranguing §altered to§ harangue   *1889a:*Erechtheus shall
2333| Shall §crossed out and replaced above by§ And   2334| MS:righteousness, and
§crossed out and replaced above by§ that turn §altered to§ turns   *P1875:*righteousness, so
turn   2335| MS:attacking Sicily,—   *P1875:*attacking Sicily!—   2336| MS:after they
recount   *P1875:*after he recounts   2337| MS:the golden §inserted above§ Fleece,
*P1875:*the far-famed Fleece,   2339| MS:'Aggression §over partial erasure§ never has the
§last two words crossed out and replaced above by two words§ yet was help §altered to§ helped
of §crossed out and replaced above by§ by   2340-41| MS:§one line expanded to two lines§
I say that Zeus §last four words crossed out and replaced below by five words§ That help or
hinder Alkibiades? §solidus added§ As §over *as*§ well make §crossed out and replaced above
by two words§ expect, should <> self,   2340| *P1875:*helps <> hinders
2341| *P1875:*self   2342| MS:up, where, §word and comma crossed out and replaced below
by§ that half   *P1875:*up, some half   2343| MS:frown should fright §last two words
altered to§ would frighten the §crossed out§ sparrows   2344| MS:§line added§ may §over
illegible word§   2345| MS:§line added in margin§   2346-48| MS:Better §crossed out

Warfare wherein I close with enemy,
2350 Call him one name and fifty epithets,
Remind you his great-grandfather sold bran,
Describe the new exomion, sleeveless coat
He knocked me down last night and robbed me of,
Protest he voted for a tax on air!
2355 And all this hate—if I write Comedy—
Finds tolerance, most like—applause, perhaps
True veneration; for I praise the god
Present in person of his minister,
And pay—the wilder my extravagance—
2360 The more appropriate worship to the Power
Adulterous, night-roaming, and the rest:
Otherwise,—that originative force
Of nature, impulse stirring death to life,
Which, underlying law, seems lawlessness,
2365 Yet is the outbreak which, ere order be,
Must thrill creation through, warm stocks and stones,
Phales Iacchos.

"Comedy for me!

---

and replaced below by§ And <> some §inserted below§ <> pole! / Best— §word and dash crossed out and replaced above by§ Hate! honest earnest and §crossed out and replaced above by§ so directest   *P1875:*/ I <> hate! / <> honest, earnest, and directest   *1889a:*/ / <> earnest and   2349| MS:wherein you §crossed out and replaced above by§ I
2350| MS:him by §crossed out§ one name, §comma crossed out§ with §inserted above§ fifty *P1875:*name and fifty   2351| MS:Remind him that §crossed out§ his great §inserted above§ grandfather sold cheese §crossed out and replaced above by§ bran,   *P1875:*Remind you his great-grandfather   2353| MS:knocked you §crossed out and replaced above by§ me <> robbed you §crossed out and replaced above by§ me   2354| MS:Protest §in margin§ Adding §crossed out and replaced above by crossed-out word, *Declare*§ he <> for the §crossed out and replaced above by§ a <> air—   *P1875:*air!
2355| MS:And §in margin§ Do all §last two words crossed out§ this—now that you §last three words crossed out and replaced above by illegibly crossed-out word and two words§ supposing I   *P1875:*And all this hate—if I   2357| MS:veneration—for you §crossed out and replaced above by§ I <> the God,   *P1875:*veneration; for <> god
2359| MS:wilder your §crossed out and replaced above by§ my extravagance,   *P1875:* extravagance—   2361| MS:night-roaming, §next word illegibly crossed out§ and §over partial erasure§ <> rest,   *P1875:*rest: 2362| MS:§illegibly crossed-out words replaced above by word, comma and dash§ Otherwise   2364| MS:And §in margin and crossed out§ Which §crossed out and restored§   2366| MS:through, earths §crossed out and replaced above by§ warm stock <> stone §last two words altered to§ stocks <> stones,

Why not for you, my Tragic masters?   Sneaks
Whose art is mere desertion of a trust!
2370 Such weapons lay to hand, the ready club,
The clay-ball, on the ground a stone to snatch,—
Arms fit to bruise the boar's neck, break the chine
O' the wolf,—and you must impiously—despise?
No, I'll say, furtively let fall that trust
2375 Consigned you!   'Twas not 'take or leave alone,'
But 'take and, wielding, recognize your god
In his prime attributes!'   And though full soon
You sneaked, subsided into poetry,
Nor met your due reward, still,—heroize
2380 And speechify and sing-song and forego
Far as you may your function,—still its pact
Endures, one piece of early homage still
Exacted of you; after your three bouts
At hoitytoity, great men with long words,
2385 And so forth,—at the end, must tack itself
The genuine sample, the Satyric Play,
Concession, with its wood-boys' fun and freak,
To the true taste of the mere multitude.
Yet, there again!   What does your Still-at-itch,
2390 Always-the-innovator?   Shrugs and shirks!
Out of his fifty Trilogies, some five

2368| MS:masters? Plain §crossed out and replaced above by§ You   *P1875:*masters? Sneaks
2369| MS:Your duty was deser §last five letters and preceding three words crossed out and
replaced above by four words§ Whose art is mere <> trust?   *P1875:*trust!
2370| MS:Your §crossed out and replaced above by crossed-out word, *Fit,* and then replaced
by§ Such arms §crossed out and replaced above by§ weapons   2371| MS:The earth-ball
§altered to§ clay-ball <> ground with soil §last two words crossed out and replaced above by
two words§ a stone   2373| MS:wolf,—which arms you §last three words crossed out and
replaced above by three words§ and you must impiously—despised §altered to§ despise?
2376| your God   *P1875:*god   2378| MS:poetry   *P1875:*poetry,
2379| MS:heroize,   *P1875:*heroize   2380| MS:speechify, and sing song, and   *P1875:*
speechify and sing-song and   2383| MS:Exacts §altered to§ Exacted <> you: that
§crossed out§ after   *P1875:*you; after   2385| MS:And so forth,— §last three words and
punctuation in margin§ No matter,— §last two words and punctuation crossed out§ at the
§over illegible erasure§ ending, tacks   *P1875:*the end, must tack
2387| MS:Conceding §altered to§ Concession, in the §last two words crossed out and replaced
above by two words§ with its wood boys'   *P1875:*wood-boys'   2389| MS:Yet, §word and
comma in margin§ there §over *There*§ <> does he §crossed out§ your

Are somehow suited: Satyrs dance and sing,
Try merriment, a grimly prank or two,
Sour joke squeezed through pursed lips and teeth on edge,
²³⁹⁵ Then quick on top of toe to pastoral sport,
Goat-tending and sheep-herding, cheese and cream,
Soft grass and silver rillets, country-fare—
When throats were promised Thasian! Five such feats,—
Then frankly off he threw the yoke: next Droll,
²⁴⁰⁰ Next festive drama, covenanted fun,
Decent reversion to indecency,
Proved—your 'Alkestis'! There's quite fun enough,
Herakles drunk! From out fate's blackening wave
Calamitous, just zigzags some shot star,
²⁴⁰⁵ Poor promise of faint joy, and turns the laugh
On dupes whose fears and tears were all in waste!

"For which sufficient reasons, in truth's name,
I closed with whom you count the Meaner Muse,
Classed me with Comic Poets who should weld
²⁴¹⁰ Dark with bright metal, show their blade may keep
Its adamantine birthright though a-blaze
With poetry, the gold, and wit, the gem,

2393| MS:Try sportiveness, a *P1875:*Try merriment, a   2395| MS:pastoral play, *P1875:*
pastoral sport,   2399| MS:he throws §altered to§ threw <> yoke: his §crossed out and
replaced above by§ next   2400| MS:IIis §crossed out and replaced above by§ Next <>
covenanted close, *P1875:*covenanted fun,   2402| MS:your 'Alkestis!' That's quite
*P1875:*your 'Alkestis!' There's quite *1889a:* your 'Alkestis'! There's   2403| MS:Content
you that §last two words crossed out and replaced above by one word§ enough! from out the
blackening *P1875:*Herakles drunk! From out fate's blackening   2404| MS:Calamitous,
faint trembles §crossed out and replaced above by§ zigzags some slow §crossed out and
replaced above by§ shot *P1875:*Calamitous, just zigzags   2405| MS:That's widen judged
to §last four words crossed out and replaced above by one word§ Poor <> of faint §last two
words inserted above§ joy, and §crossed out and replaced above by three words§ that turns
the laugh at dupes §last two words crossed out§ *P1875:*joy, and turns   2406| MS:On
dupes §last two words in margin§ <> tears and torments were in §last four words crossed out
and replaced above by two words§ were all §next word illegibly crossed out; *in* restored§
2407| MS:For these §crossed out and replaced above by§ which *P1875:*"For   2408| MS:with
what you <> Muse *P1875:*with whom you <> Muse,   2409| MS:me a §crossed out and
replaced above by§ with <> Poets, who *P1875:* with Comic Poets who   2410| MS:Dark
§in margin§ Metal §crossed out§ <> bright §inserted above§ <> show how blade *P1875:*
show their blade   2411| MS:birthright while a-blaze *P1875:*birthright though a-blaze

And strike mere gold, unstiffened out by steel,
Or gem, no iron joints its strength around,
2415   From hand of—posturer, not combatant!

"Such was my purpose: it succeeds, I say!
Have not we beaten Kallikratidas,
Not humbled Sparté?   Peace awaits our word,
Spite of Theramenes, and fools his like.
2420   Since my previsions,—warranted too well
By the long war now waged and worn to end—
Had spared such heritage of misery,
My after-counsels scarce need fear repulse.
Athenai, taught prosperity has wings,
2425   Cages the glad recapture.   Demos, see,
From folly's premature decrepitude
Boiled young again, emerges from the stew
Of twenty-five years' trouble, sits and sways,
One brilliance and one balsam,—sways and sits
2430   Monarch of Hellas! ay and, sage again,
No longer jeopardizes chieftainship,
No longer loves the brutish demagogue

2413| MS:And so §crossed out§ strike mere §inserted above§ gold—unstiffened   *P1875:*gold,
unstiffened   2414| MS:Gems §altered to§ Gem—no rough iron   *1889a:*Or gem, no iron
2415| MS:posturer not   *P1875:*posturer, not   2418| MS:humbled Sparté §over partial
erasure§   2419| MS:In §in margin§ §next word illegibly crossed out§ spite < > and his
like §punctuation illegibly crossed out and altered to period§   *1889a:*Spite < > and fools
his   2420| MS:Since §in margin§ All §crossed out§ my previsions, warranted   *P1875:*
previsions,—warranted   2421| MS:long §over illegibly erased word§ war, now all but at
an §last four words crossed out and replaced above by four words§ waged and worn to
*P1875:*war now   2422| MS:Well weighed §last two words crossed out and replaced above
by two words§ Had spared its §crossed out and replaced above by§ such §over *much*§
2423| MS:after- §word and hyphen inserted above§ counsels slow to blossom, bears fast fruit
§last six words crossed out and replaced above by four words§ scarce need not §crossed out§
fear repulse?   *P1875:*repulse.   2424| MS:Athenai, with §crossed out and replaced above
by§ taught prosperity's §altered to§ prosperity return, §word and comma crossed out§ has
2425| MS:§line added§ Cages the §last two words over two illegibly erased words§ < >
recapture: Demos   *P1875:*recapture. Demos   2426-30| MS:§lines added in margin§
2428| MS:twenty five < > trouble, §next word illegibly crossed out§ sits   *P1875:*twenty-five
2430| MS:of Hellas: ay, and wise again,   *P1875:*of Hellas! ay and, sage again,
2432| MS:longer bears the sway of §last two words crossed out and replaced above by one
word§ brutish demagogues §altered to§ demagogue   *P1875:*longer loves the

Appointed by a bestial multitude

But seeks out sound advisers.   Who are they?

2435   Ourselves, of parentage proved wise and good!

To such may hap strains thwarting quality,

(As where shall want its flaw mere human stuff?)

Still, the right grain is proper to right race;

What's contrary, call curious accident!

2440   Hold by the usual!   Orchard-grafted tree,

Not wilding, race-horse-sired, not rouncey-born,

Aristocrat, no sausage-selling snob!

Nay, why not Alkibiades, come back

Filled by the Genius, freed of petulance,

2445   Frailty,—mere youthfulness that's all at fault,—

Advanced to Perikles and something more?

—Being at least our duly born and bred,—

Curse on what chaunoprockt first gained his ear

2433| MS:a reckless §crossed out and replaced above by§ bestial multitude,   *1889a:*multitude
2434| MS:But takes the best and worst §last five words crossed out and replaced above by four words§ seeks out sound true §crossed out§ advisors   2435| MS:If not whose §last three words crossed out and replaced above by two words§ Ourselves, of parentage was §crossed out and replaced above by§ proved   2436| MS:To such §last two words inserted above§ There §crossed out§ may < > strains, and §crossed out§ thwarts of quality,   *P1875:*strains thwarting quality,   2437| MS:As where are §crossed out and replaced above by§ shall wanting §altered to§ want its §inserted above§ flaws §altered to§ flaw in §crossed out and replaced above by§ mere < > stuff?   *P1875:*(As < > stuff?)   2438| MS:But §crossed out and replaced above by§ Still, < > right kind §crossed out and replaced above by§ grain is common §crossed out and replaced above by§ proper < > race,   *P1875:*race;
2439| MS:What's §in margin§ The §crossed out§ contrary were §crossed out and replaced above by dash and word§ —call   *P1875:*contrary, call   2441| MS:wilding, racer-bred §altered to§ race horse-sired not bloodless brute §last two words crossed out and replaced above by one word§ rouncey-born,   *P1875:*race-horse-sired, not
2442| MS:§illegibly crossed-out word in margin§ Aristocrat, and §crossed out§ not §altered to§ no Huperbolos-bred §crossed out§ sausage-selling   2443| MS:Nay, §word and comma in margin§ Why shall §last two words crossed out and replaced above by one word§ why
2444| MS:freed §altered to§ free from §crossed out and replaced above by§ of   *P1875:*freed
2445| MS:Frailty, and §crossed out and replaced above by word and dashes§ —say— youthfulness < > fault?   *P1875:*say, youthfulness < > fault,—   *1889a:*Frailty,—mere youthfulness   2446| MS:Why not prove Perikles   *P1875:*Renewed to Perikles   *1889a:* Advanced to   2447| MS:least the §crossed out and replaced above by§ our
2448| MS:For all that §last three words crossed out and replaced above by three words§ Curse on those §crossed out§ what chaunoprocktoi gained < > ear §crossed out and restored§ gra §last three letters crossed out§   *P1875:*chaunoprockt first gained

And got his . . . well, once true man in right place,
2450 Our commonalty soon content themselves
With doing just what they are born to do,
Eat, drink, make merry, mind their own affairs
And leave state-business to the larger brain.
I do not stickle for their punishment;
2455 But certain culprits have a cloak to twitch,
A purse to pay the piper: flog, say I,
Your fine fantastics, paragons of parts,
Who choose to play the important! Far from side
With us, their natural supports, allies,—
2460 And, best by brain, help who are best by birth
To fortify each weak point in the wall
Built broad and wide and deep for permanence
Between what's high and low, what's rare and vile,—
They cast their lot perversely in with low
2465 And vile, lay flat the barrier, lift the mob

2449| MS:his help! §word and punctuation crossed out and replaced above by punctuation, word and comma§ ...well, True man once §marked for transposition to follow *well,*§ *P1875:* true   2450| MS:commonalty glad §crossed out and replaced above by§ soon 2451| MS:are fit §crossed out and replaced above by§ born   2453| MS:the proper §crossed out and replaced above by§ larger brain! §exclamation point over question mark§ *1889a:*brain   2454| MS:§line added§   2455| MS:But §in margin§ While the true §last three words crossed out and replaced below by one word§ certain culprits, those §comma and word crossed out and replaced below by two words§ have a with §crossed out and replaced below by crossed-out word, *have*§ a §inserted above and crossed out§ cloak 2456| MS:A §in margin§ And §crossed out§ purse <> piper,— §next four words illegibly crossed out§ flog *P1875:*piper: flog   2457| MS:The §over illegibly erased word§ clever fellows §last two words crossed out and replaced above by two words§ fine fantastics, men §crossed out and replaced above by§ paragons <> parts, fine folk §last two words crossed out§ *P1875:*Your fine   2458| MS:chose <> importants §altered to§ important <> from help §crossed out§ side *P1875:*choose   2459| MS:us, §inserted above§ their §next word illegibly crossed out§ natural   2460| MS:And, §word and comma in margin§ The §crossed out§ best §over partial erasure§ by Birth §crossed out and replaced above by§ brain, help, them the §comma and last two words crossed out and replaced above by one crossed-out word and comma, *us,*§ who are §last two words inserted above§ best §over partial erasure§ by Brain, §crossed out and replaced above by§ birth, *P1875:*birth   2461| MS:To buttress up each §last three words crossed out and replaced above by two words§ fortify each <> wall §illegibly crossed-out word inserted above§   2463| MS:Between the §crossed out and replaced above by§ what's high <> low, §last two words over partial erasures§ the §crossed out and replaced above by§ what's   2464| MS:low §over partial erasure§ 2465| MS:vile, break down §last two words crossed out and replaced above by two words§ lay flat §over *low*§ <> barrier, mount §crossed out and replaced above by§ lift

    To dizzy heights where Privilege stood firm.

    And then, simplicity become conceit,—

    Woman, slave, common soldier, artisan,

    Crazy with new-found worth, new-fangled claims,—

2470   These must be taught next how to use their heads

    And hands in driving man's right to mob's rule!

    What fellows thus inflame the multitude?

    Your Sokrates, still crying 'Understand!'

    Your Aristullos,—'Argue!'   Last and worst,

2475   Should, by good fortune, mob still hesitate,

    Remember there's degree in heaven and earth,

    Cry 'Aischulos enjoined us fear the gods,

    And Sophokles advised respect the kings!'

    Why, your Euripides informs them—'Gods?

2480   They are not! Kings? They are, but . . . do not I,

---

^{2466|} MS:where Privilege stands §altered to§ stood firm, §comma altered to colon§ *P1875:*
firm.   ^{2466-67|} MS:§between these two lines§ Preaching up §last two words crossed out
and replaced above by two words§ By §next word illegibly crossed out§ virtue latent in the
slaves, / The woman §crossed out and replaced above by§ soldier, arts, and §crossed out§
trades, and §crossed out§ handicrafts alike; §entire two lines crossed out§
^{2467|} MS:And, once §comma and word crossed out and replaced above by word and
punctuation§ then, simplicity *P1875:*then, simplicity   ^{2468|} MS:§line added in
margin§ Woman §over *woman*§ < > common §inserted above§   ^{2469|} MS:Of undreamed
§last two words crossed out and replaced above by two crossed-out words, *new discovered*§ Crazy
§over *crazy*§ with new-found §last three words inserted above§ worth new fangled §inserted
above§ and §crossed out§ claims, to correspond, §last two words and comma crossed out and
replaced above by crossed-out word and punctuation, *match,—*§ *P1875:*new-found worth,
new-fangled claims,—   ^{2470|} MS:Proceed to teach worth §last four words crossed out
and replaced below by five words§ These must be taught next < > use its §crossed out§ their
wits §crossed out§ heads   ^{2471|} MS:hands as well, §last two words and comma inserted
below§ in prompt assertion o §last letter and preceding three words crossed out and replaced
above by one word§ drive man's *P1875:*hands in driving man's   ^{2472|} MS:Mob's rule.
§last two words and period crossed out§ What fellows §inserted below§ < > multitude?—
*P1875:*multitude?   ^{2473|} MS:Why, §word and comma in margin§ Your §crossed out§
Sokrates *P1875:*Your Sokrates   ^{2474|} MS:And §in margin§ Your §crossed out§
Aristullos *P1875:*Your Aristullos   ^{2475|} MS:If, §crossed out and replaced above by§
Should, < > mob §inserted above§ still they §crossed out§ hesitate,   ^{2476|} MS:in Heaven
< > Earth, *P1875:*heaven < > earth,   ^{2477|} MS:Cry §over illegible erasure§ < >
enjoined the §crossed out and replaced above by§ us, fear of §crossed out and replaced above
by§ the Gods, *P1875:*us fear < > gods,   ^{2478|} MS:respect §next word illegibly erased§
to §crossed out and replaced above by§ the Kings!'— *P1875:*kings!'
^{2479|} MS:Why §altered to§ Who here's §crossed out and replaced above by§ but Euripides
assures §crossed out and replaced above by§ informs *P1875:*Why, your Euripides
^{2480|} MS:but . . does §altered to§ do not he §crossed out§ I, *P1875:*but...do

111

Aristophanes' Apology

In "Suppliants," make my Theseus,—yours, no more,—
Fire up at insult of who styles him King?
Play off that Herald, I despise the most,
As patronizing kings' prerogative
2485 Against a Theseus proud to dare no step
Till he consult the people?'

                    "Such as these—
Ah, you expect I am for strangling straight?
Nowise, Balaustion!   All my roundabout
Ends at beginning, with my own defence.
2490 I dose each culprit just with—Comedy.
Let each be doctored in exact the mode
Himself prescribes: by words, the word-monger—
My words to his words,—my lies, if you like,
To his lies.   Sokrates I nickname thief,
2495 Quack, necromancer; Aristullos,—say,
Male Kirké who bewitches and bewrays
And changes folk to swine; Euripides,—
Well, I acknowledge!   Every word is false,
Looked close at; but stand distant and stare through,
2500 All's absolute indubitable truth

2481| MS:In §over partial erasure§ 'Suppliants,' make his §crossed out and replaced above by§ my *1889a:*In Suppliants, make   2483| MS:off the §altered to§ that Herald, he §crossed out and replaced above by§ I despises §altered to§ despise the §inserted above§
2484| MS:kings'-prerogative *P1875:*kings' prerogative   2485| MS:Against poor §crossed out and replaced above by§ a   2486| MS:<> §¶§ Such *P1875:*people? §¶§ "Such *1889a:*people?' §¶§ <>   2488| MS:Nowise, Balaustion! All this §last two words crossed out and replaced below by two words§ All my §next word inserted above and illegibly crossed out§   2489| MS:with §over illegible erasure§ <> defence! *1889a:*defence.
2491| MS:in precise §crossed out and replaced above by§ exact   2493| MS:lies §over illegible erasure§   2495| MS:necromancer: Aristullos,—well, §word and comma crossed out§ say, *P1875:*necromancer; Aristullos   2496| MS:Male §in margin§ A- §letter and hyphen crossed out§ Kirké <> and befouls §altered to§ betrays *P1875:*and bewrays
2497| MS:And so §inserted above and crossed out§ changes §altered to *change* and then restored§ folk change §inserted above and crossed out§ to swine: Euripides,— *P1875:*swine; Euripides,—   2498| MS:Well, §word and comma in margin§ What §crossed out§ I
2499| MS:but §inserted above§ stand at §crossed out and replaced above by crossed-out word, *your*§ distance, §comma crossed out and word altered to§ distant and stare §last two words inserted above§ see right §last two words crossed out§ through,

Behind lies, truth which only lies declare!
For come, concede me truth's in thing not word,
Meaning not manner! Love smiles 'rogue' and 'wretch'
When 'sweet' and 'dear' seem vapid: Hate adopts
2505 Love's 'sweet' and 'dear' when 'rogue' and 'wretch' fall flat:
Love, Hate—are truths, then, each, in sense not sound.
Further: if Love, remaining Love, fell back
On 'sweet' and 'dear,'—if Hate, though Hate the same,
Dropped down to 'rogue' and 'wretch,'—each phrase were false.
2510 Good! and now grant I hate no matter whom
With reason: I must therefore fight my foe,
Finish the mischief which made enmity.
How?   By employing means to most hurt him
Who much harmed me.   What way did he do harm?
2515 Through word or deed?   Through word? with word, wage war!
Word with myself directly?   As direct
Reply shall follow: word to you, the wise,
Whence indirectly came the harm to me?
What wisdom I can muster waits on such.
2520 Word to the populace which, misconceived
By ignorance and incapacity,

2501| MS:Behind these §crossed out and replaced above by§ lies, truths   *P1875:*truth
2502| MS:For, §word and comma in margin§ Come, now, §word and comma crossed out§
concede that truth's   *P1875:*come, concede me truth's   2503-09| MS:§in these lines all
quotation marks altered from double to single marks§   2503|MS:Meaning, not <> 'Rogue'
§altered to§ 'rogue'   *P1875:*Meaning not   2504| MS:vapid: Hate §altered to§ hate
*P1875:*vapid; Hate   *1889a:*vapid: Hate   2505| MS:'sweet' <> 'dear' §last two words
altered to§ 'Sweet' <> 'Dear,' <> 'Rogue' §altered to§ 'rogue' <> flat;   *P1875:*'sweet' <>
'dear'   *1889a:*flat: 2506| MS:Love, Hate §over partial erasure§ <> truths, §comma
inserted§ here §altered to§ then   2507| MS:if Love, §over *love*§ <> Love §over *love*§
2508| MS:On 'Sweet' <> though hate   *P1875:*'sweet' <> though Hate   2509| MS:to
'Rogue' §over *rogue*§ <> 'Wretch,'—each §over illegible word§   *P1875:*'rogue' <>
'wretch,'—each   2510| MS:who, *P1875:*whom   2511| MS:must grapple with §last
two words crossed out and replaced above by two words§ therefore fight   2512| MS:And
get him under §last four words crossed out and replaced above by four words§ Finish the
mischief which <> enmity: *P1875:*enmity.   2513| MS:employ §*ing* inserted
above§ of what §last two words crossed out§ means to §inserted above§ hurt him most §last
three words transposed to§ most hurt him   2515| MS:with word, then §crossed out and
replaced above by§ wage   2516| MS:Word to myself *P1875:*Word with myself
2517| MS:wise— *P1875:*wise,   2518| MS:§line added§   2519| MS:such! *1889a:*such.

113

Ends in no such effect as follows cause
When I, or you the wise, are reasoned with,
So damages what I and you hold dear?
²⁵²⁵ In that event, I ply the populace
With just such word as leavens their whole lump
To the right ferment for my purpose.   *They*
Arbitrate properly between us both?
They weigh my answer with his argument,
²⁵³⁰ Match quip with quibble, wit with eloquence?
All they attain to understand is—blank!
Two adversaries differ: which is right
And which is wrong, none takes on him to say,
Since both are unintelligible.   Pooh!
²⁵³⁵ Swear my foe's mother vended herbs she stole,
They fall a-laughing!   Add,—his household drudge
Of all-work justifies that office well,
Kisses the wife, composing him the play,—
They grin at whom they gaped in wonderment,
²⁵⁴⁰ And go off—'Was he such a sorry scrub?
This other seems to know! we praised too fast!'
Why then, my lies have done the work of truth,
Since 'scrub,' improper designation, means

---

²⁵²²| MS:Ends in §last two words inserted above§ Effect §altered to§ effect precised the §last
two words crossed out and replaced above by one word§ quite contrary of §crossed out and
replaced above by§ to cause   *P1875:*in no such effect as follows cause,   *CP1875:*cause
²⁵²³| MS:When §altered to§ Were I, or §inserted above§ you, or, §commas and word crossed
out§ the wise, are §crossed out and replaced above by§ but reasoned   *P1875:*When I < >
wise, are reasoned   ²⁵²⁴| MS:So §in margin§ And §crossed out§ damages so §crossed
out§ what   ²⁵²⁵| MS:In such §crossed out and replaced above by§ that < > ply that
§altered to§ the   ²⁵²⁷| MS:ferment §over partial erasure§   ²⁵³¹| MS:is—what?
*P1875:*is—blank!   ²⁵³²| MS:differ, §comma altered to exclamation point§ which
*1889a:*differ: which   ²⁵³³| MS:wrong, who §crossed out and replaced above by§ none
²⁵³⁴| MS:unintellible! No!   *P1875:*unintelligible. Pooh!   ²⁵³⁵| MS:Swear §in margin§
Tell them §last two words crossed out and replaced above by two words§ Vow that §last two
words crossed out§ his §crossed out and replaced above by two words§ my man's mother
*P1875:*my foe's mother   ²⁵³⁷| MS:all-work, justifies   *P1875:*all-work justifies
²⁵³⁸| MS:Kissing §altered to§ Kisses < > wife, and writing §last two words crossed out and
replaced above by one word§ composing < > plays §altered to§ play,—
²⁵⁴⁰⁻⁴¹| MS:§in these lines both quotation marks altered from double to single marks§
²⁵⁴⁰| MS:he really §crossed out§ such an one §last two words crossed out and
replaced above by three words§ a sorry §inserted above§ scrub?
²⁵⁴³| MS:Since 'Scrub,' in proper designation   *P1875:*'scrub,' improper designation

Exactly what the proper argument
2545 —Had such been comprehensible—proposed
To proper audience—were I graced with such—
Would properly result in; so your friend
Gets an impartial verdict on his verse
'The tongue swears, but the soul remains unsworn!'

2550 "There, my Balaustion!   All is summed and said.
No other cause of quarrel with yourself!
Euripides and Aristophanes
Differ: he needs must round our difference
Into the mob's ear; with the mob I plead.
2555 You angrily start forward 'This to me?'
No speck of this on you the thrice refined!
Could parley be restricted to us two,
My first of duties were to clear up doubt
As to our true divergence each from each.
2560 Does my opinion so diverge from yours?
Probably less than little—not at all!
To know a matter, for my very self
And intimates—that's one thing; to imply
By 'knowledge'—loosing whatsoe'er I know
2565 Among the vulgar who, by mere mistake,
May brain themselves and me in consequence,—

2544| MS:what §next word illegibly crossed out, perhaps *my*, and replaced above by§ the
2546| MS:My §crossed out and replaced above by§ To   2547| MS:in, did your   *P1875:*in;
so your   2548| MS:Hear an < > on the §altered to§ that verse   *P1875:*Gets an < > on his
verse   2549| MS:'The §quotation mark altered from double to single mark§ < > unsworn!'
*1889a:*unsworn! §emended to§ unsworn!' §see Editorial Notes§   2550| MS:summed in
that §last two words crossed out and replaced above by two words§ and said.
2553| MS:must plead §crossed out and replaced above by§ round   2554| MS:ear: with
*P1875:*ear; with   2555| MS:You int §last three letters crossed out§ angrily < > forward
'This < > me?' §quotation marks altered from double to single marks§   2556| MS:of filth
§over illegible erasure§ on < > thrice-refined!   *P1875:*of this on < > thrice refined!
2557| MS:Could §over illegible erasure§ parley but §crossed out and replaced above by§ be
2561| MS:§line added§   2562| MS:for §next word illegibly crossed out, perhaps *one's*, and
replaced below by§ my   2563| MS:thing: to §over partial erasure§   *P1875:*thing; to
2564| MS:By 'knowledge'— §quotation marks altered from double to single marks§ loosing it
for well or ill §last five words crossed out and replaced above by three words§ whatsoe'er I know
2566| MS:me §over illegible erasure§ my §crossed out and replaced above by§ in

115

That's quite another. 'O the daring flight!
This only bard maintains the exalted brow,
Nor grovels in the slime nor fears the gods!'
2570 Did *I* fear—*I* play superstitious fool,
Who, with the due proviso, introduced,
Active and passive, their whole company
As creatures too absurd for scorn itself?
Zeus?   I have styled him—'slave, mere thrashing-block!'
2575 I'll tell you: in my very next of plays,
At Bacchos' feast, in Bacchos' honour, full
In front of Bacchos' representative,
I mean to make main-actor—Bacchos' self!
Forth shall he strut, apparent, first to last,
2580 A blockhead, coward, braggart, liar, thief,
Demonstrated all these by his own mere
Xanthias the man-slave: such man shows such god
Shamed to brute-beastship by comparison!
And when ears have their fill of his abuse,
2585 And eyes are sated with his pummelling,—
My Choros taking care, by, all the while,
Singing his glory, that men recognize
A god in the abused and pummelled beast,—
Then, should one ear be stopped of auditor,

2567| MS:another. 'O §quotation mark altered from double to single mark§
2568| MS:All §crossed out and replaced above by§ No §crossed out§ other poets save §last
three words crossed out and replaced above by four words§ This only bard maintains < >
exalted one §crossed out§ brow,   2569| But §crossed out and replaced above by§ Nor
< > slime and §crossed out and replaced above by§ nor < > Gods!'   *P1875*:gods!'
2573| MS:creatures, too absurd a laughing stock? §last three words crossed out and replaced
above by three words§ for scorn itself?   *P1875*:creatures too   2574| MS:thrashing-
block'!   *P1875*:thrashing-block!'   2576| MS:honor   *1889a*:honour
2580| MS:blockhead, §word and comma inserted above§ < > chief §altered to§ thief,   *1889a:*
blockkead §emended to§ blockhead §see Editorial Notes§   2581| MS:own slave §crossed
out and replaced above by§ mere   2582| MS:Mere human §last two words crossed out§
Xanthias and §crossed out and replaced above by§ the < > such §over illegible erasure§
2583| MS:brutebeastship   *P1875*:brute-beastship   2584| MS:And §in margin§ When < >
have had §crossed out§ their   *P1875*:when   2586| MS:My §over illegible word§ < > the
time §crossed out and replaced above by§ while   *1889a:*while,   2587| MS:that you §crossed
out and replaced above by§ men   2588| MS:pummeled one §crossed out and replaced
above by§ beast,—   2589| MS:Then, let but §last two words crossed out and replaced
above by two words§ should one < > stopped by §crossed out and replaced above by§ of

116

2590 Should one spectator shut revolted eye,—
Why, the Priest's self will first raise outraged voice
'Back, thou barbarian, thou ineptitude!
Does not most license hallow best our day,
And least decorum prove its strictest rite?
2595 Since Bacchos bids his followers play the fool,
And there's no fooling like a majesty
Mocked at,—who mocks the god, obeys the law—
Law which, impute but indiscretion to,
And . . . why, the spirit of Euripides
2600 Is evidently active in the world!'
Do I stop here? No! feat of flightier force!
See Hermes! what commotion raged,—reflect!—
When imaged god alone got injury
By drunkards' frolic! How Athenai stared
2605 Aghast, then fell to frenzy, fit on fit,—
Ever the last the longest! At this hour,
The craze abates a little; so, my Play
Shall have up Hermes: and a Karion, slave,
(Since there's no getting lower) calls our friend
2610 The profitable god, we honour so,

---

²⁵⁹⁰| MS:Or one §last two words in margin§ Spectator turn aside §last two words crossed out and replaced above by one word§ shut *P1875:*Should one spectator ²⁵⁹¹| MS:Why, §word and comma in margin§ the §over *The*§ very §crossed out§ Priest §altered to§ Priest's self §inserted above§ shall §crossed out and replaced above by crossed-out word, *first*§ would first §last two words inserted above§ raise the §crossed out§ outraged *P1875:*self will first raise ²⁵⁹²| MS:'Back, thou §inserted above§ Barbarian §altered to§ barbarian, what an ignorance §last three words crossed out and replaced above by two words§ thou ineptitude! ²⁵⁹³| MS:best the §crossed out and replaced above by§ our ²⁵⁹⁴| MS:prove the §crossed out and replaced above by§ its ²⁵⁹⁶| MS:And perfect §crossed out and replaced above by three words§ there's the §crossed out§ no fooling comes of august §last three words crossed out and replaced above by two words§ like god's majesty *P1875:*like a majesty ²⁵⁹⁷| MS:the God *P1875:*god ²⁵⁹⁸| MS:but §over *an*§ ²⁵⁹⁹| MS:And . . why, §crossed out and replaced above by illegibly crossed-out word, perhaps *straight*, and then restored§ the *P1875:*And...why ²⁶⁰¹| MS:here? No—feat *P1875:*here? No! feat ²⁶⁰²| MS:See Hermes! What *P1875:*what ²⁶⁰⁴| MS:frolic! How Athenai gazed §crossed out and replaced above by§ stared ²⁶⁰⁵| MS:frenzy §over partial erasure§ ²⁶⁰⁷| MS:little. §period altered to semi-colon§ That same §last two words crossed out and replaced above by two words§ so my *P1875:*so, my ²⁶⁰⁸| MS:a human §crossed out and replaced above by word and dash§ Karion— §over *karion*§ slave *P1875:*a Karion, slave, ²⁶⁰⁹| MS:calls the God §last two words crossed out§ our friend ²⁶¹⁰| MS:§line added§ The Profitable God <> honor *P1875:*profitable god <> honour

117

Whatever contumely fouls the mouth—
Bids him go earn more honest livelihood
By washing tripe in well-trough—wash he does,
Duly obedient! Have I dared my best?
2615 Asklepios, answer!—deity in vogue,
Who visits Sophokles familiarly,
If you believe the old man,—at his age,
Living is dreaming, and strange guests haunt door
Of house, belike, peep through and tap at times
2620 When a friend yawns there, waiting to be fetched,—
At any rate, to memorize the fact,
He has spent money, set an altar up
In the god's temple, now in much repute.
That temple-service trust me to describe—
2625 Cheaters and choused, the god, his brace of girls,
Their snake, and how they manage to snap gifts
'And consecrate the same into a bag,'
For whimsies done away with in the dark!
As if, a stone's throw from that theatre
2630 Whereon I thus unmask their dupery,
The thing were not religious and august!

"Of Sophokles himself—nor word nor sign
Beyond a harmless parody or so!
He founds no anti-school, upsets no faith,
2635 But, living, lets live, the good easy soul
Who,—if he saves his cash, unpoetlike,
Loves wine and—never mind what other sport,
Boasts for his father just a sword-blade-smith,

2611| MS:fouls the §last two words over illegible words§ mouth,   *P1875:*mouth—
2612| MS:And §crossed out§ Bids §over *bids*§ < > go §inserted above§ earn an §crossed out
and replaced above by§ more   2613| MS:well-trough—which he does, §last three words
crossed out and replaced above by one word§ wash §*he does* restored and comma retained§
2615| MS:Still, no §last two words in margin§ There's old §last two words crossed out§
Asklepios, deity   *P1875:*Asklepios, answer!—deity   2623   MS:the God's   *P1875:*god's
2627| MS:§line added§ bag §over illegible word§   2628| MS:And do away with whimsies
§last five words crossed out and replaced below by five words§ For whimsies done away with
2632-34| MS:"Of < > nor breath §crossed out and replaced above by§ sign! /
He   *P1875:*sign / Beyond < > so! / He   2635| MS:soul,   *P1875:*soul
2638| MS:Had §crossed out and replaced above by§ Boasts

118

Proves but queer captain when the people claim,
2640 For one who conquered with 'Antigone,'
The right to undertake a squadron's charge,—
And needs the son's help now to finish plays,
Seeing his dotage calls for governance
And Iophon to share his property,—
2645 Why, of all this, reported true, I breathe
Not one word—true or false, I like the man.
Sophokles lives and lets live: long live he!
Otherwise,—sharp the scourge and hard the blow!

"And what's my teaching but—accept the old,
2650 Contest the strange! acknowledge work that's done,
Misdoubt men who have still their work to do!
Religions, laws and customs, poetries,
Are old? So much achieved victorious truth!
Each work was product of a life-time, wrung
2655 From each man by an adverse world: for why?
He worked, destroying other older work

2639| MS:Proved §altered to§ Proves <> queer §over illegible erasure§ soldier when <> people claimed §altered to§ claim, *P1875:*queer captain when 2640| MS:For him §crossed out and replaced above by§ one who §over illegible erasure§ conquered with §last two words inserted above§ who compassed right §last three words crossed out and replaced above by two crossed-out words, *ordered so*§ 'Antigone,' 2642| MS:needs his §crossed out and replaced above by§ the <> now in writing §last two words crossed out and replaced above by two words§ to finish 2643| MS:dotage §over illegible word§ so, he wants §last three words crossed out and replaced above by two words§ calls for 2645| MS:Why, §word and comma crossed out and replaced above by word and comma§ Now, of <> true, §over partial erasure§ repeat §crossed out§ I *P1875:*Why, of 2646| MS:Not §in margin§ One word— much more, embellish true with false? §last six words and question mark crossed out and replaced above by seven words and punctuation§ true or false, I like the man,—! *P1875:*one <> man! *1889a:*man. 2647| MS:For §in margin and crossed out§ Sophokles lives, and §crossed out and restored§ lets *1889a:*lives and 2648| MS:Otherwise,—I bear not §last three words crossed out and replaced above by§ sharp <> scourge in vain! §last two words crossed out and replaced below by four words§ and hard the hand! *P1875:*the blow! 2649| MS:And I should use my right §last six words crossed out and replaced above by six words§ And what's my teaching but scourging, §word and comma crossed out and dash inserted§ —Accept what's old, *P1875:*"And <> accept the old, 2650| MS:Contest what's new §crossed out and replaced above by§ strange!—which means, §last two words and comma crossed out§ Acknowledge work, that's done, *P1875:*Contest the strange! acknowledge work that's 2651| MS:still the §altered to§ their 2652| MS:poetries, §over illegible erasure§ 2656| They §crossed out and replaced above by§ He <> older §inserted above§

Which the world loved and so was loth to lose.
Whom the world beat in battle—dust and ash!
Who beat the world, left work in evidence,
2660 And wears its crown till new men live new lives,
And fight new fights, and triumph in their turn.
I mean to show you on the stage: you'll see
My Just Judge only venture to decide
Between two suitors, which is god, which man,
2665 By thrashing both of them as flesh can bear.
You shall agree,—whichever bellows first,
He's human; who holds longest out, divine:
That is the only equitable test.
Cruelty?   Pray, who pricked them on to court
2670 My thong's award?   Must they needs dominate?
Then I—rebel.   Their instinct grasps the new?
Mine bids retain the old: a fight must be,
And which is stronger the event will show.
O but the pain!   Your proved divinity
2675 Still smarts all reddened?   And the rightlier served!
Was not some man's-flesh in him, after all?
Do let us lack no frank acknowledgment
There's nature common to both gods and men!
All of them—spirit?   What so winced was clay.
2680 Away pretence to some exclusive sphere

2661| MS:Fight <> fights, once more triumph   *P1875:*And fight <> fights, and triumph
2662| MS:show that §crossed out and replaced above by§ you   *P1875:*stage! you'll   *1889a:*
stage: you'll   2663| MS:The Just   *P1875:*My Just   2664| MS:is God   *P1875:*god
2665| MS:flesh may §crossed out and replaced above by§ can bear: *P1875:*bear.
2666| MS:You §in margin§ Both §crossed out§ shall agree whichever   *P1875:*agree,—
whichever   2667| MS:human: who <> longest §inserted above§ <> divine. is he: §last
two words and colon crossed out§   *P1875:*human; who <> divine: 2668| MS:test!
*1889a:*test.   2669| MS:Cruelty? Pray who   *CP1875:*Cruelty? Pray, who §not B§
2670| MS:award? They §altered to§ they needs must §last three words transposed to§ must they
needs   *P1875:*award? Must   2671| MS:Then §in margin§ And §crossed out§ I—rebel!
Their   *1889a:*rebel. Their   2674| MS:'O   *P1875:*O   2675| MS:all over §crossed out
and replaced above by§ purpled!' And   *P1875:*all reddened? And
2676| MS:mans flesh   *P1875:*man's-flesh   2677| MS:no §next word illegibly crossed out
and replaced below by§ frank acknowledgement—   *P1875:*acknowledgment
2679| MS:of you—spirit <> clay!   *P1875:*of them—spirit   *1889a:*clay.
2680| MS:to the §crossed out and replaced above by§ some

Cloud-nourishing a sole selected few
Fume-fed with self-superiority!
I stand up for the common coarse-as-clay
Existence,—stamp and ramp with heel and hoof
2685 On solid vulgar life, you fools disown.
Make haste from your unreal eminence,
And measure lengths with me upon that ground
Whence this mud-pellet sings and summons you!
I know the soul, too, how the spark ascends
2690 And how it drops apace and dies away.
I am your poet-peer, man thrice your match.
I too can lead an airy life when dead,
Fly like Kinesias when I'm cloudward bound;
But here, no death shall mix with life it mars.

2695 "So, my old enemy who caused the fight,
Own I have beaten you, Euripides!
Or,—if your advocate would contravene,—
Help him, Balaustion! Use the rosy strength!
I have not done my utmost,—treated you
2700 As I might Aristullos, mint-perfumed,—
Still, let the whole rage burst in brave attack!
Don't pay the poor ambiguous compliment
Of fearing any pearl-white knuckled fist
Will damage this broad buttress of a brow!

2681| MS:Cloud-nourishing you §crossed out and replaced above by§ a <> few, *P1875:*few
2684| MS:Every hour's §last two words crossed out§ Existence   2685| MS:disown! *1889a:*
disown.   2687| MS:lengths upon the §altered to§ that ground with me §last five words
transposed to§ with me upon that ground   2688| MS:mud pellet sung <> summoned
*P1875:*mud-pellet sings <> summons   2689| MS:the spirit §crossed out and replaced
above by two words and commas§ soul, too   2691| MS:match! *1889a:*match.
2693| MS:§line added§ when I'm §next two words illegibly crossed out§ cloudward-bound:
*P1875:*cloud-ward bound; *1889a:*cloudward bound;   2694| MS:But mean §crossed out
and replaced below by word and dash§ here—no <> mars! *P1875:*here, no *1889a:*mars.
2695| MS:"So, you §crossed out§ my old §inserted above§   2697| MS:What has your
advocate to contravene? *P1875:*Or,—if your advocate would contravene,—
2698| MS:him, Balaustion! Use your rosy *P1875:*him, Balaustion! Use the rosy
2703| MS:pearl white *P1875:*pearl-white   2704| MS:Will crash through this broad
§next word illegibly crossed out and replaced above by§ buttress *P1875:*Will damage this

²⁷⁰⁵ Fancy yourself my Aristonumos,

Ameipsias or Sannurion: punch and pound!

Three cuckoos who cry 'cuckoo'! much I care!

They boil a stone!   *Neblaretai! Rattei!"*

Cannot your task have end here, Euthukles?

²⁷¹⁰ Day by day glides our galley on its path:

Still sunrise and still sunset, Rhodes half-reached,

And still, my patient scribe! no sunset's peace

Descends more punctual than that brow's incline

O'er tablets which your serviceable hand

²⁷¹⁵ Prepares to trace.   Why treasure up, forsooth,

These relics of a night that make me rich,

But, half-remembered merely, leave so poor

Each stranger to Athenai and her past?

For—how remembered!   As some greedy hind

²⁷²⁰ Persuades a honeycomb, beyond the due,

To yield its hoarding,—heedless what alloy

Of the poor bee's own substance taints the gold

Which, unforced, yields few drops, but purity,—

---

^{2705|}   MS:Think you are §last three words crossed out and replaced above by two crossed-out words, *Fancy yourself*§ Fancy   ^{2706|}   MS:Who say §last two words crossed out§ Ameipsias ^{2707|}   MS:§line added§ 'cuckoo'—much   *P1875:*'cuckoo'! much   ^{2708|}   MS:They §in margin§ You §crossed out§ boil   ^{2708-09|}   MS:§no rule§   *P1875:*§rule§ ^{2709|}   MS:Should §crossed out and replaced above by§ Can not   *P1875:*Cannot ^{2710|}   MS:its road §crossed out§ path: ^{2711|}   MS:sunset, Rhodes unreached §*un* crossed out and replaced above by§ half reached,   *P1875:*half-reached,   ^{2712|}   MS:scribe, no *P1875:*scribe! no   ^{2713|}   MS:Descends §in margin§ More <> that constant §crossed out§ brow's   *P1875:*more   ^{2714|}   MS:which the §crossed out and replaced above by§ your ^{2715|}   MS:trace, §comma altered to exclamation point§ §next word illegibly crossed out, perhaps *with,* and replaced above by crossed-out word, *and*§ to §inserted above§ treasure *P1875:*trace. Why treasure   ^{2716|}   MS:The §altered to§ These <> of the §over illegible word§ night that left me   *P1875:*of a night   *1889a:*that make me   ^{2717|}   MS:§word and punctuation illegibly crossed out, perhaps *True!*—§ But, §over *but*§ in §inserted above§ remembered §altered to§ remembrance merely, makes less poor   *1889a:*But, half-remembered merely, leave so poor   ^{2718|}   Whom— §word and dash crossed out and replaced above by word and comma§ None, stranger <> past.   *P1875:*past?   *1889a:*Each stranger ^{2719|}   MS:remembered! As the §crossed out and replaced above by§ some ^{2720|}   MS:Persuades his §crossed out and replaced above by§ a   ^{2722|}   MS:taint   *P1875:*taints ^{2723|}   MS:yields small store but §last three words crossed out and replaced above by three words§ some drop that's §last three words altered to three words§ few drops but   *P1875:*drops, but

So would you fain relieve of load this brain,
²⁷²⁵ Though the hived thoughts must bring away, with strength,
What words and weakness, strength's receptacle—
Wax from the store!   Yet,—aching soothed away,—
Accept the compound!   No suspected scent
But proves some rose was rifled, though its ghost
²⁷³⁰ Scarce lingers with what promised musk and myrrh.
No need of farther squeezing.   What remains
Can only be Balaustion, just her speech.

Ah, but—because speech serves a purpose still!—
_____

He ended with that flourish.   I replied,

²⁷³⁵ Fancy myself your Aristonumos?
Advise me, rather, to remain myself,
Balaustion,—mindful what mere mouse confronts
The forest-monarch Aristophanes!
I who, a woman, claim no quality
²⁷⁴⁰ Beside the love of all things loveable
Created by a power pre-eminent
In knowledge, as in love I stand perchance,
—You, the consummately-creative!   How
Should I, then, dare deny submissive trust

---

²⁷²⁴| MS:would < > fain §last two words inserted above§ relieved §altered to§ relieve this hive,
§last two words and comma crossed out§ this brain, of load,   *P1875:*relieve of load this brain,
²⁷²⁵| MS:Though §in margin§ And to §last two words crossed out§ the strong §crossed out
and replaced above by§ hived < > must §inserted above§ < > away with strength, §over
illegibly erased word§ §next word illegibly erased§   *P1875:*away, with
²⁷²⁶| MS:weakness, their receptacle—   *P1875:*weakness, strength's receptacle—
²⁷²⁸| MS:Forgives §crossed out and replaced above by§ Accept the mixture! No   *P1875:*the
compound! No   ²⁷³⁰| MS:linger   *P1875:*lingers   ²⁷³¹| MS:What §crossed out and
replaced above by§ No need you go on §last three words crossed out and replaced above by
two words§ of farther squeezing? §question mark altered to exclamation point§ What   *1889a:*
squeezing. What   ²⁷³²| MS:speech!   *1889a:*speech.   ²⁷³³⁻³⁴| MS:§no rule§
P1875:§rule§   ²⁷³⁴| MS:§line added§ §alternate five words crossed out§ So ended he, I
said—   ²⁷³⁵| MS:"Fancy myself §*my* over illegible erasure§ < > Aristonumos?"   *P1875:*
Fancy < > Aristonumos?   ²⁷⁴¹| *P1875:*by that power   *1889a:*by a power
²⁷⁴³| MS:—Yours §over partially illegible word§ the consummately-creative! §exclamation
point inserted§ then §crossed out§ How   *P1875:*—You, the
²⁷⁴⁴| MS:How §crossed out§ Should < > then, §word and comma inserted above§

²⁷⁴⁵ To any process aiming at result
Such as you say your songs are pregnant with?
Result, all judge: means, let none scrutinize
Save those aware how glory best is gained
By daring means to end, ashamed of shame,
²⁷⁵⁰ Constant in faith that only good works good,
While evil yields no fruit but impotence!
Graced with such plain good, I accept the means.
Nay, if result itself in turn become
Means,—who shall say?—to ends still loftier yet,—
²⁷⁵⁵ Though still the good prove hard to understand,
The bad still seemingly predominate,—
Never may I forget which order bears
The burden, toils to win the great reward,
And finds, in failure, the grave punishment,
²⁷⁶⁰ So, meantime, claims of me a faith I yield!
Moreover, a mere woman, I recoil
From what may prove man's-work permissible,
Imperative.   Rough strokes surprise: what then?
Some lusty armsweep needs must cause the crash

---

²⁷⁴⁵| MS:process promising §crossed out and replaced above by two words§ aiming at
²⁷⁴⁶| MS:§line added§ your works shall give the world?   *P1875:*your songs are pregnant with?
²⁷⁴⁷| MS:Result,—all §crossed out and restored§ see means—let   *P1875:*Result, all judge:
means, let   ²⁷⁴⁸| MS:those whereof the §last two words crossed out and replaced above
by two words§ aware how glory may be gained   *P1875:*glory best is gained
²⁷⁴⁹| MS:daring all §crossed out and replaced above by§ means <> end, refusing naught §last
two words crossed out§ ashamed of shame,   ²⁷⁵⁰| MS:But, firm in §last three words
crossed out and replaced above by two words§ Constant in faith, hold— §comma, word and
dash crossed out and replaced above by§ that   ²⁷⁵¹| MS:And §in margin and crossed
out§ While §crossed out and restored§   ²⁷⁵²| MS:§line added in margin§ with the plain
<> means!   *P1875:*with such plain <> means.   ²⁷⁵³| MS:Nay, if §over *in*§ results
§altered to§ result—themselves §altered to§ itself   *P1875:*result itself   ²⁷⁵⁴| MS:Means,
it may be,— §last three words and comma crossed out and replaced above by dash, three
words and question mark§ —who shall say?—to   ²⁷⁵⁵| MS:If §in margin§ There, when
§last two words crossed out and replaced above by one word§ still <> good is §crossed out
and replaced above by§ prove   *P1875:*Though still   ²⁷⁵⁶| MS:The evil §last two words
crossed out and replaced above by crossed-out word, *And,* and three words§ The bad still <>
predominate,— §over partially erased word§   ²⁷⁵⁸| MS:burden, works to   *P1875:*
burden, toils to   ²⁷⁵⁹| MS:And §over *One*§ <> the great §altered to§ grave
²⁷⁶⁰| MS:meantime, challenges that §last two words crossed out and replaced above by four
words§ claims of me a   ²⁷⁶¹| MS:Moreover, the §crossed out and replaced above by§ a
²⁷⁶⁴| MS:Some giant §crossed out and replaced above by§ lusty

2765   Of thorn and bramble, ere those shrubs, those flowers,
      We fain would have earth yield exclusively,
      Are sown, matured and garlanded for boys
      And girls, who know not how the growth was gained.
      Finally, am I not a foreigner?
2770   No born and bred Athenian,—isled about,
      I scarce can drink, like you, at every breath,
      Just some particular doctrine which may best
      Explain the strange thing I revolt against—
      How—by involvement, who may extricate?—
2775   Religion perks up through impiety,
      Law leers with licence, folly wise-like frowns,
      The seemly lurks inside the abominable.
      But opposites,—each neutralizes each
      Haply by mixture: what should promise death,

2765| MS:bramble ere <> shrubs, and those §last two words inserted above; *and* crossed out§
*1889a:*bramble, ere   2766| MS:We §over partial erasure§ <> would feast upon §last two
words crossed out and replaced above by three words§ make our crop exclusively,   *P1875:*
would have earth yield exclusively,   2767| MS:matured, §altered to *mature* and then
restored§ made §crossed out and replaced above by§ and garlands §altered to§ garlanded of
§crossed out§ for girls §crossed out§ boys   *P1875:*matured, are garland   *1889a:*matured
and garlanded   2768| MS:and boys §crossed out and replaced above by§ girls <> how
§inserted above§ they §altered to§ the want earth to §last three words crossed out§ grow
§altered to§ growth   2770| MS:No §altered to§ No <> about,—   *P1875:*about,
2771| MS:How should I grow up, drink at <> breath   *P1875:*I scarce can drink, like you, at
<> breath,   2772| MS:Just that §crossed out and replaced above by§ some
2773| MS:strange §inserted above§ matters §crossed out and replaced above by§ thing
2774| MS:To wit, the §last three words crossed out and replaced above by two words§ How,—
by involvement, none §crossed out and replaced above by§ who <> extricate,— §comma
altered to question mark§   *P1875:*How—by   2775| MS:Religion mingled with §over
illegible word; last two words crossed out and replaced above by three words§ perks up
through   2776| MS:Law §next word illegibly crossed out and replaced above by illegibly
crossed-out word§ leers §inserted above§ <> folly with §crossed out and replaced above by
two crossed-out words, *masks as*§ frowns, like §last two words inserted above§ wise, words,
§word and comma crossed out§   *P1875:*folly wise-like frowns,
2777| MS:The fair and good with §last four words crossed out and replaced above by three
words§ seemly lurks inside <> abominable,—   *P1875:*abominable.   2778| MS:These
§crossed out and replaced above by§ Since opposites,—each §crossed out and replaced above
by§ good neutralizing each §crossed out and replaced above by§ bad   *P1875:*But opposites,—
each neutralizes each   2779| MS:Surely? §word and punctuation crossed out and
replaced above by§ Haply <> mixture,—which would §last two words crossed out and
replaced above by two words§ while they §crossed out§ what late §last two words inserted
above§ promise §altered to§ promised death,   *P1875:*mixture: what should promise death,

125

2780   May haply give the good ingredient force,
        Disperse in fume the antagonistic ill.
        This institution, therefore,—Comedy,—
        By origin, a rite,—by exercise,
        Proved an achievement tasking poet's power
2785   To utmost, eking legislation out
        Beyond the legislator's faculty,
        Playing the censor where the moralist
        Declines his function, far too dignified
        For dealing with minute absurdities:
2790   By efficacy,—virtue's guard, the scourge
        Of vice, each folly's fly-flap, arm in aid
        Of all that's righteous, customary, sound
        And wholesome; sanctioned therefore,—better say,
        Prescribed for fit acceptance of this age
2795   By, not alone the long recorded roll
        Of earlier triumphs but, success to-day—
        (The multitude as prompt recipient still
        Of good gay teaching from that monitor
        They crowned this morning—Aristophanes—
2800   As when Sousarion's cart first traversed street)—
        This product of Athenai—*I* dispute,
        Impugn?   There's just one only circumstance

2780| MS:Yet yield §last two words crossed out and replaced above by two words§ May give < >
ingredient threefold life §crossed out and replaced above by§ force,   *P1875:*May haply give
< > ingredient force,   2781| MS:the §in margin§ Antagonistic §altered to§ antagonistic
ill. §period inserted§ dispersed §altered to§ Disperse in fume. §period crossed out; last three
words marked for transposition to beginning of line§   2783| *P1875:*rite; by   *1889a:*
rite,—by   2788| MS:function—far §crossed out and replaced above by§ that's too
*P1875:*function, far too   2789| MS:absurdities:—   *P1875:*absurdities;   *1889a:*
absurdities: 2790| MS:efficacy, virtue's   *P1875:*efficacy,—virtue's
2793| MS:wholesome: sanctioned   *P1875:*wholesome; sanctioned
2795| MS:By evidence §crossed out and replaced above by two words§ not alone   *P1875:*By, not
2796| MS:triumphs, but success today—   *P1875:*triumphs but, success to-day—
2797| MS:As prompt recipient still the §altered to§ The multitude §first four words marked for
transposition to follow *multitude*§   *P1875:*(The < > as   2798| MS:that §over *this*§
2800| MS:when Sousarion's cart first < > street,— §over illegible word§   *P1875:*when Sousarion's
car first < > street)—   *1889a:*street) §emended to§ cart < > street)— §see Editorial Notes§
2801| MS:This glory of Athenai *I* §inserted§ to §crossed out§ dispute,   *P1875:*This product of
Athenai—*I*   2802| MS:Impugn?— §dash crossed out§ There's §over *there's*§

Explains that!   I, poor critic, see, hear, feel;
But eyes, ears, senses prove me—foreigner!
2805 Who shall gainsay that the raw new-come guest
Blames oft, too sensitive?   On every side
Of—larger than your stage—life's spectacle,
Convention here permits and there forbids
Impulse and action, nor alleges more
2810 Than some mysterious "So do all, and so
Does no one:" which the hasty stranger blames
Because, who bends the head unquestioning,
Transgresses, turns to wrong what else were right,
By failure of a reference to law
2815 Beyond convention; blames unjustly, too—
As if, through that defect, all gained were lost
And slave-brand set on brow indelibly;—
Blames unobservant or experienceless

2803| MS:Explains— §dash crossed out§ the §crossed out and replaced above by three words§
that: I, poor critic, sees, and hears, and feels— §last five words altered to three words§ see,
hear, feel   *P1875*:that! I < > feel;   2804| MS:And §crossed out and replaced above by§
But < > prove the §crossed out and replaced above by word and dash§ me
2805| MS:May be! §last two words and exclamation point crossed out§ Who shall §inserted
above§ gainsays §altered to§ gainsay < > raw §inserted above§   2806| MS:Blames, over
§crossed out and replaced above by two words§ oft, too sensitive, §comma altered to question
mark§ On §over illegible erasure§   *P1875*:Blames oft   2807| MS:§line added§ Of §in
margin over partial erasure§ At— §word crossed out; dash retained§ larger
2808| MS:here allows §crossed out and replaced below by§ permits   2809| MS:§following
this line§ Go on to next page but one   2810| MS:mysterious 'So   *1889a*:mysterious "So
2811-12| MS:§one line expanded to two lines§ one:' which the hasty stranger §last four words
inserted above§ blame §altered to§ blames, §solidus inserted§ Because §over *because*§ < >
unquestioning, §word and comma added§   2811| *P1875*:blames   *1889a*:one:" which
2813| MS:turns the very §last two words crossed out and replaced above by three words§ what
else were right, §comma inserted; last four words marked for transposition to end of line§ to
wrong   2814| MS:of due §crossed out and replaced above by§ a
2815| MS:convention: blames o'erhastily, §word and comma crossed out§ unjustly, too—
P1875:convention; blames   2816| MS:As, §comma crossed out§ if, §word and comma
inserted above§ < > that much §crossed out§ defection §altered to§ defect < > gained
§inserted above§ were sh §last two letters crossed out§ lost,   *P1875*:lost   2817| MS:And
the §crossed out§ slave-brand indelible: §colon inserted; word marked for transposition to
follow *brow*§ on free §inserted below§ brow: §colon crossed out§   *P1875*:slave-brand set on
< > indelibly;—   2818| MS:unobservant, inexperience §last two words altered to§
unobservantly, experienceless yet §crossed out§   *P1875*:unobservant or experienceless

That men, like trees, if stout and sound and sane,
2820   Show stem no more affected at the root
By bough's exceptional submissive dip
Of leaf and bell, light danced at end of spray
To windy fitfulness in wayward sport—
No more lie prostrate—than low files of flower
2825   Which, when the blast goes by, unruffled raise
Each head again o'er ruder meadow-wreck
Of thorn and thistle that refractory
Demurred to cower at passing wind's caprice.
Why shall not guest extend like charity,
2830   Conceive how,—even when astounded most
That natives seem to acquiesce in muck
Changed by prescription, they affirm, to gold,—
Such may still bring to test, still bear away

2819| MS:That, §over illegible erasure; comma crossed out§ in the main, veracious §last four words crossed out and replaced above by six words§ men, like trees, if true and just and pure, *P1875:*if stout and sound and sane,   2820| MS:Show §in margin§ Stem §altered to§ stem grow §last two words crossed out and replaced above by two words§ Trees are §last two words crossed out and *stem* restored§   2821| By bells §crossed out and replaced above by§ bough's   2822| MS:§line added§ Of blossom §crossed out§ leaf and bell §last three words inserted above illegibly-erased word§ may §crossed out and replaced above by§ light dance §altered to§ danced *P1875:*bell, light   2823| MS:fitfulness at §crossed out and replaced below by§ in <> sport,— *1889a:*sport—   2824| MS:Than all those §last three words crossed out and replaced above by three words§ No more lie prostrate, §comma inserted§ files of §last two words crossed out and replaced above by dash and two words§ —than low §over illegible word§ meadow §crossed out; *files of* restored§ flower *1889a:*prostrate—than 2826| MS:Each §in margin§ cup §over partial erasure§ as erect §last two words crossed out§ again, §word and comma inserted above§ with no less sweet to show §last six words crossed out and replaced above by three illegibly crossed-out words, perhaps *the meadow shriek*§ o'er ruder §inserted above§ meadow-wreck *P1875:*Each head again o'er   2827| MS:Of §in margin§ Than §crossed out and replaced above by crossed-out word, *From*§ thorn and §over illegible erasure§ thistle while §altered to *when* and crossed out and replaced above by§ that 2828| MS:Demurred §last three letters crossed out and restored§ <> at any §crossed out and replaced above by§ passing   2829| MS:shall §over partial erasure§ <> extend then, §word and comma crossed out and replaced above by§ like   2830| MS:Conceive that §crossed out and replaced above by word, comma and dash§ how,— <> when §over partial erasure§   2831| MS:Men §crossed out and replaced above by two words§ That natives seem all §crossed out and replaced above by§ to acquiescent §altered to§ acquiesce in sights mere §last two words crossed out§ muck   2832| MS:they affirm, to §last three words over illegible erasures§   2833| MS:They §crossed out and replaced above by§ Such may not §crossed out and replaced above by§ still <> test, and §crossed out and replaced above by§ still

Safely and surely much of good and true
²⁸³⁵ Though latent ore, themselves unspecked, unspoiled?
Fresh bathed i' the icebrook, any hand may pass
A placid moment through the lamp's fierce flame:
And who has read your "Lemnians," seen "The Hours,"
Heard "Female-Playhouse-seat-Preoccupants,"
²⁸⁴⁰ May feel no worse effect than, once a year,
Those who leave decent vesture, dress in rags
And play the mendicant, conform thereby
To country's rite, and then, no beggar-taint
Retained, don vesture due next morrow-day.
²⁸⁴⁵ What if I share the stranger's weakness then?
Well, could I also show his strength, his sense

Untutored, ay!—but then untampered with!

I fancy, though the world seems old enough,
Though Hellas be the sole unbarbarous land,
2850   Years may conduct to such extreme of age,
And outside Hellas so isles new may lurk,
That haply,—when and where remain a dream!—
In fresh days when no Hellas fills the world,
In novel lands as strange where, all the same,
2855   Their men and women yet behold, as we,
Blue heaven, black earth, and love, hate, hope and fear,
Over again, unhelped by Attiké—
Haply some philanthropic god steers bark,
Gift-laden, to the lonely ignorance
2860   Islanded, say, where mist and snow mass hard
To metal—ay, those Kassiterides!
Then asks: "Ye apprehend the human form.
What of this statue, made to Pheidias' mind,
This picture, as it pleased our Zeuxis paint?
2865   Ye too feel truth, love beauty: judge of these!"

2847| MS:Untutored, ay— §crossed out and replaced above by§ true! but all §crossed out and replaced above by§ then,—untampered   *P1875:*Untutored, ay!—but then untampered
2847-48| MS:§no ¶ called for§   *P1875:*§¶§   2848| MS:Now, Poet! §last two words and punctuation crossed out and replaced above by crossed-out word and comma, *For,* and two words and comma§ I fancy   2849-50| MS:§lines marked for transposition§
2850| MS:Years might §crossed out and replaced above by§ may   2851| MS:And §in margin§ Outside §altered to§ outside may continents and §last three words crossed out and replaced above by four words§ such §crossed out§ Hellas such new isles exist §crossed out§ may brood,— §crossed out and replaced above by§ lurk   *P1875:*lurk,   *1889a:*outside Hellas so isles new may   2852| MS:where remains §altered to§ remain <> dream,— §comma altered to exclamation point§   2853| MS:fresh §over illegible erasure§
2855| MS:Their §crossed out and then rewritten above over illegible word§
2856| MS:Blue §in margin§ This §crossed out§ heaven, and §crossed out and replaced above by§ black earth, learn §crossed out and replaced above by§ and loves, hates, hopes and fears, §last five words altered to§ love, hate, hope and fear,   2858| MS:Suppose some <> god steered bark   *P1875:*Haply some <> god steers bark,   2859| MS:lonely §over partial erasure§   2861| MS:ay, §word and comma inserted above§ those far §crossed out§ Kassiterides, §comma altered to exclamation point§   2862| MS:Saying §crossed out and replaced above by two words and colon§ Then spoke: "Ye   *P1875:*Then asks: 'Ye   *1889a:*asks: "Ye   2865| MS:too have §crossed out and replaced above by§ feel truth, and §crossed out and replaced above by§ love   *P1875:*these!'   *1889a:*these!"

Such strangers may judge feebly, stranger-like:
"Each hair too indistinct—for, see our own!
Hands, not skin-coloured as these hands we have,
And lo, the want of due decorum here!
2870 A citizen, arrayed in civic garb,
Just as he walked your streets apparently,
Yet wears no sword by side, adventures thus,
In thronged Athenai! foolish painter's-freak!
While here's his brother-sculptor found at fault
2875 Still more egregiously, who shames the world,
Shows wrestler, wrestling at the public games,
Atrociously exposed from head to foot!"
Sure, the Immortal would impart at once
Our slow-stored knowledge, how small truths suppressed
2880 Conduce to the far greater truth's display,—
Would replace simple by instructed sense,
And teach them how Athenai first so tamed
The natural fierceness that her progeny
Discarded arms nor feared the beast in man:

2866| MS:Such §in margin§ The §crossed out§ strangers might judge <> stranger-like—
*P1875:*strangers may judge <.> stranger-like: 2867| MS:"The §crossed out and replaced
above by§ Each hair is §crossed out and replaced above by§ too   *P1875.*'Each   *1889a.*"Each
2868| MS:The §crossed out and replaced above by§ Hands, skin not §last two words marked
for transposition and hyphen added to *skin*, forming§ not skin-coloured <> the hand §last
two words altered to§ these hands before §crossed out and replaced above by two words§ we
have! *P1875:*have,   2869-77| MS:§lines added in margin§   2869| MS:And—what
§crossed out and replaced above by§ lo the <> here!—   *P1875:*And lo, the <> here!
2870| MS:This §crossed out and replaced above by§ A   2871| MS:he once §crossed out§
walked your §inserted above§   2872| MS:thus §over partial erasure§ *P1875:*thus,
2873| MS:thronged Athenai: that's a §last two words crossed out and replaced above by two
words§ fie on painter's-freak! *P1875:*thronged Athenai! foolish painter's-freak!
2874| MS:And §in margin§ While §crossed out§ here's *P1875:*While here's
2876| MS:The §altered to§ Shows   2877| *P1875:*foot!'   *1889a:*foot!"
2878| MS:Sure, §word and comma in margin§ The §altered to§ the kind §crossed out§
Immortal §over *immortal*§   2879| MS:Our §in margin§ A §crossed out§ slow-stored <>
how a §crossed out and replaced above by§ small truth §altered to§ truths
2880| MS:Conduces §altered to§ Conduce <> the §crossed out and restored§ far §inserted
above§   2881| MS:—Would §dash and word in margin§ And lend the §last three words
crossed out and replaced above by one word over partial erasure§ replace simple the §crossed
out and replaced above by§ by *P1875:*Would   2882| MS:By §crossed out and replaced
above by§ And teaching §last three letters crossed out and replaced above by§ them

131

2885 Wherefore at games, where earth's wise gratitude,
Proved by responsive culture, claimed the prize
For man's mind, body, each in excellence,—
When mind had bared itself, came body's turn,
And only irreligion grudged the gods
2890 One naked glory of their master-work
Where all is glorious rightly understood,—
The human frame; enough that man mistakes:
Let him not think the gods mistaken too!

But, peradventure, if the stranger's eye
2895 Detected . . . Ah, too high my fancy-flight!
Pheidias, forgive, and Zeuxis bear with me—
How on your faultless should I fasten fault
Of my own framing, even?   Only say,—
Suppose the impossible were realized,
2900 And some as patent incongruity,
Unseemliness,—of no more warrant, there
And then, than now and here, whate'er the time
And place,—I say, the Immortal—who can doubt?—
Would never shrink, but own "The blot escaped
2905 Our artist: thus he shows humanity."

May stranger tax one peccant part in thee,
Poet, three-parts divine?   May I proceed?

2885| MS:And how §last two words crossed out and replaced above by one word§ Wherefore
2886| MS:by as worthy §last two words crossed out and replaced above by one word§
responsive   2887| MS:For man, §word and comma altered to§ man's < > body,—each
*P1875:*body, each   2888| MS:When §inserted above§ Mind having §crossed out and
replaced above by§ had < > turn—   *P1875:*mind < > turn,   2889| MS:When §crossed
out§ And irreligion only §last two words marked for transposition§   2890| MS:naked
§inserted above over illegible erasure§   2893| MS:§line added§   2894| MS:strangers'
§altered to§ stranger's   2895| MS:Detected . . Ah < > high the §crossed out and replaced
above by§ my   *P1875:*Detected...Ah   2903| MS:place,—the just §last two words crossed
out and replaced above by three words§ I say, the immortal §altered to§ Immortal,—who
*1889a:*the Immortal—who   2904| MS:never pause, avow— §last two words and dash
crossed out and replaced above by three words§ shrink, but own 'the §altered to§ 'The
*1889a:*own "The   2905| MS:Our §in margin§ The §crossed out§ artist,—thus < >
humanity!'   *P1875:*artist: thus   *1889a:*humanity."   2906| MS:§line added§ If stranger
P1875:"May stranger   *1889a:*May   2907| MS:divine...may   *P1875:*divine? May

"Comedy is prescription and a rite."
Since when?   No growth of the blind antique time,
2910 "It rose in Attiké with liberty;
When freedom falls, it too will fall."   Scarce so!
Your games,—the Olympian, Zeus gave birth to these;
Your Pythian,—these were Phoibos' institute.
Isthmian, Nemeian,—Theseus, Herakles
2915 Appointed each, the boys and barbers say!
Earth's day is growing late: where's Comedy?
"Oh, that commenced an age since,—two, belike,—
In Megara, whence here they brought the thing!"
Or I misunderstand, or here's the fact—
2920 Your grandsire could recall that rustic song,
How suchanone was thief, and miser such
And how,—immunity from chastisement
Once promised to bold singers of the same
By daylight on the drunkard's holiday,—
2925 The clever fellow of the joyous troop
Tried acting what before he sang about,
Acted and stole, or hoarded, acting too:
While his companions ranged a-row, closed up
For Choros,—bade the general rabblement
2930 Sit, see, hear, laugh,—not join the dance themselves.
Soon, the same clever fellow found a mate,

2908| *P1875:*"'Comedy <> rite.'   *1889a:*"Comedy <> rite."   2909| MS:the §inserted
above§ blind antiquity §altered to§ antique   2910| *P1875:*'It   *1889a:*"It
2911| MS:And, §word and comma crossed out§ When §over *when*§ that §crossed out and
replaced above by§ freedom   *P1875:*fall.' Scarce   *1889a:*fall." Scarce   2912| MS:the
Olympian, §over illegible erasure; comma inserted§ games— §word and dash crossed out§
Zeus <> these: *P1875:*these;   2913| MS:Your Pythian—these   *P1875:*Your Pythian,—
these   2914| MS:Your §crossed out and replaced above by word and comma§ Isthmian,
§over partial erasure§ <> Herakles invention, they. §last two words and punctuation crossed
out§   2916| MS:But this §last two words crossed out and replaced above by two words§
Earth's day   2917| *P1875:*'Oh   *1889a:*"Oh   2918| MS:thing," §comma altered to
exclamation point§   *P1875:*thing!'   *1889a:*thing! §emended to§ thing!" §see Editorial
Notes§   2919| MS:—Did I <> or ran the words—   *P1875:*Or I <> or here's the fact—
2920| MS:that §over *the*§   2921| MS:and miser §last two words inserted above§ such,
*1889a:*such   2922| MS:how, immunity   *P1875:*how,—immunity   2924| MS:holiday,
*P1875:*holiday,—   2925| MS:joyous crew §crossed out and replaced above by§ troop
2928| MS:ranged themselves §crossed out and replaced above by§ a-row   2929| MS:For
§in margin§ The §crossed out§ Choros   2930| MS:themselves: *P1875:*themselves.

And these two did the whole stage-mimicking,
Still closer in approach to Tragedy,—
So led the way to Aristophanes,
2935 Whose grandsire saw Sousarion, and whose sire—
Chionides; yourself wrote "Banqueters"
When Aischulos had made "Prometheus," nay,
All of the marvels; Sophokles,—I'll cite,
"Oidipous"—and Euripides—I bend
2940 The head—"Medeia" henceforth awed the world!
"Banqueters," "Babylonians"—next come you!
Surely the great days that left Hellas free
Happened before such advent of huge help,
Eighty-years-late assistance?   Marathon,
2945 Plataia, Salamis were fought, I think,
Before new educators stood reproved,
Or foreign legates blushed, excepted to!
Where did the helpful rite pretend its rise?
Did it break forth, as gifts divine are wont,
2950 Plainly authentic, incontestably
Adequate to the helpful ordinance?
Founts, dowered with virtue, pulse out pure from source;

2932| MS:these §over *then*§   2933| MS:to tragedy §altered to§ Tragedy,—
2934| MS:And §crossed out and replaced above by§ So leading up to—Aristophanes,   *P1875:*
So led the way to Aristophanes,   2935| MS:sire   *P1875:*sire—   2936| MS:Chionides;
while §crossed out§ yourself wrote 'Banqueters'   *1889a:*wrote "Banqueters"   2937| MS:had
written §crossed out§ made Prometheus—nay,   *P1875:*made 'Prometheus,' nay,   *1889a:*
made "Prometheus," nay,   2938| MS:§line added§ marvels: Sophokles,—I'll say,   *P1875:*
marvels; Sophokles,—I'll cite,   2939| MS:Sophokles §crossed out§ 'Oidipous'— and
1889a:"Oidipous"—and   2940| MS:Euripides §crossed out§ The head,—Medeia henceforth
*P1875:*head—'Medeia' henceforth   *1889a:*head—"Medeia" henceforth   2941| MS:§line
added§ 'Banqueters,' 'Babylonians'—next   *P1875:*'Banqueters' 'Babylonians'—next
1889a:"Banqueters," "Babylonians"—next   2943| MS:such §crossed out and restored§
2944| MS:Such §crossed out§ Eighty-years §over *eighty-years*§ late §comma and word inserted
above§ assistance? Marathon   *P1875:*Eighty-years-late < > Marathon,   2946| MS:stood
ware §crossed out§ reproved,   2948| MS:Moreover, §word and comma crossed out§
When §altered to§ Whence did the §inserted above§ help §altered to§ helpful rite §inserted
above§ pretend itself §last three letters crossed out and replaced above by one word§ rise?
*P1875:*Where did   2949| MS:it §next word illegibly crossed out and
replaced above by two words and comma§ break forth   2952| MS:Springs, dowered < >
virtue, burst forth §last two words crossed out and replaced above by two words§ pulse out
pure at §crossed out and replaced above by§ from   *P1875:*Founts, dowered

'Tis there we taste the god's benign intent:
Not when,—fatigued away by journey, foul
2955 With brutish trampling,—crystal sinks to slime,
And lymph forgets the first salubriousness.
Sprang Comedy to light thus crystal-pure?
"Nowise!" yourself protest with vehemence;
"Gross, bestial, did the clowns' diversion break;
2960 Every successor paddled in the slush;
Nay, my contemporaries one and all
Gay played the mudlark till I joined their game;
Then was I first to change buffoonery
For wit, and stupid filth for cleanly sense,
2965 Transforming pointless joke to purpose fine,
Transfusing rude enforcement of home-law—
'Drop knave's-tricks, deal more neighbour-like, ye boors!'—
With such new glory of poetic breath
As, lifting application far past use
2970 O' the present, launched it o'er men's lowly heads
To future time, when high and low alike
Are dead and done with, while my airy power
Flies disengaged, as vapour from what stuff
It—say not, dwelt in—fitlier, dallied with
2975 To forward work, which done,—deliverance brave,—
It soars away, and mud subsides to dust.

2955| MS:chrystal *P1875:*crystal   2956| MS:And so forgets < > first salubrity §altered to§ salubriousness. *P1875.*And lymph forgets   2957| MS:Came Comedy to light §last two words inserted above§ < > chrystal-pure? *P1875:*Sprang Comedy < > crystal-pure?
2958| MS:"Nowise"! yourself *P1875:*'Nowise!' yourself *1889a:*"Nowise!" yourself
2959| *P1875:*'Gross *1889a:*"Gross   2960| MS:Content, successors < > slush, *P1875:*Every successor <.> slush;   2962| MS:mudlark when I *P1875:*mudlark till I
2963| MS:was it §crossed out§ I < > to §inserted above§ changed §altered to§ change
2964| MS:To §altered to§ For < > for §over to§   2967| *P1875:*"Drop < > boors!"—
1889a:'Drop < > boors!'—   2968| MS:new §over illegible erasure§ MS:As lifted *P1875:*As, lifting   2969| MS:As   2970| MS:o'er the §crossed out and replaced above by§ men's   2972| MS:with, while §crossed out and replaced above by§ yet my *P1875:*with, while my   2973| MS:from vile stuff *P1875:*from what stuff   2974| MS:—say not dwelt—but fitlier, §punctuation and last five words inserted above§ < > with, *P1875:*not, dwelt < > with *1889a:*dwelt in—fitlier   2975| MS:And §in margin§ To §crossed out§ forward §altered to§ forwards *P1875:*To forward   2976| MS:away, while mud *P1875:*away, and mud

Say then, myself invented Comedy!"

So mouths full many a famed Parabasis!
Agreed!   No more, then, of prescriptive use,
2980   Authorization by antiquity,
For what offends our judgment!   'Tis your work,
Performed your way: not work delivered you
Intact, intact producible in turn.
Everywhere have you altered old to new—
2985   Your will, your warrant: therefore, work must stand
Or stumble by intrinsic worth.   What worth?
Its aim and object!   Peace you advocate,
And war would fain abolish from the land:
Support religion, lash irreverence,
2990   Yet laughingly administer rebuke
To superstitious folly,—equal fault!
While innovating rashness, lust of change,
New laws, new habits, manners, men and things,
Make your main quarry,—"oldest" meaning "best."
2995   You check the fretful litigation-itch,
Withstand mob-rule, expose mob-flattery,
Punish mob-favourites; most of all press hard
On sophists who assist the demagogue,
And poets their accomplices in crime.
3000   Such your main quarry: by the way, you strike

---

²⁹⁷⁷| MS:then, twas I §last two words crossed out and replaced above by one word§ myself
*P1875:*invented Comedy!'   *1889a:*invented Comedy!"   ²⁹⁷⁸| MS:So says §crossed out and
replaced above by§ mouths <> famed §inserted above§
²⁹⁷⁹| MS:prescriptive §over partial erasure§   ²⁹⁸⁰| MS:Authorization and §crossed out
and replaced above by§ by   ²⁹⁸¹| MS:what accepts §crossed out and
replaced above by§ offends our §altered to§ your judgment! §punctuation inserted§ 'tis
§altered to§ 'Tis   *P1875:*offends our judgment   ²⁹⁸³| MS:turn: *P1875:*turn.
²⁹⁸⁵| MS:therefore,—work that §crossed out and replaced above by§ must stands §altered to§
stand   *P1875:*therefore, work   ²⁹⁸⁶| MS:Or stumbles §altered to§ stumble
²⁹⁸⁷| MS:object! Peace, you   *1889a:*object! Peace you   ²⁹⁸⁸| MS:And War §over *war*§
revile, §comma altered to dash§ abolish   *P1875:*war would fain abolish   ²⁹⁹¹| MS:equal
fault! §last two words over illegible erasures§   ²⁹⁹²| MS:But §crossed out and replaced
above by§ While   ²⁹⁹³| MS:laws, and §crossed out and replaced above by§ new
²⁹⁹⁴| MS:meaning §last three letters crossed out and replaced above by crossed-out word, *the,*
and then original reading restored§   ²⁹⁹⁷| MS:mob-favorites   *1889a:*mob-favourites
³⁰⁰⁰| MS:Such §in margin§ These §crossed out§ your <> quarry,—by   *1889a:*quarry: by

Ignobler game, mere miscreants, snob or scamp,
Cowardly, gluttonous, effeminate:
Still with a bolt to spare when dramatist
Proves haply unproficient in his art.
3005 Such aims—alone, no matter for the means—
Declare the unexampled excellence
Of their first author—Aristophanes!

Whereat—Euripides, oh, not thyself—
Augustlier than the need!—thy century
3010 Of subjects dreamed and dared and done, before
"Banqueters" gave dark earth enlightenment,
Or "Babylonians" played Prometheus here,—
These let me summon to defend thy cause!
Lo, as indignantly took life and shape
3015 Labour by labour, all of Herakles,—
Palpably fronting some o'erbold pretence
"Eurustheus slew the monsters, purged the world!"
So shall each poem pass you and imprint
Shame on the strange assurance.   *You* praised Peace?
3020 Sing him full-face, Kresphontes!   "Peace" the theme?
"Peace, in whom depths of wealth lie,—of the blest
Immortals beauteousest,—
Come! for the heart within me dies away,
So long dost thou delay!
3025 O I have feared lest old age, much annoy,

3004| MS:in the §crossed out and replaced above by§ his   3005| MS:aims alone <>
means, *P1875:*aims—alone <> means, *CP1875:*means—   3011| MS:The Feasters
§last two words crossed out and replaced above by one word§ 'Banqueters' *1889a:*
"Banqueters"   3012| MS:§line added§ Or 'Babylonians' *1889a:*Or "Babylonians"
3013| MS:§line added in margin§   3014| MS:Lo, §word and comma in margin§ As
§altered to§ as if §crossed out§ indignantly   3015| MS:Labor <> labor *1889a:*Labour
<> labour   3016| MS:fronted <> pretence— *P1875:*fronting <> pretence
3017| *P1875:*'Eurustheus <> world!' *1889a:*"Eurustheus <> world!"   3019| MS:the
§over illegible erasure§   3020| MS:full-face, Kresphontes! 'Peace,' sings §over illegible
erasure§ he— §caret and word added in margin§ *Insert* *P1875:*full-face, Kresphontes! 'Peace'
the theme? *1889a:*full-face, Kresphontes! "Peace" the   3021-34| MS:§these lines
composed on slip of paper attached at right margin and added between lines 3020 and 3035§
3021| MS:whom §over partially illegible word, perhaps *whose*§ *P1875:*'Peace *1889a:*"Peace
3023| MS:away *P1875:*away,   3025| MS:annoy *P1875:*annoy,

Conquer me, quite outstrip the tardy joy,
Thy gracious triumph-season I would see,
The song, the dance, the sport, profuse of crowns to be.
But come! for my sake, goddess great and dear,
3030   Come to the city here!
Hateful Sedition drive thou from our homes,
With Her who madly roams
Rejoicing in the steel against the life
That's whetted—banish Strife!"

3035   Shall I proceed?   No need of next and next!
That were too easy, play so presses play,
Trooping tumultuous, each with instance apt,
Each eager to confute the idle boast.
What virtue but stands forth panegyrized,
3040   What vice, unburned by stigma, in the books
Which bettered Hellas,—beyond graven gold
Or gem-indenture, sung by Phoibos' self
And saved in Kunthia's mountain treasure-house—
Ere you, man, moralist, were youth or boy?
3045   —Not praise which, in the proffer, mocks the praised
By sly admixture of the blameworthy
And enforced coupling of base fellowship,—

3032| MS:With Her that §crossed out and replaced above by§ who   3034| *P1875:*banish
Strife!'   *1889a:*banish Strife!"   3035| MS:Nay, Euthukles, §last two words and
punctuation crossed out and replaced above by three words and punctuation§ Shall I
proceed? what §altered to§ What need <> next?   *P1875:*"Shall <> proceed? No need <>
next!   *1889a:*Shall   3036| MS:were §over *was*§ <> so pressed §altered to§ presses on
§crossed out§ play,   3037| MS:Trooping, tumultuous <> apt   *P1875:*Trooping
tumultuous <> apt,   3038| MS:All §over illegible word§ eager <> boast!   *P1875:*Each
eager   *1889a:*boast.   3039| MS:stands §over illegible word§
3041| MS:bettered Hellas, beyond   *P1875:*bettered Hellas,—beyond
3042| MS:And §crossed out and replaced above by§ Or gem-indenture, prized of §last two
words crossed out and replaced above by two words§ sung by Phoibos' priest §crossed out and
replaced above by§ self,   *P1875:*self   3043| MS:§line added§ in Kunthia's §over illegible
erasure§ mountain §crossed out and restored§ temple §crossed out§ treasure-house   *P1875:*
treasure-house—   3044| MS:Ere this §crossed out and replaced below by§ you, man-
moralist, were §over illegible erasure§   *P1875:*man, moralist   3046| MS:By prompt
§crossed out and replaced above by§ sly <> blameworthy §marked for transposition to§
worthy blame   *P1875:*blameworthy   3047| MS:And comic §inserted above§ coupling of
all §crossed out§ basest §altered to§ base   *P1875:*And enforced coupling

Not blame which gloats the while it frowning laughs,
"Allow one glance on horrors—laughable!"—
3050 This man's entire of heart and soul, discharged
Its love or hate, each unalloyed by each,
On objects worthy either; earnestness,
Attribute him, and power! but novelty?
Nor his nor yours a doctrine—all the world's!
3055 What man of full-grown sense and sanity
Holds other than the truth,—wide Hellas through,—
Though truth, he acts, discredit truth he holds?
What imbecile has dared to formulate
"Love war, hate peace, become a litigant!"—
3060 And so preach on, reverse each rule of right
Because he quarrels, combats, goes to law?
No, for his comment runs, with smile or sigh
According to heart's temper, "Peace were best,
Except occasions when we put aside
3065 Peace, and bid all the blessings in her gift

3048| MS:No §altered to§ Not blame, which <> frowningly §altered to§ frowning laughs
*P1875:*blame which <> laughs, 3049| MS:Laughs. Not a §last three words crossed out
and replaced above by punctuation and three words§ "Just this one *P1875:*"Allow one
3050| MS:No! §word and punctuation in margin§ But— §word crossed out; dash inserted
above§ man's *P1875:*This man's 3051| MS:In love *P1875:*Its love
3052-53| MS:§line added and expanded to two lines§ either: earnestness §solidus added§ <>
power, §over illegible erasure; comma altered to exclamation point§ but 3052| *P1875:*
either; earnestness, 3054| MS:Earnest but novel his or yours. Nay, §word and comma
inserted below; last seven words crossed out and replaced below by six words§ Nor his nor
yours the doctrine: all *P1875:*yours a doctrine—all 3055| MS:No §in margin§ What
§crossed out§ man *P1875:*What man 3057| MS:Though word prove §crossed out and
replaced above by two illegibly crossed-out words and two words§ grow all discordant matched
with §last two words crossed out and replaced above by two words§ in the deed! *P1875:*
Though truth, he acts discredit truth he holds? *1889a:*acts, discredit 3058| MS:Shall
§over *Has*§ any sane man dared §altered to§ dare to *P1875:*What imbecile has dared to
3059| MS:litigant?" *P1875:*litigant!"— 3060| MS:so go on, reversing rules *P1875:*so
preach on, <> rule *1889a:*on, reverse each rule 3061| MS:The while §last two words
crossed out and replaced above by one word§ Because he fights, is troubled, §last three words
and punctuation crossed out and replaced above by two words and punctuation§ quarrels,
combats 3062| MS:his §over *he*§ supplements §crossed out and replaced above by two
words and comma§ comment runs 3063| MS:temper, "Peace is §crossed out and
replaced above by§ were 3064| MS:But for occasions *P1875:*Except occasions
3065| MS:Peace, brotherhood §crossed out§ and all §crossed out§ bid all §last two words
inserted above§ the blessed train §crossed out and replaced above by crossed-out word, *crew*,
last two letters of *blessed* crossed out and replaced above by *ings* and two words, forming§

Quick join the crows, for sake of Marathon!"

"Nay," you reply; for one, whose mind withstands
His heart, and, loving peace, for conscience' sake
Wants war,—you find a crowd of hypocrites
3070 Whose conscience means ambition, grudge and greed.
On such, reproof, sonorous doctrine, melts
Distilled like universal but thin dew
Which all too sparsely covers country: dear,
No doubt, to universal crop and clown,
3075 Still, each bedewed keeps his own head-gear dry
With upthrust *skiadeion*, shakes adroit
The droppings to his neighbour. No! collect
All of the moisture, leave unhurt the heads
Which nowise need a washing, save and store
3080 And dash the whole condensed to one fierce spout
On some one evildoer, sheltered close,—
The fool supposed,—till you beat guard away,

---

blessings in her gift, *P1875:*gift   3066| MS:Bid §crossed out and replaced above by§
Quick <> for sake of §last three words crossed out and replaced above by three words§ and
march to §last three words crossed out and *for sake of* restored§   3066-67| MS:§no ¶ called
for§ *P1875:*§¶§   3067| MS:"Nay," §word and punctuation in margin§ Do §crossed out§
you reply; "for §over partial erasure§ *P1875:*Nay, you reply; for *1889a:*"Nay," you
3068| MS:heart, who, §crossed out and replaced above by§ and, <> conscience-sake *P1875:*
conscience' sake   3069| MS:you §over illegible erasure§   3071| MS:On such, §last
two words and comma in margin§ reproof §over illegible erasure§ <> melts on such §last two
words crossed out§   3072| MS:like that §inserted above§ thin though §crossed out§
universal dew *P1875:*like universal but thin dew   3073-75| MS:Which §over illegible
erasure§ sparsely <> country—truth §crossed out and replaced above by§ dear, no doubt— /
Only §crossed out and replaced above by word and comma§ Still, each denizen §crossed out
and replaced above by§ bedewed <> his own §last two words inserted above§ *P1875:*Which
all too sparsely <> country: dear, / No <> clown, / Still   3074| *P1875:*doubt to
*CP1875:*doubt, to   3076| MS:shakes each d §last letter and preceding word crossed out
and replaced above by one word§ adroit §over illegible erasure§   3077| MS:to §over
illegible erasure§ <> neighbour. §period inserted§ But §over illegible erasure§ collect
*P1875:*neighbour. No! collect   3079| MS:Who nowise <> save that §crossed out and
replaced above by§ and store §over illegible erasure§ *P1875:*Which nowise
3080| MS:And pour §crossed out and replaced above by§ dash <> condensed in one *P1875:*
condensed to one   3081| MS:sheltered safe §crossed out§ close, §over partial erasure§
*P1875:*close,—   3082| MS:So he supposed, till I §crossed out and replaced above by§ you
*P1875:*Fond he supposed, till *CP1875:*supposed,—till §not B§ *1889a:*The fool supposed

And showed your audience, not that war was wrong,
But Lamachos absurd,—case, crests and all,—

3085 Not that democracy was blind of choice,
But Kleon and Huperbolos were shams:
Not superstition vile, but Nikias crazed,—
The concrete for the abstract; that's the way!
What matters Choros crying "Hence, impure!"
3090 You cried "Ariphrades does thus and thus!"
Now, earnestness seems never earnest more
Than when it dons for garb—indifference;
So there's much laughing: but, compensative,
When frowning follows laughter, then indeed
3095 Scout innuendo, sarcasm, irony!—
Wit's polished warfare glancing at first graze
From off hard headpiece, coarsely-coated brain
O' the commonalty—whom, unless you prick
To purpose, what avails that finer pates
3100 Succumb to simple scratching? Those—not these—
'Tis Multitude, which, moved, fines Lamachos,
Banishes Kleon and burns Sokrates,
House over head, or, better, poisons him.

3083| MS.showed my §crossed out and replaced above by§ your   3086| MS:But Kleon
stood §over illegible erasure§ abhorrent and accurst: *P1875:*But Kleon and Huperbolos
accurst: *1889a:*and Huperbolos were shams: 3087| MS:crazed,— §over partially
illegible word§   3088| MS:abstract: that's   *P1875:*abstract; that's   3089| MS:crying
'Hence, impure!'   *1889a:*crying "Hence, impure!"   3090| MS:You §over *I*§ said §crossed
out and replaced above by§ cried 'Ariphrades < > thus!'   *1889a:*cried "Ariphrades < > thus!"
3091| MS:earnestness is §crossed out and replaced above by§ seems   3093| MS.but—
compensative—   *P1875:*but, compensative,   3094| MS:follows, then I §crossed out and
replaced above by§ you frown indeed!   *P1875:*follows laughter, then indeed
3095| MS:—Scout inuendo < > irony,   *P1875:*Scout < > irony!—   *1889a:*innuendo
3096| MS:The polished   *P1875:*Wit's polished   3097| MS:off the headpiece, triply-coated
§altered to§ coarsely-coated   *P1875:*off hard headpiece   3098| MS:unless I §crossed out
and replaced above by§ you   3099| MS:avail were then sculled wits §last four words
crossed out and replaced above by three words§ if finer pates   *P1875:*avails that finer
3100| MS:Made sensible of §last three words crossed out and replaced above by three words§
Succumb to simple satire? Those   *P1875:*simple scratching? Those
3101| MS:'Tis §in margin§ The §crossed out§ Multitude, §over *multitude*§ if §crossed out and
replaced above by word and comma§ which, < > fine §altered to§ fines
3102| MS:And §crossed out§ banish §altered to§ Banishes < > and burn §altered to§ burns
3103| MS:or better poisons   *P1875:*or, better, poisons

Therefore in dealing with King Multitude,
3105 Club-drub the callous numskulls!   In and in
Beat this essential consequential fact
That here they have a hater of the three,
Who hates in word, phrase, nickname, epithet
And illustration, beyond doubt at all!
3110 And similarly, would you win assent
To—Peace, suppose?   You tickle the tough hide
With good plain pleasure her concomitant—
And, past mistake again, exhibit Peace—
Peace, vintager and festive, cheesecake-time,
3115 Hare-slice-and-peasoup-season, household joy:
Theoria's beautiful belongings match
Opora's lavish condescendings: brief,
Since here the people are to judge, you press
Such argument as people understand:
3120 If with exaggeration—what care you?

Have I misunderstood you in the main?
No! then must answer be, such argument,

3104| MS:with this §crossed out and replaced above by§ King Multitude, §over *multitude*§
3105| MS:numsculls! Into them   *P1875:*numsculls! In and in   3107| MS:That §in
margin§ Here §altered to§ here's is §crossed out§ a thorough hater of all §crossed out and
replaced above by§ the   *P1875:*That here they have a hater   3108| Who §in margin§
Hate §altered to§ hates < > nickname, and §crossed out§ epithet   3109| MS:illustration,
left no §last two words crossed out and replaced above by illegibly crossed-out word and one
word§ beyond   3110| MS:similarly—would I §crossed out and replaced above by§ you
*P1875:*similarly, would   3111| MS:suppose? I §crossed out and replaced above by§ You
tickled §altered to§ tickle   3112| MS:pleasures < > concomitants—   *P1875:*pleasure < >
concomitant—   3113| MS:again, I §crossed out and replaced above by§ you played
§altered to§ play off Peace—   *P1875:*again, exhibit Peace—   3114| MS:The vintager, the
festive   *P1875:*Peace, vintager and festive   3115| MS:Hare-slice-and-peasoup season,
home-delights, §crossed out and replaced above by§ household-joy,   *P1875:*household-joy;
*1889a:*Hare-slice-and-peasoup-season, household joy: 3116| MS:§line added§
3117| MS:condescensions— §altered to§ condescendings—brief,   *P1875:*condescendings:
brief,   3118| MS:are to §last two words inserted above§ judge, and arbitrate, §last two
words and comma crossed out§ you urge §crossed out§ press   3119| MS:Such §over
illegible erasure§ argument the §crossed out and replaced above by§ as < > understand,—
*P1875:*understand: 3120| MS:Be it §last two words crossed out and replaced above by
two words§ If with < > care I §crossed out and replaced above by§ you?
3121| MS:Have §over illegible erasure§ < > misunderstood §over *misunderstand*§
3122| MS:then reply must be, such §last four words crossed out and replaced above by three
words§ I answer that argument,   *P1875:*then must answer be, such argument,

142

Such policy, no matter what good love
Or hate it help, in practice proves absurd,
3125 Useless and null: henceforward intercepts
Sober effective blow at what you blame,
And renders nugatory rightful praise
Of thing or person. The coarse brush has daubed—
What room for the fine limner's pencil-mark?
3130 Blame? You curse, rather, till who blames must blush—
Lean to apology or praise, more like!
Does garment, simpered o'er as white, prove grey?
"Black, blacker than Acharnian charcoal, black
Beyond Kimmerian, Stugian blackness black,"
3135 You bawl, till men sigh "nearer snowiness!"
What follows? What one faint-rewarding fall
Of foe belaboured ne'er so lustily?
Laugh Lamachos from out the people's heart?
He died, commanding, "hero," say yourself!
3140 Gibe Nikias into privacy?—nay, shake
Kleon a little from his arrogance
By cutting him to shoe-sole-shreds? I think,
He ruled his life long and, when time was ripe,
Died fighting for amusement,—good tough hide!

3123| MS:Such earnestness §crossed out and replaced above by§ policy, <> what the §crossed
out and replaced above by§ good   3124| MS:help,—your §crossed out and replaced
above by§ in practice makes §crossed out and replaced above by§ proves   *P1875:*help, in
3125| MS:henceforward— §dash crossed out§ intercepts   3128| MS:person: the   *P1875:*
person. The   3129| MS:the true limner's   *P1875:*the fine limner's
3130| MS:rather; §punctuation altered to comma§ till §inserted above§ who would §crossed
out§ blame, had blushed— §last three words altered to§ blames, shall blush—   *P1875:*blames
must blush—   3131| MS:Leans §altered to§ Lean   3132| MS:This §crossed out and
replaced above by§ Does garment, I §crossed out and replaced above by§ fools profess for
white, proves §altered to§ prove   *P1875:*garment, simpered o'er as white, prove
3134| MS:Beyond the §crossed out and replaced above by word and comma§ Kimmerian,
Stygian," and so, "black," black, black §last two words crossed out§   *P1875:*Beyond
Kimmerian, Stygian blackness black,"   *CP1875:*Beyond Kimmerian, Stugian
3135| MS:bawl till men smile §crossed out and replaced above by§ sigh "Nearer   *P1875:*bawl,
till <> "nearer   3136| MS:follows? No §crossed out and replaced above by§ What <>
faint-rewarding §*reward* over illegible erasure§   3139| MS:commanding,—"hero," say
*P1875:*commanding, "hero," say   3140| MS:privacy?—Nay   *P1875:*nay
3142| MS:By buffeting and battery? I   *P1875:*By cutting him to shoe-sole-shreds? I
3144| MS:amusement,—well done he!   *P1875:*amusement,—good tough hide!

143

3145   Sokrates still goes up and down the streets,
       And Aristullos puts his speech in book,
       When both should be abolished long ago.
       Nay, wretchedest of rags, Ariphrades—
       You have been fouling that redoubtable
3150   Harp-player, twenty years, with what effect?
       Still he strums on, strums ever cheerily,
       And earns his wage,—"Who minds a joke?" men say.
       No, friend!   The statues stand—mudstained at most—
       Titan or pygmy: what achieves their fall
3155   Will be, long after mud is flung and spent,
       Some clear thin spirit-thrust of lightning—truth!

       Your praise, then—honey-smearing helps your friend,
       More than blame's ordure-smirch hurts foe, perhaps?
       Peace, now, misunderstood, ne'er prized enough,
3160   You have interpreted to ignorance
       Till ignorance opes eye, bat-blind before,
       And for the first time knows Peace means the power
       On maw of pan-cake, cheese-cake, barley-cake,
       No stop nor stint to stuffing.   While, in camp,
3165   Who fights chews rancid tunny, onions raw,
       Peace sits at cosy feast with lamp and fire,
       Complaisant smooth-sleeked flute-girls giggling gay.

3145| MS:streets   *1889a:*streets,   3146| MS:puts §over partial erasure§
3149| MS:been pelting §inserted above§ that   *P1875:*been fouling that
3150| MS:—Harp-player—twenty years—with §last two dashes altered to commas§   *P1875:*
Harp-player   3152| MS:wage,—who minds mere jokes? men   *P1875:*minds a joke? men
*1889a:*wage,—"Who < > joke?" men   3155| MS:after dung §crossed out and replaced
above by§ mud is thrown §crossed out and replaced above by§ flung   3157| MS:then—
might not §last two words crossed out and replaced above by two illegibly crossed-out words§
honey-smearing help §altered to§ helps your §inserted above§   3158| MS:ordure-
smirching §altered to§ ordure-smirch < > foe, §word and comma inserted above§
3160| MS:Peace— §word and dash crossed out§ You §over *you*§ have §inserted above§
3161| MS:Until §altered to§ Till men §crossed out and replaced above by§ ignorance opened
§altered to§ opens eyes   *P1875:*opes eye   3163| MS:Of eating pan-cakes, cheesecakes,
barley cakes,   *P1875:*On maw of pan-cake, cheese-cake, barley-cake,   3164| MS:stuffing:
while in   *CP1875:*stuffing. While, in   3165| MS:fights, chews   *P1875:*fights chews
3166| MS:Presence §over two illegible words§ at < > lamp and §last two words inserted above§
fireside friends, §last word and *side* crossed out; comma retained§   *P1875:*Peace sits at
3167| MS:Complaisant dancing §crossed out and replaced above by§ smooth sleeked girls each

How thick and fast the snow falls, freezing War
Who shrugs, campaigns it, and may break a shin
3170 Or twist an ankle! come, who hesitates
To give Peace, over War, the preference?
Ah, friend—had this indubitable fact
Haply occurred to poor Leonidas,
How had he turned tail on Thermopulai!
3175 It cannot be that even his few wits
Were addled to the point that, so advised,
Preposterous he had answered—"Cakes are prime,
Hearth-sides are snug, sleek dancing-girls have worth,
And yet—for country's sake, to save our gods
3180 Their temples, save our ancestors their tombs,
Save wife and child and home and liberty,—
I would chew sliced-salt-fish, bear snow—nay, starve,
If need were,—and by much prefer the choice!"
Why, friend, your genuine hero, all the while,
3185 Has been—who served precisely for your butt—
Kleonumos that, wise, cast shield away
On battle-ground; cried "Cake my buckler be,
Embossed with cream-clot! peace, not war, I choose,

side of you, *P1875:*smooth-sleeked flute-girls giggling gay. ³¹⁶⁸| MS:While thick <>
falls, freezes §altered to§ freezing crest *P1875:*How thick <> freezing War
³¹⁶⁹| MS:Of who campaigning §altered to§ campaigns <> and §inserted above§ *P1875:*Who
shrugs, campaigns ³¹⁷⁰| MS:ancle: come, §inserted above over illegible word§ who will
§crossed out§ hesitate §altered to§ hesitates *P1875:*ankle! come ³¹⁷³| MS:Only
occurred *P1875:*Haply occurred ³¹⁷⁵| MS:even Spartan §crossed out and replaced
above by two words§ his few ³¹⁷⁷| MS:he had §last two words inserted above§ answer
§altered to§ answered had been— §last two words crossed out; dash retained§ "Cakes are well,
choice, §last two words crossed out and replaced above by one word§ sweet, *P1875:*are
prime, ³¹⁷⁸| MS:are warm and §last two words crossed out and replaced above by two
words§ snug, sleek dancing girls *P1875:*dancing-girls ³¹⁸⁰| MS:temples, and §crossed
out and replaced above by§ save <> their graves, §word and comma crossed out§ tombs,
³¹⁸¹| MS:Save §in margin§ And §crossed out§ wifes §altered to§ wife <> children— §last
three letters and dash crossed out and replaced above by§ and ³¹⁸²| MS:I §in margin§
One §crossed out§ would chew tunny and §last two words crossed out and replaced above by
one word§ sliced-salt-fish, <> nay, die, *P1875:*nay, starve, ³¹⁸³| MS:needs be §crossed
out and replaced above by§ were,—any, §word and comma crossed out§ and by §inserted
above§ <> prefer ones §crossed out and replaced above by§ the *P1875:*need
³¹⁸⁶| MS:that §over illegible erasure§ ³¹⁸⁷| MS:battle-field §*field* crossed out and
replaced below by§ ground; cried "cheesecake—buckler *P1875:*cried "Cake my buckler

Holding with Dikaiopolis!"   Comedy
3190 Shall triumph, Dikaiopolis win assent,
When Miltiades shall next shirk Marathon,
Themistokles swap Salamis for—cake,
And Kimon grunt "Peace, grant me dancing-girls!"
But sooner, hardly! twenty-five years since,
3195 The war began,—such pleas for Peace have reached
A reasonable age.   The end shows all.

And so with all the rest you advocate!
"Wise folk leave litigation! 'ware the wasps!
Whoso loves law and lawyers, heliast-like,
3200 Wants hemlock!"   None shows that so funnily.
But, once cure madness, how comports himself
Your sane exemplar, what's our gain thereby?
Philokleon turns Bdelukleon! just this change,—
New sanity gets straightway drunk as sow,
3205 Cheats baker-wives, brawls, kicks, cuffs, curses folk,
Parades a shameless flute-girl, bandies filth

---

^{3189|} MS:Holding with §last two words in margin§ With any §last two words crossed out§
Dikaiarchos!" Shame on you! §last three words and punctuation crossed out§ Comedy
*P1875:*with Dikaiopolis   ^{3190|} MS:Bask better, when you win him by your words §last
three words crossed out and replaced above by two words§ to assent, §entire line crossed out
and replaced above by§ Shall triumph, should §crossed out§ Dikaiarchos win assent,   *P1875:*
triumph, Dikaipolis   ^{3191|} MS:When next Themistokles who votes for cake! §last five
words crossed out and replaced above by three words§ Miltiades shirks Marathon,   *1889a:*
When Miltiades shall next shirk   ^{3192|} MS:§line added§ swaps   *1889a:*swap
^{3193|} MS:And shouts for cau with cake and §last three words crossed out and replaced below
by three words§ and smooth sleeked dancing-girls!   *P1875:*And Kimon grunts "Peace, grant
me, dancing-girls!"   *CP1875:*me dancing-girls!" §not B§   *1889a:*grunt   ^{3194|} MS:But let
them §last two words inserted above§ make haste: twenty-five full §crossed out§ years ago
§crossed out§ since,   *P1875:*But sooner, hardly! twenty-five   ^{3195|} MS:The War
began,—your plea <> has   *1885:*war began,—such pleas <> have   ^{3196|} MS:Much the
saner §last three words crossed out and replaced above by two words§ A reasonable age.
§period inserted§ with which the victory? §last four words crossed out§ The end shows all!
*1889a:*all.   ^{3197|} MS:Why proceed? So with all you   *1885:*And so with all the rest you
^{3198|} MS:"Let men leave litigation! Ware <> Wasps!   *P1875:*"Wise folk <> ware <> wasps!
1889a:'ware   ^{3199|} MS:Who loves the law   *1889a:*Whoso loves law   ^{3200|} MS:Is mad"!
None makes that clear so   *P1875:*Wants hemlock!" None shows that so   ^{3203|} MS:§line
added§ turned Bdelukleon—just <> change   *P1875:*turns Bdelukleon! just <> change,
*CP1875:*change,—   ^{3204|} MS:Oh, §word and comma altered to§ That sanity   *P1875:*New
sanity   ^{3205|} MS:kicks, and §crossed out and replaced above by word and comma§ cuffs

With his own son who cured his father's cold
By making him catch fever—funnily!
But as for curing love of lawsuits—faugh!

³²¹⁰ And how does new improve upon the old
   —Your boast—in even abusing?   Rough, may be—
Still, honest was the old mode.   "Call thief—thief!"
But never call thief even—murderer!
Much less call fop and fribble, worse one whit
³²¹⁵ Than fribble and fop!   Spare neither! beat your brains
For adequate invective,—cut the life
Clean out each quality,—but load your lash
With no least lie, or we pluck scourge from hand!
Does poet want a whipping, write bad verse,
³²²⁰ Inculcate foul deeds?   There's the fault to flog!
You vow "The rascal cannot read nor write,
Spends more in buying fish than Morsimos,
Somebody helps his Muse and courts his wife,
His uncle deals in crockery, and last,—

---

³²⁰⁶| MS:shameless §inserted above§   ³²⁰⁹| MS:But §in margin§ As §altered to§ as <>
lawsuits *P1875:*law-suits   ³²¹¹| MS:in mere §crossed out and replaced above by§ fit
abusing?—rough *P1875:*in even abusing? Rough   ³²¹²| MS:Still §over partially illegible
word§ <> old way. "Call *P1875:*old mode. "Call   ³²¹³| MS:But §in margin§ Never
call—even thief— §last two words transposed§ a §crossed out§ murderer! *P1875:*never
*1889a:*call thief   ³²¹⁴| MS:call fopling, §last four letters and comma crossed out and
replaced above by one word§ and prater, worse *P1875:*and fribble, worse
³²¹⁵| MS:Than foppish §crossed out and replaced by§ fribble and loquacious: beat
*P1875:*Than fribble and fop! Spare neither! beat   ³²¹⁸| MS:With not one lie—lest we
pluck whip §crossed out and replaced above by§ scourge *P1875:*With no least lie, or we
³²¹⁹| MS:Does §over illegible word§ poet wants §altered to§ want <> whipping— §dash
altered to comma§ writes §altered to§ write   ³²²⁰| MS:Inculcating §altered to§ Inculcate
worse §crossed out and replaced above by§ foul morals— §word and dash crossed out and
replaced below by three words§ deeds? There's a fault *P1875:*deeds? There's the fault
³²²¹| MS:Begin! §word and punctuation crossed out and replaced above by two words and
punctuation§ And how? "The fellow could §last two words crossed out and replaced above by
two words§ rascal can *P1875:*You vow "The <> cannot   ³²²²| MS:§line added§ Spends
much §crossed out and replaced above by§ more   ³²²³| MS:helps him— §word and dash
crossed out and replaced below by three words§ his muse §altered to§ Muse and <> wife, the
while: §last two words and punctuation crossed out§   ³²²⁴| MS:deals §over *deal*§ in
anchovies—and worst, §last three words crossed out and replaced above by crossed-out word,
earthen, and two words and punctuation§ crockery, and,—last,— *P1875:*and last,—

3225 Himself's a stranger!"   That's the cap and crown
Of stinging-nettle, that's the master-stroke!
What poet-rival,—after "housebreaker,"
"Fish-gorging," "midnight footpad" and so forth,—
Proves not, beside, "a stranger"?   Chased from charge
3230 To charge, and, lie by lie, laughed out of court,—
Lo, wit's sure refuge, satire's grand resource—
All, from Kratinos downward—"strangers" they!
Pity the trick's too facile!   None so raw
Among your playmates but have caught the ball
3235 And sent it back as briskly to—yourself!
You too, my Attic, are styled "stranger"—Rhodes,
Aigina, Lindos or Kameiros,—nay,
'Twas Egypt reared, if Eupolis be right,
Who wrote the comedy (Kratinos vows)
3240 Kratinos helped a little!   Kleon's self

3225| MS:The man's §last two words crossed out and replaced above by one word; possession retained§ Himself's <> stranger!" That's §over *that's*§   3226| MS:Of satire, §last two words and comma inserted above§ That §altered to§ that's falls to pat hand and never fails; §last seven words and punctuation crossed out§ the witty §inserted above§ master-stroke! *P1875:*Of stinging-nettle, that's the master-stroke!   3227| MS:What §over partially illegible word§ of your §last two words crossed out and replaced above by word and hyphen, forming§ poet-rivals,— §altered to§ poet-rival,—besides §crossed out and replaced above by§ after "infamous," *P1875:*after "housebreaker,"   3228| MS:"Fish-eating," and a §last two words crossed out and replaced above by one word and hyphen, forming§ "midnight-footpad," and *P1875:*"Fish-gorging," "midnight footpad" and   3229| MS:Proves §over *Proved*§ not, to be §last two words crossed out and replaced above by one word and comma§ besides, <> stranger"? free of other §last three words crossed out and replaced above by two words§ Chased §over *chased*§ from *P1875:*beside   3230| MS:§line added§   3231| MS:Lo, §word and comma in margin§ That's §crossed out§ wit's   3232| MS:Kratinos downwards are §crossed out§ "strangers" every one! *P1875:*All, from Kratinos downward—"strangers" they!   3233| MS:tricks so §last two words altered to§ trick's too facile. §period altered to exclamation point§ None §over *none*§ so poor §crossed out§ raw   3234| MS:your rivals §crossed out and replaced above by crossed-out word, *fellows,* and then replaced below by§ playmates but could §crossed out and replaced above by§ has §over *have*§ catch §altered to§caught *P1875:*but have caught   3235| MS:And sent §over *send*§
3236| MS:are the §crossed out and replaced above by§ styled   3237| MS:Aegypt, §crossed out§ Aigina <> Kameiros,—bore §crossed out§ nay,   3238| MS:Twas Egypt §last two words in margin§ The blame of §last three words crossed out§ rearing §altered to§ reared (if Eupolis declares §crossed out and replaced above by two words§ be right) *P1875:*'Twas <> reared if *1889a:*reared, if <> right,   3239| MS:The man §last two words crossed out§ Who §over *who*§ <> the plays §crossed out and replaced above by§ comedy
3240| MS:helped no §crossed out and replaced above by§ a

Was nigh promoted Comic, when he haled
My poet into court, and o'er the coals
Hauled and re-hauled "the stranger,—insolent,
Who brought out plays, usurped our privilege!"
3245 Why must you Comics one and all take stand
On lower ground than truth from first to last?
Why all agree to let folk disbelieve,
So laughter but reward a funny lie?
Repel such onslaughts—answer, sad and grave,
3250 Your fancy-fleerings—who would stoop so low?
Your own adherents whisper,—when disgust
Too menacingly thrills Logeion through
At—Perikles invents this present war
Because men robbed his mistress of three maids—
3255 Or—Sokrates wants burning, house o'er head,—
"What, so obtuse, not read between the lines?
Our poet means no mischief! All should know—
Ribaldry here implies a compliment!

---

^{3241|} MS:Was he §crossed out and replaced above by§ nigh   ^{3242|} MS:My §over *The*§
^{3244|} MS:Who §over *To*§ bring §crossed out and replaced above by§ brought <> plays, the
native's §last two words crossed out and replaced above by two words§ usurped our
^{3246|} MS:last?— *P1875:*last?   ^{3247|} MS:Why §in margin over illegible erasure§ All
§altered to§ all agree never §crossed out§ to expect §crossed out and replaced above by two
words§ let folks believe §altered to§ disbelieve— *P1875:*disbelieve, *1889a:*folk
^{3248|} MS:So but frank §last two words crossed out§ laugh §altered to§ laughter but §inserted
above§ reward your §over illegible word; then crossed out and replaced above by dash and
word§ —a *P1875:*reward a   ^{3249|} MS:Repel such §crossed out and replaced above by§
your onslaughts? answer *P1875:*Repel such onslaughts—answer   ^{3250|} MS:Your §in
margin§ Such §crossed out§ fancy-fleerings? None e'er §last two words crossed out and
replaced above by two words§ Who would stooped §altered to§ stoop *P1875:*fancy-
fleerings—who   ^{3251|} MS:Nay, §crossed out§ Your §over *your*§ own §inserted above§ <>
whispered §altered to§ whisper—should disgust *P1875:*whisper,—when disgust
^{3252|} MS:Shrill through the theatre, too like §inserted above§ menace, like— §entire line
crossed out and replaced in margin by§ Too menacingly thrill Logeion through, *P1875:*
thrills <> through   ^{3253|} When "Perikles <> this §over *the*§ Spartan §crossed out and
replaced below by§ present *P1875:*At Pericles <> war— *CP1875:*At—Perikles <> war §not
B§   ^{3254|} MS:Because they §crossed out and replaced above by§ men rob §altered to§
robbed <> maids"— *P1875:*maids—   ^{3255|} MS:§line added in margin§ Or "Sokrates
<> head"— *P1875:*Or Sokrates <> head,— *CP1875:*Or—Sokrates §not B§
^{3256|} MS:obtuse, §comma altered to question mark§ Not §over *not*§ <> lines," §comma
altered to question mark§ *P1875:*obtuse, not <> lines?   ^{3257|} MS:§line added§
(Whisper your own adherents.) All *P1875:*Our poet means no mischief! "All *CP1875:*
mischief! All §not B§   ^{3258|} MS:Here §crossed out§ Ribaldry §over *ribaldry*§ here
§inserted above§ <> compliment? §question mark altered to exclamation point§

He deals with things, not men,—his men are things—
3260 Each represents a class, plays figure-head
And names the ship: no meaner than the first
Would serve; he styles a trireme 'Sokrates'—
Fears 'Sokrates' may prove unseaworthy
(That's merely—'Sophists are the bane of boys')
3265 Rat-riddled ('they are capable of theft'),
Rotten or whatsoe'er shows ship-disease,
('They war with gods and worship whirligig').
You never took the joke for earnest? scarce
Supposed mere figure-head meant entire ship,
3270 And Sokrates—the whole fraternity?"

This then is Comedy, our sacred song,
Censor of vice, and virtue's guard as sure:
Manners-instructing, morals' stop-estray,
Which, born a twin with public liberty,
3275 Thrives with its welfare, dwindles with its wane!
Liberty? what so exquisitely framed
And fitted to suck dry its life of life
To last faint fibre?—since that life is truth.
You who profess your indignation swells
3280 At sophistry, when specious words confuse

3259| MS:He §over illegible word§ <> men,—our §crossed out and replaced above by§ his
3262| MS:serve: so, §word and comma crossed out and replaced above by§ he style §altered to§
styles our §crossed out and replaced above by§ a trireme, §comma crossed out§ *P1875:*serve;
he   3263| MS:Fears §in margin§ <> may well §crossed out§ prove unseaworthy, *1889a:*
unseaworthy   3264| MS:(Translate—'His teaching is the *P1875:*(That's merely—
'Sophists are the   3265| MS:Rat-riddled ('He is capable <> theft') *P1875:*Rat-riddled
('they are capable *1889a:*theft'),   3266| MS:Rotten from §crossed out§ <> whatsoe'er
proves §crossed out and replaced above by§ shows ship-disease *P1875:*ship-disease,
3267| MS:('He worships Whirligig' and wars with gods,) §line marked for transposition to§
('He wars with gods and worships Whirligig.' *P1875:*('They war <> worship whirligig.')
*1889a:*whirligig').   3268-71| MS:You <> the §over illegible word§ <> earnest, sure?" /
This <> is Comedy, the §crossed out and replaced above by§ our *P1875:*earnest? scarce /
Supposed <> ship, / And <> fraternity?" / "This *1889a:*This   3272| MS:sure,
*P1875:*sure: 3273| MS:moral *P1875:*morals'   3276| MS:Ask §in margin§ Say
§crossed out§ rather—what <> framed, *P1875:*Liberty," what <> framed *CP1875:*Liberty?
what   3277| MS:So §in margin§ And §crossed out§ fitted   3278| MS:fibre?—for
§crossed out and replaced above by§ since <> is—truth! *P1875:*is truth! *1889a:*truth.
3279| MS:profess just §crossed out and replaced above by§ your

Deeds right and wrong, distinct before, you say—
(Though all that's done is—dare veracity,
Show that the true conception of each deed
Affirmed, in vulgar parlance, "wrong" or "right,"
3285   Proves to be neither, as the hasty hold,
But, change your side, shoots light, where dark alone
Was apprehended by the vulgar sense)
You who put sophistry to shame, and shout
"There's but a single side to man and thing;
3290   A side so much more big than thing or man
Possibly can be, that—believe 'tis true?
Such were too marvellous simplicity!"—
Confess, those sophists whom yourself depict,
(—Abide by your own painting!) what they teach,
3295   They wish at least their pupil to believe,
And, what believe, to practise! Did *you* wish

---

³²⁸¹| MS:(You cry §crossed out and replaced below by§ say, distinct before, deeds §altered to§ Deeds right and wrong— §line marked for transposition to§ Deeds right and wrong, distinct before, you say—   ³²⁸²| MS:Though all that §altered to§ that's <> veracity—   *P1875:* (Though <> veracity,   ³²⁸³| MS:Demonstrate §in margin and crossed out§ And show §last two words crossed out; *show* restored and altered to§ Show that §inserted above§ <> true §crossed out and restored§ <> of a §crossed out and replaced above by§ each
³²⁸⁴| MS:Affirmed, §word and comma in margin§ Called §crossed out§ in the §crossed out§ vulgar   ³²⁸⁵| MS:Proves §in margin§ Is not so certain §last four words crossed out and replaced above by one word and comma§ neither <> hasty §inserted above§ vulgar hold, *P1875:*Proves to be neither <> hasty hold,   ³²⁸⁶| MS:But §in margin§ May have §last two words crossed out and replaced above by one word§ shows two sides, shoot §altered to§ shoots light, show §crossed out and replaced above by§ where dark beside §crossed out§ alone *P1875:*But, change your side   ³²⁸⁷| MS:Sight §crossed out and replaced above by§ Was <> sense. *P1875:*sense)   ³²⁸⁸| MS:With §over illegible word§ you—profession, practice—all's one shout *P1875:*You who put sophistry to shame, and shout   ³²⁸⁹| MS:but one §crossed out and replaced above by crossed-out word, *only*, and then replaced above by two words§ a single <> and §inserted above§ thing, principle, §word and comma crossed out§ *P1875:*thing;   ³²⁹⁰| MS:And that's so *P1875:*A side so   ³²⁹¹| MS:*believe P1875:* believe   ³²⁹²| MS:Such §in margin§ That §crossed out§ were <> simplicity!" *P1875:* simplicity!"—   ³²⁹³| MS:Why §crossed out and replaced above by§ While those same sophists, most §over *those*§ yourself depict,— *P1875:*Confess, those sophists, whom yourself depict,   ³²⁹⁴| MS:—Abide <> painting!—what <> teach *P1875:*(—Abide <> painting!) what <> teach,   ³²⁹⁵| MS:They wished §altered to§ wish <> least their §altered to§ the pupil *P1875:*least their pupil   ³²⁹⁶| MS:§line added in margin§ And, what he believes §last three words altered to two words§ what's believed <> practice; §over illegible word§ did *P1875:*what's believed <> practise! did *CP1875:*what believe *1889a:*practise! Did

151

Hellas should haste, as taught, with torch in hand,
And fire the horrid Speculation-shop?
Straight the shop's master rose and showed the mob
3300   What man was your so monstrous Sokrates;
Himself received amusement, why not they?
Just as did Kleon first play magistrate
And bid you put your birth in evidence—
Since no unbadged buffoon is licensed here
3305   To shame us all when foreign guests may mock—
Then,—birth established, fooling licensed you,—
He, duty done, resumed mere auditor,
Laughed with the loudest at his Lamia-shape,
Kukloboros-roaring, and the camel-rest.
3310   Nay, Aristullos,—once your volley spent
On the male-Kirké and her swinish crew,—
PLATON,—So others call the youth we love,—
Sends your performance to the curious king—

3297| MS:Did you wish §last three words crossed out§ Hellas to §crossed out and replaced
below by§ should go, as taught, with §last three words inserted below§   *P1875:*should haste,
as   3298| MS:horrid 'Speculation-shop?'   *P1875:*horrid Speculation-shop?
3299| MS:Well might §last two words crossed out and replaced above by two crossed-out words
and comma, *Small need,* and then replaced by two words§ Why, straight its master rose §over
illegible erasure§ and show §altered to§ showed   *P1875:*Straight the shop's master
3300-02| MS:What <> was that §crossed out and replaced above by crossed-out word, *your,* and
then restored§ so <> Sokrates—/ Just as §last two words crossed out and replaced above by
two illegibly crossed-out words and then restored§ poor §crossed out and replaced above by§
did Kleon u §last letter crossed out§ first played §altered to§ play   *P1875:*was your so <>
Sokrates; / Himself <> they? / Just   3303| MS:And bid §over partial erasure, perhaps
bade§   3304| MS:buffoon has §crossed out and replaced above by§ is license §altered to§
licensed   3305| MS:To play the fool when <> guests will §crossed out and replaced
above by§ may see—   *P1875:*To shame us all when <> may mock—   3306| MS:Then,
§word and comma in margin§ And §crossed out§ that §crossed out and replaced above by dash
and word§ —birth   3307| MS:He, soon enough §last two words crossed out and replaced
above by two words and comma§ duty done, resumed the §crossed out and replaced above by§
mere auditor   *P1875:*auditor,   3308| MS:at the §crossed out and replaced above by§
your Lamia's filth   *P1875:*at his Lamia-shape,   3309| MS:The §crossed out§ Kukloboro's
roaring <> the §illegibly crossed-out word inserted above and replaced by§ pleasant rest!
*P1875:*Kukloboros-roaring <> the camel-rest.   3310| MS:Nay, Aristullos,—all §crossed
out and replaced above by§ once   3311| MS:the male- §last two words and hyphen inserted
above§ <> and her §altered to§ his swinish   *P1875:*and her swinish   3312| Platon,—we
§crossed out and replaced above by§ so <> the youth §last two words over illegible erasures§
we know §crossed out and replaced above by§ love—   *P1875:*PLATON <> love,—
3313| MS:to his friend §last two words crossed out§ the curious §inserted above§ King—

"Do you desire to know Athenai's knack
 At turning seriousness to pleasantry?
Read this!   One Aristullos means myself.
The author is indeed a merry grig!"
Nay, it would seem as if yourself were bent
On laying down the law "Tell lies I must—
Aforethought and of purpose, no mistake!"
When forth yourself step, tell us from the stage
"Here you behold the King of Comedy—
Me, who, the first, have purged my every piece
From each and all my predecessors' filth,
Abjured those satyr-adjuncts sewn to bid
The boys laugh, satyr-jokes whereof not one
Least sample but would make my hair turn grey
Beyond a twelvemonth's ravage!   I renounce
Mountebank-claptrap, such as firework-fizz
And torchflare, or else nuts and barleycorns
Scattered among the crowd, to scramble for
And stop their mouths with; no such stuff shames me!
Who,—what's more serious,—know both when to strike
And when to stay my hand: once dead, my foe,
Why, done, my fighting!   *I* attack a corpse?

---

*P1875:*king—   3314| MS:to taste Athenai's strength   *P1875:*to know Athenai's knack
3315| MS:At §in margin§ Of §crossed out§ turning   3316| MS:this! §next word illegibly crossed out, perhaps *The,* and replaced above by§ One Aristullos is myself §last two words crossed out and replaced above by illegibly crossed-out word §next two words illegibly erased and *is myself* restored§   *P1875:*this! One Aristullos means myself.   3317| MS:a funny §crossed out and replaced above by§ merry dog!"   *P1875:*a merry grig!"
3318| MS:Nay, it would seem as if yourself were §last seven words crossed out and replaced above by three illegibly crossed-out words, perhaps *Aristophanes was surely;* then original reading restored§   3319| MS:On §next word illegibly crossed out§ laying the §inserted above§ law down— §word marked for transposition to precede *the*§ "Tell §quotation mark and word inserted above§ lies we §crossed out and replaced above by§ I   3321| MS:yourself §*your* crossed out and restored§ step, tell §last two words altered to§ stepped, told <> stage—   *P1875:*step, tell <> stage   3322| MS:of Comedy."   *P1875:*of Comedy—
3324| MS:filth—   *P1875:*filth,   3325| MS:Abjured, from §crossed out and replaced above by§ those   *P1875:*Abjured those   3328| MS:ravage, §comma altered to exclamation point§ down to mere §last three words crossed out§ quite renounced   *P1875:*ravage! I renounce   3329| MS:—Mountebank claptrap <> firework fizz   *P1875:*Mountebank-claptrap <> firework-fizz   3332| MS:with! no   *P1875:*with; no   3333| MS:Who §over illegible erasure§ <> serious,—I §crossed out§ know both §inserted above§

I spare the corpse-like even! punish age?
I pity from my soul that sad effete
Toothless old mumbler called Kratinos! once
My rival,—now, alack, the dotard slinks
3340　Ragged and hungry to what hole's his home;
Ay, slinks thro' byways where no passenger
Flings him a bone to pick.　You formerly
Adored the Muses' darling: dotard now,
Why, he may starve!　O mob most mutable!"
3345　So you harangued in person; while,—to point
Precisely out, these were but lies you launched,—
Prompt, a play followed primed with satyr-frisks,
No spice spared of the stomach-turning stew,
Full-fraught with torch-display, and barley-throw,
3350　And Kleon, dead enough, bedaubed afresh;
While daft Kratinos—home to hole trudged he,
Wrung dry his wit to the last vinous dregs,
Decanted them to "Bottle,"—beat, next year,—
"Bottle" and dregs—your best of "Clouds" and dew!
3355　Where, Comic King, may keenest eye detect

3336| MS:No, §word and comma in margin§ I §altered to *No* and crossed out§ spare < >
corpse-like; even,— §punctuation altered to exclamation point§ punish him §crossed out and
replaced above by§ age?　*P1875:*I spare < > corpse-like even　　　3337| MS:Nay,— §word
and punctuation crossed out and replaced above by§ I　　　3338| MS:called Kratinos, §over
partial erasure§ once　*P1875:*called Kratinos! once　　　3340| MS:home—　*P1875:*home;
3341| MS:thro' streets §crossed out and replaced above by§ byways where not a §last two words
altered to§ no　　　3342| MS:bone to pick,—who formerly　*P1875:*bone, to pick. You formerly
*1889a:*bone to　　　3343| MS:darling! §punctuation altered to colon§ dotard　　　3344| MS:mob
most §last two words inserted above§　　　3345| MS:person—just §crossed out and replaced
above by word and comma§ sure, to　*P1875:*person; while,—to　　　3346| MS:Precisely to
§crossed out and replaced above by word and comma§ out, the §altered to§ these were but
§last two words inserted above§ lies, you meant to §last two words crossed out§ launched,
*P1875:*lies you launched,—　　　3347| MS:When the §crossed out and replaced above by§ a
*P1875:*Prompt, a　　　3349| MS:Full fraught < > torch flame §crossed out and replaced above
by§ display　*P1875:*Full-fraught < > torch-display　　　3350| MS:enough, denounced again:
*P1875:*enough, bedaubed afresh;　　　3351| MS:While sad §crossed out and replaced above
by§ daft < > trudged §inserted above over illegible erasure§　　　3352| MS:Gathers §altered
to§ Gathered together his last dregs of wit,　*P1875:*Wrung dry his wit to the last vinous dregs,
3353| MS:them into §*in* crossed out§ < > beats §altered to§ beat　　　3354| MS:"Bottle" in
hand §last two words crossed out and replaced above by two words and dash§ and dregs
3355| MS:Where in all this may < > eye discern　*P1875:*Where, Comic King, may < > eye detect

Improvement on your predecessors' work
Except in lying more audaciously?

Why—genius!   That's the grandeur, that's the gold—
That's *you*—superlatively true to touch—
3360   Gold, leaf or lump—gold, anyhow the mass
Takes manufacture and proves Pallas' casque
Or, at your choice, simply a cask to keep
Corruption from decay.   Your rivals' hoard
May ooze forth, lacking such preservative:
3365   Yours cannot—gold plays guardian far too well!
Genius, I call *you: dross, your rivals share;
Ay, share and share alike, too! says the world,
However you pretend supremacy
In aught beside that gold, your very own.
3370   Satire?   "Kratinos for our satirist!"
The world cries.   Elegance?   "Who elegant
As Eupolis?" resounds as noisily.
Artistic fancy?   Choros-creatures quaint?
Magnes invented "Birds" and "Frogs" enough,

---

³³⁵⁶| MS:on gross predecessors'   *P1875:*on your predecessors'   ³³⁵⁷| MS:Except—the §altered to§ their lying with §crossed out and replaced above by§ and audacity?   *P1875:*Except in lying with audacity?   *1889a:* lying more audaciously?   ³³⁵⁸| MS:But—genius? That's the glory §crossed out and replaced above by§ splendor, that's   *P1875:*Why—genius! That's the grandeur, that's   ³³⁶⁰| MS:anyhow the §altered to§ that mass   *P1875:*anyhow the mass   ³³⁶¹| MS:Turn manufacture plates for §last two words crossed out and replaced above by two words and dash§ and prove—Pallas' mail §crossed out§ casque   *P1875:*Take manufacture <> prove Pallas'   *1889a:*Takes <> proves   ³³⁶²| MS:choice has fashioned, §last two words crossed out and replaced above by one word, fell, altered to§ falls, cofferings §crossed out and replaced above by§ simply casks §altered to§ cask   *1889a:*Or, at your choice, simply a cask   ³³⁶³| MS:rivals' filth   *P1875:*rivals' hoard   ³³⁶⁴| MS:May §in margin§ Will perish, §last two words crossed out; *perish* restored§ lacking <> preservative—   1865:May ooze forth, lacking <> preservative: ³³⁶⁶| MS:Gold—I <> *you*: the rest §crossed out and replaced above by word and comma§ dross <> share: *P1875:*Genius, I <> *you*: dross <> share;   ³³⁶⁷| MS:alike, so says   *P1875:*alike, too! says   ³³⁶⁹| MS:In all beside that §over illegible word§ gold—your <> own!   *P1875:*In aught beside <> gold, your <> own.   ³³⁷⁰| MS:for a §crossed out and replaced above by§ our   ³³⁷²| MS:As Eupolis,"— §comma altered to question mark§ resounds on every side §last three words crossed out and replaced above by two words§ as noisily.   *P1875:*As Eupolis?" resounds   ³³⁷³| MS:*Artistic* fancy? §last two words and punctuation in margin§ Invention? §word and punctuation crossed out§ Choros-creatures quaint? §over partial erasure§   ³³⁷⁴| MS:§line added§

³³⁷⁵ Archippos punned, Hegemon parodied,
To heart's content, before you stepped on stage.
Moral invective?   Eupolis exposed
"That prating beggar, he who stole the cup,"
Before your "Clouds" rained grime on Sokrates;
³³⁸⁰ Nay, what beat "Clouds" but "Konnos," muck for mud?
Courage?   How long before, well-masked, you poured
Abuse on Eukrates and Lusikles,
Did Telekleides and Hermippos pelt
Their Perikles and Kumon? standing forth,
³³⁸⁵ Bareheaded, not safe crouched behind a name,—
Philonides or else Kallistratos,
Put forth, when danger threatened,—mask for face,
To bear the brunt,—if blame fell, take the blame,—
If praise . . . why, frank laughed Aristophanes
³³⁹⁰ "They write such rare stuff?   No, I promise you!"
Rather, I see all true improvements, made
Or making, go against you—tooth and nail

---

^{3375-80|}   MS:§six lines added in margin; followed by three illegibly crossed-out lines§
^{3375|}   MS:was before you with his §last five words crossed out and replaced by new line in
margin§   ^{3377|}   MS:*Moral* Invective §over partial erasure§   *P1875:*Moral invective
^{3378|}   MS:beggar, Sokrates §crossed out§ he §over illegible word§ <> cup"—   *P1875:*cup,"
^{3379|}   MS:your "Clouds" §next four words illegibly crossed out and replaced above by one
illegibly crossed-out word§ rained grime §inserted above§   *P1875:*your 'Clouds' rained
*1889a:*your "Clouds" rained   ^{3380|}   MS:Nay, what §last two words in margin§ That
§crossed out§ beat §next five words illegibly crossed out and replaced above by three words§
"Clouds" but "Konnos" muck   *P1875:*but "Konnos," muck   ^{3381|}   MS:before you poured
abuse   *P1875:*before, well-masked, you poured   ^{3382|}   MS:On Kleon and Huperbolos
§last three words crossed out and replaced above by four words§ Eukrates and Lusikles, well-
masked,   *P1875:*Abuse on Eukrates and Lusikles,   ^{3383|}   MS:and §inserted above§
Hermippos §next word illegibly crossed out§ pelt   ^{3384|}   MS:Their §in margin§ Pelt
§crossed out§ Perikles   ^{3385|}   MS:Bare-headed, boldly,—not behind <> name,   *P1875:*
Bare-headed, not safe crouched behind <> name,—   *1889a:*Bareheaded
^{3386|}   MS:Not Philonikles nor Kallistratos,   *P1875:*Philonides nor else Kallistratos,   *CP1875:*
or §not B§   ^{3387|}   MS:§line added§ threatened, then §crossed out and replaced above
by§ mask §over illegible word§ for you— §word and dash crossed out§ face,   *P1875:*
threatened,—mask   ^{3389|}   MS:praise,—then forth stood §last three words crossed out
and replaced above by three words§ why, frank laughed Aristophanes—   *P1875:*praise...why
<> Aristophanes   ^{3390|}   MS:such verses §crossed out and replaced above by two words§
rare stuff   ^{3390-91|}   MS:§¶ called for§   *P1875:*no ¶§   ^{3391|}   MS:see the §crossed out
and replaced above by§ all <> improvements made   *P1875:*improvements, made
^{3392|}   MS:making are against   *P1875:*making, go against

Contended with; 'tis still Moruchides,
'Tis Euthumenes, Surakosios, nay,
3395 Argurrhios and Kinesias,—common sense
And public shame, these only cleanse your stye!
Coerced, prohibited,—you grin and bear,
And, soon as may be, hug to heart again
The banished nastiness too dear to drop!
3400 Krates could teach and practise festive song
Yet scorn scurrility; as gay and good,
Pherekrates could follow.   *Who* loosed hold,
Must let fall rose-wreath, stoop to muck once more?
Did your particular self advance in aught,
3405 Task the sad genius—steady slave the while—
To further—say, the patriotic aim?
No, there's deterioration manifest
Year by year, play by play! survey them all,
From that boy's-triumph when "Acharnes" dawned,
3410 To "Thesmophoriazousai,"—this man's shame!
There, truly, patriot zeal so prominent
Allowed friends' plea perhaps: the baser stuff
Was but the nobler spirit's vehicle.

3393| MS:with Argurrhios, Moruchos, §last two words crossed out§ 'tis Moruchides still,
P1875:with; 'tis still Moruchides,   3394| MS:§line added§ 'Tis Euthumenes, Surakosios,
still §crossed out§ nay—   *P1875*:nay,   3396| MS:shame, that §over partial erasure§ only
cleansed §altered to§ cleanse < > stye.   *P1875*:shame, these only < > stye!
3397| MS:Coerced, prohibited; §last two words altered to *Coerce, prohibit* and then original
reading restored§ you but §inserted above and crossed out§ grinned §altered to§ grin < >
bear, §over illegible word§   *P1875*:prohibited,—you   3398| MS:as might §crossed out
and replaced above by§ may be, hugged §altered to§ hug   3399 404| MS.The < > drop! /
Did §crossed out and replaced above by§ Has your < > self improve §crossed out and replaced
above by§ advanced   *P1875*:/ < > practice < > / / / Did your < > advance   *1889a*:/ < >
practise < > / / / /   3405| MS:Save §crossed out and replaced above by§ Tasked < >
while!—   *P1875*:Task < > while—   3406| MS:But in the boasted §last four words crossed
out and replaced above by four words§ To further—say, the   3407| MS:Steady §crossed
out and replaced above by two words§ Why, there's   *P1875*:No, there's
3408| MS:§line added in margin§ play by play, §comma altered to exclamation point§ to this
man's-shame §last four words crossed out and replaced above by three words§ survey them all,
3408-09| MS:§between these two lines§ This Thesmophoriazousai of to-day, §*day* crossed out
and replaced above by§ night §entire line crossed out§   3410| MS:§line added§ To
"Thesmophoriazousai"—this   *P1875*:To "Thesmophoriazousai,"—this
3412| MS:Allowed the §crossed out and replaced above by§ friends'
3413| MS:Was §over illegible erasure§ < > vehicle: *P1875*:vehicle.

Who would imprison, unvolatilize
3415 A violet's perfume, blends with fatty oils
Essence too fugitive in flower alone;
So, calling unguent—violet, call the play—
Obscenity impregnated with "Peace"!
But here's the boy grown bald, and here's the play
3420 With twenty years' experience: where's one spice
Of odour in the hog's-lard? what pretends
To aught except a grease-pot's quality?
Friend, sophist-hating! know,—worst sophistry
Is when man's own soul plays its own self false,
3425 Reasons a vice into a virtue, pleads
"I detail sin to shame its author"—not
"I shame Ariphrades for sin's display"!
"I show Opora to commend Sweet Home"—
Not "I show Bacchis for the striplings' sake!"

3430 Yet all the same—O genius and O gold—
Had genius ne'er diverted gold from use
Worthy the temple, to do copper's work
And coat a swine's trough—which abundantly

3415| MS:A §in margin§ The §crossed out§ violet's   3416| MS:The §crossed out§ Essence,
§over *essence*§ were too §last two words inserted above; *were* crossed out§ < > in flowers
§altered to§ flower alone: *P1875:*Essence too < > alone;   3417| MS:So, call the unguent
*P1875:*So, calling unguent   3418| MS:with—"Peace"!   *P1875:*with "Peace"!
3419| MS:But—here's < > grown man §crossed out and replaced above by§ bald   *P1875:*But
here's   3420| MS:spice §over illegible erasure§   3421| MS:Of flavour §crossed out
and replaced above by§ odour in this §crossed out and replaced above by§ the hogs'-lard,
what   *P1875:*hogs'-lard? what   *1889a:*hog's-lard   3422| MS:except the §crossed out and
replaced above by§ a   3425| MS:Reasons his §crossed out and replaced above by§ a < >
into his §crossed out and replaced above by§ a   3426| MS:"I but §crossed out§ detail the
§crossed out§ sin < > not,   *P1875:*not   3427| MS:shame Ariphrades §crossed out and
replaced above by crossed-out word, *Thea*, and then restored§ for §over *to*§ < > display"—
*P1875:*display"!   3428| MS:"I strip Oporia   *P1875:*"I show Oporia   *1889a:*show Opora
3429| MS:Not, "I praise Festive Mirth—for §over illegible word, perhaps *how*§ strip her else?"
§last two words crossed out and replaced below by altered word and one word§ stripling's
sake!"   *P1875:*Not "I show Bacchis for the striplings'   3430| MS:genius, O fine gold—
*P1875:*genius and O gold—   3431| MS:O misery, what diverted   *P1875:*Had genius
ne'er diverted   3432| MS:temple, why did §last two words crossed out and replaced above
by two words§ to do mere §inserted above and crossed out§ copper's work—   *P1875:*work
3433| MS:Coating a swine's-trough,—which   *P1875:*And coat a swine's trough—which

Might furnish Phoibos' tripod, Pallas' throne!
3435 Had you, I dream, discarding all the base,
The brutish, spurned alone convention's watch
And ward against invading decency
Disguised as license, law in lawlessness,
And so, re-ordinating outworn rule,
3440 Made Comedy and Tragedy combine,
Prove some new Both-yet-neither, all one bard,
Euripides with Aristophanes
Coöperant! this, reproducing Now
As that gave Then existence: Life to-day,
3445 This, as that other—Life dead long ago!
The mob decrees such feat no crown, perchance,
But—why call crowning the reward of quest?
Tell him, my other poet,—where thou walk'st
Some rarer world than e'er Ilissos washed!

3450 But dream goes idly in the air. To earth!
Earth's question just amounts to—which succeeds,
Which fails of two life-long antagonists?
Suppose my charges all mistake! assume

3434| MS:Had furnished forth a §last two words crossed out and replaced above by one word§
Phoibos' tripod, Phoibos' §crossed out and replaced above by§ Pallas' throne? *P1875:*
Might furnish <> throne!   3435| MS:I §in margin§ dream §over partial erasure§ of
§crossed out and restored§ this man §last two words crossed out and replaced above by one
word§ one discarding   *P1875:*Had you, I dream, discarding   3436| MS:spurning poor
§crossed out and replaced above by§ tame convention's   *P1875:*spurned alone convention's
3437| MS:decency,   *1889a.*decency   3438| MS:Himself unlicensing the lawlessness,
*P1875:*Disguised as license, law in lawlessness,   3439| MS:Re-ordinating outworn rule,
and fresh   *P1875:*And so, re-ordinating outworn rule,   3440| MS:Till Comedy <>
combined §altered to§ combine,   *P1875:*Made Comedy   3441| MS:Prove §in margin§ In
§crossed out§ some <> Both-yet-Neither,—all <> bard, §over man§   *P1875:*new Both-yet-
neither, all   3443| MS:Coöperant! that §crossed out§ This §over *this*§   *P1875:*this
3444| MS:As That §over *that*§   *P1875:*that   3445| MS:This §in margin§ Breathing, as
That— §word and dash inserted above over *that*§ Life   *P1875:*This as that other—Life
*CP1875:*This, as   3446| MS:The multitude had §crossed out and replaced above by§ shall
cast no   *P1875:*The mob decrees such feat no   3447| MS:But—is such crowning fit
reward of work? §crossed out and replaced above by§ quest §crossed out and then rewritten at
end of line§   *P1875:*But—why call crowning the reward   3448| MS:other Poet
*P1875:*poet   3449| MS:than §next word illegibly crossed out§ e'er   3450| MS:But,
§over At§ that §crossed out and replaced above by§ dream   *P1875:*But dream

Your end, despite ambiguous means, the best—
3455　The only! you and he, a patriot-pair,
Have striven alike for one result—say, Peace!
You spoke your best straight to the arbiters—
Our people:　have you made them end this war
By dint of laughter and abuse and lies
3460　And postures of Opora?　Sadly—No!
This war, despite your twenty-five years' work,
May yet endure until Athenai falls,
And freedom falls with her.　So much for you!
Now, the antagonist Euripides—
3465　Has he succeeded better?　Who shall say?
He spoke quite o'er the heads of Kleon's crowd
To a dim future, and if there he fail,
Why, you are fellows in adversity.
But that's unlike the fate of wise words launched
3470　By music on their voyage.　Hail, Depart,
Arrive, Glad Welcome!　Not my single wish—
Yours also wafts the white sail on its way,
Your nature too is kingly.　All beside
I call pretension—no true potentate,
3475　Whatever intermediary be crowned,

3454| MS:end, §over illegible erasure§ despite the §crossed out§ ambiguous
3456| MS:Have §in margin§ Shall §crossed out§ strive §altered to§ striven　　3458| MS:The §crossed out and replaced above by§ Our <> end the §altered to§ this　　3459| MS:For all the §last three words crossed out and replaced below by three words§ By dint of laughter, the §comma and word crossed out and replaced below by§ and abuse, the §comma and word crossed out and replaced below by§ and lies,　*P1875*:lies　　3460| MS:And §in margin§ The §crossed out§ postures <> Oporia §emended to§ of Opora §see Editorial Notes§
3461| MS:war, for all §last two words crossed out and replaced above by one word§ despite <> twenty five　*P1875*:twenty-five　　3464| MS:§line added§ Now the　*P1875*:Now, the
3467| MS:a §inserted above§ dim futurity §altered to§ future, and §inserted above over illegible word§　　3468| MS:adversity!　*P1875*:adversity.　　3472| MS:the venture §crossed out and replaced above by two words§ white sail <> way!　*P1875*:way,　　3473| MS:Such §crossed out and replaced above by crossed-out word, *Upon*§ Your §inserted above§ natures §altered to§ nature are the §last two words crossed out and replaced above by two words§ too is kingly: all　*P1875*:kingly. All　　3474| MS:Is §altered to§ I play §crossed out and replaced above by§ call pure §inserted above and crossed out§ pretension—not the potentates— §last three words altered to§ no true potentate—　*P1875*:potentate,　　3475| MS:intermediary be crowned §last two words altered to§ they crown,　*P1875*:intermediary be crowned,

Zeus or Poseidon, where the vulgar sky
Lacks not Triballos to complete the group.
I recognize,—behind such phantom-crew,—
Necessity, Creation, Poet's Power,
3480 Else never had I dared approach, appeal
To poetry, power, Aristophanes!
But I trust truth's inherent kingliness,
Trust who, by reason of much truth, shall reign
More or less royally—may prayer but push
3485 His sway past limit, purge the false from true!
Nor, even so, had boldness nerved my tongue
But that the other king stands suddenly,
In all the grand investiture of death,
Bowing your knee beside my lowly head—
3490 Equals one moment!

Now, arise and go!
Both have done homage to Euripides!

Silence pursued the words: till he broke out—

"Scarce so! This constitutes, I may believe,

3477| MS:the §over illegible erasure§ gods. §crossed out and replaced above by§ group!
*P1875:*group. 3478| MS:But sock the §last three words crossed out and replaced above
by one word§ Recognize Force behind the phantom-crew,— *P1875:*I recognize,—behind
such phantom-crew,— 3479| MS:Necessity, Creation, Poet §altered to§ Poet's Power!—
*P1875:*Necessity, Creation, Poet's Power, 3480| MS:And if I dared §altered to§ dare
approach, have made appeal *P1875:*Else never had I dared approach, appeal
3481| MS:To Poetry, Power, Aristophanes— *P1875:*poetry, power, Aristophanes!
3482| MS:I trusted §altered to§ trust the truth's §inserted above§ <> kingliness *P1875:*But I
trust truth's <> kingliness, 3483| MS:Of §in margin§ With truth §last two words crossed
out and replaced above by one word and comma§ who, by virtue §crossed out and replaced
above by§ reason of which §crossed out and replaced above by§ much truth, he reigns §last
two words altered to§ shall reign *P1875:*Trust who 3484| MS:royally—for I would push
*P1875:*royally—may prayer but push 3485| MS:limit, put what's false afar! §over illegible
erasure§ *P1875:*limit, purge the false from true! 3487| MS:other King <> suddenly
*P1875:*king <> suddenly, 3490| MS:That shall §last two words crossed out§ Equals <>
§¶§ Now §crossed out and rewritten above§ arise *P1875:*<> §¶§ Now, arise
3491| MS:Both §in margin§ I §altered to *We* and crossed out§ have *P1875:*to Euripides!"
*1889a:*to Euripides! 3492| MS:out *P1875:*out— 3493| MS:"Not §crossed out and
replaced above by§ "Scarce <> I well believe, *P1875:*constitutes, I may believe,

161

Sufficient homage done by who defames
³⁴⁹⁵ Your poet's foe, since you account me such;
But homage-proper,—pay it by defence
Of him, direct defence and not oblique,
Not by mere mild admonishment of me!"

Defence?   The best, the only! I replied.
³⁵⁰⁰ A story goes—When Sophokles, last year,
Cited before tribunal by his son
(A poet—to complete the parallel)
Was certified unsound of intellect,
And claimed as only fit for tutelage,
³⁵⁰⁵ Since old and doating and incompetent
To carry on this world's work,—the defence
Consisted just in his reciting (calm
As the verse bore, which sets our heart a-swell
And voice a-heaving too tempestuously)
³⁵¹⁰ That choros-chant "The station of the steed,
Stranger! thou comest to,—Kolonos white!"
Then he looked round and all revolt was dead.
You know the one adventure of my life—
What made Euripides Balaustion's friend.
³⁵¹⁵ When I last saw him, as he bade farewell,

---

³⁴⁹⁵| MS:such— *P1875:*such;   ³⁴⁹⁷| MS:defence, and <> oblique *P1875:*defence
and <> oblique,   ³⁴⁹⁸| MS:Not §in margin§ by §over partial erasure§ all §crossed out§
this mild <> me!" *P1875:*by mere mild   *1889a:*me! §emended to§ me!" §see Editorial
Notes§   ³⁴⁹⁹| MS:"Defence <> only!" I   *1889a:*Defence <> only! I
³⁵⁰⁰| MS:A §in margin§ The §crossed out§ story <> when Sophokles last year— *P1875:*"A
<> When Sophokles, last year,   *1889a:*A   ³⁵⁰¹| MS:son— *P1875:*son
³⁵⁰³| MS:Was summoned as §last two words crossed out and replaced above by one word§
testified unsound *P1875:*Was certified unsound   ³⁵⁰⁴| MS:And fit to §last two words
crossed out§ claim §altered to§ claimant of §inserted above; last two words crossed out and
replaced above by two words§ calling for his childrens' tutelage,   *P1875:*And claimed as only
fit for tutelage,   ³⁵⁰⁵| MS:Incompetent by reason of old age §entire line crossed out and
replaced by§ Since old and doating and incompetent   ³⁵⁰⁷| MS:reciting—calm *P1875:*
reciting (calm   ³⁵⁰⁸| MS:the grand §crossed out§ verse <> our §inserted above§
³⁵⁰⁹| MS:too §over illegible erasure§ tempestuously, *P1875:*tempestuously)
³⁵¹⁰| MS:The clarion cry, Kolonos §last three words crossed out and replaced above by one
word§ choros-chant, "The <> steed— *P1875:*That choros-chant "The <> steed,
³⁵¹¹| MS:§line added§ Stranger,—thou *P1875:*Stranger! thou
³⁵¹³| MS:life, *P1875:*life—   ³⁵¹⁴| MS:Which made *P1875:*What made

"I sang another 'Herakles,' " smiled he;
"It gained no prize: your love be prize I gain!
Take it—the tablets also where I traced
The story first with stulos pendent still—
3520   Nay, the psalterion may complete the gift,
So, should you croon the ode bewailing Age,
Yourself shall modulate—same notes, same strings—
With the old friend who loved Balaustion once."
There they lie!   When you broke our solitude,
3525   We were about to honour him once more
By reading the consummate Tragedy.
Night is advanced; I have small mind to sleep;
May I go on, and read,—so make defence,
So test true godship?   You affirm, not I,
3530   —Beating the god, affords such test: *I* hold
That when rash hands but touch divinity,
The chains drop off, the prison-walls dispart,
And—fire—he fronts mad Pentheus!   Dare we try?

Accordingly I read the perfect piece.

3516| MS:"I made another 'Herakles,' " said §crossed out and replaced above by§ smiled
P1875:"I sang another   3517| MS:prize to gain! *P1875:*prize I gain!   3518| MS:it—
upon §crossed out§ the very §inserted above§ tablets where *P1875:*the tablets also where
3519| MS:story, with the stulos <> still: *P1875:*story first with stulos <> still—
3520| MS:psalterion too §inserted above§ should §crossed out and replaced above by crossed-
out word, *all*§ complete §altered to§ completes *P1875:*psalterion may complete
3521| MS:That, while §crossed out and replaced above by§ should <> the choros §altered to§
Choros to Old Age, *P1875:*So, should <> the ode bewailing Age,
3522| MS:Yourself may modulate *P1875:*Yourself shall modulate
3523| MS:With §over *As*§ <> Old Friend, §crossed out and replaced above by illegibly crossed-
out word, perhaps *one*, and then restored§ who *P1875:*old friend who
3525| MS:honor *1889a:*honour   3528| MS:read, and §crossed out and replaced above
by dash and word§ —so <> defence? *P1875:*defence,   3529| MS:Your test of the true
godship—did §crossed out§ you say, call §last two words crossed out§ affirm *P1875:*So test
true godship? You affirm, not I,   3530| MS:—Beating §over partial erasure§ <> affords
it? I believe *P1875:*affords such test: *I* hold   3531| MS:hands have §crossed out and
replaced above by§ once touched §altered to§ touch *P1875:*hands but touch
3532| MS:prison walls *P1875:*prison-walls   3533-34| MS:And—fire— §dashes and word
over illegible erasure§ <> May §crossed out and replaced above by§ Dare <> try? §followed
by§ End of Vol. I— *P1875:*try?" §¶§ Accordingly <> piece. *1889a:*try? §¶§

HERAKLES

AMPHITRUON

3535 Zeus' Couchmate,—who of mortals knows not me,
Argive Amphitruon whom Alkaios sired
Of old, as Perseus him, I—Herakles?
My home, this Thebai where the earth-born spike
Of Sown-ones burgeoned: Ares saved from these
3540 A handful of their seed that stocks to-day
With children's children Thebai, Kadmos built.
Of these had Kreon birth, Menoikeus' child,
King of the country,—Kreon that became
The father of this woman, Megara,
3545 Whom, when time was, Kadmeians one and all
Pealed praise to, marriage-songs with fluted help,
While to my dwelling that grand Herakles
Bore her, his bride.   But, leaving Thebes—where I
Abode perforce—this Megara and those
3550 Her kinsmen, the desire possessed my son
Rather to dwell in Argos, that walled work,
Kuklopian city, which I fly, myself,
Because I slew Elektruon.   Seeking so
To ease away my hardships and once more
3555 Inhabit his own land, for my return
Heavy the price he pays Eurustheus there—
The letting in of light on this choked world!
Either he promised, vanquished by the goad
Of Heré, or because fate willed it thus,

3535| MS:Zeus' Couchmate, who *P1875:*Zeus' Couchmate,—who
3537| MS:old as *P1875:*old, as 3539| MS:burgeoned: whereof Ares saved *P1875:*
burgeoned: Ares saved from these 3541| MS:children, Thebai *P1875:*children Thebai
3542| MS:child, §crossed out and replaced above by§ heir §crossed out and restored§
3543| MS:country—Kreon *P1875:*country,—Kreon 3544| MS:woman, Megara *P1875:*
woman, Megara, 3547| MS:When to *P1875:*While to
3552| MS: fly myself *P1875:* Kukoplian < > fly, myself, *CP1875:*Kukloplian
3553| MS:slew Elektruon: seeking *P1875:*slew Elektruon. Seeking 3556| MS:Heavy
§over partially illegible word§ 3557| MS:light upon §altered to§ on < > choaked
§inserted above§ *1889a:*choaked 3558| MS:vainquished *P1875:*vanquished

3560 The other labours—why, he toiled them through;
But for this last one—down by Tainaros,
Its mouth, to Haides' realm descended he
To drag into the light the three-shaped hound
Of Hell: whence Herakles returns no more.
3565 Now, there's an old-world tale, Kadmeians have,
How Dirké's husband was a Lukos once,
Holding the seven-towered city here in sway
Before they ruled the land, white-steeded pair,
The twins Amphion, Zethos, born to Zeus.
3570 This Lukos' son,—named like his father too,
No born Kadmeian but Euboia's gift,—
Comes and kills Kreon, lords it o'er the land,
Falling upon our town sedition-sick.
To us, akin to Kreon, just that bond
3575 Becomes the worst of evils, seemingly;
For, since my son is in the earth's abysms,
This man of valour, Lukos, lord and king,
Seeks now to slay these sons of Herakles,
And slay his wife as well,—by murder thus
3580 Thinking to stamp out murder,—slay too me,
(If me 'tis fit you count among men still,—
Useless old age) and all for fear lest these,
Grown men one day, exact due punishment
Of bloodshed and their mother's father's fate.
3585 I therefore, since he leaves me in these domes,

3560| MS:through: *P1875:*through;   3564| MS:hell—whence *P1875:*Of Hell: whence
3565| MS:have, §crossed out and replaced above by§ keep §crossed out and restored§
3566| MS:How Dirkés' had a §last two words crossed out§ husband   3569| MS:Amphion,
Zethos, born to Zeus the twins: *P1875:*twins. *1889a:*The twins Amphion <> Zeus.
3570| MS:Whereof the son—named *P1875:*This Lukos' son,—named   3571| MS:born
Kadmeian §altered to *Cadmeian* and then restored§ <> gift, *P1875:*gift,—
3572| MS:land *P1875:*land,   3573| MS:Having surprised §last two words crossed out and
replaced above by two words§ Falling upon   3575| MS:seemingly: *P1875:*seemingly;
3578| MS:Needs must he §last three words crossed out and replaced above by four words§
Seeks now to slay   3580| MS:me *P1875:*me,   3581| MS:If <> still— *P1875:*(If
<> still,—   3582| MS:age,—and <> fear one day *P1875:*age) and <> fear lest these,
3583| MS:Lest §in margin§ These, boys §crossed out§ grown up §crossed out and replaced
above by§ men, exact *P1875:*Grown men one day, exact   3584| MS:For §crossed out
and replaced above by§ Of   3585| MS:therefore—since *P1875:*therefore, since

The children's household guardian,—left, when earth's
Dark dread he underwent, that son of mine,—
I, with their mother, lest his boys should die,
Sit at this altar of the saviour Zeus
3590   Which, glory of triumphant spear, he raised
Conquering—my nobly-born!—the Minuai.
Here do we guard our station, destitute
Of all things, drink, food, raiment, on bare ground
Couched side by side: sealed out of house and home
3595   Sit we in a resourcelessness of help.
Our friends—why, some are no true friends, I see!
The rest, that are true, want the means to aid.
So operates in man adversity:
Whereof may never anybody—no,
3600   Though half of him should really wish me well,—
Happen to taste! a friend-test faultless, that!

MEGARA

Old man, who erst didst raze the Taphian town,
Illustriously, the army-leader, thou,
Of speared Kadmeians—how gods play men false!
3605   I, now, missed nowise fortune in my sire,
Who, for his wealth, was boasted mighty once,
Having supreme rule,—for the love of which
Leap the long lances forth at favoured breasts,—
And having children too: and me he gave
3610   Thy son, his house with that of Herakles
Uniting by the far-famed marriage-bed.

3586| MS:childrens <> guardian—when the earth's *P1875:*children's <> guardian,—left,
when earth's   3587| MS:mine—   *P1875:*mine,—   3589| MS:the Saviour *P1875:*
saviour   3592| MS:Here these §crossed out and replaced above by§ do   3595| MS:in
such §crossed out and replaced above by§ a   3596| MS:see: *P1875:*see!
3598| MS:Such is the schooling of §last five words crossed out and replaced above by four
words§ So operates in man adversity—   *P1875:*adversity: 3600| MS:well, *P1875:*well,—
3601| MS:taste,—a §crossed out and restored§ friend-test §*test* crossed out and replaced above
by illegibly crossed-out word, perhaps *temptation*§ faultless *P1875:*taste! a <> friend-test
faultless   3603| MS:Illustriously the *P1875:*Illustriously, the   3605| MS:now—nor
missed of fortune as to sire, *P1875:*now, missed nowise fortune in my sire,

And now these things are dead and flown away,
While thou and I await our death, old man,
These Herakleian boys too, whom—my chicks—
3615   I save beneath my wings like brooding bird.
But one or other falls to questioning
"O mother," cries he, "where in all the world
Is father gone to?   What's he doing? when
Will he come back?"   At fault through tender years,
3620   They seek their sire.   For me, I put them off,
Telling them stories; at each creak of doors,
All wonder "Does he come?"—and all a-foot
Make for the fall before the parent knee.
Now then, what hope, what method of escape
3625   Facilitatest thou?—for, thee, old man,
I look to,—since we may not leave by stealth
The limits of the land, and guards, more strong
Than we, are at the outlets: nor in friends
Remain to us the hopes of safety more.
3630   Therefore, whatever thy decision be,
Impart it for the common good of all!
Lest now should prove the proper time to die,
Though, being weak, we spin it out and live.

AMPHITRUON

Daughter, it scarce is easy, do one's best,
3635   To blurt out counsel, things at such a pass.

MEGARA

You want some sorrow more, or so love life?

3613| MS:and I have §crossed out§ await §over illegible word§   3614| MS:chicks, *P1875:*
chicks—   3618| MS:doing—when *P1875:*doing? when   3620| MS:sire: for *P1875:*
sire. For   3621| MS:stories: at < > door— *P1875:*stories; at < > door, *1889a:*doors,
3622| MS:"I wonder is it he!"—and *P1875:*All wonder "Does he come?"—and
3625| MS:thou, §comma altered to question mark§ since §crossed out and replaced above by§
—for thee *P1875:*for, thee   3626| MS:to: since *P1875:*to,—since
3627| MS:land, for guards more *P1875:*land, and guards, more   3631| MS:all, *P1875:*
all!   3636| MS:or love life so? §last word marked for transposition to follow *or*§

AMPHITRUON

I both enjoy life, and love hopes beside.

MEGARA

And I; but hope against hope—no, old man!

AMPHITRUON

In these delayings of an ill lurks cure.

MEGARA

3640 But bitter is the meantime, and it bites.

AMPIIITRUON

O there may be a run before the wind
From out these present ills, for me and thee,
Daughter, and yet may come my son, thy spouse!
But hush! and from the children take away
3645 Their founts a-flow with tears, and talk them calm
Steal them by stories—sad theft, all the same!
For, human troubles—they grow weary too;
Neither the wind-blasts always have their strength
Nor happy men keep happy to the end:
3650 Since all things change—their natures part in twain;
And that man's bravest, therefore, who hopes on,
Hopes ever: to despair is coward-like.

CHOROS

These domes that overroof,

3637| MS:life and *P1875:*life, and   3638| MS:And I: but *P1875:*And I; but
3644| MS:hush—and <> thy §altered to§ the *P1875:*hush! and
3645| MS:calm, *1889a:*calm   3647| MS:too: *P1875:*too;   3648| MS:strength,
*1889a:*strength   3650| MS:nature parts in two: *P1875:*natures part in twain;
3652| MS:ever—to <> cowardly. *P1875:*ever: to *1889a:*coward-like.

This long-used couch, I come to, having made
3655   A staff my prop, that song may put to proof
The swan-like power, age-whitened,—poet's aid
Of sobbed-forth dirges—words that stand aloof
From action now: such am I—just a shade
With night for all its face, a mere night-dream—
3660   And words that tremble too: howe'er they seem,
Devoted words, I deem.

O, of a father ye unfathered ones,
O thou old man, and thou whose groaning stuns—
Unhappy mother—only us above,
3665   Nor reaches him below in Haides' realm, thy love!
—(Faint not too soon, urge forward foot and limb
Way-weary, nor lose courage—as some horse
Yoked to the car whose weight recoils on him
Just at the rock-ridge that concludes his course!
3670   Take by the hand, the peplos, anyone
Whose foothold fails him, printless and fordone!
Aged, assist along me aged too,
Who,—mate with thee in toils when life was new,
And shields and spears first made acquaintanceship,—
3675   Stood by thyself and proved no bastard-slip
Of fatherland when loftiest glory grew.)—
See now, how like the sire's
Each eyeball fiercely fires!
What though ill-fortune have not left his race?
3680   Neither is gone the grand paternal grace!
Hellas!   O what—what combatants, destroyed

3655| MS:The §crossed out and replaced above by§ A <> song might §crossed out and replaced above by§ may   3658| MS:now—such *P1875:*now: such   3659| MS:a mere §inserted above§   3663| MS:man—and *P1875:*man, and   3665| MS:in Hades' *P1875:*in Haides'   3666| MS:(Faint *P1875:*—(Faint   3667| MS:lose heart §crossed out and replaced above by§ courage as may §crossed out§ *P1875:*courage—as 3670| MS:Hold §crossed out and replaced above by§ Take <> peplos, any §inserted above§ one *1889a:*anyone   3671| MS:fordone— *P1875:*fordone!   3672| MS:Aged—assist *P1875:*Aged, assist   3674| MS:spears and shields §transposed to§ shields and spears 3676| MS:grew.) *P1875:*grew.)—   3681| MS:Hellas—oh *P1875:*Hellas! O

In these, wilt thou one day seek—seek, and find all void!

Pause! for I see the ruler of this land,
Lukos, now passing through the palace-gate.

LUKOS

3685   The Herakleian couple—father, wife—
If needs I must, I question: "must" forsooth?
Being your master—all I please, I ask.
To what time do you seek to spin out life?
What hope, what help see, so as not to die?
3690   Is it you trust the sire of these, that's sunk
In Haides, will return?   How past the pitch,
Suppose you have to die, you pile the woe—
Thou, casting, Hellas through, thy empty vaunts
As though Zeus helped thee to a god for son;
3695   And thou, that thou wast styled our best man's wife!
Where was the awful in his work wound up,
If he did quell and quench the marshy snake
Or the Nemeian monster whom he snared
And—says, by throttlings of his arm, he slew?
3700   With these do you outwrestle me?   Such feats
Shall save from death the sons of Herakles
Who got praise, being nought, for bravery
In wild-beast-battle, otherwise a blank?
No man to throw on left arm buckler's weight,

3682| MS:seek for and   *P1875:*seek—seek, and   3683| MS:Pause for   *P1875:*Pause! for
3684| MS:Lukos §over *Lykos*§ now   *P1875:*Lukos, now   3687| MS:master—what §crossed
out and replaced above by§ all   3689| MS:see so   *P1875:*see, so   3691| MS:In Hades
<> return? How beyond §crossed out and replaced above by§ past <> pitch   *P1875:*In Haides
<> pitch,   3693| MS:Thou—casting   *P1875:*Thou, casting   3694| MS:son!
§exclamation point altered to semi-colon§   3696| MS:What §altered to§ Where <> awful
when §crossed out and replaced above by§ if §crossed out§ in §inserted above§   3697| MS:If
§in margin§ He did §inserted above§ really §crossed out§ quell and kill §crossed out and
replaced above by§ quench §over illegible word§   *P1875:*he   3698| MS:snared §over
illegible word§   3699| MS:And says <> slew.   *P1875:*And—says <> slew?   3700| MS:me?
For §crossed out and replaced above by§ Such   3701| MS:Like these §last two words crossed
out§ Shall   3702| MS:got praise §last two words inserted above§   3703| MS:blank—
*P1875:*blank?   3704| MS:throw §over illegible word§ <> weight   *P1875:*weight,

3705　Not he, nor get in spear's reach! bow he bore—
True coward's-weapon: shoot first and then fly!
No bow-and-arrow proves a man is brave,
But who keeps rank,—stands, one unwinking stare
As, ploughing up, the darts come,—brave is he.
3710　My action has no impudence, old man!
Providence, rather: for I own I slew
Kreon, this woman's sire, and have his seat.
Nowise I wish, then, to leave, these grown up,
Avengers on me, payment for my deeds.

AMPHITRUON

3715　As to the part of Zeus in his own child,
Let Zeus defend that! As to mine, 'tis me
The care concerns to show by argument
The folly of this fellow,—Herakles,
Whom I stand up for! since to hear thee styled—
3720　Cowardly—that is unendurable.
First then, the infamous (for I account
Amongst the words denied to human speech,
Timidity ascribed thee, Herakles!)
This I must put from thee, with gods in proof.
3725　Zeus' thunder I appeal to, those four steeds
Whereof he also was the charioteer
When, having shot down the earth's Giant-growth—
(Never shaft flew but found and fitted flank)

3705| MS:reach: bow　*P1875*:reach! bow　3708| MS:But standing stock-still, wh §last two
letters and preceding two words crossed out and replaced above by four words and comma§
who keeps rank, stands　*P1875*:rank,—stands　3709| MS:come, brave　*P1875*:come,—
brave　3710| MS:man,　*P1875*:man!　3711| MS:Discreteness §crossed out and
replaced above by§ Providence　3714| MS:Avenge §altered to§ Avengers them §crossed
out§ <> payment back §crossed out and replaced above by§ for　3718| MS:fellow,
Herakles,　*P1875*:fellow,—Herakles,　3719| MS:for! For §crossed out and replaced
above by§ Since <> styled　*P1875*:since　*1889a*:styled—　3721| MS:the infamies
§altered to§ infamous—for　*P1875*:infamous (for　3722| MS:words forbidden §crossed
out and replaced above by two words§ denied to　3723| MS:Timidity ascribed §last three
letters altered to form *ascription* and then original reading restored§ thee, §crossed out and
restored§ Herakles!—　*P1875*:thee, Herakles!)　3724| MS:with Gods　*P1875*:gods
3725| MS:Witness the §last two words crossed out and replaced above by one word§ Zeus
P1875:Zeus'　3728| MS:Never <> flank—　*P1875*:(Never <> flank)

Triumph he sang in common with the gods.
3730 The Kentaur-race, four footed insolence—
Go ask at Pholoé, vilest thou of kings,
Whom they would pick out and pronounce best man,
If not my son, "the seeming-brave," say'st thou!
But Dirphus, thy Abantid mother-town,
3735 Question her, and she would not praise, I think!
For there's no spot, where having done some good,
Thy country thou mightst call to witness worth.
Now, that all-wise invention, archer's-gear,
Thou blamest: hear my teaching and grow sage!
3740 A man in armour is his armour's slave,
And, mixed with rank and file that want to run,
He dies because his neighbours have lost heart.
Then, should he break his spear, no way remains
Of warding death off,—gone that body-guard,
3745 His one and only; while, whatever folk
Have the true bow-hand,—here's the one main good,—
Though he have sent ten thousand shafts abroad,
Others remain wherewith the archer saves
His limbs and life, too,—stands afar and wards
3750 Away from flesh the foe that vainly stares
Hurt by the viewless arrow, while himself
Offers no full front to those opposite,
But keeps in thorough cover: there's the point
That's capital in combat—damage foe,
3755 Yet keep a safe skin—foe not out of reach
As you are! Thus my words contrast with thine,

3729| MS:the Gods. *P1875:*gods.   3730| MS:The Kentaur-race—four-footed insolence—
*P1875:*The Kentaur-race, four-footed   *1889a:*four footed   3732| MS:Whom *P1875: Whom*
3733| MS:sayst *P1875:*say'st   3735| MS:think: *P1875:*think!   3736| MS:some deed
§crossed out§ good,   3737| MS:Note worthy, §last two words and comma crossed out§ Thy
3738| MS:allwise invention, §next illegible letter crossed out§ archer's-gear, *1889a:*all-wise
3741| MS:to fly §crossed out and replaced above by§ run,   3744| MS:off, gone <> body-
guard— *P1875:*off,—gone <> body-guard,   3745| MS:only: while whatever *P1875:*
only; while,   3746| MS:good— *P1875:*good,—   3747| MS:Though they
§crossed out and replaced above by§ he   3748| MS:More still §last two words crossed out
and replaced above by one word§ Others   3749| MS:too: stands *P1875:*too,—stands
3756| MS:are! Such the difference §next word illegibly crossed out§ I reason §last six words
crossed out and replaced above by§ Thus my words contrast with thine,

And such, in judging facts, our difference.
These children, now, why dost thou seek to slay?
What have they done thee?   In a single point
3760   I count thee wise—if, being base thyself,
Thou dread'st the progeny of nobleness.
Yet this bears hard upon us, all the same,
If we must die—because of fear in thee—
A death 'twere fit thou suffer at our hands,
3765   Thy betters, did Zeus rightly judge us all.
If therefore thou art bent on sceptre-sway,
Thyself, here—suffer us to leave the land,
Fugitives! nothing do by violence,
Or violence thyself shalt undergo
3770   When the gods' gale may chance to change for thee!
Alas, O land of Kadmos,—for 'tis thee
I mean to close with, dealing out the due
Revilement,—in such sort dost thou defend
Herakles and his children?   Herakles
3775   Who, coming, one to all the world, against
The Minuai, fought them and left Thebes an eye
Unblinded henceforth to front freedom with!
Neither do I praise Hellas, nor shall brook
Ever to keep in silence that I count
3780   Towards my son, craven of cravens—her

3758| MS:These §over illegible word§   3759| MS:thee? As §crossed out and replaced
above by§ In a single to §last three words crossed out and then *a single* restored§
3761| MS:the offsprin §last eight letters crossed out§ <> nobleness: *P1875:*dreadst <>
nobleness.   *1889a:*dread'st   3762| MS:same—   *P1875:*same,   3763| MS:die
because   *P1875:*die—because   3764| MS:A §in margin§ Death <> hands   *P1875:*death
<> hands,   3766| MS:If therefore §inserted above§ thou art th §last two letters crossed
out§ bent then §crossed out§ on   3767| MS:Thyself here <> land   *P1875:*Thyself, here
<> land,   3768| MS:Fugitives: nothing   *P1875:*Fugitives! nothing   3771| MS:for
needs §crossed out§ tis thou   *P1875:*'tis thee   3773| MS:Of §crossed out§ Revilement
<> thou def protect §last word and preceding three letters crossed out§ defend
3775| MS:all of them, §last two words crossed out and replaced above by two words§ the world
3776| MS:them till he §last two words crossed out and replaced above by one word§ and left
your §crossed out§ Thebes   3777| MS:Unblinded eyeball §crossed out and replaced
above by§ henceforth   3779| MS:to curb my tongue, since §last four words crossed out
and replaced above by four words§ keep in silence that I account §altered to§ count
3780| MS:Craven of cravens—her towards §altered to§ Towards my son, §last three words
marked for transposition to beginning of line§   *P1875:*craven

Whom it behoved go bring the young ones here
Fire, spears, arms—in exchange for seas made safe,
And cleansings of the land—his labour's price.
But fire, spears, arms,—O children, neither Thebes
3785   Nor Hellas has them for you!   'Tis myself,
A feeble friend, ye look to: nothing now
But a tongue's murmur, for the strength is gone
We had once, and with age are limbs a-shake
And force a-flicker!   Were I only young,
3790   Still with the mastery o'er bone and thew,
Grasping first spear that came, the yellow locks
Of this insulter would I bloody so—
Should send him skipping o'er the Atlantic bounds
Out of my arm's reach through poltroonery!

CHOROS

3795   Have not the really good folk starting-points
For speech to purpose,—though rare talkers they?

LUKOS

Say thou against us words thou towerest with!
I, for thy words, will deal thee blows, their due.
Go, some to Helikon, to Parnasos
3800   Some, and the clefts there!   Bid the woodmen fell
Oak-trunks, and, when the same are brought inside
The city, pile the altar round with logs,

3783| MS:land, his   *1889a:*land—his   3785| MS:you! but to §last two words crossed out and
replaced above by one word§ 'Tis myself *P1875:*myself,   3786| MS:to, nothing *P1875:*
to: nothing   3787| MS:murmur—for *P1875:*murmur, for   3788| MS:once! and <>
a-shake, *P1875:*once, and <> a-shake   3789| MS:The §crossed out§ And <> a-flicker. Were
*P1875:*a-flicker! Were   3792| MS:so *P1875:*so—   3794| MS:Out my <> poltroonery.
*P1875:*Out of my <> poltroonery!   3796| MS:purpose,—ay, §word and comma crossed
out§ <> rare §over illegible word§   3797| MS:with— *P1875:*with!   3798| MS:thee
harm §crossed out and replaced above by§ blows   3800| MS:there, bid *P1875:*there!
Bid   3801| MS:and when they bring them §last three words crossed out and replaced
above by four words§ the same are brought inside here §crossed out§ *P1875:*and, when
3802| MS:Having §crossed out and replaced above by two words and comma§ The city, piled
§altered to§ pile wood §crossed out§ the <> round about, §word and comma crossed out§ with

175

Then fire it, burn the bodies of them all,
That they may learn thereby, no dead man rules
3805 The land here, but 'tis I, by acts like these!
As for you, old sirs, who are set against
My judgments, you shall groan for—not alone
The Herakleian children, but the fate
Of your own house beside, when faring ill
3810 By any chance: and you shall recollect
Slaves are you of a tyranny that's mine!

CHOROS

O progeny of earth,—whom Ares sowed
When he laid waste the dragon's greedy jaw—
Will ye not lift the staves, right-hand supports,
3815 And bloody this man's irreligious head?
Who, being no Kadmeian, rules,—the wretch,—
Our easy youth: an interloper too!
But not of me, at least, shalt thou enjoy
Thy lordship ever; nor my labour's fruit,—
3820 Hand worked so hard for,—have! A curse with thee,
Whence thou didst come, there go and tyrannize!
For never while I live shalt thou destroy
The Herakleian children: not so deep
Hides he below ground, leaving thee their lord!
3825 But we bear both of you in mind,—that thou,
The land's destroyer, dost possess the land,
While he who saved it, loses every right.

3804| MS:may know §crossed out and replaced above by§ learn   3805| MS:'tis I, whose §crossed out and replaced above by§ by acts are §crossed out§ <> these.   *P1875:*these!
3806| MS:As for §inserted above§ <> who have §crossed out§ are   3810| MS:chance—and <> shall call to min §last three letters and preceding two words crossed out§ recollect *P1875:*chance: and   3811| MS:You are the §crossed out§ slaves, mine is the §last two words crossed out and replaced above by two words§ of a tyranny that's §line marked for transposition to§ slaves are You, of a tyranny that's mine   *P1875:*Slaves <> you of <> mine!
3812| MS:O offspring §crossed out and replaced above by§ progeny of the §crossed out§ earth   3815| MS:head—   *P1875:*head?   3816| MS:being §inserted above§   3817| MS:youth—an   *P1875:*youth: an   3819| MS:ever,—nor   *P1875:*ever; nor   3823| MS:not to that degree §last three words crossed out§ so   3824| MS:ground; and §crossed out§ leaving   *P1875:*ground, leaving   3825| MS:thou   *P1875:*thou,

I play the busybody—for I serve
My dead friends when they need friends' service most?
3830 O right-hand, how thou yearnest to snatch spear
And serve indeed! in weakness dies the wish,
Or I had stayed thee calling me a slave,
And nobly drawn my breath at home in Thebes
Where thou exultest!—city that's insane,
3835 Sick through sedition and bad government,
Else never had she gained for master—thee!

MEGARA

Old friends, I praise you: since a righteous wrath
For friend's sake well becomes a friend.   But no!
On our account in anger with your lord,
3840 Suffer no injury!   Hear my advice,
Amphitruon, if I seem to speak aright.
O yes, I love my children! how not love
What I brought forth, what toiled for? and to die—
Sad I esteem too; still, the fated way
3845 Who stiffens him against, that man I count
Poor creature; us, who are of other mood,
Since we must die, behoves us meet our death
Not burnt to cinders, giving foes the laugh—
To me, worse ill than dying, that!   We owe
3850 Our houses many a brave deed, now to pay.
Thee, indeed, gloriously men estimate
For spear-work, so that unendurable

3828| MS:busy-body since I *P1875:*busy-body—for I *1889a:*busybody   3833| MS:drawn
§over illegible word§ <> breath again §crossed out and replaced above by two words§ at
home   3834| MS:exultest: §colon and next word illegibly crossed out and replaced above
by comma and dash§ *P1875:*exultest!—city   3836| MS:she §over illegible word, perhaps
it§   3838| MS:friend: but *P1875:*friend. But   3840| MS:no harm §crossed out and
replaced above by§ injury! Hear what I §last two words crossed out and replaced above by one
word§ my advise §altered to§ advice,   3842| MS:children—how *P1875:*children! how
3844| MS:Dreadful §crossed out and replaced above by§ Sad I account §crossed out and
replaced above by§ esteem too: yet §crossed out and replaced above by§ still, <> bated
§altered to§ fated way, *P1875:*too; still <> way   3846| MS:creature: us *P1875:*creature;
us   3849| MS:that: we *P1875:*that! we *1889a:*that! We   3850| MS:pay! *P1875:*pay.

Were it that thou shouldst die a death of shame.
And for my glorious husband, where wants he
3855 A witness that he would not save his boys
If touched in their good fame thereby?   Since birth
Bears ill with baseness done for children's sake,
My husband needs must be my pattern here.
See now thy hope—how much I count thereon!
3860 Thou thinkest that thy son will come to light:
And, of the dead, who came from Haides back?
But we with talk this man might mollify:
Never!   Of all foes, fly the foolish one!
Wise, well-bred people, make concession to!
3865 Sooner you meet respect by speaking soft.
Already it was in my mind—perchance
We might beg off these children's banishment;
But even that is sad, involving them
In safety, ay—and piteous poverty!
3870 Since the host's visage for the flying friend
Has, only one day, the sweet look, 'tis said.
Dare with us death, which waits thee, dared or no!
We call on thine ancestral worth, old man!
For who outlabours what the gods appoint
3875 Shows energy, but energy gone mad.
Since what must—none e'er makes what must not be.

CHOROS

Had anyone, while yet my arms were strong,

3856| MS:since   *1889a:*thereby? Since   3857| MS:done §inserted above§ < > sake,—
*P1875:*sake,   3858| MS:—My husband here §crossed out and replaced above by§ needs
< > pattern too §crossed out and replaced above by§ here!   *1889a:*My < > here.
3861| MS:from Hades   *P1875:*from Haides   3863| MS:one: *P1875:*one!
3867| MS:these boys to §last two words crossed out and replaced above by one word§ children's
banishment—   *P1875:*banishment;   3868| MS:is wretched §crossed out and replaced
above by§ sad—involving   *1889a:*sad, involving   3869| MS:poverty:
*P1875:*poverty!   3870| MS:Since the §over illegible word§ < > for the §over illegible
word§ flying friends §altered to§ friend   3871| MS:look, they say §last
two words crossed out and replaced above by two words§ 'tis said.   3872| MS:thee dared
*P1875:*thee, dared   3873| MS:man.   *P1875:*man!   3874| MS:out-labours < > gods
allot §crossed out§ appoint,   *1889a:*outlabours < > appoint

Been scorning thee, he easily had ceased.
But we are nought, now; thine henceforth to see—
3880 Amphitruon, how to push aside these fates!

AMPHITRUON

Nor cowardice nor a desire of life
Stops me from dying: but I seek to save
My son his children.   Vain! I set my heart,
It seems, upon impossibility.
3885 See, it is ready for the sword, this throat
To pierce, divide, dash down from precipice!
But one grace grant us, king, we supplicate!
Slay me and this unhappy one before
The children, lest we see them—impious sight!—
3890 Gasping the soul forth, calling all the while
On mother and on father's father!   Else,
Do as thy heart inclines thee!   No resource
Have we from death, and we resign ourselves.

MEGARA

And I too supplicate: add grace to grace,
3895 And, though but one man, doubly serve us both!
Let me bestow adornment of the dead
Upon these children!   Throw the palace wide!
For now we are shut out.   Thence these shall share

3879| MS:henceforth §over *thenceforth*§   3883| MS:children. Well, §crossed out and
replaced above by§ Vain! <> heart   *P1875*:heart,   3885| MS:this neck §crossed out§
throat   3886| MS:divide, §over illegible word§ precipate from rock §last three words
crossed out and replaced above by four words§ dash down from precipice!   3889| MS:sight!
P1875:sight!—   3892| MS:Do what §crossed out and replaced above by§ as
3893| MS:from death §last two words inserted above§   3894| MS:And §inserted above in
margin§ I too §inserted above§ supplicate thee too, §last two words and comma crossed out§
add   *P1875*:supplicate: add   3895| MS:And, though but one man, §both commas and
last four words inserted above§ <> both, §comma altered to exclamation point§
3897| MS:children: throw the house-doors §crossed out and replaced above by§ palace
P1875:children! Throw   3898| MS:out: so these   *P1875*:out. Thence these

At least so much of wealth was once their sire's!

LUKOS

3900 These things shall be.   Withdraw the bolts, I bid
My servants!   Enter and adorn yourselves!
I grudge no peploi; but when these ye wind
About your bodies,—that adornment done,—
Then I shall come and give you to the grave.

MEGARA

3905 O children, follow this unhappy foot,
Your mother's, into your ancestral home,
Where others have the power, are lords in truth,
Although the empty name is left us yet!

AMPHITRUON

O Zeus, in vain I had thee marriage-mate,
3910 In vain I called thee father of my child!
Thou wast less friendly far than thou didst seem.
I, the mere man, o'ermatch in virtue thee
The mighty god: for I have not betrayed
The Herakleian children,—whereas thou
3915 Hadst wit enough to come clandestinely
Into the chamber, take what no man gave,
Another's place; and when it comes to help

---

³⁸⁹⁹| MS:So §altered to§ In so §inserted above§ much, at §altered to§ At least, of their sires wealth was §inserted above§ once! §line marked for transposition to§ At least In so much of wealth was once their sires! *P1875:*least so <> wealth, was *1889a:*wealth was
³⁹⁰⁰| MS:So be it open §last four words crossed out and replaced above by three words§ These things shall be: withdraw *P1875:*be. Withdraw   ³⁹⁰²| MS:but §over illegible word§
³⁹⁰³| MS:done, *P1875:*done,—   ³⁹⁰⁵| MS:children, keep §crossed out and replaced above by§ follow this sad §crossed out and replaced above by§ unhappy foot, company— §word and dash crossed out§   ³⁹⁰⁶| MS:home *P1875:*home,   ³⁹¹⁴| MS:children: while t §last letter and preceding word crossed out§ whereas *P1875:*children,—whereas
³⁹¹⁶| MS:the couch, and §last two words crossed out and replaced above by word and comma§ chamber   ³⁹¹⁷| MS:place: and *P1875:*place; and

Thy loved ones, there thou lackest wit indeed!
Thou art some stupid god or born unjust.

CHOROS

³⁹²⁰ Even a dirge, can Phoibos suit
In song to music jubilant
For all its sorrow: making shoot
His golden plectron o'er the lute,
Melodious ministrant.
³⁹²⁵ And I, too, am of mind to raise,
Despite the imminence of doom,
A song of joy, outpour my praise
To him—what is it rumour says?—
Whether—now buried in the ghostly gloom
³⁹³⁰ Below ground,—he was child of Zeus indeed,
Or mere Amphitruon's mortal seed—
To him I weave the wreath of song, his labour's meed.
For, is my hero perished in the feat?
The virtues of brave toils, in death complete,
³⁹³⁵ These save the dead in song,—their glory-garland meet!

First, then, he made the wood
Of Zeus a solitude,

---

³⁹¹⁸| MS:ones, why §crossed out and replaced above by§ there　　³⁹²²| MS:all the §crossed out and replaced above by§ its sorrow-making　*P1875:*sorrow: making
³⁹²³| MS:plectroun o'er §over illegible word§ *P1875:*plectron　　³⁹²⁶| MS:§first word illegibly crossed out and replaced above by§ Despite <> of grief §crossed out and replaced above by§ doom,　　³⁹²⁷| MS:joy, a meed of §last three words crossed out and replaced above by two words§ outpouring §altered to§ outpour my　　³⁹²⁹| MS:That he §last two words crossed out and replaced above by one word§ Whether, now <> gloom,　*P1875.*Whether—now <> gloom　　³⁹³⁰| MS:Below ground, he §last three words inserted above§ Was §altered to§ was the §crossed out§ child <> indeed　*P1875:*ground,—he <> indeed,　　³⁹³¹| MS:mortal §inserted above§ seed? §question mark altered to dash§　³⁹³²| MS:him I dedicate §crossed out and replaced above by§ weave the crown §crossed out and replaced above by three words and comma§ wreath of song　　³⁹³³| MS:is he §crossed out and replaced above by two words§ my hero　　³⁹³⁴| MS:of their §crossed out and replaced above by§ brave toils in death §last two words inserted above§　*P1875:*toils, in　　³⁹³⁵| MS:These make §crossed out and replaced above by§ save <> in song,— §last two words and punctuation inserted above§ <> glory §altered to§ glory-garland meet.　*P1875:*meet!

181

Slaying its lion-tenant; and he spread
The tawniness behind—his yellow head
3940 Enmuffled by the brute's, backed by that grin of dread.
The mountain-roving savage Kentaur-race
He strewed with deadly bow about their place,
Slaying with winged shafts: Peneios knew,
Beauteously-eddying, and the long tracts too
3945 Of pasture trampled fruitless, and as well
Those desolated haunts Mount Pelion under,
And, grassy up to Homolé, each dell
Whence, having filled their hands with pine-tree plunder,
Horse-like was wont to prance from, and subdue
3950 The land of Thessaly, that bestial crew.
The golden-headed spot-back'd stag he slew,
That robber of the rustics: glorified
Therewith the goddess who in hunter's pride
Slaughters the game along Oinoé's side.
3955 And, yoked abreast, he brought the chariot-breed
To pace submissive to the bit, each steed
That in the bloody cribs of Diomede
Champed and, unbridled, hurried down that gore
For grain, exultant the dread feast before—
3960 Of man's flesh: hideous feeders they of yore!
All as he crossed the Hebros' silver-flow
Accomplished he such labour, toiling so

3938| MS:lion-tenant: and   *P1875:*lion-tenant; and   3939| MS:behind: §colon altered to
dash§ him, §comma crossed out and word altered to§ his   3940| MS:Close covered §last
two words crossed out and replaced above by one word§ Enmuffled   3941| MS:The §over
illegible word§ < > Kentaur race   *P1875:*savage Kentaur-race   3945| MS:and the
§crossed out§ as   3947| MS:grassing   *CP1875:*grassy   3949| MS:from and   *P1875:*
from, and   3950| MS:of Thessaly that   *P1875:*of Thessaly, that   3951| MS:spot-
backed   *P1875:*spot-back'd   3952| MS:rustics—glorified   *P1875:*rustics: glorified
3954| MS:along Mount §crossed out§ Oinoé's   3955| MS:abreast beneath his §last two
words crossed out and replaced above by three words§ he brought the   *P1875:*abreast, he
3957| MS:bloody stalls §crossed out and replaced above by§ cribs   3958| MS:Champed,
and, §last two words and commas inserted above§ Unbridled, hurried §over partial erasure§
< > that flesh §crossed out§ gore   *P1875:*Champed and, unbridled   3959| MS:For §over
illegible word§ provender §crossed out and replaced above by§ grain, < > before   *P1875:*before—
3960| MS:flesh, hideous   *P1875:*flesh: hideous   3962| MS:labor   *P1875:*labour

182

For Mukenaian tyrant; ay, and more—
He crossed the Melian shore
3965 And, by the sources of Amauros, shot
To death that strangers'-pest
Kuknos, who dwelt in Amphanaia: not
Of fame for good to guest!

And next, to the melodious maids he came,
3970 Inside the Hesperian court-yard: hand must aim
At plucking gold fruit from the appled leaves,
Now he had killed the dragon, backed like flame,
Who guards the unapproachable he weaves
Himself all round, one spire about the same.
3975 And into those sea-troughs of ocean dived
The hero, and for mortals calm contrived,
Whatever oars should follow in his wake.
And under heaven's mid-seat his hands thrust he,
At home with Atlas: and, for valour's sake,
3980 Held the gods up their star-faced mansionry.
Also, the rider-host of Amazons
About Maiotis many-streamed, he went
To conquer through the billowy Euxin once,
Having collected what an armament

3963| MS:tyrant,—ay *P1875:*tyrant; ay   3965| MS:And by <> Amarous shot *P1875:*
And, by <> Amarous, shot   3966| MS:that stranger's slay §last two words crossed out;
stranger's restored and altered to§ stranger's-pest *P1875:*strangers'-pest
3967| MS:Kuknos who <> in Amphanaia—not *P1875:*Kuknos, who <> in Amphanaia:not
3968| MS:Praised by the §last three words crossed out and replaced above by four words§ Of
fame for good   3969| MS:next he came §last two words crossed out§ to the Hesperian
court, §last two words crossed out and replaced above by two words§ melodious maids
*P1875:*next, to <.> maids he   3970| MS:court-yard,—hand *P1875:*court-yard: hand
3971| MS:leaves *P1875:*leaves,   3972| MS:he has §altered to§ had slain §crossed out and
replaced above by§ killed <> dragon backed <> flame *P1875:*dragon, backed <> flame,
3973| MS:guards that unapproachable *P1875:*guards the unapproachable
3976| MS:mortals peacefulness §crossed out§ calm   3978| MS:hands he thrust, §last two
words marked for transposition§   3979| MS:with Atlas, and for *P1875:*with Atlas: and,
for   3980| MS:Supported §crossed out and replaced above by§ Lifted §crossed out§ Held
the Gods up, their §last two words inserted above; *their* crossed out and restored§ *P1875:*
gods up their   3980-81| MS:§¶ called for in margin§ *P1875:*§page ends§ *1889a:*§no ¶§
3983| MS:billowy Euxeine once *P1875:*once *1889a:*billowy Euxin

³⁹⁸⁵   Of friends from Hellas, all on conquest bent
      Of that gold-garnished cloak, dread girdle-chase!
      So Hellas gained the girl's barbarian grace
      And at Mukenai saves the trophy still—
      Go wonder there, who will!

³⁹⁹⁰   And the ten thousand-headed hound
      Of many a murder, the Lernaian snake
      He burned out, head by head, and cast around
      His darts a poison thence,—darts soon to slake
      Their rage in that three-bodied herdsman's gore
³⁹⁹⁵   Of Erutheia.   Many a running more
      He made for triumph and felicity,
      And, last of toils, to Haides, never dry
      Of tears, he sailed: and there he, luckless, ends
      His life completely, nor returns again.
⁴⁰⁰⁰   The house and home are desolate of friends,
      And where the children's life-path leads them, plain
      I see,—no step retraceable, no god
      Availing, and no law to help the lost!
      The oar of Charon marks their period,
⁴⁰⁰⁵   Waits to end all.   Thy hands, these roofs accost!—

---

³⁹⁸⁵| MS:Of every §inserted above§ friends §altered to§ friend from Hellas! all   *P1875:*Of friends <> Hellas, all   ³⁹⁸⁶| MS:gold-garnished vesture direful §last two words crossed out and replaced above by three words and hyphen§ cloaklet §altered to§ cloak, dread §over illegible word§ girdle-chase: *P1875:*girdle-chase!   ³⁹⁸⁷| MS:So deadly §last two words crossed out and replaced above by one word§ Destructive §crossed out§ to §altered to§ So Hellas   ³⁹⁸⁸⁻⁹⁰| MS:And §crossed out and restored§ <> the splendid trophy still. / And <> thousand headed   *P1875:*the trophy still— / Go <> will! / <> thousand-headed   ³⁹⁹³| MS:His arrows §crossed out and replaced above by two words§ darts a <> thence, darts §over illegible word§   *P1875:*thence,—darts   ³⁹⁹⁴| MS:Their fires §crossed out and replaced above by§ rage in that §inserted above§ <> herdsman's heart §crossed out§ gore   ³⁹⁹⁵| MS:The §crossed out and replaced above by§ Of Erutheia: ay, and many   *P1875:*Of Erutheia. Many   ³⁹⁹⁶| MS:triumph §over illegible word§ <> felicity   *P1875:*felicity,   ³⁹⁹⁷| MS:Until, for §last two words crossed out and replaced above by one word and comma§ And <> of labours §crossed out and replaced above by§ toils, he sailed §last two words crossed out§ to Hades never   *P1875:*to Haides, never   ³⁹⁹⁸| MS:tears,—he sailed, §last two words and comma inserted above§ and   *P1875:*tears, he sailed: and   ³⁹⁹⁹| MS:completely nor <> again: *P1875:*completely, nor <> again.   ⁴⁰⁰⁰| MS:house and home are §last three words crossed out and restored§   ⁴⁰⁰¹| MS:lead §altered to§ leads   ⁴⁰⁰³| MS:help, the   *P1875:*help the   ⁴⁰⁰⁴| MS:of charon §altered to§ Charon   ⁴⁰⁰⁵| MS:hands our roofs accost,   *P1875:*hands, these roofs accost!—

To thee, though absent, look their uttermost!

But if in youth and strength I flourished still,
Still shook the spear in fight, did power match will
In these Kadmeian co-mates of my age,
4010   They would,—and I,—when warfare was to wage,
Stand by these children; but I am bereft
Of youth now, lone of that good genius left!

But hist, desist! for here come these,—
Draped as the dead go, under and over,—
4015   Children long since,—now hard to discover,—
Of the once so potent Herakles!
And the loved wife dragging, in one tether
About her feet, the boys together;
And the hero's aged sire comes last!
4020   Unhappy that I am!   Of tears which rise,—
How am I all unable to hold fast,
Longer, the aged fountains of these eyes!

---

⁴⁰⁰⁶| MS:thee—though absent still, §last three words and punctuation inserted above and then *still* crossed out§ they look, their   *P1875:*thee, though absent, look their
⁴⁰⁰⁷| MS:While §crossed out§ But if I §crossed out§ in   ⁴⁰⁰⁸| MS:fight, and §crossed out and replaced above by§ if power matched   *P1875:*fight, did power match   ⁴⁰⁰⁹| MS:of §over *in*§   ⁴⁰¹⁰| MS:I would stand forth §last four words crossed out and replaced above by four words§ They would—and I, when battle §crossed out and replaced above by§ warfare   *P1875:*would,—and I,—when   ⁴⁰¹¹| MS:children: but   *P1875:*children; but   ⁴⁰¹²| MS:now—that good genius! lonely left!   *P1875:*now, lone of that good genius left!   ⁴⁰¹³| MS:Ah §crossed out§ But I pause: §last two words crossed out and replaced above by two words and colon altered to exclamation point§ hist, desist   ⁴⁰¹⁴| MS:Ah, but I see now §last five words crossed out and replaced above by seven words§ With the dress of the dead, over §last seven words crossed out§ Draped as the dead go §over *are*, last five words and comma inserted above§ <> over—   *P1875:*over,—   ⁴⁰¹⁵| MS:Children, that were, §last two words crossed out and replaced above by two crossed-out words, *of old*§ long since §last two words inserted above§ now <> discover,   *P1875:*Children long since,—now <> discover,—
⁴⁰¹⁶| MS:the hero which §last two words crossed out and replaced above by one illegibly crossed-out word§ once §over illegible erasure§ was §crossed out and replaced above by two words§ so potent Herakles—   *P1875:*potent Herakles!   ⁴⁰¹⁷| MS:Here comes the §last three words crossed out and replaced above by three words§ And the loved wife, here drags, §comma and last two words crossed out and replaced above by one word§ dragging   ⁴⁰¹⁸| MS:together,   *P1875:*together;   ⁴⁰¹⁹| MS:last.   *P1875:*last!   ⁴⁰²⁰| MS:am! The springs §last two words crossed out and replaced above by two words§ Of tears which §over illegible word§   ⁴⁰²¹| MS:Old §crossed out§ How shall §crossed out and replaced above by§ am   ⁴⁰²²| MS:§first word illegibly crossed out and replaced above by three words§ Longer, the aged

185

MEGARA

Be it so!   Who is priest, who butcher here
Of these ill-fated ones, or stops the breath
4025 Of me, the miserable?   Ready, see,
The sacrifice—to lead where Haides lives!
O children, we are led—no lovely team
Of corpses—age, youth, motherhood, all mixed!
O sad fate of myself and these my sons
4030 Whom with these eyes I look at, this last time!
I, indeed, bore you: but for enemies
I brought you up to be a laughing-stock,
Matter for merriment, destruction-stuff!
Woe's me!
4035 Strangely indeed my hopes have struck me down
From what I used to hope about you once—
The expectation from your father's talk!
For thee, now, thy dead sire dealt Argos to:
Thou wast to have Eurustheus' house one day,
4040 And rule Pelasgia where the fine fruits grow;
And, for a stole of state, he wrapped about
Thy head with that the lion-monster bore,
That which himself went wearing armour-wise.
And thou wast King of Thebes—such chariots there!
4045 Those plains I had for portion—all for thee,
As thou hadst coaxed them out of who gave birth
To thee, his boy: and into thy right hand
He thrust the guardian-club of Daidalos,—

4023| Let be, then! §last three words crossed out and replaced above by three words§ Be it so!
Who   4026| MS:lives. *P1875:*lives!   4027| MS:children we *P1875:*children, we
4028| MS:corpses, age, and §crossed out§ youth, motherhood all mixed,   *P1875:*corpses—age
<> motherhood, all mixed!   4029| MS:my boys §crossed out§ sons   4030| MS:with
my eyes <> at this   *P1875:*with these eyes <> at, this   4031| MS:you, but *P1875:*you:
but   4032| MS:laughing stock *P1875:*laughing-stock   4036| MS:used to §last two
words inserted above§ hoped §altered to§ hope   4037| MS:talk, *P1875:*talk!
4038| MS:to— *P1875:*to: 4040| MS:grow *P1875:*grow;   4041| MS:And for <>
state he   *P1875:*And, for <> state, he   4043| MS:With §crossed out and replaced above
by§ And which   *P1875:*That which   4046| MS:thou had §altered to§ hadst <> them
§over *those*§   4048| MS:guardian club *P1875:*guardian-club

Poor guardian proves the gift that plays thee false!
4050 And upon thee he promised to bestow
Oichalia—what, with those far-shooting shafts,
He ravaged once; and so, since three you were,
With threefold kingdoms did he build you up
To very towers, your father,—proud enough
4055 Prognosticating, from your manliness
In boyhood, what the manhood's self would be.
For my part, I was picking out for you
Brides, suiting each with his alliance—this
From Athens, this from Sparté, this from Thebes—
4060 Whence, suited—as stern-cables steady ship—
You might have hold on life gods bless.   All gone!
Fortune turns round and gives us—you, the Fates
Instead of brides—me, tears for nuptial baths,
Unhappy in my hoping!   And the sire
4065 Of your sire—he prepares the marriage-feast
Befitting Haides who plays father now—
Bitter relationship!   Oh me! which first—
Which last of you shall I to bosom fold?
To whom shall I fit close, his mouth to mine?
4070 Of whom shall I lay hold and ne'er let go?
How would I gather, like the brown-winged bee,
The groans from all, and, gathered into one,
Give them you back again, a crowded tear!
Dearest, if any voice be heard of men
4075 Dungeoned in Haides, thee—to thee I speak!
Here is thy father dying, and thy boys!

4049| MS:proves the §last two words inserted above§   4050| MS:And thee < > promised
he promise §last two words crossed out and replaced above by two words§ to bestow upon
*CP1875:*And upon thee < > to bestow   4051| MS:Oichalia §over partial erasure§
4052| MS:once: and *P1875:*once; and   4053| MS:up, *P1875:*up   4054| MS:So
§altered to§ To many §crossed out and replaced above by§ very < > proud man, he §last two
words crossed out§ enough *P1875:*enough, *1889a:*enough   4055| MS:Prognosticating
from *P1875:*Prognosticating, from   4059| MS:from Sparta *P1875:*from Sparté
4060| MS:That suited *P1875:*Whence, suited   4063| MS:nuptial-baths *P1875:*nuptial
baths   4071| MS:gather §inserted above§ < > bee, collect §crossed out§
4072| MS:The §in margin§ Groans of §crossed out and replaced above by§ from < > and,
gathering §altered to§ gathered *P1875:*groans   4076| MS:boys, *P1875:*boys!

And I too perish, famed as fortunate
By mortals once, through thee!   Assist them! Come!
But come! though just a shade, appear to me!
4080 For, coming, thy ghost-grandeur would suffice,
Such cowards are they in thy presence, these
Who kill thy children now thy back is turned!

AMPHITRUON

Ay, daughter, bid the powers below assist!
But I will rather, raising hand to heaven,
4085 Call thee to help, O Zeus, if thy intent
Be, to these children, helpful anyway,
Since soon thou wilt be valueless enough!
And yet thou hast been called and called; in vain
I labour: for we needs must die, it seems.
4090 Well, aged brothers—life's a little thing!
Such as it is, then, pass life pleasantly
From day to night, nor once grieve all the while!
Since Time concerns him not about our hopes,—
To save them,—but his own work done, flies off.
4095 Witness myself, looked up to among men,
Doing noteworthy deeds: when here comes fate
Lifts me away, like feather skyward borne,
In one day!   Riches then and glory,—whom
These are found constant to, I know not.   Friends,
4100 Farewell! the man who loved you all so much,

4077| MS:perish famed *P1875:*perish, famed   4078| MS:thee! Assist, then! Come!
*P1875:*thee! Assist them! Come!   4079| MS:come—though *P1875:*come! though
4082| MS:Who kills §altered to§ kill <> children, now *P1875:*children now
4083| MS:daughter—bid <> Powers *P1875:*daughter, bid <> powers   4085| MS:help,
O Zeus! if *P1875:*help, O Zeus, if   4086| MS:Be to <> children helpful *P1875:*Be, to
<> children, helpful   4088| MS:called: in vain, *P1875:*called; in vain
4090| MS:thing: *P1875:*thing!   4092| MS:night nor *P1875:*night, nor
4093| MS:Time §altered to§ Since time <> hopes *P1875:*Since Time <> hopes,—
4094| MS:them, but <> work §inserted above§ *P1875:*them,—but   4096| MS:deeds,
when *P1875:*deeds: when   4097| MS:And §crossed out§ lift §altered to§ Lifts
4098| MS:All in a §last three words crossed out and replaced above by four words§ In one day.
Riches §crossed out and restored§ <> glory, whom *P1875:*day! Riches <> glory,—whom
4099| MS:to,—I *P1875:*to, I   4100| MS:Farewell: the *P1875:*Farewell! the

188

Now, this last time, my mates, ye look upon!

MEGARA

Ha!
O father, do I see my dearest?   Speak!

AMPHITRUON

No more than thou canst, daughter—dumb like thee!

MEGARA

4105   Is this he whom we heard was under ground?

AMPHITRUON

Unless at least some dream in day we see!

MEGARA

What do I say? what dreams insanely view?
This is no other than thy son, old sire!
Here children! hang to these paternal robes,
4110   Quick, haste, hold hard on him, since here's your true
Zeus that can save—and every whit as well!

HERAKLES

O hail, my palace, my hearth's propula,—
How glad I see thee as I come to light!
Ha, what means this?   My children I behold
4115   Before the house in garments of the grave,

---

⁴¹⁰³| MS:father! do <> Speak!—   *P1875*:father, do <> Speak!   ⁴¹⁰⁶| MS:at <> in §last
two words over illegible words§   ⁴¹⁰⁷| MS:What I do <> view? §over illegible word§
P1875:What do   ⁴¹⁰⁹| MS:Here, children   *1889a*:Here children
⁴¹¹³| MS:glad to §altered to§ I   ⁴¹¹⁴| MS:this?—my   *P1875*:this? My
⁴¹¹⁵| MS:the §over illegible word§ <> grave— §over partial erasure§   *P1875*:grave,

Chapleted, and, amid a crowd of men,
My very wife—my father weeping too,
Whatever the misfortune!   Come, best take
My station nearer these and learn it all!
4120   Wife, what new sorrow has approached our home?

MEGARA

O dearest! light flashed on thy father now!
Art thou come? art thou saved and dost thou fall
On friends in their supreme extremity?

HERAKLES

How say'st thou?   Father! what's the trouble here?

MEGARA

4125   Undone are we!—but thou, old man, forgive
If first I snatch what thou shouldst say to him!
For somehow womanhood wakes pity more.
Here are my children killed and I undone!

HERAKLES

Apollon, with what preludes speech begins!

MEGARA

4130   Dead are my brothers and old father too.

4116| MS:and amid <> men   *P1875:*and, amid <> men,
4120| MS:new trouble §crossed out and replaced above by§ sorrow   4121| MS:Oh,
dearest,—light <> now,—   *P1875:*O dearest! light <> now!   4122| MS:come—art <>
thou fall §crossed out and restored§   *P1875:*come? art   4123| MS:In their supreme
extremity on friends?   *P1875:*On friends in their supreme extremity?   4124| MS:sayst
<> Father—what's the trouble §crossed out and restored§   *P1875:*say'st <> Father! what's
4125| MS:we! but, §comma crossed out§ thou   *P1875:*we!—but

HERAKLES

How say'st thou?—doing what?—by spear-stroke whence?

MEGARA

Lukos destroyed them—the land's noble king!

HERAKLES

Met them in arms? or through the land's disease?

MEGARA

Sedition: and he sways seven-gated Thebes.

HERAKLES

4135   Why then came fear on the old man and thee?

MEGARA

He meant to kill thy father, me, our boys.

HERAKLES

How say'st thou?   Fearing what from orphanage?

MEGARA

Lest they should some day pay back Kreon's death.

HERAKLES

4131| MS:sayst thou? doing what? by   P1875:say'st thou?—doing what?—by
4132| MS:Lukos, §comma crossed out§ destroyed them,—the < > king.   P1875:them—the
< > king!   4134| MS:seven gated   P1875:seven-gated
4136| MS:me, the §crossed out and replaced above by§ our

And why trick out the boys corpse-fashion thus?

MEGARA

4140   These wraps of death we have already donned.

HERAKLES

And you had died through violence?   Woe's me!

MEGARA

Left bare of friends: and thou wast dead, we heard.

HERAKLES.

And whence came on you this faintheartedness?

MEGARA

The heralds of Eurustheus brought the news.

HERAKLES

4145   And why was it you left my house and hearth?

MEGARA

Forced thence; thy father—from his very couch!

HERAKLES

And no shame at insulting the old man?

4140| MS:We have already donned these §altered to§ These wraps of death. §last four words marked for transposition to beginning of line§   *P1875:*we   4141| MS:And §inserted above§ You had §over illegible word§   *P1875:*you   4144| MS:heralds §over partial erasure§   4145| MS:why did §crossed out and replaced above by two words§ was it you §next word illegibly crossed out§ left   4146| MS:thence: thy < > couch.   *P1875:*couch!   *1889a:*thence; thy   4147| MS:And §inserted above§ No   *P1875:*no

MEGARA

Shame, truly! no near neighbours *he* and Shame!

HERAKLES

And so much, in my absence, lacked I friends?

MEGARA

4150   Friends,—are there any to a luckless man?

HERAKLES

The Minuai-war I waged,—they spat forth these?

MEGARA

Friendless,—again I tell thee,—is ill-luck.

HERAKLES

Will not you cast these hell-wraps from your hair
And look on light again, and with your eyes
4155   Taste the sweet change from nether dark to day?
While I—for now there needs my handiwork—
First I shall go, demolish the abodes
Of these new lordships; next hew off the head
Accurst and toss it for the dogs to trail.
4160   Then, such of the Kadmeians as I find

4148| MS:he *P1875:he*   4149| MS:so much, §last two words and comma inserted above§
4150| MS:Friends,—who §crossed out§ are friends §crossed out and replaced above by two
words§ there any to any §crossed out and replaced above by§ a   4151| MS:The Minuai
war < > spat on §altered to§ forth   *P1875:*The Minuai-war
4153| MS:these hell-wreaths §altered to§ hell-wraps   4154| MS:on day §crossed out and
replaced above by§ light   4157| MS:shall §inserted above§
4158| MS:new masters §crossed out and replaced above by§ lordships; then §crossed out and
replaced above by§ next   4160| MS:of those §altered to§ the

193

Were craven though they owed me gratitude,—
Some I intend to handle with this club
Renowned for conquest; and with winged shafts
Scatter the others, fill Ismenos full
4165 With bloody corpses,—Dirké's flow so white
Shall be incarnadined.   For, whom, I pray,
Behoves me rather help than wife and child
And aged father?   Farewell, "Labours" mine!
Vainly I wrought them: my true work lay here!
4170 My business is to die defending these,—
If for their father's sake they meant to die.
Or how shall we call brave the battling it
With snake and lion, as Eurustheus bade,
If yet I must not labour death away
4175 From my own children?   "Conquering Herakles"
Folk will not call me as they used, I think!
The right thing is for parents to assist
Children, old age, the partner of the couch.

AMPHITRUON

True, son! thy duty is—be friend to friends
4180 And foe to foes: yet—no more haste than needs!

HERAKLES

Why, father, what is over hasty here?

4161| MS:Were cravens §crossed out and restored and rewritten above§ *P1875:*craven
4162| MS:These §crossed out and replaced above by§ Some   4163| MS:conquest: and the
rest §last two words crossed out and replaced above by one word§ with *P1875:*conquest; and
4164| MS:Scattering §altered to§ Scatter <> Ismenus *P1875:*fill Ismenos
4165| MS:corpses,—Dirke's *P1875:*corpses,—Dirké's   4167| MS:rather §inserted above§
4168| MS:farewell *P1875:*father? Farewell   4173| MS:With §next word illegibly crossed
out and replaced above by§ snake and §over illegible word§   4174| MS:And yet *P1875:*
If yet   4176| MS:Folks *1889a:*Folk   4177| MS:The true §crossed out and replaced
above by§ right <> for fathers §crossed out and replaced above by§ parents to stand up §last
two words crossed out§ defend §crossed out§ assist   4178| MS:For §crossed out§ children
§altered to§ Children <> the §inserted above§ <> of their §altered to§ the
4179| MS:son—thy *P1875:*son! thy   4181| MS:over-hasty *1889a:*over hasty

AMPHITRUON

Many a pauper,—seeming to be rich,
As the word goes,—the king calls partisan.
Such made a riot, ruined Thebes to rob
4185 Their neighbour: for, what good they had at home
Was spent and gone—flew off through idleness.
You came to trouble Thebes, they saw: since seen,
Beware lest, raising foes, a multitude,
You stumble where you apprehend no harm.

HERAKLES

4190 If all Thebes saw me, not a whit care I.
But seeing as I did a certain bird
Not in the lucky seats, I knew some woe
Was fallen upon the house: so, purposely,
By stealth I made my way into the land.

AMPHITRUON

4195 And now, advancing, hail the hearth with praise
And give the ancestral home thine eye to see!
For he himself will come, thy wife and sons
To drag-forth—slaughter—slay me too,—this king!
But, here remaining, all succeeds with thee—

4182| MS:rich *P1875*:rich,   4183| MS:partisan: *P1875*:partisan.
4185| MS:for what *P1875*:for, what   4186| MS:spent and §last two words inserted above§
4187| MS:saw: since §crossed out and replaced above by§ and, §word and
comma crossed out and *since* restored§   4188| MS:raising up §inserted above and then
crossed out§ all your §last two words crossed out§ foes, at once §last two words crossed out
and replaced above by two words§ a multitude,   4189| MS:You make a §last two words
crossed out§ stumble <> you least expect trap §last three words crossed out and replaced
above by three words§ apprehend no snare. *P1875*:no harm.
4190| MS:not one §crossed out and replaced above by§ a   4192| MS:the right place §last
two words crossed out and replaced above by two words§ lucky spaces §altered to§ seats, where
§crossed out§ I <> some ill §crossed out§ woe   4193| MS:Had §crossed out and replaced
above by§ Was fallen <> purposely, §crossed out and replaced above by crossed-out word,
secretly, and then restored§   4194| MS:On purpose §last two words crossed out and
replaced above by two words§ By stealth   4198| MS:drag-forth—slay §altered to§
slaughter <> king: *P1875*:king!   4199| MS:For, here *P1875*:But, here

4200   Gain lost by no false step.   So, this thy town
        Disturb not, son, ere thou right matters here!

HERAKLES

        Thus will I do, for thou say'st well; my home
        Let me first enter!   Since at the due time
        Returning from the unsunned depths where dwells
4205   Haides' wife Koré, let me not affront
        Those gods beneath my roof I first should hail!

AMPHITRUON

        For didst thou really visit Haides, son?

HERAKLES

        Ay—dragged to light, too, his three-headed beast.

AMPHITRUON

        By fight didst conquer, or through Koré's gift?

HERAKLES

4210   Fight: well for me, I saw the Orgies first!

AMPHITRUON

        And is he in Eurustheus' house, the brute?

4200| MS:step. But this   *P1875:*step. So, this   4201| MS:son, §word and comma inserted above§ <> right things §crossed out and replaced above by§ matters   4202| MS:So will <> well: my   *P1875:*Thus will <> well; my   4203| MS:enter! Since it §altered to§ at 4205| MS:Haides' and §crossed out and replaced above by§ wife   4206| MS:The §altered to§ Those <> hail.   *P1875:*roof, I <> hail!   *1889a:*roof I   4207| MS:really §inserted above§   4209| MS:fight, didst conquer—or   *1889a:*fight didst conquer, or

HERAKLES

Chthonia's grove, Hermion's city, hold him now.

AMPHITRUON

Does not Eurustheus know thee back on earth?

HERAKLES

No: I would come first and see matters here.

AMPHITRUON

4215   But how wast thou below ground such a time?

HERAKLES

I stopped, from Haides, bringing Theseus up.

AMPHITRUON

And where is he?—bound o'er the plain for home?

HERAKLES

Gone glad to Athens—Haides' fugitive!
But, up, boys! follow father into house!
4220   There's a far better going-in for you
Truly, than going-out was!   Nay, take heart,
And let the eyes no longer run and run!

4212| *P1875:*holds   *1889a:*hold   4215| MS:ground all §crossed out§ such
4216| MS:I §in margin§ Stopping §last three letters crossed out and replaced above by *ed* and
comma, forming§ Stopped, to bring §crossed out and replaced above by§ see from §last three
words crossed out and *from* restored§ Haides, bringing §inserted above§ Theseus up thence.
§last two words crossed out and *up* restored§   *P1875:*stopped   4221| MS:Truly, §word
and comma inserted above§ Than §altered to§ than < > was! But take heart. §period crossed
out§   *P1875:*was! Nay, take heart,   4222| MS:and run—   *P1875:*and run!

And thou, O wife, my own, collect thy soul
Nor tremble now!   Leave grasping, all of you,
4225   My garments!   I'm not winged, nor fly from friends!
Ah,—
No letting go for these, who all the more
Hang to my garments!   Did you foot indeed
The razor's edge?   Why, then I'll carry them—
4230   Take with my hands these small craft up, and tow
Just as a ship would.   There! don't fear I shirk
My children's service! this way, men are men,
No difference! best and worst, they love their boys
After one fashion: wealth they differ in—
4235   Some have it, others not; but each and all
Combine to form the children-loving race.

CHOROS

Youth is a pleasant burthen to me;
But age on my head, more heavily
Than the crags of Aitna, weighs and weighs,
4240   And darkening cloaks the lids and intercepts the rays.

---

^{4223|} MS:o   *P1875:*thou, O   ^{4224|} MS:now! Leave holding §crossed out and replaced
above by§ grasping   ^{4225|} MS:My peplo §crossed out and replaced above by§ garments!
< > winged! §exclamation point altered to comma§ nor   ^{4227|} MS:these who   *P1875:*
these, who   ^{4229|} MS:carry you §crossed out and replaced above by§ them—
^{4230|} MS:Take up these small craft with my hands §last eight words marked for transposition
to§ Take with my hands these small craft up and   *P1875:*up, and   ^{4231|} MS:don't think
§crossed out and replaced above by§ fear   ^{4234|} MS:wealth makes difference §last two
words crossed out and replaced above by three words§ they differ in—   ^{4235|} MS:Some
§crossed out and restored§ have §over partial erasure§ < > others §crossed out and restored§
not: all love alike, §last three words and comma crossed out and replaced above by four
words§ but each and all   *P1875:*not; but   ^{4236|} MS:The human race—a children-loving
race. §entire line crossed out and replaced above by four words§ Combine to form the §last
four words crossed out and followed by a seven-word line§ And every race is a child-loving
one. §entire line crossed out and replaced above by five words§ And of all the kinds §last five
words crossed out and then six words restored§ Combine to form the children-loving race.
^{4237|} MS:pleasant §inserted above§ < > me: *P1875:*me;   ^{4237-38|} MS:§between these
two lines§ Pleasant to bear §last three words crossed out§   ^{4238|} MS:on §crossed out and
restored§ < > head, lies heavily §last two words crossed out and replaced above by two crossed-
out words, *weighs incessantly; lies heavily* restored and then *lies* replaced above by *more*§
^{4239|} MS:Beyond §crossed out and replaced above by§ Than   ^{4240|} MS:darkening
§inserted above§ < > intercepts the gaze §crossed out and replaced above by§ rays.

198

Never be mine the preference
Of an Asian empire's wealth, nor yet
Of a house all gold, to youth, to youth
That's beauty, whatever the gods dispense!
4245   Whether in wealth we joy, or fret
Paupers,—of all God's gifts most beautiful, in truth!

But miserable murderous age I hate!
Let it go to wreck, the waves adown,
Nor ever by rights plague tower or town
4250   Where mortals bide, but still elate
With wings, on ether, precipitate,
Wander them round—nor wait!

But if the gods, to man's degree,
Had wit and wisdom, they would bring
4255   Mankind a twofold youth, to be
Their virtue's sign-mark, all should see,
In those with whom life's winter thus grew spring.
For when they died, into the sun once more
Would they have traversed twice life's racecourse o'er;

4240-41| MS:§¶ called for in margin§   *P1875:*§no ¶§   4241| MS:preference §crossed out
and restored§ choice §crossed out§   4243| MS:house brimful of §last two words crossed
out and replaced above by one word§ all gold, to §crossed out and replaced above by three
crossed-out words, *in place of*, then *to* restored§ youth, to youth   4244| MS:That's §crossed
out and replaced above by illegibly crossed-out word and comma, perhaps *Most*, and then
restored§ beauty, §over illegible word, perhaps *beauties*§ beyond all §last two words crossed out
and replaced above by two words§ whatever the Gods dispense: *P1875:*gods dispense!
4246| MS:In poverty, still §last three words crossed out and replaced above by six words§
Paupers: of all God's gifts most < > in §inserted§ truth.   *P1875:*Paupers,—of < > truth!
4247| MS:hate: *P1875:*hate!   4248| MS:adown!   *P1875:*adown,   4249| MS:Nor
§over illegible word§ should §inserted above and crossed out§ never §altered to§ ever by
§over illegible erasure§ < > town,   *P1875:*town   4250| MS:elate §over illegible erasure§
4251| MS:wings, on §last two words inserted above§ the §crossed out§ ether, on wings §last two
words crossed out§ precipitate,   4252| MS:§first word illegibly crossed out§ Wander < >
round—not wait!   *P1875:*round—nor wait!   4253| MS:gods' §apostrophe crossed out§
< > degree   *P1875:*degree,   4255| MS:Mankind a §last word and *kind* inserted§
4256| MS:Their §in margin§ Virtue's §next word illegibly crossed out§ sign-mark, pl §last two
letters crossed out§ all   *P1875:*virtue's   4257| MS:winter changed to §last two words
crossed out and replaced above by two words§ thus grew spring: *P1875:*spring.
4259| MS:they emerge, §word and comma crossed out and replaced above by two words§ have
traversed twice run §crossed out§ life's < > o'er: *P1875:*o'er;

4260   While ignobility had simply run
      Existence through, nor second life begun.
      And so might we discern both bad and good
      As surely as the starry multitude
      Is numbered by the sailors, one and one.
4265   But now the gods by no apparent line
      Limit the worthy and the base define;
      Only, a certain period rounds, and so
      Brings man more wealth,—but youthful vigour, no!

      Well! I am not to pause
4270   Mingling together—wine and wine in cup—
      The Graces with the Muses up—
      Most dulcet marriage: loosed from music's laws,
      No life for me!
      But where the wreaths abound, there ever may I be!
4275   And still, an aged bard, I shout Mnemosuné—
      Still chant of Herakles the triumph-chant,
      Companioned by the seven-stringed tortoise-shell
      And Libuan flute, and Bromios' self as well,
      God of the grape, with man participant!
4280   Not yet will we arrest their glad advance—
      The Muses who so long have led me forth to dance!
      A paian—hymn the Delian girls indeed,
      Weaving a beauteous measure in and out

4261| MS:begun: *P1875*:begun.   4266| MS:base §over illegible word§ define, *P1875*: define;   4267| MS:Only the §crossed out§ a <> rounds to full §last two words crossed out§ and *P1875*:Only, a <> rounds, and   4268| MS:And §crossed out§ Brings man
4269| MS:pause §over illegible word§   4270| MS:together,— wine and wine in cup,— §last six words and punctuation inserted above§ *P1875*:together—wine <> cup—
4271| MS:§solidus and line added§ the §altered to§ The <> the muses §altered to§ Muses
4272| MS:Making the sweetest of companionships §crossed out and replaced above by two words§ all company! §last six words crossed out and replaced above by seven words§ Most dulcet—marriage: loosed from music's laws *P1875*:dulcet marriage <> laws,
4273| MS:me! apart from music's laws! §last four words and exclamation point crossed out§
4274| MS:be, *P1875*:be!   4275| MS:still, the §crossed out and replaced above by§ an <> I §inserted above§ shouts §altered to§ shout forth §crossed out§ Mnemosune— *P1875*:shout Mnemosuné—   4276| MS:Still sing §crossed out and replaced above by four words§ chant the triumph chant §last three words crossed out§ of Herakles the triumph-song, §last two words crossed out and restored; last word altered to *triumph-chant*§   4278| MS:And Libuan §over *Libyan*§   4282| MS:paian §over partial erasure§ hymn *P1875*:paian— hymn   4283| MS:Weaving the §crossed out and replaced above by§ a

His temple-gates, Latona's goodly seed;
4285　And paians—I too, these thy domes about,
From these grey cheeks, my king, will swan-like shout—
Old songster!　Ay, in song it starts off brave—
"Zeus' son is he!" and yet, such grace of birth
Surpassing far, to man his labours gave
4290　Existence, one calm flow without a wave,
Having destroyed the beasts, the terrors of the earth.

LUKOS

From out the house Amphitruon comes—in time!
For 'tis a long while now since ye bedecked
Your bodies with the dead-folk's finery.
4295　But quick! the boys and wife of Herakles—
Bid them appear outside this house, keep pact
To die, and need no bidding but your own!

AMPHITRUON

King! you press hard on me sore-pressed enough,
And give me scorn—beside my dead ones here.
4300　Meet in such matters were it, though you reign,
To temper zeal with moderation.　Since
You do impose on us the need to die—
Needs must we love our lot, obey your will.

4284| MS:seed: *P1875:*seed; 　4205| MS:paians §inserted above§ I too, f §last letter crossed out§ these *P1875:*paians—I 　4286| MS:From these grey cheeks,— §last four words and punctuation inserted above§ my §over partial erasure§ *P1875:*cheeks, my 4287| MS:songster,—ay, it starts off well §crossed out§ in song brave— §last six words transposed to§ in song it starts off brave— *P1875:*songster! Ay 4288| MS:"Zeus son *P1875:*"Zeus' son 　4294| MS:the peplos §last word crossed out and replaced above by two words§ dead folk's finery *P1875:*dead-folk's finery. 4296| MS:this palace §crossed out and replaced above by§ house,—keep *P1875:*house, keep 4297| MS:die and §last two words inserted above§ < > own! to die §last two words crossed out§ *P1875:*die, and 　4298| MS:enough! §exclamation point altered to comma§ 4299| MS:And §over illegible erasure§ < > beside the §crossed out and replaced above by§ my < > here! *P1875:*here. 　4300| MS:Meet §over illegible erasure§ 4301| MS:moderation: since *P1875:*moderation. Since 　4303| MS:love §over illegible word§ < > lot, and do §last two words crossed out and replaced above by one word§ obey

LUKOS

Where's Megara, then?   Alkmené's grandsons, where?

AMPHITRUON

4305 She, I think,—as one figures from outside,—

LUKOS

Well, this same thinking,—what affords its ground?

AMPHITRUON

—Sits suppliant on the holy altar-steps,—

LUKOS

Idly indeed a suppliant to save life!

AMPHITRUON

—And calls on her dead husband, vainly too!

LUKOS

4310 For he's not come, nor ever will arrive.

AMPHITRUON

Never—at least, if no god raise him up.

4304| MS:then? Alkemena's grandson, §last two words and comma inserted above§ Where?
§altered to§ where?   P1875:then? Alkemené's   4306| MS:And this <> affords p §last
letter crossed out§ ground?   P1875:Well, this   4308| MS:Idly enough
§crossed out and replaced above by§ indeed   4309| MS:—And, §comma crossed out§
calls <> her §inserted above§ <> too!   P1875:too!
4310| MS:And he's <> come §over illegible word§   P1875:For he's

202

LUKOS

Go to her, and conduct her from the house!

AMPHITRUON

I should partake the murder, doing that.

LUKOS

We,—since thou hast a scruple in the case,—
4315   Outside of fears, we shall march forth these lads,
Mother and all.   Here, follow me, my folk—
And gladly so remove what stops our toils!

AMPHITRUON

Thou—go then! March where needs must! What remains—
Perhaps concerns another.   Doing ill,
4320   Expect some ill be done thee!
                     Ha, old friends!
On he strides beautifully! in the toils
O' the net, where swords spring forth, will he be fast—
Minded to kill his neighbours—the arch-knave!
I go, too—I must see the falling corpse!
4325   For he has sweets to give—a dying man,
Your foe, that pays the price of deeds he did.

CHOROS

Troubles are over!   He the great king once

4313| MS:partake you §crossed out and replaced above by§ the   4314| MS:We then §crossed out and dash inserted§ since <> case—   *P1875:*We,—since <> case,—
4315| MS:Outside §*Out* over partial erasure§   4316| MS:all §over illegible word§ <> me §over illegible word§ <> folk!— §exclamation point crossed out§   4317| MS:gladly §inserted above§ so, what <> our toils §inserted above§ task, remove! §over partial erasure§   *P1875:*so remove what <> our toils!   4319| MS:Perhaps §in margin§ Concerns §altered to§ concerns
4320| MS:friends—   *P1875:*friends!   4321| MS:he goes §crossed out and replaced above by§ strides beautifully—in   *P1875:*beautifully! in   4324| MS:see <> falling §last two words inserted above§   4327| MS:over! He, the <> once,   *P1875:*He the   *1889a:*once

Turns the point, tends for Haides, goal of life!
O justice, and the gods' back-flowing fate!

AMPHITRUON

4330 Thou art come, late indeed, where death pays, crime—
These insults heaped on better than thyself!

CHOROS

Joy gives this outburst to my tears!   Again
Come round those deeds, his doing, which of old
He never dreamed himself was to endure—
4335 King of the country!   But enough, old man!
Indoors, now, let us see how matters stand—
If somebody be faring as I wish!

LUKOS

Ah me—me!

CHOROS

This strikes the keynote—music to my mind,
4340 Merry i' the household!   Death takes up the tune!
The king gives voice, groans murder's prelude well!

LUKOS

O, all the land of Kadmos! slain by guile!

4329| MS:O §over illegible word, perhaps *He*§   4331| MS:These §over illegible word§ < >
thyself. *P1875:*thyself!   4332| MS:tears: again *P1875:* tears! Again   4335| MS:old
friends §crossed out and replaced above by§ man!   4336| MS:matters fare §crossed out
and replaced above by§ stand—   4337| MS:If Someone §altered to§
somebody there §crossed out§ be   4339| MS:strikes up a §last two words crossed out and
replaced above by three words and dash§ the key note *P1875:*keynote

CHOROS

Ay, for who slew first?   Paying back thy due,
Resign thee! make, for deeds done, mere amends!
4345   Who was it grazed the gods through lawlessness—
Mortal himself, threw up his fool's-conceit
Against the blessed heavenly ones—as though
Gods had no power?   Old friends, the impious man
Exists not any more!   The house is mute.
4350   Turn we to song and dance!   For, those I love,
Those I wish well to, well fare they, to wish!

Dances, dances and banqueting
To Thebes, the sacred city through,
Are a care! for, change and change
4355   Of tears to laughter, old to new,
Our lays, glad birth, they bring, they bring!
He is gone and past, the mighty king!
And the old one reigns, returned—O strange!
From the Acherontian harbour too!
4360   Advent of hope, beyond thought's widest range!
To the gods, the gods, are crimes a care,
And they watch our virtue, well aware
That gold and that prosperity drive man

---

⁴³⁴³| MS:who slayed §crossed out and replaced above by§ slew   ⁴³⁴⁴| MS:thee, go
§crossed out§ making §altered to§ make <> mere §over illegible word and inserted above§
*P1875:*thee! make   ⁴³⁴⁷| MS:one   *P1875:*ones   ⁴³⁴⁸| MS:Gods have no <> Old
§over illegible word§ friend §altered to§ friends   *P1875:*Gods had no   ⁴³⁴⁹| MS:is dum
§last three letters crossed out§ mute.   ⁴³⁵⁰| MS:dance. For those   *P1875:*dance! For,
those   ⁴³⁵²| MS:dances, and   *P1875:*dances and   ⁴³⁵³| MS:Are a care to §last four
words crossed out and replaced above by one word§ To <> sacred §inserted above§
⁴³⁵⁴| MS:The sacred one §last three words crossed out and replaced above by one word§
Concern §crossed out and replaced by three words§ Are a care: for change   *P1875:*care! for,
change   ⁴³⁵⁵| MS:From §crossed out and replaced above by§ Of <> laughter, from
§crossed out§ old   ⁴³⁵⁶| MS:Our §over illegible word§ lays, to §crossed out and replaced
above by§ a birth   *P1875:*lays, glad birth   ⁴³⁵⁷| MS:and past §last two words and comma
inserted above§   ⁴³⁵⁸| MS:And by right §last two words inserted
above and crossed out§ the old §over illegible erasure§ king—the true, returns §last four
words crossed out and replaced above by four words§ one reigns, returning—strange!
*P1875:*returned—O strange!   ⁴³⁶⁰| MS:gods are   *1889a:*gods, are
⁴³⁶²| MS:aware! §exclamation point crossed out§   ⁴³⁶³| MS:man §over *men*§

Out of his mind—those charioteers who hale
4365   Might-without-right behind them: face who can
Fortune's reverse which time prepares, nor quail?
—He who evades law and in lawlessness
Delights him,—he has broken down his trust—
The chariot, riches haled—now blackening in the dust!

4370   Ismenos, go thou garlanded!
Break into dance, ye ways, the polished bed
O' the seven-gated city!   Dirké, thou
Fair-flowing, with the Asopiad sisters all,
Leave your sire's stream, attend the festival
4375   Of Herakles, one choir of nymphs, sing triumph now!
O woody rock of Puthios and each home
O' the Helikonian Muses, ye shall come
With joyous shouting to my walls, my town
Where saw the light that Spartan race, those "Sown,"
4380   Brazen-shield-bearing chiefs, whereof the band
With children's children renovates our land,
To Thebes a sacred light!

4364| MS:of their §crossed out and replaced above by§ his §over illegible word§ minds
§altered to§ mind < > charioteers that §crossed out and replaced above by§ who
4365| MS:Might without right   *P1875:*Might-without-right   4366| MS:prepares nor
*P1875:*prepares, nor   4367| MS:and to §crossed out and replaced above by§ in
4368| MS:him. He   *P1875:*him,—he   4369| MS:haled,—now blackened §altered to§
blackens in   *P1875:*haled—now blackening in   4369-70| MS:§no ¶ called for§   *P1875:*
§¶§   4370| MS:garlanded, *P1875:*garlanded!   4372| MS:city; Dirka, thou §over
illegible word§   *P1875:*city! Dirké   4373| MS:the Asopiad nymphs, come §last two words
crossed out, marked to restore, and then replaced above by one word and comma§ sisters, all
*P1875:*sisters all,   4374| MS:the triumph-festival §altered to§ festival
4376| MS:and ye §crossed out and replaced above by§ each   4377| MS:Of Heliconian
Muses com §last three letters crossed out§ ye   *P1875:*O' the Helikonian Muses, ye
4378| MS:With mirth and §last two words crossed out and replaced above by one word§ joyous
< > to Thebes, §word and comma crossed out§ my towers §crossed out and replaced above
by§ walls   4379| MS:Where §next word illegibly crossed out and replaced above by§ saw
the < > that < > those §last three words over illegible words§
4380| MS:The band of those brazen shielded §last three words altered to§ Those Brazen shield
§last six words crossed out and replaced above by one word§ Brazen-shield-bearing ones
whereof   *P1875:*Brazen-shield-bearing chiefs, whereof   4382| MS:A sacred-light.
§period inserted§ unquestionable §crossed out§ To §over illegible word§ Thebes. §line
marked for transposition to§ To Thebes a sacred light.   *P1875:*light!

O combination of the marriage rite—
Bed of the mortal-born and Zeus, who couched
⁴³⁸⁵ Beside the nymph of Perseus' progeny!
For credible, past hope, becomes to me
That nuptial story long ago avouched,
O Zeus! and time has turned the dark to bright,
And made one blaze of truth the Herakleidan might—
⁴³⁹⁰ His, who emerged from earth's pavilion, left
Plouton's abode, the nether palace-cleft.
Thou wast the lord that nature gave me—not
That baseness born and bred—my king, by lot!
—Baseness made plain to all, who now regard
⁴³⁹⁵ The match of sword with sword in fight,—
If to the gods the Just and Right
Still pleasing be, still claim the palm's award.

Horror!
Are we come to the self-same passion of fear,
⁴⁴⁰⁰ Old friends?—such a phantasm fronts me here
Visible over the palace-roof!
In flight, in flight, the laggard limb
Bestir! and haste aloof

---

^{4383|} MS:the nuptial couch §last two words crossed out and replaced above by two words§
marriage rite—   ^{4384|} MS:Bed That §crossed out§ of the mortal-born §last four words
inserted above§ And   *P1875:*and   ^{4386|} MS:credible, §next two words illegibly crossed
out and replaced above by two words§ past hope becomes   *P1875:*hope, becomes
^{4387|} MS:avouched,— §dash crossed out§   ^{4388|} MS:O Zeus, §comma altered to
exclamation point§ but time <> bright   *P1875:*O Zeus! and time <> bright,
^{4389|} MS:truth the §last two words inserted above§   ^{4390|} MS:His who   *P1875:*His, who
^{4391|} MS:abode, the deep down §last three words crossed out and replaced above by one
word§ the palace-cleft.   *P1875:*the nether palace-cleft.   ^{4394|} MS:—Baseness apparent
now §last two words crossed out and replaced above by two words§ made plain to us, now §last
two words inserted above; *now* crossed out, then restored and marked for transposition to
follow *who*§ who regards §altered to§ regard   *P1875:*to all, who   ^{4395|} MS:The battle,
§word and comma crossed out and replaced above by two words§ match of sword to §crossed
out and replaced above by§ with <> in §inserted§   ^{4396|} MS:to §over illegible word,
perhaps *of*§ <> the Right   *P1875:*the Just and Right   ^{4397|} MS:Still please, §word
and comma crossed out§ claim   *P1875:*Still pleasing be, still claim
^{4401|} MS:palace-roof? §question mark altered to exclamation point§   ^{4402|} MS:the
sluggish §crossed out and replaced above by§ laggard   ^{4403|} MS:Bestir and stand
§crossed out and replaced above by§ haste   *P1875:*Bestir! and

207

From that on the roof there—grand and grim!
4405 O Paian, king!
Be thou my safeguard from the woeful thing!

IRIS

Courage, old men! beholding here—Night's birth—
Madness, and me the handmaid of the gods,
Iris: since to your town we come, no plague—
4410 Wage war against the house of but one man
From Zeus and from Alkmené sprung, they say.
Now, till he made an end of bitter toils,
Fate kept him safe, nor did his father Zeus
Let us once hurt him, Heré nor myself.
4415 But, since he has toiled through Eurustheus' task,
Heré desires to fix fresh blood on him—
Slaying his children: I desire it too.

Up then, collecting the unsoftened heart,
Unwedded virgin of black Night! Drive, drag
4420 Frenzy upon the man here—whirls of brain
Big with child-murder, while his feet leap gay!
Let go the bloody cable its whole length!

4404| MS:on the roof §last three words inserted above§ 4405| MS:king— *P1875:*king!
4406| MS:Avert §crossed out and replaced above by four words§ Be thou my safeguard from
me §crossed out§ the 4407| MS:men, beholding this §crossed out and replaced above
by§ here *P1875:*men! beholding 4409| MS:Iris: for to <> come no *P1875:*Iris: since
to <> come, no 4410| MS:Wage §over illegible word§ wage §crossed out and replaced
above by§ war 4411| MS:Whom they §last two words crossed out§ Of §crossed out and
replaced above by§ From <> and of §crossed out and replaced above by§ from <> sprung
§over illegible word§ <> say— *P1875:*say. 4412| MS:For till <> toils *P1875:*Now, till
<> toils, 4415| MS:he passed §last two words inserted above§ Eurustheus' labours
through, *P1875:*he has toiled through Eurustheus' task, 4416| MS:Heré is minded
§last two words crossed out and replaced above by one word§ desires <> fix §next word
inserted above and illegibly crossed out§ fresh §inserted above§ 4417| MS:From his own
veins §last four words crossed out and replaced above by three words and colon§ Slaying his
children 4418| MS:Up §crossed out and replaced above by illegibly crossed-out word and
then restored§ 4419| MS:virgin §next word illegibly crossed out, perhaps *thou* or *then*§ of
black Night!—drive—drag *P1875:*black Night! Drive, drag 4421| MS:Bringing §crossed
out and replaced above by two words§ Big with <> while the feet *P1875:*while his feet
4422| MS:Let out §crossed out and replaced above by§ go <> length, *P1875:*length!

So that,—when o'er the Acherousian ford
He has sent floating, by self-homicide,
His beautiful boy-garland,—he may know
First, Heré's anger, what it is to him,
And then learn mine.   The gods are vile indeed
And mortal matters vast, if he 'scape free!

⁴⁴²⁵

MADNESS

Certes, from well-born sire and mother too
Had I my birth, whose blood is Night's and Heaven's;
But here's my glory,—not to grudge the good!
Nor love I raids against the friends of man.
I wish, then, to persuade,—before I see
You stumbling, you and Heré! trust my words!
This man, the house of whom ye hound me to,
Is not unfamed on earth nor gods among;
Since, having quelled waste land and savage sea,
He alone raised again the falling rights
Of gods—gone ruinous through impious men.
Desire no mighty mischief, I advise!

⁴⁴³⁰

⁴⁴³⁵

⁴⁴⁴⁰

4423| MS:that, when he sends floating §last three words crossed out§ o'er <> Acherousian §inserted above§ *P1875:*that,—when   4424| MS:Of Acherou §last seven letters and preceding word crossed out and replaced above by six words§ He has sent floating, by self-homicide,   4425| MS:boy-garland, he   *P1875:*boy-garland,—he   4426| MS:First, Here's §over illegible word§   4428| MS:scape   *P1875:*'scape   4429| MS:True, from a well born sire   *P1875:*Certes, from well-born sire   4430| MS:Had §over *Have*§
4431| MS:good;   *P1875:*good!   4433| MS:wish then to dissuade §altered to§ persuade, before   *P1875:*wish, then, to persuade,—before   4434| MS: You stumble §last two words crossed out and replaced above by five words§ The false step, you did, Heré and, §crossed out§ trust   *P1875:*You stumbling, you and Heré! trust
4435| MS:man, because §crossed out and replaced above by two words§ the house <> me on the house §last three words crossed out and replaced above by one word§ to,   4436| MS:nor with the §last two words crossed out§ gods among.   *P1875:*among;
4437| MS:But having tamed land §last two words crossed out and replaced above by two words§ quelled waste §*land* restored§ trackless §crossed out and replaced above by§ and <> sea   *P1875:*Since, having <> sea,   4440| MS:Do §in margin§ You, now, §last three words crossed out and replaced above by one word§ Desire I advise §last two words inserted above and crossed out§ no <> mischiefs   *P1875:*mischief

IRIS

Give thou no thought to Heré's faulty schemes!

MADNESS

Changing her step from faulty to fault-free!

IRIS

Not to be wise, did Zeus' wife send thee here.

MADNESS

Sun, thee I cite to witness—doing what I loathe to do!
4445 But since indeed to Heré and thyself I must subserve,
And follow you quick, with a whizz, as the hounds a-hunt with the huntsman,
—Go I will! and neither the sea, as it groans with its waves so furiously,
Nor earthquake, no, nor the bolt of thunder gasping out heaven's
    labour-throe,
Shall cover the ground as I, at a bound, rush into the bosom of Herakles!
4450 And home I scatter, and house I batter,
Having first of all made the children fall,—
And he who felled them is never to know
He gave birth to each child that received the blow,

4441| MS:Give not you §last two words crossed out and replaced above by two words§ thou no
<> faulty §inserted above; crossed out and then rewritten above§ schemes, §comma altered
to exclamation point§ and mine! §last two words and punctuation crossed out§
4442| MS:I §crossed out and replaced above by dash§ change §altered to§ Changing your way
§last two words crossed out and replaced above by two words§ her step   *P1875:*Changing
4443| MS:did §over illegible word§   4444| MS:Helias d §last letter and preceding word
crossed out and replaced above by three words§ Sun, I cite §over illegible word§ to §crossed
out and restored§ <> doing what unwillingly I do!   *P1875:*Sun, thee I <> doing what I
loathe to do!   4445| MS:But if verily §last two words crossed out and replaced above by
three words§ since I indeed <> thyself must needs subserve,   *P1875:*since indeed <> thyself
I must subserve,   4446| MS:follow thee §crossed out and replaced above by§ you
4447| its §inserted above§ <> so furious §altered to§ furiously,   4448| MS:the
thunderbolt of §last two words transposed to§ bolt of thunder
4450| MS:home I shatter, and   *P1875:*home I scatter, and   4451| MS:made his children
*P1875:*made the children   4452| MS:who killed them never shall §last two words crossed
out and replaced above by three words§ is never to   *P1875:*who felled them

Till the Madness, I am, have let him go!

⁴⁴⁵⁵ Ha, behold! already he rocks his head—he is off from the starting-place!
Not a word, as he rolls his frightful orbs, from their sockets wrenched in
    the ghastly race!
And the breathings of him he tempers and times no more than a bull in
    act to toss,
And hideously he bellows invoking the Keres, daughters of Tartaros.
Ay, and I soon will dance thee madder, and pipe thee quite out of thy
    mind with fear!
⁴⁴⁶⁰ So, up with the famous foot, thou Iris, march to Olumpos, leave me
    here!
Me and mine, who now combine, in the dreadful shape no mortal sees,
And now are about to pass, from without, inside of the home of Herakles!

CHOROS

Otototoi,—groan!
Away is mown
⁴⁴⁶⁵ Thy flower, Zeus' offspring, City!
Unhappy Hellas, who dost cast (the pity!)
Who worked thee all the good,
Away from thee,—destroyest in a mood
Of madness him, to death whom pipings dance!

---

^{4454|} MS:the Madness I am have   *P1875:*the Madness, I am, have   ^{4455|} MS:behold,
already he shakes §crossed out and replaced above by§ rocks   *1889a:*behold! already
^{4456|} MS:word as   *P1875:*word, as   ^{4457|} MS:the §over illegible word, perhaps *those*§ <>
tempers §over illegible word§ <> toss—   *P1875:*toss,   ^{4458|} MS:he §inserted above§
<> Keres, §over illegible word§ daughter §altered to§ daughters <> Tartaros. §over illegible
erasure§   ^{4459|} MS:madder and <> quite out of thy mind §last five words inserted above§
frantic §crossed out§ with   *P1875:*madder, and   ^{4463-64|} MS:§one line expanded to two
lines§ groan! one and all §last three words crossed out§ §solidus added§ away §altered to§ Away
P1875:§two lines merged into one line§ Otototoi,—groan! Away is mown   *1889a:*§restored to
two lines§   ^{4465|} MS:§two lines merged into one line§ Plucked is §last two words crossed
out§ thy §altered to§ Thy flower, §next word illegibly crossed out§ city §altered to§ City; / Zeus'
offspring, §last two words and comma marked for transposition to follow *flower*§ bemoan!—
§crossed out§   *P1875:*offspring, City!   ^{4466|} MS:And thee, too, Hellas <> cast §over
illegible word and rewritten above§   *P1875:*Unhappy Hellas   ^{4468|} MS:thee,—destroyed
§altered to§ destroyest in this §crossed out and replaced above by§ a   ^{4469|} MS:Of
Madness whom §altered to *him* and then altered to original reading§ her pipings dance!
§exclamation point inserted§ to death. §last two words marked for transposition to follow *whom*
and period crossed out§   *P1875:*Of Madness him, to death whom pipings   *1889a:*madness

211

4470 There goes she, in her chariot,—groans, her brood,—
And gives her team the goad, as though adrift
For doom, Night's Gorgon, Madness, she whose glance
Turns man to marble! with what hissings lift
Their hundred heads the snakes, her head's inheritance!
4475 Quick has the god changed fortune: through their sire
Quick will the children, that he saved, expire!
O miserable me! O Zeus! thy child—
Childless himself—soon vengeance, hunger-wild,
Craving for punishment, will lay how low—
4480 Loaded with many a woe!

O palace-roofs! your courts about,
A measure begins all unrejoiced
By the tympanies and the thyrsos hoist
Of the Bromian revel-rout!
4485 O ye domes! and the measure proceeds
For blood, not such as the cluster bleeds
Of the Dionusian pouring-out!

4470| MS:There she is gone §last three words crossed out and replaced above by two words§ goes she, Night's §over illegible word§ Gorgon §last two words crossed out§ in <> her gift §crossed out and replaced above by§ brood,—   4471| MS:her team §last two words over illegible erasures§   4472| MS:Upon destruction §last two words crossed out and replaced above by two words§ For mischief §crossed out and replaced above by§ doom, Night's Gorgon §last two words inserted above§ of the Night §last three words crossed out and replaced above by two words§ Madness, she   4473| MS:marble,—with *P1875:*marble! with
4474| MS:The hundred snaky things her head's §over illegible erasure§ *P1875:*Their hundred heads the snakes, her   4475| MS:changed happiness to woe §last three words crossed out and replaced above by four words§ fortune: thro' their sire *P1875:*through
4476| MS:expire. *P1875:*expire!   4477| MS:me! O Zeus—thy *P1875:*me! O Zeus! thy
4478| MS:himself, soon <> hunger wild, *P1875:*himself—soon <> hunger-wild,
4479| MS:punishment will lay thee low *P1875:*punishment, will lay how low—
4480| MS:With much disaster. §last two words and period crossed out and replaced above by three words and exclamation point§ many a woe! *P1875:*Loaded with
4481| MS:§solidus added§ O ye §crossed out and replaced above by crossed-out word, *the*§ palace-roofs,— §*palace* crossed out and restored§ the §crossed out and replaced above by§ your *P1875:*palace-roofs! your   4482| MS:A §over illegible word§ measure leads off §last two words crossed out and replaced above by one word and comma§ begins *P1875:* begins all   4483| MS:the drums' glad tap, §last three words and comma crossed out and replaced above by one word§ tympany §altered to§ tympanies   4484| MS:And §crossed out and replaced above by§ Of   4485| MS:domes—and *P1875:*domes! and

Break forth, fly, children! fatal this—
Fatal the lay that is piped, I wis!
4490 Ay, for he hunts a children-chase—
Never shall Madness lead her revel
And leave no trace in the dwelling-place!
Ai ai, because of the evil!
Ai ai, the old man—how I groan
4495 For the father, and not the father alone!
She who was nurse of his children,—small
Her gain that they ever were born at all!

See! See!
A whirlwind shakes hither and thither
4500 The house—the roof falls in together!
Ha, ha, what dost thou, son of Zeus?
A trouble of Tartaros broke loose,
Such as once Pallas on the Titan thundered,
Thou sendest on thy domes, roof-shattered and wall-sundered!

MESSENGER

4505 O bodies white with age!—

CHOROS

What cry, to me—
What, dost thou call with?

4489| MS:piped, to-day §crossed out§ I   4490| MS:a children's-chase §altered to§
children-chase—   4491| *P1875:*madness *1889a:*shall Madness   4493| MS:ai—
because §over partially illegible word§ *P1875:*ai, because   4494| MS:ai, and §crossed
out§ the   4495| MS:I groan §last two words crossed out§ for §altered to§ For < > and, not
< > alone,— §punctuation altered to exclamation point§ *P1875:*and not
4496| MS:§first two words illegibly crossed out and replaced above by one word§ She < > his
boys. §word and period crossed out and replaced above by word, comma and dash§ children
4497| MS:The §crossed out and replaced above by§ Her   4498| MS:See! See! the walls are
sundered, §last four words and comma crossed out§   4501| MS:thou—Son
§altered to§ son *P1875:*thou, son   4503| MS:as Pallas thundered once on the Titan
§last six words transposed to§ once Pallas on the Titan thundered *P1875:*thundered,
4504| MS:on the domes, §over illegible word, perhaps *walls*§ roof- < > wall- §last
two words and hyphens inserted above§ *P1875:*on thy domes

MESSENGER

There's a curse indoors.

CHOROS

I shall not bring a prophet: you suffice.

MESSENGER

Dead are the children.

CHOROS

Ai ai!

MESSENGER

Groan! for, groans
Suit well the subject.   Dire the children's death,
4510   Dire too the parent's hands that dealt the fate.
No one could tell worse woe than we have borne.

CHOROS

How dost thou that same curse—curse, cause for groan—
The father's on the children, make appear?
Tell in what matter they were hurled from heaven
4515   Against the house—these evils; and recount
The children's hapless fate, O Messenger!

4506| MS:in-doors!   *P1875:*indoors!   *1889a:*indoors.   4507| MS:suffice!   *1889a:*suffice.
4508| MS:Dead are §last two words inserted above§ The §altered to§ the children! < >
Groan—for groans   *P1875:*ai! §¶§ Groan! for, groans   *1889a:*children. §¶§ Ai
4509| MS:subject! Dire   *1889a:*subject. Dire   4512| MS:same curse—curse §last three
words crossed out and restored§ cause   *P1875:*curse—curse, cause   4514| MS:were urg
§last three letters crossed out§ hurled   4515| MS:evils,—and   *P1875:*evils; and

MESSENGER

The victims were before the hearth of Zeus,
A household-expiation: since the king
O' the country, Herakles had killed and cast
⁴⁵²⁰ From out the dwelling; and a beauteous choir
Of boys stood by his sire, too, and his wife.
And now the basket had been carried round
The altar in a circle, and we used
The consecrated speech.   Alkmené's son,—
⁴⁵²⁵ Just as he was about, in his right hand,
To bear the torch, that he might dip into
The cleansing-water,—came to a stand-still;
And, as their father yet delayed, his boys
Had their eyes on him.   But he was himself
⁴⁵³⁰ No longer: lost in rollings of the eyes;
Outthrusting eyes—their very roots—like blood!
Froth he dropped down his bushy-bearded cheek,
And said—together with a madman's laugh—
"Father! why sacrifice, before I slay
⁴⁵³⁵ Eurustheus? why have twice the lustral fire,
And double pains, when 'tis permitted me
To end, with one good hand-sweep, matters here?

---

⁴⁵¹⁷| MS:The sacrifice §altered to§ sacrifices §crossed out and replaced above by§ victims were
§over *was*§   ⁴⁵¹⁸| MS:To purify the dwelling §last four words crossed out and replaced
above by three words and colon§ A household expiation   *P1875:*household-expiation
⁴⁵²⁰| MS:dwelling: and   *P1875:*dwelling; and   ⁴⁵²²| MS:been §next word illegibly
crossed out and replaced above by§ carried abound §altered to§ round
⁴⁵²⁵| MS:Just as he was about to §altered to§ To bear the torch, §last four words marked for
transposition to beginning of line 4526§   *P1875:*about, in his right hand,
⁴⁵²⁶| MS:In §altered to§ in his right hand §last four words marked for transposition to end of
line 4525§ and §crossed out and replaced above by three words§ that he might dip into
*P1875:*To bear the torch, that   ⁴⁵²⁷| MS:cleansing-water—came <> stand-still.   *P1875:*
cleansing-water,—came <> stand-still;   ⁴⁵²⁹| MS:Had §over illegible word§
⁴⁵³⁰| MS:longer—lost §over illegible word§ <> eyes—   *P1875:*longer: lost <> eyes;
⁴⁵³²| MS:bushy bearded cheek: *P1875:*bushy-bearded cheek,   ⁴⁵³³| MS:And §over
illegible word§ said,—together <> laugh,—   *P1875:*laugh—   *1889a:*said—together
⁴⁵³⁴| MS:"Father—why §over illegible word followed by illegibly crossed-out punctuation§
sacrifice before   *P1875:*"Father! why sacrifice, before   ⁴⁵³⁵| MS:Eurustheus?—why
*P1875.*Eurustheus? why   ⁴⁵³⁶| MS:double trouble— §word and dash crossed out and
replaced above by word and comma§ pains, <> tis   *P1875:*'tis

215

Then,—when I hither bring Eurustheus' head,—
Then for these just slain, wash hands once for all!
4540 Now,—cast drink-offerings forth, throw baskets down!
Who gives me bow and arrows, who my club?
I go to that Mukenai.   One must match
Crowbars and mattocks, so that—those sunk stones
The Kuklops squared with picks and plumb-line red—
4545 I, with my bent steel, may o'ertumble town."
Which said, he goes and—with no car to have—
Affirms he has one! mounts the chariot-board,
And strikes, as having really goad in hand!
And two ways laughed the servants—laugh with awe;
4550 And one said, as each met the other's stare,
"Playing us boys' tricks? or is master mad?"
But up he climbs, and down along the roof,
And, dropping into the men's place, maintains
He's come to Nisos city, when he's come
4555 Only inside his own house! then reclines

4538| MS:Then, §word and comma in margin§ when §over *Then*§ <> hither §inserted above§
bring hither §crossed out and replaced above by illegibly crossed-out word§ Eurustheus'
head, indeed, §word and comma crossed out§   *P1875:*Then,—when <> head,—
4539| MS:Then §crossed out§ for §altered to§ For <> slain, I wash   *P1875:*Then for <> slain,
wash   4540| MS:Pour away now §last three words crossed out and replaced above by
three words§ Now—shed forth §crossed out§ drink-offerings forth, §word and comma
inserted above§ throw down baskets §last two words transposed; exclamation point inserted
after *down*§ now §crossed out§   *P1875:*Now,—cast drink-offerings
4542| MS:that Mukenai! One must take §crossed out§ match   *1889a:*that Mukenai. One
4543| MS:mattocks §over partially illegible word§ <> that those   *P1875:*that—those
4544| MS:The Kuklops squared §crossed out and replaced above by§ ranged §crossed out and
squared restored§ <> and plumb §over illegible word§ line red,—   *P1875:*plumb-line red—
4545| MS:with §over illegible word§ <> town!"   *1889a:*town."   4546| MS:Which said,
§last two words crossed out and restored§ <> and,— §word over partially illegible word and
comma§ with no chariot there,— §last two words and punctuation crossed out and replaced
above by three words and dash§ car to have—   *1889a:*and—with   4547| MS:§first two
words illegibly crossed out, perhaps *Says that,* and replaced above by one word§ Affirmed he
had one—mounts   *P1875:*Affirms he has one! mounts   4548| MS:strikes—as <> hand,
§comma crossed out and replaced by exclamation point§   *P1875:*strikes, as
4549| MS:laugh, §comma crossed out§ with §over illegible word§ fear §crossed out and
replaced above by§ awe—   *P1875:*awe;   4550| MS:said—as <> the §over *this*§ <> stare—
*P1875:*said, as <> stare,   4551| MS:tricks?—or   *P1875:*tricks? or   4553| MS:And
dropping <> place maintains   *P1875:*And, dropping <> place, maintains   4554| MS:to
Nisos' City   *P1875:*to Nisos city   4555| MS:Only §in margin§ Inside <> house! then
§over illegible word§ he rests §last two words crossed out§ reclines   *P1875:*inside

On floor, for couch, and, as arrived indeed,
Makes himself supper; goes through some brief stay
Then says he's traversing the forest-flats
Of Isthmos; thereupon lays body bare
4560   Of bucklings, and begins a contest with
—No one! and is proclaimed the conqueror—
He by himself—having called out to hear
—Nobody!   Then, if you will take his word,
Blaring against Eurustheus horribly,
4565   He's at Mukenai.   But his father laid
Hold of the strong hand and addressed him thus:
"O son, what ails thee?   Of what sort is this
Extravagance?   Has not some murder-craze,
Bred of those corpses thou didst just despatch,
4570   Danced thee drunk?"   But he,—taking him to crouch,
Eurustheus' sire, that apprehensive touched
His hand, a suppliant,—pushes him aside,
Gets ready quiver, and bends bow against
His children—thinking them Eurustheus' boys
4575   He means to slay.   They, horrified with fear,
Rushed here and there,—this child, into the robes

4557| MS:supper: goes <> stay, *P1875:*supper; goes *1889a:*stay   4558| MS:says, he's
<> forest flats *P1875:*says he's <> forest-flats   4559| MS:Of Isthmos: thereupon §over
whereupon§ *P1875:*Of Isthmos; thereupon   4560| MS:bucklings and begins §over
illegible word§ *P1875:*bucklings, and   4561| MS:and was proclaimed *P1875:*and is
proclaimed   4563| MS:you believe §crossed out and replaced above by two words§ will take
4564| MS:Bellowing at §last two words crossed out and replaced above by two words§ Blaring
against Eurystheus *P1875:*against Eurustheus   4565| MS:father §next word illegibly crossed
out, perhaps *held*§ laid §over illegible word§   4566| MS:Hold of §last two words inserted
above§ the §over *The*§ strong §over partial erasure§ <> thus *P1875:*thus: 4567| MS:thee?
Of §inserted§ <> what §over partial erasure§   4568| MS:Extravagance? Has §over
illegible word§   4569| MS:Bred §inserted above§ Of those §next word illegibly crossed
out and replaced above by§ corpses thou hast §crossed out and replaced above by§ didst just
dispatched §altered to§ despatch, *P1875:*of   4570| MS:he—taking *P1875:*he,—taking
4571| MS:sire, a suppliant §last two words crossed out and replaced above by
two words§ who apprehensive *P1875:*sire, that apprehensive   4572| MS:hand a
*P1875:*hand, a   4573| MS:quiver and *P1875:*quiver, and   4575| MS:He §over
illegible word§ <> slay. They—horrified <> fear *P1875:*slay. They, horrified <> fear,
4576| MS:Rushed, one this, one that way;— §last five words crossed out and replaced above by one
illegibly crossed-out word and four crossed-out words and comma, *one way and another,* and then
replaced below by three words and comma§ here and there,—this §over illegible word§ child
§inserted below§ into *P1875:*Rushed here <> child, into

O' the wretched mother—this, beneath the shade
O' the column,—and this other, like a bird,
Cowered at the altar-foot.   The mother shrieks
4580 "Parent—what dost thou?—kill thy children?"   So
Shriek the old sire and crowd of servitors.
But he, outwinding him, as round about
The column ran the boy,—a horrid whirl
O' the lathe his foot described!—stands opposite,
4585 Strikes through the liver; and supine the boy
Bedews the stone shafts, breathing out his life.
But "Victory!" he shouted—boasted thus:
"Well, this one nestling of Eurustheus—dead—
Falls by me, pays back the paternal hate!"
4590 Then bends bow on another who was crouched
At base of altar—overlooked, he thought—
And now prevents him, falls at father's knee,
Throwing up hand to beard and cheek above.
"O dearest!" cries he; "father, kill me not!
4595 Yours I am—your boy: not Eurustheus' boy
You kill now!"   But he, rolling the wild eye
Of Gorgon,—as the boy stood all too close
For deadly bowshot,—mimicry of smith
Who batters red-hot iron,—hand o'er head

4578| MS:other like <> bird   *P1875:*other, like <> bird,   4579| MS:altar-foot; And the
<> shrieks §over illegible word§   *P1875:*altar-foot. The   4581| MS:Shrieks §over *Shrieked*§
<> old man §crossed out and replaced above by§ sire, and servants in a §last three words
crossed out§ crowd   *P1875:*Shriek the <> sire and   4582| MS:outwinding §over partial
erasure§   4583| MS:boy—as if the §last three words crossed out and replaced above by
two words§ a horrid whirl §over illegible word§   *P1875:*boy,—a   4584| MS:opposite—
*P1875:*opposite,   4585| MS:liver! and <> the corpse §crossed out§ boy   *1889a:*liver; and
4586| MS:stone shaft §altered to§ shafts <> his blood §crossed out§ life.   4587| MS:But
"Victory" he shouted, boasted thus—   *P1875:*shouted! boasted thus: *1889a:*But "Victory!"
he shouted—boasted   4588| MS:one youngster §crossed out and replaced above by§
nestling <> Eurystheus   *P1875:*of Eurustheus   4591| MS:About the §last two words
crossed out and replaced above by three words§ At base of altar's §altered to§ altar base
§crossed out§ overlooked §over *o'erlooked*§   *P1875:*altar—overlooked   4593| MS:cheek of
him,   *P1875:*cheek above.   4594| MS:dearest"—cries he—"father   *P1875:*dearest!" cries
he "father   *1889a:*he; "father   4595| MS:not Eurystheus'   *P1875:*not Eurustheus'
4596| MS:he rolling <> wild wild §crossed out§ eye   *P1875:*he, rolling   4597| MS:stood
§over illegible word§   4598| MS:For deadly §last two words over illegible erasures§
4599| MS:iron,—over §crossed out and replaced above by two words§ hand o'er

4600 Heaving his club, on the boy's yellow hair
Hurls it and breaks the bone.   This second caught,—
He goes, would slay the third, one sacrifice
He and the couple; but, beforehand here,
The miserable mother catches up,
4605 Carries him inside house and bars the gate.
Then he, as he were at those Kuklops' work,
Digs at, heaves doors up, wrenches doorposts out,
Lays wife and child low with the selfsame shaft.
And this done, at the old man's death he drives;
4610 But there came, as it seemed to us who saw,
A statue—Pallas with the crested head,
Swinging her spear—and threw a stone which smote
Herakles' breast and stayed his slaughter-rage,
And sent him safe to sleep.   He falls to ground—
4615 Striking against the column with his back—
Column which, with the falling of the roof,
Broken in two, lay by the altar-base.
And we, foot-free now from our several flights,
Along with the old man, we fastened bonds
4620 Of rope-noose to the column, so that he,
Ceasing from sleep, might not go adding deeds
To deeds done.   And he sleeps a sleep, poor wretch,
No gift of any god! since he has slain

4600| MS:hair §over *head*§   4601| MS:bone, this <> caught,   *P1875:*bone. This <>
caught,—   4602| MS:the §inserted above§   4603| MS:beforehand §over illegible
word§   4605| MS:the door §crossed out and replaced above by§ gates §altered to§ gate.
4606| MS:But he <> Kuklop's §altered to§ Kuklops'   *P1875:*Then he   4607| MS:at,
upheaves §*up* marked for transposition to follow *doors*§ door §altered to§ doors
4608| MS:And §crossed out and replaced above by§ Lays <> child low §over *lay*§ prostrate
§crossed out§ with one §crossed out and replaced above by two words§ the selfsame
4609| MS:And §over illegible word§ <> drives—   *P1875:*drives;   4612| MS:And §crossed
out§ Swinging §over *swinging*§   4613| MS:Herakles' §apostrophe inserted§ in the §last
two words crossed out§ breast   4614| MS:safe §inserted above§ into §*in* crossed out§
sleep: he   *P1875:*sleep. He   4616| MS:Which column, §word and comma inserted
above§ with   *P1875:*Column which, with   4617| MS:altar base.   *P1875:*altar-base.
4618| MS:And §over illegible word§   4620| MS:he   *P1875:*he,   4621| MS:sleep
might   *P1875:*sleep, might   4622| MS:sleeps, the unhappy man, §last three words
crossed out and replaced above by four words§ a sleep, poor wretch,   *P1875:*sleeps a
4623| MS:A sleep §last two words crossed out§ No §over *no*§ <> god—since   *P1875:*god! since

219

Children and wife.   For me, I do not know
4625   What mortal has more misery to bear.

CHOROS

A murder there was which Argolis
Holds in remembrance, Hellas through,
As, at that time, best and famousest:
Of those, the daughters of Danaos slew.
4630   A murder indeed was that! but this
Outstrips it, straight to the goal has pressed.
I am able to speak of a murder done
To the hapless Zeus-born offspring, too—
Prokné's son, who had but one—
4635   Or a sacrifice to the Muses, say
Rather, who Itus sing alway,
Her single child.   But thou, the sire
Of children three—O thou consuming fire!—
In one outrageous fate hast made them all expire.
4640   And this outrageous fate—
What groan, or wail, or deadmen's dirge,
Or choric dance of Haides shall I urge
The Muse to celebrate?

Woe! woe! behold!
4645   The portalled palace lies unrolled,

4624| MS:wife. Nor §crossed out and replaced above by two words and comma§ For me
4629| MS:Of §over *The*§ those the   *P1875:*those, the   4630| MS:that—but   *P1875:*that!
but   4631-33| MS:Outstrips < > pressed / And §crossed out and replaced above by two
words§ To the < > offspring too—   *P1875:* / I < > done / < > offspring, too—
4634| MS:Procne's   *CP1875:*Prokné's   4635| MS:say,   *P1875:*say   4636| MS:Who
Itys < > alway.   *P1875:*Rather, who Itus < > alway,   4637| MS:His §over illegible word§
single child,— §over illegible word§ but thou the   *P1875:*Her single child! But thou, the
*1889a:*child. But   4638| MS:children §inserted above§ < > fire—   *P1875:*fire!—
4639| MS:Hast §crossed out§ In < > expire!   *1889a:*expire.   4640| MS:And §in margin§
This < > fate   *P1875:*this < > fate—   4641| MS:groan or wail or deadmen's §inserted
above§ dirge   *P1875:*groan, or wail, or < > dirge,   4642| MS:of Hades §altered to§
Haides   4644| MS:Woe—woe—behold! the show §last two words crossed out§   *P1875:*
Woe! woe! behold!   4645| MS:§word illegibly crossed out in margin§ The §next word
illegibly crossed out§ portaled §crossed out and restored§ palace doors unfold §last two words

This way and that way, each prodigious fold!
Alas for me! these children, see,
Stretched, hapless group, before their father—he
The all-unhappy, who lies sleeping out
4650　The murder of his sons, a dreadful sleep!
And bonds, see, all about,—
Rope-tangle, ties and tether,—these
Tightenings around the body of Herakles
To the stone columns of the house made fast!

4655　But—like a bird that grieves
For callow nestlings some rude hand bereaves—
See, here, a bitter journey overpast,
The old man—all too late—is here at last!

AMPHITRUON

Silently, silently, aged Kadmeians!
4660　Will ye not suffer my son, diffused
Yonder, to slide from his sorrows in sleep?

---

crossed out and replaced above by one crossed-out word, *each,* and replaced above by two
words and dash§ lies unrolled— *P1875:*unrolled, *1889a:*portalled ⁴⁶⁴⁷| MS:me—
these *P1875:*me! these ⁴⁶⁴⁹| MS:The §over illegible word§ ⁴⁶⁵¹| MS:see, ties
ands §altered to§ and tether §last three words marked for transposition to line 4652 to follow
tangle§ all about— *P1875:*about,— ⁴⁶⁵²| MS:§line added§ tether,— §comma and dash
inserted§ these ⁴⁶⁵³| MS:Tightenings around §last two words over partial erasures§ < >
Herakles, *P1875:*of Herakles ⁴⁶⁵⁴| MS:Fastened §crossed out§ To §over *to*§
⁴⁶⁵⁵| MS:Ah, §word and comma crossed out§ But §over *but*§ here comes— §last two words
crossed out; dash retained§ like some §inserted above, crossed out and replaced above by§ a
⁴⁶⁵⁶| MS:For §over illegible erasure§ callow young §crossed out§ nestlings, some *1889a:*
nestlings some ⁴⁶⁵⁷| MS:See, §word and comma in margin§ Here §altered to§ here comes,
§crossed out; comma retained§ a < > over-passed §altered to§ over-past, *1889a:*overpast,
⁴⁶⁵⁹| MS:Kadmeian elders—silently—silently— §last four words crossed out and replaced
above by six words§ Silently, will ye not §last three words crossed out and replaced above by
one word§ silently, aged Kadmeians, *P1875:*aged Kadmeians! ⁴⁶⁶⁰| MS:Silently
§crossed out and replaced above by three words§ Will ye not suffer the man, §last two words
crossed out and replaced above by two words; comma retained§ my son ⁴⁶⁶¹| MS:In
sleep §last two words crossed out and replaced above by word and comma§ Yonder, to forget
§crossed out and replaced above by two words§ slide from < > sorrows there §crossed out§ in

221

CHOROS

And thee, old man, do I, groaning, weep,
And the children too, and the head there—used
Of old to the wreaths and paians!

AMPHITRUON

⁴⁶⁶⁵   Farther away!   Nor beat the breast,
Nor wail aloud, nor rouse from rest
The slumberer—asleep, so best!

CHOROS

Ah me—what a slaughter!

AMPHITRUON

                   Refrain—refrain!
Ye will prove my perdition.

CHOROS

                   Unlike water,
⁴⁶⁷⁰   Bloodshed rises from earth again.

AMPHITRUON

Do I bid you bate your breath, in vain—

4662| MS:And §in margin§ Thee, too, §word and comma crossed out§ old §over illegible word§ man, I lament for, w groan for §last four words and letter crossed out and replaced above by five words§ bewail §crossed out§ do I groaning weep   *P1875:*man, do I, groaning, weep,   4663| MS:too, and the §inserted above§   4664| MS:To the victor— §last three words and dash crossed out and replaced above by four words§ Of old to the < > paeans! *P1875:*paians!   4665| MS:away!—nor *P1875:*away! Nor
4667| MS:asleep, and §crossed out§ so   4668| MS:slaughter §next word illegibly crossed out§ . . §¶§ Refrain *P1875:*slaughter! §¶§ Refrain   4669| MS:will §next four words illegibly crossed out and replaced above by three words§ prove my perdition! §¶§ For §crossed out§ Unlike §over *unlike*§ *1889a:*perdition. §¶§ Unlike
4670| MS:The §crossed out§ Bloodshed §over *bloodshed*§ < > again! *1889a:*again.

222

Ye elders?   Lament in a softer strain!
Lest he rouse himself, burst every chain,
And bury the city in ravage—bray
4675   Father and house to dust away!

CHOROS

I cannot forbear—I cannot forbear!

AMPHITRUON

Hush! I will learn his breathings: there!
I will lay my ears close.

CHOROS

What, he sleeps?

AMPHITRUON

Ay,—sleeps!   A horror of slumber keeps
4680   The man who has piled
On wife and child
Death and death, as he shot them down
With clang o' the bow.

CHOROS

Wail—

AMPHITRUON

Even so!

---

⁴⁶⁷²| MS:elders? Lament §over *lament*§ <> softer §over illegible word§ strain   *P1875:*strain!
⁴⁶⁷³| MS:burst §over *break*§   ⁴⁶⁷⁴| MS:ravage— §over illegible word, perhaps *ruin*§ break
and bray   *P1875:*ravage—bray   ⁴⁶⁷⁵| house and all §last two words crossed out and
replaced above by two words§ to dust   ⁴⁶⁷⁷| MS:Hush—I   *P1875:*Hush! I
⁴⁶⁸⁰⁻⁸¹| MS:§one line expanded to two lines§ piled §solidus added§ On §over *on*§
⁴⁶⁸³| MS:With o' the bow!—clang!— §last four words marked for transposition to§ clang o'
the bow!—all there was to drown §last five words crossed out and replaced above by one word

CHOROS

—The fate of the children—

AMPHITRUON

Triple woe!

CHOROS

4685 —Old man, the fate of thy son!

AMPHITRUON

Hush, hush!   Have done!
He is turning about!
He is breaking out!
Away! I steal
4690 And my body conceal,
Before he arouse,
In the depths of the house.

CHOROS

Courage!   The Night
Maintains her right

---

and exclamation point§ Wail! / The §crossed out§ §¶§ Wail!— §¶§ Even so!—   *P1875:*bow.
§¶§ Wail— §¶§ <> so!   4684| MS:woe!   *1889a:*woe §emended to§ woe! §see Editorial
Notes§   4685| MS:The §altered to§ the fate of thy son,— §comma altered to exclamation
point§ old §altered to§ Old man, §dash and last two words marked for transposition to
beginning of line§   4686| MS:Hush, Hush—Have   *P1875:*Hush, hush! Have
4687-88| MS:§one line expanded to two lines§ about— §solidus added§ and waking up— §last
three words and dash crossed out and replaced above by four words and dash§ He is breaking
out—   4687| *P1875:*about!   4688| *P1875:*out!   4689-90| MS:§one line expanded
to two lines§ Away! I will hide this §last three words crossed out and replaced above by three
words§ steal §solidus added§ And §over *and*§ my body of mine, §last two words crossed out
and replaced above by one word§ conceal,   4691-92| MS:§one line expanded to two lines§
arouse, §solidus added§ In §over *in*§ <> house!   4692| *1889a:*house.
4693-94| MS:§one line expanded to two lines§ Courage! The §inserted above§ Night maintains
her right,   4693| *P1875:*Courage! The Night   4694| *P1875:*Maintains her right

224

4695   On the lids of thy son there, sealed from sight!

AMPHITRUON

See, see!   To leave the light
And, wretch that I am, bear one last ill,
I do not avoid; but if he kill
Me his own father, and devise
4700   Beyond the present miseries
A misery more ghastly still—
And to haunt him, over and above
Those here who, as they used to love,
Now hate him, what if he have with these
4705   My murder, the worst of Erinues?

CHOROS

Then was the time to die, for thee,
When ready to wreak in the full degree
Vengeance on those
Thy consort's foes
4710   Who murdered her brothers! glad, life's close,
With the Taphioi down,
And sacked their town

4695| MS:thy son son there   *P1875:*thy son there   4696| MS:see! to leave both life and
§last three words crossed out and replaced above by one word§ the   *P1875:*see! To
4697| MS:After such roils §last three words crossed out and replaced above by one word§ And,
<> one woe more, §last two words and comma crossed out and replaced above by one word§
last   4698| MS:I nowise §crossed out and replaced above by two words§ do not avoid;—
but   *P1875:*avoid; but   4700| MS:the actual §crossed out and replaced above by§ present
4702| MS:And have §crossed out§ to   4703| MS:The Erinues here §last three words
crossed out and replaced above by two words§ Those here that, as <> love   *P1875:*here who,
as <> love,   4704| MS:he shall §crossed out§ have   4707| MS:When about §crossed
out and replaced above by§ ready to avenge thy wife's §last three words crossed out and
replaced above by four words§ wreak §over illegible word§ in the full
4708-09| MS:§one line expanded to two lines§ those §solidus added§ Thy §over *thy*§
4710| MS:Who §over illegible word§   4711-12| MS:§one line expanded to two lines§ When
slain were §last two words crossed out and replaced above by four illegibly crossed-out words
and then replaced below by one word§ quelled §*were* restored§ the Taphioi's §altered to§
Taphioi, sacked §over illegible word§ their §last two words crossed out and restored§ town
4711| *P1875:*With the Taphioi down,   4712| *P1875:*And sacked their town

225

Clustered about with a wash of sea!

AMPHITRUON

To flight—to flight!
4715   Away from the house, troop off, old men!
Save yourselves out of the maniac's sight!
He is rousing himself right up: and then,
Murder on murder heaping anew,
He will revel in blood your city through!

CHOROS

4720   O Zeus, why hast, with such unmeasured hate,
Hated thy son, whelmed in this sea of woes?

HERAKLES

Ha,—
In breath indeed I am—see things I ought—
Æther, and earth, and these the sunbeam-shafts!
4725   But then—some billow and strange whirl of sense
I have fallen into! and breathings hot I breathe—
Smoked upwards, not the steady work from lungs.
See now!   Why bound,—at moorings like a ship,—
About my young breast and young arm, to this
4730   Stone piece of carved work broke in half, do I

4713| MS:with this §altered to *the*, crossed out and replaced above by§ a
4714| MS:To §over *In*§ <> to §over *in*§   4717| MS:up—and   *P1875*:up: and
4719| MS:A §altered to§ He   4720| MS:hast thou hated past all bounds §last five words
crossed out and replaced above by comma, four words and comma§ with such §inserted
above§ unmeasured hate,   4721| MS:Of §crossed out§ Hated §over illegible word§ this
§crossed out§ thy son, §comma inserted§ so— §word and dash crossed out§ whelmed
4722| MS:Hah,—   *1889a:*Ha,—   4723| MS:ought,—   *P1875:*ought—
4724| MS:earth, and §over illegible word§   4725| MS:then—what §crossed out and
replaced above by§ some <> and horrid §crossed out and replaced above by§ strange
4726| MS:into—and   *P1875:*into! and   4728| MS:now! Why am I unchosed §last three
words crossed out and replaced above by three words§ bound,—at moorings <> ship—
*P1875:*ship,—   4729| MS:About thy §crossed out and replaced above by§ my <> and this
§crossed out and replaced above by§ young arm, do I §last two words crossed out§ to
4730| MS:On this §last two words crossed out§ Stone §over *stone*§

Sit, have my rest in corpses' neighbourhood?
Strewn on the ground are winged darts, and bow
Which played my brother-shieldman, held in hand,—
Guarded my side, and got my guardianship!
4735 I cannot have gone back to Haides—twice
Begun Eurustheus' race I ended thence?
But I nor see the Sisupheian stone,
Nor Plouton, nor Demeter's sceptred maid!
I am struck witless sure!   Where can I be?
4740 Ho there! what friend of mine is near or far—
Some one to cure me of bewilderment?
For nought familiar do I recognize.

AMPHITRUON

Old friends, shall I go close to these my woes?

CHOROS

Ay, and let me too,—nor desert your ills!

HERAKLES

4745 Father, why weepest thou, and buriest up

4731| MS:rest with §crossed out§ in   4733| MS:Which used §over illegible word§ played §altered to§ play brother-shieldman   *P1875:*Which played my brother-shieldman
4734| MS:guardianship. *P1875:*guardianship!   4735| MS:cannot §inserted above§ have §next two words and punctuation illegibly crossed out§ gone back §over partially illegible word§ <> Hades §altered to§ Haides   4736| MS:Run thence the doubles §last four words crossed out and replaced above by two words§ Begun §crossed out and replaced above by crossed-out word, *Commenced,* and then restored§ Eurustheus' race; course, begun again §last three words crossed out and replaced above by three words§ I ended §over illegible word§ thence? *P1875:*race I   4737| MS:the Sisupheian rock §crossed out§ stone,
4739| MS:struck mad, §crossed out and replaced above by§ witless   4740| MS:there, what *P1875:*there! what   4741| MS:To cure §last two words crossed out and replaced above by one word§ Some   4742| MS:Certainly, I §last two words crossed out and replaced above by five words§ For nought of old §last two words crossed out§ familiar do I
4744| MS:and I likewise §last two words crossed out and replaced above by two crossed-out words, *with these*§ let me go §crossed out and replaced above by word, comma and dash§ too
4745| MS:buriest up this §last two words crossed out; *up* restored and rewritten above§

Thine eyes, aloof so from thy much-loved son?

AMPHITRUON

O child!—for, faring badly, mine thou art!

HERAKLES

Do I fare somehow ill, that tears should flow?

AMPHITRUON

Ill,—would cause any god who bore, to groan!

HERAKLES

4750   That's boasting, truly! still, you state no hap.

AMPHITRUON

For, thyself seest—if in thy wits again.

HERAKLES

Heyday!   How riddlingly that hint returns!

AMPHITRUON

Well, I am trying—art thou sane and sound!

4746| MS:eyes, up from §inserted above§ thus §last three words crossed out§ aloof th §last two letters crossed out§ so   4747| MS:child! for, woes and all, mine— §last four words and dash crossed out and replaced above by two words and comma§ faring badly   *P1875:*child!—for   4749| MS:Ill,— §comma crossed out§ would   *P1875:*Ill,—would   4750| MS:truly—still you   *P1875:*truly! still, you   4751| MS:For thyself   *P1875:*For, thyself   4752| MS:§line added§   4753| MS:§line added§ thou sound and sane §last three words transposed to§ sane and sound   *P1875:*sound!

HERAKLES

Say if thou lay'st aught strange to my life's charge!

AMPHITRUON

⁴⁷⁵⁵ If thou no more art Haides-drunk,—I tell!

HERAKLES

I bring to mind no drunkenness of soul.

AMPHITRUON

Shall I unbind my son, old men, or what?

HERAKLES

And who was binder, tell!—not *that,* my deed!

AMPHITRUON

Mind that much of misfortune—pass the rest!

HERAKLES

⁴⁷⁶⁰ Enough! from silence, I nor learn nor wish.

---

⁴⁷⁵⁴| MS:Say §over partial erasure§ if you §crossed out and replaced above by§ thou lay'st
§over illegible word§ aught new §crossed out and replaced above by illegibly crossed-out word
and then restored§ to   *P1875:*aught strange to   ⁴⁷⁵⁵| MS:thou art
no more Hades-drunk §altered to§ Haides-drunk   *P1875:*thou no more art Haides-drunk
⁴⁷⁵⁷| MS:Shall I set free §last two words crossed out and replaced
above by one word§ unbind   ⁴⁷⁵⁸| MS:not §crossed out and restored§
⁴⁷⁶⁰| MS:Or silence, then §last three words crossed out and replaced above by three words§
Enough: from silence, < > nor seek §crossed out§ wish.   *P1875:*Enough! from

229

AMPHITRUON

O Zeus, dost witness here throned Heré's work?

HERAKLES

But have I had to bear aught hostile thence?

AMPHITRUON

Let be the goddess—bury thine own guilt!

HERAKLES

Undone!   What is the sorrow thou wilt say?

AMPHITRUON

4765   Look!   See the ruins of thy children here!

HERAKLES

Ah me!   What sight do wretched I behold?

AMPHITRUON

Unfair fight, son, this fight thou fastenedst
On thine own children!

HERAKLES

What fight?   Who slew these?

4761| MS:dost see §crossed out and replaced above by two words§ witness here
4763| MS:goddess—hide §crossed out§ bury   4764| MS:Woe's me! §last two words and exclamation point crossed out and replaced above by one word and exclamation point§ Undone! <> sorrow, wilt thou say?   *P1875:*sorrow thou wilt say?
4765| MS:Look!—See the §over *these*§   *P1875:*Look! See   4766| MS:what <> behold! *P1875:*me! What <> behold?   4768| MS:children! §over partial erasure§

AMPHITRUON

Thou and thy bow, and who of gods was cause.

HERAKLES

⁴⁷⁷⁰   How say'st?   What did I?   Ill-announcing sire!

AMPHITRUON

—Go mad!   Thou askest a sad clearing up.

HERAKLES

And am I also murderer of my wife?

AMPHITRUON

All the work here was just one hand's work—thine!

HERAKLES

Ai ai—for groans encompass me—a cloud!

AMPHITRUON

⁴⁷⁷⁵   For these deeds' sake do I begroan thy fate.

HERAKLES

Did I break up my house or dance it down?

---

⁴⁷⁶⁹| MS:of Gods   *P1875:*gods   ⁴⁷⁷⁰| MS:sayest < > I?—O §last letter crossed out§ Ill-announcing   *P1875:*say'st < > I? Ill-announcing   ⁴⁷⁷¹| MS:mad!—Thou < > clearing-up! *P1875:*mad! Thou < > clearing up!   *1889a:*up.   ⁴⁷⁷²| MS:What— §word and dash crossed out§ And §over and§   ⁴⁷⁷³| MS:hand's work   *P1875:*hand's work   ⁴⁷⁷⁴| MS:for §over illegible word§   ⁴⁷⁷⁵| MS:do §inserted above§ I too §crossed out§ begroan < > fate!   *1889a:*fate.

231

AMPHITRUON

I know just one thing—all's a woe with thee.

HERAKLES

But where did the craze catch me? where destroy?

AMPHITRUON

When thou didst cleanse hands at the altar-flame.

HERAKLES

4780   Ah me! why is it then I save my life—
Proved murderer of my dearest ones, my boys?
Shall not I rush to the rock-level's leap,
Or, darting sword through breast and all, become
My children's blood-avenger? or, this flesh
4785   Burning away with fire, so thrust away
The infamy, which waits me there, from life?

Ah but,—a hindrance to my purposed death,
Theseus arrives, my friend and kinsman, here!
Eyes will be on me! my child-murder-plague
4790   In evidence before friends loved so much!
O me, what shall I do?   Where, taking wing
Or gliding underground, shall I seek out

A solitariness from misery?
I will pull night upon my muffled head!
4795 Let this wretch here content him with his curse
Of blood: I would pollute no innocents.

THESEUS

I come,—with others who await beside
Asopos' stream, the armed Athenian youth,—
Bring thy son, old man, spear's fight-fellowship!
4800 For a bruit reached the Erechtheidai's town
That, having seized the sceptre of this realm,
Lukos prepares you battle-violence.
So, paying good back,—Herakles began,
Saving me down there,—I have come, old man,
4805 If aught, of my hand or my friends', you want.
What's here?   Why all these corpses on the ground?
Am I perhaps behindhand—come too late
For newer ill?   Who killed these children now?
Whose wife was she, this woman I behold?
4810 Boys, at least, take no stand in reach of spear!

4794| MS:pull darkness on me §altered to§ my with §crossed out§ muffled head— *P1875:* pull night upon my <> head!   4795| MS:Let §in margin§ §next word illegibly crossed out and replaced above by illegibly crossed-out word§ this <> content §over partially illegible word§ him §last two words inserted above§ <> curse— *P1875:*curse   4796| MS:Of blood: §last two words and colon inserted above§ <> innocents! *1889a:*innocents.   4798| MS:armed §over partially illegible word§   4799| MS:man, §next word illegibly crossed out§ spear's fight-fellowship. *P1875:*fight-fellowship!   4801| MS:That Lukos, §word and comma crossed out and replaced above by two words§ having §next word illegibly crossed out§ seizing §altered to§ seized this realms sceptre, sets §last four words crossed out and replaced above by five words and comma§ the sceptre of this realm, *P1875:*That, having   4802| MS:Upon you §last two words crossed out and replaced above by two words§ Lukos prepares <> battle-violence; *P1875:*battle-violence.   4805| MS:If you want §over partially illegible word§ aught of <> friends'. *P1875:*If aught, of <> friends,' you want. *CP1875:*friends', you §not B§   4807| MS:perhaps §inserted above§ behind-hand *P1875:* behindhand   4808| MS:newer §inserted above§ evils that have §last three words crossed out and replaced above by one word§ ills §altered to§ ill?   Who §over *who*§   4809| MS:wife <> she §last two words over illegible erasures§ <> woman that §crossed out§ I behold? §over illegible word§   4810| MS:For §crossed out§ boys §altered to§ Boys <> least, are not stationed §last three words crossed out and replaced above by three words§ take no stand in sp §last two letters crossed out§ reach

233

Some other woe than war, I chance upon.

AMPHITRUON

O thou, who sway'st the olive-bearing height!—

THESEUS

Why hail'st thou me with woeful prelude thus?

AMPHITRUON

Dire sufferings have we suffered from the gods.

THESEUS

4815   These boys,—who are they thou art weeping o'er?

AMPHITRUON

He gave them birth, indeed, my hapless son!
Begot, but killed them—dared their bloody death.

THESEUS

Speak no such horror!

AMPHITRUON

Would I might obey!

4811| MS:other kind §crossed out and replaced above by§ woe <> upon!   *1889a:*upon.
4812| MS:Oh, thou, who hast the <> height,—   *P1875:*O thou, who sway'st the <> height!—
4815| MS:they, thou   *1889a:*they thou   4816| MS:birth, he gave it, §last three words
crossed out and replaced above by one word§ indeed, my poor boy §last two words crossed out
and replaced above by two words§ hapless son!   4817| MS:Begot, these and despatched
§last three words crossed out and replaced above by two words§ but killed <> their §over
illegible word§ bloody §inserted above§   4818| MS:Speak §over illegible word, perhaps
Say§ <> §¶§ Would I could §crossed out and replaced above by§ might

THESEUS

O teller of dread tidings!

AMPHITRUON

Lost are we—
4820   Lost—flown away from life!

THESEUS

What sayest thou?
What did he?

AMPHITRUON

Erring through a frenzy-fit,
He did all, with the arrows dipt in dye
Of hundred-headed Hudra.

THESEUS

Heré's strife!
But who is this among the dead, old man?

AMPHITRUON

4825   Mine, mine, this progeny—the labour-plagued,
Who went with gods once to Phlegraia's plain,
And in the giant-slaying war bore shield.

4820| MS:§¶§ What §crossed out and restored§ hast §crossed out and replaced above by§ sayest thou say? §word crossed out; punctuation retained§   4822| MS:all with   *P1875:*all, with   4823| MS:Of the §crossed out§ hundred headed hudra §altered to§ Hudra *P1875:*hundred-headed   4825| MS:labour-plagued—   *P1875:*labour-plagued, 4826| MS:Who §over illegible word§ <>Phlegraia's   *P1875:*to Phlegruia's §emended to§ Phlegraia's §see Editorial Notes§   4827| MS:And §in margin§ Bore buckles §crossed out and replaced above by§ shield! §last two words marked for transposition to end of line§ in the giant-slaying band §crossed out§ war   *P1875:*bore   *1889a:*shield.

THESEUS

Woe—woe!   What man was born mischanceful thus!

AMPHITRUON

Thou couldst not know another mortal man
4830   Toil-weary, more outworn by wanderings.

THESEUS

And why i' the peploi hides he his sad head?

AMPHITRUON

Not daring meet thine eye, thy friendliness
And kinship,—nor that children's-blood about.

THESEUS

But *I* come to who shared my woe with me!
4835   Uncover him!

AMPHITRUON

O child, put from thine eyes
The peplos, throw it off, show face to sun!
Woe's weight well matched contends with tears in thee.
I supplicate thee, falling at thy cheek

4828| MS:§first word illegibly crossed out, perhaps *Alas*, and replaced above by two words§
Woe—woe! what   *P1875:*woe! What   4829| MS:You §crossed out and replaced above by§
Thou could §altered to§ couldst <> another wearied §crossed out and replaced above by§
mortal more §altered to§ man   4830| MS:With toil more §last three words crossed out
and replaced above by three words§ Toil-weary, and §crossed out§
more out-worn §inserted above§   *1889a:*outworn   4831| MS:And wherefore into §last
two words crossed out and replaced above by two words§ why i'   4833| MS:children's
blood about!   *P1875:*children's-blood   *1889a:*about.   4834| MS:But I have §crossed
out§ come <> my §inserted above§   *P1875:*But *I*   4836| MS:peplos §over *peploi*§
4837| MS:well-matched   *P1875:*well matched

And knee and hand, and shedding this old tear!
4840   O son, remit the savage lion's mood,
Since to a bloody, an unholy race
Art thou led forth, if thou be resolute
To go on adding ill to ill, my child!

THESEUS

Let me speak!   Thee, who sittest—seated woe—
4845   I call upon to show thy friends thine eye!
For there's no darkness has a cloud so black
May hide thy misery thus absolute.
Why, waving hand, dost sign me—murder's done?
Lest a pollution strike me, from thy speech?
4850   Nought care I to—with thee, at least—fare ill:
For I had joy once!   *Then,*—soul rises to,—
When thou didst save me from the dead to light!
Friends' gratitude that tastes old age, I loathe,
And him who likes to share when things look fine,
4855   But, sail along with friends in trouble—no!
Arise, uncover thine unhappy head!
Look on us!   Every man of the right race
Bears what, at least, the gods inflict, nor shrinks.

HERAKLES

Theseus, hast seen this match—my boys with me?

4840| MS:son—remit <> savage §inserted above§ *P1875:*son, remit   4841| MS:to §over
for§ a §last two words inserted above§   4842| MS:forth §over illegible word§
4845| MS:call on §altered to§ upon   4847| MS:thy <> thus §last two words over illegible
words§   4848| MS:me murder's *P1875:*me—murder's   4850| MS:ill— *P1875:*ill:
4851| MS:For I had §last two words over illegible words§ <> once!—*then* §altered to§ *Then,*—
soul §over illegible word§ *P1875:*once! *Then*   4853| MS:age, I ha §last two letters and
preceding word crossed out§ I   4854| MS:And whenever §crossed out and replaced
above by three words§ him who likes <> look well §crossed out and replaced above by§ fine,
4855| MS:But—sail *P1875:*But, sail   4858| MS:what the gods, at least, inflict, unshamed
§crossed out§ nor *P1875:*what, at least, the gods inflict, nor
4859| MS:my children §crossed out and replaced above by two words§ boys with

237

THESEUS

⁴⁸⁶⁰ I heard of, now I see the ills thou sign'st.

HERAKLES

Why then hast thou displayed my head to sun?

THESEUS

Why? mortals bring no plague on aught divine.

HERAKLES

Fly, O unhappy, this my impious plague!

THESEUS

No plague of vengeance flits to friends from friends.

HERAKLES

⁴⁸⁶⁵ I praise thee.   But I helped thee,—that is truth.

THESEUS

And I, advantaged then, now pity thee.

4860| MS:of, §next two words illegibly crossed out, perhaps *ills thou*§ now   4861| MS:then
wouldst §crossed out and replaced above by§ hast   4862| MS:Why? Mortals cannot mar no
work of Gods. §last seven words crossed out and replaced above by three crossed-out words,
Bring man you§ Mortals bring no plague on aught divine! §last seven words inserted above§
*P1875:*mortals   *1889a:*divine.   4863| MS:unhappy, me—an impious   *1889a:*unhappy,
this my impious   4864| MS:No such destroyer §last two words crossed out and replaced above
by one word§ avenger §crossed out and replaced above by three words§ plague of vengeance
4865| MS:praise §next word illegibly crossed out and replaced above by§ thee! §over illegible
word§ But < > helped you §crossed out and replaced above by§ thee   *1889a:*thee. But

HERAKLES

—The pitiable,—my children's murderer!

THESEUS

I mourn for thy sake, in this altered lot.

HERAKLES

Hast thou found others in still greater woe?

THESEUS

4870   Thou, from earth, touchest heaven, one huge distress!

HERAKLES

Accordingly, I am prepared to die.

THESEUS

Think'st thou thy threats at all import the gods?

HERAKLES

Gods please themselves: to gods I give their like.

THESEUS

Shut thy mouth, lest big words bring bigger woe!

4868| MS:sake, other lot than once §last four words crossed out and replaced above by four words§ in this altered lot.   4869| MS:thou §inserted above§

4870| MS:earth touchest <> one §over *an*; then *a* written above *one* and crossed out§   *P1875:* earth, touchest   4871| MS:Accordingly I   *P1875:*Accordingly, I

4872| MS:Thinkst   *P1875:*Think'st   4873| MS:themselves: the §crossed out and replaced above by§ to gods their like give I!   *P1875:*themselves: to gods I give their like.

4874| MS:Hold §crossed out and replaced above by§ Shut thy tongue §crossed out and replaced above by§ mouth—lest <> words brings §altered to§ bring   *P1875:*mouth, lest

HERAKLES

4875   I am full fraught with ills—no stowing more!

THESEUS

Thou wilt do—what, then?   Whither moody borne?

HERAKLES

Dying, I go below earth whence I came.

THESEUS

Thou hast used words of—what man turns up first!

HERAKLES

While thou, being outside sorrow, schoolest me.

THESEUS

4880   The much-enduring Herakles talks thus?—

HERAKLES

Not the so much-enduring: measure's past.

THESEUS

—Mainstay to mortals, and their mighty friend?

4875| MS:no stowage left §last two words crossed out and replaced above by two words§
stowing more!   4876| MS:moody §inserted above§ borne? by wrath? §last two words and
punctuation crossed out§   4880| MS:much-enduring Herakles, talks thus?   *P1875:*much-
enduring Herakles talks thus?—   4881| MS:so-much enduring < > past!   *P1875:*so
much-enduring < > past.   4882| MS:friend! §exclamation point altered to question mark§

HERAKLES

They nowise profit me: but Heré rules.

THESEUS

Hellas forbids thou shouldst ineptly die.

HERAKLES

4885 But hear, then, how I strive by arguments
Against thy teachings!   I will ope thee out
My life—past, present—as unliveable.
First, I was born of this man, who had slain
His mother's aged sire, and, sullied so,
4890 Married Alkmené, she who gave me birth.
Now, when the basis of a family
Is not laid right, what follows needs must fall;
And Zeus, whoever Zeus is, formed me foe
To Heré (take not thou offence, old man!
4895 Since father, in Zeus' stead, account I thee),
And, while I was at suck yet, frightful snakes
She introduced among my swaddling-clothes,—
That bedfellow of Zeus!—to end me so.
But when I gained the youthful garb of flesh,
4900 The labours I endured—what need to tell?
What lions ever, or three-bodied brutes,

4884| MS:Hellas would not allow a foolish death §last six words crossed out and replaced above by five words§ forbids thou shouldst ineptly die.   4885| MS:then §over illegible word§
4886| MS:Against your §crossed out and replaced above by§ thy teaching. §word and punctuation altered to§ teachings! I   4890| MS:she < > me §last two words inserted above§ birth. to me. §last two words and punctuation crossed out§   4892| MS:right, needs must what follows §last two words marked for transposition to precede *needs*§
4893| MS:is §over illegible word§   4894| MS:To Heré,— §over partial erasure§ oh take §last two words crossed out§ take   *P1875:*To Heré (take   4895| MS:Since §over partial erasure§ < > thee,—   *P1875:*thee)   *1889a:*thee),   4897| MS:swaddling clothes   *P1875:* swaddling clothes,   4898| MS:— §dash in margin§ That <.> Zeus,—to   *P1875:*That < > of Zeus!—to   4900| MS:labors   *P1875:*labours   4901| MS:lions §over illegible word§

241

Tuphons or giants, or the four-legg'd swarms
Of Kentaur-battle, did not I end out?
And that hound, headed all about with heads
4905   Which cropped up twice, the Hudra, having slain—
I both went through a myriad other toils
In full drove, and arrived among the dead
To convoy, as Eurustheus bade, to light
Haides' three-headed dog and doorkeeper.
4910   But then I,—wretch,—dared this last labour—see!
Slew my sons, keystone-coped my house with ills.
To such a strait I come! nor my dear Thebes
Dare I inhabit: and, suppose I stay?
Into what fane or festival of friends
4915   Am I to go? My curse scarce courts accost!
Shall I seek Argos? How, if fled from home?
But say—I hurry to some other town!
And there they eye me, as notorious now,—
Kept by sharp tongue-taunts under lock and key—
4920   "Is not this he, Zeus' son, who murdered once

4902| MS:four legged §next word illegibly crossed out and replaced above by§ swarms, §comma crossed out§ *P1875*:four-legg'd   4903| MS:That §crossed out and replaced above by two words§ Of That §crossed out§ Kentaur-swarming battle §last two words crossed out and replaced above by three words§ Of Kentaur combat §last three words crossed out; *Kentaur* and *battle* restored§ Of Kentaur-battle §last two words and comma rewritten for clarification and inserted above§   4904| MS:about, and §comma and word crossed out and replaced above by§ with   4908| MS:That I might at §last four words crossed out and replaced above by three words§ To convoy, as Eurustheus' biddings, being §apostrophe and last two words crossed out and replaced above by one word illegibly crossed out, perhaps *asks,* crossed out and replaced by three words§ bade, to light   *P1875*:as Erustheus   *CP1875*:as Eurusteus   4909| MS:three headed <> door-keeper.   *P1875*:three-headed <> doorkeeper.   4910| MS:But last I §last two words crossed out and replaced above by two words, *I have;* last two words replaced by two words and punctuation§ then I,—wretch,—I have §last two words crossed out§ dared <> labour: here §colon and word crossed out§ —see!   4911| MS:sons, and put key done to §last five words crossed out and replaced above by dash and one word§ —keystone-coped *P1875*:sons, keystone-coped   4912| MS:come: nor   *P1875*:come! nor   4913| MS:inhabit . . yet, if §last two words crossed out and replaced above by two words§ and, suppose I remain §crossed out§ stay?   *P1875*:inhabit,—and   *1889a*:inhabit: and   4914| MS:what temple §crossed out and replaced above by§ fane of friends or festival §last four words marked for transposition to§ or festival of friends   4915| MS:scarce §inserted above§   4917| MS:But come,—I <> town? §question mark altered to dash and then altered to exclamation point§ *P1875*:But say, I   *1889a*:say—I   4918| MS:they have an §last two words crossed out§ eye me, §over *on*§ the §crossed out§ as <> now,   *P1875*:now,—

Children and wife?   Let him go rot elsewhere!"
To any man renowned as happy once,
Reverses are a grave thing; but to whom
Evil is old acquaintance there's no hurt
4925   To speak of, he and misery are twins.
To this degree of woe I think to come:
For earth will utter voice forbidding me
To touch the ground, and sea—to pierce the wave,
The river-springs—to drink, and I shall play
4930   Ixion's part quite out, the chained and wheeled!
And best of all will be, if so I 'scape
Sight from one man of those Hellenes,—once
I lived among, felicitous and rich!
Why ought I then to live?   What gain accrues
4935   From good-for-nothing, wicked life I lead?
In fine, let Zeus' brave consort dance and sing,
Stamp foot, the Olumpian Zeus' own sandal-trick!
What she has willed, that brings her will to pass—
The foremost man of Hellas pedestalled,
4940   Up, over, and down whirling!   Who would pray
To such a goddess?—that, begrudging Zeus
Because he loved a woman, ruins me—

Lover of Hellas, faultless of the wrong!

THESEUS

This strife is from no other of the gods
₄₉₄₅ Than Zeus' wife; rightly apprehend, as well,
Why, to no death—thou meditatest now—
I would persuade thee, but to bear thy woes!
None, none of mortals boasts a fate unmixed,
Nor gods—if poets' teaching be not false.
₄₉₅₀ Have not they joined in wedlock against law
With one another? not, for sake of rule,
Branded their sires in bondage? Yet they house,
All the same, in Olumpos, carry heads
High there, notorious sinners though they be!
₄₉₅₅ What wilt thou say, then, if thou, mortal-born,
Bearest outrageously fate gods endure?
Leave Thebes, now, pay obedience to the law
And follow me to Pallas' citadel!
There, when thy hands are purified from stain,
₄₉₆₀ House will I give thee, and goods shared alike.
What gifts I hold too from the citizens
For saving twice seven children, when I slew
The Knosian bull, these also give I thee.
And everywhere about the land are plots

_{4943|} MS:of Hellas,—faultless <> wrong. *P1875:*of Hellas, faultless <> wrong!
_{4945|} Than Heré: rightly *P1875:*Than Zeus' wife; rightly _{4946|} MS:death thou <>
now, *P1875:*death—thou <> now— _{4947|} MS:thy grief §crossed out§ woes!
_{4948|} MS:For none of *P1875:*None, none of _{4950|} MS:in marriage §crossed out and
replaced above by§ wedlock _{4951|} MS:another? Not disagreed their sires §last three
words crossed out and replaced above by four words§ for sake of rule *P1875:*not, for <>
rule, _{4952|} MS:With shams §last two words crossed out and replaced above by two
words§ Branded their _{4954|} MS:notorious t §crossed out§ sinners <> be. *P1875:*be!
_{4955|} MS:if, mere §crossed out and replaced above by word and comma§ thou *P1875:*if thou
_{4956|} MS:Thou §next word illegible§ at those fortunes §last five words crossed out and
replaced above by three words and dash§ Bearest outrageously fate *P1875:*fate gods
_{4957|} MS:Leave Thebes, then, in obedience <> law, *P1875:*Leave Thebes, now, pay
obedience *1889a:*law _{4958|} MS:follow with §crossed out and replaced above by§ me
_{4959|} MS:There, having purified thy hands from *P1875:*There, when thy hands are purified
from _{4962|} MS:saving fou §last three letters crossed out and replaced above by§ twice
_{4963|} MS:The Knossian <> thee,— *P1875:*The Knosian <> thee.

4965   Apportioned me: these, named by thine own name,
Shall be henceforward styled by all men—thine,
Thy life long; but at death, when Haides-bound,
All Athens shall uphold the honoured one
With sacrifices, and huge marble heaps:
4970   For that's a fair crown our Hellenes grant
Their people—glory, should they help the brave!
And I repay thee back this grace for thine
That saved me, now that thou art lorn of friends—
Since, when the gods give honour, friends may flit:
4975   For, a god's help suffices, if he please.

HERAKLES

Ah me, these words are foreign to my woes!
I neither fancy gods love lawless beds,
Nor, that with chains they bind each other's hands,
Have I judged worthy faith, at any time;
4980   Nor shall I be persuaded—one is born
His fellows' master! since God stands in need—
If he is really God—of nought at all.
These are the poets' pitiful conceits!
But this it was I pondered, though woe-whelmed—
4985   "Take heed lest thou be taxed with cowardice

4967| MS:long, but <> Hades-bound, §altered to§ Haides-bound, *P1875:*long; but
4968-69| MS:§lines transposed§   4968| MS:honored one: *P1875:*honoured one
4969| MS:heaps, *P1875:*heaps: 4970| MS:a rare §over illegible word; then crossed out and replaced above by§ fair crown the §crossed out and replaced above by§ our Hellenes give §crossed out§ grant   4971| MS:Their §next three words illegibly crossed out and replaced above by three words§ people—glory should §over partially illegible word§ they helped §altered to§ help *P1875:*glory, should   4972| MS:repay thee back §last three words inserted above§ <> grace of §crossed out§ for   4974| MS:Since, §over illegible erasure; comma inserted§ <> gods do §crossed out and replaced above by§ give honor <> flit— *P1875:*honour <> flit: 4975| MS:For a *P1875:*For, a   4977| MS:For §crossed out§ I nor §crossed out and replaced above by§ neither   4978| MS:Nor—that with chains §last two words inserted above§ they fasten §crossed out and replaced above by§ bind *P1875:*Nor, that   4979| MS:time, *P1875:*time;   4980| MS:be made believe §last two words crossed out and replaced above by one word and dash§ persuaded   4981| MS:master: since <> need *P1875:*master! since <> need—   4982| MS:he is really §last three words inserted above§ <> of nobody §crossed out§ nought   4983| MS:pitiful §over partially illegible word§ conceits. *P1875:*conceits!   4985| MS:lest I be *P1875:*lest thou be

Somehow in leaving thus the light of day!"
For whoso cannot make a stand against
These same misfortunes, neither could withstand
A mere man's dart, oppose death, strength to strength.
4990   Therefore unto thy city I will go
And have the grace of thy ten thousand gifts.
There!   I have tasted of ten thousand toils
As truly—never waived a single one,
Nor let these runnings drop from out my eyes:
4995   Nor ever thought it would have come to this—
That I from out my eyes do drop tears.   Well!
At present, as it seems, one bows to fate.
So be it!   Old man, thou seest my exile—
Seest, too, me—my children's murderer!
5000   These give thou to the tomb, and deck the dead,
Doing them honour with thy tears—since me
Law does not sanction.   Propping on her breast,
And giving them into their mother's arms,
—Re-institute the sad community
5005   Which I, unhappy, brought to nothingness—
Not by my will!   And, when earth hides the dead,
Live in this city!—sad, but, all the same,
Force thy soul to bear woe along with me!

---

^{4987|}   MS:whoso mortal born, withstand §last three words crossed out and replaced above by
five words§ cannot make a stand against   ^{4988|}   MS:Mortals §crossed out and replaced
above by two words§ These same   ^{4990|}   MS:I will go therefore §altered to§ Therefore
unto thy city §last four words marked for transposition to beginning of line§
^{4992|}   MS:There, I   *P1875:*There! I   ^{4994|}   MS:eyes—   *P1875:*eyes!   *1889a:*eyes:
^{4995|}   MS:Nor did I think it   *P1875:*Nor ever thought it   ^{4996|}   *P1875:*tears! Well!
*1889a:*tears. Well!   ^{4998|}   MS:thou seest my exile— §last four words marked for
transposition and then original reading retained§ this my flight, §last three words and comma
inserted below and crossed out§   ^{4999|}   MS:Seest me—my own children's   *P1875:*Seest
too, me   *CP1875:*Seest, too, me—my children's   ^{5001|}   MS:Doing them §last two words
over partial erasure and illegible word§ honor   *1889a:*honour
^{5002|}   MS:sanction— §dash altered to exclamation point§ lay them propped §last three words
crossed out and replaced above by three words, the first two illegibly crossed
out§ Propping < > her §inserted above§   *1889a:*sanction. Propping   ^{5006|}   MS:will! And
when < > hides the §crossed out§ each corpse, §last two words crossed out; *the* restored and
rewritten above with one word§ dead,   *P1875:*will! And, when   ^{5007|}   MS:city,—
§punctuation altered to exclamation point§ sorrowful, §crossed out and replaced above by
dash, word and comma§ —sad   ^{5008|}   MS:Force §crossed out and restored§

246

O children, who begat and gave you birth—
5010 Your father—has destroyed you! nought you gain
By those fair deeds of mine I laid you up,
As by main-force I laboured glory out
To give you,—that fine gift of fatherhood!
And thee, too, O my poor one, I destroyed,
5015 Not rendering like for like, as when thou kept'st
My marriage-bed inviolate,—those long
Household-seclusions draining to the dregs
Inside my house! O me, my wife, my boys—
And—O myself, how, miserably moved,
5020 Am I disyoked now from both boys and wife!
O bitter those delights of kisses now—
And bitter these my weapons' fellowship!
For I am doubtful whether shall I keep
Or cast away these arrows which will clang
5025 Ever such words out, as they knock my side—
"Us—thou didst murder wife and children with!
Us—child-destroyers—still thou keepest thine!"
Ha, shall I bear them in my arms, then? What
Say for excuse? Yet, naked of my darts
5030 Wherewith I did my bravest, Hellas through,
Throwing myself beneath foot to my foes,
Shall I die basely? No! relinquishment
Of these must never be,—companions once,

5009| MS:children, he your father, §last three words and comma crossed out and replaced by
dash§ <> and <> you §last two words inserted above§ *1889a:*children, who
5010| MS:Your father, §last two words and comma inserted above§ Has §altered to§ has
*1889a:*father—has 5011| MS:By my §crossed out and replaced above by§ those
5012| MS:out— §dash crossed out§ 5014| MS:And §over partial erasure§
5015| MS:keptst *P1875:*kept'st 5017| MS:Watching at home, see §last four words
crossed out and replaced above by five words§ Household-seclusions draining to the dregs
5018| MS:me—my *P1875:*me, my 5019| MS:oh *P1875:*And—O
5020| MS:Am §over illegible word§ <> dis-yoked now §inserted above§ *P1875:*disyoked
5021| MS:those §over illegible word§ 5022| MS:weapon's §altered to§ weapons'
5023| MS:doubtful— §dash crossed out and replaced above by§ whether 5025| MS:Ever
these §crossed out and replaced above by§ such <> out as *P1875:*out, as
5027| MS:Us,—child-destroyers, still *P1875:*Us—child-destroyers—still
5030| MS:bravest §over partial erasure§ 5032| MS:basely? No! they §last word and next
illegible word crossed out§ relinquishment 5033| MS:these, must *P1875:*these must

We sorrowfully must observe the pact.
⁵⁰³⁵   In just one thing, co-operate with me
Thy sad friend, Theseus!   Go along with him
To Argos, and in concert get arranged
The price my due for bringing there the Hound!
O land of Kadmos, Theban people all,
⁵⁰⁴⁰   Shear off your locks, lament one wide lament,
Go to my children's grave and, in one strain,
Lament the whole of us—my dead and me—
Since all together are fordone and lost,
Smitten by Heré's single stroke of fate!

THESEUS

⁵⁰⁴⁵   Rise up now from thy dead ones!   Tears enough,
Poor friend!

HERAKLES

            I cannot: for my limbs are fixed.

THESEUS

Ay: even these strong men fate overthrows.

HERAKLES

Woe!
Here might I grow a stone, nor mind woes more!

---

⁵⁰³⁴| MS:And ever §last two words crossed out§ we §altered to§ We sorrowfully §inserted above§
< > pact!   *1889a:*pact.   ⁵⁰³⁵| MS:In §in margin§ just §inserted above§ One < > cooperate
*P1875:*one < > co-operate   ⁵⁰³⁶| MS:Thy poor friend   *P1875:*Thy sad friend
⁵⁰³⁹| MS:all— §over illegible word§   *P1875:*all,   ⁵⁰⁴¹| MS:grave, and in one word §crossed
out and replaced above by§ strain   *P1875:*grave and, in < > strain,   ⁵⁰⁴²| MS:me!   *P1875:*
me—   ⁵⁰⁴³| MS:lost—   *P1875:*lost,   ⁵⁰⁴⁴| MS:fate.   *P1875:*fate!   ⁵⁰⁴⁵| MS:ones!
tears enough! §punctuation crossed out and replaced by comma§   *P1875:*ones! Tears
⁵⁰⁴⁷| MS:overthrows!   *1889a:*overthrows.   ⁵⁰⁴⁸| MS:Pheu!   *P1875:*Woe!

THESEUS

5050   Cease!   Give thy hand to friendly helpmate now!

HERAKLES

Nay, but I wipe off blood upon thy robes.

THESEUS

Squeeze out and spare no drop!   I take it all!

HERAKLES

Of sons bereaved, I have thee like my son.

THESEUS

Give to my neck thy hand!   'tis I will lead.

HERAKLES

5055   Yoke-fellows friendly—one heart-broken, though!
O father, such a man we need for friend!

AMPHITRUON

Certes the land that bred him boasts good sons.

HERAKLES

Turn me round, Theseus—to behold my boys!

5050| MS:Cease: give *P1875:*Cease! Give   5051| MS:robes! *1889a:*robes.
5052| MS:drop, I *P1875:*drop! I   5053| *P1875:*son! *1889a:*son.   5054| MS:Give
§over partially illegible word§ < > hand: 'tis *P1875:*hand! 'tis   5055| MS:Yoke fellows
*P1875:*Yoke-fellows   5056| MS:father! such *1889a:*father, such
5057| MS:Ay, for the < > him, boasts < > sons! *P1875:*Certes, the < > him boasts *1889a:*
Certes the < > sons.   5058| MS:Theseus, turn §altered to§ Turn me round
§last three words marked for transposition to beginning of sentence§

THESEUS

What? will the having such a love-charm soothe?

HERAKLES

5060 I want it; and to press my father's breast.

AMPHITRUON

See here, O son! for, what I love thou seek'st.

THESEUS

Strange!   Of thy labours no more memory?

HERAKLES

All those were less than these, those ills I bore.

THESEUS

Who sees thee grow a woman,—will not praise.

HERAKLES

5065 I live low to thee?   Not so once, I think.

THESEUS

Too low by far!   "Famed Herakles"—where's he?

5059| MS:Now, wherefore §last two words crossed out and replaced above by four words§ What, will the having §over partially illegible word§ <> love charm soothe? §over illegible word§ *P1875:*What? will <> love-charm   5060| MS:it: and *P1875:*it; and   5061| MS:seekst! *P1875:*seek'st! *1889a:*seek'st.   5063| MS:bore! *1889a:*bore.   5064| MS:sees you grow <> praise! *P1875:*sees thee grow *1889a:*praise.   5065| MS:Do §crossed out§ I <> so §inserted above§ once—I think! *P1875:*once, I *1889a:*think.   5066| MS:far! famed §altered to§ Famed Herakles—where's *P1875:*far! "Famed Herakles"—where's

HERAKLES

Down amid evils, of what kind wast *thou?*

THESEUS

As far as courage—least of all mankind!

HERAKLES

How say'st, then, *I* in evils shrink to nought?

THESEUS

5070   Forward!

HERAKLES

    Farewell, old father!

AMPHITRUON

                Thou too, son!

HERAKLES

Bury the boys as I enjoined!

AMPHITRUON

               And *me*—
Who will be found to bury now, my child?

5069| MS:say'st then, *I* am §crossed out and replaced above by two words§ in evils shrink §over *shrunk*§   *P1875:*say'st, then   5070| MS:too, Son!   *P1875:*son!   5071-73| MS:Bury < > *me?*— / Myself! §¶§ When   *P1875: me*— / Who < > child? /   *1889a:* / / Myself. §¶§ When

HERAKLES

Myself.

AMPHITRUON

When, coming?

HERAKLES

When thy task is done.

AMPHITRUON

How?

HERAKLES

5075 I will have thee carried forth from Thebes
To Athens.   But bear in the children, earth
Is burthened by!   Myself,—who with these shames
Have cast away my house,—a ruined hulk,
I follow—trailed by Theseus—on my way;
And whoso rather would have wealth and strength
5080 Than good friends, reasons foolishly therein.

CHOROS

And we depart, with sorrow at heart,
Sobs that increase with tears that start;

5074| MS:How? §¶§ I will send §crossed out and replaced above by§ have
for thee courage §last three words inserted above§ to Athens §last eight words crossed out§ I
< > carried from §altered to§ forth   5079| MS:And whosoever wishes to obtain §last
three words and *ever* crossed out and replaced above by four words§ rather would have wealth
§over partially illegible word§   5080| MS:Riches or power rather §last four words crossed
out§ than §altered to§ Than   *P1875:*therein!   *1889a:*therein.
5081| MS:And §altered to§ and we depart, with §altered to§ With sorrow at heart,
§last four words and comma marked for transposition to beginning of line§   *P1875:*And we
depart, with sorrow at heart,   5082| MS:with §over illegible word§

The greatest of all our friends of yore
We have lost for evermore!

———————

5085   When the long silence ended,—"Our best friend—
Lost, our best friend!" he muttered musingly.
Then, "Lachares the sculptor" (half aloud)
"Sinned he or sinned he not? 'Outrageous sin!'
Shuddered our elders, 'Pallas should be clothed:
5090   He carved her naked.' 'But more beautiful!'
Answers this generation: 'Wisdom formed
For love not fear!'   And there the statue stands,
Entraps the eye severer art repels.
Moreover, Pallas wields the thunderbolt
5095   Yet has not struck the artist all this while.
Pheidias and Aischulos?   Euripides
And Lachares?   But youth will have its way.
The ripe man ought to be as old as young—
As young as old.   I too have youth at need.
5100   Much may be said for stripping wisdom bare.

"And who's 'our best friend'?   You play kottabos;
Here's the last mode of playing.   Take a sphere

———————————————————————————————

5083| MS:The best of our §last three words crossed out and replaced above by three words§ greatest of all <> yore, *1889a:*yore   5084| MS:§following this line§ (L. D. I. E. / June 17. '73.) §see Editorial Notes§   5085| MS:§line added§ friend,— *P1875:*friend—
5086| MS:"Lost §over partial erasure§ <> friend, he repeated §crossed out and replaced below by§ muttered *P1875:*Lost <> friend!" he   5086-87| MS:§¶ called for in margin§ *P1875:*§page ends§ *1889a:*§no ¶§   5087| MS:Then—"Lachares <> sculptor"—(half *P1875:*Then, "Lachares <> sculptor" (half   5088| MS:Sinned *P1875:*"Sinned
5089| MS:elders 'Pallas *P1875:*elders, 'Pallas   5090| MS:naked.'—'And §crossed out and replaced above by§ 'But <> beautiful' *P1875:*naked.' 'But <> beautiful!'
5093| MS:eye, severer *P1875:*eye severer   5094| *P1875:*thunderbolt, *1889a:*thunderbolt
5096| MS:and Aischulos—Euripides *P1875:*and Aischulos? Euripides   5097| MS:And Lachares! But <> way! *P1875:*And Lachares? But <> way.   5098| MS:man is both §last two words crossed out and replaced above by four words§ ought to be as old and §crossed out and replaced above by§ as   5100| MS:bare! §over partially illegible word§ *1889a:*bare.
5101| MS:And who's the great §crossed out and replaced above by§ best friend? §over *man*§ You know §crossed out and replaced above by§ play kottabos? *P1875:*"And who's 'our best friend'? You <> kottabos;   5102| MS:playing: take *P1875:*playing. Take

253

With orifices at due interval,
Through topmost one of which, a throw adroit
5105 Sends wine from cup, clean passage, from outside
To where, in hollow midst, a manikin
Suspended ever bobs with head erect
Right underneath whatever hole's a-top
When you set orb a-rolling: plumb, he gets
5110 Ever this benediction of the splash.
An other-fashioned orb presents him fixed:
Of all the outlets, he fronts only one,
And only when that one,—and rare the chance,—
Comes uppermost, does he turn upward too:
5115 He can't turn all sides with the turning orb.
Inside this sphere of life,—all objects, sense
And soul perceive,—Euripides hangs fixed,
Gets knowledge through the single aperture
Of High and Right: with visage fronting these
5120 He waits the wine thence ere he operate,
Work in the world and write a tragedy.
When that hole happens to revolve to point,
In drops the knowledge, waiting meets reward.
But, duly in rotation, Low and Wrong—
5125 When these enjoy the moment's altitude,
His heels are found just where his head should be!
No knowledge that way!   *I* am moveable,—
To slightest shift of orb make prompt response,
Face Low and Wrong and Weak and all the rest,
5130 And still drink knowledge, wine-drenched every turn,—
Equally favoured by their opposites.
Little and Bad exist, are natural:
Then let me know them, and be twice as great
As he who only knows one phase of life!

5106| MS:mannikin   *P1875:*manikin   5111| MS:fixed—   *P1875:*fixed:
5113| MS:rare's < > chance,   *P1875:*chance,—   *CP1875:*rare   5114| MS:too—   *P1875:*
too: 5116| MS:objects sense   *P1875:*objects, sense   5119| MS:with face set §last two
words crossed out and replaced above by one word§ visage   5123| MS:reward;   *P1875:*
reward.   5124| MS:and Wrong   *P1875:*and Wrong—   5125| MS:Do these < >
altitude?   *P1875:*When these < > altitude,   5126| MS:be—   *P1875:*be!
5129| MS:rest   *P1875:*rest,   5130| MS:still §inserted above§

5135   So doubly shall I prove 'best friend of man,'
      If I report the whole truth—Vice, perceived
      While he shut eyes to all but Virtue there.
      Man's made of both: and both must be of use
      To somebody: if not to him, to me.
5140   While, as to your imaginary Third
      Who, stationed (by mechanics past my guess)
      So as to take in every side at once,
      And not successively,—may reconcile
      The High and Low in tragi-comic verse,—
5145   He shall be hailed superior to us both
      When born—in the Tin-islands! Meantime, here
      In bright Athenai, I contest the claim,
      Call myself Iostephanos' 'best friend,'
      Who took my own course, worked as I descried
5150   Ordainment, stuck to my first faculty.

      "For listen! There's no failure breaks the heart,
      Whate'er be man's endeavour in this world,
      Like the rash poet's when he—nowise fails
      By poetizing badly,—Zeus or makes
5155   Or mars a man, so—at it, merrily!
      But when,—made man,—much like myself,—equipt

5135| MS:—Prove §in margin§ Nay, twice as §last three words crossed out and replaced above by four words§ doubly also far more truly §last three words crossed out§ 'the best <> man' *P1875:*So doubly shall I prove 'best <> man,' 5136| MS:If I do justice by perceiving §last four words crossed out and replaced above by four words and dash§ report the whole truth 5138 40| MS:Man's <> use. / There! §word and punctuation crossed out and replaced above by word and comma§ While, As §altered to§ as <> Third— *P1875:*use / To <> me. / <> imaginary Third 5141| MS:Who's stationed—by <> guess— *P1875:* Who,—stationed (by <> guess) *1889a:*Who, stationed 5142| MS:Tak §last three letters crossed out§ So <> once *P1875:*once, 5143| MS:successively, and reconcile *P1875:* successively,—may reconcile 5144| MS:in Tragicomedy, §altered to§ Tragicomic verse *P1875:*tragicomic verse,— *1889a:*tragi-comic 5146| MS:the Tin-islands! meanwhile §altered to§ Meantime, here— *P1875:*here 5147| MS:In rough §altered to§ Rough Athenai—I *P1875:*In bright Athenai, I 5148| MS:Call myself §last two words in margin§ Of being §last two words crossed out§ Iostephanos' 5149| MS:Who §over illegible word§ 5150| MS:faculty! *1889a:*faculty. 5151| MS:For, listen *P1875:*"For *1889a:*"For listen 5155| MS:mars the §crossed out and replaced above by§ a 5156| MS:But the made man,—myself, now,—say, equipt *P1875:*But when,—made man, much like myself,—equipt

For such and such achievement,—rash he turns
Out of the straight path, bent on snatch of feat
From—who's the appointed fellow born thereto,—
5160   Crows take him!—in your Kassiterides?
Half-doing his work, leaving mine untouched,
That were the failure.   Here I stand, heart-whole,
No Thamuris!

             "Well thought of, Thamuris!
Has zeal, pray, for 'best friend' Euripides
5165   Allowed you to observe the honour done
His elder rival, in our Poikilé?
You don't know?   Once and only once, trod stage,
Sang and touched lyre in person, in his youth,
Our Sophokles,—youth, beauty, dedicate
5170   To Thamuris who named the tragedy.
The voice of him was weak; face, limbs and lyre,
These were worth saving: Thamuris stands yet
Perfect as painting helps in such a case.
At least you know the story, for 'best friend'
5175   Enriched his 'Rhesos' from the Blind Bard's store;

5157| MS:achievement,—had I turned   *P1875:*achievement,—rash he turns
5159| MS:fellow, born   *P1875:*fellow born   5160| MS:him!— §punctuation inserted§ < >
Kassiterides,— §comma altered to question mark§   *P1875:*your Kassiterides?
5162| MS:failure! Here   *1889a:*failure. Here   5163| MS:No Thamuris! §¶§ Well
*CP1875:*No Thamuris! §¶§ "Well §not B§   5164| MS:Has love §crossed out and replaced
above by§ zeal < > for your own §crossed out and replaced above by§ best Euripides   *P1875:*
for 'best friend' Euripides   5165| MS:observe last §crossed out and replaced above by§
our honor   *P1875:*observe the honour   5166| MS:in the Poikilé?   *P1875:*in our Poikilé?
5167| MS:You §over partially illegible word§ < > know, §comma altered to question mark§
Once §over *once*§ < > stage   *P1875:*stage,   5168| MS:Sang §in margin§ And touched the
§crossed out§ lyre   *P1875:*and   5169| MS:Our §in margin§ Sophokles,—glorious
§crossed out and replaced above by word and comma§ youth §following this line§ (Go on to
next page)   5170-87| MS:§these lines composed on verso of leaf bearing ll. 5138-69§
5171| MS:of him §inserted above§ < > weak,—they say,—§last two words and following
punctuation crossed out§ face   *P1875:*weak; face   5172| MS:These they §crossed out
and replaced above by§ we have saved, and Thamuros   *P1875:*These were worth saving:
Thamuros   *1889a:*saving: Thamuris   5174| MS:Well, now— §last two words and dash
crossed out and replaced above by two words§ At least < > for §over illegible erasure§ your
friend   *P1875:*for 'best friend'   5175| MS:store—   *P1875:*store;

So haste and see the work, and lay to heart
What it was struck me when I eyed the piece!
Here stands a poet punished for rash strife
With Powers above his power, who see with sight
5180   Beyond his vision, sing accordingly
A song, which he must needs dare emulate.
Poet, remain the man nor ape the Muse!

"But—lend me the psalterion!   Nay, for once—
Once let my hand fall where the other's lay!
5185   I see it, just as I were Sophokles,
That sunrise and combustion of the east!"

And then he sang—are these unlike the words?

Thamuris marching,—lyre and song of Thrace—
(Perpend the first, the worst of woes that were
5190   Allotted lyre and song, ye poet-race!)

Thamuris from Oichalia, feasted there
By kingly Eurutos of late, now bound
For Dorion at the uprise broad and bare

Of Mount Pangaios (ore with earth enwound
5195   Glittered beneath his footstep)—marching gay
And glad, Thessalia through, came, robed and crowned,

5176| MS:§line added§ Well, go and <> work, of Rumphilos §last two words crossed out§ and
P1875:So haste and   5177| MS:What was it §last two words transposed to§ it was <> piece?
§punctuation altered to exclamation point§   5181| MS:he is fond to §last three words
crossed out and replaced above by three words§ must needs dare emulate!   *1889a*:emulate.
5182| MS:Had he §last two words crossed out and replaced above by one word and comma§
Poet, remained §altered to§ remain <> nor tried §crossed out and replaced above by§ ape
5183| MS:But   *P1875*:"But   5184-85| MS:§between these two lines an entire line illegibly
crossed out§   5186| MS:the East!   *P1875*:east!"   5187| MS:§following this line§
Thamuris marching &c (Next page)   5188-239| MS:§throughout this section,
B first wrote *Thamyris* and then altered the spelling to *Thamuris*§   5188| MS:marching—
lyre   *P1875*:marching,—lyre   5189| MS:were, *1889a*:were
5190| MS:song, the §crossed out and replaced above by§ ye   5192| MS:kingly Eurytus
§altered to§ Eurutus   *P1875*:y kingly   *CP1875*:By   *1889a*:kingly Eurutos
5194| MS:Of Mount Pangaios, (ore   *1889a*:Of Mount Pangaios (ore   5195| MS:beneath
the §crossed out and replaced above by§ his footstep) marching   *P1875*:footstep)—marching

From triumph on to triumph, mid a ray .
Of early morn,—came, saw and knew the spot
Assigned him for his worst of woes, that day.

5200 Balura—happier while its name was not—
Met him, but nowise menaced; slipt aside,
Obsequious river to pursue its lot

Of solacing the valley—say, some wide
Thick busy human cluster, house and home,
5205 Embanked for peace, or thrift that thanks the tide.

Thamuris, marching, laughed "Each flake of foam"
(As sparklingly the ripple raced him by)
"Mocks slower clouds adrift in the blue dome!"

For Autumn was the season; red the sky
5210 Held morn's conclusive signet of the sun
To break the mists up, bid them blaze and die.

Morn had the mastery as, one by one
All pomps produced themselves along the tract
From earth's far ending to near heaven begun.

5215 Was there a ravaged tree? it laughed compact
With gold, a leaf-ball crisp, high-brandished now,
Tempting to onset frost which late attacked.

5197| MS:mid the §crossed out and replaced above by§ a   5200| MS:Balyra §altered to§
Balura   5201| MS:aside *1889a:*aside,   5206| MS:Thamuris marching made
§crossed out and replaced above by§ laughed "Each §over *each*; quotation mark inserted§ < >
foam," §quotation mark inserted§ *P1875:*Thamuris, marching, laughed < > foam"
5207| MS:Sparklingly As §over *as* and marked for transposition to beginning of line§ < > by,
P1875:(As sparklingly < > by)   5209| MS:season, and its §last two words crossed out and
replaced above by two words§ red the *P1875:*season; red   5210| MS:Bore the §last two
words crossed out and replaced above by two words§ Held with §crossed out and *the* restored§
conclusive *P1875:*Held morn's conclusive   5211| MS:Which §crossed
out and replaced above by§ To broke §altered to§ break < > up, bade §altered to§ bid
5212| MS:mastery, as one *P1875:*mastery as, one   5216| MS:gold, that leaf-ball crisp it
brandished *P1875:*gold, a leaf-ball crisp, high-brandished

Was there a wizened shrub, a starveling bough,
A fleecy thistle filched from by the wind,
5220   A weed, Pan's trampling hoof would disallow?

Each, with a glory and a rapture twined
About it, joined the rush of air and light
And force: the world was of one joyous mind.

Say not the birds flew! they forebore their right—
5225   Swam, revelling onward in the roll of things.
Say not the beasts' mirth bounded! that was flight—

How could the creatures leap, no lift of wings?
Such earth's community of purpose, such
The ease of earth's fulfilled imaginings,—

5230   So did the near and far appear to touch
I' the moment's transport,—that an interchange
Of function, far with near, seemed scarce too much;

And had the rooted plant aspired to range
With the snake's license, while the insect yearned
5235   To glow fixed as the flower, it were not strange—

No more than if the fluttery tree-top turned
To actual music, sang itself aloft;
Or if the wind, impassioned chantress, earned

The right to soar embodied in some soft
5240   Fine form all fit for cloud-companionship,

5219| MS:wind— *P1875*:wind,   5220| MS:disavow— *P1875*:disallow?
5221| MS:Each had a   *P1875*:Each, with a   5222| MS:it in the rush   *P1875*:it, joined the
rush   5223| MS:force; the   *P1875*:force: the   5225| MS:Swam revelling <> things;
P1875:Swam, revelling <> things.   5226| MS:flight.   *P1875*:flight—
5227| MS:creature   *P1875*:creatures   5229| MS:imaginings,   *P1875*:imaginings,—
5231| MS:transport, that   *P1875*:transport,—   5232| MS:much,   *P1875*:much;
5233| MS:That if §last two words crossed out and replaced above by two words§ And had
5235| MS:glow as §crossed out§ fixed <> the §inserted above§ flowers §altered to§ flower
5238| MS:chantress §over *chanter*§   5239| MS:The §over illegible erasure§

And, blissful, once touch beauty chased so oft.

Thamuris, marching, let no fancy slip
Born of the fiery transport; lyre and song
Were his, to smite with hand and launch from lip—

5245 Peerless recorded, since the list grew long
Of poets (saith Homeros) free to stand
Pedestalled mid the Muses' temple-throng,

A statued service, laurelled, lyre in hand,
(Ay, for we see them)—Thamuris of Thrace
5250 Predominating foremost of the band.

Therefore the morn-ray that enriched his face,
If it gave lambent chill, took flame again
From flush of pride; he saw, he knew the place.

What wind arrived with all the rhythms from plain,
5255 Hill, dale, and that rough wildwood interspersed?
Compounding these to one consummate strain,

It reached him, music; but his own outburst
Of victory concluded the account,
And that grew song which was mere music erst.

5260 "Be my Parnassos, thou Pangaian mount!
And turn thee, river, nameless hitherto!

5241| MS:Touch §crossed out and replaced above by word and comma§ And, blissful once the §crossed out and replaced above by§ touch   *P1875:*blissful, once
5242| MS:Thamuris marching, let §over *set*§   *P1875:*Thamuris, marching
5243| MS:transport: lyre   *P1875:*transport; lyre   5244| MS:lip   *P1875:*lip—
5245| MS:As none recorded since   *P1875:*Peerless recorded, since   5246| MS:poets,
§comma altered to parenthesis§ (saith §next word illegibly crossed out and replaced above
by§ Homeros, §comma altered to parenthesis§   5247| *P1875:*Pedestaled   *1889a:*
Pedestalled   5248| *P1875:*laureled   *1889a:*laurelled   5249| MS:for he §crossed out
and replaced above by§ we see §over *saw*§   5251| MS:face   *P1875:*face,
5255| MS:Hill and §crossed out§ dale and < > rough §inserted above§   *P1875:*Hill, dale, and
5257| MS:music: but   *P1875:*music; but   5258| MS:account   *P1875:*account,
5260| MS:my Parnassas §altered to§ Parnassos < > Mount;   *P1875:*mount!

Famed shalt thou vie with famed Pieria's fount!

"Here I await the end of this ado:
Which wins—Earth's poet or the Heavenly Muse." . . .

5265 But song broke up in laughter.   "Tell the rest
Who may! *I* have not spurned the common life,
Nor vaunted mine a lyre to match the Muse
Who sings for gods, not men!   Accordingly,
I shall not decorate her vestibule—
5270 Mute marble, blind the eyes and quenched the brain,
Loose in the hand a bright, a broken lyre!
—Not Thamuris but Aristophanes!

"There!   I have sung content back to myself,
And started subject for a play beside.
5275 My next performance shall content you both.
Did 'Prelude Battle' maul 'best friend' too much?
Then 'Main-Fight' be my next song, fairness' self!
Its subject—Contest for the Tragic Crown.
Ay, you shall hear none else but Aischulos
5280 Lay down the law of Tragedy, and prove
'Best friend' a stray-away,—no praise denied
His manifold deservings, never fear—

5262| MS:thou be §crossed out and replaced above by§ vie with that Pierian *P1875:*with
famed Pieria's   5263| MS:Here <> ado— *P1875:*ado: *1889a:*"Here   5264| MS:the
Heavenly Muse.... *1889a:*the Heavenly Muse."...   5265| *P1875:*rest, *1889a:*rest
5266| MS:Who cares? I <> life *P1875:*Who may! *I* <> life,   5268| MS:gods not men.
Accordingly *P1875:*gods, not men! Accordingly,   5271| MS:in my hand the bright, the
broken *P1875:*in the hand a bright, a broken   5272-73| MS:§rule called for and then
crossed out§   5273| MS:"Come, as §crossed out§ I have §inserted below§ sung §over
sing§ *P1875:*"There! I   5274| MS:§line added in margin§ started a §crossed out§
subject <> besides *P1875:*beside.   5275| MS:next song shall §altered to§ should §last
two words crossed out and replaced above by two words§ performance shall <> you equally
§crossed out§ both.   5276| MS:Did §in margin§ The §crossed out§ 'Prelude-Battle'
mauled §altered to§ maul your friend too *P1875:*maul 'best friend' too   5277| MS:next
play, fairness' *P1875:*next song, fairness'   5278| MS:Its §in margin§ For §crossed out§
subject—contest <> tragic crown: §last three words altered to§ Contest <> Tragic Crown:
*P1875:*the Tragic Crown.   5279| MS:hear §over *have*§ <> else than §crossed out and
replaced above by§ but   5280| *P1875:*tragedy *CP1875:*of Tragedy   5281| MS:Your
friend a *P1875:*'Best friend' a   5282| MS:deservings: never *P1875:*deservings, never

Nor word more of the old fun!   Death defends.
Sound admonition has its due effect.

5285   Oh, you have uttered weighty words, believe!
Such as shall bear abundant fruit, next year,
In judgment, regular, legitimate.
Let Bacchos' self preside in person!   Ay—
For there's a buzz about those 'Bacchanals'

5290   Rumour attributes to your great and dead
For final effort: just the prodigy
Great dead men leave, to lay survivors low!
—Until we make acquaintance with our fate
And find, fate's worst done, we, the same, survive

5295   Perchance to honour more the patron-god,
Fitlier inaugurate a festal year.
Now that the cloud has broken, sky laughs blue,
Earth blossoms youthfully.   Athenai breathes.
After a twenty-six years' wintry blank

5300   Struck from her life,—war-madness, one long swoon,
She wakes up: Arginousai bids good cheer.

5283| MS:No word <> death defends—   *P1875:*Nor word <> Death defends!   *1889a:*
defends.   5284| MS:And you, Balaustion, §last two words crossed out and replaced above
by two words§ my §crossed out§ admonition have §altered to§ has your §crossed out and
replaced above by§ its §crossed out and then rewritten§   *P1875:*Sound admonition
5285| MS:have said a §last two words crossed out and replaced above by one word§ uttered
weighty thing §crossed out§ words   5287| MS:legitimate—   *P1875:*legitimate.
5288| MS:When §in margin§ For §crossed out§ Bacchos shall §crossed out and replaced above
by apostrophe and word, forming§ Bacchos' self preside §altered to§ presides <> person.
Ay—   *P1875:*Let Bacchos' <> preside <> person! Ay—   5289| MS:about the §altered
to§ those "Bacchanals"   *P1875:*those 'Bacchanals'   5290| MS:to Euripides §crossed out§
your   5291| MS:effort—Oh, §word and comma crossed out and replaced above by§ still
the   *P1875:*effort: just the   5292| MS:Most dead <> low,   *P1875:*Great dead <> low!
5293| MS:—Until they §crossed out and replaced above by§ we <> with the thing   *P1875:*
with our fate   5294| MS:find, its worst done, they §crossed out and replaced above by§ we
survive, the same, §last two words and commas marked for transposition to follow *we*§
*P1875:*find, fate's worst   5295| MS:To §in margin§ We'll §crossed out§ see who honors
most §altered to§ more   *P1875:*Perchance to honor more   *1889a:*honour
5296| MS:inaugurates <> year!   *P1875:*inaugurate <> year.
5297| MS:For §crossed out and replaced above by§ Ay, the dark cloud <> broken—sky
*P1875:*Now that the cloud <> broken, sky   5298| MS:youthfully! Athenai breathes
*P1875:*breathes!   *1889a:*youthfully. Athenai breathes.   5299| MS:After the §crossed out
and replaced above by§ a twenty six <> blank—   *P1875:*twenty-six <> blank
5300| MS:swoon,—   *P1875:*swoon,   5301| MS:up,—Arginousai cries §crossed out and
replaced above by§ bids Good Cheer!   *P1875:*up: Arginousai <> good cheer!   *1889a:*cheer.

We have disposed of Kallikratidas;
Once more will Sparté sue for terms,—who knows?
Cede Dekeleia, as the rumour runs:
5305 Terms which Athenai, of right mind again,
Accepts—she can no other.   Peace declared,
Have my long labours borne their fruit or no?
Grinned coarse buffoonery so oft in vain?
Enough—it simply saved you.   Saved ones, praise
5310 Theoria's beauty and Opora's breath!
Nor, when Peace realizes promised bliss,
Forget the Bald Bard, Envy! but go burst
As the cup goes round and the cates abound,
Collops of hare with roast spinks rare!
5315 Confess my pipings, dancings, posings served
A purpose: guttlings, guzzlings, had their use!
Say whether light Muse, Rosy-finger-tips,

5302| MS:of Kallikratidas— *P1875:*of Kallikratidas;   5303| MS:for pence— §word and
dash crossed out and replaced above by word, comma and dash§ terms
5304| MS:Cede Dekeleia, so the < > runs— *P1875:*Cede Dekeleia, as the < > runs:
5305| MS:Terms which §last two words in margin§ Athenai, now in her §last three words
crossed out and replaced above by one word§ of   5306| MS:other! then §crossed out and
replaced above by§ Peace declared— §altered to§ declare— *P1875:*declared,   *1889a:*other.
Peace   5307| MS:labours borne §over partially illegible word§ thee fruit   *P1875.*labours
borne their fruit   5308| MS:Was all the §last two words crossed out§ coarse < > so much
§last two words inserted above§ in   *P1875:*Grinned coarse < > so oft in
5309| MS:you,—saved,—I say— §last two words and dash crossed out§ all praise   *P1875:*you!
saviours—praise   *1889a:*you. Saved ones, praise   5310| MS:§line added§ To rolls and
peasoup and Oporia's charms §crossed out§ breadth!   *P1875:*Theoria's beauty and   *1889a:*
and Opora's §emended to§ breath! §see Editorial Notes§   5311| MS:So, §word and
comma in margin§ And §crossed out§ when < > bliss—   *P1875:*Nor, when < > bliss,
5312-14| MS:§two lines expanded to three lines§ Think of my own worth §last three words
crossed out and replaced above by seven words and solidus§ the Bald Bard, Envy, and go
burst. / *When* §crossed out and replaced below by§ *For the wine* §crossed out and replaced
above by§ *cup goes round, / And the cakes abound,* slices §altered to§ *Slices of hare, and* §altered to§
And eel-fry rare!   5312| *P1875:*Forget the < > Envy! but go burst
5313| *P1875:*As the < > round, and the cates abound,   *1889a:*round and
5314| *P1875:* Collops of hare, with roast spinks rare!   *1889a:*hare with   5315| MS:piping
dancing damsels served   *P1875:*pipings, dancings, posings served   5316| MS:A §in
margin§ Their §crossed out§ purpose, and Oporia's §last two words crossed out and replaced
above by two words§ my Elaphion's pranks had use!   *P1875:*purpose: guttlings, guzzlings, had
their use!   5317| MS:Say §over illegible erasure§ whether the §crossed out§ < > Muse
Rosy-finger-tips §over *muse rosy-finger-tips*§   *P1875:*light Muse, Rosy-finger-tips,

Or 'best friend's' heavy-hand, Melpomené,
Touched lyre to purpose, played Amphion's part,
5320 And built Athenai to the skies once more!
Farewell, brave couple!   Next year, welcome me!"

No doubt, in what he said that night, sincere!
One story he referred to, false or fact,
Was not without adaptability.
5325 They do say—Lais the Corinthian once
Chancing to see Euripides (who paced
Composing in a garden, tablet-book
In left hand, with appended stulos prompt)
"Answer me," she began, "O Poet,—this!
5330 What didst intend by writing in thy play
Go hang, thou filthy doer?"   Struck on heap,
Euripides, at the audacious speech—
"Well now," quoth he, "thyself art just the one
I should imagine fit for deeds of filth!"

5318| MS:Or that §crossed out and replaced above by§ his hard-handed, §altered to§ Hard-heavy-hand, §*heavy-* inserted above§ his §word and preceding comma crossed out§ Melpomené,   *P1875:*Or 'best friend's' Heavy-hand, Melpomené,   *1889a:*heavy-hand
5319| MS:Best touch §altered to§ touched psalterion— §dash altered to comma§ play §altered to§ played   *P1875:*Touched lyre to purpose, played   5320| MS:built §over *build*§ Athenai §over partially illegible word§ <> skies again §crossed out§ once   5321| MS:Farewell, Balaustion, welcome me!" §punctuation inserted§ next §altered to§ Next year, §last two words and comma marked for transposition to precede *welcome*§ §next word illegibly crossed out, perhaps *too*§ §following last line§ (Go on to next page)   *P1875:*Farewell, brave couple! Next
5321-22| MS:§no rule§   *P1875:*§rule§   5322-37| MS:§these lines composed on verso of leaf bearing ll. 5289-321§   5322| MS:said he was §last two words crossed out and replaced above by two words and comma§ that night, sincere.   *P1875:*sincere!
5323| MS:That §crossed out and replaced above by *The*, then altered to§ One <> to, §over illegible erasure§ first of all,   *P1875:*to, false or fact,   5325| MS:They do say §last two words crossed out and replaced above by one word§ fable—Lais   *P1875:*They do say—Lais
5326| MS:see Euripides, who   *P1875:*see Euripides (who   5328| MS:left §inserted above over *right*§ <> with the §crossed out§ <> stulos there §crossed out§ prompt, §over partial erasure§   *P1875:*prompt)   5329| MS:began "O <> this: *P1875:*began, "O <> this!   5331| MS:'Go hang, thou filthy doer!' " Struck   *P1875:*Go hang, thou filthy doer?" Struck §emended to§ *doer?*" Struck §see Editorial Notes§
5332| MS:at his audaciousness, §comma crossed out; last two words altered to§ the audacious speech,   *P1875:*speech—   5333| MS:he "thyself   *P1875:*he, "thyself

5335 She laughingly retorted his own line
"What's filth,—unless who does it, thinks it so?"

So might he doubtless think.   "Farewell," said we.

And he was gone, lost in the morning-grey
Rose-streaked and gold to eastward.   Did we dream?
5340 Could the poor twelve-hours hold this argument
We render durable from fugitive,
As duly at each sunset's droop of sail,
Delay of oar, submission to sea-might,
I still remember, you as duly dint
5345 Remembrance, with the punctual rapid style,
Into—what calm cold page!

                                   Thus soul escapes
From eloquence made captive: thus mere words
—Ah, would the lifeless body stay!   But no:
Change upon change till,—who may recognize
5350 What did soul service, in the dusty heap?
What energy of Aristophanes
Inflames the wreck Balaustion saves to show?
Ashes be evidence how fire—with smoke—
All night went lamping on!   But morn must rise.

5337| So did he §following this line§ And he was gone &c &c   *P1875:*So might he
5338| MS:morning-grey,   *1889a:*morning-grey   5339| MS:Streaked rose §last two words
transposed and altered to§ Rose-streaked   5340| MS:the §over illegible word§
5341| MS:We turn to §last two words crossed out and replaced above by one word§ rendered
*P1875:*render   5343| MS:sea's-might, §altered to§ sea-might,
5344| MS:remembered <> duly wrought   *P1875:*remember <> duly dint
5345| MS:Remembrance with <> style   *P1875:*Remembrance, with <> style,
5346| MS:escapes, §comma crossed out§   5347| MS:§line added§ captive,   thus   *P1875:*
captive: thus   5348| MS:Thus body §last two words crossed out§ —Ah <> the lifeless
§last two words inserted below§   5350| MS:service in <> heap—   *P1875:*service, in <>
heap?   5351| MS:What §over illegible word§   5352| MS:In lifeless words §last three
words crossed out and replaced above by three words§ Inflamed the wreck Balaustion saved
§altered to§ saves   *P1875:*Inflames   5353| MS:Just §over *The* and then crossed out§
ashes §altered to§ Ashes for evidence how flame §crossed out and replaced above by§ fire—
and smoke—   *P1875:*Ashes be evidence   *1889a:*fire—with smoke—
5354| MS:on! but §altered to§ But morning comes, §last word and preceding three letters
crossed out and replaced above by two words§ must rise;   *P1875:*rise.

⁵³⁵⁵ The poet—I shall say—burned up and, blank
Smouldered this ash, now white and cold enough.

Nay, Euthukles! for best, though mine it be,
Comes yet.   Write on, write ever, wrong no word!

Add, first,—he gone, if jollity went too,
⁵³⁶⁰ Some of the graver mood, which mixed and marred,
Departed likewise.   Sight of narrow scope
Has this meek consolation: neither ills
We dread, nor joys we dare anticipate,
Perform to promise.   Each soul sows a seed—
⁵³⁶⁵ Euripides and Aristophanes;
Seed bears crop, scarce within our little lives;
But germinates,—perhaps enough to judge,—
Next year?

Whereas, next year brought harvest time!
For, next year came, and went not, but is now,
⁵³⁷⁰ Still now, while you and I are bound for Rhodes
That's all but reached—and harvest has it brought,

---

⁵³⁵⁵| MS: and—blank *P1875:*and, blank, *1889a:*blank   ⁵³⁵⁶| MS:enough! *P1875:*
enough.   ⁵³⁵⁷| MS:Nay, Euthukles, the §crossed out and replaced above by§ for best
comes yet, §last two words crossed out§ though   *P1875:*Nay, Euthukles! for
⁵³⁵⁸| MS:Patience §crossed out and replaced above by two words§ Comes yet! <> ever, miss
§crossed out and replaced above by§ wrong   *P1875:*yet. Write   ⁵³⁵⁹| MS:Add, though
§crossed out and replaced above by§ first <> jollity must go §last two words crossed out and
replaced above by§ went too,   ⁵³⁶⁰| MS:mood that §crossed out and replaced above by§
which   *P1875:*mood, which   ⁵³⁶¹| MS:Departed also . . §word and punctuation crossed
out and replaced above by word and period§ likewise. Sight §over *sight*§ of narrowed §altered
to§ narrow   ⁵³⁶²| MS:this §over illegible erasure§ <> consolation—neither ills, *P1875:*
consolation: neither *1889a:*ills   ⁵³⁶³| MS:joys, we *1889a:*joys we
⁵³⁶⁴| MS:Answer §crossed out and replaced above by§ Perform <> Each has sown the
§crossed out and replaced above by§ his seed—   *P1875:*promise. Each soul sows a seed—
⁵³⁶⁵| MS:§line added§ and Aristophanes—   *P1875:*and Aristophanes;
⁵³⁶⁶| MS:Seed §in margin§ Will §crossed out§ bear §altered to§ bears fruit—scarce <>
lives—   *P1875:*bears crop, scarce <> lives;   ⁵³⁶⁷| MS:§line added§ judge—   *P1875:*
judge,—   ⁵³⁶⁸| MS:year! §¶§ As if §last two words crossed out and replaced below by one
word and comma§ Whereas   *P1875:*year? §¶§ Whereas   ⁵³⁶⁹| MS:Ah, §word and
comma in margin§ But §crossed out§ next   *P1875:*For, next
⁵³⁷¹| MS:reached,— §comma altered to exclamation point§ and *1889a:*reached—and

Dire as the homicidal dragon-crop.
Sophokles had dismissal ere it dawned,
Happy as ever; though men mournfully
5375   Plausive,—when only soul could triumph now,
And Iophon produced his father's play,—
Crowned the consummate song where Oidipous
Dared the descent mid earthquake-thundering,
And hardly Theseus' hands availed to guard
5380   Eyes from the horror, as their grove disgorged
Its dread ones, while each daughter sank to ground.

Then Aristophanes, on heel of that,
Triumphant also, followed with his "Frogs":
Produced at next Lenaia,—three months since,—
5385   The promised Main-Fight, loyal, license-free!
As if the poet, primed with Thasian juice,
(Himself swore—wine that conquers every kind
For long abiding in the head) could fix
Thenceforward any object in its truth,
5390   Through eyeballs bathed by mere Castalian dew,

---

⁵³⁷²| MS:the crop §altered to§ dragon-crop! §punctuation inserted§ of §crossed out§ homicidal §over partial erasure and marked for transposition to follow the§ *1889a:*dragon-crop. ⁵³⁷⁴| MS:ever: yet §crossed out and replaced above by§ though *P1875:*ever; though ⁵³⁷⁵| MS:§line added§ Next year,—when *P1875:*Plausive,—when ⁵³⁷⁶| MS:§line added in margin§ ⁵³⁷⁷| MS:consumate piece §crossed out and replaced above by§ song when §altered to§ where ⁵³⁷⁸| MS:Died §crossed out and replaced above by§ Dared the dread death §last two words crossed out and replaced above by one word§ descent <.> earthquake, thundering, *P1875:*earthquake-thundering, ⁵³⁷⁹| MS:And §crossed out and replaced above by two words§ While even Theseus' while his §last two words crossed out§ hand §altered to§ hands bade horror off §last two words crossed out§ darkness help *P1875:*And hardly Theseus' hands availed to guard ⁵³⁸⁰| MS:From §crossed out§ eyes §altered to§ Eyes, too §inserted above§ unequal, as the Grove *P1875:*Eyes from the horrow, as their grove ⁵³⁸¹| MS:ones, and each *P1875:*ones, while each ⁵³⁸²| MS:And §crossed out and replaced above by§ Then ⁵³⁸³| MS:his "Frogs": *P1875:*his "Frogs:" §emended to§ "Frogs": §see Editorial Notes§ ⁵³⁸⁴| MS:§line added§ Produced §in margin over illegible word§ Brought out §last two words crossed out§ at ⁵³⁸⁵| MS:licence-free? §punctuation altered to exclamation point§ *1889a:*license-free! ⁵³⁸⁶| MS:Who judged §last two words in margin§ As if §last two words crossed out§ the <> juice,— *P1875:*As if the <> juice, ⁵³⁸⁷| MS:(Himself §parenthesis inserted§ ⁵³⁸⁸| MS:head— §dash altered to parenthesis§ could eye *P1875:*could fix ⁵³⁹⁰| MS:Through filmed balls *P1875:*Through eyeballs

267

Nor miss the borrowed medium,—vinous drop
That colours all to the right crimson pitch
When mirth grows mockery, censure takes the tinge
Of malice!

      All was Aristophanes:
5395   There blazed the glory, there shot black the shame.
Ay, Bacchos did stand forth, the Tragic God
In person! and when duly dragged through mire,—
Having lied, filched, played fool, proved coward, flung
The boys their dose of fit indecency,
5400   And finally got trounced to heart's content,
At his own feast, in his own theatre
(—Oh never fear! 'Twas consecrated sport,
Exact tradition, warranted no whit
Offensive to instructed taste,—indeed,
5405   Essential to Athenai's liberty,
Could the poor stranger understand!) why, then—
He was pronounced the rarely-qualified
To rate the work, adjust the claims to worth,
Of Aischulos (of whom, in other mood,
5410   This same appreciative poet pleased
To say "He's all one stiff and gluey piece
Of back of swine's neck!")—and of Chatterbox
Who, "twisting words like wool," usurped his seat

5391| MS:the ruddier §crossed out and replaced above by§ fictive medium *P1875:*the
borrowed medium 5393| MS:Where mirth turns mockery *P1875:*When mirth grows
mockery 5394| MS:malice! §¶§ All §over *all*§ <> Aristophanes, *P1875:*was Aristophanes:
5395| MS:shame! *1889a:*shame. 5396| MS:did present §crossed out and replaced above
by two words§ stand forth the *P1875:*forth, the 5397| MS:mire, *P1875:*mire,—
5398| MS:fool and coward, found *P1875:*fool, proved coward, flung 5399| MS:boy's
*P1875:*boys 5400| MS:got thrashed to *P1875:*got trounced to 5402| MS:(—Oh,
§parenthesis inserted§ never fear! The §crossed out and replaced above by§ 'Twas consecrated
play §crossed out and replaced above by§ sport, *1889a:*(—Oh never 5403| MS:whit
§over illegible word§ 5406| MS:understand at all!— §dash altered to parenthesis§
*P1875:*understand!) why, then— 5407| MS:rarely qualified *P1875:*rarely-qualified
5408| MS:the §over illegible word§ claim *1889a:*claims 5409| MS:Of Aischulos and who
usurped his seat §last five words crossed out and replaced above by five words§ of whom, in other
mood, *P1875:*Of Aischulos (of 5410-13| MS:§lines added in margin§ 5410| MS:same
§inserted above§ <> Poet *P1875:*poet 5411| MS:To say §last two words in margin§
5412| MS:neck!"—and the new-comer *P1875:*neck!")—and the Chatterbox *1889a:*and of

In Plouton's realm: "the arch-rogue, liar, scamp
5415 That lives by snatching-up of altar-orts,"
—Who failed to recognize Euripides?

Then came a contest for supremacy—
Crammed full of genius, wit and fun and freak.
No spice of undue spite to spoil the dish
5420 Of all sorts,—for the Mystics matched the Frogs
In poetry, no Seiren sang so sweet!—
Till, pressed into the service (how dispense
With Phaps-Elaphion and free foot-display?)
The Muse of dead Euripides danced frank,
5425 Rattled her bits of tile, made all too plain
How baby-work like "Herakles" had birth!
Last, Bacchos,—candidly disclaiming brains
Able to follow finer argument,—
Confessed himself much moved by three main facts:
5430 First,   if you stick a "Lost his flask of oil"
At pause of period, you perplex the sense—
Were it the Elegy for Marathon!
Next, if you weigh two verses, "car"—the word,
Will outweigh "club"—the word, in each packed line!
5435 And—last, worst fact of all!—in rivalry
The younger poet dared to improvise

Chatterbox   5414-17| MS:In <> realm—the rash Euripides. / Then   *P1875*:realm: "the
arch-rogue, liar, scamp / §lines 5415-16 added§   5419| MS:No over §crossed out§ spice <>
undue §inserted above§ spite to §crossed out§ spoil §altered to§ spoiled the §crossed out and
replaced above by§ olios dish   *P1875*.spite to spoil the dish   5420| MS:all-sorts   *P1875*:all
sorts   5421| MS:sings §over *sang*§   *P1875*:sang   5422| MS:Till §in margin§ While,
§word crossed out; comma retained§ <> service, (how   *P1875*:service (how   5423| MS:With
poor Elaphion and each §crossed out and replaced above by§ free   *P1875*:With Phaps-
Elaphion   5425| MS:tiles, exposed her charms, §last three words and comma crossed
out§ made   5426| MS:And showed the way that §last five words crossed out and replaced
above by three words§ How baby-work like 'Herakles' had   *P1875*:like "Herakles" had
5428| MS:follow the fine argument,—   *P1875*:follow finer argument,—   5430| MS:stuck
on 'Lost <> oil'   *P1875*:stick a 'Lost   *1889a*:a "Lost <> oil"   5431| MS:At §over illegible
erasure§ <> period—you   *P1875*:period, you   5432| MS:for Marathon.   *P1875*:for
Marathon!   5433| MS:two §over partial erasure§ <> 'car'—the   *1889a*:verses, "car"—the
5434| MS:outweigh 'club'— <> word, each packed in each.   *P1875*:word, each word-packed
line!   *1889a*:outweigh "club"— <> word, in each packed line!   5435-36| MS:§one line
expanded to two lines§ And last, the younger rival improvised   *P1875*:§lines 5435-36 added§

Laudation less distinct of—Triphales?
(Nay, that served when ourself abused the youth!)
Pheidippides? (nor that's appropriate now!)
5440 Then,—Alkibiades, our city's hope,
Since times change and we Comics should change too!
These three main facts, well weighed, drew judgment down,
Conclusively assigned the wretch his fate—
"Fate due" admonished the sage Mystic choir,
5445 "To sitting, prate-apace, with Sokrates,
Neglecting music and each tragic aid!"
—All wound-up by a wish "We soon may cease
From certain griefs, and warfare, worst of them!"
—Since, deaf to Comedy's persistent voice,
5450 War still raged, still was like to rage.   In vain
Had Sparté cried once more "But grant us Peace
We give you Dekeleia back!"   Too shrewd
Was Kleophon to let escape, forsooth,
The enemy—at final gasp, besides!

5437| MS:of Triphales   *P1875:*of Triphales—   *1889a:*of—Triphales?   5438| MS:—Nay,
§dash altered to parenthesis§ that was §crossed out and replaced above by§ served <> youth—
§dash altered to parenthesis§   *P1875:*youth!)   5439| MS:Pheidippides—nor §dash
altered to parenthesis§ <> now!— §dash altered to parenthesis§   *P1875:*Pheidippides—(nor
*1889a:*Pheidippides? (nor   5440| MS:Then, Alkibiades <> hope—   *P1875:*Then,—
Alkibiades <> hope,   5441| MS:Since §in margin§ For §crossed out§ times <> we satirists
change   *P1875:*we Comics should change   5442| MS:facts, you see, prove capital, §last
four words crossed out and replaced above by five words§ well weighed, drew judgment down,
5443| MS:assigned our friend his   *P1875:*assigned the wretch his   5444| MS:All come,
§last two words and comma crossed out and replaced above by two words and punctuation§
"Gained him" the Mystic Choros sagely sang §last three words crossed out and replaced above
by three words§ choir admonished sage, §over illegible erasure§   *P1875:*"Fate due" admonished
the sage Mystic choir,   5445| MS:Thus §crossed out and replaced above by word and
punctuation§ "By sitting, prate-apace, by §crossed out and replaced above by§ with   *P1875:*
"To sitting   5446| MS:and true §crossed out and replaced above by§ each Tragic aids."
§altered to§ aid."   *P1875:*tragic aid!"   5447| MS:—Well wound up   *P1875:*—All wound-up
5448| MS:From all our griefs <> of all §crossed out and replaced above by§ them!"   *P1875:*
From certain griefs   5449| MS:Since, spite of §last two words crossed out and replaced
above by two words§ deaf to   *P1875:*—Since   5450| MS:raged, §over illegible word§ <>
to be §crossed out and replaced above by§ rage. §period inserted§ In §over *in*§ vain,   *P1875:*
vain   5451| MS:Had Sparté §over *Sparta*§ <> "For gift of Peace   *P1875:*more "For
granted Peace   *1889a:*more "But grant us Peace   5452| MS:back!" §punctuation
inserted§ again §crossed out§ But no!   *P1875:*back!" Too shrewd   5453| MS:Kleophon
was too wise §crossed out and replaced above by§ shrewd to let escape   *P1875:*Was Kleophon
to let escape, forsooth,   5454| MS:gasp, forsooth!   *P1875:*gasp, besides!

⁵⁴⁵⁵ So, Aristophanes obtained the prize,
And so Athenai felt she had a friend
Far better than her "best friend," lost last year;
And so, such fame had "Frogs" that, when came round
This present year, those Frogs croaked gay again
⁵⁴⁶⁰ At the great Feast, Elaphebolion-month.
Only—there happened Aigispotamoi!

And, in the midst of the frog-merriment,
Plump o' the sudden, pounces stern King Stork
On the light-hearted people of the marsh!
⁵⁴⁶⁵ Spartan Lusandros swooped precipitate,
Ended Athenai, rowed her sacred bay
With oars which brought a hundred triremes back
Captive!

And first word of the conqueror
Was "Down with those Long Walls, Peiraios' pride!
⁵⁴⁷⁰ Destroy, yourselves, your bulwarks! Peace needs none!"
And "We obey" they shuddered in their dream.

But, at next quick imposure of decree—
"No longer democratic government!

---

^{5456|} MS:so, Athenai *P1875:*so Athenai   ^{5457|} MS:Far worthier than the poet, lost <>
year, *P1875:*Far better than her "best friend," lost <> year;   ^{5458|} MS:And so
§crossed out and replaced above by§ such had fame, §last two words marked for
transposition; comma crossed out§ one month §altered to§ months ago §last three words
crossed out§ "The §over *the*§ Frogs," that *P1875:*And so, such <> had "Frogs" that
^{5459|} MS:those §over illegible word§   ^{5460|} MS:the Great <> Elaphebolion month.
*P1875:*great <> Elaphebolion-month.   ^{5461|} MS:Also §crossed out and replaced above
by word and dash§ Only   ^{5462|} MS:And §crossed out and replaced above by word and
comma§ Lo, in <> of this §crossed out and replaced above by§ much frog-merriment,
*P1875:*And, in <> of the frog-merriment,   ^{5463|} MS:As when, §last two words and
comma crossed out and replaced above by§ Plump <> sudden, plump §crossed out and
replaced above by word and comma§ lo, descends King *P1875:*sudden, pounces stern King
^{5464|} MS:marsh, §comma altered to exclamation point§   ^{5466|} MS:Ended Athenai, as he
beat §last three words crossed out and replaced above by one word§ rowed <> sacred
§inserted above§   ^{5467|} MS:which rowed her §last two words crossed out and replaced
above by two words§ brought a   ^{5468|} MS:Captive. §¶§ And §over *and*§ *P1875:*Captive!
§¶§ And   ^{5469|} MS:those Long Walls §over illegible erasure§ <> pride, §comma altered
to exclamation point§   ^{5470|} MS:Yourself destroy your *P1875:*Destroy, yourselves, your
^{5473|} MS:"No more of democratic *P1875:*"No longer democratic

Henceforth such oligarchy as ourselves
⁵⁴⁷⁵ Please to appoint you!"—then the horror stung
Dreamers awake; they started up a-stare
At the half-helot captain and his crew
—Spartans, "men used to let their hair grow long,
To fast, be dirty, and just—Socratize"—
⁵⁴⁸⁰ Whose word was "Trample on Themistokles!"

So, as the way is with much misery,
The heads swam, hands refused their office, hearts
Sunk as they stood in stupor. "Wreck the Walls?
Ruin Peiraios?—with our Pallas armed
⁵⁴⁸⁵ For interference?—Herakles apprised,
And Theseus hasting? Lay the Long Walls low?"

Three days they stood, stared,—stonier than their walls.

Whereupon, sleep who might, Lusandros woke:
Saw the prostration of his enemy,
⁵⁴⁹⁰ Utter and absolute beyond belief,
Past hope of hatred even. I surmise
He also probably saw fade in fume
Certain fears, bred of Bakis-prophecy,
Nor apprehended any more that gods
⁵⁴⁹⁵ And heroes,—fire, must glow forth, guard the ground

5479| MS:just—Sokratize,"— *P1875*:just—Socratize"— 5482| MS:heads turned §crossed out and replaced above by§ swam 5483| MS:Died §crossed out and replaced above by§ Sunk 5484| MS:with the §crossed out and replaced above by§ our Goddess armed *P1875*:our Pallas armed 5486| MS:And §in margin§ Theseus §next two words illegibly crossed out and replaced above by two words§ swift §crossed out§ haste §altered to§ hasting? Pull §crossed out and replaced above by§ Lay < > Walls down §crossed out and replaced above by§ low?" 5487| MS:stood, thus §crossed out and replaced above by§ stared 5488| MS:woke— *P1875*:woke: 5489| MS:of the §crossed out and replaced above by§ his 5491| MS:even. §period inserted§ Some §over *some*, then crossed out and replaced above by§ I 5492| MS:also §inserted above§ 5493| MS:§line added§ Certain old §crossed out§ fears, and §comma and word crossed out and replaced above by two words§ bred of Bakis-phrophecy §altered to§ Bakis-prophecy, *P1875*:fears, bred 5494| MS:that §over *the*§ 5495| MS:heroes would §crossed out and replaced above by two words§ needs must < > forth, and §crossed out§ guard *P1875*:heroes,—fire, must

272

Where prone, by sober day-dawn, corpse-like lay
Powerless Athenai, late predominant
Lady of Hellas,—Sparté's slave-prize now!
Where should a menace lurk in those slack limbs?
5500   What was to move his circumspection?   Why
Demolish just Peiraios?

                "Stay!" bade he:
"Already promise-breakers?   True to type,
Athenians! past and present and to come—
The fickle and the false!   No stone dislodged,
5505   No implement applied, yet three days' grace
Expire!   Forbearance is no longer-lived.
By breaking promise, terms of peace you break—
Too gently framed for falsehood, fickleness!
All must be reconsidered—yours the fault!"

5510   Wherewith, he called a council of allies.
Pent-up resentment used its privilege,—
Outburst at ending: this the summed result.

"Because we would avenge no transient wrong

5496| MS:Where §over illegible erasure§ lay §crossed out and replaced above by§ prone, < > sober daylight, corpse like prone §crossed out§ lay   *P1875:*sober day-dawn, corpse-like
5498| MS:of Hellas,—Sparta's §altered to§ Sparté's < > now.   *P1875:*now!
5498-99| MS:§¶ called for in margin§   *P1875:*§no ¶§   5499| MS:Where was the §last two words crossed out and replaced above by two words§ should a menace lurked §altered to§ lurk
5500| MS:was to §last two words inserted above§ moved so much §last two words and preceding letter crossed out§ our circumspection here?   *P1875:*move his circumspection? Why
5501| MS:just Peiraios? "Stay!" cried §crossed out and replaced above by§ bade   *P1875:*just Peiraios? §¶§ "Stay!" bade   5503| MS:Athenians,—that's— §crossed out and replaced above by§ still—past, present and < > come,   *P1875:*Athenians! past, and present, and < > come,—   *1889a:*past and present and < > come—   5505| MS:applied, and §crossed out and replaced above by§ yet < > days' expire! §word and punctuation crossed out and replaced above by§ grace   5506| MS:§line added in margin§ Expire? Forbearance   *P1875:*Expire! Forbearance   5507| MS:Then, §word and comma in margin and crossed out§ Broken the §last two words crossed out and replaced above by two words§ And, breaking   *P1875:*By breaking   5509| MS:All is to §last two words crossed out and replaced above by two words§ must be reconsider §altered to§ reconsidered. Yours < > fault!"—   *P1875:*reconsidered— yours < > fault!"   5512| MS:Outburst: at ending, this   *P1875:*Outburst at ending: this

But an eternity of insolence,
5515   Aggression,—folly, no disasters mend,
Pride, no reverses teach humility,—
Because too plainly were all punishment,
Such as comports with less obdurate crime,
Evadable by falsehood, fickleness—
5520   Experience proves the true Athenian type,—
Therefore, 'tis need we dig deep down into
The root of evil; lop nor bole nor branch.
Look up, look round and see, on every side,
What nurtured the rank tree to noisome fruit!
5525   We who live hutted (so they laugh) not housed,
Build barns for temples, prize mud-monuments,
Nor show the sneering stranger aught but—men,—
Spartans take insult of Athenians just
Because they boast Akropolis to mount,
5530   And Propulaia to make entry by,
Through a mad maze of marble arrogance
Such as you see—such as let none see more!
Abolish the detested luxury!
Leave not one stone upon another, raze
5535   Athenai to the rock! Let hill and plain
Become a waste, a grassy pasture-ground

5515| MS:disaster mends, §last two words and comma altered to§ disasters mend   *P1875:*
mend,   5516| MS:reverse §altered to§ reverses can §crossed out§ teach
5517| MS:too manifest were punishment—   *P1875:*too plainly were all punishment,
5518| MS:crime—   *P1875:*crime,   5519| MS:Evadible   *1889a:*Evadible
5520| MS:§two words illegibly crossed out in margin, perhaps *Tis by*§ Experience §altered to
experience and then restored§ proves the §last two words crossed out and restored§
5522| MS:nor branch nor twig.   *P1875:*nor bole nor branch.   5523| MS:Look round you
§crossed out and replaced above by§ and see extend, on   *P1875:*Look up, look round and
see, on   5524| MS:rank plant to poison §crossed out and replaced above by§ noisome
*P1875:*rank tree to   5525| MS:hutted— §dash altered to parenthesis§ so they laugh—
§dash altered to parenthesis§   5526| MS:Take §crossed out and replaced above by§ Build
<> mud monuments,   *P1875:*mud-monuments,   5528| MS:Spartans are warred on §last
three words and preceding two letters crossed out and replaced above by two words§ is
outraged §*is* crossed out and *Spartans are* restored§ by Athenai's pride   *P1875:*Spartans take
insult of Athenia just   *CP1875:*of Athenians §not B§   5529| MS:Since her sons §last
three words crossed out and replaced above by two words§ Because she boast §altered to§
boasts   *P1875:*Because they boast   5531| MS:And §crossed out and replaced above by§
Through   5533| MS:luxury,   *P1875:*luxury!   5535| MS:rock! Let §over *let*§
5536| MS:waste, a §crossed out and replaced above by§ mere grassy   *P1875:*waste, a grassy

Where sheep may wander, grazing goats depend
From shapeless crags once columns! so at last
Shall peace inhabit there, and peace enough."

5540 Whereon, a shout approved "Such peace bestow!"

Then did a Man of Phokis rise—O heart!
Rise—when no bolt of Zeus disparted sky,
No omen-bird from Pallas scared the crew,
Rise—when mere human argument could stem
5545 No foam-fringe of the passion surging fierce,
Baffle no wrath-wave that o'er barrier broke—
Who was the Man of Phokis rose and flung
A flower i' the way of that fierce foot's advance,
Which—stop for?—nay, had stamped down sword's assault!
5550 Could it be *He* stayed Sparté with the snatch
"Daughter of Agamemnon, late my liege,
Elektra, palaced once, a visitant
To thy poor rustic dwelling, now I come?"

Ay, facing fury of revenge, and lust
5555 Of hate, and malice moaning to appease
Hunger on prey presumptuous, prostrate now—

5537| MS:sheep shall §crossed out and replaced above by§ may wander, and the §last two words crossed out and replaced above by dash and word§ —haply goats *P1875:*wander, grazing goats   5538| MS:columns: so *P1875:*columns! so   5539| MS:Peace shall §last two words marked for transposition and altered to§ Shall peace <> enough!" *P1875:* enough."   5540| MS:Whereat §altered to§ Whereon   5541| MS:Until §crossed out and replaced above by two words§ Then did <> Phokis rose §altered to§ rise   5542| MS:Rose §altered to§ Rise   5544| MS:Rose §altered to§ Rise—when all §crossed out and replaced above by§ mere <> argument had stemmed *P1875:*argument could stem   5546| MS:Baffled <> wrath- §word and hyphen inserted above§ <> o'er the §crossed out§ barrier *P1875:*Baffle   5548| MS:of that §crossed out and replaced above by§ fierce advancing foot *P1875:*fierce foot's advance,   5549| MS:Had stopped not for—stamped down mere §crossed out and replaced above by§ the sword's assault— *P1875:*Which—stop for?—nay, had stamped down sword's assault!   5550| MS:it be, §last two words and comma inserted above§ he stay Sparta §last two words altered to§ stayed Sparté <> the Choros §crossed out§ snatch *P1875:*be *He*   5553| MS:dwelling, here I come!" *P1875:*dwelling, now I come?"   5553-54| MS:§no ¶ called for§ *P1875:*§¶§   5554| MS:For all the §last three words crossed out and replaced above by two words§ Ay, facing <> revenge, the §crossed out and replaced above by§ and   5555| MS:hate, the §crossed out and replaced above by§ and

Full in the hideous faces—last resource,
You flung that choric flower, my Euthukles!

And see, as through some pinhole, should the wind
5560   Wedgingly pierce but once, in with a rush
Hurries the whole wild weather, rends to rags
The weak sail stretched against the outside storm—
So did the power of that triumphant play
Pour in, and oversweep the assembled foe!
5565   Triumphant play, wherein our poet first
Dared bring the grandeur of the Tragic Two
Down to the level of our common life,
Close to the beating of our common heart.
Elektra?   'Twas Athenai, Sparté's ice
5570   Thawed to, while that sad portraiture appealed—
Agamemnonian lady, lost by fault
Of her own kindred, cast from house and home,
Despoiled of all the brave inheritance,
Dowered humbly as befits a herdsman's mate,
5575   Partaker of his cottage, clothed in rags,
Patient performer of the poorest chares,
Yet mindful, all the while, of glory past
When she walked darling of Mukenai, dear
Beyond Orestes to the King of Men!

5580   So, because Greeks are Greeks, though Sparté's brood,
And hearts are hearts, though in Lusandros' breast,
And poetry is power, and Euthukles

---

^{5557|} MS:the threatening §crossed out and replaced above by§ hideous   ^{5558|} MS:He
flung that choros-flower §altered to§ Choros-flower *P1875:*that choric flower *1889a:*You flung
^{5563|} MS:did §inserted above§   ^{5565|} MS:wherein Euripides §crossed out§ our dead
friend first *P1875:*our poet first   ^{5567|} MS:of the §crossed out and replaced above by§
our   ^{5568|} MS:of the §crossed out and replaced above by§ our   ^{5569|} MS:Electra?
Nay, §word and comma crossed out and replaced above by§ 'Twas <> Sparta §altered to§
Sparté's   ^{5570|} MS:Thawed at, the §last two words crossed out and replaced above by
word and comma§ to, <> sad §inserted above§   ^{5573|} MS:all that §over *the*§ brave
*P1875:*all the brave   ^{5574|} MS:humbly §inserted above§ <> herdsman's humble §crossed
out§ mate,   ^{5580|} MS:Then §crossed out and replaced above by word and comma§ So, <>
Sparta's §altered to§ Sparté's   ^{5581|} MS:in Lukandros' *CP1875:*in Lusandros'

Had faith therein to, full-face, fling the same—
Sudden, the ice-thaw!   The assembled foe,
5585   Heaving and swaying with strange friendliness,
Cried "Reverence Elektra!"—cried "Abstain
Like that chaste Herdsman, nor dare violate
The sanctity of such reverse!   Let stand
Athenai!"

         Mindful of that story's close,
5590   Perchance, and how,—when he, the Herdsman chaste,
Needs apprehend no break of tranquil sleep,—
All in due time, a stranger, dark, disguised,
Knocks at the door: with searching glance, notes keen,
Knows quick, through mean attire and disrespect,
5595   The ravaged princess!   Ay, right on, the clutch
Of guiding retribution has in charge
The author of the outrage!   While one hand,
Elektra's, pulls the door behind, made fast
On fate,—the other strains, prepared to push
5600   The victim-queen, should she make frightened pause
Before that serpentining blood which steals
Out of the darkness where, a pace beyond,
Above the slain Aigisthos, bides his blow

5583| MS:to, full face, §last two words and commas inserted above§ <> the flower! at foot—
§exclamation point and last two words crossed out; dash retained§   P1875:full-face <> the
same—   5584| MS:ice-thaw: the §punctuation and word altered to§ ice-thaw! The
5586| MS:Cried "Hands off, from Elektra!"—cried "Abstain—   P1875:Cried "Reverence
Elektra!"—cried "Abstain   5587| MS:chaste §over illegible erasure§ Herdsman,—nor
dare §inserted above§   P1875:chaste Herdsman, nor   5588| MS:let be   P1875:reverse!
Let stand   5589| MS:story's end,   P1875:story's close,   5590| MS:herdsman
P1875:the Herdsman   5591| MS:tranquil time §crossed out and replaced above by§
sleep,—   5593| MS:door,—with   P1875:door: with   5594| MS:And §crossed out
and replaced above by§ Knows <> disrespect   P1875.disrespect,   5595| MS:princess:
§colon altered to exclamation point§ while §crossed out and replaced above by word and
comma§ Ay, <> clutch §over illegible word; crossed out and then rewritten§
5596| MS:guiding §inserted above§   5597| MS:of all outrage! while that §last two words
crossed out and replaced above by one word§ one sure §inserted above and crossed out and
while restored§ hand,   P1875:of the outrage! While   5599| MS:fate, the   P1875:fate,—
the   5600| MS:victim when §crossed out and replaced above by§ should she makes
§altered to§ make a frightened   P1875:victim-queen, should <> make frightened
5601| MS:blood that breaks §last two words crossed out and replaced above by one word§ which
5603| MS:slain Aigisthos, waits his   P1875:slain Aigisthos, bides his

Dreadful Orestes!

              Klutaimnestra, wise

5605 This time, forbore; Elektra held her own;

Saved was Athenai through Euripides,

Through Euthukles, through—more than ever—me,

Balaustion, me, who, Wild-pomegranate-flower,

Felt my fruit triumph, and fade proudly so!

5610 But next day, as ungracious minds are wont,

The Spartan, late surprised into a grace,

Grew sudden sober at the enormity,

And grudged, by daybreak, midnight's easy gift;

Splenetically must repay its cost

5615 By due increase of rigour, doglike snatch

At aught still left dog to concede like man.

Rough sea, at flow of tide, may lip, perchance,

5605| MS:This §over *The*§ <> forebore: Elektra <> own. *P1875:*forbore; Elektra <> own;
5606| MS:Athenai save §altered to§ Saved was §last two words marked for transposition to beginning of line§ <> Euripides? §question mark altered to exclamation point§ *P1875:* through Euripides,   5607-09| MS:§lines added in margin§   5607| MS:Through Euthukles—adventuring for me, §last three words crossed out and replaced above by five words§ through, more than ever, me— *P1875:*Through Euthukles, through—more <> ever—me,   5608| MS:me, §word and comma inserted above§ who, §over illegible word§ the §crossed out§ Wild-pomegranate-flower, §over *wild-pomegranate-flower*§   5609| MS:Felt the §crossed out and replaced below by§ my <> triumph, faded <> so. *P1875:*triumph and fade <> so! *CP1875:*triumph, and §not B§   5610| MS:next §next word illegibly crossed out, perhaps *morn*, and replaced above by§ day   5611| MS:§line added§ Yielding to what seems weakness—oversight §entire line crossed out and replaced by new line in margin§ Showed us §last two words inserted above and then crossed out§ The Spartans, §altered to *Spartan's* and then altered to§ Spartan thus, §word and comma crossed out and replaced above by§ late §over *mind*§   5612| MS:After concession of some hard won grace §entire line crossed out and replaced by new line in margin§ sudden-sober *P1875:*sudden sober
5613| MS:Grudged on review, must repay its cost §entire line crossed out and replaced by new line in margin§ by day light §last two words crossed out and replaced below by illegibly crossed-out word and then replaced above by one word§ dawn-break <> gift: *P1875:*day-break <> gift; *1889a:*daybreak   5614| MS:§line added in margin§   5615| MS:By some §crossed out and replaced above by§ due <> doglike snap §altered to§ snatch   5616| MS:left them §crossed out and replaced above by§ dogs to §next word illegibly crossed out and replaced above by§ concede like men. *P1875:*dog <> man.   5617| MS:Just as §crossed out and replaced above by§ so the §altered to§ The §last three words crossed out§ Rough §inserted above over illegible word§ <> tide, perchance §inserted above and crossed out§ may

Smoothly the land-line reached as for repose—
Lie indolent in all unquestioned sway;
5620 But ebbing, when needs must, all thwart and loth,
Sea claws at sand relinquished strugglingly.
So, harsh Lusandros—pinioned to inflict
The lesser penalty alone—spoke harsh,
As minded to embitter scathe by scorn.

5625 "Athenai's self be saved then, thank the Lyre!
If Tragedy withdraws her presence—quick,
If Comedy replace her,—what more just?
Let Comedy do service, frisk away,
Dance off stage these indomitable stones,
5630 Long Walls, Peiraian bulwarks!   Hew and heave,
Pick at, pound into dust each dear defence!
Not to the Kommos—*eleleleleu*

5618| MS:land-line—reached out §crossed out and replaced above by§ as for §over illegible erasure and illegibly crossed-out word inserted above§ repose—   *P1875:*land-line reached   5619| MS:With §crossed out and replaced above by§ Lie indolent §over *indolence*§ of §crossed out and replaced above by§ in < > sway: §colon over illegible erasure§   *P1875:*sway;   5620| MS:Which §crossed out and replaced above by§ But, ebbing, since §crossed out and replaced above by§ when < > must, §next word illegibly crossed out and replaced above by§ all   *P1875:*But ebbing   5621| MS:Sea §inserted above§ Bites §crossed out and replaced above by two words§ It §crossed out§ claws at the §crossed out§ sand: relinquished strugglingly:—   *P1875:*sand relinquished strugglingly.   5622| MS:So, §word and comma over illegible erasure§ < > Lusandros, buffered §crossed out and replaced above by three words§ pinioned bound tethered §last two words crossed out§ to inflict §following word added in margin and crossed out§ pinioned   *P1875:*harsh Lusandros—pinioned   5623| MS:alone—thus §crossed out§ spoke   5624| MS:As §in margin§ Minded §altered to§ minded to more §crossed out§ embitter   5626| MS:Let §in margin; crossed out and replaced above by§ If Tragedy has withdrawn §last two words crossed out and replaced above by one crossed-out word, *bestowed;* then *withdrawn* restored and altered to§ withdraw < > presence, still, §word and comma crossed out§ now— §crossed out and replaced above by§ then,—   *P1875:*withdraws < > presence—quick,   5627| MS:§word illegibly crossed out in margin§ If < > her,—as would seem, §last three words and comma crossed out§ what   5628| MS:Let Comedy §over illegible erasure§ in service §last two words inserted above and crossed out§ do thorough §crossed out§ service—flute §crossed out and replaced above by§ frisk   *P1875:*service, frisk   5629| MS:off the §crossed out§ stage the §altered to§ these   5630| MS:Long Walls, Peiraian §over partial erasure§ bulwarks, §comma altered to exclamation point§ Hew §over *hew*§   5631| MS:at, and §crossed out§ pound in §inserted above§ to < > defence   *P1875:*into < > defence!   5632| MS:Not §altered to§ No to the §last two words crossed out and replaced above by one crossed-out word, *whining;* then *Not to the* restored§ kommas §altered to§ Kommas—elelelelu, §first four letters crossed out and then rewritten above; comma crossed out§   *P1875: elelelelu*

279

With breast bethumped, as Tragic lyre prefers,
But Comedy shall sound the flute, and crow
5635   At kordax-end—the hearty slapping-dance!
Collect those flute-girls—trash who flattered ear
With whistlings and fed eye with caper-cuts
While we Lakonians supped black broth or crunched
Sea-urchin, conchs and all, unpricked—coarse brutes!
5640   Command they lead off step, time steady stroke
To spade and pickaxe, till demolished lie
Athenai's pride in powder!"

Done that day—
That sixteenth famed day of Munuchion-month!
The day when Hellas fought at Salamis,
5645   The very day Euripides was born,
Those flute-girls—Phaps-Elaphion at their head—
Did blow their best, did dance their worst, the while
Sparté pulled down the walls, wrecked wide the works,
Laid low each merest molehill of defence,
5650   And so the Power, Athenai, passed away!

---

⁵⁶³³| MS:§solidus and line added in margin§ With §over *with*§ breasts §altered to§ breast
bethumped, §over partial erasure§ as §next word illegibly crossed out and replaced above by
two words§ Tragic §over illegible word§ lyre   ⁵⁶³⁴| MS:§line added§ But Comedy §over
comedy§ < > sound §over illegible word§ < > and laugh   *P1875:*and crow   ⁵⁶³⁵| MS:But
§crossed out and replaced below by§ With Kordax §over *kordax*§ and the §next word illegibly
crossed out and replaced above by§ hearty   *P1875:*At kordax-end—the
⁵⁶³⁶| MS:Collect the §altered to§ those   ⁵⁶³⁷| MS:whistlings, and §inserted above§ < >
eye full §crossed out§ with caper-cuts,   *1889a:*whistlings and < > caper-cuts
⁵⁶³⁹| MS:Sea-urchin, shells §crossed out and replaced above by§ conchs < > all,—unpricked,—
§marked for transposition to beginning of line and then original reading retained§ coarse
*P1875:*all, unpricked—coarse   ⁵⁶⁴⁰| MS:Command them §altered to§ they < > off dance
§crossed out and replaced above by§ step   ⁵⁶⁴¹| MS:Of §crossed out and replaced above
by three words§ To spade and pickaxe, mattock, §word and comma crossed out§ till < > lies
§altered to§ lie   ⁵⁶⁴³| MS:sixteenth §altered to§ Sixteenth < > Munuchion-month,
*P1875:*sixteenth < > Munuchion-month!   ⁵⁶⁴⁶| MS:flute-girls—poor Elaphion   *P1875:*
flute-girls—Phaps-Elaphion   ⁵⁶⁴⁷| MS:while,   *P1875:*while   ⁵⁶⁴⁸| MS:Sparta
§altered to§ Sparté < > walls, destroyed §crossed out and replaced above by two crossed-out
words, *laid low*§ wrecked wide §last two words inserted above§   ⁵⁶⁴⁹| MS:§line added§
Laid low §last two words in margin§ §next two words illegibly crossed out§ each mere §altered
to§ merest   ⁵⁶⁵⁰| MS:And §next word illegibly crossed out and replaced below by§ so

We would not see its passing.   Ere I knew
The issue of their counsels,—crouching low
And shrouded by my peplos,—I conceived,
Despite the shut eyes, the stopped ears,—by count
5655 Only of heart-beats, telling the slow time,—
Athenai's doom was signed and signified
In that assembly,—ay, but knew there watched
One who would dare and do, nor bate at all
The stranger's licensed duty,—speak the word
5660 Allowed the Man from Phokis!   Nought remained
But urge departure, flee the sights and sounds,
Hideous exultings, wailings worth contempt,
And press to other earth, new heaven, by sea
That somehow ever prompts to 'scape despair.

5665 Help rose to heart's wish; at the harbour-side,
The old grey mariner did reverence
To who had saved his ship, still weather-tight
As when with prow gay-garlanded she praised
The hospitable port and pushed to sea.
5670 "Convoy Balaustion back to Rhodes, for sake
Of her and her Euripides!" laughed he.

Rhodes,—shall it not be there, my Euthukles,
Till this brief trouble of a life-time end,

---

⁵⁶⁵¹| MS:I §altered to§ We <> passing! Ere §over *ere*§   *1889a:*passing. Ere   ⁵⁶⁵²| MS:§line added§ The yesterday's §crossed out§ §next two words and comma illegibly crossed out and replaced above by four words, comma and dash§ Issue of their counsels   ⁵⁶⁵³| MS:And §over illegible erasure§ <> peplos, I conceived,—   *P1875:*peplos,—I conceived,   ⁵⁶⁵⁵| MS:telling so §crossed out§ the slow §inserted above§   ⁵⁶⁵⁷| MS:assembly,—I did know at least   *P1875:*assembly,—ay, but knew there watched   ⁵⁶⁵⁸| MS:That thou §last two words crossed out and replaced above by two words§ Onc man wouldst §altered to§ would   *P1875:*One who would   ⁵⁶⁵⁹| MS:licenced §inserted above§ duty, speak the single §crossed out§ word word unspoke §last two words inserted below and crossed out§   *P1875:* licensed duty,—speak   ⁵⁶⁶⁰| MS:from Phokis! What remained   *P1875:*from Phokis! Nought remained   ⁵⁶⁶²| MS:wails just worth   *P1875:*wailings worth   ⁵⁶⁶⁴| MS:despair! §exclamation point altered to question mark§   *P1875:*despair.   ⁵⁶⁶⁴⁻⁶⁵| MS:§no ¶ called for§   *1889a:*§¶§   ⁵⁶⁶⁵| MS:wish: at   *P1875:*wish; at   ⁵⁶⁶⁶| MS:mariner had reverence   *P1875:*mariner did reverence   ⁵⁶⁶⁷| MS:For who   *P1875:*To who   ⁵⁶⁶⁸| MS:with prore gay-garlanded   *P1875:*with prow gay-garlanded   ⁵⁶⁷¹| MS:and of Euripides   *P1875:*and her Euripides

That solitude—two make so populous!—
5675 For food finds memories of the past suffice,
May be, anticipations,—hope so swells,—
Of some great future we, familiar once
With who so taught, should hail and entertain?
He lies now in the little valley, laughed
5680 And moaned about by those mysterious streams,
Boiling and freezing, like the love and hate
Which helped or harmed him through his earthly course.
They mix in Arethousa by his grave.
The warm spring, traveller, dip thine arms into,
5685 Brighten thy brow with!   Life detests black cold.

I sent the tablets, the psalterion, so
Rewarded Sicily; the tyrant there
Bestowed them worthily in Phoibos' shrine.
A gold-graved writing tells—"I also loved
5690 The poet, Free Athenai cheaply prized—
King Dionusios,—Archelaos-like!"

And see if young Philemon,—sure one day
To do good service and be loved himself,—
If he too have not made a votive verse!
5695 "Grant, in good sooth, our great dead, all the same,
Retain their sense, as certain wise men say,
I'd hang myself—to see Euripides!"
Hands off, Philemon! nowise hang thyself,
But pen the prime plays, labour the right life,
5700 And die at good old age as grand men use,—

5674| MS:In solitude *P1875:*That solitude   5675| MS:That the mere memories   *P1875:*
For food finds memories   5677| MS:Of that great   *P1875:*Of some great
5682| MS:course: *P1875:*course.   5685| MS:cold! *1889a:*cold.
5685-86| MS:§no ¶ called for§   *P1875:*§¶§   5687| MS:Rewarded Sicily: the Tyrant
*P1875:*Rewarded Sicily; the tyrant   5689| MS:Gold-graved a §last two words marked for
transposition and altered to§ A gold-graved < > tells—this other loved   *P1875:*tells—"I also loved
5691| MS:King Dionusios,—Archelaos-like! *P1875:*King Dionusios,—Archelaos-like!"
5691-92| MS:§no ¶ called for§   *P1875:*§¶§   5695| MS:"If in < > sooth our   *P1875:*"Grant,
in < > sooth, our   5698| MS:off, Philemon, nowise   *P1875:*off, Philemon! nowise

Keeping thee, with that great thought, warm the while,—
That he does live, Philemon!   Ay, most sure!
"He lives!" hark,—waves say, winds sing out the same,
And yonder dares the citied ridge of Rhodes
5705 Its headlong plunge from sky to sea, disparts
North bay from south,—each guarded calm, that guest
May enter gladly, blow what wind there will,—
Boiled round with breakers, to no other cry!
All in one choros,—what the master-word
5710 They take up?—hark!   "There are no gods, no gods!
Glory to God—who saves Euripides!"

5701| MS:while *P1875:*while,—   5703| MS:lives",—hark *P1875:*lives!" hark
5706| MS:south bay,—guarded calms *P1875:*south,—each guarded calm   5708| MS:Boiling
with breakers—to <> other sound! *P1875:*Boiled round with breakers, to <> other cry!
5709| MS:one Choros,—his the *P1875:*choros,—what the   5710| MS:up,—hark *P1875:*
up?—hark   5711| MS:to God,—who <> Euripideds §altered to§ Euripides!" *P1875:*to
God—who §following last line of poem§ L. D. I. I. RB / (Begun about August 11—ended /
Saturday, Nov. 7. '74.   Mers, Picardy.) §see Editorial Notes§

ARISTOPHANES' APOLOGY

Emendations to the Text

The following emendations have been made to the 1889a copy-text:

l. 112: In 1889a, the apostrophe in *'Neath* was inverted; the correct MS-1875 reading is restored.

l. 660: In 1889a, the comma after *frown* was omitted; to indicate the grammatical parallel between *quenched* and *struck* in the following line, the MS-1875 reading is restored.

l. 951: The MS clearly reads *Set*; the compositors in 1875 misread the MS and introduced the word *Let*, which is far less sensible idiomatically. The MS reading is restored.

l. 1197: The speech of Strattis ends after *thyme!* and should be marked with a single closing quotation mark. The MS has double quotation marks, and P1875 has the correct single quotation mark; 1889a has no punctuation, though a space for it remains. The P1875 reading is restored.

l. 1217: In 1889a, the necessary initial single quotation mark is missing, though space for it remains. The MS has double quotation marks here, and P1875 has the correct single quotation mark. The P1875 reading is restored.

l. 1279: As a new paragraph of a continuing quoted speech, the line should begin with double quotation marks (Balaustion is quoting Aristophanes), but 1889a has no punctuation. The MS-1875 reading is restored.

l. 1353: In MS-1875, a comma follows *Ay*; no punctuation appears in 1889a, though a space for it remains. The MS-1875 reading is restored.

l. 1392: In each text of the poem, B has made errors involving the various quotation marks needed to signify changing speakers. The problem persists through several hundred lines, requiring a series of emendations. At this point, Balaustion is quoting Aristophanes, but Aristophanes is also quoting himself, recounting what he said earlier in the evening. This line should thus begin with triple quotation marks, and the double quotation marks after *Strattis* should be a single quotation mark to close the first recalled remark.

l. 1428: In 1889a, this line ends with double quotation marks; since Aristophanes' recollected speech ends here, the line should end with a single closing quotation mark, as in P1875. The P1875 reading is restored.

l. 1429: As a new paragraph in Balaustion's quotation of Euripides, this line should begin with double opening quotation marks, as it does in P1875; 1889a has no punctuation here. The P1875 reading is restored.

l. 1430: As in l. 1429, this line requires double opening quotation marks, but 1889a lacks them; the P1875 reading is restored.

l. 1432: This line begins Aristophanes' quotation of what others said about him, so the line must begin with triple quotation marks. P1875 inaccurately indicates the interior quotation with only a single opening quote, while 1889a has double quotation marks; the necessary additional quotation mark is inserted.

l. 1455: Here end the words of the *company* (mentioned in l. 1430) that began at l. 1432. The line should end with a single closing quotation mark, as in P1875; the P1875 reading is restored.

l. 1465: As with the case at l. 1392, Balaustion is quoting Aristophanes, who is quoting what he himself said earlier in the evening. Triple quotation marks are needed before *Both*, and only a single closing quotation mark is required after *praised*. The necessary punctuation is inserted.

l. 1466: This line recommences Aristophanes' quotation of himself, and so must begin with a single quotation mark, rather than the double quotation marks in 1889a.

l. 1498: Following the convention that alternates single and double quotation marks every time one adds a further layer of embedded speech, the single opening quotation mark before *Raise* in all texts should be double. Aristophanes is still remembering and quoting what he said to his friends earlier (see ll. 1521-24), and these words he had imagined as what Euripides' works preached.

l. 1499: See the preceding entry; the words Aristophanes imputed to Euripides' works end after *Hermes*, so double closing quotation marks are required, not the single one found in all texts.

l. 1528: Aristophanes quotation of his speech to his friends, which began at l. 1466, ends here (see ll. 1521ff.); the line should end with a single closing quotation mark. MS-1875 has double quotation marks here, and 1889a has no punctuation; the correct single closing quotation mark is inserted.

l. 1529: Balaustion quotes what Aristophanes said to her after arriving at her house. The line should begin with double quotation marks, because this is a new (one-line) paragraph of her quotation; 1889a has no punctuation here.The MS-1875 reading is restored

l. 1544: In all copies of 1888-89a collated, the punctuation after *Since* appears as a fragmentary period; this is probably a remnant of the correct mark, a comma. The MS-1875 reading is restored.

l. 1603: The word-order in 1889a, *Aught had I spoken,* disrupts the grammar of this line and the preceding one; the MS-1875 reading, *Aught I had spoken,* is restored.

l. 1892: This line ends with an imaginary title, indicated by the single quotation mark before *Threttanelo.* The closing quotation mark, present in MS-1875, is missing in 1889a; the MS-1875 reading is restored.

l. 1914: The necessary question mark at the end of this line, present in MS-1875, disappeared in 1889a; the MS-1875 reading is restored.

ll. 2135, 2137: Since Aristophanes has made Euripides defend himself in his own words, correctly indicated by the quotation marks in ll. 2114 and 2115, the imaginary words of Euripides' Choros must be enclosed in double quotation marks. The punctuation is correct in 1875, but MS and 1889a have single quotation marks; the P1875 reading is restored.

l. 2189: Aristophanes has been quoting his own imagined answer since l. 2175; this line ends the embedded speech and requires the closing single quotation mark that is present in MS-1875. The correct punctuation is restored.

l. 2549: The necessary closing quotation mark at the end of this line is present in MS-1875, but missing in 1889a; the MS-1875 reading is restored.

l. 2580: MS-1875 read *blockhead* where 1889a erroneously prints *blockkead*; the correct spelling is restored.

l. 2800: The MS reading *cart* is clearly correct, as is explained in the Editorial Notes; the printed texts read *car.* The MS reading is restored. Also, in all copies of 1888-89a collated, the punctuation at the end of the line has disintegrated; the final dash found in MS-1875 is restored.

l. 2838: MS-1875 have the correct comma after *Lemnians,* but there is no punctuation here in 1889a; to ensure that *seen* is kept parallel with *read,* the comma is restored.

l. 2918: 1889a lacks the required closing quotation mark; the MS reading is restored.

l. 3460: MS-1875 read *Oporia,* both here and in l. 3428; the copy-text corrects to *Opora* in l. 3428, but not in l. 3460. In a letter to his publisher, B asked that the reading in 3460 be corrected to *Opora,* and this change was made in the second impression of 1888-89 (see *Preface*, III, above; note also the identical correction at l. 5310).

l. 3498: In 1889a, the double quotation marks required to close Aristophanes' speech are omitted; the MS-1875 reading is restored.

l. 4684: In MS-1875, the line ends with an exclamation mark after *woe*, there is no punctuation at this point in 1889a. As a complete utterance by Amphitruon, the partial line requires some closing mark; the MS-1875 reading is restored.

l. 4826: Though B's MS correctly reads *Phlegraia's*, the compositors of P1875 misread the first *a* as a *u*. The error went uncorrected in 1875 and 1889a; the MS reading is restored.

l. 5310: The apparent MS reading *breadth* was probably intended to be *breath*, as in the source Aristophanes is quoting; see the Editorial Notes. The extensive corrections and revisions to this portion of the MS make a reading of *breath* plausible, and the word is substituted here.

l. 5331: Lais (mentioned in l. 5325) is asking a question of Euripides; but the words she is quoting, which are indicated by italics, are imperative, not interrogative. Thus the question mark and quotation marks at the end of the utterance should be in roman face rather than the italic of P1875-1889. The punctuation is changed to roman face.

l. 5383: The MS correctly places the colon at the end of the line after the quotation marks, but P1875 reverses the order; no correction was made in 1875 or 1889a. The MS reading is restored.

B was erratic in using quotation marks to indicate the titles of plays; we have regularized his citations, sometimes inserting punctuation where none was present in the collated texts. These emendations occur in ll. 508, 958, 1005, 1330, 1331, 1639, 1641, 1746, 2138, 2266, 2332, 2481, 2838, and 2839.

In addition, the compositors of 1888-89 frequently used B's paragraph breaks to divide one page from another. As a consequence, certain interruptions and shifts in the discourse disappeared in the copy-text. We have restored paragraph breaks lost in this way in *Aristophanes' Apology* at ll. 141-42, 452-53, 476-77, 573-74, 959, 1278-79, 1429-30, 1528-29, 2241-42, 2893-94, 3120-21, 3196-97, 3498-99, 3682-83, 5337-38.

Composition

Aristophanes' Apology, Browning's longest poem except for *The Ring and the Book* and *Sordello*, was written in two installments. The *Transcript from*

Euripides mentioned in the full title was done first, in London, and the manuscript dated "June 17. '73." On 16 July 1873 Alfred Domett recorded in his diary: "Browning repeated (as we crossed the Park) the whole plot of the *Hercules Furens* of Euripides, which he had just been translating, collating 4 editions as he went along. He gave it afterwards in *Aristophanes's Apology*"(*The Diary of Alfred Domett,* ed. E. A. Horsman [Oxford, 1953], 99). The rest of the poem, though apparently begun and finished in London (DeVane, *Hbk.*, 376), was mostly written at Mers in Normandy, then a "straggling village" where Browning was staying for a summer holiday in an isolated cliff-top house overlooking the "open sea" (Orr, *Life,* 293). The whole manuscript was dated as follows: "Begun about August 11—ended Saturday, Nov. 7. '74. Mers, Picardy." The remarkably rapid production of such a long and exhaustively researched poem suggests that it was written under pressure of strong feelings. He told Carlyle: "I felt in a manner bound to write it, so many blunders about Aristophanes afloat, even among the so-called learned" (*William Allingham: A Diary,* ed. H. Allingham and D. Radford [London, 1907], 240). The greatest "blunder" was probably the common Victorian assumption that Aristophanes was too obscene to be thought a major poet. "Indeed," wrote Browning to Swinburne, "I am no enemy of that Aristophanes—all on fire with invention,—and such music!" (5 February 1881; Hood, 193).

His intensive study of Aristophanes began soon after he finished the *Transcript.* On 3 August 1873 he wrote from St Aubin to Annie Egerton-Smith: "I bathed yesterday, and found the water warm and pleasant. Repeating that process, seeing Milsand, and reading Aristophanes will be my portion for the next six weeks, I suppose and hope" (Hood, 158). Such a reading program would not have attracted his dead wife, whose favorite Greek author had been Aristophanes' satiric victim, Euripides. On 3 April 1832 she had written in her diary: "I told him [her classical mentor H. S. Boyd] of my having read every play of Euripides; and he seemed very much surprised, and called me 'a funny girl' " (*The Unpublished Diary of Elizabeth Barrett Barrett 1831-1832,* ed. P. Kelley and R. Hudson [Athens, OH, 1969], 43). Ten years later (10 March 1842) she told him: "Aristophanes I took with me to Devonshire—& after all I do not know much more of *him* than three or four of his plays may stand for" (*Correspondence,* 5.257). Although on 23 March 1846 she found a few lines of his worth mentioning in a letter (*Peace* 1158-71; *Correspondence,* 12.171), she evidently disliked Aristophanes. In 1857 she made her otherwise unconventional heroine Aurora Leigh dismiss the relatively inoffensive *Daphnis and Chloe* as an "obscene text" (*Aurora Leigh,* 1.828-89); and Balaustion surely spoke for Mrs. Browning when she denounced the "obscenity" of *Lysistrata,* and "for such reasons . . . did not go to see" his *Thesmophoriazusae* (see ll. 416-56 below).

So the emotional pressures behind *Aristophanes' Apology* were probably conflicting ones: an urge to defend his wife's beloved poet against all his detractors, from Aristophanes to A. W. von Schlegel (in his lectures *On Dramatic Art and Literature,* republished in a new edition 1871), and a simultaneous urge to defend Aristophanes against Victorian prudery. Thus as with "Mr. Sludge 'The Medium'" and *Prince Hohenstiel-Schwangau* (see this edition, 6.452-54, 10.242-47) this was in part an *Apology* for a man of whom Robert and Elizabeth had taken different views. Clearly she was much in his mind when he wrote the poem. Like the portrait of Euripides, in whose "impassive presence" (see l. 1592 below) Balaustion argues with Aristophanes, a portrait of Mrs. Browning figured significantly in Domett's recollections of her husband at this time. Four days before their conversation about Euripides' *Heracles* in the Park, Domett wrote: "Looking at the copy of his wife's portrait by Richmond . . . he [Browning] said 'That was taken when she was at her best,' and that 'the eyes were very like.'" He then quoted a remark by a believer in phrenology, that the "organs of Imagination" were larger in her head than in her husband's. On the latter's response to the *Heracles* Domett commented: "Browning . . . was full of the pathos of the scenes in Euripides where Heracles becomes conscious of what he has done" (*The Diary of Alfred Domett,* ed. E. A. Horsman [Oxford, 1953], 97-100). Heracles has just killed his wife and children, and perhaps these scenes brought back to Browning some feelings of responsibility for his wife's early death. That might help to explain Mrs. Orr's remark: "Large tears fell from [his eyes], and emotion choked his voice, when he first read aloud the transcript of the *Herakles* to a friend, who was often privileged to hear him" (Orr, *Life,* 294). Presumably the Balaustion of this poem was meant to be his most speaking portrait of his wife—and not only as a poet and brilliant classical scholar. Four years later (February 1877) Domett noted: "I had happened to say, looking at Mrs. Browning's portrait, 'She looks all intellect.' 'Ah, she was much more than *that!*' he said, musingly and with feeling"(*The Diary of Alfred Domett,* ed. E. A. Horsman [Oxford, 1953], 181).

Sources

"As for *Aristophanes,*" Browning wrote to Furnivall 23 January 1882, "—the allusions require a knowledge of the Scholia, besides acquaintance with the 'Comicorum Graecorum Fragmenta,' Athenaeus, Alciphron, and so forth, not forgotten. But I wrote in France, at an out of the way place, with none of these books" (Hood, 208; *Browning's Trumpeter: The Correspondence of Robert Browning and Frederick J. Furnivall 1872-1889,* ed. W. S. Peterson [Washington D. C., 1979], 48). Those who find Balaustion's memory incredible should ponder this evidence of her creator's, since the details drawn from those and many other books prove surprisingly accurate. The identification of individual sources was notably pioneered by C. N. Jackson in "Classical Elements in Browning's *Aristophanes' Apology*" (*Harvard Studies in Classical Philology* 20 [1909], 15-73), by T. L. Hood in "Browning's Ancient Classical Sources" (*Harvard Studies in Classical Philology* 33 [1922], 78-180), and by F. M. Tisdel in "Browning's *Aristophanes' Apology*" (*University of Missouri Studies* [1927], 1-46). Besides explaining classical and other allusions, the notes in the present edition aim to show precisely how Browning handled his sources, especially in "transcribing" the *Heracles.* Here he seems chiefly to have used A. Nauck's *Euripidis Tragoediae, Editio Altera* (Leipsig, 1866), and F. A. Paley's *Euripides, With an English Commentary* (London, 1857-1860), both of which he possessed. But he occasionally consulted other editions and was boldly eclectic in deciding which text to follow at any one point, which reading or suggested emendation to translate.

He was understandably irritated by the reviewers' sneers at his Greek scholarship: "somebody, wholly a stranger to me, reviewing it in the *Athenaeum,* observed (for fun's sake, I suppose) that it was 'probably written after one of Mr. Browning's Oxford Symposia with Jowett.' Whereupon half a dozen other critics reported the poem to be 'the transcript of the talk of the Master of Balliol'—whom I have not set eyes on these four years, and with whom I never had a conversation about Aristophanes in my life. Such a love of a lie have the verminous tribe!" (Hood, 171; *Athenaeum* No. 2177, 17 April 1875, 513-14). The gradual exclusion of classics from ordinary education had already gone far enough to create the assumption that only a don could know much about ancient Greek literature, so Browning's knowledge must be second-hand. Today that exclusion is so complete that any unacknowledged quotation from a Greek author can be mistaken for surreptitious plagiarism. But it is slightly misleading to speak like T. L. Hood of "Browning's direct borrowings from ancient sources" (DeVane, *Hbk.,* 377). Wordsworth did not *borrow* from the daffodils. All poets tend to write about their personal experience, and for those like Shelley, Tennyson, Browning, Matthew Arnold, and Clough, Greek literature was an essential part of that experience. Mrs. Orr remarked on

Browning's "deep feeling for the humanities of Greek literature, and his almost passionate love of the language" (Orr, *Life*, 294); and at least one purpose of *Aristophanes' Apology* was to share such feelings with Greekless readers. The *Heracles* transcript tried to express his own experience of that play without disguising its historical remoteness in time, language, and style from everything Victorian. And the whole poem was clearly meant to be an equally historical reconstruction of Athenian life around the end of the fifth century B.C. This required much supporting evidence from extant literary and historical texts, and the way he incorporated such evidence seamlessly into his monologue, by numerous tacit references to his authorities, was among his most brilliant achievements.

Text and Publication

The Balliol Manuscript (MS)   The manuscript of *Aristophanes' Apology* in the Balliol College Library (MS 389; *Reconstruction*, E18) is clearly the compositional MS, subjected to considerable revision by B and used by the compositors at Spottiswoode and Company in 1874. The MS consists of 200 leaves of lined paper, including a separate title page and a leaf for the epigraph. The wide spacing of the lined paper that B used provided him with sufficient room for additional lines of verse to fit between existing lines. In the variant listings such revisions are noted with the editorial comment §line added§. The pages were numbered throughout by the printer and also contain names of several compositors.

It is evident that B composed the poem in two parts. The first section contains 112 leaves of verse. Throughout this section B numbered alternate leaves in the pattern of other Balliol manuscripts, such as *Balaustion's Adventure* (this edition, Volume 10) and *The Inn Album* (Volume 13), and composed only on the recto of each leaf. On the whole, these pages display B's clear and steady hand with a controlled interspersal of corrections and added lines. A 7-line passage is written on the verso of leaf 24a, and heavier revision starts after leaf 38 with inserted lines placed vertically in the margin on four different pages. The most extensive revision occurs where a passage of thirty lines is added on the verso of leaf 46 with nine additional lines written vertically along the inner margin (ll. 2843-881). B gives careful instructions to the printer for the order of these added lines by numbering the leaves 46, 46/3 and 46/2. Then his usual numbering system continues through leaf 56, concluding with l. 3533, where the original publication plan would have concluded the first of two volumes (see below).

The next section of 86 leaves contains the *Herakles* "transcript" and Balaustion's conclusion. Here, B begins numbering anew and two folios are incorrectly numbered 24. Following l. 5084, B inserts a familiar feature of the Balliol MSS, the letters "L. D. I. E.," standing for *Laus Deo in excelsis*, "Praise God in the highest," and B provides the date of "June 17. '73." In the final 21 leaves, there is much disorder in B's numbering system caused by heavy revision and a mix of previously written pages. B's page 33 is also numbered 57 in his hand and crossed out. Several pages in this concluding section contain as many as three of his crossed out and altered numbers, showing that the material was rearranged more than once. Differences in pen-point and style of writing indicate a rush of creativity and at least two stages of composition. This is substantiated by an 18-line addition preceding the lines familiarly known as "Thamuris Marching" (ll. 5188-262) and a 16-line passage preceding l. 5338. The manuscript concludes with l. 5711 followed by B's comment, "Begun about August 11—ended / Saturday, Nov. 7. '74. Mers, Picardy."

The Balliol MS is more sparsely punctuated than the published work. This is especially true regarding end-line punctuation and commas for appositive phrases, both added during the typesetting of the first edition. The poem includes long passages of stichomythia as well as many instances in which one speaker quotes another, and B did not always keep meticulous track of his quotation marks. Lines 1399, 1432 and 1465, for example, require triple quotation marks to indicate this complicated process of speakers quoting themselves and others. In the MS, two words were clearly misread by the printer at lines 951 and 2800 and emendations have been made to correct these and other errors.

The Turnbull Proofs (P1875) One important set of proof sheets for the first edition of *Aristophanes' Apology* has survived; it is housed in the Alexander H. Turnbull Library in Wellington, New Zealand. The presence of the inscription "For Press" in B's hand indicates that these page proofs were the last he corrected. Beyond the revisions that occurred between the MS and the printed readings of this document, the Turnbull proofs contain forty-three hand alterations. Of these, twenty-eight are in B's hand and sixteen are not. B's corrections are indicated in our variant listings as *CP1875*. Since all but one of these sixteen non-authorial changes was accepted by B for the first edition and for *1889a*, we also include them as *CP1875* entries, with the editorial comment §not B§. The numerous proofreaders' instructions to change spacing, correct turned letters, and the like are not recorded in our variant lists.

There is clear evidence that B and his publishers expected to issue *Aristophanes' Apology* in two volumes, the first ending with the present l. 3533, and the second comprising the transcript of *Herakles* and the conclusion of Balaustion's tale. But in the Turnbull proofs, the words "In Two Volumes" and "Vol. I" are cancelled on the title-page, and the notation "End of Vol. I—" after l. 3533 in the MS was not set in type at all.

The First Edition (1875)   *Aristophanes' Apology* was published in a single bulky volume on 15 April 1875. Both B and his publisher may have anticipated a good sale for the book, since it proclaimed itself as a continuation of the story of Balaustion, whose first outing in 1871 had been a pleasant success (see this edition, 10.219-220). If Smith did order more than his standard 1500 copies, it might account for the continued availability of the first edition over the ensuing years; *Aristophanes' Apology* was still listed among B's available volumes in the advertisements bound into the early volumes of the 1888-89 edition.

The Poetical Works (1889a)   In revising for the collected edition of 1888-1889, B made numerous small changes to the text of *Aristophanes' Apology* and added a total of six lines to the poem. He also attempted to correct the complex punctuation he used to indicate different voices and quoted speeches, but he seems to have introduced as many errors as he corrected. His proofreading of this part of the thirteenth volume of 1888-1889 was not up to his usual standard, and several obvious compositors' errors went uncorrected in the first impression. But one somewhat celebrated correction was made for the second impression of 1888-1889, the changing of *Oporia* to *Opora* in l. 3460 (see p. xv and *Emendations to the Text*, above).

Browning's Concept of the "Transcript": His Theory and Practice

Besides such familiar meanings of the verb *transcribe* as "copy in writing" and "transliterate," the Oxford English Dictionary gives one dating from 1639: "translate or render accurately in another language"; and describes Browning's use of the noun *transcript* in the subtitle of *Balaustion's Adventure* (1871) as a "? *nonce-use*" to mean: "A verbal or close translation or rendering." What Browning really meant by the word then is not easily inferred from the version of Euripides' *Alcestis* included in that poem. The first line of that version ("O Admeteian domes where I endured" [*Balaustion's Adventure,* 366; this edition, 10.23]) was an almost word-for-word equivalent of the Greek, even to the use of "domes" to represent the similar-sounding cognate word δώματα; and Greek names like *Apollon, Phoibos, Asklepios, Admetos, Moirai,* and so forth were accurately transliterated, on a principle first adopted by Browning in "Artemis Prologizes" (1842; this edition, 3.224). But the translation as a whole was far from literal, being supposedly based, not on a text, but on Balaustion's memory of a stage-performance: "plain I told the play, / Just as I saw it; what the actors said, / And what I saw, or thought I saw the while" (*Balaustion's Adventure,* 246-48; this edition, 10.18). In fact, within ten lines she had started reporting rather than translating Apollo's direct speech ("Then told how Zeus had been the cause of all . . ."), and the rest of the Transcript frequently paraphrased, abbreviated, or otherwise adapted its original. But by 1873, when Browning started making his next "transcript," the ambiguous word had evidently developed a much stricter meaning in his mind. It now meant a translation that came as close as possible to the original *wording.* This involved, first, systematically transliterating familiar names and words in their Greek rather than their Latin spelling, (e.g., *Phoibos* not *Phoebus*). Here it needs pointing out, despite critical disapproval of Browning's "strange spelling" (DeVane, *Hbk.,* 117), that it was much more authentic than the usual spelling. It is only a freak of history that we expect to see our Greek words Latinized; and it is only on grounds of "accessibility" in "a work of reference aimed at a general (as well as a specialist) readership" that the latest *Oxford Classical Dictionary* (1996) defends its retention of "the more familiar form" (viii).

Besides a more accurate spelling of Greek names and words, the transcript theory had also come to imply some approximation to the original style, word-order, and syntax. Browning was already moving in practice towards the theory of translation that he formulated four years later, in the preface to *The Agamemnon of Aeschylus Transcribed* (1877; 1888-1889a edition, 13.261-67). That theory was designed to give Greekless readers some idea what Greek literature was really like, in form as well as content: "If, because of the immense fame of the following Tragedy [the *Agamemnon*], I wished to acquaint myself with it, and could only do so by the help of a translator, I should require him to be literal at every cost save that of absolute violence to our language.

The use of certain allowable constructions which, happening to be out of daily favor, are all the more appropriate to archaic workmanship, is no violence: but I would be tolerant for once—in the case of so immensely famous an original,—of even a clumsy attempt to furnish me with the very turn of each phrase in as Greek a fashion as English will bear." This excluded all "amplifications and embellishments," especially any attempt "to brighten up a passage" by eliminating inelegant repetitions of words. Nor did his theory encourage any attempt to reproduce the original music or sound-effects: "if I obtained a mere strict bald version of thing by thing, or at least word pregnant with thing, I should hardly look for an impossible transmission of the reputed magniloquence and sonority of the Greek; and this with the less regret, inasmuch as there is abundant musicality elsewhere, but nowhere else than in his poem the ideas of the poet." In "transcribing" the *Heracles*, Browning often broke these rules, as the notes will show. But he generally obeyed them in trying to reproduce "the very turn of each phrase in as Greek a fashion as English will bear"—sometimes rather more than English would bear. Within his period, the "transcript" theory partially aligned Browning with Francis Newman, whose *Iliad of Homer, Faithfully Translated* (1856) was unfairly ridiculed in Matthew Arnold's *On Translating Homer* (1861), for "the oddness of his diction" (*The Complete Prose Works of Matthew Arnold*, ed. R. H. Super [Ann Arbor, 1960-77], 1.141). "It is *all* odd," replied Newman. "But that is just why people want to read an English Homer,—to know all his oddities, exactly as learned men do. He is the phenomenon to be studied" (F. W. Newman, *Homeric Translation in Theory and Practice: A Reply to Matthew Arnold* [London, 1861], 59).

Form

Aristophanes' Apology* has been called "nearly the formless compendium that its title implies" (Irvine and Honan, 475). Certainly its form is obscured by the unusually complicated use the poet makes of the dramatic monologue. Balaustion's speech includes, among other things, the dictated narrative of a long, argumentative dialogue between her and Aristophanes, during which she had read aloud a whole tragedy by Euripides, and Aristophanes had responded by improvising a poem of his own. But through all the complications (which demand constant attention to single and double quotation-marks) one may perhaps dimly discern a thematic pattern in the work, analogous to that of its companion-piece, *Balaustion's Adventure*. In the *Adventure*, everything centered on the "transcribed" *Alcestis,* a play about a wife who dies to save her husband's life, and is then brought back to life herself by Heracles. The life-saving theme was repeated in the framing narrative, where Balaustion saved the lives of a boatful of Rhodians as well as her own, by reciting that play on the steps of Heracles' temple at Syracuse. In the *Apology,* everything seems to center similarly on the *Heracles,* a play where the life-saving hero goes mad and kills his wife and children. In the framing narrative the reading of that play is Balaustion's final "defense" of Euripides (see ll. 3496-528 and nn. below). So much is clear enough. But how does the theme of the play relate to the rest of the poem? Presumably by symbolizing the madness of civil war, particularly the Peloponnesian War, in which Greeks who had fought like brothers against the Persians, had for twenty-seven years been fighting one another. It ended with the total defeat and occupation of Athens. There Browning's poem starts, and Balaustion proposes to spend the whole voyage to Rhodes (i.e., the whole monologue) in re-enacting that "tragedy" of the fall of Athens (see ll. 167-73 below). It is then re-enacted in two ways: symbolically in the stage-tragedy of family-murder, and more literally but indirectly in the picture of Athenian decadence since the Persian wars that emerges from Balaustion's argument with Aristophanes. He attributes that decadence to demagogues like Cleon and sceptics like Socrates and Euripides. She evidently regards Aristophanes himself as both symptom and cause of a general moral decline.

Some such pattern may well have been intended; but it is only vaguely worked out, and the precise relevance of the theatrical tragedy to the historical one is left unclear. In killing his own family Heracles might be thought to symbolize either Greece herself, or Athens, or even Pericles, the architect of Athenian glory who by his imperialism provoked the war, and thus "pulled down such glory on [Athenian] heads!" (see ll. 102-3 below). Whatever Heracles himself was actually meant to stand for, his final tribute to friendship, as he starts off from Thebes to Athens with one arm round Theseus' neck, would fit in with the idea that the play was meant to parallel that internecine war within the Greek family of city-states: "And who so rather would have wealth and strength / Than good friends, reasons foolishly therein" (ll. 5079-80 below).

Title] *Apology* Used in the sense of the Greek word ἀπολογία (= speech in defense).
Epigraph] B adapts an Aristophanic fragment ("When you sacrifice a bit of carrion, you won't be able to invite me"), presumably to imply his disgust at Aristophanes' obscenities (Meineke, 2.1201, No. ciii).

1] *Wind, wave, and bark, bear Euthukles and me*   The monologue is spoken by Balaustion (βαλαύστιον = wild pomegranate-flower) while sailing from Athens with her husband Euthukles (see *Balaustion's Adventure*, 265-74; this edition, 10.18-19) to her native island, Rhodes. The name Euthukles (Εὐθυκλῆς = famously straightforward) was that of a comic poet quoted by Athenaeus (3.124b). Traditionally, a Greek *u* becomes a *y* in English, and a *k* becomes a *c*; but B transliterates Greek words more exactly.

2] *not sorrow but despair*   They are leaving Athens for good around 404 B.C., the year of its final defeat by the Spartans, who occupied the city and destroyed its fleet and fortifications.

4] *Athenai*   Ἀθῆναι, the Athenian name for Athens.

6] *repugnant orbs*   Eyes reluctant to see. The tragic diction recalls the passage in Sophocles (*Oedipus Tyrannus* 1270, 1369-85) where Oedipus stabs out the κύκλοι (= circles) of his eyes so as not to see the truth about himself.

9] *Haides*   Hades, the god of the Underworld. B retains the Attic or Athenian Greek spelling, Ἅιδης, which suggests the meaning "unseen."

19] *Koré*   κόρη (= Maiden), the name under which Hades' wife Persephone was worshipped at Athens.

20] *watery plural vastitude*   The odd phrase echoes Shakespeare's "multitudinous seas" (*Macbeth*, 2.2.63), Aeschylus' κυμάτων ἀνήριθμον γέλασμα (= innumerable laughter of the waves, *Prometheus Bound* 90) and Plato's πολὺ πέλαγος τοῦ καλοῦ (= many/great sea of beauty) in *Symposium* 210 d4. Unlike its English equivalent *many*, the Greek adjective πολύς can be used with a singular noun. Hence perhaps B's *plural*.

23] *glaucous*   Bluish grey-green, the color associated with Athene the patron goddess of Athens, whose Homeric epithet is γλαυκῶπις, often translated "grey-eyed".

29] *Attiké*   Ἀττική, Attica, the country round Athens.

34] *Pallas*   Pallas Athene.

35] *Helios' island-bride*   A phrase adapted from Pindar's reference to Rhodes as "Helios' bride" (*Olympian Odes* 7.14). Pindar then relates how the sun-god Helios, granted possession of the island by Zeus, had seven sons by the eponymous nymph Rhodos (Ῥόδος), and his three grandsons gave their names to the island's three cities.

36] *Zeus' darling*   As were nearly all attractive women in Greek mythology. But B was possibly remembering the sanctuary of Zeus, mentioned by Pindar in the same Ode, on the highest mountain in Rhodes, Atabyrion.

45-46] *Above all crowding . . . solitude*   The passage recalls Plato's *Symposium* (211 b5-e4) where the soul ascends from the Many to the

One, from the love of beautiful people and things to the eternal "Idea" of Beauty, accessible only by thought.

48, 58] *"assert the wise"* A semi-colloquial reference to expert opinion, as in *Symposium* 185 c5: "διδάσκουσι οἱ σοφοί (= the wise teach us)."

50] *O nothing doubt, Philemon!* An allusion to a statement in the *Life of Euripides* (one of the brief biographies that survive with the work of most ancient writers) included in Nauck's edition (vii.104-8): "And Philemon loved him [Euripides] so much that he actually said something like this about him: 'If in truth the dead had consciousness . . . as some say, I'd have hanged myself [ἀπηγξάμην ἂν] to see Euripides.'" Strictly, the syntax should imply a so-called "unfulfilled condition in the past," i.e., that he would otherwise have gone to join Euripides long ago; but B later translates Philemon's words (see ll. 5695-97 below) almost as though the condition might possibly be fulfilled: *"Grant, in good sooth, our great dead, all the same / Retain their sense, as certain wise men say, / I'd hang myself to see Euripides!"* In fact, though this Philemon did come from Syracuse (hence Balaustion's interest in him), he was probably not born until 360 B.C., and Balaustion was speaking around 404 B.C. The fragment just quoted also appeared in Meineke (4.48).

53] *rose-smit* Struck with rose-color. The names Rhodos and Rhodes come from ῥόδον (= rose), a flower common on the island.

71] *Peiraios* An anomalous transliteration of Πειραιεύς, the port of Athens.

74] *flute-girls* According to Plutarch (*Life of Lysander*, 15), the Spartan general Lysander had the destruction of the Athenian fleet and fortifications accompanied by music from flute-girls specially collected for the purpose.

79-80] *long double range / Themistoklean* Themistocles, the Athenian general largely responsible for the defeat of the Persians at Salamis, also built the two "Long Walls" between Athens and Piraeus, four miles away.

89] *Dikast and heliast* Δικαστής, ἡλιαστής. Both words mean "juryman," a type satirized in Aristophanes' *Wasps*; but nearly all the types listed here were taken from his comedies. In *Knights* 61, for instance, the *demagogue* Cleon is a *sham-prophecy-retailer* (cf. *Peace* 1047, *Birds* 960); and *altar-scrap-snatcher* paraphrases an Aristotophanic term of abuse, βωμολόχος (e.g., *Knights* 1058).

98] *psaltress* Female player of psaltery or harp. See l. 1562n. below.

99] *Athenai's harlotry* Flute-girls often doubled as prostitutes at parties, as implied in Plato's *Symposium* (176 e).

101] *kordax-step* A dance mentioned by Aristophanes (*Clouds* 537-

40), as a form of obscenity (like making the actors wear "large, red-tipped" leather phalluses) that he claims to have excluded from his comedies. According to a scholiast (*Scholia,* 107) the dance involved "an indecent movement of the loins."

102]   *Die then, who pulled such glory on your heads!*   Pericles (c.495-429 B.C.), the Athenian statesman who created the visible "glory" of Athens, e.g., by building the Parthenon (a temple of Athena), but was blamed by Aristophanes and others for provoking the war with Sparta by his imperialistic policy. The image of pulling down a temple on to the heads of its worshippers, linked with the thunder-image, was possibly suggested by Milton's Samson in the temple of Dagon: "those two massie Pillars / With horrible convulsion to and fro / He tugg'd, he shook, till down they came and drew / The whole roof after them with burst of thunder / Upon the heads of all who sate beneath" (*Samson Agonistes,* 1648-52).

106]   *Prove thee Olympian*   Show that you really deserve Zeus's title, "the Olympian," applied to him by Aristophanes for "hurling thunder and lightning and throwing Greece into confusion" (*Acharnians* 530-31). Zeus, the chief god on Olympus, specialized in thunderbolts. Despite B's policy of exact transliteration, *Olympian* is *here* spelt with a *y* not a *u* in the MS—perhaps because the adjectival ending is English not Greek.

108-11]   *Build me . . . yon west extravagance*   The notion of an Athens existing eternally in the mind squares with Plato's theory of Ideas; but the link with sunset suggests that B was thinking of Shelley's *Hellas,* 1084-89: "Another Athens shall arise, / And to remoter time / Bequeath, like sunset to the skies, / The splendour of its prime; / And leave, if nought so bright may live, / All earth can take or Heaven can give."

109]   *Pheidias*   The sculptor, painter, and architect (c. 490-493 B.C.) employed by Pericles to build the Parthenon and generally beautify Athens.

112]   *Propulaia*   Προπύλαια (= before the gate), the roofed marble entrance to the Acropolis.

113]   *grade*   Step (Latin *gradus*).

114]   *Pnux*   Πνύξ, a hill just west of the Acropolis, where the Assembly met (as in Aristophanes' *Acharnians* 20-42).

   Bema   βῆμα (= stepping-up place), speakers' platform.

117]   *Sparté*   Σπάρτη (= Sparta).

118]   *Chasmed in the crag . . . our Theatre*   The Athenian theatre of Dionysus was in a hollow on the southern slope of the Acropolis.

119] *purple* An expensive dye used for the clothes of the rich and powerful and, as here, for theatrical costumes.

Staghunt-month Elaphebolion (ἐλαφηβολιών = Stag-shooting), the Athenian month roughly equivalent to March-April.

120] *Dionusia* The Great Dionysia, a festival of Dionysus at which plays were performed in a competition for tragic and comic poets.

121] *Aischulos, Sophokles, Euripides* The order is chronological. Aeschylus (?525/4-456/5 B.C.) won thirteen first prizes, Sophocles (?496-406 B.C.) eighteen, and Euripides (c. 485-406 B.C.) only four in his lifetime, one after his death.

124] *Their noble want the unworthy* Lest their nobility lack the challenge of unworthiness in others (a quasi-Greek use of a neuter adjective as an abstract or collective noun).

126] *his ape* His subhuman imitator.

127] *antic* Grotesque.

128] *Hermippos to pelt Perikles* According to Plutarch (*Life of Pericles,* 32), the comic poet Hermippus prosecuted Pericles' mistress Aspasia for impiety, and also accused her of making assignations for Pericles with free-born women.

129] *Kratinos to swear Pheidias* Cratinus was a rival comic poet satirized by Aristophanes (*Knights* 526-33). Plutarch mentions him (*Life of Pericles,* 13) as a critic of Pericles' building-programme, adding that "the comic poets" joined in the political campaign against both Pericles and Pheidias which led to the latter's imprisonment on a charge of stealing gold intended for his statue of Athena (*Life of Pericles,* 31).

130] *Eruxis* A man called in Aristophanes' *Frogs* 932-34 a "horse-cock" (ἰππαλεκτρυών, a word used by Aeschylus in a fragment of his *Myrmidons; Fragmenta,* 43, No. 134). Nothing else is known about him, but a scholiast explained that Eruxis was "slandered as ugly and unpleasant" (*Scholia,* 301); and the word *eruxis* (ἔρυξις) means a "belch" or "vomit." Here it is probably used as a name for Alfred Austin, a minor poet and critic who had long been "flea-biting" B (DeVane, *Hbk.,* 382) and who became the target of "Pacchiarotto, and How He Worked in Distemper" (1876). See this edition, 13.137-65 and nn.

131] *mop and mow* Sneering grimaces.

132-34] *a dog-faced dwarf . . . hierarchy* Anubis, one of the divine guardians of the dead in Egyptian religion, originally pictured as a jackal, later as a man with a dog's head. Austin was only five feet tall.

136-37] Why *should not . . . Momos as thou Zeus?* In Lucian's *Assembly of the Gods* (10) Momos, the god of Criticism, complains to Zeus about the admission of foreigners to the Greek hierarchy. He then asks Anubis: "And who are you, you dog-faced Egyptian?. . . How do you think you can be a god if you bark?" Accepting that paradox, Balaustion asks: "If a dog can become a god, why shouldn't Eruxis become the god of Criticism, and Euripides the chief god of Poetry?"

138-40]   *thy Makaria . . . low contention"*   B adapts the words of Heracles' daughter Macaria, in Euripides' *Children of Heracles* (593-96), when about to be sacrificed to ensure the victory of the Athenian army: "If those of us mortals who are going to die will have worries there too, I don't know where one can turn; for death is usually thought the best cure for evils."

147]   *Those Furies in the Oresteian song*   In the third play of Aeschylus' *Oresteia*, the Furies who pursue Orestes for killing his mother are found asleep and snoring in Apollo's temple at Delphi (*Eumenides* 46-56).

158]   *Bruise and not brain the pest*   B's image was probably suggested by Shakespeare's "We have scotch'd the snake not kill'd it" (*Macbeth*, 3.2.12).

160]   *the Three*   Aeschylus, Sophocles, Euripides.

161]   *How Klutaimnestra hated*   In Aeschylus' *Agamemnon* (1372-1447) Clytaemnestra claims to have killed her husband in revenge for his sacrifice of her daughter Iphigenia, and for all his infidelities.

161-62]   *pride / Of Iokasté*   Ἰοκάστη, the Greek spelling (four syllables, as required here for the scansion) of Oedipus' mother/wife, Jocasta. In Sophocles' *Oedipus Tyrannus* (1070, 1078-79) Oedipus misinterprets her reluctance to face the truth about his parentage as snobbishness.

162-63]   *Medeia clove / Nature asunder*   By murdering her own children in Euripides' *Medea* (1079-81).

165]   *prevent the humbling hand*   Anticipate (Latin *praevenio*) the humiliating effect of outside forces, like defeat by the Spartans.

166]   *Our petty passions purify their tide*   Anachronistically, Balaustion paraphrases the famous statement of Aristotle (born 384 B.C.) that Tragedy "effects, through pity and fear, the purification [κάθαρσις] of emotions like these" (*Poetics*, 1449b 27-28). The meaning of *catharsis* here is disputed, but B seems to follow Milton's interpretation in his Preface to *Samson Agonistes*: "by raising pity and fear, or terror, to purge the mind of those and such like passions, that is to temper and reduce them to just measure."

171]   *Peplosed and kothorned*   Wearing the πέπλος (= rich, formal robe) and κόθορνος (= high boot with thick soles) commonly used by actors in Greek Tragedy.

173]   *Lent for the lesson*   An allusion to Aeschylus' doctrine of πάθει μάθος (= learning by suffering; see also *The Agamemnon of Aeschylus*, 190).

Choros, I and thou   The tragic chorus, increased by Sophocles from twelve to fifteen members, represented the reactions of "ordinary people" to the extraordinary experiences of the heroes and heroines, usually royal.

174-76]   *piteous . . . terrible*   Another reference to Aristotle (see l. 166 above).

176]   *Phrunichos*   One of the earliest tragic poets. When Miletus was captured by the Persians in 494 B.C., most of its men killed and its women and children enslaved, Phrynichus produced a play about it at Athens; but "the whole audience burst into tears and they fined him a thousand drachmas for reminding them of sufferings that they felt to be their own" (Herodotus, *Histories*, 6.21).

178]   *smart-place freshly frayed*   Sore spot rubbed open again.

182]   *prologue*   Used in its technical sense as the first section of a tragedy, whether monologue or dialogue, which announced the theme and starting-point of the action.

185]   *my first*   I.e., *Balaustion's Adventure*, in which she described from memory a performance of Euripides' *Alcestis*, first at Syracuse and later at Athens to four friends (*Balaustion's Adventure*, 1-5; this edition, 10.9).

193-98]   *For fear Admetos . . . statue start / Alcestis*   The play ends with Heracles urging the reluctant Admetus to touch the veiled woman that he claims to have won as a prize in a wrestling contest. When Admetus finally touches her, he finds that she is his resurrected wife (*Alcestis* 1117-26, *Balaustion's Adventure*, 2314-22; this edition, 10.102). The *statue* was possibly suggested by that of Hermione in Shakespeare's *Winter's Tale* (5.3.21-100).

199]   *streamlet*   The Ilissus, a setting probably borrowed from Plato's dialogue, *Phaedrus* 229a 1-3.

202]   *Baccheion*   The temple of Bacchus (= Dionysus).

204]   *boatman-spider*   An aquatic insect usually called a water-boatman.

205]   *Lenaia*   From ληνός (= wine-vat) a festival of Dionysus around January which included dramatic competitions.

206]   *Euripides had taught "Andromedé"*   Since each poet produced his own play, which meant training the chorus and actors, διδάσκω (= teach) was the technical term for producing. The *Andromeda* has survived chiefly in passages burlesqued by Aristophanes, e.g., *Thesmophoriazusae* 1015-1115.

207]   *"Kresphontes"*   Only fragments of this play survive.

208]   *Someone from Phokis*   An inventive use of a statement by Plutarch (*Life of Lysander*, 15): "when the victorious Spartans and their allies were considering a proposal to 'make slaves of the Athenians, demolish their city, and turn their country into pastureland for sheep . . . a certain Phocian sang the opening chorus of Euripides' *Electra*. . . . All hearts were softened, and it seemed barbarous to annihilate so famous a city, which had produced such men [i.e. as Euripides]." B calls that Phocian Euthukles, and elaborates the incident towards the end of the poem (ll. 5500-5609 below).

211] *the masters let the slaves / Do Bacchic service* The Spartans allow the Athenians to celebrate the Dionysia; see l. 120 above.

213] *that trilogy* *Bacchae, Iphigenia in Aulis,* and a lost play, *Alcmaeon in Corinth,* now thought to have been produced in 405 B.C., which slightly spoils B's time-scheme.

214] *no Euripides* He had died 407-6 B.C.

222] *prore* Prow. B gets as close as he can to the word πρώρα used by Euripides, e.g., *Helen* 1563.

227-30] *his own Amphitheos . . . a visitor* The visitor was Aristophanes. In his *Acharnians* (46-58), Amphitheos (Ἀμφίθεος = "god on both sides," since both priest and great-grandson of Demeter) is told by the gods to arrange a peace with Sparta (*Scholia,* 4). Apart from the *deity-dung* alliteration, his only link with *dung* is that another Aristophanic peace-maker, the hero of *Peace,* flies up to heaven on a dung-beetle. Though "immortal," Amphitheus has to apply to the magistrates for a "travelling allowance," but is turned down. Aristophanes is *like* him, in being a strange mixture of earthly and divine.

238] *Thrace* The name of a vaguely defined northern region of Greece, here used for Macedonia, where Euripides spent his last years at the court of King Archelaus. B was probably remembering the story told in the *Life of Euripides,* about "a village called Thrace [Θρᾳκῶν = of Thracians] in Macedonia": Euripides got the Thracian villagers pardoned for killing and eating one of the King's hounds, but was later torn to pieces and devoured by that very hound's puppies (Nauck, vi.47-58).

245] *tripod* The three-legged stool from which the priestess at Delphi delivered oracles. In both Sophocles' *Oedipus Tyranus* 82-83, and Euripides' *Hippolytus* 806-7, returning from Delphi with a laurel wreath implied that one brought good news .

248] *Speak good words* An adaptation of the liturgical command εὐφήμει (= speak well, i.e., speak words of good omen or be silent), to mean: "I hope it's not bad news?"

249] *He is crowned* The prize for winning the tragedy competition was a crown of ivy.

261] *stade* στάδιον, a measure of length equalling 606.75 English feet. The racecourse at Olympia was exactly one stade long, so the word came to mean a single course in a race.

263] *diaulos* δίαυλος (= double pipe or channel), a double course, where the racer ran back from the *stade's end* to the starting point.

hundred plays Poetic licence. Euripides is said to have written ninety-two, of which about eighty titles are known.

271] *Girded* Jeered at.

274] *We drop our ballot-bean* We vote.

278] *took on him command* He was sent as a general with Pericles to suppress the revolt of Samos (441 B.C.), but Pericles told him: "You know how to write poetry, but you don't know how to be a general" (Athenaeus, 13.604d).

279] *Got laughed at* B expurgates the point of the anecdote, which was to illustrate Sophocles' homosexuality and verbal dexterity. The laugh that he raised at a party was not derisive but admiring. Having ingeniously contrived to kiss a blushing boy, he boasted to the others: "Pericles said I didn't know how to be a general [στρατηγεῖν] but how was that for a stratagem [στρατήγημα]?"

284] *A sea-cave suits him* "They say he furnished a cave on Salamis which had an airhole towards the sea, and spent all his days there to escape the crowds; which is why he takes most of his similes from the sea" (Nauck, vi.59-62). See *The Times* of 2 February 1998 for the identification of this cave by the archaeologist Yannis Lolos with a Stone Age cave overlooking Peristeria Bay.

285] *a bookish store* Nauck observed: "Euripides is mentioned among the few private individuals who collected a library for themselves, nor does he himself make any secret of this bookish equipment" (Nauck, xxvii.11-13; cf. Athenaeus, 1.3a). Aristophanes made him boast of having dosed tragedy with an extract of books (*Frogs* 943).

286] *Shadow of an ass* A proverbial phrase used in *Wasps* 191 to describe a pointless controversy. A scholiast explains: "a man hired a donkey to carry his luggage while he walked from Athens to Megara. When it got hot at mid-day, he took down his luggage to make some shade for himself. The donkey-driver objected that his contract was for carrying luggage, not providing shade, and the resultant argument was taken to court" (*Scholia*, 140). B may also have known No. 392 in the Tauchnitz *Aesopicae Fabulae* (1868), entitled "Shadow of an ass ["Ονου σκιά]," where both men wanted to get into the donkey's shadow, and they argued about their exclusive rights to do so.

290] *Phoinissai* The only one of the three to survive (c. 412-408 B.C.).

290-91] *the Match / Of Life Contemplative with Active Life* I.e., the *Antiope*. "Zethus surrounded [Thebes] with a strong wall, while his brother amused himself with playing on his lyre. Music and verses were disagreeable to Zethus, and, according to some, he prevailed upon his brother no longer to pursue so unproductive a study" (Lemprière, 673). It was far from unproductive in another version of the myth, where Amphion's music drew the stones into their places. But B's subtitle for the play followed Nauck: "In the *Antiopa* Euripides meant to defend the study of liberal arts against the calumnies of its enemies; for he set forth a contest between Zethus and Amphion in which Zethus studied how to produce good crops and praised the active life . . . while Amphion championed inactivity, music, and wisdom" (Nauck, xxvii.5-10).

294] *o'er the entire man* Translating ἀμφίβροτος (= round the man), the adjective used in Homer (e.g., *Iliad* 2.389) to differentiate the large oval shield from the smaller round one.

299] *Whatever renovation flatter age* Whatever forms of recreation tempt the elderly. Perhaps B was expressing his own determination to keep working at sixty-two.

302] *Macedonian Archelaus* See l. 238n. above.

311] *phorminx* A Homeric word for the lyre or cithara, the seven-stringed plucking instrument. Though Euripides was associated with a new type of music, the word stands simply for his tragic poetry.

312] *Clashed thence* I.e., sang to a pizzicato accompaniment on that instrument. The odd verb possibly imitated the use of κλάζω (= clash, clang) by Euripides himself in a lyric addressed to Apollo: "and you clash on a lyre, singing paeans" (*Ion* 905-6).

'*Alkaion*' Apparently a mistake (in both MS and first edition) for "Alkmaion"; see l. 213 above. B's ultimate source was the scholium to *Frogs* 67, quoting a record that "after Euripides died, his son of the same name produced at Athens *Iphigenia in Aulis, Alcmaeon, Bacchae*." Only fragments of the *Alcmaeon* survive.

*maddened '*Pentheus*' up* In the *Bacchae* Pentheus, King of Thebes, is fanatically opposed to the cult of Dionysus. "'Now Dionysus,' says the god to himself (849-51) 'let's punish him. First send him out of his mind, by injecting light-headed madness.'" The quotation marks round Pentheus' name were probably suggested by a note in Paley's edition of Euripides (2.395): "The *Bacchae* of Euripides appears also to have been known by the name of the *Pentheus*, under which title Stobaeus twice quotes it."

317] *Agathon* The most famous tragic poet after "the Three" (born c. 445 B.C.). See ll. 120, 121 and nn. above. He gave the party described in Plato's *Symposium*, and Nauck mentioned Euripides' enjoyment of Agathon's company in Macedon (Nauck, xix.5-6), quoting Aelian's story (*Varia Historia* 13.4) of how Euripides got drunk at a party, and started hugging and kissing the forty-year-old Agathon.

319] *young Euripides* The poet's son.

320] *Mounuchia* A hill northeast of Piraeus, with a harbor directly below it (possibly mentioned here because the Theatre of Dionysus was on the hill's northwest flank).

324-25] *their favourite . . . 'City of Gapers'* In *Knights* 1263 Aristophanes replaces the stock phrase, "city of Athenians" (Ἀθηναίων) by the rhyming one, "city of Gapenians" (Κεχηναίων), coined from a verb meaning "gape foolishly, in wonder or expectation."

328] *Glauketes* Mentioned by Aristophanes (*Peace* 1008) as one of the gourmands crowding round a stall selling eels from Lake Copae in Boeotia.

Morsimos A man much ridiculed by Aristophanes (*Knights* 402, *Peace* 803, *Frogs* 151) but always as a bad tragic poet. Did B mean to imply that Morsimos was a tragic failure in every kind of competition?

329-30] *Kopaic eel . . . cooked his prize* Eels, and ways of cooking them, are discussed at length in Athenaeus (7.297c-300c). In Aristophanes' *Acharnians* 962, a Copaic eel (ἔγχελυς) is priced at only three drachmas, but is also apostrophized in a parody of Admetus' words about his dead wife (*Acharnians* 893-94, *Alcestis* 367-68, *Balaustion's Adventure*, 876-77; this edition, 10.43).

331] *proper conger-fashion* Athenaeus quotes a caricature of a cook who boasts of having dealt perfectly with a conger-eel (γόγγρος): not smothering it with cheese or herbs, but simply baking it so gently that it looked exactly as if it were still alive (7.288 c-e).

331-32] *oil / And nettles . . . foam-fish-kind* A recipe quoted in Athenaeus for cooking a fish "which the Ionians call ἀφρός (= foam)" (7.285b-c).

333] *triremes* τριήρεις, warships with three banks of oars.

334] *Arginousai* Small islands south of Lesbos, where the Athenian fleet decisively defeated the Spartans in 406 B.C.; but bad weather prevented the rescue of casualties and the recovery of dead bodies. The victorious commanders were tried and condemned collectively, an illegal procedure resisted only by Socrates (Plato, *Apology* 32b), and the six who failed to escape arrest were all executed, including the son of Pericles.

336] *Mikon* A painter whose fresco of Amazons fighting on horseback is mentioned in Aristophanes (*Lysistrata* 678-79).

Thessalian mime B anglicizes μῖμος (= imitator, actor, actress), possibly remembering Athenaeus' story (13.607c-e) of "Thessalian dancing-girls" who performed practically naked to entertain some serious-minded delegates, including a grave philosopher who came to blows with the auctioneer when passionately bidding for a flute-girl. As a painter wedded to his art, Micon is perhaps meant to be acting equally out of character.

337] *Lais* A famous prostitute from Corinth. According to Lemprière (316-17) her clients and lovers included Alcibiades, Demosthenes, and Diogenes, and she was finally murdered by jealous wives in Thessaly—though not, it seems, before teaching her technique to at least one *Thessalian mime.*

338] *Leogoras* Mentioned by Aristophanes (*Clouds* 109) as a breeder of Φασιανοί, which the context requires to mean "Phasian horses." But the word usually means "Phasian birds," i.e., pheasants. Athenaeus tried to solve the problem by suggesting that Leogoras bred both horses and pheasants (9.387a).

blood-mare koppa-marked Pedigree mare branded with the early Greek letter *koppa* (later displaced by *kappa* = *k*) to show that it came from Corinth (Κόρινθος), so supposedly descended from the winged horse, Pegasus (see *Clouds* 23, where Aristophanes puns on the term).

339] *six talents* Six times the cost of building a trireme, more than enough to buy an expensive house.

341] *A choeni . . . wine* Nearly a litre of neat wine from Mende in northern Greece . A comic writer quoted by Athenaeus called that wine good enough to make "the gods themselves wet their soft beds" (1.29d). Wine was usually drunk much diluted with water.

342] *dine on herbs!* Before losing his bet Leogoras had a reputation for gluttony (Athenaeus, 9.387a).

349] '*The Female Celebrators of the Feast*' *Thesmophoriazusae* Θεσμοφοριάζουσαι (= women celebrating the Thesmophoria [a festival of Demeter]), produced 411 B.C. Athenaeus mentions a "second *Thesmophoriazousae*" (1.29a) which Meineke assumed (2.1074-75) to have been, not *the old play chopped and changed,* but a quite new one, intended as a sequel to the first. B, however, makes it a rewriting of the original play, produced around the time of Euripides' death (406 B.C.). The prominence of alcohol and sex in B's portrait of Aristophanes was doubtless encouraged by the first of the fragments from the "second Thesmophoriazusae" included by Meineke (2.1076): "Nor will I allow anyone to drink Pramnian, Chian, Thasian, Peparethian, or any other wine that stimulates the ἔμβολος" [= anything pointed so as to be easily thrust in, a peg, stopper (Liddell and Scott, 1996)].

357-58] *women, moved / By reason of his liking Krateros* I.e., by resentment at his homosexuality. Nauck's edition of Euripides quoted Suidas: "Others related that he was torn to pieces, not by hounds, but by women when he was going at dead of night to visit Archelaus' boyfriend, Craterus; for he had that sort of love-life too" (Nauck, xxi).

359] *He was loved by Sokrates* The *Life* called him "a ἑταῖρος [= comrade, companion, disciple] of Socrates" (Nauck, v.10). Balaustion implies that Euripides would hardly have turned from such a friendship to an affair with Craterus. B was probably remembering Plato's *Symposium*, which illustrates (219 b-d) Socrates' indifference to Alcibiades' famous sex-appeal.

362]   *Arridaios . . . Krateues*   B paraphrases a story in Nauck (xxi, n. 30) that these two poets, Macedonian and Thessalian respectively, were jealous of Euripides, so bribed the King's Master of Hounds to set them on to him.

364]   *Protagoras*   The most famous of the Sophists (Σοφισταί = teachers of wisdom, i.e., professional teachers of rhetoric, public speaking, science etc.). The *Life of Euripides* called him a "student of Protagoras" (Nauck, v.9). Balaustion smiles at the idea of competition between a poet of such high culture and a couple of regional scribblers.

365]   *Phu* φῦ, an exclamation used by Aristophanes both to imitate the act of blowing and to express disgust. Here B adapts it to express contemptuous dismissal.

Comic Platon   I.e., Plato the writer of comedy, not Plato the philosopher. The story is in Athenaeus (13.557e), where Sophocles' joke is neater: "Yes, he's a misogynist in his tragedies, but in bed he's a philogynist."

371-72]   *Arethousian Nikodikos' wife . . . simply seventy-five*   An alternative to the Craterus story (see l. 358n. above) quoted by Nauck (xxi, n. 30) from Suidas. The *Life* gives the poet's age as "more than seventy" (Nauck, v-vi).

376]   *'The Festivals'* Ἑορταί, a lost comedy in which Plato had "stigmatized" Euripides (Meineke, 1.170).

379]   *a second treat*   I.e., the "second" *Thesmophoriazusae* (see l. 349 above).

381]   *assisted at*   Used in the sense of the French *assister* (= attend, be present at).

383-86]   *cuttlefish . . . foul dreams*   B was evidently recalling three passages in Athenaeus: "the cuttlefish, when pursued, emits mud [θολός] and hides in it" (7.323 d-e); "*phukidas* [φυκίδας = fishes that live in seaweed], the *alphestes*, and the red-skinned scorpion . . ." (7.282a); and a third passage explaining that the *alphestes* was a type of fish usually seen in pairs, "one following the tail of another," for which reason the word had become a term of abuse for sodomites (7.281f). Thus "mud" and "foul dreams" at "midnight" were used to imply Aristophanes' obscenity.

387-88]   *so could not I, / Balaustion, say*   I.e., that I "assisted at" the *Thesmophoriazusae*.

388]   *"Lusistraté"*   Aristophanes' *Lysistrata* (411 B.C.), in which the

women force their husbands to make peace, by refusing sexual inter-
course until they do.

389]   *"people's privilege"*   I.e., the democratic right to satirize the rich
and powerful in comedy. Disgusted by *Lysistrata*, Balaustion refused to
go to any more of Aristophanes' plays, though everyone kept telling
her what a splendid thing Athenian Comedy was.

391]   *Coëval with our freedom*   According to Aristotle (*Poetics* 1448a 31-
32) the Megarians claimed to have invented Comedy "at the time when
Democracy was born among them"; hence Meineke (1.20) called Com-
edy an "associate and foster-child of popular government."

397]   *stranger*   Used in the sense of "foreigner" (a Rhodian, not a na-
tive Athenian). The Greek word ξένος covers both meanings.

401]   *Kleons*   From the *Acharnians* onwards, the demagogue Cleon
was one of Aristophanes' favorite targets.

408]   *gust*   Gusto.

409]   *wine-lees*   An allusion to the probable origin of Greek Comedy
in the songs of a κῶμος (= procession of drunken revellers). The hero
of Aristophanes' *Peace*, Trygaeus, is so named from τρύξ (= wine-lees)
or τρύγη (= vintage); and in *Acharnians* 499-500 Aristophanes calls
Comedy "Trugedy" (τρυγῳδία), as a jocular counterpart to Tragedy. A
scholiast explained the coinage: "because, instead of masks, comic ac-
tors smeared their faces with wine-lees" (*Scholia*, 15); but Athenaeus of-
fered a slightly different explanation: "because Comedy was invented
at the time of the vintage" (2.40).

411]   *Phuromachus*   Mentioned in *Ecclesiazusae* 22 as having proposed
a decree for the segregation of sexes in theatre audiences, and of free
women from prostitutes (*Scholia*, 683).

417]   *Waves, said*   I.e., by her favorite poet, Euripides: "The sea
washes away all the evils of mankind" (*Iphigenia in Tauris* 1193).

420]   *one appalled at Phaidra's fate*   Aristophanes. In *Frogs* 1043-44
Aeschylus is made to claim moral superiority to Euripides, saying: "*I
didn't write about whores like Phaedra . . . and nobody can say I ever
wrote about a woman in love.*" Phaedra, in Euripides' *Hippolytus*, is pas-
sionately in love with her stepson. But there (375-432), as Balaustion
points out, Phaedra is the chaste and innocent victim of the goddess
Aphrodite—though her innocence is slightly reduced when she writes
a suicide-letter falsely accusing the chaste Hippolytus of trying to rape
her (856-86).

422-25]   *serpent . . . lambency of honeyed tongue*   Though the serpent-
image seems to come from Gen. 3:1-5 (see ll. 2088-91 below), the hon-
eyed tongue has a Euripidean basis in Phaedra's rejection of the

Nurse's pragmatic arguments as "too fine words . . . pleasant to the ear" (486-89). The word *lambent* means literally, "licking."

431] *the Scythian's whip* In *Thesmophoriazusae* (which contains a coarse joke about Phaedra) a Scythian archer with a whip stands guard over Euripides' elderly relative, Mnesilochus, arrested for attending the women-only festival in female costume to defend the poet against the women's charges of defaming them (153, 930-1225).

438-39] *Salabaccho* A notorious prostitute mentioned in *Thesmophoriazusae* 805. B casts her as Lysistrata's semi-allegorical maid, Διαλλαγή (= Reconciliation) in *Lysistrata* 1114-20, and assumes that she performed in the nude—a reasonable inference from the context, where the negotiations over disputed territory are conducted through punning allusions to Reconciliation's legs, buttocks, and pudenda (1157-75).

445] *Pattern-proposing* Example-setting, exemplary (*propose* used in its Latin sense of "set forth").

450] *Aristeides . . . Miltiades* Athenian generals who defeated the Persian invaders at the battle of Marathon (490 B.C.). Aristeides' moral reputation made him known as "the Just."

451] *golden tettix* Describing early Athenian society, Thucydides remarked (*History*, 1.6): "It is not long since older men of the upper classes stopped tying up their hair in a bun on top of their heads, with a clasp of golden tettixes" (τεττίγων = grasshoppers, cicalas). In *Clouds* 984-86 and *Knights* 1331-34 these symbols of native origin are associated with the good old days of the Μαραθωνόμαχοι (= fighters at Marathon).

452] *Kleophon* A politician who earned popularity by introducing a dole for poor citizens. Aristophanes described him (*Thesmophoriazusae* 805) as worse than the prostitute Salabaccho. See l. 438n. above.

467] *Pnux* See l. 114n. above.

    kordax-dance See l. 101n. above.

469] *muck* For B's previous use of this word to express disgust, see "Mr. Sludge, 'the Medium,'" 755-57 (this edition, 6.318).

481] *true lightning* The image was probably suggested by the *Life* (Nauck, vi.43): "and they say that both Euripides' tombs were struck by lightning." Nauck commented: "in which story, whether fact or fiction, the ancients recognized the highest divine testimony that this poet was dear to the gods beyond all the rest" (Nauck, xxii, n. 32).

485-86] *beetle . . . menace heaven* An allusion to Aristophanes' *Peace*, where Trygaeus flies up to heaven on a dung-beetle, which had previously rolled around or "*trundled*" (περικυλίσας) a dung-ball with its feet (*Peace*, 7).

488]   *statue in the theatre*   A proposal that was duly implemented (Nauck, xxiii, n. 37; Pausanius, *Description of Greece*, 1.21.1).

489]   *Bring the poet's body back*   A request firmly refused by the Macedonians (Nauck, xxii, n. 35).

491]   *Alkamenes*   An Athenian sculptor (c. 440-400 B.C.), described by Pausanias as "second in skill to Pheidias" (*Description of Greece*, 5.10.8).

491-92]   *the music-witch, / The songstress-seiren*   After mentioning the statue of Euripides in the theatre, Pausanias goes on: "and it is said that after Sophocles' death the Spartans invaded Attica; and their leader dreamt he saw Dionysus, telling him to pay the customary honors of the dead to the new Siren, which he took to mean Sophocles and his poetry; and it is still their custom to represent the inspiration of prose-works and poems as a Siren" (*Description of Greece* 1.21.1). The *Life of Sophocles* states (15): "and some say that they also put a siren on his tomb." B was possibly encouraged to do the same for Euripides by a story in the *Life of Euripides* (Nauck, vii.84-86): when accused of halitosis (στόμα δυσῶδες = bad-smelling mouth) the poet replied: "What blasphemy! [εὐφήμει = say nothing profane!] My mouth is sweeter than honey and Sirens" [i.e. than their song]. See Homer, *Odyssey* 12.157-200.

492]   *meed of melody*   As a reward for his music. The elliptical wording was perhaps the price of the quasi-musical assonance and alliteration on *k*, *s*, and *me*: *Alkamenes . . . music-witch . . . songstress-seiren . . . meed of melody*.

493]   *Thoukudides*   Thucydides, the historian (c. 455-400 B.C.) famous for his history of the Peloponnesian War. The *Life* (Nauck, vi.36-39) quoted four lines of verse "by Thucydides the historian or Timotheus the lyric poet," inscribed on Euripides' empty tomb at Athens.

497]   *vest*   Vesture, clothing.

504]   *Singing . . . its own song*   I.e., by reading aloud his *Heracles* (see ll. 3525, 3534, 5084 below).

508-9]   *"Alkestis," which saved me, / Secured me—you*   In *Balaustion's Adventure* Balaustion had saved her own and her companions' life, and also won the love of Euthukles by reciting the *Alcestis* from memory to the previously hostile Syracusans (265-74; this edition, 10.18).

510]   *pardon of Admetos*   For selfishly allowing his wife Alcestis to die instead of him.

512]   *huge gratitude*   For bringing Alcestis back to life, by wrestling with Death for her.

513]   *Club . . . lion-fleece*   A club and the skin of the Nemean Lion (the victim of his first Labor) were both parts of his usual costume.

514]   *next new labour*   The next of the Labors, or apparently impossible tasks imposed on him by Eurystheus: to tame the man-eating horses of Diomedes.

514-15]   *"height o'er height . . . decree!"*   Not an echo of Longfellow's "Excelsior," but B's paraphrase of Euripides, where Heracles describes his destiny as always going "πρός αἶπος (= up a steep slope)" (*Alcestis* 500, *Balaustion's Adventure*, 1119-20; this edition, 10.53).

516-18]   *He helps us . . . Alkestis helped*   The capitalized *He* marks Heracles' status as demi-god: a son of Zeus, admitted after death to Olympus. In *Balaustion's Adventure*, 1773, Heracles is called "the Helper," a phrase used in Liddell and Scott (1871) to translate ὁ Παράκλητος (= The Paraclete) in the New Testament. Did B mean to suggest an analogy between the Greek demi-god and the divine human being of Christianity who also overcame death?

517]   *He*   Euripides, not Heracles (here capitalized as line-starter only).

522]   *"Herakles"*   Conjecturally dated 414 B.C., and later known as *Heracles Mainomenos* or *Hercules Furens*, i.e., Heracles going mad.

524]   *Somebody, I forget who*   No record of his name has survived.

531]   *We have not waited to acquaint*   We have already acquainted.

532]   *we can prologuize*   Balaustion summarizes Euripides' prologue (HL 1-59; see ll. 3535-99 below).

533]   *Eurustheus*   King of Tiryns in Argos, who imposed the Labors on Heracles. In Euripides' version of the myth, they were the price demanded by Eurystheus for letting Heracles' father, Amphitryon, return from exile (HL 13 21; see ll. 3548-59 below).

536]   *Haides*   See l. 9n. above.

537]   *triple-headed hound*   Cerberus, the watchdog of the Underworld.

537-38]   *which sun should see . . . whose darkness*   The image elaborates Euripides' words: "he has gone to the house of Hades, to bring up the three-formed dog to the light" (HL 24-25).

    the Fear   The fearful creature. B imitates the adaptability of Greek, where φόβος can mean either "fear" or "an object of fear."

540]   *Lukos*   A usurper from Euboea who has seized power in Thebes (the scene of the play) by killing its ruler, Creon.

542]   *the land's loved one*   Heracles.

543]   *Megara*   Daughter of Creon, ruler of Thebes.

547]   *Father*   Heracles' (human) father, Amphitryon.

555]   *the Three in funeral garb*   The reader naturally assumes that these are the *Father and wife and child* of l. 547; but it turns out that there are three children not one (HL 1023), and it is these three who are later put in *funeral garb* (HL 329-33, 548). Perhaps the confusion is meant to be Balaustion's—a credible lapse of an otherwise incredible memory.

560] *Suddenly, torch-light! knocking at the door* The ill-timed irruption of Aristophanes seems modelled on that of Alcibiades in Plato's *Symposium.* After Socrates' serious speech about Heavenly Love, "Suddenly there was a knocking on the outer door, and a loud noise as of revellers [κωμαστῶν, etymologically connected with *Comedy*], and we could hear the voice of a flute-girl . . . a little later we heard the voice of Alcibiades in the courtyard, very drunk and shouting loudly" (*Symposium*, 212 c6-d4).

562] *Komos-cry* Singing of a κῶμος (= procession of Bacchic revellers), from which Comedy probably developed.

563] *Raw-flesh red, no cap upon his head* A not too *unintelligible* reference to the phalluses worn by comic actors, which were "red at the tip" in *Clouds* 539.

564] *Dionusos, Bacchos, Phales, Iacchos* The first, second, and fourth were alternative names for Dionysus, god of wine and fertility. Phales was a personified phallus, called by Aristophanes "fellow-reveller of Bacchus" (*Acharnians* 263-64).

565] *kid-skin* Wine-bag made of kid-skin (now presumably empty and dropped by its owner).

567] *Our Rhodian Jackdaw-song* Apparently a reference to the cryptic begging-songs called κορωνίσματα (= crow-songs) quoted from Hagnocles of Rhodes by Athenaeus: "Good people, give to the crow whatever each of you has in his hands" (8.359e-360b). B specifies the grey-headed crow or jackdaw, doubtless because of its acquisitive habits.

575] *Fifteen* B gives the number of a tragic chorus, possibly forgetting that in comedy it was twenty-four (the number of birds identified in *Birds* 297-304).

577] *the Three* The actors (who regularly doubled parts). According to Aristotle's brief history of drama: "Aeschylus first changed the number of actors from one to two. Sophocles made it three" (*Poetics* 1449a 15-19).

    Mnesilochos See l. 431n. above.

578-79] *Toxotes* Τοξότης (= Archer), the *Scythian* (see l. 431 above).

    and who . . . Monkeyed our Great and Dead The actor who aped Euripides.

580] *Masks were down* They had taken off the masks worn in all dramatic performances.

585-87] *fifty-drachma fine . . . walk bare* Apparently a vague reminiscence of a statement in a book owned jointly by B and EBB (*Recon-*

struction, A1888), John Potter's *Antiquities of Greece* (1820), 2.309, that women could be fined a thousand drachmas for appearing naked in public, the fines being posted on a plane-tree (F. M. Tisdel, "Browning's *Aristophanes' Apology*," *University of Missouri Studies* [1927] 3, 30).

588-89]   *Elaphion*   Ἐλάφιον (= little deer), a dancing-girl told by Euripides in *Thesmophoriazusae* 1172-75 to distract the Scythian's attention by dancing a Persian dance "with her dress tucked up" (ἀνακόλπασον).

593]   *more Peiraios-known*   Better known in the Piraeus district, which was full of foreign immigrants, including prostitutes like one mentioned in Alciphron (1.6.2) that all "the seaside youths go to revel with."

   Phaps   Φάψ (= wild pigeon), a relevant nickname, since doves were sacred to Aphrodite, the goddess of sex.

594-96]   *Tripped at the head . . . and foremost*   Elaphion's proximity to Aristophanes, implying the meretricious side of his character, again recalls Plato's *Symposium* 212 d, where the drunk Alcibiades is "led in and supported" by a flute-girl.

598]   *Archon's feast*   The dinner given by the state-official (ἄρχων = ruler) in charge of the dramatic festival.

601]   *baldness,—all his head one brow*   In *Peace* 767-74 Aristophanes tells the bald men in the audience to vote for the prize to be awarded to "the Baldhead . . . the noblest of poets, who has the forehead of a Man!"

604]   *dark-leaved chaplet*   The crown of ivy marking his victory in the theatre.

611   *vinous foam*   The image, followed by the marine one of a ship's figurehead, hints at sexuality, since Aphrodite (Ἀφροδίτη) means "sprung from the sea-foam."

614]   *Hephaistos*   The god of arts and crafts (as well as fire). His most famous artifact was the Shield of Achilles (*Iliad* 18.478- 613).

615]   *his gay brother*   That other son of Zeus, Heracles, whose "gay cheer" had so impressed Balaustion in *Balaustion's Adventure* (1046; this edition, 10.50).

615-16]   *imbrue that path . . . conqueror*   I.e., stain the sea purple (the color of kings and conquerors) along its path. "Purple" (πορφύρεος) was a stock Homeric epithet for the sea, e.g., in *Iliad* 1.481-82: "and as the ship went, the purple wave roared loudly along the keel." Another ingredient of B's image may have been the delightful story in Pollux (*Onomasticon* 1.45-47) of how Heracles, helped by his dog and stimulated by love for a Tyrian nymph, invented purple dye.

618]   *sense too plainly snuffed*   Sensuality all too easy to smell.

624-25]   *as the god . . . snakes*   Just as the infant Heracles grasped the snakes sent by Hera to kill him in his cradle. The snake-image for physical appetites again recalls Genesis (see ll. 422-25n. above, 2088-91n. below).

631-32]   *They had been wreathing . . . entry*   Notably in the person of Elaphion.

635]   *Hail, house, the friendly*   The unEnglish use of the definite article would be quite normal in Greek.

638]   *Victory's self*   The ostensible compliment to Balaustion's beauty indicates his own egotism: he sees her as a personification of his own victory, like the statue of Νίκη on the Acropolis. But that, according to Pausanias (*Description of Greece*, 3.15.7) was wingless, and "upsoaring" suggests the more usual representation of the goddess as winged.

641]   *rose-glow*   See l. 53n. above.

642]   *the Isle's unguent*   A perfumed ointment from Rhodes (used by a wife in *Lysistrata* 944 as an excuse for delaying sexual intercourse).

642-43]   *some diminished end / In* ion   A Greek noun-ending to indicate an affectionate diminutive (= dear little). The whole passage simulates the linguistic facility shown in Aristophanic comedy, e.g., in the invention of comic words.

643]   *Kallistion*   Little most beautiful.

644-50]   *Kubelion . . . Balaustion*   The meanings would be: *Kubelion* = violet; *Melittion* = bee; *Phibalion* = fig; *Korakinidion* = young raven; *Nettarion* = duckling; *Phabion* (diminutive of Phaps)   = pigeon, dove; *Rhoidion* = pomegranate; *Balaustion* = pomegranate-flower.

651]   *Folk have called me Rhodian*   The *Life of Aristophanes* included in Meineke stated: "Some people say he was a Rhodian from Lindus" (1.543).

652]   *if Helios wived*   See l. 35n. above.

653]   *As Pindaros sings somewhere*   In his *Olympian Odes*, vii.

655]   *phorminx*   See l. 311n. above.

       boy   The usual address for a domestic slave (παῖ), as in *Clouds* 18.

656-57   *baulk an ode . . . wing*   Stop me improvising an ode that is just taking off, i.e., is on the tip of my tongue.

658]   *frays*   Frightens away.

659]   *Superb*   Used in the Latin sense: proud, haughty.

660]   *Pho*   An exclamation expressing contemptuous rejection, but here used more like *faugh* or *foh* to express disgust, and perhaps associated by B with φῦ, which may conceivably have both those meanings in *Lysistrata* 295, 305.

       Komos   See l. 562n. above.

662]   *cheekband*   A cloth band (φορβειά) worn round the head and face of a flute-player, as in *Wasps* 582, to support the cheeks. The αὐλός, though usually translated "flute" (hence *fluting*) was really an end-blown, reeded pipe, quite unlike the side-blown, reedless modern flute.

663] *cuckoo-apple* A literal translation of κοκκύμηλον (= plum). The reader naturally assumes that cuckoo-apples were supposed to cause dumbness, but no evidence seems to have been traced for such a belief. B was probably remembering a remark in Athenaeus (2.49f-50a) that in Rhodes cuckoo-apples were called sloes, a fruit which is "laxative and ejects food." True to the scatological element in Aristophanic comedy, B makes Aristophanes hint that the chorus are shit-scared of the girl from Rhodes.

664] *Thasian* Wine from Thasos, recommended in Athenaeus (1.28e) as an instant cure for any kind of worry.

665] *Threttanelo* An onomatopoeic word for strumming a lyre, used in Aristophanes' *Plutus* 290 and 296 to express drunken euphoria, like that of the Cyclops in *Odyssey* 9.360-62.

666] *Neblaretai* νεβλάρεται (= it is brought to an end), a one-word fragment from Aristophanes' lost comedy, *Banqueters* Δαιταλεῖς; quoted and explained by Meineke (2.1046, xl-xli; see also C. Dahl, *MLN* 72 [1957], 271-73). B uses the word to mean: "Everything stops!"

666-67] *this earth-and-sun / Product* Balaustion, as a product of Helios and the island of Rhodes.

667] *looks wormwood . . . bitter herbs* B imitates a favorite idiom of Aristophanes: "looking mustard" or "cress" or "origanum" (*Knights* 631, *Wasps* 455, *Frogs* 603).

669] *By the cabbage* μὰ τὴν κράμβην, an oath, possibly Ionian, which is discussed in Athenaeus (9.370b-c).

670] *Chrusomelolonthion* χρυσομηλολόνθιον (= little golden beetle), an endearment addressed to a girl like Elaphion in *Wasps* 1341.

671] *Girl-goldling-beetle-beauty* An attempt to bring out the separate components of the same Greek word. *Girl* may be B's euphemism for the μηλο- (= apple) component, which (as μᾶλα) refers in *Lysistrata* 155 to "naked Helen's breasts."

674] *Artamouxia* The Scythian Archer's pronunciation of Artemisia, the name assumed by Euripides when, disguised as an old woman, he uses Elaphion to divert the Archer's attention from his prisoner (*Thesmophoriazusae* 1200-1). See ll. 588-89n. above.

675] *Hermes* The god of luck.

681] *goat's breakfast* An allusion to *Plutus* 295: "and you he-goats will have breakfast." The speaker, posing as Polyphemus leading out his flocks in the *Odyssey* (9.312-16), is leading a chorus of impoverished farm-workers to a promised land of wealth. Since he has just told them to follow "ἀπεψωλημένοι" (= with their foreskins retracted), and since he-goats (τράγοι) were proverbially lecherous, their "breakfast" had sexual implications. Thus B's allusion was a private joke for classicists, which could mean something different to Greekless Victorian readers: Elaphion punished for her *cowardice* by being sent off to feed the goat.

681-82]   *Fare afield / Ye circumcised of Egypt*   A delicate allusion to an Aristophanic pun: "To the plain, ye ψωλοί" (*Birds* 507), where the word for "plain" can also refer to female genitals, and ψωλοί can mean either "circumcised" or "with foreskin retracted." B prudently follows the one scholiast who missed the joke and simply remarked: "there were many circumcised in the days of the Egyptians" (*Scholia*, 222). But the unexplained allusion makes little sense in the context.

   pigs to sow   B's thoughts have apparently gone back to the same passage in the *Plutus,* where the speaker (now posing as Circe, who in *Odyssey* 10.282-83 turned her lovers into pigs) tells the chorus: "Follow your mother, pigs!" (*Plutus* 315).

683]   *the Priest's*   I.e., the house of the Archon managing the festival of Dionysus, and so acting as his priest (see l. 598n. above).

   to the crows   ἐς κόρακας, a common phrase for "go to hell!"

688-90]   *beat the sacred brow . . . Phoibos' bay*   I.e., he is protected from browbeating by his Bacchic crown of ivy (see l. 604 above), as well as by one of laurel, (sacred to Apollo, the god of poetry and music).

695]   *birds' wings, beetles' armour*   For *Birds* and *Peace* respectively.

696]   *three-crest skull-caps*   Helmets. B was probably remembering *Birds* 94, where the Hoopoe is asked: "What are those feathers [on your head]? What kind of three-crest helmet τριλοφία is that?"

   three days' salt-fish-slice   The "three days" rations" (σιτία τριῶν ἡμερῶν) issued to soldiers (*Acharnians* 197, *Peace* 312).

697]   *Three-banked ships*   Triremes (see l. 333 above).

   for these sham-ambassadors   I.e., war-ships will be wasted on transport for diplomats like those satirized in *Acharnians* 61-114, where the name of the Persian envoy, Pseudo-Artabas (= False-Measure) possibly suggested the *sham.*

700]   *Archinos and Agurrhios*   Identified by the scholiast (*Scholia*, 286) as the probable targets of *Frogs* 367-68 ("the politician who, once ridiculed in comedy . . . starts nibbling away at the comic poets' fees"): "for these men, when in charge of the public treasury, reduced the pay of comic writers, because they had been ridiculed in comedy." Discussing such economies, Meineke called Agyrrhius "a most worthless fellow [*futilissimus homo*] who tried to undermine the power and dignity of comedy, so that he could cut poets' pay" (Meineke, 1.42).

scrape your flint Be skinflints, mean and stingy.

701] *Flay your dead dog* An inappropriate approximation to "flog a dead horse," for the meaning required here is: "Flay your flayed dog," (i.e. go on making cuts even when there is nothing left to cut). Since just such a proverbial phrase (κύνα δέρειν δεδαρμένην) is quoted in *Lysistrata* 158, why did not B use it? Presumably because that passage was about use of a dildo.

702] *loss of leather* I.e., of "leather hanging down" (σκύτινον καθειμένον), the phrase used in *Clouds* 538 to describe the phallus worn by each chorus-member.

703] *We lose the boys' vote* The phrase quoted in the previous note is followed by the words: "to make the boys laugh" (τοῖς παιδίοις ἵν' ἦ γέλως, *Clouds* 539).

705] *baldhead* See l. 601n. above.

706] *Kudathenaian and Pandionid* The names are recorded in the first sentence of the *Life of Aristophanes* (Meineke, 1.542). He boasts of them because the first (his deme, i.e., district or community) means "glory of Athens," and the second (his tribe) was taken from that of a legendary king of Athens.

710] *'Manners and men,'* I.e., distinguishing between behavior and individuals, between generalized and personal satire; a reference to legal restrictions on Comedy, such as the decree mentioned by the Scholiast on *Birds* 1297: "that nobody should be attacked in comedy by name" (*Scholia*, 238). Such restrictions were discussed by Meineke (1.40-41).

711] *'Step forward, strip for anapaests!'* Quoted from *Acharnians* 627, where the words introduce the Parabasis (Παράβασις = a stepping forward), a regular part of Old Comedy which was in anapaestic meter. Here the chorus addressed the audience, speaking for the poet himself. The "stripping" (ἀποδύντες) implied both preparing for action, and divesting themselves of their stage characters so that the poet could explain his satiric purpose.

712] *No calling naughty people by their names* See l. 710n. above.

714] *chick-pease . . . plums* Thrown at the audience, like the barley-corns in *Peace* 962, or the nuts mentioned but not thrown in *Wasps* 58-59.

715] *Salabaccho* See l. 438n. above. The very name is enough to make Balaustion turn away in disgust (*As I turned*).

718] *Phrunichos, Choirilos!* Early tragic poets, here addressed contemptuously, (though Aeschylus' *Persae* may have owed something to Phrynichus' *Phoenissae*).

718-19] *had Aischulos / So foiled you at the goat-song?* Would Aeschylus have beaten you at tragedy (τραγῳδία = goat-song)? Athenaeus quotes a statement that "Aeschylus wrote his tragedies when drunk" (1.22a).

721-28]   *Kratinos*   In 423 B.C. he beat Aristophanes' *Clouds* with his *Putine* Πυτίνη (= flask covered with plaited willow twigs). An epigram quoted by Athenaeus (2.39c) makes Cratinus say: "Wine is a great horse for a fine poet, but you'll never produce anything good if you drink water."

724]   *style*   Stylus (στῦλος), a pointed implement for writing on wax tablets, with a blunt end used for erasing. In a revised parabasis (*Clouds* 523-24) Aristophanes said the play had given him more work than any of the others.

730-31]   *Thasian . . . Mendesian, merely*   In a passage of Athenaeus (1.29d-e) where Thasian was called "by far the best of all wines," Cratinus was quoted referring to an οἰνίσκος (= young or little wine) from Mende.

732]   *High priest*   The official in charge of the Dionysia. See ll. 598n. and 683n. above.

742-43]   *Good Genius*   ἀγαθὸς δαίμων (= Good Spirit, i.e., Good Fortune) to whom it was usual to drink at the end of a party. *Wasps* 525 stresses that this toast was drunk in neat wine (ἄκρατος = unmixed), and in Athenaeus (15.693c) a character in comedy is quoted as saying, rather like Aristophanes here: "draining that neat Good Daemon has completely shattered me."

745]   *that*   The still unspecified "something" of l. 741.

750]   *laughed*   An image possibly suggested by Aeschylus (see l. 20n. above).

765-66]   *our sophists . . . accidents*   A slight anachronism: the philosophical distinction between "substance" and "accident" was first developed by Aristotle (born about the time of Aristophanes' death).

768]   *cinct*   Girded, armed, equipped.

769]   *satyr sportive*   Obscenely playful, like the lecherous goat-legged attendants on Dionysus called satyrs.

   boss and spike   Like the boss or the spike at the center of a shield.

780]   *Good Genius!*   Balaustion repeats the phrase Aristophanes had used in a purely alcoholic sense (see l. 743 above), but restores its religious meaning (good divine spirit), and applies it to the poet almost in the English sense of *genius*.

793]   *learned in the laurel*   I.e., with an understanding of poetry.

794]   *lyric shell or tragic barbiton*   Apparently meant to suggest poetry in the two parts of a tragedy, the musical choruses and the dramatic dialogue, where the music was purely verbal. The first lyre was made by Hermes from the shell of a tortoise (χέλυς), a word used for a lyre in Euripides' *Alcestis* 447. The near-synonym *barbiton* (βάρβιτος = multi-stringed instrument) had just been used by Aristophanes in *Thesmophoriazusae* 137, when ridiculing the tragic poet Agathon.

797]   *how pulses flame a patriot-star*   How a patriot-star (= Aristophanes) sends out pulses of flame.

799]   *would she trust no meteor-blaze*   If only she would stop trusting transient and delusive forms of guidance.

806-25]   *Once, in my Rhodes . . . she sees now*   Balaustion's improbable story is a parable adapted from the myth of Andromeda (the subject of a painting by Caravaggio, a print of which hung over B's desk in his youth). It subtly rebukes Aristophanes for burlesquing Euripides' (lost) *Andromeda* in *Thesmophoriazusae* 1009-1159.

809]   *Who snatched*   Anyone who snatched (Greek often omits the antecedent of a relative).

813]   *Tuphon . . . mount*   Typhon or Typhoeus was a hundred-snake-headed monster punished for warring against the gods by imprisonment under Mount Etna.

817]   *a certain female child*   Balaustion. See l. 777 above.

829]   *He taught you tragedy!*   Aristophanes responds derisively to her veiled rebuke. Capitalized as for a god, *He* means not the semi-divine sea-creature of her parable, i.e., Aristophanes, but her wholly divine poet, Euripides; and *taught* is used in its technical sense (see l. 206n. above) to mean: "So he made you learn his *Andromeda* by heart, as if you had been a member of his cast!"   Hence Aristophanes' next question, since only men were allowed to act speaking parts (as opposed to mute ones like Elaphion's).

831]   *comic visor*   The grotesque mask worn by actors in comedy.

837]   *quite new Comedy*   The historical Aristophanes was a great innovator in the genre. Though his first nine plays represent what is known as Old Comedy, his last two, *Ecclesiazusae* and *Plutus*, belong to a class now labelled Middle Comedy, in which the Parabasis disappears, the chorus-role is much reduced, and so is the concern with specifically Athenian politics and society. In so-called New Comedy (c. 323-263 B.C.) costumes became more realistic, and plots more concerned with ordinary private life.

839]   *Elaphionize*   Behave like Elaphion in *Thesmophoriazusae*. See l. 588-89n. above.

845-46]   *Sousarion*   The legendary inventor of comedy, said to have come from Megara. The only surviving fragment of his work, quoted by Meineke, ends: "Women are a bad thing, but all the same, fellow-citizens, one can't live in a house without something bad—for it's a bad thing both to marry and not to marry" (Meineke, 2.3).

847]   *Chionides*   The first writer of comedy, mentioned by Aristotle (*Poetics* 1448a 34). Meineke took this to mean that "he was the most ancient of those whose comedies were both written down and worked out with some artistry, which is what I think those people meant who called him the protagonist of the old comedy" (Meineke, 1.28).

848-50]   *This club . . . mere polished steel*   An image possibly developed from Dryden's "Original and Progress of Satire": "there is still a vast difference betwixt the slovenly butchering of a man, and the fineness of a stroke that separates the head from the body, and leaves it standing in its place" (*Essays of John Dryden,* ed. W. P. Ker [New York, 1961], 2.93).

853]   *pashed*   Crushed, smashed.

855]   *last year unfortunate*   See l. 349n. above.

873]   *the orb*   Balaustion reverts to her image of the *patriot-star* (see l. 797 above).

880]   *My 'Grasshoppers'*   No trace has been found of any such play by Aristophanes; but the title and plot (described in ll. 1041-1112 below) are perfectly consistent with his known works.

881]   *'Little-in-the-Fields'*   The Rural Dionysia, referred to in *Acharnians* 250 as τὰ κατ' ἀγροὺς Διονύσια (= the in-the-fields Dionysia). The *Little* marks B's knowledge that the City Dionysia was also called the "Great (μεγάλα) Dionysia."

899]   *such tough work tasks soul*   The sequence of stressed monosyllables notably exemplify B's metrical onomatopoeia.

901]   *demiourgos!*   δημιουργός (= craftsman, maker), here used in the Platonic sense of Creator of the visible world; Plato, *Republic* 7.530a.

909]   *Ameipsias*   A rival comic poet whose *Connus* (Κόννος = Beard) beat Aristophanes' *Clouds* into third place when Cratinus came first in 423 B.C.; and whose *Comastae* (Κωμασταί = Revellers) beat *Birds* into second place in 414 B.C.

910]   *Salaminian cave*   A sneer at Euripides. See l. 284n. above.

915]   *dared and done*   From the last line of Christopher Smart's "A Song to David," also used in the first line of B's *La Saisiaz* (1878) and in other poems.   For the importance of Smart and this phrase to B, see the "Parleying with Christopher Smart," this edition, 16.48-57, 199-201; and *La Saisiaz*, this edition, 14.

916]   *clap-to*   Slam shut.

919]   *sky-scud*   Scudding clouds in the sky.

921]   *late*   Lately.

937]   *either*   Body or soul.

Iostephanos   ἰοστέφανος (= violet-crowned), an epithet applied to Aphrodite, goddess of beauty and love, to the Graces, and as here by Pindar (fragment 76) to Athens. Aristophanes twice quotes Pindar's application of the word to Athens (*Acharnians* 637, *Knights* 1329), both times to contrast the city's image and reputation with the actual folly of its citizens.

941]   *Kleophon*   A demagogue who persistently opposed peace with Sparta. Hence the last words of *Frogs* (1532): "And let Cleophon and anyone else who wants to, go and fight in his own country [i.e. Thrace, from which his mother was said to come]."

943]   *Dekeleia*   A small part of Attica occupied by the Spartans, which they offered to hand back, when negotiating for peace.

943-44]   *Kleonumos*   Another anti-peace politician, satirized as a ῥίψασπις (= one who throws away his shield in battle) in *Clouds* 353, *Wasps* 19-24, *Birds* 1473-81.

946]   *Orestes*   Observed by the chorus of *Birds* (1487-93) mugging passers-by in unlighted districts at night.

947]   *He wants your cloak as you his cudgelling*   A rather too elliptical version of "He wants to take your cloak from you as he wants you to take a beating from him," i.e., he wants to give you a beating in exchange for your cloak.

948]   *Melanthios*   A tragic poet seen queuing for Copaic eels in *Peace* 1005-14, and lamenting his failure to get one in words said to parody his own *Medea*. In *fat with fish* B possibly imitates Aristophanes' coined word for people like Melanthius, ἰχθυολύμης (= fatal to fish, *Peace* 814).

951]   *Parabasis*   See l. 711n. above.

952]   *agape at either end*   A combination of two Aristophanic terms of abuse, χαυνοπολίτης (= gaping citizen, *Acharnians* 635, see ll. 324-25 above); and χαυνόπρωκτος (= gaping-arsed, *Acharnians* 104). In his copy of T. A. Buckley's translation of Euripides B wrote: "If I could but spit in the face of this χαυνόπρωκτος!" He wrote it at the end of Buckley's Introduction, which after many sneering criticisms of Euripides' work concluded: "the study of Aristophanes is indissolubly connected with that of our author . . . the burlesque writer is greater than the tragedian" (F. M. Tisdel, "Browning's *Aristophanes' Apology*," *University of Missouri Studies* [1927], 2; *Reconstruction*, A889: *The Tragedies of Euripides, literally translated by Theodore Alois Buckley* [London, 1887], 2.xi).

958]   *'Wasps'*   A satire (422 B.C.) on old men who served on juries for the fee, and on Cleon, who used them to punish his political opponents. The chorus of jurors appeared as angry wasps.

963]   *'Wine-lees-poet'*   Writer of comedy. See l. 409n. above.

964-67]   *Less blunt . . . at his best*   The comparisons are with contemporary comic poets discussed and quoted by Meineke.

964]   *Telekleides*   Meineke called him   "a bitter opponent of Pericles," and quoted a fragment complaining that the Athenians had put themselves completely in Pericles' power (Meineke, 1.86).

964-65]   *less obscene / Than Murtilos*   The words σκῶμμα ἀσελγές (= filthy joke) occur in a fragment attributed to Myrtilus (Meineke,

2.418); one of his lost plays (Τιτανόπανες) was thought by Meineke (1.100-1) to be about pederasts.

965] *Hermippos* Murtilos's brother, mentioned disparagingly in *Clouds* 557. That his plays were *obscene* was probably inferred by B from Meineke's belief "that Hermippus produced a book of indecent poems," and from Meineke's association of a word used by Hermippus (σεσαλακωνισμένην) with Aristophanes' Salabaccho and with male homosexuals (Meineke, 1.96, 98-99 ; see l. 448 above).

966] *In elegance for Eupolis himself* Meineke wrote of a "sublimity in Eupolis' poetry, marvellously combined with the charms of grace and elegance" (Meineke, 1.108). For Aristophanes, however, Eupolis was "a wicked man who wickedly [κακὸς κακῶς] distorted my *Knights*" (*Clouds* 554-55).

967] *pungent as Kratinos* See ll. 721-28n. above. On the epigram there quoted Plutarch commented: "some comic poets seem to temper their own pungency [πικρίαν] by making jokes against themselves" (Meineke, 1.47).

970] *in Megara* See ll. 845-46n. above.

970-82] *Some funny village-man . . . our Comedy* Freely paraphrased from an early account of the origin of Comedy in Meineke (1.538).

973] *phyz* Physiognomy, face.

974] *mounted cart* Some partly obliterated words in an inscription were conjecturally deciphered by Bentley to read: "since the time when comedies were carried about on carts" [ἐν ἀπήναις], which Meineke called "hardly credible" (1.25).

983] *Mullos . . . Euetes* Names included by Meineke in a list of "the most ancient comic poets in Attica" (Meineke, 1.18)

987] *Morucheides . . . Surakosios* Archons 440-439 and 416-415 B.C. respectively (F. M. Tisdel, "Browning's *Aristophanes' Apology*," *University of Missouri Studies* [1927], 32), periods during which personal satire in comedy and the writing of comedy by members of the Areopagus council were legally prohibited (Meineke, 1.40-43). Syracosius was cast in *Birds* 1297 as a jay (κίττα), i.e., a silly chatterer.

988] *No more naming citizens* See l. 710n. above.

996] *Tragic Trilogy* The three tragedies produced by each competing poet—though these did not necessarily form a trilogy in the modern sense of dealing with a single subject, like the *Oresteia* of Aeschylus.

999] *the contemptuous fourth* The satyric play (a kind of burlesque) that normally followed the three tragedies. It had a chorus of satyrs, half-animal creatures of the wild with an insatiable appetite for wine and sex.

1003] *some five such* The only one to survive complete is the *Cyclops* (perhaps 412 B.C.) burlesquing the Polyphemus episode in *Odyssey* 9.105-542.

1005-6] *"Alkestis"* Produced 438 B.C. after *Cretan Women, Alcmaeon in Psophis,* and *Telephus.* Its only "satyric" features were a semi-comic slanging-match between Admetus and his father, a tipsy Heracles, and a happy ending.

1010] *Sokrates, meteors, moonshine* In *Clouds* 227 Socrates explains his suspension from a crane in a basket as facilitating research into "τὰ μετέωρα πράγμστα" (= meteoric things, though the Greek adjective means, not meteors, but "up in the air, celestial, astronomical"). In *Clouds* 171-72 Socrates was pictured "gaping upwards" (κεχηνώς) to study "the paths and revolutions of the moon."

'Life's not Life' In *Alcestis* 521 Admetus, asked if his wife is still alive, replies: "She is and is no longer." In *Frogs* 1082 Euripides' heroines are accused of saying that "living is not being alive" (οὐ ζῆν τὸ ζῆν), and *Frogs* 1477 parodies a fragment of Euripides' lost *Polyidus*: "but who knows if living is dying?" (*Fragmenta,* 560, No. 638).

1011] *'The tongue swore . . . remains,'* Hippolytus 612, which Aristophanes has just parodied in *Thesmophoriazusae* 275-76.

1013] *digested* In a physical as well as mental sense. True to Aristophanes' scatological humor, B makes him hint that such literary products are mere excreta.

head low and heels in heaven In *Acharnians* 410 Euripides is said to be writing poetry ἀναβάδην, which the scholiast (*Scholia,* 14) interprets to mean ἄνω τοὺς πόδας ἔχων (= having his feet up, i.e., simply lying down); but B makes those words imply a position as topsy-turvy as the poet's ideas (cf. l. 2152 below).

1022] *leek-and-onion-plait* *Frogs* 621-22 implies that being beaten with "leek or horn-onion' is relatively painless.

1029] *'The Birds'* An allegorical fantasy (414 B.C.), more lyrical than anything he had produced before, and generally admired for its poetry.

1040-1121] *"Grasshoppers . . . Tragic, Comic, Lyric excellence!* This comedy seems to have been dreamt up by B, on the basis of Aristophanes' extant works. Thus its allegorical fantasy is in the manner of *Birds,* and its title presupposes Aristophanes' association of the Tettix with the good old days and with the upper classes (see l. 451 above). The grasshoppers' leading role in the action may also have been suggested by the fable told in Plato's *Phaedrus* (258e-259d), that the Tettixes were once men who, after the birth of the Muses, were so entranced by music and poetry that they could spend their lives singing, without needing any food or drink.

1042] *Alkibiades* An aristocratic politician (c. 451-404 B.C.) remarkable for his good looks and intellectual brilliance.
1043] *Triphales* Τριφάλης (= three-phallus, i.e., oversexed), the title of a lost play by Aristophanes thought to have satirized Alcibiades (Meineke, 2.1163) for his sexual excesses, an aspect of his character implied in Plato's *Symposium* (219 a-d).
   Trilophos Τρίλοφος (= three-crest), like a Homeric helmet, i.e., a War-hero.
1044] *Whom I called Darling-of-the-Summertime* The hyphenated name suggests that B was trying to invent some typical Aristophanic coinage, perhaps Θερείφιλος (dear to Summer), on the analogy of Theophilus (Θεόφιλος = dear to God), and θερείποτος (= drinking, i.e., watered in summer).
1047] *Autochthon* Αὐτόχθων (= of the land itself), i.e., of native origin, aboriginal, the status indicated by wearing a golden tettix. See l. 451n. above.
1048] *sip the dew* According to Aristotle (*History of Animals*, iv, 532b) "the grasshopper . . . feeds only on dew."
1053] *Taügetan* Adjective of Taygete, a nymph from whom the Spartans claimed descent. A mountain-range west of Sparta, mentioned by the Spartans in *Lysistrata* 117, was named after her.
1056] *morbifies* Makes diseased or unhealthy. B adapts the biblical precept (Colossians 3:5) already adapted by Tennyson ("St. Simeon Stylites," 176-77) to: "Mortify your flesh."
1064] *Cockered no noddle up* Pampered no head, i.e., brain.
   A, b, g A, β, γ, the first three letters of the Greek alphabet (= the English A B C).
1066] *Ruppapai* In *Frogs* 1069-73 Aeschylus accuses Euripides of teaching young men to chatter, and the crews of state-galleys to argue with their officers; whereas in the old days their only linguistic skill was "to ask for barley-bread, and say ῥυππαπαῖ," a rhythmical cry to help rowers keep time.
1067-68] *take your ease . . . tier beneath* A quasi-Aristophanic pun, since "do one's ease" or "ease oneself" were euphemisms for "defecate."
1072] *Gathered the tunic well about the ham* A concern for decency adapted from *Clouds* 973-74, in a similar account of ancient schooling.
1073] *Remembering 'twas soft sand* A cryptic line explained by *Clouds* 975-76: "Then, when they got up, they had to smooth [the sand], taking care not to leave an imprint [of their bottoms and private parts] for lovers of young boys to study."
1075] *cross his legs* Forbidden in *Clouds* 983.
1076-77] *myrtle bough . . . sing for supper* In *Clouds* 1355-73 the father

tells his son after supper to sing a song by the early poet, Simonides (556-468 B.C.), and then to take a myrtle wreath and recite something from Aeschylus; but the son replies that music with drinks is out of fashion, that Simonides was a bad poet, and that Aeschylus was "full of noise." When told to produce something clever and up to date, he recites a bit of Euripides about a brother having intercourse with his sister (from the lost play, *Aeolus*).

1078]   *Mitulené*   An anomalous transliteration (corresponding to the later Latin spelling, *Mitylene*) of Μυτιλήνη (*Mutilene* = Mytilene), the chief city of Lesbos. Pittacus of Mytilene was one of the Seven Sages. As a reforming legislator, he doubled the penalty for alcohol-related offences (one punishment for the drinking and one for the crime)—hence presumably Aristophanes' prejudice against him. B was evidently thinking of Plato's *Protagoras* (338e-347a), where a lost poem of Simonides (*Greek Lyric III*, ed. and tr. D. A. Campbell [London, 1991], 432-37) questioning the truth of Pittacus' dictum, "it is not easy to be good" is exhaustively discussed.

1079-81]   *Jumped into hedge . . . scratched them in again*   A parable apparently invented by B to express Aristophanes' contempt for subtle and inconclusive moral arguments, such as Plato attributed to the sophists in the *Protagoras*.

1080]   *Oedipous*   Οἰδίπους (= swollen-foot). Oedipus was so named from the effect of having his feet pinned together when exposed as a child). See l. 6n. above.

1082]   *Phaidras*   See l. 420n. above.

Augés   Auge was the mother of Telephus, the subject of a lost play by Euripides, much ridiculed by Aristophanes in *Acharnians* (415-48) because its hero appeared in rags, and his mother, "giving birth in a temple" (Nauck, xxxvii).

Kanakés   Canace, daughter of Aeolus, was the incestuous sister mentioned in ll. 1076-77 above.

1084]   *Marathon*   A district of Attica where the Athenians defeated the Persians in 490 B.C. In *Clouds* 985-86 the old type of education was said to have bred the men who fought at Marathon, and the famous victory symbolized for Aristophanes all the old-fashioned values (*Acharnians* 692-701, *Knights* 781-82).

1085]   *Antistrophé*   The second section of a choral ode, metrically corresponding with the strophe, or first section.

praise of Peace   The theme of the chorus in *Peace* 1127-71.

1088-89]   *Romp with one's Thratta . . . bathing*   Paraphrased from that chorus (1138-39): "kissing the Thratta (τὴν Θρᾷτταν =Thracian slave-girl) while the wife is washing herself."

1092]   *Thasian grape*   See l. 664n. above.

1095]   *Pour peasoup*   In *Peace* 1136 "roasting the chickpeas" is done while kissing Thratta.

1096]   *tunic at his heels*   See l. 565n. above. The substitution of "tunic" for "kid-skin" implies that wine leads to sex.

1098]   *Parabasis*   See l. 711n. above.

1100-17]   *None of the self-laudation . . . good taste*   The self-laudatory Parabasis of the "Grasshoppers" seems modelled on that of *Peace* (735-74)

1109]   *Bald-head*   See l. 601n. above, and *Peace* 767-74.

     Aigina's boast   From the "Life of Aristophanes" in Meineke (1.543): "Some say that he was Aeginetan."

1114-15]   *dinner . . . Prutaneion*   B was probably thinking of Socrates who, when required at his trial to propose an alternative to the death-penalty, suggested that he should be given free meals in the Prytaneion Πρυτανεῖον (= Town Hall; Plato, *Apology*, 36d).

1120]   *one more gird at old Ariphrades*   He had girded (jeered) at him in *Knights* 1284-85 as   "abusing his own tongue in filthy pleasures, licking up the revolting dew of brothels," and repeated the charge in *Wasps* 1280-83. B bowdlerizes cunnilingus into cannibalism.

1121]   *scorpion-like . . . human flesh*   Scorpions are actually insectivores, not man-eaters; but B's train of thought may perhaps be traced to *Thesmophoriazusae* 524-30, where the chorus, shocked by the shamelessness of the disguised Mnesilochus, parodies the proverb: "There's a scorpion under every stone" (cf. Athenaeus, 15.695d, No. 20). Mnesilochus has just been describing (505-16) how a wife tried to convince her husband that a baby imported in a basket was her own: "Look, his penis is just like yours, all twisted [στρεβλὸν] like a pine-cone." Hence, perhaps, the *tail-twist* metaphor that follows (see *OED, tail,* sb. 5c).

1122]   *Ever finds out some novel infamy*   See *Knights* 1282-83: "not just wicked, or I shouldn't have noticed it, nor even just totally wicked—but he has invented a new type of wickedness."

1125]   *each tail-twist at ink-shed time*   I.e., each twisted thing about him, once I put pen to paper (or rather, stylus to wax tablet). In *Frogs* 775 there is a similar sneer at Euripides' λυγισμοί καὶ στροφαί (= twists and turns). But see also l. 1121 above for a possible double entendre.

1129]   *Housebreakers!*   I.e., my audience were a lot of villains anyway. In *Frogs* 770-76 Euripides is said to have been a mad success in Hades with an audience of "thieves, bag-snatchers, parricides, and housebreakers (τοιχωρύχοι)." Later (*Frogs* 807-8) Aeschylus is said to have gone down badly with the Athenians—"perhaps he thought them a lot of housebreakers." Thus B's Aristophanes presents himself as another fine artist misjudged by a rotten audience.

1130] *This pattern-purity* This paragon of purity, i.e., "*Grasshoppers.*"

1131] *Rural Dionusia* τά κατ' ἀγροὺς Διονύσια (= the in-the-fields Dionysia), mentioned in *Acharnians* 250, as opposed to the great city festival.

1132] *Ameipsias* See l. 909n. above.

the genuine stuff The coarse material of traditional comedy.

1134-35] *Karkinos . . . spinning-tops* Καρκίνος (= Crab), author of 160 tragedies, but was also a dancer, as were his sons. Aristophanes had ridiculed the family in *Wasps* 1505-15.

1137] *boys' frank laugh* See l. 703n. above.

1143] *exomis* ἐξωμίς (= one-sleeved vest), worn by working men, like the male chorus in *Lysistrata* 662, or the slaves in *Wasps* 444; here symbolizing the popular appeal of comedy, where a *purple sleeve* would imply its gentrification (see l. 119n. above).

1145] *plaits* Tricks, dodges: an old sense of the word, possibly adopted here because it hints at the female chorus's hairdo, while offering alliteration with *please*, and also with the Greek πλόκος (= braided hair) and πλοκή (= a complication in a dramatic plot).

1148] *No Parachoregema* Not just a παραχορήγημα (= a small subsidiary chorus added to the cast for a single episode, like the chorus of children in *Peace* 114-49; *Scholia*, 174), but two full choruses, one female, one male.

1150] *Aristullos* Mentioned in *Ecclesiazusae* 646-50 and *Plutus* 314-15 as having once had his face smeared with dung; but the former passage seems to satirize the free sex advocated in Plato's *Republic* (5.457c-465b), and Meineke accepted that in both passages Aristullos meant Plato himself (Meineke, 1.287-8; 2.1162).

1151] *His plan* Not quite Plato's plan, which merely proposed equality of opportunity for women (*Republic* 5.454d 7- 455e 2); though it explicitly accepted the possibility of "ἀρχούσας" as well as "ἄρχοντας" i.e., female as well as male "rulers" (vii 540c 5).

1152] *'A-field, ye cribbed of cape!'* B's version of *Birds* 507: "ψωλοὶ πεδίονδε (= To the plain, with foreskins retracted!)" See ll. 681-82n. above. Knowing that πεδίον (= plain) could also mean the female genitals, B prudently inserted *plough*, barely hinting at the meaning of ψωλοὶ by *cribbed of cape*, which ostensibly means "wearing shorter cloaks than women, i.e., men," but implicitly "with *capes* off."

1153-54] *exempt from service . . . boys cried 'Brave!'* Almost meaningless in an innocently agricultural context; for this time B contrives no double meaning to conceal the point of *Birds* 507. The *stupendous show* of *exemption from service* must be some stage-business with the male chorus's leather phalluses to express the erectile failure predicted in *Ecclesiazusae* 619-20: "If old men like us have to mate with ugly women first, how can we expect our penises not to fail, before reaching the point you mention [i.e. of mating with pretty ones]?" The *boys'* reaction follows from *Clouds* 538-39 (see l. 703 above).

1157]   *board and binding-strap*   In *Thesmophoriazusae* 930-31 the Toxotes is told to tie Mnesilochus on to a board. See ll. 577-78n. above.

1159]   *both shrewish wives*   According to the *Life* in Nauck's edition, Euripides found his first wife (Mnesilochus' daughter Choerile) "undisciplined" and divorced her, then married a second wife, and found her even worse (Nauck, vi.65-72).

1160]   *'Gravity'* . . . *'Sophist-lore'*   See l. 364n. above. The sophists were seen by Plato as unscrupulous arguers, and satirized in *Clouds* both for that, and for subverting morality and religion by foolish scientific theories. The allegorical names recall the paired personifications of Just and Unjust Argument in *Clouds,* and the prostitute playing Reconciliation in *Lysistrata* (See ll. 438-39n. above).

1161]   *hetairai*   ἑταίραι (= girl-friends), often in the sense of prostitutes.

1163]   *Murrhiné*   Μυρρίνη (= Myrtle [sacred to Aphrodite]), the name of the wife who tantalizes her husband in *Lysistrata* 850-955.

        Acalanthis   Ἀκαλανθίς (= greenfinch), the name of a prostitute in Alciphron's *Letters of Parasites* 28.3.64.

1163-64]   *beautiful / Their whole belongings*   An allusion to Opora Ὀπώρα (= end of summer, fruit-time) and Theoria Θεωρία (= play-going or games-watching) personified attendants of Peace presented, according to the scholiast, "as prostitutes" (*Scholia,* 187) in *Peace* 520-26, where Theoria is complimented on her pretty face and sweet breath. The other *belongings* were doubtless inferred by B from those of Reconciliation in *Lysistrata* 1155-70 (see ll. 438-39 above).

1166]   *nuts and sweetmeats on the mob*   See l. 714n. above.

1168]   *Kalligeneia, the frank last-day rite*   Καλλιγένεια (= producer of beautiful babies), a sacrifice made to Artemis on the third day of the Thesmophoria (Alciphron, *Letters of Farmers,* 37.3.39; *Thesmophoriazusae* 80). The *frank* (i.e. obscene) character of the rite, was possibly inferred by B from Alciphron's *Letters of Prostitutes,* 19.2.4, where Glycera swears "by Calligeneia, in whose temple I now am." Cf. *Oxford Classical Dictionary* (3rd ed., ed. S. Hornblower and A. Spawforth [Oxford, 1996]), 1509: "The Festival included obscenity . . . Otherwise, the secrets of the Thesmophoria have been well kept."

1171]   *chorus-cap*   I.e., speaking through the chorus, in the Parabasis.

1172]   *your hands to your faces!*   I.e., cover your faces in shame.

1173-74] *Summon no more . . . places* Paraphrased from a fragment of the Second *Thesmophoriazusae* (see l. 349 above): "Stop invoking the curly-haired Muses or calling the Olympian Graces to join your chorus; for they are here, as the Producer can tell you" (Meineke, 2.1086, No. 16, where Meineke explains that Aristophanes is boasting to his uninspired rivals).

1177] *choragos* χοραγός, the rich citizen who paid the expenses of the chorus and the whole production. Scrupulously authentic, B used the Athenian form of the word, though *choregus* (χορηγός) has always been more familiar in English.

mutes / And flutes Non-speaking extras like Murrhine and Acalanthis, and flute-girls (see l. 99 above).

1182] *Lusandros* Lysander (Λύσανδρος), the Spartan general who later occupied Athens.

1183] *Euboia* One of Athens' most useful tributary allies, which had revolted against her in 411 B.C.

1184] *the Confederation* The Delian League, an alliance of Greek cities originally formed to fight off the Persians, but later made by Pericles more like an Athenian empire.

1185] *The Great King's Eye* βασιλέως ὀφθαλμός, confidential adviser to the Persian King, as deputy overseer of the realm. In *Acharnians* 91-124 he is the wily diplomat, Pseudo-Artabas. See l. 697n. above.

1187] *Kompolakuthes* κομπολακύθης (= boaster), a word applied in *Acharnians* 588-89 to Lamachus, a general representing the war-policy. Appearing with a huge plume on his helmet, he is asked "What ever bird did that come from? A Compolacuthes?" Hence B's *peacock*, taken from an earlier passage in the same play (*Acharnians* 63).

1189] *Strattis* A prolific writer of Old Comedy, a *friend* of Aristophanes in the sense of being a fellow-parodist of Euripides.

1191] *klepsudra* κλεψύδρα (= water-clock), mentioned in *Wasps* 857-58 as a speech-timer in law-courts, not a cooking-timer, as here; and the *click* sounds more like modern clockwork than dropping water.

1192-94] *shark's-head . . . cocks'-brain-sauce* In Athenaeus (7.286a) the Rhodian γαλεός (= a kind of shark) is called worth stealing at the cost of your life, if you can't afford to buy it. Athenaeus (2.67 c-d) also mentions *Sphettian vinegar* in a culinary context, quoting Aristophanes in a quasi-medical one (*Plutus* 720). *Silphium* (juice of the laserwort) occurs often in Aristophanes, notably in *Ecclesiazusae* 1165-71, where it figures, together with γαλεο- (= shark) among the linguistic ingredients of a seven-line comic polysyllable, used to describe the gourmet-menu of a public feast. The *cocks'-brain-sauce* probably came from another luxury menu in Athenaeus which included a kid's head, boiled whole, followed by young cockerels (ἀλεκτρυόνων νεοσσοί) and a tit-bit prepared with silphium (4.147d).

1197]   *Salt without thyme*   I.e., witty but not spicy. Thinking of supper, Strattis employs a culinary image, possibly suggested to B by a neighbouring passage in Athenaeus (3.79d-e) explaining that vinegar and thyme make the gastric juice (χυμός) more acid, whereas figs and other foods make it more salty.

1200]   *Kleonclapper*   An alliterative coinage implying not applause of Cleon (see l. 401 above) but, in an earlier sense of *clap*, striking him resounding blows.

1205]   *crocus-vested*   Agathon, notorious for his effeminacy, had in *Thesmophoriazusae* 136-38 worn a dress dyed with saffron (made from crocus stigmas). See l. 317n. above.

1206-26]   *When suddenly . . . night resumed him*   See ll. 741 and 745 above. Thus B dramatizes a single sentence of the *Life of Euripides* in Nauck: "And they say that even Sophocles, hearing that Euripides had died, stepped forward himself in a dark grey [φαιῷ] cloak, and led in his chorus and actors ungarlanded at the proagon [προαγών = ceremonial parade of actors etc. before a dramatic contest], and the audience burst into tears" (Nauck, vi.43-46).

1208]   *Babaiax*   βαβαιάξ, an exclamation of surprise, used in *Acharnians* 64 in response to the Persian diplomat's outlandish dress.

1209]   *Aristullos*   I.e., Plato. See l. 1150 above.

1210]   *question touching Comic Law*   At the end of Plato's *Symposium* Socrates "was left arguing with Aristophanes and Agathon, and forcing them to agree that it took the same talents to write Comedy and Tragedy" (323 d3-5).

1213]   *Strattis . . . the sneak*   Because he himself had parodied the *Philoctetes* of Sophocles (the *majesty* to whom he is now showing such reverence).

1230-31]   *in extreme old age . . . gods for visitants*   B was probably remembering Plutarch's *Life of Numa*, 4: "And there is a story, for which much evidence has been preserved to this day, that Asclepius was entertained as a guest by Sophocles even during his lifetime."

1232-34]   *Why did he . . . crown of gold?*   The story is told in the ancient *Life of Sophocles* (xii): "When this golden crown was stolen from the Acropolis, Heracles told Sophocles in a dream to search an empty house on the right as he went in—where it had been hidden. He reported it to the people, received the one-talent reward which had been advertised, and dedicated a shrine to Heracles the Informer[ʽΗρακλῆς Μηνυτής]."

1232-41]   *Herakles . . . the Judge*   In Cicero's version of the story (*De*

Divinatione, i.54) Μηνυτής (= Informer) is correctly translated into Latin as *Index*. Perhaps B misread it there as *Iudex* (= Judge), or perhaps it was so misprinted in his edition of Cicero. Otherwise his three references to a *judge* seem pointless.

1235] *He who restored Akropolis the theft* Restored the stolen goods to the Acropolis, i.e., Sophocles.

1237] *certain other crowns* Ivy-crowns for winning tragic contests. See l. 249n. above.

1238] *who now visits Herakles* I.e., the dead Euripides. But why should he visit Heracles, who was not, as B seems to imply, one of the judges in Hades? Presumably because in *Frogs* 35-118 Dionysus does indeed visit Heracles to ask him the quickest route to Hades, so that he can rejoin his favorite poet, Euripides. Heracles tells him how to get there, though in his view Euripides' poetry is "simply rotten stuff"(ἀτεχνῶς γε παμπόνηρα, 106).

1239-41] *Medeia . . . Euphorion* Euripides came only third with *Medea* in 431 B.C. Sophocles came second, and Aeschylus' son Euphorion came first, with a play possibly written by his father.

1245-49] *Put capitally . . . to sea* In *Peace* 695-99 Trygaeus says: "Sophocles is becoming Simonides . . . now that he's old and rotten, he'd sail on a hurdle to make some money." Simonides (556-468 B.C.), according to the scholiast, "seems to have been the first to introduce meanness into music, and write songs for money" (*Scholia*, 192).

1250] *Philonides* A writer of Old Comedy often quoted in Athenaeus. He produced Aristophanes' first play, *Banqueters*, under his own name (Meineke, 1.102).

 Kallistratos Another producer of early plays by Aristophanes. He may have written comedies himself.

1253-54] *turned priest . . . Alkon* From a corrupt passage in the *Life of Sophocles* (11): "He held the priesthood of halon [ἄλων = threshing-floor], who Hero . . . with Asclepius . . ." Meincke emended the inappropriate word to the name Alcon (Ἀλκων), a son of Ares (Lemprière, 30); and B's *half-hero* was presumably meant as an extra sneer: Heroes (Ἥρωες) were normally thought half-human, half-divine, but Alcon was barely a quarter-divine.

1254-55] *visited . . . Asklepios' self* See ll. 1230-31n. above.

1257-59] *Iophon's the manager . . . sonship* Sophocles' son Iophon wrote tragedies himself. He won first prize in 435 B.C., and came second to Euripides in 428 B.C. In *Frogs* 78-79 Aristophanes implied that Iophon's plays were written by his father. The hint here of bad feeling between the two was probably suggested by the story in the *Life of Sophocles* (13) that he "presented Iophon in a play being jealous of him, and accusing him before other members of his clan, of suffering from senile dementia."

1260]   *dozen-dozen prodigies*   He was said to have written more than 120 plays.

1262]   *ten years later*   They were born c. 496 and c. 485 respectively.

1264]   *good-natured*   A translation of εὔκολος, as Aristophanes calls him in *Frogs* 82.

1265]   *no bad panegyric*   I.e., Sophocles' theatrical gesture at Euripides' death. B's scansion requires the fourth letter to be an accented long *e* (ή), as in the word it comes from πανήγυρις (= public festival or assembly).

1281]   *what sophists style—the wall of sense*   The thought is Platonic (from the phenomenal world of appearances Aristophanes glimpses the real world of Ideas); the image was possibly suggested by the famous cave-simile of *Republic* 7.515a-b, where the prisoners see only the shadows of people and things passing behind a wall (τειχίον). Just before *Aristophanes' Apology* was written, Plato's simile had been given a new slant in the "Conclusion" to Pater's *Renaissance* (1873): "Experience . . . is ringed round for each one of us by that thick wall of personality through which no real voice has ever pierced on its way to us, or from us to that which we can only conjecture to be without."

1288]   *Should life . . . death, the rest*   As suggested by Euripides (see l. 1010 above).

1294]   *two years since . . . "Ploutos"*   The surviving *Plutus* was not produced until 388 B.C.; this was an earlier *Plutus*, discussed by Meineke (2.1130-31) as Πλοῦτος πρότερος, produced in 408 B.C.

1295]   *the cold grave-bearded bard*   According to the *Life* in Nauck (v.25-26, vi.62-63) Euripides "grew a long beard," and "looked gloomy, abstracted, austere, and laughter-hating."

1305]   *But those Art leans on lag*   Unless artists fail to move forward.

1309]   *This step decides your foot from old to new*   Your foot decides to take this innovating step.

1310-13]   *Proves you relinquish . . . veritable men think, say and do*   B seems to assume that the first *Plutus* went much further than the surviving second one towards the relative realism of New Comedy (see l. 837 above).

1317]   *while day craved no flame*   While daylight made such artificial brilliance unnecessary.

1319]   *Horses*   I.e., *Knights* (Ἱππεῖς = horsemen), but the actual title would not have supported the charge that these four plays were on non-human subjects.

1321]   *The new adventure for the novel man*   A thought conceivably inspired by the name of the greatest New Comedy writer, Menander (Μένανδρος) which might fancifully be derived from μένω (= await) and ἀνδρός, part of ἀνήρ (= a man).

1330]   *Antiope*   See ll. 290-91n. above.

1331]   *Phoinissai*   See l. 290n. above.

1332-33]   *great and awful Victory / Accompany my life*   A slightly inaccurate quotation from the final choruses of both *Phoenissae* (1764-65) and *Orestes* (1691-93): "O greatly reverend (μέγα σεμνὴ) Victory, may you hold fast to my life, and never cease to crown me."

1333]   *Maketis*   Μακέτις (= Macedonian land).

1340]   *Pentelikos*   A mountain ten miles from Athens, from which white marble was quarried for the Parthenon.

1343]   *would it*   If it tries to.

1348]   *Archon*   See l. 598n. above.

1351]   *Good Genius*   See ll. 742-44n. above.

1352]   *Strattis*   See l. 1189n. above.

1354-74]   *She who evolves superiority . . . by the Muse*   This view of Comedy neatly combines B's evolutionary theory (first outlined in *Paracelsus* 5.872-84, this edition, 1.264-65) of failure as a germ of success with Plato's theory of Ideas.

1362-73]   *perfect man . . . the fine form . . . high-and-fair exists / In that ethereal realm*   According to Plato each individual on earth is a poor imitation of a perfect Form or Idea (᾽Ιδέα) existing eternally in heaven, but perceptible only by the mind (*Republic* 6.507b). In Plato's *Symposium* 210 such perception is the end-product of a process beginning with the love of physically beautiful people. Strattis makes it begin with a comic reaction to *ugsome* (= ugly, loathsome) ones, whose *divergency from* the ideal *type* is simply the effect of their having come down to *earth,* instead of flying about heaven, as all souls originally do (Plato's *Phaedrus* 235b-c).

1374]   *Lift*   Lifted (poetic past participle).

1380]   *Lamachos*   See l. 1187n. above.

1382]   *Philokleon*   Φιλοκλέων (= lover of Cleon), the old man obsessed with jury-sitting in *Wasps*. See l. 958n. above.

1384]   *dikast*   See l. 89n. above.

1384]   *obol*   The smallest silver coin, worth a sixth of a drachma (= about three of the halfpenny coins current in UK until 1984).

1385]   *Paphlagonian*   Παφλαγών (= splutterer, blusterer), a name under which Cleon was satirized in the *Knights*.

1387]   *Trugaios, Pisthetairos, Strepsiades*   Τρύγαιος (= harvester), Πεισθέταιρος or Πεισέταιρος (= persuasive friend), Στρεψιάδης (= twister), names of the heroes of *Peace, Birds,* and *Clouds* respectively.

1402]   *substitute thus things for words*   B imitates a favorite Greek antithesis between the real and the ostensible, practice and preaching, deed and word, (ἔργον and λόγος).

1408]   *Barrier about . . .*   The slightly odd metaphor, apparently expressing the Muse's "instruction" to *her poet* rather than *man's soul*, implies that Tragedy isolates and displays in an ideal form deliberately differentiated from everyday life, the heroic potential of the human spirit.

1411]   *Pour to . . . ministrant*   I.e., drink a toast to Euripides.

1412]   *Hippolutos*   Hero and title of of the play about Phaedra (produced 429 B.C.). See l. 420n. above.

1413]   *Ariphrades*   See l. 1120n. above.

1414]   *Bellerophon*   Hero of a lost play by Euripides (Nauck, xxiv; *Fragmenta*, 443-53), presumably mentioned here because like *Hippolytus* he suffered for his purity when a married woman fell in love with him; and like Heracles, the hero of the play to be "transcribed," successfully completed some impossible tasks (see Homer, *Iliad* 6.160-90).

1415]   *Kleonumos*   See ll. 943-44n. above.

1416]   *his Theseus . . . man once more*   When, after being rescued from Hades by Heracles, he showed his gratitude by dissuading his rescuer from suicide, and giving him sanctuary in Athens (HL 1214-1418, see also ll. 4844-5070 below).

1417]   *Alkibiades*   See ll. 1042-43n. above.

1422-26]   *But some god's . . . sphere*   Aristophanes' self-aggrandizing tribute to Euripides seems to conceal sly mockery of Balaustion's favorite play,—in which Admetus is enabled to "*scape necessity* by Alcestis' *self-sacrifice,* and Heracles' *power.*"

1426]   *By power displayed, forbidden this strait sphere*   By a display of power which is not allowed in this narrow world.

1429]   *The Thasian! All, the Thasian, I account!*   I reckon all that must be the result of drinking too much.

1439]   *Struck to the heart by lightning*   See l. 481n. above.

1439-42]   *Sokrates / Would question us . . . his friend*   Socrates (whose teaching-method was cross-questioning, would have bored them with literary criticism until they wished him as dead as Euripides (see l. 359 above).

1443]   *Agathon*   See ll. 317n. and 1205n. above.

1456-57]   *Nikias*   A conscientious politician (c. 470-413 B.C.), opposed like Aristophanes to Cleon and his war policy, but unlucky enough to be left in sole command of the Syracusan expedition. He missed the last chance of getting the defeated Athenian army out of Sicily, because of a *moon-eclipse,* "being rather too much addicted to divination and that sort of thing" (Thucydides, *History,* 7.50); and was was ridiculed for it in *Knights* 28-34.

1460] *hail onset in the blast* Gladly mistake the trumpet-call for the order to attack.

1461] *alalé* ἀλαλή, a battle-cry. In Paley's edition of Euripides (3.137), a few pages after the *Heracles,* the use of this word in *Phoenissae* 335 was annotated: "properly a cry of joy, but here . . . of wailing." If B's eye fell on that note, it may have suggested this curious idea of a sound-signal mistaken for its opposite, and of *their joyous answer.*

1464] *amain* With full force.

1467] *Lord of Tears* A reminiscence of EBB's words in "Wine of Cyprus," 89-92, already quoted as epigraph to *Balaustion's Adventure:* "Our Euripides, the human, / With his droppings of warm tears."

1468] *Priest* See l. 683n. above.

1471] *Either of which who serving, only serves* Whoever serves either *function of the god,* serves that function only (a baffling piece of English that would be much clearer in inflected Greek).

1482] *Hermai* Ἑρμαῖ, images of Hermes, in the form of quadrangular stone pillars with a head on top and a phallus below, which stood all over Athens in temples and private porches. On the night before the disastrous Sicilian Expedition (415 B.C.) their "faces" were mutilated by persons unknown, and Alcibiades was suspected of complicity. Thucydides (*History,* 6.27) only mentioned πρόσωπα (= faces or fronts), but B's neatly topical image requires the *homelier symbol of asserted sense* (l. 1485) to have been the main target; and for this he could have cited Plutarch (*Life of Alcibiades,* 18) who used the verb ἀκρωτηριάζω (= cut off extremities or projecting parts). Though he also mentioned πρόσωπα, this may have meant, not "faces of the heads" but "fronts of the pillars."

1487] *freak* Used in the old sense of "capricious prank." Thucydides went on to say (6.28) that other statues had been mutilated "by young men in drunken sport [μετὰ παιδιᾶς καὶ οἴνου]."

1492] *no more than our City* According to Thucydides (*History,* 6.28), the Athenians took the mutilation of the Herms "very seriously" and immediately offered large rewards for information about the perpetrators.

1499] *Evirate* Castrate, emasculate.

1501] *argute* Subtle, artful, ingenious.

1505-8] *From Lais . . . no reply* The *tale* was in Athenaeus (13.582c-d): Lais, the prostitute (see l. 337n. above) saw Euripides in a garden, equipped with writing-tool (γραφεῖον) and writing-tablet, and asked him why, in *Medea* 1346, he made Jason call his wife an αἰσχροποιός (= doer of shameful things). Astonished at her impudence, Euripides replied, "What are you, woman, if not an αἰσχροποιός?" She laughingly quoted a line from his own *Aeolus,* parodied in *Frogs* 1475: "What is shameful, if it does not seem so to those who do it?" (*Fragmenta*, 368, No. 19).

1511-12] *Does none remain . . . sophist-skill?* A half-serious challenge to Balaustion.

1513-24] *No sun . . . Euripides* B plays, as in "Numpholeptos," with the optical fact that all colors are contained in white light. But these colors cannot be seen in the sun itself, only in the clouds at sunset. Balaustion should be a *serviceable cloud* to reveal the spectrum of Euripides, especially its *rosy* component (see l. 53 above).

1520] *was lost to us* Which was lost to us (B's frequent omission of the relative).

1523] *clasp that cloud* I.e., embrace Balaustion, with a mocking allusion to Ixion, who was punished in Hades for trying to seduce what looked like the goddess Hera, but turned out to be a cloud.

1527] *watch* Stay awake (as if keeping a vigil for the divine Euripides).

1528] *Accompany!* A direct command to Balaustion, on the strength of his quasi-royal crown. He keeps trying to treat her as an Elaphion.

1530-33] *In honest language . . . will that do?* A reaction to her look of distrust.

1534] *strike conviction* A punning use of the phrase to imply: "convict of lying."

1543] *pledged my Genius* Another pun: on the English and Greek senses of *Genius* (see ll. 742-44 above).

1545] *One of us declared* See l. 779-80 above.

1555] *freckled face* Another detail from the *Life* in Nauck: "he was said to have had φακούς (= moles or freckles) on his face" (Nauck, v.25-26).

all but breath, I hope A catty reference to the charge of halitosis (see ll. 491-92n. above).

1559] *Flat-nose, Sophroniskos' son* Socrates. His portrayal on drinking-mugs seems to be B's inference from English Toby mugs, and from Alcibiades' comparison of Socrates in Plato's *Symposium* 215b, 216d to images of the bibulous, snub-nosed satyr Silenus.

1560] *what's this lies below* I.e., below his portrait.

1561] *graver* Stylus; see l. 724n. above.

1562] *psalterion* ψαλτήριον (= plucking musical instrument, harp).

screwed I.e., tuned.

1563-65] *Whereon he tried . . . lad's delight* In *Frogs* 1314-18 Aeschylus parodies certain musical effects in Euripides' lyrics, multiplying by six the first syllable of εἰλίσσετε (= spin) to εἰειειειειειλίσσετε and continuing with a complicated pattern of alliteration on *l* and *k*). B reproduces what he can of that parody in English, with a little help from Tennyson's "Lady of Shalott," 107.

1566]   *Aischulos*   See l. 121n. above. In *Frogs* 1474 Dionysus similarly prefers Aeschylus to Euripides.

    bronze-throat   An imitation of χαλκεόφωνος (= bronze-voiced), applied by Homer (*Iliad* 5.785) to Stentor, who shouted as loud as fifty men, and by Hesiod (*Theogony* 311) to Cerberus, there not just three but "fifty-headed."

    eagle-bark at blood   An allusion to *Prometheus Vinctus* 1021-22, where Prometheus' liver is to be devoured by the "winged dog of Zeus, the bloody eagle."

1569]   *'Frenzied Hero'*   Originally called simply *Heracles*, the tragedy was later subtitled *Mainomenos* (Μαινόμενος = raving mad), as in Nauck's and Paley's editions, which B owned.

1571]   *Papuros*   πάπυρος (= papyrus, a kind of reed from which Greek books were usually made).

1574]   *'Antiope'*   See ll. 290-91n. above. According to the scholium on *Frogs* 53, the *Antiope* was produced shortly before *Frogs,* and was one of Euripides "good [καλῶν]" plays (*Scholia,* 276).

1579]   *stranger*   Used in the sense of "foreigner" (ξένος covers both meanings). See l. 397n. above.

1580]   *call it*   If you call it. A reference to l. 1552.

1581]   *the Daimon*   Δαίμων (= divine spirit, god), i.e., Euripides. See ll. 742-44n. above.

1587]   *So you but suffer*   So long as you allow.

1588-89]   *the bolt . . . iron malice*   B was probably remembering *Alcestis* 5-6, where the Cyclopes, famous as iron-workers, are called the makers of Zeus's thunderbolts.

1592]   *yon impassive presence*   The portrait of Euripides.

1601]   *Silk breaks lightning's blow*   I can trace no Greek source for this general statement. Perhaps B's prophetically knowledgeable heroine cites the fact that silk is a non-conductor of electricity, to imply that the "merest female child" (see l. 777 above), dressed in the softest silk, can ward off Aristophanes' thunderbolts (see ll. 1587-88 above).

1609]   *Solon*   Athenian legislator and poet (c. 640-c. 558 B.C.).

1610-11]   *'Let none revile . . . revile thyself!'*   The *saw* is mentioned in a scholium on Demosthenes: "The law of Solon forbade speaking evil of the dead, even if provoked by insults from the dead man's children" (E. Ruschenbusch, "Σόλωνος Νόμοι," *Historia* 9 [1966], 116).

1612-15]   *him who made Elektra*   Euripides, whose heroine says she wants to speak her mind over Aegisthus' corpse, but is ashamed to insult the dead (*Electra* 900-2).

1622]   *Olympiad*   The four-year interval between Olympic festivals.

1623]   *froze*   The slightly odd metaphor was possibly meant to imitate the Greek use of ψυχρός (= cold) as a pejorative term in literary criticism.

1631]   *Lenaia*   See l. 205n. above.

1644]   *man of Mitulené*   See l. 1078n. above.

1648]   *your own test*   I.e., Euripides' test, e.g., in *Hippolytus* 428-30, where Phaedra says "Time shows up the bad ones among mortals [κακοὺς θνητῶν ἐξέφηνε . . . χρόνος]" and 1051-52, where Hippolytus appeals to the verdict of "Time the informer [μηνυτὴν χρόνον]." Cf. a fragment of his *Antiope*: "They say that Justice is the daughter of Time" (*Fragmenta*, 425, No. 222).

1657]   *hide head safe . . . flung its stone*   An image used by Pheres to his son in *Alcestis* 679-80: "you won't get away like that after hurling such impudent words at me."

1658]   *turn cheek*   The gospel phrase (Matt. 5:39) is one of B's relatively few anachronisms.

1659]   *flogged*   A metaphor for harsh literary criticism quite in Aristophanes' character: see *Frogs* 633-70, where Xanthius and Dionysus are both flogged, to find out which is the god.

1661-70   *splotch . . . immerded*   A literal, onomatopoeic realization of "mud-slinging" reminiscent of "Mr. Sludge, 'the Medium,'" 755-70 (this edition, 6.318-19).

1662]   *slab*   Semi-solid, sticky (like the gruel in *Macbeth*, 4.1.32).

1670]   *immerded*   Covered with excrement.

1672]   *I'll engage*   I bet.

1674]   *Eruxis*   See l. 130n. above.

1679]   *pin-point*   Small and unimportant; but perhaps used here with a thought of "push-pin," a children's game (*play*) used by English writers as a type of triviality.

1682]   *'twas no dwarf he heaved Olumpos at*   In the war between the giants and the gods mountains were used as missiles—though Zeus would hardly have *heaved* the mountain that he lived on.

1686]   *Strattis might steal from*   I.e., garbage suitable for a minor comic poet like Strattis to plagiarize. See l. 1189n. above.

1702-3]   *beyond less puissant . . . declare*   More than anyone without my divine eloquence could express.

1707-12]   *detecting . . . God*   Realizing that the *thought* of such demagogues is based on religious error.

1716]   *just on him*   Just on my natural ally, Euripides, the *fellow-fighter* of l. 1730.

1720]   *not by flagellating foe*   These words replace what B had originally written in the MS: "not as I laughing say." The deleted words help to clarify the train of thought, which contrasts the way Euripides *cham-*

pioned truth directly with Aristophanes' own indirect way of doing so: laughing at *falsehood*. But the whole passage remains opaque, chiefly because it makes such complicated use of the dramatic monologue form. Balaustion is relating to Euthukles how she asked Aristophanes *why* he had left in his works a *mixture-monument* to the fact (expressed by him in the first person singular, and in words ascribed to him by her) that he concentrated on attacking a fellow-champion of truth, Euripides.

1721]   *With simple rose and lily*   When revising his MS for publication, B must have found he had repeated himself by writing: "With whips of leeks and onions" (see l. 1022 above), and substituted, in the first edition, this less apt and authentic metaphor for good-humored satire.

1722]   *bowze*   An early spelling of *booze.*

1725-26]   *No, the balled fist . . . till brain flew*   Another unhappy result of the strain put on the dramatic monologue: the sadistic violence of the image, suitable enough in the mouth of Aristophanes, sounds quite wrong in Balaustion's. The number of MS corrections around here suggests that B was dissatisfied with the whole passage.

1729]   *he displeased me*   I just didn't like Euripides.

1733-34]   *no taunt . . . studies books*   In *Frogs* 943 Euripides is made to boast of having introduced "chatter from unfamiliar books." See l. 285n. above.

1736]   *uses . . . phrase of daily life*   In *Frogs* 924-59 Euripides mocks Aeschylus' tragic diction as inflated and unintelligible, but calls his own "democratic," since he "introduced domestic incidents that we're used to and actually experience," and made "women, slaves, masters, young girls, and old women" do the talking.

1737]   *His mother was a herb-woman*   Nauck's edition of Euripides lists all the passages where Aristophanes jeers at him because his mother, Cleito, sold vegetables (Nauck, xi; *Acharnians* 457, 478, *Knights* 19, *Thesmophoriazusae* 456, *Frogs* 840).

1739]   *Kephisophon*   A slave of Euripides, said to have "worked with him, especially on his lyrics . . . and also slept with his wife" (*Scholia*, 302). In *Frogs* 944 Euripides claims to have improved on Aeschylus' tragic diction by "mixing in some Cephisophon"—perhaps with a pun on the word μίγνυς (= mixing), which often implied sexual intercourse. Aristophanes made similar jokes about Cephisophon in *Frogs* 1408, 1452-53.

1743]   *Sicilian cheese*   Athenaeus mentions cheese as a special product of Sicily (1.27d), and it is Sicilian cheese that a dog is accused of stealing in *Wasps* 838. But the point here is simply the wildness of Aristophanes' fantasies.

1752]   *Beside . . . Wine-lees-song*   Such lies can be discounted as comic licence. See l. 409n. above.

1757]   *man of Phokis*   B identifies his Euthukles with the "certain Phocian" in Plutarch's *Life of Lysander*, 15, who dissuaded the Spartans and their allies from totally demolishing Athens, by reciting the opening chorus of Euripides' *Electra* (167-68). See l. 208n. above. A Phocian's opinion might have some reflected authority, since his country, though small, contained the Delphic oracle; but Aristophanes' attitude here to "foreigners" was consistent with the Athenian treatment of metics (μέτοικοι) i.e., resident aliens.

1761]   *strangers*   See l. 1579n. above.

1771-73]   *Eats . . . hugs as hugely . . . talks nonsense*   Was B remembering Swift's intoxicated Yahoos who "sometimes hug, and sometimes tear one another . . . howl, and grin, and chatter, and then fall asleep in the Mud" (*Gulliver's Travels* [Oxford 1986], 266)?

1777]   *to its crow-kindred*   I.e., to hell, with a pun on "go to the crows"; see l. 683n. above.

1777-78]   *leave philosophy / Her heights serene*   Probably an anachronistic echo of Lucretius' *sapientum templa serena* (= serene temples of the wise) from which an Epicurean philosopher looks down on the errors of ordinary mortals (*De rerum natura*, 2.7-13).

1784-87]   *Coëval with the birth . . . downfall of the pair*   See l. 391n. above. The Greek *Prolegomena de Comoedia* began by attributing the differences berween Old, Middle, and New Comedy to the curbs on free speech (ἰσηγορία) which resulted from the replacement of democracy by oligarchies and tyrannies (*Scholia*, xiii-iv).

1790]   *'They are not, no, they are not!'*   Quoted from a fragment of Euripides' lost *Bellerophon*: "Does anyone say that there are gods in heaven? There are not, there are not —unless anyone on earth is fool enough to accept the old story" (*Fragmenta*, 445, No. 286, 1-3).

1793]   *black mother-earth*   B combines Homer's γαῖα μέλαινα (= black earth [*Iliad* 2.699]) with the name of the goddess of agriculture, Demeter (Δημήτηρ = earth mother).

1804]   *phyz*   Physiognomy, i.e., face. See l. 409n. above.

1807]   *sunk their crest*   Were crestfallen.

1812]   *hunks*   An Elizabethan term of abuse for a mean or stingy character.

1815]   *man of parts*   Chief actor, chorus-leader (with a pun on the usual English sense of the phrase: a man of abilities).

1817]   *mount cart*   See l. 974n. above.

     be persons   Act parts.

1825]   *steel . . . civil speech*   See ll. 848-50n. above.

1827] *ribroast* Thrash or cudgel severely.

1828] *Sousarion* See ll. 845-46n. above.

1829] *acceding* Taking office as King of Comedy.

1833] *crabtree* Probably suggested by the "grievous Crab-tree Cudgel" used by Giant Despair to beat Christian and Hopeful "fearfully" (J. Bunyan, *Pilgrim's Progress* [Oxford, 1984], 93).

1835] *stickled* Contended, stuck out for, insisted on.

1838] *fig-leaf* Athenaeus (1.9a) mentions a delicacy called θρῖον, a kind of omelette served in fig-leaves (1.9a); but B may have intended an Aristophanic pun on the Biblical sense of the English word (Gen. 3:7).

1842] *Not who* Not the man who (an omission of the antecedent common in Greek).

tells of untaxed figs I.e., a "sycophant" or informer (συκοφάντης = fig-revealer), a word tentatively explained in Plutarch's *Life of Solon*, 24, to mean one who informed on breakers of the law prohibiting the export of figs from Attica.

1843] *ellops-fish* ἔλ(λ)οψ, an unidentified fish, possibly the sturgeon, compared, in a mock-epic poem about a dinner quoted by Athenaeus, to the "ambrosia that the blessed, eternal gods feast on" (4.136b).

1844] *gives a pheasant . . . wife* Presumably as an aid to seduction—a train of thought possibly started by a quotation from Menander's *Concubine* in Athenaeus, just before a section on pheasants: "he runs up to her, saying, 'I've bought these pigeons for you'"(14.654b; Meineke, 4.182).

1848] *so the thing / Lay sap* So long as it's something that undermines.

1851] *Pnux* See l. 114n. above.

1852] *Palaistra* παλαίστρα (= wrestling-school), but here, as in *Frogs* 729, meaning a center of traditional education.

1854] *bring contempt on oaths* See l. 1011n. above.

1855 *despise the Cult* The capital letter suggests a reference, not to religious worship in general, but to the cult of Demeter in the Mysteries of Eleusis, scornfully dismissed by Euripides in *Frogs* 889-90: "There are other gods to whom *I* pray."

1859] *bray* Bruise, pound, crush to powder.

1860] *Lamachos* See l. 1187n. above.

1861] *Kleon* See l. 401n. above.

1862-64] *Shaft pushed no worse . . . spiteless rustic mirth* Shaft of wit no less forceful for its brilliance, so that nobody could doubt it was meant as much more than a joke.

1873] *jabber argument, chop logic* Challenged by Aeschylus in *Frogs* 964-75 to a comparison of what they taught their students (μαθητὰς), Euripides claims to have taught his "to think, by introducing rational argument and speculation into my art, so that now they can understand and make distinctions between all things."

1873-74]   *pore / On sun and moon*   Though Socrates was not interested in physical science, other sophists were, so Socrates was caricatured in *Clouds* 217-25, suspended in a basket, saying "walk on air and think about the sun."

1874]   *worship Whirligig*   In *Clouds* 374-81 Socrates explains thunder as resulting from cloud-collisions caused, not by Zeus, but by Upper-Air Dinos (Δῖνος Αἰθέριος = whirling of the ether, the new Supreme Power).

1875]   *your tragedian*   Euripides.

1880]   *moon he maunders of*   An unfair charge apparently inspired by English romantic poetry. Euripides seldom mentions the moon, though it does shine "all night" in *Alcestis* 451, "dance" in *Ion* 1080, "drive a chariot" in *Supplices* 991-92, and become the sun's "daughter" in *Phoenissae* 175-76 (instead of his sister, as in Hesiod's *Theogony* 371-74).

1883]   *flesh rebuked*   Flesh that rebuked.

1884]   *Excess*   An allusion to the words inscribed on Apollo's temple at Delphi μηδὲν ἄγαν (= nothing in excess; Plato, *Protagoras* 343b).

  Glauketes   See l. 328n. above.

1885]   *Chairephon*   A friend of Socrates, described in *Clouds* 504 as looking "half-dead," and in a scholium as "thin and pale and wasted away by his philosophical studies" (*Scholia,* 104-5).

1886]   *understander*   Supporter (with a pun on the usual meaning of the word).

1889]   *cheesecakes Peace may chew*   In *Acharnians* 1126 Dicaeopolis celebrates his private peace by eating, among other things, the "cheese-backed circle of a cake [πλακοῦντος τυρόνωτον . . . κύκλον]."

1891]   *Pnux*   See l. 114n. above.

1892]   *dance 'Threttanelo the Kuklops drunk!'*   See l. 665n. above.

1895]   *No naming names*   See l. 710n. above.

1898]   *Don't throw away hard cash*   See l. 700n. above.

1900-5]   *Then Kleon . . . play at all*   Based on *Acharnians* 378-82 and the scholiast's explanation of the passage (*Scholia,* 13): that Cleon prosecuted Aristophanes on two charges: the first of ἀδικία (illegal action) against the people and the Council, by satirizing in his *Babylonians* properly elected and appointed officials like Cleon, before an audience which included aliens (ξένοι); and the second for "ξενία," i.e., for being an alien himself, and yet producing plays, a privilege reserved for Athenian citizens.

1905-7]   *Egyptian . . . Lindian*   See l. 651n. above. According to Suidas (*The Suda,* [formerly known as Suidas' *Lexicon*], ed. I. Bekker

[Berlin, 1854], 1.170) Aristophanes was "a Rhodian or Lindian, (some said an Egyptian, others a Camiran)"; and the *Life of Aristophanes* (Meineke, 1.543) adds Aegina to the list of suggested ethnic origins. Lindus, and Balaustion's birthplace, Camirus were independent Doric cities on Rhodes.

1913]   *my triumph*   The first edition read "its triumph," i.e., the day-star's. The 1889 correction makes it clearer that Aristophanes is using the sun as an image for himself and his supremacy.

1914]   *quench his beams*   In the first edition these words were fol-lowed by a question-mark, which seems necessary to the sense and grammar. The words themselves were probably suggested by Shake-speare's *Midsummer-Night's Dream* 2.1.161-62: "But I might see young Cupid's fiery shaft / Quenched in the chaste beams of the watery moon," which suited Aristophanes' picture of himself as a full-blooded, virile sun contrasted with the *blood-thinned . . . purity* of the moon-maundering Euripides (see ll. 1880-82 above).

1915]   *Aias*   Αἴας, the Homeric name of the hero better known as Ajax, whose shield was "made of seven bull-hides" (ἑπταβόειον). See *Iliad* 7.219-22.

1917]   *soft and sure*   A slightly puzzling phrase, perhaps determined by the alliteration. The first adjective may imply sentimentality, the sec-ond, a wish to play safe. B's Aristophanes is apparently able to *foretell* how the Victorian Mrs. Grundy will downgrade his literary achieve-ment just because of its obscenities.

1918]   *breathe against his brightest*   Breathe complaints against him when at his brightest.

1919]   *'So let be, we pardon you!'*   If only you'll stop it, we'll forgive you.

1920]   *Till the minute mist hangs a block*   Until a slight haze suspends a sort of sunshade in the sky.

1921]   *'twilight mild and equable'*   I.e., such *dullards* would prefer his genius bowdlerized.

1923]   *ramped*   Reared up on its hind legs with its front paws in the air, like a "lion rampant" in heraldry.

1924]   *gendered*   Copulated.

1928]   *Thearion*   A baker mentioned by Plato in *Gorgias* 518b and by Aristophanes in a fragment burlesquing the first lines of Euripides' *Hecuba*: "I am come from Thearion's breadshop, where the baking-ovens dwell" (Meineke, 2.946, No. 7).

1932]   *Kilikian loaves*   Called "large and dirty" in a fragment of Plato Comicus quoted by Athenaeus (3.110d).

1933]   *horseflesh branded San*   I.e., a σαμφόρας (= San-carrying horse). *San* (σάν) was the old Doric name for *sigma*, the letter *s*. Strepsiades suffers equal *heart-break* about his son's taste for these expensive horses (*Clouds* 121-22, 1298). See l. 338n. above.

1934]   *Menippos*   A horsebreeder and horsetrader mentioned in *Birds* 1293 as nicknamed "Swallow" (Χελίδων) because, according to the scholiast, that was his brand-mark (*Scholia*, 238).

1935]   *pretty daughter Kepphé*   Did B misread κέπφε (= "you silly man," vocative masculine) in *Plutus* 912 as Κέπφη, and assume it was a girl's name?

1936]   *Sporgilos*   A man described in *Birds* 299-300 as a bird, by a pun on κηρύλος (= halcyon) and κειρύλος, a comic coinage which ought to mean "haircutter" (from κείρω = cut hair). The Scholiast quotes Plato Comicus: "Sporgilus' barber's shop, a most hateful brothel" (*Scholia*, 217, Meineke, 2.662).

1937-39]   *Out with . . . your exchange?*   I.e., do you want me to come out with a play about a small tradesman's private affairs (the typical content of New Comedy) rather than treat larger issues of education and politics, as I do in plays like *Clouds* and *Birds?*

1939]   *Muse of Megara*   See ll. 845-46n. above.

1940]   *weasel-lap*   Baby-food for weasels.

1941]   *wild-boar's marrow*   I.e., meat for heroes, who traditionally hunted wild boars, like the one that gashed Odysseus in *Odyssey* 19.447-51.

   Cheiron   The wise Centaur who tutored Achilles.

1942]   *Ariphrades*   See l. 1120n. above.

1945]   *fancy*   I.e., taste.

1947]   *Rocky Ones*   A literal translation of οἱ Κραναοί, as, according to Herodotus (*Histories*, 8.44), the Athenians were originally named, and as they are called in *Birds* 123.

1950-63]   *that first feud . . . misery*   Very like the feud between Fra Lippo Lippi and his otherworldly critics ("Fra Lippo Lippi," 174-98; this edition, 5.188-89).

1953]   *'Death . . . better Life'*   See l. 1010n. above.

1956]   *well-side violet-patch*   One of the joys of peace mentioned in *Peace* 577-78.

1957]   *club-feast*   In England, an annual feast of members of a benefit-club, or a parish, like the "club-walking" in Hardy's *Tess of the d'Urbervilles* (ch. 2). Here the term was probably meant to translate πανδαισία, used by Aristophanes (*Peace* 565) a few lines before the *violet-patch*. For this word (compounded of "all" + "feast") the scholiast suggested several possible meanings, including: "a dinner at which each brings food for himself, and puts it into a common pool," so that everybody shares everything (*Scholia*, 188). B would have known of such meals from Athenaeus (8.362e) under the term ἔρανοι, which can also mean clubs or societies.

1958]   *Roast thrushes*   Mentioned as a delicacy by Athenaeus (2.64f). In *Clouds* 339 Strepsiades speaks enviously of people who "gulp down bird-flesh of thrushes."

hare-soup   *Wasps* 709 implies that eating hare is the essence of good living.

pea-soup   In *Peace* 1136 roasting chick-peas is a peace-time pleasure best combined with kissing .

1959]   *Peparethian*   See l. 349n. above.

1962]   *look fig-juice*   B's varies the Aristophanic idiom, "look cress etc." (see l. 667n. above). The use of figs as a curdling-agent was probably suggested by Athenaeus, 2.67e, where vinegar is said to make some things curdle (συνιστάνει) and 2.68a, where a list of seasonings ends with "cress, fig-leaves, ὀπός [= the acid juice of a fig-tree, used as rennet]."

1967]   *I need particular discourtesy*   See ll. 1747-51 above.

1980]   *Salamis*   The island near which the Persians were decisively defeated in September 480 B.C. The *Life* in Nauck began: "The poet Euripides . . . was born on Salamis . . . when the Greeks fought the naval battle against the Persians" (Nauck, v.1-4).

1981]   *Themistokles*   See l. 80n. above.

1985]   *the unruptured chain*   An image probably adapted from the "golden chain" (σειρὴν χρυσείην) by which Zeus challenged all the gods and goddesses to drag him down (Homer, *Iliad* 8.19-26).

1986-88]   *Aischulos . . . Pindaros . . . Theognis . . . Homeros*   See l. 121n. above. Pindar (518- after 446 B.C.) was the first great writer of lyric odes. Theognis (? 6th century B.C.) wrote short epigrams in elegiac couplets. Homer (who may or may not have existed as an individual poet) was traditionally regarded as the author of two epics, the *Iliad* (about 750 B.C.) and the *Odyssey* (perhaps a generation later).

1990]   *Ah, people,—ah, lost antique liberty*   The apostrophe to the Hellenic people merely interrupts the main statement: *Hellas lost antique liberty.*

1991-2012]   *We lived . . . Zeus takes umbrage else*   Beneath all the exclamations the argument goes like this: "In the good old days we *ourselves* (i.e., Athenians) were content with the blessings of our own beautiful country, an oasis of culture in a desert of *barbarism*, without any of the imperialist ambitions that provoked the Peloponnesian War. It was enough for us to defend ourselves, and humbly enjoy the generosity of the gods. The trouble started when the religious scepticism of the sophists and their poetic spokesman Euripides broke the implicit bargain with the gods: human worship in return for divine protection."

347

1995] *barbarians* Non-Greeks (especially Persians). According to Strabo (*Geography* 14. 2.28) the word βάρβαρος (= barbarian) was originally an onomatopoeic term (of abuse) for the noises made by foreigners trying to speak Greek, and then became a "general ethnic name to distinguish between Greeks" and everyone else.

2005] *humanism* Feeling for humanity, humane behavior.

2006] *escapes* Used in the Elizabethan sense of peccadillos, usually sexual ones like "The escapes of Jupiter, the wanton delights of Venus, and the amorous deceits of Cupid" (T. Lodge, 1596 [*OED*, sb. 7]).

2009-12] *Bacchos . . . Aphrodité . . . Zeus* Here Aristophanes echoes that "primitive religionist," Guido (*The Ring and the Book* 11.1913-73; this edition, 9.232-34).

2011-12] *Provided . . . Zeus takes umbrage else* Zeus was the god of oaths (ὅρκιος) and also of strangers (ξένιος), i.e., of hospitality.

2013] *had I been there to taste!* Aristophanes was probably born between 460 and 450 B.C., but the date commonly given in B's day was 448 B.C.

2014] *Perikles . . . Olumpian* See l. 106n. above.

2015-16] *an Olumpos . . . above Akropolis* E.g., the sculptures on the Parthenon, which represented, among other things, the Olympian gods' war with the Giants.

2017-18] *Wisely so spends . . . cut-throat projects* Pericles' building programme was largely financed by contributions from members of the Delian League, an alliance of Greek cities originally formed for war against the Persians.

2018-19] *Who carves . . . Who writes* I.e., in these degenerate days.

2018] *Promachos* Πρόμαχος (= fighting for, defending), an epithet of Athena. The Athena Promachus was a colossal bronze statue by Pheidias on the Acropolis, dating from about 456 B.C. The *Oresteia* of Aeschylus was produced in 458 B.C.

2026] *gor-crow* Carrion crow (a bird mentioned by the Pope in *The Ring and the Book* 10.578; this edition, 9.94).

2028] *Kimon* The son of Miltiades (see l. 450n. above), famous for defeating the Persian fleet in 466 B.C. Unlike the *starveling crew* of sophists he was described in Plutarch as "above criticism in appearance, tall with thick curly hair" and "attractive and obliging" in manner (*Life of Miltiades*, 5).

Boulé Βουλή (= council), the senate or upper house in the Athenian constitution, consisting of 500 specially appointed male citizens.

2030] *altar-base and temple-step* The council-chamber contained a sanctuary of the goddess Cybele.

2033] *'Wise men'* The original meaning of σοφισταί (= sophists). See l. 364n. above.

Prodikos A famous sophist from Ceos, admired as much as Socrates by the chorus of *Clouds* (360-61), but dismissed with contempt by that of *Birds* (690-92). A religious sceptic or atheist, he appeared in Plato's *Protagoras* 315d lying in bed "wrapped up in sheepskins and great numbers of bedclothes," and was mentioned in Plutarch's *Moralia* 791e as a "thin, unhealthy, and usually bedridden young man." The contrast between astronomical dogmatism possibly came from Lucian's *Icaromenippus* 6 8-11, where scientists who, "from age or laziness had very bad eyesight, claimed to be able to see to the ends of the sky, measured the sun, and set foot in regions beyond the moon."

2035] *way Theseia . . . Tripods' way* An illustration of feebleness evidently inspired by Pausanias, who, after after relating a prodigious feat of strength performed by Theseus on his first arrival in Athens (*Description of Greece*, 1.19.1-2), went on to remark (1.20.1): "And there is a street called Tripods leading away from the *Prytaneion*" (see ll. 1114-15n. above). Recalling from Thucydides' *History*, 2.15 that this building was allegedly founded by Theseus, B apparently assumed the existence of a ὁδός Θησεία (= Thesean Way or Theseus Street) very near it.

2037-38] *he's* It is.

Aeginas's bigness As big as the island of Aegina: B's adaptation of the statement attributed to Anaxagoras (c. 500-428 B.C.), and ridiculed in Lucian's *Icaromenippus* 7.22-23, that the sun was a "flaming mass of red-hot stone or metal, bigger than the Peloponnese" (Diogenes Laertius, *Lives of the Philosophers*, 2.8).

wheels no whit . . . wants a steed I.e., Prodicus's scientific explanation replaces the myth that the sun travels from east to west in a horse-drawn chariot.

2039] *Protagoras* See l. 363n. above.

2040] *Explains what virtue, vice . . . mean* In Plato's *Protagoras* 318e-320b the sophist claims to make his students good citizens, but Socrates doubts if such virtue (ἀρετή) can be taught.

2042-43] *on either side . . . something is to say* According to Diogenes Laertius (*Lives of the Philosophers*, 9.51) Protagoras "was the first to say that there were two mutually contradictory λόγους [= things to be said, arguments] about everything."

2045] *kottabos* κότταβος, a game played at drinking-parties, discussed at length in Athenaeus (15.665b-668f), and included among the joys of peace by Aristophanes (*Peace* 342). It involved throwing wine left in a wine-cup into a metal basin so as to make an audible splash.

2046] *whether moon-spots breed* In Lucian's *Icaromenippus* (7) scientists "are ready to swear that the moon is inhabited," and his *True History* 1.22 describes how those all-male inhabitants *breed*: "when pregnant by other males, they carry the embryos in the calves of their legs [γαστοκνημία = womb of the shin, i.e., calf], give birth to them dead, and bring them to life by exposing them to the wind with their mouths open."

2047] *keep Choes* Celebrate Χόαι (= pourings or drink-offerings), part of a late-February festival of Dionysus, at which celebrators competed in draining five-litre containers (χόοι) of wine. In *Acharnians* 960-61 Dicaeopolis is invited to such a celebration.

2048] *Why should I like my wife who dislikes me?* Aristophanes assumes, like most Victorians, that religious belief is the basis of all morality.

2050] *in your teeth* In flat contradiction of your beliefs.

2052] *What and where are they?* Protagoras was quoted as saying: "About the gods, I can know neither that they exist nor that they do not exist" (Diogenes Laertius, *Lives of the Philosophers*, 9.51).

2054-55] *scramble down . . . as a bull.* Zeus took the form of a swan to seduce Leda, of a bull to seduce Europa.

2060] *Zeus distilling pickle through a sieve* A bowdlerized version of *Clouds* 373: "Zeus urinating through a sieve."

2061] *Theorus* A politician called a perjuror in *Clouds* 400, so a living proof that thunderbolts were not sent as punishments by Zeus.

2064] *the atmosphere* See l. 1874n. above.

2068] *"Necessity"* The chorus-leader in *Euripides' Alcestis* (962-66) says that after much literary, astronomical, and philosophical research he has "found nothing stronger than Necessity [Ἀνάγκη]."

2071] *Whether gnats . . . head or tail* Asked in *Clouds* 155-65 "whether gnats sing through their mouths or their tails," Socrates says "their tails," and Strepsiades comments: "So the rump is the gnat's trumpet [σάλπιγξ]."

2074] *hemlock* The poison by which Socrates was executed.

bull's-blood In *Knights* 81-84 drinking bulls' blood like Themistocles is suggested as the manliest way to commit suicide. The scholiast explains: "on the pretext of sacrificing a bull to Artemis he caught its blood in a cup, gulped it down, and died instantly" (*Scholia*, 36).

2075] *the Olumpian* See l. 106n. above.

2076] *they* The sophists.

2077-79] *Anaxagoras . . . thy teaching* See ll. 2037-38n. above. Plutarch's *Life of Pericles* says he "admired Anaxagoras enormously," and was saved from superstition (δεισιδαιμονία) by his scientific teaching (5, 6). Lemprière stated (43) that Anaxagoras "gave scientific accounts of eclipses," but B was probably recalling Plutarch's *Life of Nicias*, 23, which after describing his "great fear" of the *moon-eclipse* (see ll. 1456-57n. above) called Anaxagoras "the first man to give the clearest and boldest account of the shinings and shadowings [καταυγασμῶν καὶ σκιᾶς] of the moon."

2080]   *Zeus nods: man must reconcile himself*   If Pericles, as Olympian Zeus, pronounces in favor of such "madmen," we ordinary mortals must put up with it. There is a pun on *nods*, which alludes first to the majestic, Olympus-shaking nod that confirms Zeus's decision in Homer's *Iliad* 1.524-30, and secondly to Horace's *Ars Poetica* 359: "good Homer nods [*dormitat* = becomes drowsy, i.e., makes occasional mistakes]."

2081]   *Charon's-company*   I.e., the hellish sophists (since Charon was the ferryman in Hades, as in *Frogs* 189).

2082]   *as we wish*   An imitation of *Acharnians* 446: "Good luck to you, and to Telephus—what I'd like for him [ἁγώ φρονῶ]."

2084]   *sesame*   Included among seasonings in Athenaeus (2.68a), and among the good things of life in *Wasps* 676.

2085]   *Brilesian*   Of Mount Brilessus or Brillettus, just north of Athens.

2086]   *Bacchis*   A prostitute who writes and receives letters in Alciphron's *Letters of Prostitutes,* and also figures in a story told by Athenaeus (13.594b-c).

2087]   *You . . . young man?*   Presumably addressed to his slave.

2088]   *Pho!*   See l. 660n. above.

2088-91]   *that panniered ass . . . quench thirst*   An Aesop-type fable, but not to be found in the 1868 Tauchnitz collection of *Aesopicae Fabulae.* The nearest approach to it there is No. 135, "Donkey carrying divine image [ὄνος βαστάζων ἄγαλμα]"—who thinks that passers-by are worshipping him, not the image on his back. B seems to have made the image a rather unAesopic personification of Youth, adding a persuasive *serpent* from Gen. 3:1-6, and the *swap* of something *priceless* for mere physical satisfaction from the sale of a birthright for a mess of pottage in Gen. 25:29-34.

2093]   *Spartanizes*   Imitates the Spartans in their austerity. B was perhaps anglicizing λακωνίζω, or λακεδαιμονιάζω, a word used by Aristophanes in his lost *Babylonians* (Meineke, 2.983, No. 33).

2096]   *learn ere act*   Cf. "Grammarian's Funeral" 77: "That before living he'd learn how to live" (this edition, 6.132).

2100]   *Plataian help*   I.e., vital help when most needed. The Plataeans were the only allies to fight alongside the Athenians at Marathon (490 B.C.). In *Frogs* 693-96 Aristophanes approves of rewarding such loyalty by giving Plataean refugees Athenian citizenship when their own city was destroyed.

2101]   *all right and tight*   Smartly lined up, like army recruits.

2103]   *Would cheat*   That would cheat.

2105]   *Saperdion*   Σαπέρδιον (= little fish of the Nile), mentioned in Athenaeus as the nickname of a prostitute better known as Phryne (13.591c).

    the Empousa   A monster called a "demonic apparition" in a scholium to *Frogs* 293, where she appears in rapid succession as "cow, a mule, a most beautiful woman, and a bitch."

2111-12]   *him we style / The Muses' Bee*   See *Life of Sophocles*: "Many others have imitated one previous or contemporary writer, but only Sophocles culls the brightest flowers from all of them; for which reason he was called the Bee . . . So Aristophanes says, "a honeycomb sat on him," and elsewhere, "Sophocles' mouth dripped with honey" (*Life of Sophocles* 20; cf. M. R. Lefkowitz, *The Lives of the Greek Poets* [London, 1981], 163).

2113]   *a Kimberic robe*   Κιμβερικόν, a type of female clothing mentioned in *Lysistrata* 45 and 52; apparently made of expensive material imported from Asia Minor.

2114]   *"I, his successor,'"*   Euripides is made to defend his own poetic policy, as in *Frogs* 939f.

2117]   *Are heroes men? . . . scarce as much*   B paraphrases Nauck's introduction: "Euripides' characters are not remarkable for courage or strength of mind, but quite ordinary, as if he had taken them straight from domestic life on to the stage. Sometimes they are wicked or morally contemptible" (Nauck, xxxvii).

2119]   *ragged, sick, lame, halt and blind*   Nauck continues: "He is criticized by Aristophanes for presenting kings and heroes dressed in rags or lame."

2120]   *Do they use speech? . . . market-phrase*   In *Frogs* 1058 Euripides puts it more briefly: "one must speak like a human being [ἀνθρωπείως]."

2123-24]   *womankind . . . match the male*   See l. 1736n. above.

2126-27]   *the very slave . . . honest, kind and true*   Like the peasant who, though married to Electra, renounces his conjugal rights, which makes Orestes say: "I have seen a high mind in the body of a poor man" (Euripides, *Electra* 34-46, 369-72).

2129-30]   *I paint men as they are . . . as they should be*   A distinction drawn, not by Euripides himself, but by his rival; see Aristotle's *Poetics* 1460b 33-34, quoted by Nauck (xxxvii, n. 83): "Sophocles said he represented people as they ought to be, but Euripides, as they were."

2131]   *Women and slaves*   The normal view of them is clear from Aristotle's *Poetics* 1454a 20-22: "An [individual] woman may be good, and so may a slave, although the first of these [classes] is perhaps inferior and the second wholly worthless."

2134-37]   *while my Choros cants . . . all things there!*   A parody of the religious humility expressed in some choruses of his predecessors, e.g., Aeschylus' *Prometheus Vinctus* 526-33: "May Zeus, who controls all things, never set his power against my judgement . . . nor may I sin in words"; or Sophocles' *Oedipus Tyrannus* 863-68: "May it always be my fate to be reverent and holy in all words and deeds, obedient to the laws which step high through the upper air, fathered by Olympus alone . . . ."

2138] *'Herakles' may help* I.e., I may find a suitable quotation in this MS of his *Heracles* (see ll. 1560-71 above).

2140] *He read . . . "There are no Gods"* He could not actually have *read* these *very words* in the *Heracles,* but only in the *Bellerophon* (see l. 1790 n. above). Unless B had forgotten the exact source, he must have meant Aristophanes to show his dishonesty by pretending to *read* what he could only have inferred from *Heracles* 1345-46 (ll. 4981-83 below), where Heracles dismisses accounts of the gods' immoral behavior as "the wretched stories of poets."

2143] *what man likes be man's sole law!* An idea more topical for B than for Aristophanes: "Doing as One Likes" had been the subject of a chapter in Matthew Arnold's *Culture and Anarchy* (1869).

2145] *by your roundabout* By a circuitous route: since freedom means escape from law, and your only law is to do what you like, you can only *reach freedom* by denying your natural instincts.

2147] *"Necessity"* See l. 2068n. above.

2152] *A-sitting with my legs up!* In *Acharnians* 399-400 Euripides is said to be writing a tragedy ἀναβάδην, which the scholiast explains (*Scholia,* 14) as "sitting with his feet up on a high place." Though the word may imply no more than lying on his back, B exploits the hint of a posture as topsy-turvy as the poet's arguments.

2153] *casts in calm* Calmly throws in (adverbial use of the adjective, as often in Greek).

2154] *Apollon* Ἀπόλλων (= Apollo, the god of poetry, whom a poet should especially revere.)

2156] *that roseate world* I.e., of poetry. B seems to echo Sidney's *Apology for Poetry*: "Nature never set forth the earth in so rich tapestry as poets have done—neither with pleasant rivers, fruitful trees, sweet-smelling flowers . . . Her world is brazen, the poets only deliver a golden" (*English Critical Essays xvi-xviii Century*, ed. E. D. Jones [Oxford, 1922], 7).

2161] *enthusiastic* Used in its Greek sense, i.e., "inspired by a *god*" (ἔνθεος), as the poet is called in Plato's *Ion* 534b.

2164] *emballed by* Enclosed in the sphere of (like the "silver sphere" of Shelley's "To a Skylark," 22, a poem from which B's Aristophanes seems to borrow his imagery.

2168]   *Truth, for all beauty!   Beauty, in all truth*   Another surprising echo—of Keats's "Ode on a Grecian Urn" 49-50.

2173]   *So much assistance*   I.e., so much *Plataian help* (l. 2100 above).

2175]   *feed the crows*   A variant on "go to the crows" (see l. 683 n. above), which originally meant, "may your dead body be eaten by the crows," the worst fear of the Homeric warrior (see *Iliad* 1.4-5, 22.335-354).

2181]   *all's concocted upstairs, heels o'er head*   See l. 2152n. above.

2184]   *wife's friend Kephisophon*   See l. 1739n. above.

2185]   *cramp*   Obscure, unintelligible.

2191]   *shag-rag*   Ragged.

2193]   *Pity and terror*   The emotions that Aristotle thought tragedy should arouse. He also called Euripides "the most tragic of the poets" (*Poetics* 1449b 27-28; 1453a 29).

2210]   *Kuthereia* Κυθέρεια, a name of Aphrodite, from the island on which she landed when born from the sea-foam.

2225]   *plethron* πλέθρον (= about 100 English feet).

2227-29]   *parent-right . . . wife's submission*   Questions argued out, for instance, between Pheres and Admetus in *Alcestis* 630-738, and between Jason and Medea in *Medea* 1323-404.

2235]   *for a trireme, good*   Rich enough to pay for a naval trireme, in discharge of his duty as a a citizen.

2237]   *Chresphontes or Bellerophon*   Heroes of tragedies by Euripides which survive only in fragments.

2239]   *turn the drachmas o'er*   Hand over the money I owe.

2240]   *chiton* χιτών (= tunic or vest).

2243]   *he rarely gained a prize*   He came first only four times in his lifetime.

2245]   *Ions, Iophons*   The poets he beat into third and second place respectively with his *Hippolytus* in 428 B.C. See ll. 1257-59n. above. In *Peace* 834-35 Trygaeus reported that on his flight to heaven he had seen Ion, transformed after death into a star.

2249]   *Aristullos*   I.e., Plato, our chief authority for what Socrates said and did. See l. 1150n. above.

2254]   *Euphorions*   Euphorion was said to have won prizes with tragedies written by his father, Aeschylus; in 431 B.C. he defeated both Sophocles and Euripides (whose plays included the *Medea*).

2258]   *Archelaos*   See l. 238n. above.

2265-66]   *he who wrote / "Erechtheus"*   In the surviving fragments of Euripides' *Erechtheus* two political points are made: that the population of a state should be wholly indigenous, and that a ruler should sacrifice his private feelings to the public good. The first excludes foreign immigrants: "A resident alien is like a bad joint in carpentry—he calls himself a citizen, but doesn't behave like one." The second point is the main theme of the play: Erechtheus, when King of Athens, is told by the Delphic oracle that he can defeat an invading army by sacrificing his daughter. The longest fragment (360) argues arithmetically that "the fall of one man's house is not more important than that of a whole city, nor even equally important" (*Fragmenta*, 467, 11-13, 19-21).

2267]   *Kleophon*   See ll. 452n. and 941n. above.

2269]   *this*   I.e., the influence of sophistry spread by Euripides.

2282]   *franker phrase*   E.g., "easily beaten."

2292]   *Marathonian muscle*   See l. 1084n. above.

2294]   *How did I fable?*   What imagery did I use?

2294-98   *mash / To mincemeat . . . Pound in their mortar . . . dainty dish*
In *Peace* 259 War sends for a "pestle [ἀλετρίβανος]" to pound the Greek cities, and in 247 Megara is told that it will be "made mincemeat [καταμεμυττωτευμένα]." Both images are culinary.

2300-1]   *who pleads throng and press / O' the people*   Who pleads popular support.

2303]   *tans hides so*   Cf. *Peace* 647-48: "and the man who did it was a leather-seller [βυρσοπώλης]." See l. 401n. above.

2304]   *Huperbolos*   Another demagogue, accused in *Clouds* 1065-66 of making great profits "out of lamps by his wickedness," which he did, according to the scholiast, by mixing his copper with lead (*Scholia*, 658).

2305]   *Eukrates*   In *Knights* 129 an oracle predicts that the first tradesman-demagogue to seize power will be a "στυππειοπώλης," a seller of hemp (for ropes, not drugs), identified by the scholiast (*Scholia*, 38) as Eucrates, nicknamed Στύππαξ because of his trade.

2305-6]   *Lusikles*   The second in the line of tradesman-demagogues, in *Knights* 132 called "a sheep-seller [προβατοπώλης]," identified by the scholiast (*Scholia*, 38) as "Callias, but some say he means Lysicles."

2306]   *Kephalos*   Sarcastically described in *Ecclesiazusae* 248-54 as "a potter who's no good at making cups, but splendid at remoulding the constitution."

2307]   *Diitriphes*   Mentioned in *Birds* 798-800 as having risen "from nothing to become a very important horsecock [ἱππαλεκτρυών; see l. 130n. above], though his wings were only made of wicker." He made flasks covered with wickerwork, the carrying straps of which were called "wings" (πτερά; *Scholia*, 227).

2308]   *Nausikudes*   A dealer in barley-groats who is sneered at in *Ecclesiazusae* 426. According to Socrates (Xenophon's *Memorabilia* 2.7.6), Nausikydes earned great wealth by his trade.

2309]   *more, their mates*   What's more, we also "choose" their friends (by a process known in recent English politics as "cronyism").

2322]   *Cloudcuckooburg*   Νεφελοκοκκυγία (= Cloud-Cuckoo-Land), the bird-utopia founded by Peisetairus and Euelpides in *Birds* 819). Ostensibly an escape from Athens, it also satirizes Athenian politics.

2324] *rules* A verb, of which the subject is Tereus (a word-order less confusing in inflected Greek).

2326] *Tereus . . . Triple-Crest* a king of Thrace who, after raping his sister-in-law Philomela and cutting out her tongue, was changed into a hoopoe, while she and her sister (according to the Greek version of the myth) became a swallow and a nightingale respectively. In *Birds* 94 he appears as a hoopoe, wearing on his head what Euelpides calls a τριλοφία (= triple crest). See l. 1043n. above.

2327] *and bring the gods to terms* Under the treaty finally negotiated with the Olympian gods, Peisetairus marries Zeus's daughter Basileia (βασιλεία = kingly power), with whom he returns, "brandishing the winged thunderbolt of Zeus" (*Birds* 1714).

2331] *Palaistra-tool* Academic weapon. See l. 1852n. above.

2332] *'Erechtheus'* A legendary king of Athens, whose political idealism was celebrated in Euripides' play of that name (see ll. 2265-66n. above).

 Amphiktuon Ἀμφικτύων (= dweller around, neighbouring state), another legendary king of Athens, brother of Hellen ("Ελλην, the eponymous hero of the Greeks), and founder of the Amphictyonic League, a religious association of Greek states based on Delphi.

2335] *attacking Sicily* I.e., the Sicilian Expedition against Syracuse (415 B.C.), which ended in a disastrous defeat for Athens.

2336] *Choros* The Chorus-leader, hence the singular "he."

2337] *How Phrixos rode the ram . . . Fleece* Aristophanes imagines a typical tragic chorus, moralizing the myth of Phrixus and Helle, who escaped from their cruel stepmother on a winged ram with a golden fleece—until Helle fell into the sea, hence named the Hellespont. Presumably her fall, like the defeat of Xerxes in Aeschylus' *Persae* (where she is mentioned four times) would be seen as punishment for *Aggression* (i.e. *hubris*).

2340] *Alkibiades* The chief advocate of the Expedition.

2341] *Pheidias* See l. 109n. above.

2344] *Eagles . . . their lord* The eagle was sacred to Zeus. See l. 1566n. above.

2346] *Priapos* A god of sex and fertility, whose image was used in gardens to scare off birds and thieves with his huge *pole* (phallus), like the "red stake projecting from the obscene groin" in Horace's *Satire* 1.8.1-7.

2352] *exomion* Diminutive of ἐξωμίς (= shoulder out), a one-sleeved tunic worn by poor working men, and by Philocleon's slaves in *Wasps* 444.

2354]   *Protest*   Used in the Latin and earlier English sense of "solemnly declare."

2361]   *Adulterous*   No specific adultery was attributed to Dionysus, whose "amours were not numerous" (Lemprière, 101), and whose legitimate children included Hymenaeus, the god of marriage; but sexual licence was a traditional element of Dionysus' festival, the Dionysia.

2367]   *Phales Iacchos*   See l. 564n. above.

2386]   *Satyric Play*   See l. 999n. above.

2387]   *wood-boys*   As creatures of the wild, Satyrs were especially associated with forests and hills.

2389-90]   *your Still-at-itch . . . innovator*   Your Euripides, with his passion for innovation.

2391]   *fifty . . . five*   Nauck spoils the neat proportion by listing the titles of eight satyric dramas by Euripides (Nauck, xxv). See l. 1003n. above.

2393]   *grimly*   Grim-looking.

2397]   *rillet*   A tiny stream (diminutive of *rill*).

2398]   *Thasian*   See l. 664n. above.

2399]   *Droll*   Comic production.

2402]   *your 'Alkestis'*   See ll. 1005-6n. above.

2411]   *adamantine*   The primary meaning of the Greek adjective (ἀδαμάντινος) is "of steel, steely."

2414]   *no iron joints its strength around*   Without any iron joints around it.

2417]   *Kallikratidas*   A Spartan admiral, drowned when defeated by the Athenian fleet at the battle of Arginusae (406 B.C.).

2419]   *Theramenes*   Satirized in *Frogs* 533-41 as a shifty politician who "always rolls over to the sheltered side of the boat." According to Thucydides (*History*, 8.89), Theramenes was among those who criticized the peace mission to Sparta, "fearing, as they said . . . that in the absence of the majority it might do some harm to the City."

2425-27]   *Demos . . . Boiled young again*   Adapted from *Knights* 1321, where the Sausage-Seller says: "By boiling Demos down [Δῆμον ἀφεψήσας] I've made him beautiful instead of ugly," an allusion to Medea's method of rejuvenating an old ram.

2429]   *One brilliance and one balsam*   I.e., looking and smelling superb, as after a bath.

   sways   A pun on two meanings of the word: rules as a *Monarch*, but also swings from one opinion to another, a common criticism of Athenian democracy.

2434]   *seeks out sound advisers*   Apparently a reference to the oligarchic government of the Four Hundred in 411 B.C.

2438] *the right grain is proper to right race* Good character naturally goes with good birth.

2441] *rouncey* An ordinary riding-horse.

2442] *sausage-selling snob* The adjective echoes the Sausage-Seller (ἀλλαντοπώλης) who replaces Cleon in *Knights*. The noun is used in its early sense (from 1832) of a common or vulgar member of the lower classes.

2443] *Alkibiades* See notes to 1042, 1043.

2448] *chaunoprockt* χαυνόπρωκτος (= loose-arsed [from the practice of sodomy]), an abusive adjective coined by Aristophanes in *Acharnians* 104, 106, and here turned into a noun. See l. 952n. above.

2449] *And got his . . .* A less Victorian Aristophanes would have replaced the dots by πέος (= penis), a word used some lines later in the same play (*Acharnians* (158).

2454] *I do not stickle for their punishment* I don't insist on punishing the common people.

2474] *Aristullos* See l. 1150n. above.

2476] *there's degree in heaven and earth* B was doubtless remembering Shakespeare's Ulysses (*Troilus and Cressida* 1.3.109-10) "Take but degree away, untune that string, / And hark what discord follows."

2480] *They are not!* See l. 1790n. above.

2480-82] *do not I . . . styles him King* In Euripides' *Suppliants* 399-405 a herald, just arrived in Athens, sensibly asks: "Who is the king [τύραννος] of the country?" and Theseus replies: "You were wrong from the start, stranger, to ask for a king here—for the city is not ruled by one man, but is a free one."

2484] *patronizing* Advocating, supporting (without the modern sense of condescension).

2496] *Kirké* Κίρκη (= Circe); see l. 682n. above.

2501] *truth which only lies declare* Cf. "Don't let truth's lump rot stagnant for the lack / Of a timely helpful lie to leaven it!" ("Mr. Sludge, 'the Medium,'" 1305-6; this edition, 6.342).

2517] *word to you, the wise* Aristophanes plays anachronistically with the English expression, "verb. sap.," which abbreviates a Latin one found in Plautus and Terence: *verbum sapienti sat est* (= a word is enough for a wise person, i.e., to understand something without a full explanation).

2526] *leavens their whole lump* Another anachronism: see 1 Cor. 5:6.

2535] *mother vended herbs* See l. 1737n. above.

2536-38] *his household drudge . . . the play* See l. 1739n. above.

2540] *a sorry scrub* A contemptible creature (eighteenth-century slang).

2549]   *'The tongue swears . . . unsworn!'*   See l. 1011n. above.

2553]   *round*   Whisper.

2554-55]   *with the mob . . . 'This to me?'*   Aristophanes means: In my plays I put my side of the argument to the mob, just as Euripides has put his. He then thinks (or pretends to think) that Balaustion has taken him to mean: "I am *now* pleading with a typical member of the mob," and has taken offence.

2574]   *Zeus? I have styled him . . . thrashing-block*   In *Frogs* 756 Dionysus' slave Xanthias calls Zeus his ὁμομαστιγίας (= fellow-deserver of whipping).

2575]   *my very next of plays*   I.e., Frogs (405 B.C.).

2584]   *of his abuse*   Of hearing him abused.

2585]   *his pummelling*   Both Xanthias and Dionysus are beaten to discover which is really the slave and which the god (*Frogs* 628-39).

2602-4]   *Hermes . . . imaged god . . . drunkards' frolic*   See l. 1482n. above.

2607]   *my Play*   Fuddled with Thasian, Aristophanes has now forgotten about his *Frogs* and started talking about his *Plutus*.

2608]   *have up Hermes*   Bring him up for trial. He was the god of thieves, tricksters, and dishonest tradesmen.

    a Karion, slave   A slave called Karion (Καρίων = little Carian) a common name for slaves in Comedy.

2609]   *calls our friend / The profitable god*   In *Plutus* 1156 Karion calls Hermes a παλιγκάπηλον (= buyer-and-seller, i.e., someone who buys things and sells them at a profit).

2610]   *we honour so*   Whom we honor by imitating his dishonesty, however much we insult him.

2612-13]   *Bids him . . . tripe in well-trough*   In Aeschylus' *Prometheus Bound* 942 Hermes calls himself the servant (διάκονος) of Zeus. In *Plutus* 1169-70 Karion tells him to make himself serviceable (διακονικός) by washing some tripe at the well.

2615-20]   *Asklepios . . . to be fetched*   The god of medicine. See l. 1230-31n. above.

2619]   *belike*   Perhaps, possibly.

2621]   *memorize*   Commemorate.

2622]   *set an altar up*   Apparently B's combination of two statements in the *Life of Sophocles* (11-12) that he was "a priest of Alcon who [was] a hero with Asclepius," and that "he founded a temple to Heracles the Informer"; see ll. 1232-34n. above.

2624]   *trust me to describe*   He did so in *Plutus* 653-747, where Plutus is cured of his blindness by Asclepius.

2625]   *choused*   Cheated.

    his brace of girls   His daughters, Iaso and Panacea, mentioned in *Plutus* 701-2.

2626] *Their snake* One of two sacred ones, whose hiss Karion imitates in *Plutus* 689-90.

2627] *'consecrate . . . into a bag'* An expression used of the priest in *Plutus* 681.

2628] *for whimsies done away with* I.e., a liturgical euphemism for the theft of anything that take the priest's fancy.

2629] *a stone's throw from that theatre* The sanctuary of Asclepius was above the Theatre of Dionysus on the west slope of the Acropolis.

2630] *I thus unmask their dupery* The irreverence of the whole description, e.g., Karion's "tremendous fart" at the god's approach (*Plutus* 696-99) is cited to prove that Aristophanes is no *superstitious fool* (l. 2570 above).

2632] *nor word nor sign* I.e., of criticism by Aristophanes.

2633] *a harmless parody or so* E.g., *Plutus* 635-36, quoted from Sophocles' *Phineus*.

2635] *good easy soul* In *Frogs* 82 Sophocles is described as εὔκολος (= easy-going, contented).

2636] *saves his cash* See ll. 1245-49n. above.

2637] *loves wine and . . . other sport* See l. 279n. above.

2638] *sword-blade-smith* The *Life of Sophocles* begins (1: 3-5): "Sophillus [his father], was not, as Aristoxenus says, a sword-maker [μαχαιροποιός]] . . . but owned slaves who were copper-smiths or carpenters."

2639] *Proves but queer captain* See l. 278n. above.

2639-41] *when the people claim . . . squadron's charge* The *Hypothesis* (= introductory notes) to Sophocles' *Antigone* by Aristophanes of Byzantium states (15-17): "They say that Sophocles was thought worthy of the generalship in Samos after distinguishing himself by producing *Antigone*."

2642] *needs the son's help . . . finish plays* See ll. 1257-59n. above.

2663] *My Just Judge* Aeacus, one of the judges of the dead in the Underworld, who "justly [δικαίως]" beats both Dionysus and Xanthias to see which of them is the god (*Frogs* 641-43); see l. 1659n. above.

2685] *you fools* Which you fools.

2693] *Kinesias* Parodied in *Birds* 1372-1409 as typical of the new school of dithyrambic poetry (for choral singing). His vapid song begins with words borrowed from Anacreon: "I fly up on light wings to Olympus," and goes on to elaborate that image of poetic inspiration, until Peisthetaerus exclaims (1382): "Do stop singing and tell me what you mean!"

2697] *contravene* Contradict me.

2698] *rosy* One more patronizing pun on her nationality. See l. 53n. above.

2700]   *Aristullos, mint-perfumed*   Aristyllus, i.e., Plato (see l. 1150n. above), was said to have once had his face smeared with dung. So in *Ecclesiazusae* 646-47 Blepyrus is told: "If Aristyllus were to kiss you, . . . you'd smell of mint   [καλαμίνθη, with a pun on μίνθος = dung]."

2705-6]   *my Aristonumos, / Ameipsias or Sannurion*   Rivals and critics of Aristophanes. See l. 909n. above. According to the *Life of Aristophanes* (Meineke, 1.542-43) Aristonymus and Ameipsias "jeered at Aristophanes" because he produced his first plays under the names of Callistratus and Philonides. Meineke says (1.263) that Sannurion ridiculed Aristophanes, and was called by him a ᾁδοφοίτης (= frequenter of Hades), because he was so thin that he always looked at death's door.

2707]   *Three cuckoos who cry 'cuckoo'*   In *Acharnians* 598 Lamachus is said to have been elected, not "by the people," as he is about to claim, but by "three cuckoos" (= people who voted again and again). The phrase *cry cuckoo* roughly equates with the Greek κοκκύζω, though that word is also used in *Frogs* 1380 merely to mean "sing out," as a signal to let go of the scales. Here B uses it to suggest not merely senseless repetition, but also calling someone a fool (one meaning of the English word *cuckoo*).

2708]   *boil a stone*   A metaphor based on λίθον ἕψεις (= "you're boiling a stone," i.e., wasting your time), an expression used by Philocleon in *Wasps* 280, when rejecting pleas for mercy. That allusion aptly concludes Aristophanes' attack on Euripides, since nine lines later (*Wasps* 289) the wasp-chorus mention a new target for their rage: one of "the traitors in Thrace" (there aimed at Brasidas, but here naturally recalling Euripides; see l. 238n. above).

    Neblaretai! I've finished! (I.e., that ends my indictment of Euripides; see l. 666n. above.)

    Rattei! ῾Ράττει, a word not found in Aristophanes, but mentioned by Meineke (2.1046) when explaining *Neblaretai* (Νεβλάρεται). See l. 666n. above. Meineke quoted Photius' definition of this second word: "exclamation of people enjoying themselves and dancing," i.e., something like "Whoopee!" Here it marks Aristophanes' reversion to his festive mood.

2725]   *strength*   Balaustion's point (personal memories are non-transferable), and her image (memory = honey, wording = wax) are clear enough; but the train of thought between *honey* and *strength* requires a knowledge of Samson's riddle about honey in a lion's carcase to explain it: "Out of the strong came forth sweetness" (Judg. 14:14)— and also to explain the transition to the lion-fable in l. 2738 below.

2728]   *suspected*   I.e., too faint to prove its existence. The flower-scent image seems to echo Shelley's poem "Music, when soft voices die" (3-6).

2737-38]   *mouse confronts / The forest-monarch*   In the Aesop fable,

"Lion and Mouse" (No. 98 in *Aesopicae Fabulae* [Leipsig, 1868], 47-48), the lion "smiled" when the mouse promised to return the favor of his release, but was duly rescued by the mouse when tied by hunters to a tree. Thus Balaustion implies that her advice might save Aristophanes from condemnation by later critics.

2742] *knowledge . . . love* An antithesis central to *Paracelsus*, e.g., 2.384-85 (this edition, 1.126).

2757] *order* Rank or class of person, i.e., in this case a poetic genius.

2766] *those flowers / We fain would have earth yield* Those flowers (of *good*) that we want earth to yield.

2770] *isled about* Isolated, as a foreigner, from the climate of opinion in which natives live.

2774] *who may extricate?* A rhetorical equivalent of the adjective, "inextricable."

2775] *perks up* Raises its head, shows itself.

2790] *By efficacy* Parallel to *By origin, by exercise* (l. 2783).

2791] *fly-flap* Instrument for driving off flies.

2800] *Sousarion* See ll. 845-46n. above.

    car cart, wagon; an allusion to the tradition, accepted by Bentley but judged "hardly credible" by Meineke (1.25) that the comedies invented by Susarion were staged and "carried about on wagons [ἐν ἀπήναις]."

2805-6] *Who shall gainsay . . . too sensitive?* Is B hinting that Victorian horror of Aristophanes' obscenity is equally caused by ignorance of a foreign culture?

2812] *Who bends the head unquestioning* I.e., to current *convention*.

2817] *slave-brand set on brow indelibly* I.e., a genius like Aristophanes is considered beneath contempt.

2821] *submissive dip* An almost metaphysical image for a temporary response to the "low" tastes of a popular audience.

2825] *blast* No longer the light breeze that makes leaves and blossoms merely *dance,* but a dangerous gale threatening *meadow-wreck.* The first image has given place to another, possibly suggested by Horace's *Odes* II x 9-12, where the *ingens pinus* (huge pine) is more vulnerable to winds than humbler vegetation.

2832] *prescription* I.e., tradition.

2833] *Such* Such charitably critical foreigners.

2838] *"Lemnians"* A lost Aristophanes comedy. B had two possible reasons to make Balaustion disapprove of it: Dindorf thought it was a satire on Euripides' *Hypsipyle*; and Meineke thought it was all about a "foul superstition" which appealed to the Athenians' "lusts" by its "all-night orgies" (Meineke, 2.1096-97).

"The Hours" Another lost play by Aristophanes, a satire, according to Meineke (2.1170), on another "foul" cult, that of Sabazius, whose all-night orgies made Sosias keep falling asleep in *Wasps* 9.

2839] *"Female-Playhouse-seat-Preoccupants,"* A "transcription" of Σκηνὰς Καταλαμβανοῦσαι (= Women Seizing Theatres), another of Aristophanes' lost comedies. Meineke guessed from the title that "the women, who were not allowed to watch comedies, preoccupied [*preoccuparent*] seats in the theatre before the men came in (Meineke, 2.1140-41)."

2840-42] *once a year . . . play the mendicant* As the Emperor Augustus was said by Suetonius to have done (*Life of Augustus,* 91). B used that story again in "Imperante Augusto Natus Est," 126-30 (*Asolando* [1889]).

2846] *could I also show* Apparently a wish: "may I also share!" The *should I also share* of the first edition reads more confidently, as the apodosis of the conditional clause in l. 2845: "If I share the weakness I should also share the strength."

2854] *as strange* I.e., as strange as the idea of a world not filled by Hellas.

2856] *black earth* See l. 1793n. above.

2857] *Attiké* See l. 29n. above.

2858] *philanthropic* In the Greek sense of the word φιλάνθρωπος (= loving human beings).

2861] *Kassiterides* Κασσιτερίδες (= Tin-Islands), used generally of north-western tin-producing regions, especially the Scillies and Cornwall, but here suggesting the British Isles.

2863] *Pheidias* See l. 109n. above.

2864] *Zeuxis* A famous painter (5th century B.C.), relevant here because his picture of Eros is alluded to in *Acharnians* 991-92, and because he was said to have given a picture of Pan to Euripides' host, King Archelaus.

2865] *judge of these!* Balaustion appeals, in effect, to what Pater's article on "Coleridge's Writings" (1866) had called the "relative spirit"; but the anachronism was defensible, since Pater had found the "germ" of that spirit in the dictum of Heraclitus (c. 540-480 B.C.): πάντα ῥεῖ (= everything flows, i.e., is in a state of flux).

2872] *wears no sword* According to Thucydides (*History,* 1.6) the Athenians were the first among the Greeks to drop the habit of wearing arms, a point used by Matthew Arnold to prove that fifth-century Athens was more "modern" than Elizabethan England ("The Modern Element in Literature"[1857], *The Complete Prose Works of Matthew Arnold,* ed. R. H. Super [Ann Arbor, 1960-77], 1.24).

2874] *brother-sculptor* Perhaps Pheidias' older contemporary, Myron, a specialist in athlete-statues like the Discobolus (Δισκοβόλος = Discus-Thrower), of which B could have seen the copy in Rome. But he was evidently still thinking of the same passage in Thucydides, which continued: "And the Spartans . . . were the first to strip naked [for the Games] and, undressing in public [ἐς τὸ φανερόν], to anoint themselves with oil after exercise" (*History*, 1.6).

2876-77] *public games, / Atrociously exposed* Thucydides added (*History*, 1.6): "but in ancient times, even at the Olympic Games, athletes wore loin-cloths to cover their private parts, and it is not many years since that stopped." Thus Victorian prudery could even be seen as a throwback to primitivism.

2878] *the Immortal* The *philanthropic god* of l. 2858.

2890-92] *One naked glory . . . human frame* Balaustion anticipates B's protest at the outcry against his son Pen's nude Joan of Arc (12 May 1886): "I am ashamed at the objection taken by some of the critics to the Eve-like simplicity of Pen's peasant-girl" (Hood, 247). See Irvine and Honan, 487-88, and the notes to the "Parleying with Francis Furini" in this edition, 16.216-17.

2897] *your faultless* A quasi-Greek use of a neuter adjective as an abstract noun; see l. 124n. above.

2906] *tax* Criticize.

2912] *your games . . . Olympian, Zeus gave birth to these* The Olympic Games were held at Olympia, the main sanctuary of Zeus in Greece, and were held at his four-yearly festivals there from 776 B.C.

2913] *institute* Used in the Latin sense of *institutum* (a neuter past participle passive serving as noun = something established by). The Pythian Games, held in honor of Phoebus Apollo at Delphi, were reorganized as early as 582 B.C.

2914] *Isthmian* Held on the Isthmus of Corinth in honor of Poseidon. Lemprière said they were "instituted" in 1326 B.C., but later discontinued until Theseus "reinstituted them in honor of Neptune, whom he publicly called his father" (Lemprière, 302). Historically they dated from the 580s B.C.

Nemeian Held in the sanctuary of Zeus at Nemea, and founded, according to one tradition, by Heracles after killing the Nemean lion. They dated from c. 573 B.C.

2919] *Or I misunderstand, or* "Either I misunderstand or"; B imitates the Greek use of the same word, ἤ, for both "either" and "or." Balaustion's debating-point about the *late* development of Comedy was probably suggested by Aristotle's *Poetics* (1449a 38-1449b 2): "The origins of Comedy are not known, because it was not at first taken seriously; for it was at a late date [ὀψέ ποτε, probably around 465 B.C.] that the archon sanctioned a chorus of comic players."

2920]   *that rustic song*   According to *Poetics* 1448a 37-38, the Megarians took the word *Comedy* (Κωμῳδία)to mean "village-song," deriving it, "not from κωμάζειν [= to revel] but from κώμη [= village], because comic players went wandering around villages, being driven in disgrace [ἀτιμαζομένους] from the city." Balaustion refers back to Aristophanes' own account of the birth of Comedy in ll. 1792-1829 above.

2935]   *Sousarion*   See ll. 845-46n. above. The chronology inscribed on the Parian Marble dates his origination of Comedy in Attica between 581 and 560 B.C.

2936]   *Chionides*   See l. 847n. above.

   "Banqueters"   Δαιταλεῖς, Aristophanes' first comedy, which won second prize in 427 B.C.

2937]   *"Prometheus"*   *Prometheus Bound* (Δεσμώτης), traditionally attributed to Aeschylus, but possibly completed or even composed by someone else after his death in 456 B.C. B seems to assume a much earlier date for it, perhaps because it has been thought to refer to a great eruption of Mount Etna in 478 B.C.

2939]   *"Oidipous"*   Οἰδίπους (– Swollen-Foot). Balaustion is again on shaky ground: the date of the Οἰδίπους Τύραννος (= *Oedipus the King*) is unknown, but was possibly not long after 430 B.C.—so *Banqueters* (427 B.C.) may conceivably have come first.

2940]   *"Medeia"*   See ll. 162-63n. above. It was produced in 431 B.C.

2941]   *"Babylonians"*   Aristophanes' second comedy, produced 426 B.C., but also lost.

2942]   *days that left Hellas free*   I.e., from Persian domination.

2943]   *huge help*   One of many sarcastic references to Aristophanes' claim that Comedy might bring *Plataian help*, l. 2100 above; a claim possibly suggested by the *Prolegomena de Comoedia* (*Scholia*, xvii Ixa 22-25): "and since the city derived great help [μεγάλας ὠφελείας] from this [the public shaming of wrongdoers in Comedy], they decreed that poets should be free to satirize anyone they liked."

2944-51]   *Eighty-years-late . . . helpful ordinance?*   A figure hardly confirmed by the dates of the events mentioned: Marathon 490 B.C., Plataea 479 B.C., Salamis 480 B.C.; *new educators* were satirized in the first production of *Clouds* (423 B.C.); *exception* was taken to *foreign legates* in *Acharnians* (425 B.C.). The *eighty* was possibly taken out of context by B from two clauses in Meineke's lengthy discussion of Susarion and the early development of Comedy: "for the next eighty years after Susarion Comedy made so little noise that we hear of no progress or advances in the new art"; and "finally, eighty years after Susarion . . . the art of comedy rose again" (Meineke, 1.25-26).

2948]   *pretend its rise*   Claim to have risen.

2955-59]   *brutish . . . bestial*   A reply to Aristophanes' emphasis on the animal aspects of early comedy, e.g., *disguised their forms / With skins, beast-fashion,* (ll. 1803-4 above), and on his own preference for *the earth-spasm, when the lion ramped / And the bull gendered* (ll. 1923-24 above).

2963-64]   *Then was I first . . . cleanly sense*   A boast made, for instance, in *Clouds* 537-40.

2977]   *myself invented Comedy!*   A claim supported by the *Life of Aristophanes:* "He seems to have been the first to guide Comedy, which was still wandering in its ancient ways, towards something more useful and dignified, when Cratinus and Eupolis were just hurling unduly violent and disgusting abuse" (Meineke, 1.542).

2978]   *many a famed Parabasis!*   E.g., *Acharnians* 628-58, where he calls himself "the best poet . . . giving to best advice"; or *Wasps* 1015-50, where he "swears by Dionysus that no one has ever heard a better comedy than this one." See l. 711n. above.

2985-86]   *will . . . warrant . . . work . . . stand . . . stumble . . . worth*   A type of alliterative word-play dear to Aristophanes as well as B.

2995]   *check . . . litigation-itch*   Notably in *Wasps.*

2996-97]   *mob-rule . . . mob-flattery . . . mob-favourites*   E.g., in *Acharnians.*

2998]   *sophists*   E.g., in *Clouds.*

2999]   *poets their accomplices*   In all the satire on Euripides, from *Acharnians* to *Thesmophoriazusae.*

3001]   *snob*   See l. 2442n. above.

3009]   *not thyself Augustlier than the need*   She need not call anyone as grand as Euripides to appear in person as a witness: it is enough to cite his works.

3009-10]   *century / Of subjects*   Hundred tragic themes and characters (perhaps with a pun on the "subjects" of an *august* king). See l. 263n. above.

   dared and done   See l. 915n. above.

3011-12]   *"Banqueters" . . . "Babylonians"*   See ll. 2936n. and 2941n. above.

3012]   *played Prometheus*   An ingenious pun: pretended to *enlighten earth* by the gift of fire, science, and technology, as described in Aeschylus' *Prometheus Bound* 442-506; and also claimed to be as great a play as that one.

3015]   *Labour by labour, all of Herakles*   The Labors imposed on Heracles by Eurystheus are described by the chorus of Euripides' *Heracles,* 359-424; ll. 3936-95 below.

3021-34] *"Peace, in whom depths . . . banish Strife"* A fairly close translation of fragment 453, from Euripides' lost *Cresphontes* (*Fragmenta*, 499-500).

3033-34] *against the life / That's whetted* That is whetted against the life (again a quasi-Greek word-order, though not that of the original, which is: "Strife in whetted rejoicing steel").

3040] *unburned by stigma* Unstigmatized. Unlike *brand* in English, the Greek word *stigma* has nothing to do with burning, only with pricking or tattooing, e.g., as a mark of disgrace; but B had the excuse that Liddell and Scott (1871) still gave one meaning of the verb στίζω (used in *Frogs* 1511) as: "*to burn a mark in, to brand*, of runaway slaves."

3041] *bettered* Made better, improved.

3042] *gem-indenture* State of being indented (= embossed, inlaid) with jewels.

3043] *Kunthia's mountain treasure-house* A slightly inaccurate phrase: Κυνθία (anglicized as Cynthia) was a name for Artemis, as in Keats's *Endymion*; but she had no special connection with poetry. The word was actually a feminine adjective of Mount Cynthus in Delos, the birthplace of both Artemis and Phoebus Apollo, the god of poetry. B was evidently recalling *Clouds* 594-97: "Lord Phoebus of Delos, inhabiting the high-peaked Cynthian [Κυνθίαν] rock."

3044] *Ere you . . . or boy?* Euripides' first play was produced in 455 B.C., Aristophanes,' in 427 B.C.

3066] *Marathon* Here used to symbolize the unquestionable priority of national defense. See l. 450n. above.

3071] *universal crop and clown* I.e., to any fool. The first noun is presumably used in the sense (*OED*, sb. 15) of "a person wearing his hair cropped short," e.g., a slave or laborer; and the second, of an "ignorant peasant."

3076] *skiadeion* σκιάδειον (= sunshade, parasol, from σκιά = shadow). In *Birds* 1508, 1550 a *skiadeion* is jokingly mentioned as a means of escaping divine observation; but B, conscious that *umbrella* (from *umbra* = shade) should also mean "sunshade," lets the Greek equivalent offer protection against the downpour of *reproof* and *sonorous doctrine*.

3084] *Lamachos . . . case, crests and all* See l. 1187n. above. In *Acharnians* 572-86 Lamachus appears fully armed, with a Gorgon on his shield and his helmet crested with huge plumes, asking mock-heroically, "Who has roused the Gorgon from its case [σάγμα (= covering of a shield)]?" The pacifist-hero Dicaeopolis borrows one of the plumes to make himself sick in the upturned shield, explaining: "I'm sick of crests!"

3086] *Kleon* See ll. 89n. and 401n. above.

Huperbolos   See l. 2304n. above.

3087]   *Nikias*   See ll. 1456-57n. above.

3089]   *Choros crying "Hence, impure!"*   Like the chorus of initiates in *Frogs* 354-70: "Keep away from our dances . . . whoever is not pure in mind!"

3090]   *Ariphrades*   See l. 1120n. above.

3095]   *scout*   Reject with scorn.

3097]   *coarsely-coated*   I.e., thick-headed.

3100]   *Those—not these*   Aim at the former (*hard headpieces*) not the latter (*finer pates*). B copies the Greek use of ἐκεῖνος (= that), and οὗτος (= this) to indicate further or nearer words in a sentence.

3102-3]   *burns Sokrates, / House over head*   Burns Socrates' house over his head. In *Clouds* 1484-85 Strepsiades goes off to "burn the house [οἰκίαν] of those idle talkers," i.e., Socrates and his associates.

3103]   *or, better, poisons him*   B thus implicitly blames Aristophanes for the execution of Socrates, by poisoning with hemlock, in 399 B.C.

3105]   *Club-drub*   Thump with a club.

callous   I.e., thick-skinned, insensitive.

3114]   *cheesecake-time*   See l. 1889n. above.

3115]   *Hare-slice-and-peasoup-season*   See l. 1958n. above.

3116]   *Theoria*   Θεωρία (= the sending of a state-ambassador; θεωρός = spectator) to watch the festival Games in another Greek city; hence a symbol of friendly relations between Greek cities, and of shared celebration. In *Peace* 523-27 Theoria is personified as a beautiful girl-attendant on Peace. The *beautiful belongings* there praised are her face and her breath. See ll. 1163-64n. above.

3117]   *Opora*   Ὀπώρα (= late summer, fruit-time, fruit), personified in *Peace* 523 as another girl-attendant of Peace. Her *lavish condescendings* ironically reflect the scholiast's note (*Scholia,* 187) that both girls were presented "as prostitutes [ὡς πόρνας]."

3131]   *apology*   Defense (the meaning of the Greek word ἀπολογία).

3133]   *Acharnian charcoal*   An image possibly suggested by *Acharnians* 321, where Dicaeopolis, threatened by the rage of the chorus, exclaims: "What a black piece of burning charcoal [μέλας θυμάλωψ] has flared up among you!"

3134]   *Kimmerian*   Like the land of the Cimmerians, where the sun never shines, but "baleful night is spread over wretched mortals" (*Odyssey* 11.14-19).

Stugian   Like the darkness of Styx, the River of Hatred in Hades.

3138-39]   *Lamachos . . . "hero," say yourself*   He died (414 B.C.) as one of the generals in the Sicilian Expedition. Praising Homer's moral influence in *Frogs* 1034-39, Aristophanes makes Aeschylus say: "he taught many other good men, of whom the hero Lamachus was one."

3140] *Gibe Nikias into privacy?* It was under his sole command that the Sicilian expedition ended in disaster. See ll. 1456-57n. above.

3141-44] *Kleon . . . good tough hide* An allusion to Aristophanes' constant gibes at Cleon for being a tanner. His death in the battle of Amphipolis (422 B.C.) showed rather less *toughness* than Balaustion implies. At Brasidas' surprise attack (according to Thucydides, *History*, 5.10): "Cleon, who had never intended to stand his ground, immediately ran away, and was caught and killed by a Myrcinian peltast."

3146] *Aristullos* See l. 1150n. above.

3148] *Ariphrades* See l. 1120n. above.

3149-50] *that redoubtable / Harp-player* In *Wasps* 1278 it is not Ariphrades, but his brother Arignotus that is called a "superlative harpist [κίθαραοιδότατος]"; but a scholium to *Ecclesiazusae* 129 (*Scholia*, 316) describes Ariphrades himself as a "filthy harpist [αἰσχρὸς κιθαρῳδός]."

3165] *rancid tunny, onions raw* In *Acharnians* 1099-1101, where Lamachus and Dicaeopolis order a soldier's and a peacetime civilian's dinners respectively, Lamachus calls for "salt with thyme, onions, and a fig-leaf full of rotten dried fish."

3167] *flute-girls* See l. 99n. above.

3168] *How thick and fast . . . freezing War* The passage contrasting the two menus ends with Lamachus saying (*Acharnians* 1141): "Oh dear, it's snowing! Things look wintry."

3173] *Leonidas* The Spartan commander of the Greeks who fought off the Persian invaders in the narrow mountain-pass of Thermopylae (480 B.C.), until all the defenders were killed. Their heroism was celebrated in a famous epigram of Simonides (*Greek Lyric III*, ed. and tr. D. A. Campbell [London, 1991], 540, No. 22b).

3179-81] *to save . . . home and liberty* A paraphrase of the cry heard at the battle of Salamis in Aeschylus' *Persae* 402-4: "Come, children of the Greeks, free your fatherland, free your children, your wives, the seats of your fathers' gods, and the tombs of your ancestors."

3186] *Kleonumos* See ll. 943-44n. above.

3191] *Miltiades* See l. 450n. above.

3192] *Themistokles* See ll. 79-80n. above.

3193] *Kimon* See l. 2028n. above.

3194-95] *twenty-five years since, / The war began* Since it began in 431 B.C., B seems to imply that this conversation (and the production of the second *Thesmophoriazusae*) took place in 406 B.C.

3196] *The end shows all* An echo of Hector's comment on the Trojan War in Shakespeare's *Troilus and Cressida* 4.5.224-26: "The end crowns all, / And that old common arbitrator, Time, / Will one day end it."

But the thought resembles that of Sophocles' *Oedipus Tyrannus* 1528-30: "Looking to see that final day, call no mortal happy before he passes the end of his life without suffering anything painful."

3198]   '*ware the wasps*   Beware of politically biased jurymen like the spiteful wasp-chorus in *Wasps*.

3199]   *heliast-like*   See l. 89n. above.

3200]   *Wants hemlock*   Is asking for capital punishment; see l. 2074n. above.

3203]   *Philokleon*   Φιλοκλέων (= Lover of Cleon). See l. 1382n. above.

  Bdelukleon   Βδελυκλέων (= Loather of Cleon): Philocleon's son in *Wasps*. From l. 1129 onwards the comedy becomes pointless farce. The son converts his father to his own way of life, as a young man about town.

3205]   *cheats baker's wives*   A female bread-seller (ἀρτοπῶλις) complains that he has knocked ten obols' worth of bread off her shelves (*Wasps* 1389-91).

3206]   *Parades . . . flute-girl*   He has "stolen her from his son's party" and invites her to hold his leather phallus (*Wasps* 1341-44).

3206-7]   *bandies filth / With his own son*   In a cryptic comparison of the flute-girl to a torch (*Wasps* 1373-75) one scholiast detects a reference to her pubic hair (*Scholia,* 165).

3207-8]   *cured his father's cold / By making him catch fever*   An image possibly suggested by the Vaccination Acts of 1871 and 1874 (the year B wrote *Aristophanes' Apology*).

3209]   *faugh!*   Exclamation of disgust and contempt.

3214]   *fribble*   An unimportant, frivolous person.

3222]   *Morsimos*   See l. 328n. above.

3223]   *Somebody . . . courts his wife*   I.e., Cephisophon; see l. 1739n. above.

3224]   *His uncle deals in crockery*   A comic variation on the herb-selling-mother theme. See l. 1737n. above.

3225]   *stranger*   See l. 1579n. above.

3227]   *housebreaker*   See l. 1129n. above (though in *Frogs* the word is used to abuse, not a *poet-rival,* but two tragic poets' audiences).

3228]   *Fish-gorging*   See l. 948n. above.

  midnight footpad   See l. 946n. above.

3232]   *from Kratinos downwards*   The point of Balaustion's sarcasm is that Cratinus was both a member and a taxiarch (= commander) of the Oeneis tribe at Athens, so could not have been less of a foreigner. See Meineke, 1.46, and l. 129n. above.

3236-37]   *You too . . . Kameiros*   See ll. 651n. and 1905-7n. above.

3238]   *Egypt reared, if Eupolis be right*   Egyptian was one of several nationalities attributed to Aristophanes. Meineke suggested (1.111-2) that a fragment of Eupolis complaining about the popularity of foreign poets with Athenian audiences was specifically aimed at Aristophanes as "Rhodian by birth," but it is not clear why B linked Eupolis with the "Egyptian" theory here. In Athenaeus (6.229e) Heliodorus of Athens is quoted as saying that Aristophanes was born in the Egyptian city of Naucratis.

3239-40]   *Who wrote . . . helped a little*   You (Aristophanes), who wrote the comedy (*Knights*) which Cratinus swears he helped you a little to write. The *little* help was the comparison of Cratinus to a river in *Knights* 526-28, an image which, according to the scholiast (*Scholia,* 52), Cratinus had first used in praise of himself, and which Aristophanes had ridiculed by making it a river of urine. Balaustion innocently ignores that implication, and treats it as a simple case of plagiarism.

3241]   *nigh promoted Comic*   Promoted almost to the status of a comic poet (κωμικός), i.e., showed the same absurd xenophobia.

3241-44]   *when he haled . . . our privilege*   See ll. 1900-5n. above.

3250]   *fancy-fleerings*   I.e., jeers based on fancy rather than fact.

3252]   *Logeion*   Λογεῖον (= speaking-place, stage), theatre.

3253-54]   *Perikles invents . . . three maids*   A summary of *Acharnians* 524-29: "Some drunk young men went and stole a prostitute called Simaetha from Megara; and then the Megarians . . . retaliated by stealing two prostitutes of Aspasia's; and that's how the war that burst out over the whole of Greece was started—by three tarts. And that's why Olympian Pericles showed his wrath with thunder and lightning, and threw all Greece into turmoil." According to Plutarch (*Life of Pericles,* 24) Pericles' mistress Aspasia was highly educated, much valued by him for her political wisdom, and visited by Socrates and his friends for philosophical discussions; but also kept a brothel.

3255]   *wants burning, house o'er head*   Ought to have his house burnt down on him. See ll. 3102-3n. above.

3267]   *whirligig*   See l. 1874n. above.

3273]   *stop-estray*   Preventer of straying from the path of virtue.

3274]   *born a twin with public liberty*   See ll. 391n., 1784-87n. above.

3286]   *change your side*   If you look at it from another angle.

   shoots light, where dark alone   For the image, central to B's thinking, see *The Ring and the Book* 1.1363-65 (this edition, 7.56): "Shifted a hair's-breadth shoots you dark for bright, / Suffuses bright with dark, and baffles so / Your sentence absolute for shine or shade."

3293-94]   *depict . . . painting*   B assumes the reader's awareness that *depict* comes from Latin *pingere* (= paint).

371

3298] *Speculation-shop* B's translation of φροντιστήριον (= thinking-place), Socrates' schoolhouse, which is set on fire by Strepsiades in *Clouds* (94, 128, 1484). See ll. 3102-3n. above.

3302-5] *Just as did Kleon . . . may mock* See ll. 1900-5n. above.

3308-9] *Lamia-shape . . . camel-rest* In *Wasps* 1031-35 Cleon was described as having "the voice of a torrent that had mothered destruction, and the stink of a seal, and the unwashed balls of a Lamia [Λάμια = fabulous man-eating monster], and the rump of a camel."

3309] *Kukloboros* Κυκλόβορος (= with devouring eddies), the name of a river in Attica, which only flowed in winter. See scholiast (*Scholia,* 38) to *Knights* 137, where Cleon is said to sound like it.

3310] *Aristullos* See l. 1150n. above.

3311] *male-Kirké and her swinish crew* The image used for this attack on Plato's homosexuality came from *Plutus* 302-15, where the reference to Aristyllus is associated with Circe's transformations of men into pigs (see l. 682n. above). In Plato's own *Symposium* (191e-192b) Aristophanes jocosely praises homosexuals as more "manly" than heterosexuals.

3312] *PLATON* Πλάτων = Plato.

3313-15] *Sends your performance . . . pleasantry* From the *Life of Aristophanes*: "And they say that, when King Dionysius wanted to learn about Athenian politics, Plato sent him the poetry of Aristophanes, and advised him to find out about Athenian politics by studying his plays" (Meineke, 1.544; *Scholia,* xvii 59-63).

3316-17] *One Aristullos means myself . . . merry grig* I.e., Plato dismisses the attack on himself as just good fun.

3321] *When forth yourself step, tell us from the stage* E.g., in the Parabasis of *Clouds* (518f), *Wasps* (1015f), or *Peace* (734f).

3325] *those satyr-adjuncts* See ll. 101n. and 1153-54n. above.

3330] *nuts and barleycorns* See l. 714n. above.

3334-35] *once dead . . . attack a corpse?* Cf. *Clouds* 549-50: "When Cleon was at his greatest, I hit him in the stomach, but I hadn't the heart to do it again, or jump on him when he was lying dead."

3337-38] *I pity from my soul . . . Kratinos* In *Knights* 526-34 Aristophanes reproached his audience for "not pitying" Cratinus in his old age. See ll. 129n. and 721-28n. above.

3341] *passenger* Passer by.

3353] *"Bottle"* I.e., Πυτίνη (= wine-flask), the title of Cratinus' play, which beat Aristophanes' *Clouds* in 423 B.C.

3361] *Pallas's casque* The punning image for high art and divine protection was doubtless suggested by Cratinus's charge that Phidias embezzled gold intended for his statue of Pallas Athene (see l. 129n. above).

3367] *share and share . . . says the world* Possibly an allusion to the proverbial saying "κοινὰ τὰ φίλων" (= the possessions of friends are held in common; Plato, *Republic* 4.424a 1-2, *Phaedrus*, 279c).

3370-72] *Kratinos . . . Eupolis* Included in Meineke's list of the "brightest stars of comic poetry" (Meineke, 1.43).

3374] *Magnes* Mentioned in Aristotle's *Poetics* 1448a 34 as one of the earliest comic poets; and in Aristophanes' *Knights* 520-23, as having won more prizes than any of his competitors, with choruses that imitated "the sounds of plucking instruments, of fluttering wings, . . . of gall-insects, and were dressed in frog-colors"—thus anticipating his own *Birds* and *Frogs*.

3375] *Archippos punned* Athenaeus quotes (14.329b-c) a fragment of Archippus' comedy, *Fish*, about *Thrattai* (Θρᾷτται = 1. Thracian girls 2. small sea-fishes). Editing this fragment, Meineke says (2.719): "I have capitalized those words on which the poet plays ambiguously."

Hegemon parodied According to Aristotle's *Poetics* 1448a 12-13), "Hegemon of Thasos was the first who wrote parodies."

3377-79] *Eupolis exposed . . . grime on Socrates* Based on Scholia to *Clouds* 96 (*Scholia*, 85-86): "Eupolis attacked Socrates more than Aristophanes did in the whole of the *Clouds* [when he wrote] 'But Socrates, when passed the winecup, stole it'" (c.f. Meineke, 2.552, No. ix).

3380] *what beat "Clouds" but "Konnos,"* See l. 909n. above.

3382] *Eukrates and Lusikles* See l. 2305-6n. above.

3383] *Telekleides* A comic poet who won his first prize at the Dionysia around 445 B.C. Meineke called him "a bitter opponent of Pericles," and quoted a fragment protesting against his dictatorial power (Meineke, 1.86).

Hermippos See l. 965n. above. Meineke (1.91) quoted some lines of Hermippus calling Pericles "a king of Satyrs" and a cowardly general.

3384] *Kumon* An unknown name, though it appears in B's MS. He probably meant to write *Kimon*, i.e., Κίμων, traditionally transliterated *Cimon* (see l. 2028n. above). In Plutarch's *Life of Cimon*, 15, Pericles is mentioned as being "in power [δυναμένου]" and then some lines of Eupolis attacking Cimon are quoted. But nowhere in the fragments of either Teleclides or Hermippus, or in Meineke's comments on them (1.86-99; 2.361-417) can I trace any mention of Cimon. Perhaps a rare case of B "nodding."

3386] *Philonides or else Kallistratos* See l. 1250n. above, and the *Life of Aristophanes:* "Being very cautious when he started, he produced his first plays through Callistratus and Philonides" (Meineke, 1.543).

3393-94]   *Moruchides . . . Surakosios*   See ll. 710n. and 987n. above.

Euthumenes   Mentioned by Meineke as the last archon under whom the decree against personal abuse in comedy remained in force (Meineke, 1.40).

3395]   *Agurrhios*   See l. 700n. above.

Kinesias   The odd man out in this company of anti-comedy legislators. Aristophanes had parodied him in *Birds* 1372-1415 as a vapid dithyrambic poet. Unless B has got his names confused, he must mean Balaustion to regard even that type of poetry as an improvement on the *sty* of Aristophanic comedy.

3400]   *Krates*   Mentioned in Aristotle's *Poetics* 1449b 7-9 as "the first at Athens to give up the iambic form [i.e., the personal lampoon], and compose general stories or plots [λόγους ἢ μύθους]", a passage quoted and discussed by Meineke (1.59-60). In *Knights* 537-41 Aristophanes praises Crates for "holding out against the angry abuse of his audience" and for his "most witty inventiveness"—exemplified by his Θηρία (= Animals). In this lost comedy, wrote Meineke (2.237), he "presented animals conversing rationally with human beings, and urging them not to eat meat."

3401]   *gay*   One instance of his gaiety (*festivitatis*) given by Meineke (1.61) was that Crates was "the first Attic poet to bring characters on to the stage drunk."

3402]   *Pherekrates*   Mentioned by Meineke (1.66) as another comic poet whose "type of humor was not bitter or spiteful, but full of *hilaritatis* [= cheerful gaiety]."

3409]   *"Acharnes"*   A transliteration of Ἀχαρνῆς (= Acharnians), the Greek title of Aristophanes' earliest surviving play, produced 425 B.C., when he was probably about twenty.

3414]   *Who would*   Anyone who wishes to.

3419]   *grown bald*   See l. 601n. above.

3427]   *Ariphrades*   See l. 1120n. above.

3428]   *Opora*   See l. 3117n. above.

Sweet Home   An anachronistic echo of J. H. Payne's popular song, "Home, sweet home" (1823), here implying the delights of coming home from war.

3429]   *Bacchis*   A prostitute-correspondent in Alciphron's *Letters of Prostitutes.* See l. 2086n. above.

for the stripling's sake   See l. 703n. above.

3430]   *O genius and O gold*   Balaustion refers back to l. 3358 above.

3431-35]   *Had genius . . . Had you*   If only genius had . . . if only you had (an "unfulfilled" conditional clause that ends, for lack of apodosis, as an exclamatory wish).

3434]   *Phoibos' tripod*   See l. 245n. above.

3443-45]   *this, reproducing Now . . . dead long ago*   I.e., Aristophanic Comedy deals with the present, Euripidean Tragedy resurrects the past.

3448]   *Tell him . . . where thou walk'st*   A reverent apostrophe to the dead Euripides, asking him to *tell* Aristophanes what matters more than winning dramatic competitions.

3449]   *Ilissos*   A river that flowed close to Athens; see l. 199n. above.

3470-71]   *Hail, Depart . . . Glad Welcome!*   Probably suggested by Catullus' words to his dead brother (101.10), *ave atque vale* (= hail and farewell). Balaustion implies her *wish* that Euripides' works may be welcomed by posterity.

3472]   *Yours also wafts the white sail on its way*   You too, despite all you say against him, wish Euripides a safe voyage to future fame. The *white sail* presumably symbolizes his survival, as that of Theseus should have been signalled on his return from killing the Minotaur (only he forgot to change the black one, so his father thought he was dead).

3476-77]   *Zeus or Poseidon . . . Triballos*   In *Birds* 1565-95 Poseidon heads a divine delegation, including the new democrat god, Triballus, to negotiate a peace between Olympus and Cloud-Cuckooland. The final terms include the marriage of Peisthetaerus to Zeus's daughter Basileia (Βασιλεία = *kingly* power, i.e., that of a *true potentate*). See l. 2327n. above. Triballus (Τριβαλλός = outlandish tribesman from Thrace) is "the most barbarous of all gods" (*Birds* 1573), hence the *vulgar sky*.

3483]   *Trust who*   Trust a man who.

3484-85]   *push / His sway past limit*   Persuade him to transcend his limitations.

3487]   *the other king*   Euripides.

3489]   *Bowing your knee*   Making you kneel in respect for the dead.

3494]   *by who defames*   By one who defames, i.e., Balaustion is being unfair to Aristophanes.

3500-6]   *When Sophokles . . . this world's work*   See the end of the story quoted in ll. 1257-59n. above: "he replied: 'If I am Sophocles, I am not out of my mind, and if I am out of my mind I am not Sophocles.'" And he then read out his *Oedipus*" (*Life of Sophocles* 13).

3510-11]   *"The station of the steed . . . white!"*   An alliterative version of *Oedipus at Colonus* 668-70: "to the best cattlefold of this well-horsed country you have come, stranger, to white Colonus."

3513]   *the one adventure of my life*   I.e., *Balaustion's Adventure*. See l. 185n. above.

3516]   *another 'Herakles'*   A hint of the contrast between the cheerful "Helper" of the *Alcestis* and the psychopathic murderer of the *Heracles*.

3517]   *It gained no prize*   Nothing is known about this play's production (perhaps around 417 B.C.), or reception.

3519]   *stulos pendent*   Stylus attached to it. See l. 724n. above.

3520]   *psalterion*   See l. 1562n. above.

3521]   *the ode bewailing Age*   I.e., the choral lyric in *Heracles* 637-54 on the theme: "I hate miserable, murderous old age."

3522]   *modulate*   Used in the sense of the Latin *modulor* (= sing, play) but possibly with a hint of adapting himself to the spirit of the dead poet.

3525-26]   *We were about . . . consummate Tragedy*   See ll. 503-4 above.

3530]   *Beating the god*   See l. 2585n. above.

3531-33]   *when rash hands . . . mad Pentheus*   An allusion to Euripides' *Bacchae* (443-48, 509-10, 613-45, 849-51) where when Pentheus imprisons Dionysus, he easily escapes, shatters the palace in an earthquake, starts a fire, then calmly confronts the king and sends him mad. See l. 312n. above.

3533]   *And—fire—he*   Transformed to fire, he.

3534]   *the perfect piece*   A recent editor of the *Heracles* "would hesitate" to call it quite that, but "finds it easy to understand . . . the loving attention" it has received from eminent Greek scholars, and himself judges it "a great play with a serious theme, the sudden downfall of the good and glorious" (G. W. Bond, *Euripides' Heracles, with Introduction and Commentary* [Oxford, 1981], v).

3535-5084]   *Herakles*   B possessed five different editions of Euripides' complete works (*Reconstruction*, 77-78). For this transcript he seems to have chiefly used the two most recent ones: August Nauck's two-volume *Euripidis Tragoediae* (Leipsig,1866) [*Reconstruction*, A890], acquired by May 1871; and F. A. Paley's three-volume *Euripides, with an English Commentary*, (London,1857-60) [*Reconstruction*, A886]. Where the Greek text was disputed, he apparently translated whichever reading he liked best, tending to prefer the traditional text to editorial emendations. As he put it later, when explaining his policy for *The Agamemnon of Aeschylus Transcribed* (1889a edition, 13.263): "following no editor exclusively, I keep to the earlier readings so long as sense can be made out of them, but disregard, I hope, little of importance in recent criticism." Here he was perhaps influenced by the fact that his two oldest editions of Euripides were associated with his wife. Thus the second volume of *Euripidis Tragoediae XIX* (a Greek text with a parallel Latin translation printed in Heidelberg in 1599) had belonged to EBB, and contained notes in her handwriting (*Reconstruction*, A895); and J. Barnes's *Tragoediae XX* (Oxford 1812), a set of six charming little volumes, had been inscribed by her: "Elizabeth Barrett and Robert Browning" (*Reconstruction*, A893).

When comparing B's transcript with the Greek original, line-numbers are preceded by HN (the 1866 Nauck edition), HP (the Paley edition), or HL (the Greek text of the Loeb edition, by D. Kovacs, 1998). The Loeb edition is referred to chiefly as a standard modern text, where there is no question of B's having translated a different reading; i.e., where all three texts read the same. These notes do not refer to or quote from the excellent Loeb translation. For all the translations in these notes the present editor must take sole responsibility.

3535] *Zeus' Couchmate* A curious boast: Amphitryon means, not that he has slept with Zeus, but that Zeus has slept with his wife Alcmena, thus fathering Heracles.

3538, 3544, 3549] *this . . . this . . . this* B reproduces the use of Greek demonstrative adjectives to imply gestures, when explaining the scene to the audience, or identifying characters on stage (HL 4, 9, 14).

3538] *Thebai* Θῆβαι = Thebes, the scene of the play.

where the earth-born spike / Of Sown-ones burgeoned Cadmus, the mythical founder of Thebes, killed a dragon and sowed its teeth in the earth, thus producing a crop of armed men called Spartoi (Σπαρτοί = Sown-ones), who immediately started fighting one another. The survivors became the ancestors of the Theban nobles. B translates στάχυς (= ear of corn) as *spike*, possibly because his lexicon equated the Greek word with the Latin *spica* (hence the use of *spike* in that sense by Langland and other English poets). The Spartoi were supposed to have a spear-head as a birth-mark.

3539] *Ares* The god of war.

3541] *Kadmos built* Which Cadmus built.

3547] *that grand* Literally, "the famous" (ὁ κλεινὸς, HL 12).

3550] *the desire possessed my son* I.e., "my son desired" (HL 13-16). By changing the grammatical subject, B makes "leaving" a "hanging participle," and obscures the meaning.

3552] *Kuklopian* Made by the Cyclopes, workmen of Hephaestus; see l. 4544n. below.

which I fly, myself From which I myself am exiled. The Greekless reader seems expected to guess that φεύγω (= flee from) can have this special meaning (HL 16).

3553] *Elektruon* The father of Alcmena, to whom Amphitryon was engaged. In one version of the myth, her *fiancé* threw a stick to round up some cattle: it bounced off a cow's horn and killed his prospective father-in-law (Lemprière, 41).

3556] *Eurustheus* King of Tiryns in Argos, who prescribed the Labors of Heracles.

3557] *letting in of light on this choked world* I.e., "taming the earth"

(HL 20). B's fine image to translate ἐξημερῶσαι was possibly inspired by Paley's gloss on the word (HP 20): "to make a clearing in a woodland by cutting a road through it"—which suggested a derivation, not from ἥμερος (= tame) but from ἡμέρα (= day).

3559]   *Here*   Hera, Zeus's wife, whose implacable hatred of Heracles from birth is usually attributed to prejudice against all her husband's extra-marital offspring—though this one's name (Ἡρακλῆς) appears to mean: "glorious through Hera." See *Oxford Classical Dictionary* (3rd ed., ed. S. Hornblower and A. Spawforth [Oxford, 1996]), 684).

3561]   *Tainaros*   A cave on a cape in the Peloponnese, regarded as an entrance into Hades.

3563]   *three-shaped*   B tries to soften the inaccuracy of τρισώματον (= three-bodied, HL 24) to describe the three-headed Cerberus

3566]   *Dirke*   A woman changed into a spring and river near Thebes. See l. 4165n. below.

  a Lukos   A man called Lycus (B's conscientious rendering of τις . . . Λύκος [= a certain Lycus, HL 27]).

3569]   *Amphion, Zethos*   See ll. 290-91n. above.

3571]   *Euboia's gift*   B's sarcastic version of "coming from Euboea" (HL 32).

3572]   *Kreon*   Then King of Thebes.

3574]   *akin to Kreon*   Heracles' wife Megara was Creon's daughter.

3577]   *This man of valour*   With Nauck and Paley B follows the MS reading: ὁ κλεινὸς οὗτος (= this famous, glossed as "said ironically," HP 38), though sometimes emended, as in HL 38, to ὁ καινὸς οὗτος (= this new).

3582]   *Useless old age*   "A useless old man" (HL 42). B's curious change was possibly meant as an exclamation of frustration.

3584]   *their mother's father*   Creon.

3585]   *domes*   B's rather misleading semi-transliteration of δώμασι (= houses, HL 44).

3586-87]   *when earth's / Dark dread he underwent*   "When he entered the black darkness of the earth" (HL 45-46).

3591]   *Conquering*   I.e., to commemorate his conquest of.

  the Minuai   Inhabitants of Orchomenus, one of Thebes' rivals in Boeotia.

3592]   *guard our station*   Watchfully maintain our position ("guard these seats," HL 51), fearing to leave the altar which should give us sanctuary.

3594]   *sealed out*   The precise meaning of ἐσφραγισμένοι (HL 53). Lycus has put his seal on their house, to show that he now owns it.

3595]   *resourcelessness of help*   Not English, but close to the Greek of
HL 54: ἀπορίᾳ σωτηρίας (= resourcelessness of safety).

3602]   *raze the Taphian town*   In revenge for the Taphians' killing of
Alcmena's brothers.

3604]   *speared*   I.e., with a spearhead birthmark; see l. 3538n. above.

   play men false   Slightly more critical of the gods than the original
(HL 62): "none of divine things is clear [σαφές] to human beings." But
perhaps B was remembering the use of τὸ σαφές elsewhere in Euripi-
des (*Orestes* 397) to mean "the (plain) truth."

3608]   *Leap the long lances*   A fine phrase to which B contributed only
the alliteration (HL 65).

3611]   *the far-famed*   The indefinite article *a* might have made the
sense of HL 68 clearer: Megara includes among past blessings her fa-
ther's arrangement of a splendid marriage for her.

3622-23]   *all a-foot . . . the fall*   I.e., they all jump up to kneel before
him.

3625]   *Facilitatest*   An almost too literal translation of ἐξευμαρίζει (=
make light or easy). In this context (HL 81) the meaning seems to be:
"what hope or plan can you suggest to make our predicament easier to
bear?"

3630]   *decision*   A word of rather narrower meaning than γνώμην
here (HL 85), which implies not just intention, but assessment of the
situation.

3632]   *Lest now should prove the proper time to die*   HL86: "lest death is
ready," i.e., inevitable.

3635   *blurt out counsel*   Advise without adequate thought.

3636]   *want*   Need.

3639]   *these*   I.e., such.

3640]   *it bites*   The literal meaning of δάκνει (HL 94); but the
metaphorical use of the word to express sharp mental pain is quite
common in Greek.

3644-45]   *take away / Their founts a-flow with tears*   A precise equiva-
lent of the original (HL 98-99), i.e., stop them crying.

3646]   *Steal them by stories—sad theft*   B's alliteration neatly supports
the conceit that the *founts* are stolen; but he cannot reproduce Euripi-
des' pun (HL 100) on the two senses of the verb κλέπτω (= 1. steal and
2. cheat, deceive).

3650]   *all things change—their natures part in twain*   HL 104: "all things
change two ways from each other"—an equally cryptic way of saying
that opposites like happiness and misery perpetually alternate with
one another.

379

3653] *CHOROS* Of old men. B marks the change (HL 107) from iambic to lyric meter by changing from blank to irregular rhymed verse; but does not try to imitate the exact correspondence between strophe and antistrophe (HL 107-18, 119-30) characteristic of Greek tragic lyrics.

domes See l. 3585n. above. But B has no excuse for the misleading translation here (HL 107), since the original word is not δώματα but μέλαθρα (= roofs, house).

3654] *long-used couch* "Aged bed," HL 108. But the adjective (γεραιὰ) here implies connection with an old man (γέρων), i.e., Amphitryon, and the "bed" means where he now has to sleep: on the bare ground.

3655-57] *that song may . . . dirges* B freely elaborates his five-word original (HL 110-11): "a singer of laments, like a hoary bird."

3657-61] *words that stand aloof . . . I deem* Another elaboration (HL 112-14): "words only, and a night-faced phantom of nocturnal dreams, tremulous, but still eager [i.e., to help]." Here, as throughout the Transcript, when literal translation becomes impossible, or the text is uncertain, B evidently feels free to improvise his own variations on Euripidian themes.

3663-65] *whose groaning stuns . . . thy love!* "Unhappy mother, who groans for your husband in the house of Hades" (HL 116-18). The rhyme for "unfathered ones" is dearly bought.

3670] *peplos* See l. 171n. above.

3671] *printless* HL 124: ἀμαυρὸν ἴχνος (= faint footstep). Since the adjective can mean "faint" visually, as well as physically, and the noun can mean either "footstep or footprint," B exploits the ambiguities of both languages to suggest a foot too feeble to leave any visible traces.

fordone Exhausted.

3672] *Aged . . . me aged* B replicates the common Greek trick of word-repetion (γέρων ... γέροντα, HL 126), but not the balancing phrase in the next line: νέα νέῳ (= young . . . young).

3673] *when life was new* An imaginative rendering justified by the two meanings of νέος, "young" and "new."

3675-76] *no bastard-slip . . . glory grew* A rhyme-dictated elaboration of "not a disgrace to the most glorious fatherland" (HL 127-30). The *slip* is used in the botanical sense of an alien growth grafted on to a tree.

3681] *what—what* The repetition is in the Greek (HL 136).

combatants Not the full meaning of ξυμμάχους (HL 135) which is: "men to fighting together with or alongside one, i.e., allies."

3681-82] *destroyed . . . void!* HL 136-7: "will you be deprived of, when you have lost these!"

3686-87]   *If needs I must . . . all I please, I ask*   Taking χρή (HL 141) in its usual meaning of "it is necessary, one must," B makes little sense of this passage; but the word can also mean, "it is fitting or proper, one should," as it does here. Lycus starts with a conventional phrase like "if I may ask," then corrects himself, and rudely asserts the rights of conquest.

3691]   *Haides*   See l. 9n. above.

past the pitch   Over the top, excessively (using *pitch* in its old sense of "highest point, top." HL 146: ὑπὲρ τὴν ἀξίαν (= beyond what it's worth).

3692]   *Suppose*   Supposing.

3694]   *As though . . . god for son*   B follows a conjectural reading (HP 149): "that Zeus, sharing your marriage, begat a new god for you."

3696]   *the awful*   A literal translation of "τὸ σέμνον" (HL 151). See ll. 1332-33 above.

was . . . wound up   The slightly incongruous translation of κατείργασται (= has been accomplished, HL 151) was probably due to B's instinct for alliteration.

3697]   *the marshy snake*   The many-headed Lernaean Hydra, which instantly replaced any heads cut off, and was also helped by a crab sent by Hera.

3698]   *the Nemeian monster*   A lion whose skin was impenetrable, except by its own claws; so Heracles used them to flay it, after throttling it with his bare hands, and thus acquired the most famous part of his costume.

3700]   *outwrestle*   B retains the ἐξ (= out) prefix in ἐξαγωνίζεσθε (HL 155), though the compound means no more than "struggle hard," without the "surpassing" sense of the *out-* prefix in English.

3706]   *shoot first and then fly!*   A lively translation of "having a bow . . . he was ready for flight" (HL 160-61).

3709]   *ploughing up, the darts come*   A neat clarification of a puzzling original: "faces the swift furrow of the spear" (HL 163-64).

3710]   *impudence*   Used in the sense of Latin *impudentia*, and of the Greek original, ἀναίδειαν (= shamelessness, HL 165). Αἰδώς (= shame) was seen as the basis of all morality.

3711]   *Providence*   Used in the Latin sense of "foresight, prudence," to translate εὐλάβεια (HL 166), which was regarded by the Greeks as a virtue, and personified in Euripides' *Phoenissae* 782 as "the most useful of gods."

3716-17]   *'tis me / The care concerns*   It's my job. B follows the stock dictionary translation of ἐμοὶ μέλει: "there is a care to me" (HL 171).

3725-29]   *Zeus' thunder . . . with the gods*   HL 177-80: "I call to witness Zeus' thunderbolt and the four-horse chariot, standing in which he

[Heracles] fitted winged missiles into the flanks of the earth-sprung Giants, and celebrated victory with the gods." Heracles helped Zeus and the Olympian gods fight off the attack of the Giants (Γίγαντες = Earth-born).

3731]   *Pholoé*   A mountain in Arcadia, where Heracles fought against the Centaurs.

        vilest   HL 182: κάκιστε = worst; but here, where Lycus has questioned Heracles' courage, it means "most cowardly," just as *best* in the next line (ἄριστον, HL 183) means "bravest."

3733]   *"the seeming brave"*   B makes Amphitryon quote the Greek behind l. 3702, HL 157: "he got a reputation [δόξαν = seeming, reputation], for bravery, while being nothing."

3734]   *Dirphus*   Lycus's birthplace in Euboea (an island originally inhabited by the Abantes).

3736-37]   *For there's no spot . . . witness worth*   An almost literal translation (HL 186-7), i.e., "You never showed any bravery in your own country."

3741]   *that want to run*   A livelier version of "who are not brave" (HL 191).

3750-51]   *that vainly stares . . . viewless arrow*   B struggles to convey the sense of Euripides' forced conceit: "wounding with blind [= unseen] arrows those who see" (HL 199), i.e., though not blind, they cannot see where the arrows are coming from.

3760-61]   *base . . . nobleness*   Again B fails to bring out the antithesis between κακὸς (= bad in the sense of cowardly) and ἀρίστων (= best in the sense of bravest, HL 208). See ll. 3731-32n. above.

3763-65]   *fear in thee . . . Thy betters*   HL 210-11: "your cowardice [δειλίας] . . . us the better ones [ἀμεινόνων in the sense of braver]." Once more B obscures Amphitryon's point—possibly to avoid repetition, though this would contravene the transcript-principle laid down later in his preface to the *The Agamemnon of Aeschylus* (1888-1889a edition, 13.262): "I should especially decline, what may appear to brighten up a passage—the employment of a new word for some old one—πόνος, or μέγας, or τέλος with its congeners, recurring four times in three lines . . . ."

3768]   *Fugitives*   The primary meaning of φυγάδας; but here (HL 214) the word is used in its common sense of "exiles."

3770]   *gale*   The alliterating noun sounds stranger in this context than πνεῦμα (= breath, wind) does in the Greek (HL 216).

3775]   *one to all the world*   B exaggerates "one to all the Minyae" (HL 220).

3776]   *The Minuai*   See l. 3591n. above.

3776-77]   *eye / Unblinded . . . front freedom with*   B's alliterating phrase replaces: ὄμμ' ἐλεύθερον βλέπειν (= look with a free eye (HL 221).

3779-80]   *count / Towards my son, craven of cravens—her*   The tangled word-order has no equivalent in HL 224: "finding her κακίστην [= most cowardly/bad] towards my son," i.e., in failing to protect his family.

3784]   *But fire, spears, arms*   The rhetorical repetition of this whole phrase is not in the original (HL 227), which has merely "but these things."

3789]   *And force a-flicker*   B's ingenious improvisation for HL 231: "and strength dim" (ἀμαυρόν = visually faint, metaphorically uncertain).

3792]   *this insulter*   HL 233: "this man."

3793]   *Atlantic bounds*   The Pillars of Heracles (later identified as the mountains on either side of the Straits of Gibraltar), i.e., the end of the known world.

3795-96]   *Have not the . . . talkers they?*   An admiring comment on Amphitryon's unexpected burst of eloquence. HL 236-37: "Have not the good/brave ones of mortals starting-points [ἀφορμὰς] for speeches, even if one is [generally] slow to speak?" i.e., good people can always speak well when they really need to, however taciturn they usually are.

3796]   *rare talkers*   B's ambiguous shorthand for "those who rarely talk."

3797]   *thou towerest with*   HL 238: πεπύργωσαι (= you have towered up, i.e., exalted yourself). Lycus retaliates with the favorite Greek antithesis between words and deeds.

3799]   *Helikon*   A mountain in Boeotia.

   Parnasos   Correctly spelled and accented on the last syllable (Παρνασός): a mountain north of Delphi. Lycus flaunts his barbarity by seeing these two haunts of the Muses as mere sources of timber.

3804]   *no dead man*   HL 245: "not the man who has died," i.e., Heracles.

3806]   *As for you, old sirs . . . against*   Though the line contains ten syllables, it can hardly be scanned as an iambic pentameter except by invoking Hopkins's "sprung rhythm," making a whole first foot out of *As,* and resolving the fourth into an anapaest (*who are set*).

3809-10]   *when faring ill / By any chance*   HL 250: "when it [your house] chances to suffer something"; a vague threat of future disaster.

3812-13]   *O progeny of earth . . . greedy jaw*   See l. 3538n. above.

3817]   *youth*   HN, HP 257: τῶν νέων = the young men; tentatively explained by Paley as "the young and revolutionary party" who, unlike their elders, supported the usurper.

3820]   *Hand worked . . . for*   Worked for with my hands.

3825]   *we bear both of you in mind*   Not in the original. HN, HP, HL 264-65: "since you, who have utterly destroyed this land, possess it, while he, who helped it, does not get his deserts." B's interpolation was probably suggested by a gloss quoted by Paley on HP 262: "We are not so forgetful of their father, though absent, as to consent to your crime."

3828]   *I play the busybody*   B rightly gives the idiomatic, not the literal meaning of πράσσω πολλά (= I do many things, HL 266), but hardly brings out the point of Amphitryon's question: "do you suggest that I'm interfering, when I'm simply doing my obvious duty?"

3832]   *stayed*   A literal translation of ἔπαυσα (= stopped, HL 270) would have made clearer English .

3833]   *drawn my breath . . . in*   HN, HP 271: ᾠκήσαμεν (= inhabited). To the grammatical objection that this meaning would require an imperfect instead of an aorist, Paley replied that the verb "seems to be used, as it often is, for διοικεῖν [= manage, administer]. We would have governed Thebes in a creditable way, where *you* now exult in dwelling as king over us." B seems to have borrowed Paley's word, *exult*, to translate χαίρεις (= rejoice) in the next line, but rejected his suggested interpretation ("governed"), ignored the tense-problem, and produced a near-equivalent for the simplest interpretation, "inhabited." Perhaps *nobly drawn my breath* was meant to imply that killing Lycus in such circumstances would be a relief to his conscience, rather than a burden on it.

3844]   *Sad*   HN, HP, HL 282: δεινὸν (= terrible). The change was apparently designed to underline Megara's stoical courage.

3846]   *Poor creature*   Another characterizing change. HN, HP, HL 283: σκαιὸν (= left-handed, i.e., clumsy, stupid). Cf. l. 3863 below, HL 299, where B translates the same adjective: "foolish."

3853]   *shame*   HN, HP, HL 289: "cowardice."

3854-56]   *my glorious husband . . . good fame thereby*   A fairly close translation of HN, HP 290-92 though Paley thought it needed emendation: "Now the reading ὡς could only mean 'he does not require witnesses to prove that he would not be willing to let his children live if they were cowards': which is absurd." B accepts the absurdity, which Paley had slightly reduced by equating "if they were cowards" with "if they got a reputation for cowardice [δόξαν κακὴν λαβόντας]."

3865]   *speaking soft*   A neat rendering of the (emended) reading, ὑποβαλών φίλα (= suggesting friendly things), glossed by Paley: "to try the use of a friendly compliance rather than an obstinate resistance" (HP 301).

3867]   *beg off*   A dictionary definition of παραιτησαίμεθα (HL 302), but the wrong one for this context: Megara suggests begging for the children to be exiled instead of killed, not *begging off* their exile.

3870]   *flying*   Exiled. See l. 3552n. above.

3871]   *sweet look*   I.e., warm welcome (HL 306).

3874] *outlabours* A "transcription" of ἐκμοχθεῖ (= labors to get out of, HL 309), though Paley (HP 309) called this use of it "very peculiar."
3878] *he easily had ceased* B translated the MS reading (ῥᾳδίως ἐπαύσατ᾽ ἄν, HP 313), though Nauck (HN 313) adopted the emendation: ῥᾳδίως ἔπαυσά γ᾽ ἄν (= I'd easily have stopped him).
3883] *My son his* My son's.
3893] *and we resign ourselves* Interpolated (HL 326).
3902] *peploi* Plural of πέπλος (= robe, HL 333); see l. 171n. above.
3904] *grave* HL 335: "lower earth."
3905-6] *this unhappy foot, / Your mother's* HL 336: "mother's unhappy foot."
3907] *have the power, are lords in truth* HL 337: "have power over the οὐσία" (= the being to one, i.e., what is one's own, one's substance or property). But here the word may also carry the philosophical sense attached to it by Plato and Aristotle, of basic reality.
3909] *marriage-mate* See l. 3535n. above.
3917] *place* I.e., in a marriage-bed. HL 345: "other people's beds [τἀλλότρια λέκτρα]."
3920-21] *Even a dirge . . . music jubilant.* In the choral lyrics, where the text is often disputed, and the precise meaning doubtful, B freely introduces ideas of his own, as here (HN, HP 348-49), that poetry can transmute sorrow into joy, where the Chorus says only that Apollo may follow a cheerful song by a dirge. Athenaeus (14.619c) had confused the issue by wrongly taking this passage to mean: "a dirge [αἴλινος] is sung not only in mourning but also at the happy dance."
3926] *Despite the imminence of doom* A rhyme-dictated interpolation (HL 355-56).
3928] *what is it rumour says?* Another interpolation.
3933-35] *For, is my hero . . . dead in song* HN, HP 357-58 (seven words): "and the virtues of noble labors are an ornament to the dead."
3938-40] *spread / The tawniness behind . . . that grin of dread* HN, HP 361-63: "and he covered himself round with the tawny, putting on his back the yellow head of the beast with terrible open mouth."
3941] *Kentaur-race* See l. 3731n. above.
3943] *Peneios knew* Peneus (the chief river in Thessaly) witnessed the battle.
3947] *Homolé* Another mountain in Thessaly inhabited by the Centaurs.
3949-50] *Horse-like was wont . . . that bestial crew* HN, HP 373-74: "they subdued the Thessalians' land with their horsemanship [ἱππείαις]." The puzzling inversion, with the interpolated *bestial crew* as the subject of *was*, is B's contribution.

3951]   *stag*   The Cerynitian Hind. Though female, it had golden horns.

3953]   *goddess*   Artemis, to whom Heracles presented the hind, since it had been sacred to her,

3954]   *Oinoé*   In Argolis, where Artemis was worshipped.

3955]   *chariot-breed*   I.e., horses bred for chariots, an odd coinage to translate τεθρίππων (= four-horse chariot-team, HL 380).

3957]   *Diomede*   A Thracian king, who fed his horses on human flesh. This was the Labor on which Heracles was engaged in the *Alcestis* (481-98). See *Balaustion's Adventure*, 1093-1117; this edition, 10.51-53.

3961]   *Hebros*   A river in Thrace, said to flow over golden sands.

3963]   *Mukenaian tyrant*   Eurystheus, king of Tiryns, near Mycenae. See l. 533 n. above.

3964]   *Melian*   B translates Paley's Μηλιάδα in preference to Nauck's Πηλιάδα (= Pelian; HP, HN 389). Paley explained: the "Anaurus flowed into the Melian gulf." But it rose on Mount Pelion.

3965]   *Amauros*   So spelt in B's MS—apparently a mistake for *Anauros*, as in HN, HP 390.

3967]   *Kuknos*   A son of Ares who robbed and killed travellers taking offerings to Delphi, and planned to build a temple to Apollo out of their skulls (*Oxford Companion to Classical Literature*, 2nd ed., ed. M. C. Howatson [Oxford, 1989], 164).

   Amphanaia   A region of Thessaly.

3967-68]   *not / Of fame for good to guest!*   B's humorous version of ξεινοδαίκταν (= guest/stranger-murderer, HL 391).

3969]   *melodious maids*   The Hesperides, daughters of Night who guarded a tree producing golden apples in a remote western island.

3970-71]   *hand must aim / At plucking*   A rhyme-induced complication of a simple phrase, χερὶ . . . ἀμέρξων (= in order to pluck with his hand, HL 397).

3972]   *Now he had killed*   HL 400: "having killed."

3973]   *the unapproachable he weaves*   The unapproachable tree that he weaves. The text was doubtful, but B complicated what Paley called the "simple sense . . . the dragon which guarded the sacred (unapproachable) tree by twining round it" (HP 398).

3974]   *spire*   A near-pun on the verb *spire* (= wind spirally), and the noun *spire* in its primary sense of: "a stalk or stem of a plant" (*OED*, sb. 1).

3975-77]   *into those sea-troughs . . . his wake*   HL 400-2: "entered the inmost recesses of the sea, creating calms for mortal oars."

3979]   *At home with Atlas*   An oddly cosy version of HL 405: "having come to the house of Atlas," a Titan (identified with the Atlas Mountains in north Africa) who guarded the pillars supporting the sky, and later had to hold it up himself. In a version of the myth mentioned by Paley (HP 403) Heracles temporarily relieved Atlas of this job, while he fetched him "the apples (oranges) of the Hesperides."

for valour's sake   HL 407: "by his manliness [εὐανορίᾳ, i.e., manly strength]."

3980]   *Held the gods up . . . mansionry*   HL 406-7: "held the star-faced houses of the gods."

3982, 3983]   *Maiotis . . . Euxin*   The Sea of Azov, joined to the Black Sea by a strait, the *Euxin* or Euxine (Εὔξεινον = kind to strangers, a euphemism, perhaps propitiatory, for the opposite, HN, HP 410).

3984-85]   *Having collected what an armament / Of friends*   HL 411-12: "having collected what not company of friends?" i.e., all his friends. B tries to simplify by omitting the "not," while retaining the un-English combination of an exclamation with a participle, and adds an extra difficulty by using *armament* in the obsolete sense of "an armed military force."

3986]   *that gold-garnished cloak*   I.e., the girdle of Hippolyte, queen of the Amazons.

3987]   *girl's barbarian grace*   A rhyme-led departure from HN, HP 416: "the famous spoils of the barbarian girl."

3989]   *Go wonder there, who will!*   An interpolated expansion of "famous."

3991]   *the Lernaian snake*   HL 420: "dog of Lerna." See l. 3697n. above.

3993-94]   *darts soon to slake / Their rage . . . gore*   HL 423-24: "with which he killed the three bodied herdsman" (i.e. the giant Geryon, whose cattle Heracles had to rustle).

3995]   *Erutheia*   Ἐρυθεία (= red, i.e., sunset-colored), an island in the far west. Perhaps the color suggested B's rhyme-word, *gore*

a running   The literal meaning of δρόμος, the noun used here (HL 425) for a race or contest, i.e., a Labor.

3997-98]   *never dry / Of tears*   HL 426 "of many tears [πολυδάκρυον]."

4001-5]   *And where the children's . . . end all!*   B expands, but hardly clarifies, the cryptically compressed original: "and Charon's oar awaits the childrens' no-return life-path, godless, unjust (HL 431-33)." See l. 2081n. above.

4005]   *accost*   I.e., appeal to, call for—the inappropriate word serves only to rhyme with the interpolated *uttermost*. HL 434-35: "The house looks to your hands, though you are not present."

4011-12]   *but I am bereft / Of youth now, lone of that good genius left*   B's elaboration of six Greek words (HL 440-41): "but now I am bereft of happy [εὐδαίμονος = with a good *daimon* or genius] youth."

4013]   *But hist, desist! for*   The fragment of melodrama (reminiscent of B's *A Blot in the 'Scutcheon*, this edition 4.5-60) serves to fill out the elliptical ἀλλ᾽ ἐσορῶ γὰρ (= But, for I see, HL 442).

4015-16] *Children long since . . . potent Herakles* HL 443-44: "children of the once formerly great Herakles." Paley (HP 443) found the "pleonasm" of the "formerly" (τὸ πρὶν) "remarkable," but B's word-order obscures the point: they are still Heracles' children, though he is no longer *potent.*

now hard to discover Interpolated, apparently for the rhyme.

4017-18] *dragging, in one tether / About her feet* HN, HP 445-46: "dragging the children at her feet like trace-horses (ὑποσειραίους)."

4021] *hold fast* Hold in, keep back.

4023] *Be it so!* Not a comment on Amphitryon's last words, but on the general situation. B translates εἶεν (HL 451) not as a particle meaning "well, good, proceed," but as the third plural optative of the verb *to be* (= may these things be, HL 451). Both interpretations are given in Liddell and Scott (1871).

4033] *destruction-stuff* An odd but accurate translation of διαφθοράν (= destruction), used here (HL 459) for "something to be destroyed."

4038] *For thee . . . dealt Argos to* The awkward combination of *For* and *to* has no equivalent in the Greek: "To thee he used to assign Argos" (HL 462).

4038, 4044] *dealt . . . wast* Paley suggested (HP 460) that the imperfect tenses expressed not merely the intentions, but "the actual words of Herakles in sportive play with his children," e.g., "now you are King of Thebes."

4039, 4044, 4050] *Thou . . . And thou . . . And upon thee* Megara addresses her three sons in turn.

4039] *Eurustheus* See l. 533n. above.

4040] *Pelasgia* A name given to Argos from an ancient mythic people said to have lived there.

4041] *stole* A transliteration of στολή (= clothing), used here (HL465) of a lion's skin. The English word once meant "a long robe."

4044] *Thebes—such chariots there!* B tries to dramatize the stock phrase: "chariot-loving Thebes" (HL 467).

4045] *had for portion* I.e., inherited from Creon.

4046-47] *who gave birth / To thee* B follows Paley's text (HP 469: "the man who begat thee," rejecting the conjectural emendation of "thee" to "me" (σε to με) adopted by Nauck (HN 469), which would make the grandfather, not the father, the person *coaxed.*

4048] *of Daidalos* The Cretan inventor of aeronautics, and father of Icarus. With Nauck (HN 471) B translates the MS reading Δαιδάλου (= of Daidalus) rather than Paley's δαίδαλον (= finely-wrought), though Paley stated (HP 470) that Daedalus "is nowhere recorded to have given Hercules his club."

4049] *Poor guardian proves the gift that plays thee false* B's clarification of the cryptic phrase (HL 471): ψευδῆ δόσιν (= deceiving gift).

4051] *Oichalia* A small town and country in the Peloponnese attacked and appropriated by Heracles, because Eurytus, its king, would not let him marry his daughter Iole.

what Used to translate the simple relative "which" (ἥν, HL 472), this looks strangely like a relapse into Camberwell or Peckham slang, but B certainly wrote it, possibly in its correct sense of "that which," to emphasize the antecedent (*Oichalia*).

4053-54] *did he build you up / To very towers* The literal meaning of ἐπύργου (HL 475).

4054-56] *proud . . . Prognosticating . . . would be* An alliterative elaboration of four Greek words, μέγα φρονῶν ἐπ' ἀνδρίᾳ (= thinking big on, i.e., being proud of, manliness) and of Paley's paraphrase (HP 475): "i.e. on the early development of your physical powers, and your promising youth."

4061] *gods bless* That gods bless another attempt to convey the literal meaning of εὐδαίμονα (= with a good *daimon* or guardian spirit, so happy, HL 479).

4062] *Fates* HL 481: Κῆρας (= Fates, goddesses of death, HL 481).

4066] *Befitting Haides who plays father now* The Greek is clearer: "regarding Hades as father-in-law [πενθερὸν, HL 484]." Since Hades was the god of the dead, the death-goddesses are made his daughters.

4070] *and ne'er let go* Interpolated (HL 487).

4073] *crowded* ἀθρόον = collected together, HL 489; but Liddell and Scott (1871) gives "in crowds" to translate the plural ἀθρόοι.

4075] *Dungeoned* B's image for "in the house of Hades" (HL 491).

4080] *thy ghost-grandeur* HP 494: καὶ σκιά (= even as a shade; explained by Paley: "Even though a mere ghost, and not in the body").

4098] *Riches* ὄλβος = happiness, especially worldly happiness, wealth; but the context surely requires the broader meaning (HL 511).

4100] *the man who loved you all so* much A tear-jerking expansion of ἄνδρα φίλον (= dear man or man-friend, HL 512).

4102] *Ha!* A melodramatic approach to the sound, if not quite the feeling, of ἔα, an exclamation of wonder or surprise (HL 514).

4103] *Speak!* HL 514: "or what am I to say?"

4104] *No more than thou canst* HL 315: "I do not know."

4106] *Unless . . . we see!* B follows Nauck and Paley (HN, HP 517) in attributing this line to Amphitryon, though Paley notes that "The copies continue it to Megara."

4107]   *What do I say?*   B faithfully translates the indicative φημί (HL 518), though one would have expected a deliberative subjunctive (= what am I to say?) as in HL 514, since Megara has not yet mentioned dreams. See l. 4106n. above.

4111]   *Zeus that can save*   A reference to the altar at which they are sitting. See l. 3589 above (HL 48).

4112]   *palace*   B obscures the realistic perspective by thus translating μέλαθρον (= roof, but often extended to mean the whole building). As Heracles climbs the stairs, he sees first the palace-roof, then the *propula* (πρόπυλα = gateway), and then, reaching ground-level, the children in front of the house (πρὸ δωμάτων, HL 523-25).

4112-13]   *O hail, my palace . . . as I come to light!*   As Paley explains (HP 516), Heracles appears from underground by "Charon's Staircase," a stage-property designed for such entrances from Hades.

4114]   *Ha*   See l. 4102n. above.

4120]   *Wife, what new sorrow*   The text is uncertain, but B follows Paley and Nauck (HN, HP 530). The word translated *new* (καινὸν) need not here imply an addition to existing sorrows, but probably means "novel" or "strange."

4122-23]   *fall / On*   Come upon, find.

4125]   *Undone are we!*   Curiously close to the abominable Buckley's "We are undone" (*The Tragedies of Euripides, literally translated by Theodore Alois Buckley* [London, 1887], 2.16; see l. 952n. above), which misses the point of the continuous present tense, διολλύμεσθα (HL 534): "we are in the process of being destroyed, [but you are just in time to stop it]."

4127]   *wakes pity more*   HL 536: "are more pitiable (οἴκτρὸν)," i.e., deserve more pity.

4128]   *Here are my children killed and I undone!*   B overlooks the imperfect tenses (ἔθνῃσκε . . . ἀπωλλύμην, HN, HP 537): "My children were dying [i.e. about to die] and I was being destroyed."

4129]   *speech begins*   The Greek is more straightforward: "you begin the speech" (HL 538).

4131]   *by spear-stroke whence?*   Hardly clearer than the concise original: "meeting what kind of spear?" (HN, HP 540).

4132]   *noble*   B adapts the ironical adjective in Paley's text, κλεινός (= famous, HP 541), rather than Nauck's καινός (= new, HN 541).

4133]   *disease*   A common Greek metaphor for political turmoil.

4137]   *orphanage*   Orphanhood, i.e., orphans.

4141]   *had died*   Would have died.

4146]   *couch*   A surprising lapse into poetic diction for the more vivid στρωτοῦ λέχους (= covered bed, i.e., when he was tucked up in bed, HL 555).

4151] *spat forth* The literal meaning of ἀπέπτυσαν (HL 560), i.e., dismissed with contempt.

these I.e., the plural μάχας (= battles) of HL 560, though B has turned them into a singular *war*. See l. 3591n. above.

4159] *to trail* To drag about.

4162] *handle* χειρώσομαι (= master, subdue, defeat, HL 570). Liddell and Scott (1996) derives the word from χείρων (= worse), but B assumes a connection with χείρ (= hand).

4164] *Ismenos* A river near Thebes.

4165] *Dirké* A spring and river at Thebes.

4166] *incarnadined* A verb borrowed from Shakespeare's *Macbeth*, 2.2.63 (but without its guilt-associations).

4171] *If for their father's sake they meant to die* B's puzzling expansion of "if these for their father" (HP 577), explained by Paley: "If they, the children, are going to die in their father's cause, because Lycus fears their father's valour, it becomes me also to die for them."

4177-78] *The right thing . . . couch* B follows the MS text in making Heracles the speaker, though Nauck and Paley ascribe these two lines (HN, HP 583-84) to the Chorus.

4179] *true* B's addition (HN, HP 585-86).

4183] *the king calls partisan* HN, HP 589: "the king has as allies."

4186] *flew off* διαφυγόντα (= having fled away, i.e., been dissipated, HL 592).

4187] *You came to trouble Thebes, they saw* B follows, with Nauck (HN 593) the MS reading: "You were seen coming against [ἐπελθὼν] the city," and ignores the plausible emendation adopted by Paley (HP 593): ἐσελθὼν (= entering; i.e., you must have been seen as you entered the city).

4188] *raising foes, a multitude* HL 594: "you collect foes."

4191-92] *a certain bird / Not in the lucky seats* A literal translation of the Greek (HL 596), where *seats* (ἕδραις) is a technical term for the quarter of the sky in which a bird is seen as an omen.

4195] *with praise* B translates καλῶς (= well) as explained by Paley (HP 599): "go and address good words to the hearth," where Nauck marks the adverb off by a colon to mean: "That's good" (HN 599).

4196] *eye* ὄμμα = eye; but often used, as here (HL 600), for face, i.e., "show your face to the gods of the hearth."

4199] *here remaining, all succeeds* If you stay here, all will go well.

4205] *Koré* See l. 19n. above.

4208]   *three-headed beast*   See l. 537n. above.

4210]   *Orgies* ὄργια (HL 613), i.e., the Mysteries of Eleusis. See l. 1855n. above.

4212]   *Chthonia's* Χθονίας (= of the underground goddess, HL 615).

  Hermion A city of Troezen in Argolis, mentioned by Pausanias (*Description of Greece* 2.35.10) as the site of the worship of Chthonia, near which was a ravine through which Heracles was said to have "brought up the dog from Hades."

4214]   *I would come* I.e., I wanted to come. B seems to be translating the difficult MS reading retained by Nauck (HN 617), εἰδείην (= would that I knew!) rather than Paley's ἵνα ... εἰδείην (= in order that I might know) which makes better sense.

4216]   *I stopped* ἐχρόνισα (= I spent time, delayed, HL 619).

4218]   *Gone glad to Athens—Haides' fugitive!* The original (HL 621) is simpler: "He has gone to Athens, glad to have escaped from below."

4232]   *men are men* Despite the hint that looking after children is woman's work, the original noun is ἄνθρωποι (= human beings, not specifically male, HL 633).

4236]   *Combine to form the children-loving race* The generalization, ironical in the light of subsequent events, is again clearer in the Greek: "The whole [human] race is child-loving" (HL 636).

4237]   *a pleasant burthen* B translates an old MS reading, φίλον ἄχθος, though both Nauck and Paley adopt an emendation: "Youth is a dear thing to me, but age is always a burden" (HN, HP 637).

4239]   *Aitna* The speaker implicitly compares himself to the monster Typhon, who was buried under Mount Etna.

4249]   *Nor ever* Struggling to produce a rhyming, stress-scanned equivalent for the complicated quantitative verse of a Greek choral lyric, B obscures the point made by ὤφελεν (HL 651) that old age *ought* never to have come into human life, a design-fault theoretically corrected in ll. 4253-61 below.

4257]   *life's winter thus grew spring* A pleasant image interpolated for the rhyme (HL 657).

4263]   *As surely as* B omits the following phrase, "in the clouds" (HN, HP 667), perhaps because they might interfere with astronavigation.

4268]   *but youthful vigour, no!* Interpolated to explain "increases wealth alone" (HL 772).

4269]   *I am not to pause* A partial transliteration of οὐ παύσομαι (= I shall not stop, HL 673), i.e., old age won't stop me trying to make poetry and music.

4275]   *Mnemosuné* Μνημοσύνη (= Memory personified, HL 679), the mother of the Muses, and patron goddess of bards.

4277] *tortoise-shell* χέλυς (HL 683, across which Hermes stretched strings, to make the first lyre).

4278] *Libuan* Λίβυν (= Libyan, HL 684, because made of wood from the Libyan lotus-tree).

Bromios Βρόμιος (= noisy, boisterous), a name for Bacchus. The typical time for a bard's performance was with the wine at dinner (see *Odyssey* 8.470-91).

4279] *God . . . with man participant* An oddly Christian-sounding interpolation, to suggest that wine inspires poetry. (HL 682).

4282] *A paian—hymn the Delian girls* Object, verb, subject. B slightly exaggerates the inverted word-order of the original: παιᾶνα μὲν Δηλιάδες ὑμνοῦσι (HN, HP 687-88).

paian A choral humn to Apollo, the god of poetry, born and worshipped on the island of Delos.

4284] *Latona* Leto, the mother of Apollo and Artemis. Inconsistently, B uses her Latin name.

4285] *domes* B's habitual near-transliteration of δώματα (= houses, palaces), but used here (HL 691) to translate μελάθροις (= roofs, houses). See l. 3585n. above.

4286] *will swan-like shout* B comes uncomfortably close to Buckley's version: "will I, an aged bard, shout from my hoary cheeks, swan-like" (*The Tragedies of Euripides, literally translated by Theodore Alois Buckley* [London, 1887], 2.20; see l. 952n. above). Though *shout* seems inappropriate, it translates κελαδήσω (= I will shout, HL 694) from a verb used twice by Aristophanes of a swallow's song (*Peace* 801, *Frogs* 684). For the swansong simile, cf. HL 111 and l. 3656 above.

4287] *starts off brave* B takes ὑπάρχει (HL 695) in its sense of "begins," though Paley (HP 694) chooses another one, "exists," and paraphrases: "for that which is good (a good topic) is supplied (or exists as a subject-matter) for my strains" (HP 694-95).

4291] *terrors of the earth* Perhaps borrowed from *King Lear*, 2.4.282; HN 700: "terrors of wild beasts."

4292] *Amphitruon comes* HN, HP 701; "you pass, Amphitryon."

in time! I.e., it's high time you did so.

4293] *since ye bedecked* Not quite the meaning of the present tense, κοσμεῖσθε (HL 703): "you have been bedecking."

4303] *love our lot* The alliterative phrase neatly reflects the double meaning of στέργειν (= 1. love, 2. be content with, HL 711).

4311] *raise him up* The optative ἀναστήσειε (HL 719) expresses a remote, i.e wildly improbable condition. Amphitryon is enjoying his private joke.

4315] *Outside of* Free from.

393

4318] *needs must* Although χρεών can have this meaning, it here probably means "you are fated to" (HL 726).

4321] *beautifully* B follows Paley's note (HP 728) in taking ἐς καλὸν (= to beautiful or good) as synonymous with the simple adverb καλῶς (= beautifully, well). But its meaning here may be more like: "to good purpose, at the right moment, opportunely."

4325] *sweets* Pleasures (ἡδονὰς, HL 732); but B emphasizes the word's derivation from ἡδύς (= sweet).

4329] *O ἰὼ*, an exclamation here expressing joy (HL 739).

4330] *where death pays, crime* HL 740: "where you will pay the penalty by dying."

4335] *King of the country!* I.e., when he was king of the country.

4339-40] *This strikes the keynote . . . Death takes up the tune!* B elaborates the musical image: "Now he begins a song in the house that I love to hear. Death is not far away" (HL 750-51).

4343] *who slew first?* B makes a dramatic question out of the bare statement: "for you slew" (HL 755), to parallel the question that follows (HL 757, l. 4345 below).

4345] *grazed* Slightly wounded. B gives the primary meaning of the verb χραίνω (HL 757) to suit the missile-throwing image in the next line; but the secondary sense of "stain, defile" seems more relevant to the context.

4346] *fool's-conceit* HL 758: ἄφρονα λόγον (= silly word). B's wording stresses the parallel with Ps. 14:1: "The fool hath said in his heart: There is no God."

4351] *Those I wish well to, well fare they, to wish!* HL 762 is simpler: "for [my] friends fare well, whom I wish to [do so]."

4354] *Are a care!* The stock dictionary definition of μελουσι (HL 764); but no anxiety is implied: "that's all they're thinking about now."

4357] *mighty* B seems to follow the MS reading, κλεινός (= famous) rather than the emendation καινὸς (= new) adopted by Nauck and Paley (HN 768, HP 767).

4359] *Acherontian* Adjective of Acheron, the River of Pain in the underworld.

  too A rhyme-led echo of Paley's note (HP 770): "as if the sense were, 'aye, and he has returned from the waters of Acheron too.'"

4361] *are crimes a care* See l. 4354n. above; but here the stock translation is more appropriate.

4368-69] *broken down his trust . . . dust* A rhyme-led expansion of HL 780: "he has broken the black chariot of wealth."

4370] *Ismenos* See l. 4164n. above.

4371-72] *ways, the polished bed / O' the seven-gated city!* HL 782-83:

"streets of the seven-gated city." B's puzzling *bed* was possibly suggested by the previous mention of a river.

4372]   *Dirké*   See l. 4165n. above.

4373]   *Asopiad sisters*   Daughters of Asopus, a Theban river.

4376]   *Puthios*   HN 790: Πυθίου (= the Pythian, i.e., Apollo). The reference is to Mount Parnassus.

4377]   *Helikonian*   Of Mount Helicon in Boeotia, a favorite haunt of the Muses.

4379]   *Spartan . . . Sown*   See l. 3538n. above

4385]   *nymph of Perseus' progeny*   Alcmena, daughter of Perseus' son Electryon.

4388-89]   *time has turned . . . Herakleidan might*   A rhyme-led expansion of HN, HP 805-6: "time has shown up brilliantly the strength of Heracles."

4391]   *cleft*   Interpolated, apparently for the rhyme (HL 807-8: "the nether house of Pluto."

4392]   *the lord that nature gave me*   HL 809: "Thou wast by nature a better king to me."

4393]   *That baseness born and bred*   A fine equivalent for a strange term of abuse: δυσγένεια ἀνάκτων (– an ill-birth of kings, HL 810). The antithesis between nature and *lot* (i.e. chance) was B's contribution.

4396-97]   *If to the gods . . . palm's award*   Expanded from "if justice still pleases the gods" (HL 813-14).

4398]   *Horror!*   B's interpretation of ἔα ἔα, an exclamation of surprise or displeasure (HL 815).

4404]   *grand and grim!*   Interpolated: "What an apparition I see!" (HL 817).

4405]   *Paian*   Παιάν, a title of Apollo as healer.

4409]   *to your town we come, no plague*   We have not come to hurt your town. B imitates the original word-order (HL 824).

4416]   *fresh*   B follows the MS reading, καινὸν (= new), though both Nauck and Paley adopt the emendation, κοινὸν (= kindred; HN, HP 831).

4417]   *Slaying*   The participle must be attached to *him*, as in the Greek (HL 832).

4418]   *collecting*   A literal translation of συλλαβοῦσα (= grasping together, bracing, hardening, HL 833).

4419]   *drag*   An alliterative substitute for the original "move, stir up" (κίνει, HL 837).

4422]   *Let go the bloody cable*   The image (HN 837) is of letting out sail for maximum speed.

4423]   *Acherousian*   Acherontian. See l. 4359n. above.

4424]   *self-homicide*   A conscientious attempt to replicate αὐθέντῃ (=

self-killer, i.e., one who himself kills, or who kills himself). Here (HL 839) both meanings seem present: Heracles himself (not Lycus) kills his own children, a quasi-suicidal act.

4425]   *beautiful boy-garland*   A precise translation of καλλίπαιδα στέφανον (HL 839).

4427]   *vile*   Used in the Latin sense of "cheap, unimportant" (HL 841: "nowhere," i.e., of no account).

4429]   *Certes*   Archaic word for "certainly," here used to translate μὲν (= on the one hand, HL 843). She contrasts her own good breeding with the dubious morality of the job she has been given—an amusing touch of Euripidean scepticism.

4431]   *glory*   Not quite the meaning of τιμὰς (= honors, place of honor) in HL 845. Paley explains her point (HP 844): it is no part of her high office to treat friends badly or instigate murders.

4432]   *friends of man*   Regarding Heracles as the "Helper" (see ll. 516-18n. above), B translates the MS reading, φίλους (= friends, HL 846), though bracketed by Nauck and rejected by Paley.

4441]   *faulty*   Again B prefers the MS reading, κακὰ (= bad, used sarcastically) to the emendation adopted by Nauck and Paley (HN, HP 855): κἀμὰ (= and my own).

4442]   *Changing her step . . . fault-free.*   B again translates a MS reading rejected by Nauck and Paley (HN, HP 856).

4443]   *to be wise*   An ironic pun, since σωφρονεῖν (HL 857), can express sanity as well as wisdom.

4444]   *cite*   Call—but that obvious word would have spoiled B's sound-effect.

   doing   That I am doing.

   loathe   οὐ βούλομαι (= do not wish, HL 858).

4446]   *And follow you quick*   The change to semi-anapaestic rhythms with irregular rhymes and line-lengths parallels Euripides' switch from iambic trimeters to trochaic tetrameters (from HL 855).

   with a whizz   ἐπιρροίβδην (HN 860), a word used elsewhere for the sound of a flying arrow.

4458]   *Keres*   See l. 4062n. above.

4460]   *famous*   An alliterative replacement for γενναῖον (= noble, HN, HP 872).

4466-68]   *dost cast . . . Away from thee . . . destroyest*   ἀποβαλεῖς (= you will throw away, or let fall) . . . ὀλεῖς (= you will destroy, or lose, HL 878). Since Greece has not caused the madness, the second meaning of each future verb is required to make sense.

4470]   *groans, her brood*   An imaginative rendering of ἁ πολύστονος (= the many-groan female, HL 880).

4471-72] *adrift / For doom* A gratuitously puzzling replacement for ὡς ἐπὶ λώβᾳ (= as for ill-treatment), paraphrased by Paley: "as if for mischief, as if resolved on doing injury to someone" (HP 879). But the original chorus is full of weird imagery.

4476] *that he saved* I.e., from being killed by Lycus, interpolated into HL 885) to spell out the irony of the story.

4478] *hunger-wild* Surprisingly euphemistic for ὠμοβρῶτες (= eating raw flesh, HL 887).

4482] *measure* Dance.

4482-84] *unrejoiced . . . revel-rout* I.e., as wild as a Bacchic orgy, but not so enjoyable.

tympanies A near transliteration of τυμπάνων (= drums; HN 891, HP 890).

thyrsos Inconsistently transliterated from θύρσῳ (= wand wreathed with ivy and vine-leaves, carried by Bacchic revellers).

Bromian See l. 4278n. above.

4485] *domes* δόμοι (= houses, HL 891). See l. 3585n. above

4489] *I wis!* Certainly (Old English *gewis*), a rhyme-led archaism.

4492] *and leave no trace* HL 896: ἄκραντα (= without accomplishing, i.e., to no effect).

4493] *Ai ai* αἰαῖ (HL 900), an exclamation of grief.

4496-97] *small . . . at all!* HL 902-3: "to whom children are born in vain."

4501] *Ha, ha* Not a laugh, but an unfortunate rendering of ἦ ἦ (HL 906), an exclamation calling attention to something.

4502] *Tartaros* The place of punishment in Hades.

4503] *the Titan* HL 908: "Enceladus," one of the giants who rebelled against the gods. He was killed by Pallas Athena.

4504] *domes* δόμους (= houses). See ll. 3585n. and 4485n. above.

4505] *bodies white with age* The elderly chorus.

4505-6] *What cry . . . dost thou call with?* The literal sense of the Greek (HL 910-11), i.e., What are you calling me to say?.

4507] *There's a curse indoors* "The happenings in the house are ἄλαστα [= unforgettable, abominable, HL 911]."

4508] *I shall not bring a prophet; you suffice* Paley paraphrases: "I do not want a prophet to tell me that" (HP 912).

4509] *Ai ai!* See ll. 4493n. above.

4513] *make appear* The basic meaning of ἀμφαίνεις (HL 919). The Chorus-leader asks for more details of the murders.

4516] *O Messenger* Interpolated into HL 921, though ΑΓΓ (short for ἄγγελος = Messenger) is given as the next speaker; HN 922. Such messenger-narratives were a regular feature of Greek tragedy.

4520]   *choir*   A near transliteration of χορὸς (= dance, band of dancers or singers, group, HL 925), but B exploits the English word's associations with religious ceremonial and choir-boy innocence.

4527]   *came to a stand-still*   HL 930 "Stood still in silence."

4529]   *himself*   B appears to translate the MS reading αὐτὸς (= himself), though Nauck and Paley read αὑτὸς (= the same; HN, HP 931).

4535]   *Eurustheus*   See l. 533n. above.

4541]   *Who gives me*   The literal sense of the Greek (HL 942), i.e., Who will give me?

4542]   *that Mukenai*   τὰς Μυκήνας (= the Mycenae). Paley explains the definite article (originally a demonstrative) as "denoting the celebrity of the place" (HP 943).

match   I.e., set the tools in conflict with the stonework—a puzzling translation of the straightforward λάζυσθαι (= seize, take, HL 943).

4543]   *sunk stones*   βάθρα (= foundations, HL 944).

4544]   *the Kuklops*   As workmen of Hephaestus, the god of ironwork and technology, the Cyclopes were commonly said to have built ancient walls.

4545]   *o'ertumble town*   The alliteration on *t* parallels that on σ (= *s*) in the Greek (στρεπτῳ σιδήρῳ συντριαινώσω πόλιν, HL 946).

4551]   *boys' tricks*   B stresses the derivation of παίζει (= he plays, jokes, HL 952) from παῖς (= boy).

4554]   *Nisos*   first king of Megara, at the end of the Isthmus of Corinth, on Heracles' imagined route from Thebes to Mycenae.

4560]   *bucklings*   πορπαμάτων (= clothes fastened with buckles or brooches, HL 959), as if to take part in the Isthmian Games.

4562-63]   *called out to hear /—Nobody*   I.e., called "Hear!" to an imaginary audience.

4564]   *Blaring*   Roaring.

4568]   *Extravagance*   Abnormal behavior.

4570-72]   *Danced thee drunk*   A clever equivalent for ἐβακχευσεν (= inspired thee with Bacchic frenzy, HL 966).

taking him to crouch . . . a suppliant   "Thinking it was Eurystheus' terrified father touching his hand in supplication" (HL 967-68).

4582]   *outwinding*   The literal sense of ἐξελίσσων (HL 977), i.e., overtaking him as he runs round the pillar.

4583-84]   *whirl / O' the lathe*   τόρνευμα (= lathe-work), an emendation adopted by Paley (HP 978).

4592]   *prevents*   Used in the Latin sense of "comes before" to translate φθάνει (= forestalls him, HL 986) i.e., falls at his father's feet before he has had time to shoot.

4593]   *cheek*   "Neck" (HN, HP 987).

4598] *mimicry of smith* Like a smith. The strange expression almost exactly reproduces the original words, HL 992.

4599-4601] *hand o'er head / Heaving . . . Hurls* The *h*-alliteration neatly replaces that on *k* + *x* in the Greek (HL 992-94), where it evidently simulates the sound of smashing bones.

4603] *He and the couple* I.e., him and the couple (the Greek was more grammatical; HL 995).

4606] *as he were at those Kuklops' work* As if he were at the walls of Mycenae. See l. 4544 n. above.

4608] *shaft* Arrow.

4611] *A statue* Paley saw an allusion by Euripides to "the great bronze statue of Pallas on the Acropolis" (HP 1003).

4623] *No gift of any god* B elaborates the literal meaning of οὐκ εὐδαίμονα (= not with a good genius or destiny, i.e., not happy, HL 1014)—inappropriately, since in context Heracles' sleep is undeniably the gift of the goddess Pallas.

4626] *A murder there was* Paley points out that this choral lyric is largely in dochmiacs, and quotes a statement that the dochmiac rhythm is "peculiarly . . . characteristic of Tragedy's 'entire being and essence'" (HP 1017). One would like to think that B deliberately put his first four words, *A murder there was,* in a rhythm that could be scanned as a dochmiac metron (= short-long-long-short-long). But he continued with his usual equivalent for Greek lyric meters: irregular rhymed verse.

4628] *best* B translates the puzzling MS reading, ἄριστος, though Nauck and (with misgivings) Paley adopt the emendation ἄπιστος (= unbelievable; HN 1017, HP 1018).

4629] *those, the daughters of Danaos slew* Their fifty husbands, on the wedding-night.

4630] *A murder indeed was that!* Interpolated (HL 1019).

4631] *straight to the goal has pressed* παρέδραμε (= has run past; HN, HP 1020).

4634] *Proknè's son* Itys, who was a *sacrifice to the Muses* only in the sense that his mother was turned into a singing nightingale, and that the story became useful material for poets.

4639, 4640] *outrageous fate* λυσσάδι . . . μοίρᾳ (= raving-mad fate, i.e., fated madness, HL 1024). The repetition is B's.

4642-43] *shall I urge / The Muse to celebrate?* HL 1027: "shall I sound forth?"

4645] *unrolled* A word probably suggested, not only by the rhyme, but by Paley's note (HP 1030): "the double door of the room is being opened (by the *eccyclema*) to display the bodies within." The ἐκκύκλημα (= wheel-out) was a wheeled stage-machine to display interiors.

4646]   *This way and that way, each prodigious fold!*   Expanded from five Greek words, διάνδιχα κληθρα κλίνεται ὑψιπύλων δόμων (= the bars of the high-doored house are bent in two directions; HN, HP 1029-30), interpreted by Paley to indicate "the separation of the two hinged doors in the middle."

4653]   *Tightenings*   A strange word to help represent an even stranger phrase: "many-noosed supports of knots" (HL 1035-36).

4658]   *all too late*   A possible meaning of ὑστέρῳ ποδί (= with later foot) in another context; but here (HL 1040) it makes no sense, since Amphitryon had done all he could already, in helping to immobilize the killer. The point must be that the old man moves slowly and reluctantly towards his sleeping son.

4660]   *diffused*   Used in the Latin sense of "spread out, sprawling." The original word παρειμένον (HL 1043) implies the total relaxation of exhaustion.

4661]   *slide from his sorrows in sleep*   A fine alliterative phrase to stress the prefix ἐκ (= out, out of) in ἐκλαθεσθαι κακῶν (= utterly forget his evils, HL 1044). B was possibly remembering the *Rime of the Ancient Mariner*, 293-94: "She sent the gentle sleep from Heaven, / That slid into my soul."

4663-64]   *used / Of old to the wreaths and paians*   An expansion of καλλίνικον (= beautifully victorious, triumphant, HL 1046), a key-epithet for Heracles in the play. Cf. the irony of its association with the threatened murder of his children by Lycus (HL 582, l. 4171 above).

4668]   *Refrain—refrain!*   A rhyme-led replacement for ἆ ἆ, an interjection of strong emotion (HL 1052).

4669]   *Unlike water*   Interpolated. B has also made a general statement out of the specific exclamation: "How much φόνος [= murder or blood shed in murder] spilt here rises up!" Paley refers to the "gore . . . which, being shed on the ground, is said to rise up against the murderer" (HP 1052).

4674]   *bray*   Crush to powder, as in a mortar.

4679]   *A horror of slumber*   B's phrase for "he sleeps a sleep, a deadly sleep" (HN 1060-61, HP 1061).

4684]   *Triple woe!*   B's insertion, possibly suggested by the odd phrase, τέκνα τρίγονα(= children produced at three births) used elsewhere in the play (HL 1023, l. 4638 above).

4703-4]   *who, as they used to love, / Now hate him*   Interpolated into a passage of incoherent dialogue where the text is disputed, and exact translation almost impossible. Amphitryon fears that if his son kills him too, he will have even more "kindred blood" for the *Erinyes* (the Furies who haunted murderers of close relatives) to pursue him for.

4707]   *ready to wreak*   B follows the MS reading retained by Nauck, but emended in Paley: ἔμελλες (= you were about to; HN, HP 1079). Heracles had fought the Taphians to avenge the killing of Alcmena's brothers. See l. 3602n. above.

4710]   *glad, life's close*   B's recapitulation.

4713]   *Clustered about with a wash of sea!*   A fine lyrical expansion of one word, περίκλυστον (= washed around, HL 1080), exploiting the chance resemblance of the Greek κλυσ to the English *clus* in *clustered*.

4723]   *In breath*   The literal sense of ἔμπνους; but here (HL 1089), it just means: "breathing."

4727]   *Smoked upwards*   B's imaginative rendering of μετάρσια (= up in the air, i.e., shallow, HL 1093).

4729]   *young . . . young*   νεανίαν (youthful, active, vigorous, HL 1095). The repetition is B's.

4733]   *my brother-shieldman*   HL 1099: "which bore a shield [i.e. fought in battle] beside my arms."

4735-36]   *twice / Begun Eurustheus' race*   HL 1102: "Eurustheus' *diaulos.*" See l. 263n. above. He knows that he has been to Hades and back on Eurustheus' orders—surely he hasn't started doing it all again?

4737]   *the Sisupheian stone*   The rock that Sisyphus, for his sins, had to keep rolling up a hill in Hades: it rolled down again every time he reached the top.

4738]   *Demeter's sceptred maid*   Her daughter Persephone who, as Pluto's wife, became queen of the Underworld.

4743]   *these my woes*   I.e., to Heracles, their source.

4744]   *desert your ills*   I.e., desert you in your misfortunes.

4747]   *faring badly*   Although you are faring badly. The καὶ + participle of the original clearly expresses the missing *although* (HN, HP 1113).

4750]   *boasting*   The usual meaning of κόμπος; but here (HL 1116) it simply means, "That's putting it strongly."

   state no hap   You do not say what has happened.

4752]   *Heyday!*   An archaic exclamation of surprise, used to translate the similar Greek exclamation, παπαῖ (HL 1120). B adopts Nauck's transposition of ll. 1118-19 to follow l. 1121. This appeared, not in HN (1866), which the poet possessed, but in the 1871 edition, which he must also have consulted.

4753]   *trying*   I.e., trying to find out if you are sane again.

4755]   *Haides-drunk*   HL 1119: "a Bacchus of Hades."

4756]   *I bring to mind no drunkenness of soul*   HL 1122: "I don't remember any Bacchic revel in my mind."

4759]   *Mind*   Know, be conscious of.

4760]   *Enough!* . . . *nor wish*   B follows HP 1126: "It suffices; for I do not wish to learn by silence"; explained by Paley to mean: "That is enough to know: I do not desire to learn what you do not choose to tell."

4763]   *bury*   A possible meaning of περιστέλλου (HL 1129), if Amphitryon is still trying to protect his son from the truth. Otherwise it would mean: "attend to, concentrate on," as Paley takes it (HP 1129). Either way, *guilt* is too judgemental for κακά (= bad things, i.e., misfortunes, HL 1129).

4767]   *fastenedst*   ἔσπευσας (= hastened, zealously promoted, HL 1133)). B's odd choice of verb was evidently dictated by his *f*-alliteration, to parallel the repeated π in the Greek: ἀπόλεμον, ὦ παῖ, πόλεμον ἔσπευσας.

4770]   *Ill-announcing*   κακ᾽ ἀγγέλλων (= reporting bad news, HL 1136).

4771]   *Go mad!*   Answering the question, *What did I?*— you went mad. The Greek is clearer, where both verbs are participles: "having done what? Having gone mad."

   clearing up   I.e., clarification ἑρμηνεύματα (= interpretations, things to be explained, HL 1137).

4774]   *Ai ai*   See ll. 4493n. above.

4776]   *dance it down*   ἐβάκχευσα (= raved through it like a Bacchant, HL 1142).

4780]   *save*   An unnecessarily puzzling translation of φείδομαι (= spare, HL 1146).

4782]   *rock-level's leap*   An alliterative version of "leaps from a bare rock"(HL 1148).

4783]   *through breast and all*   "To the liver"(HL 1149).

4789-90]   *Eyes will be* . . . *loved so much!*   HL 1155-56: "We shall be seen, and the pollution [μύσος] of [my] child-murder will come to the eyes of the dearest of my friends." B's *plague* neatly expresses Heracles' fear of infecting his friend's eyes with his own guilt.

4794]   *night*   HN, HP 1159: "darkness."

4795-96]   *Let this wretch* . . . *innocents*   HL 1160-62: "for I am ashamed of the evil I have done, and have no wish, by attaching blood-guilt to this man, to do [more] evil to the innocent."

4798]   *Asopos*   See l. 4373n. above.

4799]   *spear's fight-fellowship*   HL 1165: σύμμαχον δόρυ (= fighting-alongside spear). B's alliterative phrase stresses the literal meaning of the adjective normally translated: "allied."

4800]   *bruit*   Rumor, report.

   Erechtheidai   Sons of Erectheus, a mythical king of Athens.

4804]   *Saving me down there*   In rescuing me from Hades.

4814]   *sufferings . . . suffered*   B reproduces the Greek trick of combining a verb with its related noun (ἐπάθομεν πάθεα; HL 1180).

4818]   *Would I might obey!*   HL 1185: "you command the willing."

4822]   *dye*   The alliterating noun expresses a possible meaning of βαφή (= a dipping, e.g., of clothes in dye); but here (HL 1188) the word implies no change of color. See l. 3697n. above.

4823]   *Heré's strife!*   HL 1189: "This is Hera's ἀγών (= contest, struggle, battle)," i.e., this is the result of Hera's enmity.

4826]   *Phlegraia's*   HN, HP 1194: Φλεγραῖον (Phlegraion = adjective of Phlegra, a volcanic plain in Thrace, famous for its underground fire, where the Giants fought the gods).

4831]   *peploi*   πέπλοισι (= robes, HL 1199). See l. 171n. above.

4834]   *who shared my woe with me*   I.e., when Heracles rescued him from Hades. B makes what sense he can of the disputed MS reading, συναλγοῦντ᾽ (= sharing pain with, HP 1202), rejecting with Paley an emendation adopted by Nauck (HN 1202); but the present participle cannot easily be understood as a past one.

4837]   *Woe's weight . . . in thee*   The original is equally obscure: βάρος ἀντίπαλον δακρύοισιν ἁμιλλᾶται (= "a wrestling-against weight contends with tears"). Paley thought it might mean: "a weighty motive (*viz.* friendship for Theseus . . .) induces you to uncover your face as much as much as grief induces you to cover it" (HP 1205). B apparently relies on alliteration to identify the *weight.*

4838]   *falling at*   A near-literal translation of προσπίτνων (IIN 1208, HP 1207), used here in its common sense of "supplicating."

4844]   *Let me speak!*   B's gloss on the interjection εἶεν (= well, all right, HL 1214).

4845]   *eye*   ὄμμα, a word often used, as here, for "face" (HL 1215).

4850]   *Nought care I to*   I.e., I don't care if I.

4851]   *soul rises to*   ἐκεῖσ᾽ ἀνοιστέον (= one must refer back to that point, HL 1221). B's characteristic phrase is based on the literal sense of the verb ἀναφέρω (= bring up, lift up, rise).

4853]   *tastes old age*   HL 1223: "grows old," i.e., wears out.

4857]   *of the right race*   B translates εὐγενὴς (= well born), though it here probably means just "noble," without such emphasis on pedigree (HL 1227).

4860]   *sign'st*   σημαίνεις, i.e., point to (HL 1230).

4862]   *aught divine*   I.e., the sun. Euripides implicitly questions Creon's assumption in Sophocles' *Oedipus Tyrannus* 1424-28 that the sun needs protection against the pollution of Oedipus's crimes.

4872]   *at all import*   Are of any importance to.

4873]　*to gods I give their like*　I.e., I please myself as far as the gods are concerned. HL 1243: "the god is a self-willed creature (αὔθαδες) and [so am] I towards the gods."

4876]　*moody*　I.e., in your anger.

4878]　*what man turns up first*　Almost the literal sense of ἐπιτυχόντος (= man who meets, i.e., ordinary man, HL 1248).

4881]　*measure's past*　HL 1251: "one must suffer ἐν μέτρῳ[= in measure, i.e in moderation]."

4886]　*ope thee out*　Unfold to you.

4888]　*this man*　Amphitryon. See l. 3553n. above.

4892]　*what follows needs must fall*　The alliterating last word enables B to continue the building metaphor, though the original is quite literal: "the offspring must be unfortunate"(HL 1262).

4902]　*Tuphons or giants*　B follows Paley's text (HP 1272), not Nauck's, which reads: "Geryons or Giants" (HN 1272). See ll. 813n. and 3993-94n. above.

4903]　*end out*　The literal equivalent of the compound ἐξανύω, though the *out* prefix here implies "completely," and the whole verb means "finish off, wipe out, destroy" (HL 1273).

4904]　*headed all about with heads*　A vivid rendering of one word, ἀμφίκρανον (= with heads all round, HL 1274).

4905]　*Hudra*　See l. 3697n. above.

4907]　*In full drove*　B brings out a linguistic detail of his original: "and I went through droves (ἀγέλας) of a myriad other toils," where the noun for herds of cattle (ἀγέλας) is derived from the verb ἄγω (= drive) exactly as in English.

4913]　*Dare I*　HL 1282: "is it ὅσιον [= allowable by divine law] for me to."

4914]　*festival*　πανήγυριν (= assembly of a whole nation, especially for a public festival, HL 1283).

4915]　*My curse scarce courts accost*　HN, HP 1284: "I have curses not admitting conversation (εὐπροσηγόρους)." Paley explains: "It was forbidden by the law for any man to speak to a murderer before he had been expiated." B uses alliteration to carry the compressed meaning.

4919]　*Kept by sharp tongue-taunts under lock and key*　HL 1288: "locked in by bitter goads of the tongue."

4924-25]　*there's no hurt / To speak of*　HL 1293: "he feels no pain." B's qualifying version is unfortunate, in a context where the impossibility of speaking has just been emphasized (l. 4915 above).

4928]　*pierce*　One meaning of περᾶν, doubtless selected for its dynamic quality; but here (HL 1296) the word probably means just "pass across."

4929]   *to drink*   Interpolated to fill out the sense (HL 1297).

4930]   *Ixion*   Punished in Hades by being bound on a perpetually turning wheel. See l. 1523n. above.

4937]   *Stamp foot . . . own sandal-trick!*   B rejects suggested emendations to this probably corrupt line: κρούουσ᾽ Ὀλυμπίου Ζηνὸς ἀρβύλη πόδα (= "striking with shoe the foot of Olympian Zeus," HP 1304), and seems content with English as meaningless as the Greek. The general thought is that Hera should dance with joy at so triumphing over her husband's bastard.

4939]   *pedestalled*   B spells out the statue-image implicit in the original: "turning up-down [i.e. upside-down], foundations and all, the first man in Greece" (HL 1306-7).

4942-43]   *me— / Lover of Hellas*   HL 1309-10: "the benefactors of Hellas."

4944]   *strife* ἀγὼν (= struggle, contest, HL 1311), i.e., you're up against Hera—she is your opponent in this contest.

4946-47]   *Why, to no death . . . bear thy woes!*   After l. 1312 there seems to be a lacuna in the MS. B paraphrases Paley's guess at the missing words (HP 1313).

4950]   *wedlock against law*   Paley suggests an allusion to Zeus's marrying his sister, Hera (HP 1316). The *poets* (l. 4949) could then be represented by the *Homeric Hymn* to Hera (xii, 3): "sister and wife of loud-thundering Zeus."

4952]   *Branded their sires in bondage*   Cronus castrated his father, Uranus, and was later imprisoned in Tartarus by his own son, Zeus.

4953-54]   *carry heads / High*   An imaginative translation of ἠνέσχοντο (= held themselves up), though here (HL 1319) more likely used in its common sense of "held out, endured."

4957]   *the law*   Which forbade murderers to live in their own cities.

4960]   *goods shared alike*   HL 1325: "a share of my property."

4963]   *Knosian bull*   The Minotaur, a monster half-bull, half-man, that lived in the labyrinth at Knossos in Crete and, until killed by Theseus, ate seven boys and seven girls from Athens every year.

4968]   *uplift the honoured one*   I.e., raise you to honor, celebrate you.

4969]   *huge marble heaps*   HL 1332: λαίνοισι . . . ἐξογκώμασιν (= stone cairns); but B possibly sees them as tombs or temples.

4970]   *Hellenes*   To be scanned as a trisyllable, like ῞Ελληνες, though the original uses the genitive, ῾Ελλήνων (HL 1334).

4974]   *friends may flit*   HL 1338: "there is no need of friends."

4980]   *persuaded—one is born*   Persuaded that one god is born. The punctuation is confusing.

4984]   *I pondered*   I.e., I've just been thinking. The Greek aorist (e.g., ἐσκεψάμην, IIL 1347) often implies the sense of an English perfect.

4991]   *have the grace of*   A literal translation of χάριν . . . ἔχω (= I am grateful for, HL 1352). B carefully retains the repetition of the word χάριν (= grace, favor, sense of a favor received) from HL 1336, l. 4972 above.

4993]   *as truly*   I.e., as truly as I'm tasting this one (a slightly puzzling interpolation; HL 1353).

4997]   *one bows to fate*   HL 1357: "one must be a slave to fortune."

5002]   *sanction*   Allow to bury them.

5004]   *community*   Fellowship, communion (κοινωνίαν, HL 1363).

5009]   *who*   He who.

5012]   *by main-force*   B translates the MS reading, βίᾳ (HN 1369), though Paley (and Nauck in 1871) adopted the emendation, βίου (i.e. "laboring to procure for you an honorable life," HP 1369).

5019]   *miserably moved*   An alliterative version of HN, HP 1375: "how miserably I have fared!."

5021]   *bitter those delights of kisses now*   The original (HL 1376-77) implies that Heracles is kissing the dead children in the present, not the past: "O mournful pleasure of kisses, and mournful fellowship of these weapons!"

5032-34]   *No! relinquishment . . . observe the pact*   Expanded from six Greek words (HL 1385): "These [weapons] must not be abandoned, but miserably preserved."

5038]   *for bringing there the Hound!*   Here there is no equivalent in the MS for HN, HP, HL 1388: "in case I suffer something [a common euphemism for dying], being bereaved [μονούμενος = made alone of] my sons." Paley explains: "lest, if he should go alone, and without his children, he should die of grief" (HP 1386). Did B think that fear too unheroic to translate?

5040]   *lament one wide lament*   Expanded from one word: συμπενθήσατε (= join in lamenting, HL 1390).

5045]   *from thy dead ones!*   HL 1394: "O wretched man!"

5047]   *these strong men*   καὶ τοὺς σθενόντας (= even those who are strong, HL 1396).

5051]   *Nay, but I wipe*   HL 1399: μὴ . . . ἐξομόρξωμαι (= let me not wipe, or, I fear I may wipe).

5052]   *Squeeze out and spare no drop! I take it all!*   ἔκμασσε, φείδου μηδέν· οὐκ ἀναίνομαι (= wipe off, spare none of it; I don't refuse, HL 1400).

5055]   *heart-broken*   B's replacement for an understatement typical of Greek tragedy: "unfortunate" (δυστυχής, HL 1403).

5056]   *father*   HL 1404: "old man" (a phrase perhaps avoided by B because of its colloquial use).

5057]   *Certes*   See l. 4429n. above.

5059]   *will the having such a love-charm soothe?*   Gently satirical, i.e., will that really make you feel better?

5061]   *what I love thou seek'st*   I.e., you ask for what I want too.

5062]   *Strange! Of thy labours no more memory?*   I.e., have you so forgotten all you've been through in the past that you make such a fuss about this now?

5063]   *I bore*   That I bore.

5065]   *I live low to thee?*   A literal translation of HL 1413: ζῶ σοὶ ταπεινός (= have I lived for you to despise me?).

5067]   *Down amid evils*   I.e., when I found you suffering in Hades.

5068]   *as courage*   As courage goes.

5070]   *old father!*   Again B avoids the literal translation: "old man" (HN, HP 1418). See l. 5056n. above.

5073]   *When, coming*   Coming when? The comma obscures the meaning of πότ᾽ ἐλθών (HL 1420).

When thy task is done   HN, HP 1420: "when you have buried the children"—which the textual critic Dindorf found "surprising and almost absurd." Paley explained the difficulty by "supposing the words of the speakers to be mutually interrupted. Amphitryon was going to ask, 'And who is to take care of *me*?' To which Hercules replies, '*I* will have you brought to Athens, when you shall have buried my children.'" B ingeniously evades the problem by a deliberately ambiguous phrase that could mean either, "when you've buried the children," or "when you've ended your life."

5074]   *have thee carried forth*   Again deliberately ambiguous: either as a corpse for burial, or as a guest for whom transport has been arranged.

5077-78]   *hulk . . . trailed*   HL 1424: ἐφολκίδες (= small boats towed by a ship). The image here is full of irony, since Heracles has previously applied it to his own small sons (HL 631, ll. 4230-31 above). B's *hulk* is particularly apt, because it resembles the main stem (ὀλκ from ἕλκω = draw, drag, pull) of ἐφολκίδες; because *hulk* has been conjecturally derived from ὀλκάς (= a towed ship, merchantship); and because it developed in English the secondary meanings of a dismantled ship, and a great, shambling person.

5083-84]   *The greatest of all our friends . . . evermore!*   A rhyme-led expansion of HN, HP 1428: "having lost the greatest of dear things [τὰ μέγιστα φίλων, rather than τοὺς μείστους φίλων (= the greatest of friends)]." The neuter expression may widen the reference here to include the losses of Alcmena and the children; but Paley comments: "a well-known idiom. The chorus speak of the departure of Heracles as of the loss of their greatest friend" (HP 1428).

5085]   *Our best friend*   Euripides.

5087]   *Lachares the sculptor*   No sculptor of that name appears to be on record. Perhaps, leafing through his Athenaeus, B came across these words: "Lachares then made Athena naked" (γυμνὴν Ἀθηνᾶν τοτ᾽ ἐποίησε Λαχάρης; Athenaeus, 9.405f). They actually referred to the stripping of gold from the statue of Athena on the Acropolis by Lachares the general in 296 B.C.; but B may have read no further. Taken in their literal sense, the words may have started a train of thought from his favorite picture, Caravaggio's *Andromeda*, to Furini's painting of Andromeda, and the whole question of the female nude in art. (See ll. 806-25n. and 2890-92n. above; and the notes to B's "Parleying with Francis Furini," this edition, 16.216-17).

5094]   *Pallas wields the thunderbolt*   A missile normally associated with her father, Zeus; but according to Lemprière (381) Minerva-Athene "could hurl the thunders of Jupiter."

5101]   *kottabos*   See l. 2045n. above.

5102]   *last*   Latest.

        Take a sphere   Cf. the "glass ball" image in *The Ring and the Book* 1.1359-65 (this edition 7.56).

5105]   *clean passage*   So that it passes clean through.

5126]   *His heels . . . head should be!*   See l. 2152n. above.

5135]   *'best friend of man,'*   Aristophanes claims for himself the title given to Heracles (l. 4882 above, HL 1252) and then transferred to Euripides (ll. 5085-86 above).

5140]   *your imaginary Third*   See ll. 3440-45 above.

5146]   *Tin-islands*   See l. 2861n. above. Balaustion's *dream* of a poet who *made Comedy and Tragedy combine* (l. 3440 above) presumably pointed to Shakespeare.

5148]   *Iostephanos*   See l. 937n. above.

5163]   *Thamuris*   A poet mentioned in *Iliad* 2.594-600: "Dorium, where the Muses met the Thracian Thamyris, as he was walking from Oichalia, from the house of Eurytus the Oichalian, and stopped him singing; for he had boasted that he would win a singing-contest even with the Muses themselves, the daughters of aegis-bearing Zeus; but they in anger disabled him [by blindness] and made him forget how to play the lyre." By *"no Thamuris!"* Aristophanes means that he is still as good a poet as ever, precisely because he has not offended the Muses by *leaving . . . untouched* the type of poetry that they inspired him to write.

5166]   *Poikilé*   Ποικίλη (= many-colored), i.e., the *Stoa Poikile*, the Painted Colonnade in the *Agora* at Athens.

5169-73]   *Our Sophokles . . . such a case*   Paraphrased from the *Life of Sophocles* (5): "And they say that only in his *Thamyris* did he ever take up a lyre and play it—hence the painting of him with a lyre in the Painted Colonnade."

5171]   *The voice of him was weak   Life of Sophocles,* 4: "Among his many innovations in the tragic contests, he first stopped the custom of the poet's acting, because of his own weakness of voice [μικροφωνία]."

5175]   *Enriched his 'Rhesos'. . . store* The story of the *Rhesus,* a tragedy (doubtfully) attributed to Euripides, was based on *Iliad* 10, and Paley called it "remarkable as being the only extant Greek drama, the plot of which is taken from the direct action of the *Iliad"* (*Euripides, With an English Commentary,* 1.vii). Homer was said to have been blind. The play contains an account by Rhesus' mother, the Muse Terpsichore, of Thamyris' crime and punishment (916-25).

5177]   *eyed* Was this odd verb suggested by the legend that one of *Thamyris'* eyes was blue-grey and the other, black (*Fragmenta,* 181)? If so, perhaps those eyes also suggested the *Powers above his power*— the blue-grey (γλαυκός) symbolizing the sky and "blue-grey-eyed (γλαυκῶπις) Athena," and the black one, Thamyris' mental and finally physical blindness.

5183]   *psalterion* See l. 1562n. above.

5185]   *just as I were* Just as if I were.

5186]   *That sunrise and combustion of the east!* I.e., that dawn of poetry.

5187]   *And then he sang . . .* The meter of this song (terza rima), its sunrise-opening, and its Roman-triumph imagery all suggest the possible influence of Shelley's "The Triumph of Life."

5188]   *marching* Why that verb to represent the ἰόντα (= going) of *Iliad* 2.596? Perhaps because Thamyris' name (Θάμυρις) scans as an anapaest. Anapaests were traditionally a marching meter, and "marching anapaests" were the original meter used in tragedy for the first entrance of the Chorus (c.g., in Aeschylus' *Persae*). Thus *marching* specially suited a pioneer of lyric poetry. See also l. 711n. above.

5189]   *Perpend* Ponder upon, think about.

5191-93]   *Thamuris from Oichalia . . . bound / For Dorion* See ll. 4051n. and 5163n. above.

5193-95]   *at the uprise . . . footstep* Elaborated from the account of the same incident in *Rhesus* 921-22: "we Muses came to the gold-clodded [χρυσόβωλον] Pangaean crag of earth." Pangaeus was a mountain in Thrace, famous for its gold-mines. Paley's note on the passage (*Euripides, With an English Commentary,* 1.60) quoted from Apollodorus the brash terms offered by Thamyris: "if he won the contest, he could have sexual intercourse with all the Muses; if he lost, they could deprive him of whatever they liked."

5200]   *Balura—happier while its name was not* According to Pausanias

(*Description of Greece*, 4.33.3) the river Balura (Βαλύρα) was so named from "Thamyris' having thrown away [ἀποβαλόντος] his lyre there when blinded."

5205] *thrift that thanks the tide* I.e., gratefully economical use of the river-water for irrigation, etc.

5210] *signet* Authentic sign, promise.

5213] *pomps* Grand features of the landscape. B was perhaps remembering not only the "memorable pomp" of a similar dawn-scene in Wordsworth (*The Prelude*,4.324) but also the word's Greek source, πομπή (= escort, solemn procession). Thus the scenery may represent the crowds lining the route of Thamyris' triumphant progress.

5220] *Pan* The goat-legged god of the countryside.

5243] *fiery transport* The apocalyptic state of mind foreshadowed by the "combustion of the east" (l. 5186 above).

5246] *Homeros* ῞Ομηρος (= Homer); presumably an allusion to *Homeric Hymns* 25.2-5: "It comes from the Muses . . . that there are poets [ἀοιδοί = singers] . . . on earth . . . And happy is he whom the Muses love. Sweet is the voice that flows from his mouth."

5253] *he saw, he knew the place* For the intuitive recognition of the scene of a fatal contest, cf. B's "Childe Roland to the Dark Tower Came," 175-202: "This was the place! . . . I saw them and I knew them all" (this edition, 5.255-56).

5256] *these* These rhythms.

5260] *Be my Parnassos* The mountain associated with the worship of the Muses. See ll. 5193-95n. above.

5261] *river* The future Balura; see l. 5200n. above.

5262] *Pieria's fount* Hippocrene, the fountain sacred to the Muses on Mount Helicon, here called *Pierian* because the Muses were said to have been born in Pieria, a region of Macedonia on the northern slopes of Mount Olympus.

5263] *ado* The word implies that the contest is a tiresome formality with a foregone conclusion.

5265] *song broke up in laughter* Aristophanes stops improvising his quasi-Sophoclean song (l. 5185 above) and laughingly leaves its completion to someone else.

5268] *sings for gods, not men* In *Odyssey* 22.346-49 the bard Phemius, pleading for his life, tells Odysseus: "it will cause you pain in future if you kill me, a poet who sings to gods and men . . . and is worthy to sing to you, as to a god."

5273] *sung content back to myself* Sung myself back into a good mood.

5274] *a play beside* I.e., *The Frogs*, which will present a poetry-contest between Aeschylus and Euripides.

5276] '*Prelude-Battle*' Προαγών (= preliminary contest), the title of a lost play of Aristophanes. According to Meineke (2.1137) it ridiculed "the solemnity of tragic poets and especially Euripides."

5281] *"Best Friend"* See ll. 5085-86 above.

5289] *buzz* Much talk.

'*Bacchanals*' The *Bacchae*, found after Euripides' death in Macedonia, and produced by his son (or nephew) Euripides. See ll. 213n. and 312n. above.

5301-2] *Arginousai . . . Kallikratidas* See l. 2417n. above.

5304] *Dekelea* A district of Attica, only 14 miles from Athens, occupied by the Spartans in 413 B.C.

5306] *Peace declared* I.e., if peace is declared, once peace is declared—a conditional or proleptic use of a participle common in Greek. In fact, the Athenian victory at Arginusae (406 B.C.) was followed by the destruction of their fleet at Aegospotami (405 B.C.), and when peace came (404 B.C.), it was on Spartan terms.

5310] *Theoria . . . Opora* See ll. 1163-64n. and 3117n. above.

breath B's manuscript, which was taken by the compositors to read *breadth*, is much corrected at this point, and the *d* in this word belongs to one of the cancelled readings. It is likely that B meant to write *breath* here, since Aristophanes is clearly alluding to *Peace* 525-26 (though it was actually Theoria, not Opora, who was there complimented on her sweet breath).

5312] *Bald Bard* See l. 601n. above.

5314] *hare* See l. 1958n. above.

spinks Finches, especially chaffinches, mentioned as food (under their rather similar Greek name of σπίνοι) by Athenaeus (2.65c) and by Aristophanes (*Birds* 1079).

5316] *guttlings, guzzlings* Gluttonous eating, drinking.

5317] *Rosy-finger-tips* B coins a name suitable for a prostitute out of Homer's epithet for dawn (ῥοδοδάκτυλος = with rosy fingers), while still teasing Balaustion as a "rosy" Rhodian (see l. 2698n. above).

5318] *Melpomené* The Muse of Tragedy.

5319] *Amphion* See ll. 290-91n. above.

5322] *No doubt . . . sincere!* Cf. "For Blougram, he believed, say, half he spoke" ("Bishop Blougram's Apology," 980; this edition, 5.329).

5323] *One story he referred to* See ll. 337n. and 1505-8n. above.

5328] *stulos* See l. 724n. above.

5345] *punctual* Always keeping up with her dictation (probably used also in the Latin sense of "puncturing, pricking," with the sharp end of the stylus.

5348] *Ah, would the lifeless body stay!* Balaustion was about to equate written words with the lifeless body of spoken ones, and say: only the *mere words* remain, the dead body of speech. But she interrupts herself, realizing that not even that will remain—if only it could! For the lifeless words in wax will be obliterated by others, just as human bodies end up as an unrecognizable pile of bones (a *dusty heap*, l. 5350).

5353] *fire—with smoke* I.e., intellectual brilliance obscured, as she sees it, by moral turpitude.

5356] *ash, now white and cold enough* I.e., the wax tablet, symbolizing both the failure of the written word to represent lively speech, and of the cremated body to represent life.

5357] *Nay, Euthukles!* Don't put away your recording equipment yet.

5362-64] *neither ills / We dread . . . Perform to promise* Cf. A. H. Clough, "Say not the struggle nought availeth," 5: "If hopes were dupes, fears may be liars."

5372] *homicidal dragon-crop* See l. 3538n. above.

5374] *Happy as ever* See l. 2635n. above.

5375] *Plausive* Applauding.

5376] *Iophon produced his father's play* A reasonable assumption by B; though it now seems that *Oedipus at Colonus* was produced by the poet's grandson, Sophocles the Younger (401 B.C.). See ll. 1257-59n. above.

5378] *mid earthquake-thundering* Cf. *Oedipus at Colonus* 1606: κτύπησε μὲν Ζεὺς χθόνιος (= Zeus [the thunderer] crashed from the earth)— which Oedipus took as a signal that he must descend a "precipitous path" (1590), taking only Theseus with him.

5379-80] *hardly Theseus' hands . . . the horror* Cf. *Oedipus at Colonus* 1647-50: "we came away, and, turning round in a short time, saw from far off—one man nowhere to be seen, and the other, the king himself, holding his hand to his head to shield his eyes, as if some terrible thing had appeared, unbearable to look at."

5380-81] *as their grove disgorged / Its dread ones* B's gloss on the passage, probably suggested by Pausanias (*Description of Greece*, 1.30: 4): "and a region called Colonus Hippius is pointed out, said to be the first place in Attica visited by Oedipus . . . and an altar of Poseidon Hippius [ʽΙππιος = of horses] and Athena Hippia . . . and the grove [ἄλσος] of Poseidon . . . ."

5381] *each daughter* Antigone and Ismene, who had been looking after their blind father.

5383] *"Frogs"* The comedy with which Aristophanes won first prize at the Lenaea in 405 B.C. See l. 205n. above.

5385] *Main-Fight* I.e., *Frogs.* See l. 5277 above.

    loyal I.e., true to his promise of fair criticism (ll. 5277-87 above).

    license-free Free from licentiousness.

5386] *Thasian juice* See ll. 664n., 730-31n., and 1429n. above.

5390] *Castalian dew* Water from the Castalian spring on Mount Parnassus, which was sacred to Apollo and the Muses, and said to inspire any poet who drank from it.

5391] *medium* Liquid used by artists for mixing paints (the image here transferred from visual art to poetry).

5399] *The boys* See ll. 703n. and 1153-54n. above.

5400] *trounced to heart's content* See l. 2585n. above.

5411-12] *"He's all one stiff and gluey . . . swine's neck!"* Expanded from a fragment of Aristophanes (Meineke, 2.1193, No. lxxii): "For I think he's like κόλλοψ [= thick skin on the top of a pig's neck]"—so called, says the note, "because κόλλα [= glue] is made from it."

5412] *Chatterbox* I.e., Euripides, accused by Aeschylus in *Frogs* 1069 of having "taught gossip and chatter."

5413] *"twisting words like wool"* In *Frogs* 1297 Aeschylus calls Euripides' poetry "ἱμονιοστρόφόυ μέλη [= songs of a rope-twister]," which a scholiast took to mean what a man might sing as he hauled up buckets of water (*Scholia*, 309); but B tries to retain the notion of twisting. The *wool* was perhaps suggested partly by alliteration, and partly by an isolated fragment of Aristophanes (Meineke, 2.1216, No. ccxxvi): "he used to tease out wool."

5413-15] *usurped his seat . . . altar-orts,"* Having won the contest, Aeschylus thus dismisses Euripides: "Mind you don't let that criminal liar and βωμολόχος [= a lurker round altars, looking for scraps] ever sit in my chair, even by mistake" (*Frogs* 1520-23).

5417] *Then came a contest* B transposes the order of events in the play, presumably for rhetorical purposes.

5420] *Mystics matched the Frogs* The lyric odes are sung by two independent choruses, first the Frogs, with the imitative refrain, *Brekekekex koaxkoax* (209-50), and then the Initiates of the Mysteries of Demeter, Persephone, and Dionysus (from 316).

5421] *Seiren* See ll. 491-92n. above.

5423] *Phaps-Elaphion* See l. 588-89n. above.

5424] *The Muse of dead Euripides* In *Frogs* 1304-8, before parodying Euripides' lyrics, Aeschylus says: "Bring me the lyre—and yet what need of a lyre for a poet like this? Where's that girl that rattles the potsherds [ἡ τοῖς ὀστράκοις κροτοῦσα, i.e., dances with castanets]? Here, Muse of Euripides, these are just the right songs for you to accompany."

frank Free from concealment, i.e., naked.

5426] *How baby-work like "Herakles" had birth!* Remembering, perhaps, the terms of Thamyris' challenge to the Muses (see ll. 5193-95n.

above), B makes Aristophanes suggest that the tragedy was inspired by sex with a prostitute-Muse.

5430]   *"Lost his flask of oil"* ληκύθιον ἀπώλεσεν (= lost his little oil-flask). Aeschylus tells Euripides, "I'll destroy your prologues with a little oilflask" (*Frogs* 1200), and does so by making him recite six of his prologues, and each time interrupting him, before the end of the third line, with those two Greek words. That they fitted in both metrically and grammatically implied that Euripides' versification was monotonous, and the words themselves may have had sexual connotations (*Frogs*, ed. K. Dover [Oxford, 1993], 337-39).

5431]   *pause of period*   Pause in the sentence. The words were neatly inserted at the metrical caesura.

5433-34]   *Next, if you weigh . . . packed line!*   In *Frogs* 1365-67 Aeschylus has Euripides' poetry "weighed" against his own. Both poets speak lines of verse into a pair of scales, and Aeschylus' "chariot on chariot, corpse on corpse" is judged weightier than Euripides' "club heavy with iron" (1402-5).

5437]   *Triphales*   I.e., Alcibiades. See l. 1043n. above. In *Frogs* 1422-23 the two poets are asked for their opinion of Alcibiades, then in exile. Euripides condemns him as a self-seeking politician, Aeschylus, less directly, as a lion who must be humored.

5438]   *(Nay, that served when ourself abused the youth!)*   Balaustion's pointed question ("Triphales?") addressed to the absent Aristophanes, meant: "shall we call Alcibiades by the name you gave him?" Aristophanes' imagined reply (using the royal "we"), implies that he has simply moved with the times and changed his mind.

5439]   *Pheidippides?*   I.e., would you like to call him Pheidippides, the trendy young man who becomes Socrates' student in *Clouds*? In *Symposium* 221 b2-3 Alcibiades quotes a remark about Socrates in *Clouds* 362 ("you swagger along, throwing your eyes sideways"); which possibly made B think that Pheidippides was a caricature of Alcibiades.

5444-46]   *"Fate due . . . tragic aid!"*   A paraphrase of *Frogs* 1491-95.

5447-48]   *—All wound-up . . . worst of them!*   *Frogs* 1531-32: "For thus we should cease altogether from grievous woes and armed conflict."

5452]   *Dekeleia*   See l. 943n. above.

5453]   *Kleophon*   See l. 941n. above.

5458-59]   *such fame had "Frogs" . . . croaked gay again*   According to one *Hypothesis* of *Frogs,* "the play was so admired for its parabasis that it was actually produced again" (*Frogs*, ed. K. Dover [Oxford, 1993], 114).

5460]   *the great Feast, Elaphebolion-month*   See ll. 119n. and 120n. above.

5461] *Aigispotamoi* A small river in the Thracian Chersonese, near which the Athenian fleet was surprised and destroyed by the Spartans. The spelling, though in B's MS, is a curious cross between the traditional Latin/English *Aegispotami* and the Greek *Aigospotamoi*.

5462-64] *frog-merriment . . . people of the marsh!* An allusion to Aesop's *Fables.* The foolish *merriment* recalls No. 350 in the Tauchnitz edition (Leipsig, 1868), where the frogs joyfully celebrate the Sun's wedding— until one of them asks: "If the Sun by himself already burns up the forest and the earth, what good can we expect, if he marries and has a son just like him?" Their *King* seems to come indirectly from No. 37, where the frogs ask Zeus for a king, and he sends them, first a log, then an eel, and then a water-snake, which starts catching and eating them one by one. In Caxton's English version (1484) the water-snake (ὕδρα) becomes a heron, in L'Estrange's (1692) either a stork or a serpent, in Croxall's (1804), which B may have read in his nursery, a stork.

5465] *Lusandros* See ll. 74n. and 1182n. above

5466] *sacred bay* I.e., the Great Harbor at Piraeus. The word *sacred* was possibly suggested by a sentence in Plutarch. Describing how Lysander captured the fleet of 180 triremes at Aegispotami, by attacking when the crews were ashore, he mentioned that one of the sacred state-galleys (ἡ Πάραλος) escaped capture (*Life of Lysander*, 11).

5469] *"Down with those Long Walls, Peiraios' pride!* See l. 80n. above. B paraphrases the first of the peace-terms offered by the Spartan authorities: "Demolish the Piraeus and the Long Walls . . . " (*Life of Lysander*, 14).

5472-73] *next quick imposure . . . democratic government!* Plutarch: "So Lysander . . . immediately set about changing their constitution. And when they stubbornly and angrily resisted, he sent a message to the people that he had caught them breaking the peace-terms, since the Walls were still standing after the date when they should have been demolished" (*Life of Lysander*, 15).

5477] *half-helot* The Helots were the slave-underclass in Sparta. Lysander was of noble, though not of royal birth, but was "brought up in poverty," and was found to have been poor at his death (*Life of Lysander*, 2, 30).

5478] *let their hair grow long* Plutarch's *Life of Lysander* begins by describing a statue of Lysander "with very long hair according to the ancient custom . . . for it is not true . . . that the Spartans . . . let their hair grow long to celebrate what they have achieved" (*Life of Lysander*, 1).

5479] *Socratize* The fourth *Hypothesis* (plot-summary) of *Clouds* begins: "A father wants his son to socratize [σωκρατίζειν = become a student of Socrates, behave like him]." In *Birds* 1281-82 a similar verb,

Σωκρατέω, is used to mean "be Spartan-mad [λακωνομανέω] . . . be long-haired, hungry, and dirty"; criticisms of Socrates based on his capacity for Spartan endurance of hunger and cold, as praised by Alcibiades in Plato, *Symposium* 219e.

5480] *"Trample on Themistokles!"* I.e., by demolishing his legacy, the Long Walls (see l. 80n. above).

5484-86] *Pallas . . . Herakles . . . Theseus* The patron goddess, hero, and legendary king of Athens.

5492] *fade in fume* Go up in smoke.

5493] *Bakis* A Boeotian oracle-monger whose prophecies were often quoted at times of national emergency. The one that should have worried Lysander most went like this: "But when . . . with mad hope they lay waste shining Athens, Justice will snuff out strong Insolence, the son of Hubris" (Herodotus, *Histories* 8.77).

5530] *Propulaia* See l. 112n. above.

5534-37] *raze / Athenai . . . grazing goats* The landscape of B's "Love among the Ruins" (this edition, 5.163-66) is blended here with Plutarch: "and some say that a motion to enslave the Athenians was actually brought forward among the allies, when also Erianthus the Theban proposed to demolish the city and turn the country into pastureland for sheep" (*Life of Lysander*, 15).

5541] *Then did a Man of Phokis rise* Plutarch continued: "But at a later meeting of the alliance-leaders over drinks, when a certain Phocian recited the opening chorus of Euripides' *Electra*, which begins: 'I have come, Electra, daughter of Agememnon, to your rustic dwelling' [*Electra* 167-68], all their hearts were softened and they felt it would be cruel to annihilate such a famous city, which produced such men [as Euripides]" (*Life of Lysander*, 15). The anonymous Phocian was not just appealing to Athens' literary reputation. In the play *Electra*, daughter of a great king who has been murdered by his wife and her lover, has been married off to a peasant, who scrupulously refuses to humiliate the poor princess still further by exercising his conjugal rights (*Electra* 43-46). The Phocian implies that the Spartans should show equal respect for Athens in her fall. B calls the Phocian "Euthukles." See l. 1757n. above.

5542] *disparted* Split asunder.

5551-52] *late my liege, / Electra, palaced once* B's glosses on the text (*Electra* 167-68).

5560] *Wedgingly* Like a wedge.

5562] *sail* I.e., piece of sailcloth used for weatherproofing.

5566] *Tragic Two* Aeschylus and Sophocles, who had written about Electra in the *Choephori* and the *Electra* respectively.

5575] *clothed in rags* Euripides' Electra asks the Chorus if the rags she wears are suitable for the "royal daughter of Agamemnon" (*Electra* 185-87).

5576] *chares* Chores. Electra first enters carrying a pot on her head, to fetch water (140).

5579] *the King of Men* ἄναξ ἀνδρῶν, the stock epithet for Agamemnon in Homer.

5588] *such reverse* I.e., a city that has suffered such a reverse of fortune.

5592] *a stranger* Electra's brother Orestes arrives in disguise from Phocis, where he has been safely brought up, to avenge his father's murder by killing his mother Clytaemnestra and her lover Aegisthus. Electra first describes her brother and his friend Pylades as ξένοι (= strangers, *Electra* 216).

5598] *pulls the door behind* Electra lures her mother into the cottage where Orestes is waiting, by sending a message that she has just had a baby. She then follows her mother in, and helps to kill her (*Electra* 650-60, 1139-46, 1224-25).

5603-4] *hides his blow / Dreadful Orestes* I.e., Orestes bides his time to deliver his blow (a climactic word-order common in Greek).

5604-5] *Klutaimnestra . . . Electra held her own* I.e., Sparta thought better of murder and Athens survived; but at this point the Electra-Athens analogy stops working: though Athens like Electra has been betrayed by its closest relations (its own politicians), Sparta has not committed anything like Clytaemnestra's original crime. Both sides shared responsibility for the war between fellow-Greeks.

5612] *enormity* An ironical pun on the two meanings of the word: 1. a departure from the norm, 2. a monstrous error or crime.

5622] *pinioned to inflict* Prevented from inflicting.

5624] *embitter scathe by scorn* Add insult to injury.

5632] *Not to the Kommos* Not to the accompaniment of the κόμμος (= beating of breasts in grief), a feature of Greek tragedy defined by Aristotle (*Poetics* 1452b 24-25) as "a lament shared by the chorus and the actors on stage."

eleleleleu In *Birds* 364 ἐλελελεῦ is evidently a battle-cry; but in Aeschylus' *Prometheus Bound* 877 ἐλελεῦ is a cry of pain. B seems to intend the latter sense, remembering the use of the related verb ἐλελίζω, in *Birds* 213 and Euripides' *Helen* 1111, for the nightingale's mournful song. But his four-*el* version of the three-*el* cry may also be meant to imply Lysander's *scorn*, (l. 5624 above) for his defeated enemy's war-cry.

5635] *kordax* See l. 101n. above.

5636] *flute-girls* See l. 74n. above.

5639] *Sea-urchin . . . unpricked* Probably suggested by the story in Athenaeus (3.91) of the Spartan who was offered a sea-urchin or sea-hegehog at a feast. Not knowing how to deal with it, he "popped it in his mouth, shell and all, and tried to chew it with his teeth." Finding this very difficult, he refused "to be soft" and spit it out, but swore never to eat one again.

5643-44] *That sixteenth famed day . . . Salamis* B conflates two passages of Plutarch: "When Lysander had taken over all the Athenians' ships but twelve, and their walls, on the sixteenth day of Munuchion month, on which they had defeated the barbarians in the naval battle at Salamis, he started planning to change their constitution" (*Life of Lysander*, 15); "So Lysander, . . . having sent for many flute-girls from the town, and collected all that were in the camp, started demolishing the walls and burning the triremes to the music of flutes" (*Life of Lysander*, 15). The 16th of Munuchion (Μουνυχιών, the tenth month in the Athenian calendar) was around the beginning of April.

5645] *The very day Euripides was born* Nauck quoted Plutarch *Moralia* 717c: "Euripides was born on the day when the Greeks were fighting the naval battle at Salamis against the Medes" (Nauck, x). The *Life* only gives the year of his birth in Salamis, adding "when the Greeks fought the naval battle against the Persians" (Nauck, v.2-4).

5646] *Phaps-Elaphion* See ll. 588-89n. and 593n. above.

5653] *peplos* See l. 171n. above; but the word could also refer, as here, to an ordinary item of women's clothing.

5658] *bate* Reduce in importance or binding force, i.e., minimize, disregard.

5659] *The stranger's licensed duty* As a resident alien (μέτοικος) a Phocian, though without civic rights, had civic duties, e.g., paying taxes, doing military service etc.

5660] *the Man from Phokis* Euthycles. See ll. 208n., 1757n., and 5541n. above.

5667] *To who had saved his ship* I.e., Balaustion, who had saved it in *Balaustion's Adventure*, by describing a stage-performance of Euripides' *Alcestis*.

5669] *The hospitable port* Syracuse, made hospitable by her recitation. See *Balaustion's Adventure*, 2698-2704; this edition, 10.117.

5677] *we* That we.

5678] *who so taught* Euripides. See l. 206n. above.

5679] *little valley* B makes the most of Nauck's notes on the *Life*, here translating *convallis* in a quotation from Ammianus Marcellinus (Nauck, xxi.32).

5680]   *those mysterious streams*   B allegorizes Nauck's quotation from Pliny (*Natural History* 31:19): "In Macedonia, not far from the tomb of the poet Euripides, two streams flow together, one very healthy to drink, the other lethal."

5683]   *Arethousa*   Nauck (xxi) had quoted Plutarch's remark (*Life of Lycurgus*, 31): "Euripides was buried at Arethusa [the name of a town] in Macedonia"; but B makes it a river, doubtless remembering the famous myth of the nymph Arethusa (though she ended up as a river-spring on the island of Ortygia, in the harbor of Syracuse).

5686]   *the psalterion*   See l. 1562n. above.

5687]   *Sicily*   I.e., Syracuse (on its SE coast).

the tyrant there   Dionysius I, who seized power in 405 B.C., but was a patron of the arts and literature.

5691]   *Archelaos*   See l. 238n. above.

5692]   *Philemon . . . Euripides*   See l. 50n. above.

5699]   *the prime plays*   He wrote 97, and was almost as successful as Menander.

labour the right life   Struggle to lead a good life. Surviving fragments of Philemon show a great concern with morality. Thus the first fragment in Meineke begins: "O how wicked is the nature of Man, on the whole! Otherwise he would never have needed any law" (Meineke, 4.3).

5700]   *good old age*   According to various sources, he died at 97, 99, or 101; see *Oxford Classical Dictionary* (3rd ed., ed. S. Hornblower and A. Spawforth [Oxford, 1996]).

5704-6]   *citied ridge of Rhodes . . . each guarded calm*   An imaginative picture possibly based on Strabo's *Geography* (14.2.5): "The city of the Rhodians lies on the eastern ἀκρωτήριον [= topmost or extreme part of anything, e.g., a mountain-peak or promontory], and with its harbors and roads and walls and other facilities incomparably surpasses other cities. It is also admirable . . . in its arrangements for shipping, which gave it sea-power over a long period." Strabo went on to say something even more relevant to B's theme: "The present city was built during the Peloponnesian War, by the same architect, they say, as the Piraeus; but the Piraeus no longer exists, having been destroyed . . . by the Spartans, who demolished the Long Walls . . ." (14.2.9).

5708]   *boiled round with breakers*   Was B remembering Herodotus (*Histories* 7.188, where Xerxes fleet is destroyed after Salamis by a storm "when the sea boiled up" (θαλάσσης ζεσάσης)?

to no other cry   Crying out the same thing (*He lives!*).

5710-11]   *There are no gods . . . Glory to God*   See l. 1790n. above. Balaustion interprets Euripides' *master-word* as a declaration, not of atheism, but of monotheism. And B makes her final *He lives!* sound (like

Virgil's "Messianic" *Eclogue* iv) almost prophetic of Christianity. Thus her *Glory to God* can also be read as B's own thanksgiving for the completion of his long poem, corresponding with the "L. D. I. E." (his acronym for *Laudate Dominum . . . In Excelsis* = praise the Lord in the highest; Vulgate Psalms 148:1) which he had written at the end of his *Heracles*-transcript manuscript, would also write at the end of his *Agamemnon*-transcript, and may have meant to write at the end of *Aristophanes' Apology* itself, though what he actually wrote was "L. D. I. I." (see *Text and Publication*, above).